The Resonant Brain: A Themed Issue Dedicated to Professor Stephen Grossberg

The Resonant Brain: A Themed Issue Dedicated to Professor Stephen Grossberg

Guest Editors

Birgitta Dresp-Langley
Luiz Pessoa

Basel • Beijing • Wuhan • Barcelona • Belgrade • Novi Sad • Cluj • Manchester

Guest Editors

Birgitta Dresp-Langley
Centre National de la
Recherche Scientifique
UMR 7357 CNRS
Université de Strasbourg
Strasbourg
France

Luiz Pessoa
Department of Psychology
University of Maryland
College Park
United States

Editorial Office
MDPI AG
Grosspeteranlage 5
4052 Basel, Switzerland

This is a reprint of the Special Issue, published open access by the journal *Information* (ISSN 2078-2489), freely accessible at: www.mdpi.com/journal/information/special_issues/The_Resonant_Brain.

For citation purposes, cite each article independently as indicated on the article page online and as indicated below:

Lastname, A.A.; Lastname, B.B. Article Title. *Journal Name* **Year**, *Volume Number*, Page Range.

ISBN 978-3-7258-3738-0 (Hbk)
ISBN 978-3-7258-3737-3 (PDF)
https://doi.org/10.3390/books978-3-7258-3737-3

© 2025 by the authors. Articles in this book are Open Access and distributed under the Creative Commons Attribution (CC BY) license. The book as a whole is distributed by MDPI under the terms and conditions of the Creative Commons Attribution-NonCommercial-NoDerivs (CC BY-NC-ND) license (https://creativecommons.org/licenses/by-nc-nd/4.0/).

Contents

About the Editors vii

Birgitta Dresp-Langley and Luiz Pessoa
Editorial to the Special Issue "The Resonant Brain: A Themed Issue Dedicated to Professor Stephen Grossberg"
Reprinted from: *Information* 2025, *16*, 234, https://doi.org/10.3390/info16030234 1

Gerry Leisman and Paul Koch
Resonating with the World: Thinking Critically about Brain Criticality in Consciousness and Cognition
Reprinted from: *Information* 2024, *15*, 284, https://doi.org/10.3390/info15050284 3

Birgitta Dresp-Langley
The Grossberg Code: Universal Neural Network Signatures of Perceptual Experience
Reprinted from: *Information* 2023, *14*, 82, https://doi.org/10.3390/info14020082 31

Adam Reeves
The Psychometric Function for Focusing Attention on Pitch
Reprinted from: *Information* 2023, *14*, 279, https://doi.org/10.3390/info14050279 46

Baingio Pinna, Jurģis Šķilters and Daniele Porcheddu
Accentuation as a Mechanism of Visual Illusions: Insights from Adaptive Resonance Theory (ART)
Reprinted from: *Information* 2025, *16*, 172, https://doi.org/10.3390/info16030172 60

Amedeo D'Angiulli, Christy Laarakker and Derrick Matthew Buchanan
An ART Tour de Force on Mental Imagery: Vividness, Individual Bias Differences, and Complementary Visual Processing Streams
Reprinted from: *Information* 2024, *15*, 59, https://doi.org/10.3390/info15010059 98

Sasha Petrenko, Daniel B. Hier, Tayo Obafemi-Ajayi, Erik J. Timpson, William E. Marsh, Michael Speight, et al.
Analyzing Biomedical Datasets with Symbolic Tree Adaptive Resonance Theory
Reprinted from: *Information* 2024, *15*, 125, https://doi.org/10.3390/info15030125 121

Jagmeet S. Kanwal
From Information to Knowledge: A Role for Knowledge Networks in Decision Making and Action Selection
Reprinted from: *Information* 2024, *15*, 487, https://doi.org/10.3390/info15080487 151

Wen-Ran Zhang
Global Realism with Bipolar Strings: From Bell Test to Real-World Causal-Logical Quantum Gravity and Brain-Universe Similarity for Entangled Machine Thinking and Imagination
Reprinted from: *Information* 2024, *15*, 456, https://doi.org/10.3390/info15080456 185

Michela Balconi and Laura Angioletti
Inter-Brain Hemodynamic Coherence Applied to Interoceptive Attentiveness in Hyperscanning: Why Social Framing Matters
Reprinted from: *Information* 2023, *14*, 58, https://doi.org/10.3390/info14020058 225

Michela Balconi, Davide Crivelli and Federico Cassioli
"We Will Let You Know": An Assessment of Digital vs. Face-to-Face Job Interviews via EEG Connectivity Analysis
Reprinted from: *Information* 2022, *13*, 312, https://doi.org/10.3390/info13070312 238

About the Editors

Birgitta Dresp-Langley

Prof. Dr. Birgitta Dresp-Langley holds a Ph.D. in Cognitive Science from Paris Descartes University. She currently is a Full CNRS Research Professor/Directeur de Recherche CNRS Titulaire at the Centre National de la Recherche Scientifique in France. Her research interests are centered on perceptual processes, cognition, and the philosophy of Artificial Intelligence (AI).

Luiz Pessoa

Prof. Dr. Pessoa is a Full Professor of Psychology at the University of Maryland and a Director of the Maryland Neuroimaging Center. His research interests are centered on behavioral and functional MRI methods used to study cognition and emotion, with an emphasis on the interactions between cognitive and emotional brain systems.

Editorial

Editorial to the Special Issue "The Resonant Brain: A Themed Issue Dedicated to Professor Stephen Grossberg"

Birgitta Dresp-Langley [1,*] and Luiz Pessoa [2]

[1] Centre National de la Recherche Scientifique (CNRS) UMR7357, CNRS-Université de Strasbourg, F-67081 Strasbourg, France
[2] Department of Psychology and Maryland Neuroimaging Center, University of Maryland, College Park, MD 20742, USA; pessoa@umd.edu
* Correspondence: birgitta.dresp@cnrs.fr

This Special Issue offers a collection of research and model approaches to fundamental principles, mechanisms, and model architectures closely linked to the conceptual foundations of contemporary neural network research laid down by Stephen Grossberg [1] and his colleagues. Their pioneering conceptual work and models have since inspired and been explored further in state-of-the-art interdisciplinary research [2–7]. Analyzing and explaining brain mechanisms and data is considered a key to understanding cognition, with the overarching goal of explaining how the human mind arises from cooperative and competitive mechanisms through the step-by-step integration of information into brain representations. Information may be defined, in the context of this topical issue, in terms of either external physical information or internally encoded signals and emotions. Integration is achieved by mechanisms that may be pre-conscious, sub-conscious, and, ultimately, fully conscious [7,8], achieving cognitive representations across hierarchically organized layers of brain processing. The articles in this collection are directly relevant to topics ranging from the quest for explainable and predictive Artificial Intelligence (AI) [9] to the conscious representation of complex visual configurations in variable contexts [10] by the human brain. A unified understanding of how our brains see [11], hear [12], and feel [5,6] in order to learn about and know the world and to effectively interact with it clarifies how autonomous adaptive intelligence is achieved [13]. The research collected in this Special Issue is mostly concerned with mechanistic approaches to adaptive behavior. These can help solve large-scale problems in machine learning, AI, and robotics [14]. Brains embody universal developmental codes and laws found in all living cells and synapses [15], from the most primitive to the most advanced. These laws govern networks of interacting cells to support development and learning in all species, from mollusks to humans. Brain evolution across species has culminated in humans' unique ability to study their own minds and to understand how minds derive meaning from an inherently ambiguous world—a skill that helps us adapt to changing environments. Despite the general advocacy for developing AI systems, significant limitations exist. A major one is the missing conceptual link between cognitive neuroscience and AI. While breakthroughs in AI often are claimed to be inspired by cognitive neuroscience, this is, however, most often not the case. Leveraging the most recent advances in cognitive neuroscience to emulate technology for novel solutions in machine learning and AI was a major part of Grossberg's work, despite an inevitable contradiction: the pursuits of cognitive neuroscience and AI are, by nature, distinct. Cognitive neuroscience aims at clarifying mechanisms of cognition in living brains by studying neural activities linked to specific mental and behavioral states [16]. AI, on the other hand, is

Received: 7 March 2025
Accepted: 12 March 2025
Published: 16 March 2025

Citation: Dresp-Langley, B.; Pessoa, L. Editorial to the Special Issue "The Resonant Brain: A Themed Issue Dedicated to Professor Stephen Grossberg". *Information* **2025**, *16*, 234. https://doi.org/10.3390/info16030234

Copyright: © 2025 by the authors. Licensee MDPI, Basel, Switzerland. This article is an open access article distributed under the terms and conditions of the Creative Commons Attribution (CC BY) license (https://creativecommons.org/licenses/by/4.0/).

a black box approach aimed at predicting outcomes on the basis of algorithms that most often do not even remotely take into account the workings of the biological brain [17].

Conflicts of Interest: The authors declare no conflict of interest.

References

1. Grossberg, S. *Conscious Mind, Resonant Brain: How Each Brain Makes a Mind*, onlineed; OxfordAcademic: NewYork, NY, USA, 2021. [CrossRef]
2. Kellman, P.J.; Shipley, T.F. A theory of visual interpolation in object perception. *Cogn. Psychol.* **1991**, *23*, 141–221. [CrossRef] [PubMed]
3. Groberg, S.; Williamson, J.R. A neural model of how horizon tal and inter laminar connections of visual cortex develop into adult circuits that carryout perceptual groupings and learning. *Cereb. Cortex* **2001**, *11*, 37–58. [CrossRef] [PubMed]
4. Pilly, P.K.; Grossberg, S. How do spatial learning and memory occur in the brain? Coordinated learning of entorhinal grid cell sand hippocampal place cells. *J. Cogn. Neurosci.* **2012**, *24*, 1031–1054. [CrossRef] [PubMed]
5. Pessoa, L. Précis on The Cognitive-Emotional Brain. *Behav. Brain Sci.* **2015**, *38*, e71. [CrossRef] [PubMed]
6. Damasio, A.R. *The Feeling of What Happens: Body and Emotion in the Making of Consciousness*; Houghton Mifflin Harcourt: Boston, MA, USA, 1999.
7. Dresp-Langley, B. Why the brain knows more than we do: Non-conscious representations and the irrole in the construction of conscious experience. *Brain Sci.* **2011**, *2*, 1–21. [CrossRef] [PubMed]
8. Singer, W. Consciousness and the structure of neuronal representations. *Philos. Trans. R. Soc. B* **1998**, *353*, 1829–1840.
9. Dresp-Langley, B. The Grossberg Code: Universal Neural Network Signatures of Perceptual Experience. *Information* **2023**, *14*, 82. [CrossRef]
10. Pinna, B.; Škilters, J.; Porcheddu, D. Accentuation as a Mechanism of Visual Illusions: Insights from Adaptive Resonance Theory(ART). *Information* **2025**, *16*, 172. [CrossRef]
11. Ptito, M.; Bleau, M. Bouskila. The Retina: A Window into the Brain. *Cells* **2021**, *10*, 3269. [CrossRef] [PubMed]
12. Reeves, A. The Psychometric Function for Focusing Attention on Pitch. *Information* **2023**, *14*, 279. [CrossRef]
13. Sternberg, R.J. A theory of Adaptive Intelligence and Its Relation to General Intelligence. *J. Intell.* **2019**, *7*, 23. [CrossRef] [PubMed]
14. Sandini, G.; Sciutti, A.; Morasso, P. Artificial cognition vs. artificial intelligence for next-generation autonomous robotic agents. *Front. Comput. Neurosci.* **2024**, *18*, 1349408. [CrossRef] [PubMed]
15. Leisman, G.; Koch, P. Resonating with the World: Thinking Critically about Brain Criticality in Consciousness and Cognition. *Information* **2024**, *15*, 284. [CrossRef]
16. Churchland, P.S.; Sejnowski, T.J. *The Computational Brain*; MIT Press: Cambridge, MA, USA, 2016.
17. Goh, W.W.B.; Kabir, M.N.; Yoo, S.; Wong, L. Ten quick tips for ensuring machine learning model validity. *PLoS Comput. Biol.* **2024**, *20*, e1012402. [CrossRef] [PubMed]

Disclaimer/Publisher's Note: The statements, opinions and data contained in all publications are solely those of the individual author(s) and contributor(s) and not of MDPI and/or the editor(s). MDPI and/or the editor(s) disclaim responsibility for any injury to people or property resulting from any ideas, methods, instructions or products referred to in the content.

Article

Resonating with the World: Thinking Critically about Brain Criticality in Consciousness and Cognition

Gerry Leisman [1,2,*] and Paul Koch [†]

[1] Movement and Cognition Laboratory, Department of Physical Therapy, University of Haifa, Haifa 3498838, Israel
[2] Resonance Therapeutics Laboratory, Department of Neurology, University of the Medical Sciences, Havana 11600, Cuba
[*] Correspondence: g.leisman@alumni.manchester.ac.uk; Tel.: +972-52-420-5643
[†] Deceased.

Abstract: Aim: Biofields combine many physiological levels, both spatially and temporally. These biofields reflect naturally resonant forms of synaptic energy reflected in growing and spreading waves of brain activity. This study aims to theoretically understand better how resonant continuum waves may be reflective of consciousness, cognition, memory, and thought. Background: The metabolic processes that maintain animal cellular and physiological functions are enhanced by physiological coherence. Internal biological-system coordination and sensitivity to particular stimuli and signal frequencies are two aspects of coherent physiology. There exists significant support for the notion that exogenous biologically and non-biologically generated energy entrains human physiological systems. All living things have resonant frequencies that are either comparable or coherent; therefore, eventually, all species will have a shared resonance. An organism's biofield activity and resonance are what support its life and allow it to react to stimuli. Methods: As the naturally resonant forms of synaptic energy grow and spread waves of brain activity, the temporal and spatial frequency of the waves are effectively regulated by a time delay (T) in inter-layer signals in a layered structure that mimics the structure of the mammalian cortex. From ubiquitous noise, two different types of waves can arise as a function of T. One is coherent, and as T rises, so does its resonant spatial frequency. Results: Continued growth eventually causes both the wavelength and the temporal frequency to abruptly increase. Two waves expand simultaneously and randomly interfere in an area of T values as a result. Conclusion: We suggest that because of this extraordinary dualism, which has its roots in the phase relationships of amplified waves, coherent waves are essential for memory retrieval, whereas random waves represent original cognition.

Keywords: resonance; brain; consciousness; criticality; entrainment; continuum theory; biofield

Citation: Leisman, G.; Koch, P. Resonating with the World: Thinking Critically about Brain Criticality in Consciousness and Cognition. *Information* 2024, *15*, 284. https://doi.org/10.3390/info15050284

Academic Editor: Luis Martínez López

Received: 26 February 2024
Revised: 13 April 2024
Accepted: 15 May 2024
Published: 17 May 2024

Copyright: © 2024 by the authors. Licensee MDPI, Basel, Switzerland. This article is an open access article distributed under the terms and conditions of the Creative Commons Attribution (CC BY) license (https://creativecommons.org/licenses/by/4.0/).

1. Introduction

1.1. Resonating with the World

The present study aims to integrate consciousness and cognition as a function of resonance, defined as an effect that is amplified when two systems are in harmony. A tuning fork set to 440 Hz, or tuned to concert pitch "A", as is currently done in symphony orchestras, would have a second fork vibrate in sympathy with or in phase with it if one were to tap it. If we were to silence the first tuning fork, we would still be able to hear the vibrations coming from the fork that we did not touch. We might say that the second fork is experiencing an induced sympathetic resonant vibration or frequency. Both forks are tuned to the exact same frequency. We are aware of instances where people have broken glass with just their voices. Whoever wants to try it should lightly tap the glass with a nail or finger and then listen for the glass's natural resonance or pitch. The next step would be to sing a long note in the person's voice. Until the glass is broken, the vibration's amplitude will increase steadily. Alternatively, a suspension bridge In Tacoma, Washington, built with steel and concrete, fell in 1940. On November 1 of that year, the bridge experienced a modest, seemingly negligible vibration along with a constant wind of about 45 mph. Unfortunately, some areas of the bridge's resonant frequency coincided with the vibration's frequency. The vibration increased until it reached a destructive resonance frequency, which caused the bridge to collapse. There is a video of the event available [1].

A big steel and concrete bridge was demolished by resonance in one instance, while a glass was broken in another. In light of this, we may destroy a minuscule object, perhaps a living bacterium. We might be able to modify the biological liquid crystal using a unique electronic signal, but this would require a device of some sort. A tool designed to cause a resonant vibration in a cell or other living entity was patented by James Bare [2–4]. For instance, a 100 Hz input would cause the resonating cell to output 100 pulses per second, similarly for 200 Hz, and so forth. Once the matching frequency is found that will entrain with the input frequency, we can start looking for the "magic frequency" 1 Hz at a time. One high and one low input frequency are required, with the higher frequency being 11 times greater than the lower or the 11th harmonic [5], where microorganisms start to break apart. The application matters a lot. Cancer cells of a certain type are sensitive to frequencies between 100,000 and 300,000 Hz [6,7].

We have long wondered how a biologically based machine could be built with billions of neurons that could outperform several of the most sophisticated computers. The brain has significant processing capability and nearly infinitely expandable storage [8–10]. The idea that the brain may tune itself to a level where it can be excitable without disorder in a manner analogous to a phase transition has recently been supported. Our neurological systems have a propensity to maintain a balance between rest and chaos. Information processing is optimized when there is a state of flux between quiescence and chaos [11]. This brings up the notion of criticality in the context of the resonance of living entities.

1.2. Schumann Resonance and Living

The "Schumann Resonance", often referred to as the "Earth's heartbeat" Refs. [12–14], is a naturally occurring electromagnetic resonance frequency in the Earth's electromagnetic field. Winfried Otto Schumann predicted it mathematically in 1952. The Schumann Resonance occurs due to the space between the Earth's surface and the ionosphere acting as a resonant cavity for electromagnetic waves.

The primary frequency of the Schumann Resonance is around 7.83 Hz Ref. [12], though it can vary slightly. It is influenced by various factors such as solar activity, lightning activity, and ionospheric conditions. Some people believe that these resonances can have effects on human health and consciousness, although scientific research in this area is ongoing and often controversial [12,13]. Some propose that these resonances may have an impact on our circadian rhythms [15] and overall well-being [13], but conclusive evidence is still lacking here as well.

The idea of resonance in relation to consciousness often refers to theories proposing that certain frequencies or patterns of electromagnetic activity in the brain might correlate with particular states of consciousness. For instance, some research suggests that brain wave frequencies, such as those associated with alpha, beta, delta, and theta waves, may correspond to different cognitive states, such as relaxation, alertness, deep sleep, or meditative states [16].

Some proponents of consciousness theories suggest that external electromagnetic fields, including the Schumann Resonance or other natural and artificial electromagnetic fields, could potentially influence or resonate with the brain's electromagnetic activity, leading to alterations in consciousness or cognitive states [17,18]. However, it is important to note that these ideas often remain speculative and are subject to ongoing scientific investigation and debate.

While there is interest in exploring the potential links between electromagnetic phenomena and consciousness, conclusive evidence for direct causation or significant influence remains elusive. Further interdisciplinary research involving neuroscience, physics, and psychology is needed to better understand the complex relationship between electromagnetic fields and consciousness. We will, however, attempt to integrate what is known about resonance related to both consciousness and cognition.

1.3. Resonance in Cognitive–Motor Interaction

Resonance in human motor function refers to the synchronization or amplification of movement patterns in response to external stimuli or internal processes. This concept is often studied in the context of biomechanics, neuroscience, and motor control to understand how the nervous system coordinates and modulates movements.

One example of resonance in motor function is the phenomenon of entrainment, where rhythmic external stimuli, such as music or a metronome, can synchronize and influence the timing and rhythm of movements. This is commonly observed in activities like dancing, where individuals coordinate their movements to the beat of the music.

Internal processes, such as emotions or intentions, can also influence motor resonance. For instance, when observing someone performing a specific action, mirror neurons in the observer's brain may fire, leading to a mirroring or resonance of the observed movement within the observer's own motor system. This phenomenon is thought to play a role in empathy, imitation, and social interaction.

Resonance can also occur within the motor system itself. When certain movement patterns or muscles are activated, there can be a tendency for nearby muscles or movement patterns to resonate or become activated as well. This can be advantageous for efficiency in movement execution but can also contribute to unintended movements or muscle co-activation in some cases.

Overall, resonance in human motor function involves the synchronization, amplification, or modulation of movement patterns in response to various internal and external factors. Understanding these mechanisms is crucial for optimizing movement control, rehabilitation strategies, and enhancing motor performance, but most importantly for cognitive function [19].

1.4. Criticality and Consciousness

The relationship between criticality and consciousness is a complex and multifaceted topic that spans various disciplines, including philosophy, psychology, neuroscience, and even physics. Briefly, *criticality* in physics refers to the point at which a system undergoes a phase transition, exhibiting properties that are neither completely ordered nor completely disordered. Criticality often refers to a state of a system where it operates at a point of instability or sensitivity, often at the boundary between order and chaos. Systems at criticality often display scale invariance, where patterns repeat across different scales. In neuroscience, criticality is a concept that describes the state of neuronal networks when they are balanced between order and disorder. It suggests that the brain operates most efficiently by optimizing information processing and is most adaptable when it is in a state of criticality.

In bringing these two concepts together, one area of interest is in exploring whether criticality in neural networks is somehow related to or necessary for consciousness. Some researchers hypothesize that consciousness may emerge from the dynamic patterns of neural activity that occur at the critical point [20]. In this view, criticality could be a fundamental property of neural systems that gives rise to conscious experience. However, this is still a highly debated and speculative area of research.

Furthermore, criticality and consciousness intersect in discussions about the nature of complex systems, emergence, and the relationship between physical processes and subjective experience. Understanding how criticality in neural networks or other complex systems might contribute to or correlate with consciousness could potentially shed light on the mysteries of the mind. However, it is essential to approach these topics with caution and rigorous scientific inquiry due to their complexity and the many unanswered questions surrounding them.

The relationship between criticality and consciousness lies in the idea that the brain, as a complex system, may operate near criticality to facilitate flexible and adaptive cognitive processes, including those associated with consciousness. Some researchers [21] propose that critical brain dynamics may be necessary for the emergence of conscious experiences, as they allow for the integration of information across different brain regions and the generation of complex patterns of activity.

However, the precise mechanisms by which criticality and consciousness are related are still not fully understood and remain the subject of ongoing research and debate. It is an exciting area of inquiry that continues to push the boundaries of our understanding of the brain and the mind.

1.5. Criticality in Consciousness and Cognition

Consciousness and cognition are fascinating aspects of human existence that ought to be broken down. Consciousness, for our purposes, refers to the subjective awareness of ourselves and the world around us [22]. It involves our thoughts, perceptions, feelings, and experiences. Consciousness refers to the state or quality of being aware of and able to perceive one's surroundings. It involves a range of cognitive processes, including attention, perception, memory, and self-awareness. Despite decades of research, the nature of consciousness remains one of the most challenging problems in science and philosophy. There are various theories about consciousness, including the integrated information theory [16], the global workspace theory [16], and panpsychism [16], each offering different perspectives on how consciousness arises and functions. A more in-depth discussion is beyond the scope of the present paper.

Consciousness is often described as the "hard problem" in philosophy because it is challenging to understand how subjective experiences arise from physical processes in the brain. *Cognition* refers to the mental processes involved in acquiring, processing, storing, and using information. It encompasses a wide range of mental activities, including perception, attention, memory, language, reasoning, and problem solving.

These two concepts are deeply intertwined. Consciousness is closely related to cognition because our conscious experiences are shaped by our cognitive processes, and vice versa. For example, our perception of the world around us is influenced by our cognitive abilities to interpret sensory information, and our conscious thoughts can influence our cognitive processes like attention and memory. Researchers in neuroscience, psychology, philosophy, and other fields continue to explore the relationship between consciousness and cognition, seeking to understand how they interact and how they emerge from the underlying biological mechanisms of the brain.

Criticality in cognition and consciousness refers to the idea that these processes exhibit a state of dynamic balance between order and chaos, where they operate at an optimal point between too much rigidity and too much randomness.

In cognitive science, criticality suggests that the brain operates near a phase transition point where it can quickly adapt to changing circumstances and efficiently process information. This state is often associated with complex behaviors, learning, and creativity. It is like the brain is finely tuned to the edge of chaos, where it can both maintain stability and exhibit flexibility.

Similarly, in consciousness studies, criticality implies that consciousness emerges from the collective activity of neurons operating at this critical state. This perspective suggests that consciousness is not a binary phenomenon but rather a continuous spectrum that emerges from complex interactions within the brain.

Understanding criticality in cognition and consciousness is crucial for unraveling the mysteries of how our minds work and how consciousness arises from neural processes. It provides insights into phenomena such as learning, memory, decision making, and even disorders like epilepsy or schizophrenia, where deviations from criticality may occur.

2. Resonating with the Brain in Consciousness and Cognition

2.1. Thinking Critically about Brain Criticality in the Context of Resonance

Complex systems that are on the verge of a phase change between randomness and order are said to be in a critical state. There is a unique improvement in information-processing abilities in this kind of system, and we might even speculate that the brain may play a key role in it. Criticality, computation, and cognitive processes are beginning to show linkages. We can better grasp the nature of cognition and neural processing by comprehending the concept of criticality.

Neurons that fire simultaneously link together, according to Hebb [23]. We now understand that neurons seek a key set point and regime when they functionally join with others [11]. Ma and colleagues have backed the idea that criticality is subject to active regulation. Criticality is mediated by inhibitory neurons in both Ma and colleagues' models and in our own [24–26]. Larger brain networks seem to be regulated by these neurons. According to Koch and Leisman [25], the function of criticality is to develop a computational model that may be used to optimize information processing, including the storing and transmission of intricate sensory patterns and parts of memory.

Power laws serve as the foundation for the majority of measurements in clinical neurophysiology and psychophysics. These power laws are used to separate background activity from noise using a variety of methodologies, such as the Fast Fourier Transform, signal averaging techniques, coherence, dipole source localization, and Hilbert–Huang transforms, among others. The exponent relation is a good substitute for direct use in information processing. We might want to look into biofield physiology as a way of explaining the process of living to better comprehend the relationship between criticality, resonance, consciousness, "awakeness", awareness, and integrated brain function.

2.2. Critical Biofield Systems and Information

Biological systems generate a variety of fields that are only partially diffused so that they can more effectively self-regulate and organize their physiology. This is done to make physiological organization more efficient. Alterations to physiological regulatory systems can be brought about by biofields in a manner that is comparable to alterations brought about by molecular control systems. Electroencephalograms (EEGs) and magnetoencephalograms (MEGs) are two examples of the types of biofields that can cause changes in the synchronization of the brain's electrical activity (EEG).

It has been demonstrated that biofields are made up of forces that are dispersed across a broad region and can encode information [27,28]. These pressures, which also affect physiology, can control and affect the physiology of tissues and cells. As a complementary function of physiological coherence for metabolic processes, biofields coordinate the integration of several different levels of physiological activity, both temporally and spatially [29]. This is done as a result of a biofield's ability to maintain physiological coherence. When referring to the qualities that constitute a living creature, the terms "biofield activity" and "resonance" can be used interchangeably in this context because they mean the same thing.

Analyzing the functional connection while at rest using MRI helps us understand the brain's functioning architecture better. The technique depends on slow correlations in the blood oxygen level-dependent signal (BOLD) (e.g., 0.01–0.1 Hz) in the brain. These gradual correlation patterns have been utilized to identify functional networks and to explain how they grow, alter with age, differ between people, and get disrupted in disease [30–36]. Though the fundamental mechanisms remain unclear, it is thought that delayed BOLD fluctuations and their associations represent brain processes [37,38].

Two distinct types of often-seen dynamics in the brain may be related to two separate underlying systems or processes. The pacemaker may affect dynamics that show a narrow band-limited power [39]. For example, the dominant occipitally recorded EEG alpha rhythm during restful wakefulness may be generated by an alpha pacemaker. A particular subset of thalamocortical neurons with inherent rhythmic bursting at alpha frequencies and gap junction couplings make up alpha pacemakers [40]. Even though this model of oscillating resting-state activity is well supported, e.g., [39,41], the most commonly recognized hypothesis in the field holds that brain activity propagates within an anatomically limited small-world network to produce correlations [42,43]. Scale-free dynamics, or 1/f dynamics, are predicted by this model [44–46]. Large events are rare, whereas little events are frequent in 1/f dynamics because of the inverse relationship between event amplitude and frequency. More specifically, as frequency is increased, even by a small exponent, power can change inversely ($P \propto 1/f^{\beta}$, with exponents ranging from 0 to 3) [47]. Though they can also happen in other noncritical systems, complex dynamic systems possess 1/f dynamics when operating at a critical point, when ordered and disordered phases of the system are balanced [48,49]. The 1/f features of many neural signals, including local field potentials, have supported the development of brain activity models critically operating by self-organizing properties [50–52].

A high level of sensitivity to particular stimuli, and by extension, particular signal frequencies, is necessary for coherent physiology. This sensitivity is required, among other things, for the effective coordination and integration of internal biological systems. Coherent physiology requires not just the efficient coordination and integration of the body's internal biological systems, but also a significant sensitivity to particular stimuli and, as a result of this, particular signal frequencies. Exogenous energy that is generated either biologically or non-biologically appears to be vulnerable to and entrains human physiological systems, according to a significant body of research in this area. During physiological activity, it is possible to collect measurements of electrical and magnetic fields; however, this may lead to confusion, since metabolic processes or the outcomes of physiological action are not completely known [30,31].

It is recognized that there will eventually be shared resonance, both within and between individual species, because all living things resonate at comparable or coherent frequencies. In the neurosciences, resonance theory has long been noted. Crick and Koch [32], Fries [33,34], and Koch [35] have studied the concept of resonance. According to Fries, a critical component of the nervous system's operation is brain synchronization, resonance, or "communication through coherence".

2.3. Consciousness as a Function of Resonance

Resonance is thought by many theorists to contribute to conscious states. According to Dehaene's global workspace theory, integrated conscious activity is the outcome of long-distance connections between synchronous and resonant cortical areas [35,36]. By claiming that while consciousness, which is associated with being awake and aware, is a function of resonance, it is not always a property of all resonant states, Grossberg [37] extended the idea of brain-communication-based resonance. Phase changes in resonance were also considered vital for understanding brain function by Freeman and Vitiello [38]. When Pockett proposed an electromagnetic field theory based on the synchronization from movement feedback when differentiating between conscious and non-conscious fields, she raised the significance of resonance in understanding integrated brain activity [39,40]. Others have developed further resonance-based theories of brain integration, such as Bandyopadhyay and colleagues' [41] Fractal Information Theory [42–44]. As a result, albeit still in theory and without practical application, resonance's importance in comprehending brain communication systems has begun to gain some traction.

The concept of resonance is intimately connected to awareness, inter-regional connections or disconnections in the brain, and its integrative function. It can be used to describe synchrony, vibration, or harmony more broadly. Similar resonance patterns can be found in the brain's synchronized electrical cycles. Resonance's significance in fostering integrated brain activity must also be properly understood in the context of death.

3. Resonating with Life (and Death): Gaps in Current Understanding

One of the numerous hypotheses that try to explain life and living is the assumption that life function comes from organized computer-like activity in the brain's neural networks that are connected with mental states. Another notion is that the temporal binding of information in these networks is associated with synchronous oscillations between the cortex and thalamus. How we consciously think may be impacted by the complexity of neural computing.

Death itself is not noteworthy until a clinical definition is required. However, it is more important to comprehend the mechanisms at play during a lack of consciousness. Although death seems to us to be a real event and an undeniable state, a corpse, whether human or otherwise, continues its life functions even after it has been proven to be dead. There is minimal disagreement that the person is dead despite a few isolated cells, nests, or cell subnetworks that continue to function.

As we continue, the argument becomes more challenging, since, despite the brain having "died", peripheral bodily organs like the heart, lungs, liver, and others still function due to modern developments. In the past, we had thought that the body perished when the entire brain expired, and consequently, physical functions ceased. Nevertheless, the development of modern technology has made it difficult for us to determine the precise moment of death. The constituent components of conscious or micro-conscious entities need to combine to provide us with the vividness of the conscious experience, bringing us to the combination problem.

3.1. The Combination Problem in General Resonance Theory

Can components of lower-level micro-consciousness join together to produce higher-level macro-consciousnesses? According to the suggested explanation, distinct brain regions may undergo bandwidth phase shifts and changes in the speed of information transmission between regions through common resonance in the context of mammalian consciousness. More complicated variations of consciousness may form as a result of this phase transition, and the nature and content of those varieties will rely on the specific combination of component neurons that are present at any one time. To distinguish this perspective from emergent materialism, we can provide a more thorough understanding of the comparative development and categorization of consciousness and propose that in all physical processes, awareness appears as a continuum of increasing richness. This can be referred to as a metasynthesis, and it is also known as general resonance theory.

3.2. Everything Has a Unique Resonance

Everything in the universe is always changing and evolving. Certain frequencies cause even seemingly immovable things to vibrate, oscillate, or resonate. As a result, everything is genuinely oscillating, and coordinated oscillation between two states is what defines resonance. Different oscillating processes often start vibrating at the same frequency when their frequencies are close enough [45]. Sometimes they "sync" in unexpected ways that accelerate and enrich the flow of energy and information. By examining this occurrence, significant insights into the nature of consciousness—both to humans and other mammals, and on a more basic level—may be gained. Using a range of resonant examples from biology, physics, chemistry, and neuroscience, the authors of [35] aimed at describing the nature of synchrony in the experience of consciousness, and have included certain species of fireflies that start to flash their bioluminescent parts in unison when they are in large groups. Mammalian awareness and the ability of human brains to fire large numbers of neurons at specific frequencies are believed to be closely related to various forms of neural synchronization [32–36]. We always see the same face of the moon because its spin precisely matches its orbit around the planet. When photons with the same frequency and power are discharged simultaneously, a laser is produced. At this point, it can be helpful to consider how resonance and synchrony differ concerning our inquiries.

3.3. What Is Resonance and Synchrony?

Resonance or synchronization is the propensity for several processes to move in unison, or oscillate, at the same or at a similar frequency. Synchrony, also known as the harmonic oscillator theory or complex network theory, is the study of how connected oscillators behave around one another.

The following two queries are raised by numerous instances of resonance: how do the constituent elements of resonant structures—a phrase that refers to any grouping of resonating components—interact with one another, and, once achieved, how do they reach resonance? Examining each question individually, we need to pay close attention to the two examples above by examining (1) the significant neural synchronization in mammalian brains and (2) the synchronization of flashes in fireflies.

The sort of communication between each resonant structure will vary depending on the scenario being studied, and in many resonance cases, clear conclusions are difficult to derive. Each firefly has access to visual signals, but it is also likely that it has access to olfactory, chemical, and perhaps electrical or magnetic stimuli. One of the two examples of intricate resonant structures we can utilize is fireflies. Based on empirical studies, it seems that a key factor in how firefly populations coordinate the synchronization of their bioluminescent flashing is through visual perception [45].

It is less clear how each neuron communicates with the others when neuronal synchronization occurs in the brain. Neural synchronization that happens too quickly, relying solely on electrochemical neuronal communication, is known as electrical field gamma synchrony; it requires electrical field signaling, according to Freeman's studies of the brains of rabbits and cats. As noted by Freeman and Vitiello [38], the beta and gamma bands of carrier waves often re-synchronize over large distances in minuscule time lags, according to high-temporal-resolution EEG readings, providing evidence for a variety of intermittent spatial patterns. Axodendritic synaptic transmission, the predominant mechanism for brain interactions, should cause the EEG oscillations to experience distance-dependent delays because of successive synaptic delays and restricted propagation velocities. The coherence of global brain gamma "synchrony" cannot be adequately explained by gap junction coupling alone, according to Craddock et al. [46]. However, what is currently known suggests strongly that shared resonance plays a critical role in the development of mammalian consciousness, including human consciousness.

3.4. How Is Shared Resonance Attained in Resonating Structures?

How do entities that are in communication with one another through resonance modify their resonance frequencies to reach resonance with one another? In many circumstances, entities that are initially unsynchronized manage to become entrained. What driving forces are behind these processes?

We may compare the mechanisms that enable firefly synchrony to conscious human activities in terms of how fireflies time their flashes. For instance, our brains send a series of neuronal pulses to our fingers when we wish to lift them, causing the desired action. Similar to fireflies, it is conceivable that when a fly decides to flash its lights, its brain sends an electrical pulse to its abdomen. At that point, there are chemical and physiological mechanisms supporting the fly's bioluminescence.

It might seem unusual to attribute intent to fireflies. Nonetheless, it would make sense that fireflies would be aware of and able to intentionally manage their physiological functions, especially those associated with large organs such as their light-producing organ. Their actions are intricate and show a variety of "behavioral correlates of consciousness". By comparing the different neurological and behavioral similarities between humans and other mammals, we may recognize that fireflies probably only have a basic level of conscious awareness without implying that they have anything close to the depth of human consciousness.

Based on the supposition that fireflies possess a primitive kind of consciousness, compared to human consciousness, we may provide a high-level explanation for how their flashes are synchronized without considering the intricacies of sub-level mechanisms. This makes an explanation relatively simple: the body obeys the will of the brain, in the same way that any conscious activity in a person, dog, cat, etc. would be explained. However, the synchronized flashing of fireflies without intellect or consciousness can also be explained. Strogatz and his colleagues proposed that firefly synchrony can be explained by intrinsic biological oscillators that naturally synchronize with nearby additional oscillators [45].

It would be difficult to argue that individual neurons want to be in synchrony, but there is evidence for some form of neuronal consciousness, however basic in comparison to whole-brain consciousness. How is it that neurons synchronize swiftly and regularly? Although numerous indications point to different kinds of field effects, these are still unknown. How this communication occurs in each neuron, allowing them to quickly adjust their electrical cycles to meet rapidly changing macroscopic patterns, is still unknown.

Keppler [47] focused on phase changes observed in mammalian brains and the general "criticality" in which these brains appear to be, meaning that they are very sensitive to even minute changes. It is possible to think of the brain mechanisms underlying conscious activities as a complicated system that functions close to a key point of a phase transition. With appropriate stimulation, the brain can transition from a disordered phase with irregular dynamics and spontaneous activity to an ordered phase with long-range connectivities and stable attractors.

The idea of a "phase transition" could be significant when thinking about the combination problem and macro-consciousness. Phase transitions include the freezing of water into ice and the condensation of water vapor into droplets. Similar to brain states, neural states can oscillate in reaction to seemingly unimportant inputs. Dehaene [36] provides evidence in favor of the theory that mammalian consciousness depends on phase transitions.

Fries describes a trio of the cognitive frequencies of specific electrical brain wave combinations [33,34]. He notes that gamma-band synchronization carries out the attended stimuli's selective communication, beta-band synchronization mediates top-down attentional influences, and a 4 Hz theta rhythm resets the gamma band regularly. Because nature is made up of numerous lawful processes, each will resonate at different frequencies. Additionally, processes that are close to one another may eventually synchronize and resonate at the same frequency.

4. Criticality of Resonating Consciousness
4.1. Interaction of Physical Systems and Consciousness

Hunt [48] and Schooler and associates [49] proposed a set of psychophysical ideas that would clarify how consciousness and physical systems interact. They elaborate on why it is that resonance is essential for establishing macro-scale awareness by combining several micro-conscious entities at different organizational levels.

Without subscribing to panpsychism or panexperientialism [50–53], we can state that connected consciousness is significantly primitive in the vast bulk of matter, with maybe only an electron's or an atom's primitive humming of awareness. However, in certain kinds of groupings of matter, as in sophisticated biological life forms, awareness can grow notably richer in comparison to the bulk of matter [54,55].

All objects could be considered to be at least somewhat conscious based on the observable behavior of electrons, atoms, molecules, bacteria, paramecia, mice, bats, and rats. An emergentist perspective contends that consciousness appeared where it had not before existed and arose at a specific period in the history of each species that experiences consciousness. Panpsychism is the opposing position to this theory.

Panpsychism contends that rather than emerging, matter and the mind have always been connected, and vice versa (these two sides of the same coin are equally significant). However, the mind, which is constantly connected to all matter, is typically quite primitive. Only a very small amount of consciousness exists within an electron or an atom. But as matter becomes more complex, so too does the mind, and vice versa. Nevertheless, in this situation, complexity does not matter. Instead, it is the result of stronger internal and external connections that resonate. A mathematical version of the concept was developed by Hunt [50,54], emphasizing how resonant connections result in larger-scale consciously aware beings and how relevant characteristics may be characterized and measured.

Although we will not go into great detail here, (see [48,50,52,55], supported by others [49,51,53]), according to Tononi and Koch [53], within the context of the integrated information theory, elementary particles are either charged or not. As a result, a proton has one positive charge, an electron has one negative charge, and a photon, which is a carrier of light, has no charge at all. According to Tononi and Koch, charge is a feature that these particles have. A charge is just present in uncharged materials; it does not arise from them. They reason that consciousness is no different. Matter is arranged to give rise to consciousness. It is ingrained in the system's architecture. It is a characteristic of complicated things that cannot be boiled down to the operations of more basic attributes.

When two entities resonate at the same frequency, they bond or join together in a variety of ways. Such common resonance and binding may sometimes lead to the blending of different characteristics of cognitive, perceptual, and motor elements into a more cohesive whole, depending on the entities under discussion [9]. According to the quantum field theory, at the most basic level, matter is more akin to a standing wave of concentrated energy. Each of these waves is regional in both distribution (spatially) and time (temporally).

Since matter is fundamentally wave-like, it is easy to understand how information transference, and ultimately the emergence of macro-conscious forms, are associated with shared resonance. All physical processes are fueled by waves of various kinds, at least partially. Waves collaborate instead of competing when multiple entities resonate at the same frequency. This leads to significantly faster energy and information transfers between the components of whatever resonant structure we are observing, as well as a much wider bandwidth. Subsequently, the information flows merge into a larger harmonic, and the resonant wave shapes of the micro-conscious organism become coherent rather than occurring out of phase (decoherently).

Furthermore, Christof Koch [35] suggested that feedback pathways may play a crucial role in producing a type of standing wave or resonance in the brain network if the information is amplified and sustained in the brain by top-down attention. Beyond the degree of synchronization generated by sensory input alone, neurons can coordinate their spiking activity if they receive more local and widespread feedback. This amplifies their postsynaptic impact in comparison to when they activate independently. On this basis, a significant network of neurons may be developed that is capable of exerting an impact throughout the cortex and between lower brain structures. This would be the slow mode upon which conscious awareness rests, according to Koch.

Expanding on Koch's theories, Fries [33,34] proposed a "communication through coherence" theory. Fries [34] offered the following example of shared resonance concerning neural resonance/coherence: Inputs happen at various times during the excitability cycle due to a lack of coherence, and their effective connection will be consequently reduced. Nonetheless, inputs will spread faster and over a wider bandwidth if they fall within the same excitability cycle.

Through a variety of biophysical information pathways, organisms gain from faster information sharing. More macro-scale levels of consciousness can emerge thanks to these speedier and richer information flows than would be feasible in similar-scale structures like sand heaps or rocks because biological structures are more active and more interconnected than rocks or sand. However, the kind of interconnectivity that is required has to be predicated on resonance processes, which usually cause a phase shift in the information flow rate as a result of the conversion of incoherent structures into coherent ones.

We know that gamma synchrony being a main neurological correlate of consciousness in human brains is a notion supported by Dehaene [36]. He was particularly interested in certain "signatures of consciousness", such as late-onset gamma synchrony [56]. However, a combination of gamma and lower harmonic frequencies is frequently linked to mammalian consciousness [34]. This common resonance creates an electromagnetic field that, through certain neuronal electrochemical firing patterns, might act as the source of macro-conscious information [39,57–60]. Gamma synchrony is used as an example of how more neurons get incorporated into the common gamma synchrony, which Hameroff [56] refers to as "the conscious pilot". This is backed up by other slower-frequency waves [34]. However, when the shared gamma synchrony recedes from specific neurons, it allows those neurons to return to their previous resonance state, resulting in a more localized pattern.

To entrain additional neurons, this moving large-scale wave absorbs them into a semi-stable gamma wave pattern. This allows the pace of information interchange to shift from being mostly electrochemical to electromagnetic and allows the capacity for information processing of the several micro-conscious entities made up by those neuron clusters to be combined into a macro-conscious entity. The larger harmonic is entrained with the smaller-scale harmonics through this process; hence, all of the constituents' "windows" are opened to one another, facilitating more fluid information transmission. The pace of change of macro-consciousness is precisely the same as that of its constituent neurons and associated fields. Figure 1 shows an example of such a procedure.

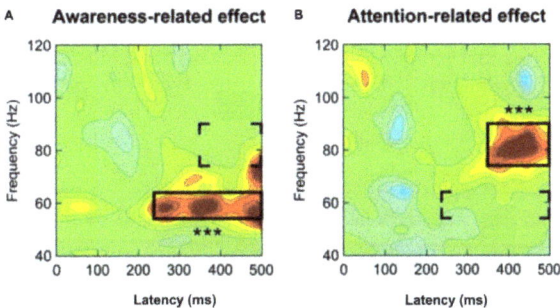

Figure 1. Division of human gamma-band activity in response to a mild visual stimulus into components associated with awareness (**A**) and attention (**B**). When attention is focused on the stimuli, there is strong gamma-band activity 200–250 ms after the stimulus initially appears. This is noteworthy because gamma-band activity associated with putative stimulus awareness started 350 ms post stimulus onset, and this was followed by gamma activity in a higher-frequency zone associated with stimulus-driven selective attention. Given this, while it may not be a reliable indicator of conscious experience, the probability of being aware of the stimuli appears to be correlated with local gamma-band activity in sensory cortical areas starting 200–250 ms after stimulus initiation. Regardless of whether the stimulus was attended to or not, it evoked mid-frequency activity in the gamma range (between 54 and 64 Hz) with a latency of approximately 240 milliseconds post stimulus (left panel). A 350 ms lag was seen in high-frequency gamma-band activity (approximately 76–90 Hz) if spatial (selective) attention was directed toward the stimulus (right panel). The three stars in each panel stand for the effects in the framed regions that are of utmost importance. Either the awareness effects in the regions included in brackets receive attention-related effects, or the awareness effects in the left panel receive attention-related effects (right panel). [Modified from Wyart and Tallon-Baudry [61]; Figure 3C is theirs].

Whitehead [62] indicated that the many become one and are augmented by one. In other words, lower-level entities are employed to create a new, higher-level entity; however, the lower-level entities are not eliminated during the binding process. Rather, they are bound into the new entity, hence increasing the number of entities by one. The many increase one by one until they achieve unity. Numerous subsidiary micro-conscious entities are included when the "conscious pilot" circumnavigates the brain; these numerous aspects of consciousness merge into a single dominating consciousness, leaving the subsidiary consciousnesses alone.

4.2. Connecting Biofield Resonance and Consciousness

Numerous natural phenomena, especially biological ones, appear to critically exist on the cusp of order and chaos [63–67]. It has been demonstrated that criticality-tuned models display brain-like dynamics [68,69], which has given rise to the Critical Brain Hypothesis [70–72]. A variety of helpful informational characteristics are displayed by systems that are tuned to criticality, facilitating the effective dissemination of and receptivity to information [73–76]. For instance, using data from the human connectome, Marinazzo and colleagues showed that information is maximized in an Ising scheme [77,78] at the critical temperature and that, beyond criticality, a law of marginal decreasing returns is attained [79]. These concepts have been expanded upon to more widely imply that critical systems are advantageous to evolution, since they are better at responding to their surroundings and guaranteeing their survival [80,81]. The Ising model is simple and applicable to numerous systems, including the integrated information theory (IIT).

Consciousness can be defined in the context of IIT either by top-down processing or phenomenologically [82–84]. Integrated information measures how processes inside a system interact and restrict one another in emergent, non-reducible ways. This enables us to quantify the characteristics of a system that its parts are unable to describe. For a system to be both highly connected and informative, it must find a balance between segregating forces that serve to distinguish the system and integrating forces that provide new types of information that are not nonexistent within the individual components. These precise characteristics are predicted to appear in Ising models at the beginning of a phase transition, close to the critical temperature.

It should be noted that there is nothing novel about the connection between IIT and the concept of criticality. Kim and Lee have observed that, in a Kuramoto model, criticality and EEG are connected. This describes synchronization [85–87]. The generalized Ising model, which simulates brain dynamics by displaying phase transitions and critical spots, is the simplest model linked to empirical pairwise correlation data [77,88]. Its dynamics have recently been shown to resemble those of the brain, leading to the development of the Critical Brain Hypothesis [89–91].

Criticality may be useful for optimizing the brain's capacity to process information [92], for understanding learning [93], and for memory [25,94,95]. It has also been observed [79] that when characterizing consciousness using IIT with an Ising model as a substrate, "consciousness" experiences a phase shift at criticality in the studied neural network motifs. This suggests, not least because of studies pointing to a possible crucial role of the brain, that "consciousness" might merely be the product of the brain's innate propensity to self-organize towards criticality. Further research into the interdependencies between the two hypotheses in patient and simulation data is made possible by the apparent synergy between the Critical Brain Hypothesis and IIT.

4.3. Grossberg's Input Regarding the Connection between Awareness and Biofield Resonance

How to account for our qualia, or phenomenal experiences, or the mental states that correlate to our experiences, is the difficult problem of consciousness. These could be regarded as the fundamental elements of conscious experience. The study of subjective experience, which originated with Wilhelm Wundt's introspective approach in the late 1800s, is a similar concept in psychology. To answer this problem, a theory of consciousness needs to model how emergent properties (such as self-organization, chaos theory, and self-referentiality theories) of different brain systems interact to incorporate specific features of each conscious psychological experience. In this instance, emergent features function more as a research guide than as an analytical tool. This is achieved by Grossberg's [96] adaptive resonance theory, or ART. Advanced brains may be able to learn to pay attention to, recognize, and predict things and events in a changing environment on their own, according to the cognitive and neurological theory known as ART. As part of its explanation of the mechanical linkages between the processes of consciousness, learning, expectancy, attention, resonance, and synchronization, ART has projected that "all conscious states are resonant states". It offers functional as well as mechanical interpretations of the data, covering a wide range of topics, from the dynamics of conscious perceptual, cognitive, and cognitive–emotional experiences to the synchronization of individual spikes. With the advancement of ART-related science, it is now possible to categorize the brain resonances underlying conscious perceptions of seeing, hearing, experiencing, and knowing. This classification can provide insight into psychological and neurological data in both healthy and sick people. Moreover, not all brain dynamics can be characterized by ART, and not all resonances result in consciousness. Important elements of these explanations of conscious and unconscious processes include the cerebral cortex's organization into distinct cell layers (laminar computing) and the brain's global layout into computationally complementary cortical processing streams (complementary computing).

4.4. Formulating a Theory Linking the Conscious Mind and Resonant Brain Dynamics

Consider a theory in which the interactions of brain mechanisms produce dynamical states that approach the spatiotemporal dynamics and patterning of the resonant neural representations representing discrete conscious qualia, or the parametric properties of these qualia. Additionally, suppose that these resonant states produce observable data about these experiences that come from human subjects' non-invasive neurobiological and psychological experiments, and that these data are consistent with data from various types of neurobiological studies, including multiple-electrode neurophysiological studies on monkeys exposed to the same stimuli. Let us also assume that these resonant states resemble the qualities of the subjective reports of these qualia.

Considering their significant similarities to a variety of data types and experienced qualia, one could argue that these dynamical resonant states are more than just "neural correlates of consciousness" [97]. Instead, they are psychologically grounded, mechanical representations of the qualia that constitute each conscious experience. Strong proof that these brain representations are the sources and maintainers of these conscious sensations would be provided if there were a correlation of this kind between the detailed characteristics of conscious qualia and detailed brain representations for a significant enough body of psychological data. Such a theory would have yielded a hypothesis connecting the conscious mind to brain dynamics. Until the brain–mind connection hypothesis is validated, a "theory of consciousness" cannot be declared.

Should a scientist or philosopher maintain—despite a hypothesis of connection—that a theory of the hard problem cannot contribute to its solution until one can "see red" or "feel fear", then no scientific theory can aspire to resolve the hard problem. This is because current research only explains the dynamical processes involved in the experience of distinct conscious qualia using a mechanical theoretical framework. However, just as the theory of relativity transformed our understanding of space and time and the quantum theory of matter, so too can a well-founded, albeit slowly evolving, theory of consciousness fundamentally transform our understanding of consciousness as it begins to explain an increasing number of distinct psychological, neurobiological, and even biochemical processes. The process of measuring our minds has limits, just like quantum theories. We cannot personally enter a neuron that is involved in conscious experience, just as we cannot personally ride an electron. Despite their limited capacity for empathy, physicists believe they have a solid understanding of the physical world since they can explain and predict enough of it.

4.5. The Conscious Mind and Resonant Dynamics Are Linked by the Adaptive Resonance Theory

Many psychological data concerning an individual's conscious experiences, including their spatiotemporal dynamics, can be explained by ART, in addition to the psychological processes and physiological underpinnings of dynamic brain states whose characteristics resemble the subjective elements of unique conscious experiences. Additionally, ART determines which brain regions these states might occur in and how they might all originate from a single set of identical neural mechanisms, even though these dynamical states each perform distinct functional tasks and are adaptable to different brain regions.

In a dynamic state known as resonance, interactions between top-down and bottom-up pathways produce reciprocal excitatory feedback signals that amplify and synchronize neuronal firings throughout the brain network. Grossberg [96] refers to this type of dynamical state as "adaptive resonance". These synchronized cells frequently oscillate in synchrony with one another through their activity. Resonant cell activity also highlights some cells for attention processes, providing insight into how the brain stores attended events. Because learning can occur within the adaptive weights or long-term memory (LTM) traces that are present at the synapses of these pathways, it is known as an adaptive resonance. Separate conscious qualia, according to ART, may arise as emergent, or interactive, characteristics of specialized neural networks when various specialized anatomies experience an adaptive resonance and receive distinct kinds of input from the brain and the environment. Specifically, ART suggests that in addition to the ability to identify these sensations, brain resonances also serve as parametric components of conscious experiences of feeling, hearing, and seeing.

Most likely, not every cell that maintains an adaptive resonance represents the conscious elements of an event. The capacity to detect psychological discriminations (such as color or fear) that are components of conscious experience is restricted, according to ART, to cells that can only do so at specific brain processing stages. This is supported by neurophysiological data about perceptual experiences [98], which have been described and, in some cases, even predicted by neural models [99]. If resonance is a more general concept than consciousness, then a theory about this more general concept would have to explain why this is the case as well as how conscious states arise from that broader function. Accordingly, it is false to say that "all resonant states are conscious states", despite ART's prediction that "all conscious states are resonant states". Brain dynamics can also happen in the absence of resonance potential, particularly during the formation of motor and spatial representations. Certain conscious experiences might not be supported in this situation.

It is important to remember that awareness was not the initial intended application of ART, even though it can shed light on the brain's underpinnings of conscious experiences. Instead, it was intended to provide predictions and insights for large-scale databases pertaining to the understanding of learning, perception, emotion, and cognition in psychology and neuroscience. Reviewing aspects of how ART explains data whose features naturally lead to brain representations of conscious qualia is important to build a self-contained exposition, and in particular to allow for new data explanations and predictions about ART. It is also interesting that the current work accounts for a far greater amount of awareness-related evidence than prior research employing ART or any other concept does. It goes beyond summarizing ART; it accomplishes more than that. A large number of the conclusions regarding consciousness that the article makes also depend on the synthesis of different but concurrent streams of modeling research that are compiled into a single piece. Examining the salient characteristics of these several modeling streams is necessary to provide a self-contained description of their synthesis. To distinguish it from its forebears, this synthesis and expansion of the ART model is known as the conscious ART, or cART, model.

No other theory has been able to explain the functional significance of a wide range of neurobiological and psychological data, both normal and clinical, until the present cART theory. This holds regardless of whether one is interested in the hard problem or whether one's definition of the hard problem precludes any scientific theory.

4.6. The Conflict between Stability and Adaptability and Lifelong Learning

Throughout their lives, humans can quickly assimilate vast amounts of new information and integrate it into coherent conscious experiences that aid in the development of a sense of identity. All it takes to be amazed by this ability is to see an opera once, after which we can recall a great deal of information about it, including conscious moments of seeing, hearing, feeling, and knowing. Humans can pick up new information quickly without losing sight of what they already know, even in situations where we are unaware of how the laws of any given environment alter or evolve. When forgetting of this kind does happen, it is called catastrophic forgetting.

The phrase "stability–plasticity conundrum" was originally used by Grossberg [100] to describe how the brain learns new information rapidly and reliably without losing track of previously learned information. ART was created to explain how brains deal with the stability–plasticity dilemma. Over time, it has evolved into a neurological and cognitive theory that explains how the brain can learn to predict, identify, and pay attention to objects and events on its own in a changing environment, thereby preventing catastrophic forgetting. Of all the existing theories of cognition and neurology, ART offers the widest range of predictions and explanations.

How does the ART tale involve consciousness? ART allowed for the discovery of mechanical connections between learning, expectation, attention, resonance, and synchronization processes in the brain to explain psychological facts about seeing, hearing, experiencing, and knowing. The stability–plasticity problem was thus handled. Because similar resonances were seen in the spatiotemporal patterning of cell activity inside networks of feature detectors, it became evident from these findings that they also displayed parametrical properties of individual conscious experiences. The functional units of the brain's short-term memory (STM) and long-term memory (LTM) are distributed patterns across networks of feature-selective cells, as early mathematical studies have demonstrated [101]. Subsequent studies have demonstrated how these dispersed patterns facilitate synchronous resonant states that direct attention toward the brain's key information-representative characteristics, like feature patterns that reflect the parametric characteristics of distinct conscious experiences. These discoveries over several decades contributed to an increasing understanding of the connections among consciousness, learning, expectation, attention, resonance, and synchrony processes (CLEARS).

According to ART, any brain representation that resolves the stability–plasticity paradox uses a variation of the CLEARS process [96]. The reasons for why "all conscious states are resonant states", that a large number of animals are intentional beings that pay attention to salient objects, and that brains are capable of learning both many-to-many and many-to-one maps—representations that provide us with extensive information about specific objects and events—are all explained by CLEARS mechanisms.

Bhatt et al. and others claim that ART is responsible for achieving these qualities [102,103]. More specifically, when a top-down anticipation and a bottom-up input pattern sufficiently match, a synchronous resonant state incorporates an attentional focus. This also explains how top-down attentive matching may help to resolve the stability–plasticity conundrum by focusing attention on salient combinations of cues, known as critical feature patterns, which characterize how attention may operate via a form of self-normalizing "biased competition". This resonance's capacity to accelerate learning suppresses unobserved outliers that might have led to catastrophic forgetting and incorporates the attended critical feature pattern into the top-down expectations that the recognition categories read out, as well as the bottom-up adaptive filters that activate them. Adaptive resonance comes from this source.

Research in the fields of psychology and neurobiology has confirmed several connections between the mechanisms represented in the CLEARS mnemonic. For instance, ART predictions for somatosensory learning [104,105] and auditory learning [106] are consistent with the link between attention and learning. From the normal and abnormal aspects of human and animal perception and cognition to the spiking and oscillatory dynamics of hierarchically organized laminar thalamocortical and corticocortical networks in multiple modalities, ART has been continuously developed to explain and predict ever-larger behavioral and neurobiological databases [100].

4.7. Why Not AI Representations?

We must explain why artificial intelligence (AI) and artificial neural network techniques are not a part of the paradigm being supported and developed here to fully justify our position. While being a major advocate of energy-based models, Yann LeCun [107] has given less attention to probabilistic graphical models that give a probability to each potential combination of relevant components that could exist. He has employed "energy-based models (EBM)" that establish a connection between energy and configurations that eliminate the need for suitable normalization of probability distributions. Such systems must be trained to be discriminative to associate lower energy with acceptable configurations and higher energies with bad configurations. While we briefly describe the overall problem with AI models below, the main issue is that they are undoubtedly artificial and not very intelligent in comparison with human neurocognitive functions [108].

It has been commonly thought that the mind functions in the brain similarly to a computer [108]. These theories overlook aspects of neurophysiology that conflict with the process of modeling the brain computationally. Glial cells comprise around 80% of the brain; at all levels of neural processes, such as dendritic–dendritic processing, electrotonic gap junctions, cytoplasmic/cytoskeletal activity, and living conditions (the brain is alive!), these cells demonstrate broad apparent randomness. Moreover, the emergence theory does not contain any testable hypotheses. We may process cognitive events when we have some degree of volitional control or coordination, knowledge of our senses and experiences (i.e., cognition), or both. Consciousness emerges spontaneously; no threshold or reason is required. The idea that the human brain functions similarly to a computer has been advanced for nearly fifty years by psychologists, linguists, and neuroscientists who study human behavior. Examining how the infant's brain develops refutes the computer analogy. Computers are guided in everything they do by algorithms. But that is not how people operate as individuals do.

In light of this, why do so many researchers discuss mental health and cognition using language that sounds like it was generated by a computer system? It is difficult, if not impossible, to comprehend intelligent human behavior without the problematic information processing (IP) model. A flawed syllogism with two reasonable premises and a fallacious conclusion forms the basis of the IP paradigm. The idea that all computers are capable of intelligent behavior is the first tenable assumption.

The idea that all computers contain information processors is a second tenable assumption. The erroneous conclusion: every organism capable of information processing is capable of intelligent action. Beyond technical terms, it is counterproductive to assume that simply because computers analyze data, so should humans. Historians will probably see the IP metaphor in the same way that we do with mechanical and hydraulic analogies when it is finally abandoned. Rather than utilizing a model more closely associated with physical ideas such as resonance to observe and quantify occurrences, let us employ a more intelligent and natural approach to "artificial intelligence".

5. Coherence in Resonance

Fries [34] uses his communication through coherence (CTC) paradigm to explain how resonance among various brain regions has a part in "selected communication" (i.e., when coherent and resonant, the "windows" are open; when incoherent and not resonant, they are closed). Furthermore, coherence enables certain neurons to synchronize with the main resonance frequency. Fries [34] states that communication requires coherence. When there is a lack of coherence, the excitability cycle experiences random inputs, which reduces effective connectivities. A postsynaptic neural group responds mostly to the coherent presynaptic group when it receives inputs from many presynaptic groups. Selective communication is thus accomplished by selective coherence.

A lack of coherence causes inputs to come at random times during the excitability cycle, which lowers effective connectivities. If one group of synaptic inputs, which collectively create one neural representation, can elicit postsynaptic excitation followed by inhibition, then further synaptic inputs will be unable to enter the cell because inhibition will have prevented that from happening. Consequently, these additional inputs are unable to inhibit themselves, and they cannot communicate the neuronal image that they generate. By entraining the postsynaptic neuronal group's perisomatic inhibition and instructing it to follow its rhythm, this tactic creates a selective or exclusive communication channel. Figure 2 is an example of optimizing inter-regional brain communication.

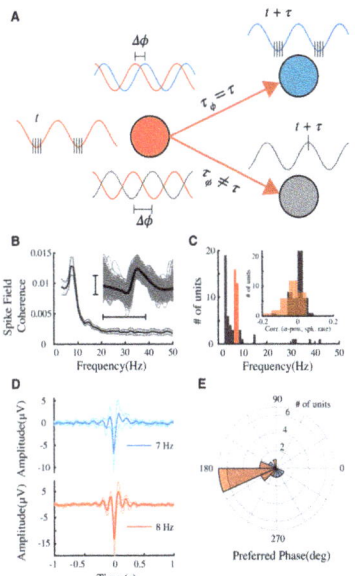

Figure 2. Diagram demonstrating the concept of communication through rhythm. (**A**) If neurons preferentially fire at a particular phase of an oscillation and the oscillations at two sites are coherent with a phase delay matching the conduction delay between them, spikes generated at the excitable phase in one region will arrive at the excitable phase in the downstream region. The construction of a communication line between two coherent zones is a feasible application for these periodic bursts of peak gain. On the other hand, if the phase and latency are not the same, spikes that occur outside of the excitable phase are less likely to result in firing (**B**) Average spike-field coherence (SFC) spectrum, with a distinct peak in the alpha band (f = [7, 8] Hz) for the average SFC spectrum across all units. The mean waveform (black) and individual spike waveforms (grey) for a single example unit are shown in the inset. The horizontal scale bar is 1.5 ms; the vertical scale bar is 10 SD. (**C**) Peak frequency histogram for each unit. Distributions of correlations between instantaneous firing rate and LFP alpha power are shown in the inset. For alpha coherent units (orange), alpha power and spike rate are generally negatively associated, while for all other units (grey), there is no correlation. (**D**) Spike-triggered average for the units at f = [7, 8] Hz with the maximum SFC. Multiple-cycle alpha oscillations are observed. (**E**) Phase preference for the alpha coherent units. (adapted from Chapeton et al. [109], with permission).

It is now thought that small organisms merged to create the organelles of highly developed eukaryotic cells, such as mitochondria, which subsequently came together to form multicellular organisms [110]. It seems plausible that life acquired the ability to incorporate subjective perceptions into hierarchically nested groups of more advanced consciousness at the same time that it obtained the ability to unite various living units into more complicated solitary life forms. The hypothesis that was suggested by Zeki and Bartel [111,112] to explain how consciousness develops from neuronal activity in the brain relies on this hierarchical view of awareness.

Zeki and Bartel [111,112] contend that the brain arranges multiple conscious experiences hierarchically to produce a single, cohesive experience using processing rate variations in various visual system components. They proposed that consciousness exists on three different hierarchical levels in the brain: unified consciousness, which corresponds to the experience of the individual experiencing the perception; micro-consciousness, which corresponds to the diverse visual system levels (for example, V4 processes color and V5 motion); and macro-consciousness, which combines numerous aspects of the system (e.g., color binding to motion).

Zeki further suggests that there is a specific temporal order in which each of these nested levels of awareness happens, with the lower-order levels coming before and influencing the higher-order ones. The reason for this is that the lower-order levels are more fundamental. Zeki's model can be explained as follows [112]. According to Zeki, there are three distinct hierarchical levels of awareness: micro-, macro-, and united consciousness. One level must depend on the presence of the level below it. One might imagine a temporal hierarchy at each level. For the micro-consciousness level, this has been demonstrated, since color and motion are perceived differently. Zeki [110] claims that it has been demonstrated that binding across characteristics takes longer than binding within attributes at the level of macro-consciousnesses". "Myself" is the perceiving individual, the product of individual temporal hierarchies of micro- and macro-consciousnesses leading to a final, combined consciousness.

The smallest sentient observers may be found exclusively in the inorganic world at the atomic and molecular levels. Life's evolution may have given rise to the capacity to organize conscious observers into hierarchies within other conscious observers, with each level embracing a more macroscopic perspective based on the (rudimentary) level of awareness intrinsic to atoms and molecules. When the organism's unified dominating experience occurs, this process ultimately reaches its greatest level.

Zeki divides his suggested levels into chronological sequences, with higher-order events taking place later in time. In other words, Zeki's hypothesis suggests that different brain regions that are involved in consciousness may go through the same experiences for slightly different times and for varied lengths of time, with the ultimate unified awareness involving the longest moments/duration of experience.

6. Integrating Consciousness and Cognition through Resonance

There is evidence that shared electrical resonance is probably the origin of this combination [33,34]. This shared electrical resonance may also be preceded and led by a shared quantum entanglement resonance. The largely unchanging physical structures can support several states of consciousness because of the constantly shifting energy and information fluxes that overlay the typically stable physical structures. This is excellently shown by Fries [33], who challenges whether brain communication is dependent on neuronal synchronization, suggesting that the communication pattern could be altered by dynamic shifts in synchronization. Stable structures are the "backbone" of conscious processes, according to Fries. He thinks that the fundamental components of cognition are these adaptive modifications to the brain's communication system, which are reinforced by the more inflexible anatomical structure, but operate through activity waves.

Constraints on the common resonance states may prevent physical materials from generating macro-consciousness. Situations that are disorganized and non-resonant hinder the exchange of information spatially. Dominant consciousness—like the waking consciousness that people experience—needs large-scale common resonance. There exists a hierarchy of resonance in brain networks [113,114]. Even when higher-level resonance, which represents more degrees of integration, is temporarily absent (such as during a seizure, sleep, or death), lower-level resonance may still exist, necessitating less information integration (death, in which case lower-level resonances may continue for some time but will also, before too long, dissipate). Small spaces may prevent physical materials from developing macro-awareness [113,114].

These mechanisms may account for the observed phenomenon of important brain regions synchronizing at regional levels during seizures in the absence of global consciousness [115]. Characterizing conscious experiences during absence seizures is often challenging since higher levels of organization lose their characteristic synchrony while lower-level systems (local and individual clusters of neurons) remain in synchrony [25,27,116]. Since resonance reflects the physical structure's dynamics, changes in resonance and awareness states do not affect the stability of the physical structure.

Some additional examples supporting the importance of resonance supporting physiological processes associated with consciousness and cognition might include a dyskinesic individual's symptoms being eradicated by light filters. We have also included references to the effects of transcranial DC magnetic stimulation (tDCS) on consciousness and cognition, which, although beyond the scope of the present paper, has garnered enough recent support to better understand the relation between resonance and physiological function [117–119].

7. Cortical Activity Waves as a Vehicle for Consciousness and Cognition

7.1. Continuum Waves in Consciousness and Cognition

The concept of "continuum waves" is not a well-established term in cognitive science or neuroscience. However, if we interpret it in a broader sense as referring to the continuous flow of neural activity and information processing in the brain, we can explore how it might relate to thought processes. In cognitive neuroscience, thoughts are understood to emerge from complex patterns of neural activity and information processing within the brain. This activity involves the coordinated firing of neurons across various brain regions, forming intricate networks that give rise to cognitive processes such as perception, attention, memory, reasoning, and problem solving.

If we consider "continuum waves" as metaphorically representing the dynamic and continuous nature of neural activity, we can think of thoughts as emerging from the modulation and interaction of these waves within the brain. Different types of thoughts, such as memories, emotions, or abstract reasoning, may correspond to distinct patterns or frequencies of neural oscillations and connectivity.

Furthermore, the concept of continuum waves could also encompass the idea that thoughts exist on a spectrum, ranging from automatic and subconscious processes to deliberate and conscious ones. Just as waves in the ocean vary in intensity and frequency, thoughts can vary in their level of awareness and control.

Overall, while the term "continuum waves" may not have a direct counterpart in cognitive science, we can conceptualize how the continuous flow of neural activity and information processing in the brain underlies the generation and modulation of thoughts across different domains of cognition.

7.2. Continuum Analysis Applied to Consciousness and Cognition

Mammalian brains differ from reptile brains in that they have a layered anatomy [120], which implies that possessing this structure has some evolutionary advantage. We here propose that the layered cortex structure permits a time delay in the interconnections between its layers and that this temporal lag efficiently controls brain activity waves, which are cortical tissue's resonant modes and the electrochemical energy they store. When enough energy is stored, these waves expand as they move to locations that are substantially farther from their origin than the normal axonal length, and they interact with most of the cells in their path until they reach their saturated amplitude.

The forgoing is grounded on the revolutionary continuum analysis of Wilson and Cowan [121,122], applied to a simple two-filamentary layered system separated by a uniform time delay in space and undergoing modest temporal variations [123]. In the Wilson–Cowan model, all other components are driven by synaptic flux into hypothetical "continuum elements", acting as reservoirs of energy; flux and stored energy are connected via what is compared to a "leaky capacitor". The energy is stored in the excitatory (e) and inhibitory (i) activities of the constituent cells, which are considered to be of these two types. The internal energy of each species is considered independently. Elements can be connected in four distinct ways: e-e, i-i, i-e, and i-e. The afferent species is indicated by the first index, while the efferent species is shown by the second index. The length of the typical connection probability of each afferent species is termed the connection range, which is the amount of time that decreases with distance along the layers [121].

The neuronal continuum can be impacted by waves of spreading and rising activity [124,125]. When one element exhibits some excess of excitatory activity, the return i-e connections lower the excitatory surplus in the originating element, while the e-i connections to adjacent elements raise the inhibitory activity. Oscillations are linked to an overcorrection, as is often the case. Meanwhile, e-e and i-i linkages stimulate development and proliferation by way of transmission to additional elements. Since the factors governing wavelength and frequency are essentially constant and only vary through synaptic modulation, this approach does not meet the requirements for carriers of cognitive processes [126].

Due to the phase relations necessary for the amplification of waves, the delay adds control. The wave is now generated as before by an excitatory surplus element, but it separates in two, with one half propagating to the opposite layer with a delay of T. The relationship between activity and flux in the second layer leads to a phase shift approximating $\pi/2$. A similar procedure is followed to return to the original layer. Amplification occurs only when the total phase shift is an even multiple of π. Consequently, the link between the delay and the angular temporal frequency of the favored wave is multivalued.

$$\omega T = (n + \frac{1}{2})\pi \quad n = 0, 1, \ldots \tag{1}$$

The integer n that yields the fastest growth—which is initially exponential—is the one selected in each given scenario [127]. The chosen mode typically becomes observably dominant at this growth rate. Nonetheless, both modes expand at those values of T where their growth rates are equivalent, and this situation continues until T reaches a point when the new mode takes precedence. When it comes to activity waves, the propagation speed increases with the wavelength, and the wavelength is a single-valued function of frequency. As a result, the waves move through space at various speeds and occupy various locations, creating a highly erratic pattern of activity in between.

7.3. The Wilson–Cowan Equations

The relative active percentages A_{sl} $s = e, i, l = 0,1$ at time t of the various species in the two layers, within an element centered at position x, are the dependent variables in our model (there are four in total).

$$\frac{\partial}{\partial t} A_{sl} + A_{sl} = S(N_{sl}) \tag{2}$$

Here, N reflects the synaptic flux into the element from all other elements, weighted by the inter-layer signal latency, and by the connection probability decreasing with distance.

$$N_{sl}(x,t) = \sum_{u=e,i} \sum_{m=0,1} \int_{-\infty}^{\infty} B_{us,ml} A_{u,m}(X, t - T_{ml}) e^{\frac{-|X-x|}{\sigma_{us,ml}}} \tag{3}$$

The connection coefficients $B_{us,ml}$ possess, when the cells are in the same position laterally, a cell of species u and layer m, with an afferent connection probability that is proportionate to the species and layer in question.

The connection probability between the afferent element at position X and the element at location x, which decreases with lateral distance, is described by the exponent; the connection range $\sigma_{us,ml}$ is considered to exclusively depend on the afferent species. All inter-layer connection parameters and connections within the layers, in this calculation, are assumed to be the same in both directions. Delay T_{ml} applies only if m and l relate to different layers when it equals T. A typical synapse's synaptic energy is represented by the attention parameter F. T and F remain constant here and the integral encompasses all of the space, whereas the sums cover both the species and strata.

The sigmoid function S must be used as a flow limiter, since, when all cells are active, the total stored energy cannot vary, nor can it decrease when none are. Since it is assumed that both species and layers have an equilibrium activity level, which is taken to be $\frac{1}{2}$, the active fractions fall between $-\frac{1}{2}$ and $\pm\frac{1}{2}$. When the synaptic flux is zero, S's functional form is zero with a slope of one. A decrease toward the equilibrium with a time constant of unity is represented by the second term in (2).

7.4. Numerical Results

$$N_{sl}(x,t) = \sum_{u=0,1} \sum_{m=e,i} \int_{-\infty}^{\infty} dX B_{us,ml} A_{u,m}(X, t - T_{ml}) e^{\frac{-|X-x|}{\sigma_{us,ml}}} \qquad (4)$$

The excitatory active fraction is considered to have been subjected to a δ-function impulse with amplitude of 0.0001 (above equilibrium) at time zero, and the first time step is carried out analytically to seed all the points. A convergence test is included in the Runge–Kutta–Fehlberg (RKF) method, which is used to simultaneously solve the equations in (2). A cubic spline integrated analytically is used to compute the integral in (3) at each function evaluation (using discrete approaches results in spurious spectral lines). The same-layer inhibitory connection range acts as the spatial unit and is used to represent all other ranges.

The 2048 amplitudes are written at intervals of several time steps in temporary files to account for the time delay; linear interpolation is employed to obtain the intermediate values required for the RKF test. To avoid end effects, the computation is terminated when a detectable signal reaches the final point. Fast Fourier Transform (*fft*) is used after every time step; this establishes the connection between wavelength λ is λ = 256/k and spectral variable k.

The findings for two values of delay are shown in Figures 3 and 4. Only positive amplitudes are displayed for clarity's sake. Since the neural refractory period is longer, the negative amplitudes are slightly bigger [121].

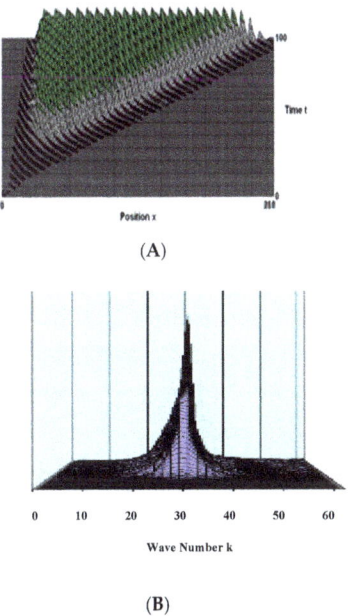

(A)

(B)

Figure 3. (**A**) The wave produced at time zero by a very slight variation (0.0001) in the excited fraction in an element located at layer 0 position. Here, we see the exponential growth of the wave amplitude in the stimulated layer, which is driven by the flux limit to saturation, with a maximum amplitude of around 0.4. Time units are decay durations, while spatial units are the same-layer inhibitory range. (**B**) The identical wave's spectral intensity is a function of time and wave number k (into the diagram). In the same layer, the connection parameters are the following: $B_{ee} = 3.5$, $B_{ei} = 5.9$, $B_{ie} = -4.8$, $B_{ii} = -2.5$, $\sigma_e = 1.25$, $\sigma_i = 1.0$; for opposite layers, $B_{ee} = 3.0$, $B_{ei} = 1.1$, $B_{ie} = B_{ii} = -1.0$, $\sigma_e = \sigma_{ii} = 0.6$. The attention factor $F = 0.45$, and the time delay $T = 2.4$.

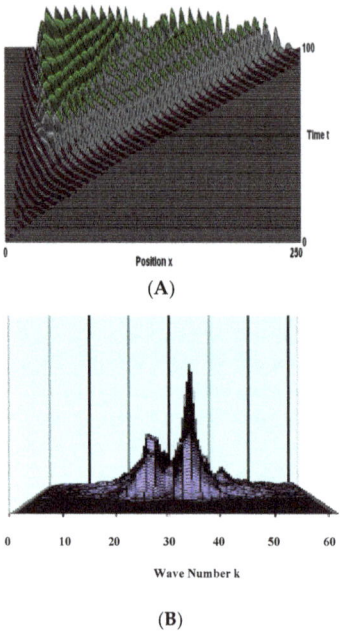

(A)

(B)

Figure 4. Here, the parameters are the same as in Figure 3, except the delay T is 3.6 decay periods. The initial noise now generates two waves, with different wavelengths. The propagation speed increases with increasing wavelength so that the waves occupy different spatial regions. There is erratic activity in the intermediate space. The energy is spread between the two spectral peaks, as shown by their lesser amplitudes. Later on, a non-linear interference excites other waves with shorter wavelengths.

Figure 4 shows the scenario at a different value, in contrast.

The wave in Figure 3 is coherent due to its regularity and narrow spectral peak. Despite the random position of the starting noise, active and inactive elements behave in lockstep when they are one wavelength apart. Two waves are produced under the parameters shown in Figure 4; they propagate at different speeds and occupy various spatial regions, have different growth rates, and have different wavelengths. There is erratic activity in the middle space. Figure 5 depicts the influence the delay has:

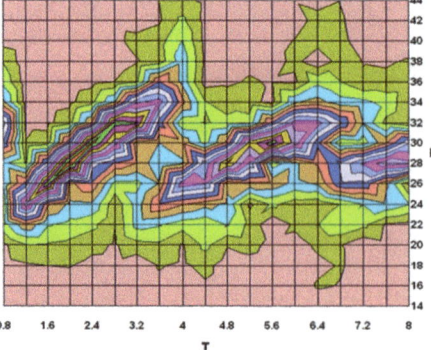

Figure 5. An example of a contour plot showing the spectral intensity against delay for a set of studies with constant delays after stimulation (80 decay periods). The remaining variables are the same as those in the figures that came before.

The preferred wavelength when just one wave is growing is a (decreasing) function of delay; altering the delay reorganizes the neurons into a subset that they were previously arranged into. Because the linked group is reconstituted (almost exactly) upon repeating a value of T, this procedure can be compared to a memory search. Regarding the theories of memory storage, we remain neutral and do not make any assumptions about the relationship between the waves and semantic content. However, since our simplistic model closely resembles the real cortex, these theories need to account for activity waves, which are the corresponding resonant modes.

8. Conclusions: Resonance Signatures Allow Us to Adapt and Effectively Interact with Our Environment

A multitude of delays and ensuing rhythms are possible due to the human cortex's six layers. There is currently no explanation for the different electroencephalographic frequency bands' origins [128,129]. It is evident that the current theory directly addresses that issue.

Since the location of the irregular wave pattern is fixed in only concerning the origin, the random placement of the first stimulus affects when two waves are produced. As a result, there are a wide variety of potential neuronal firing patterns in these situations. In the spirit of the continuum analysis, which divides cells into components, there are relatively fewer, but still a huge number of options, if each subset of individual cortical cells reflects a unique thought. There are about 106 billion such possibilities for about 20 billion cortical cells.

This hypothesis does not explain how these patterns are "decoded" into a combination of memories from the past and the semantic content of various wave memories or conscious awareness. It might, however, provide as an illustration of how cognitive research can benefit from the study of brain tissue as organized resonating media.

Each part of one's brain and body probably has its own resonance signature. These signals can fluctuate subtly from moment to moment, possibly fluctuating around the average frequency value. It has been hypothesized that the major cause of conscious experiences is the process by which our brains learn new knowledge about an ever-changing reality throughout our entire lives. Developing resonant states between bottom-up and top-down processes, learning top-down expectations, matching them with bottom-up data, and concentrating our attention on the predicted information clusters as they come to a consensus between what is expected and what is real in the outside world are examples of some of these processes.

Every conscious experience in the brain is thought to be a resonant condition, and learning, sensation, and their associated cognitive representations are caused by these resonant situations (see Grossberg [116]). As we gain more knowledge about the environment, our sensory and cognitive representations of it can hold true, according to Grossberg's idea. Our bodies can unlearn irrelevant learned maps as our motor and spatial representations develop from childhood to adulthood. This happens as a result of the brain trying to keep up with the body's changes. We conclude that procedural memories are not conscious because resonance cannot be produced by the inhibitory matching processes that underpin spatial and motor actions. Resonance, then, is the language that enables effective communication with our external and inner environments as well as with other people. Activity waves are how criticality is governed; but what governs them?

Author Contributions: Conceptualization, G.L. and P.K.; Methodology, G.L. and P.K.; Software, P.K.; Validation, G.L. and P.K.; Formal analysis, G.L. and P.K.; Investigation, G.L. and P.K.; Data curation, G.L. and P.K.; Writing—original draft, G.L. and P.K.; Writing—review & editing, G.L.; Visualization, G.L. and P.K. All authors have read and agreed to the published version of the manuscript.

Funding: This research received no external funding.

Institutional Review Board Statement: Not applicable.

Informed Consent Statement: Not applicable.

Data Availability Statement: No new data were created or analyzed in this study. Data sharing is not applicable to this article.

Conflicts of Interest: The author declares no conflict of interest.

References

1. Tacoma Bridge. Available online: https://www.youtube.com/watch?v=3mclp9QmCGs (accessed on 18 March 2023).
2. Bare, J.E. Resonant Frequency Therapy Device. US Patent 6,221,094, 24 April 2001. Available online: https://patents.google.com/patent/US5908441A/en (accessed on 16 May 2023).
3. Bare, J.E. Resonant Frequency Therapy Device. US Patent 5,908,441, 1 June 1999. Available online: https://patents.google.com/patent/US6221094B1/en (accessed on 16 May 2023).
4. Bare, J.E. Resonant Frequency Therapy Device. US Patent 8,652,184, 18 February 2014. Available online: https://patents.google.com/patent/US8652184B2/en (accessed on 16 May 2023).
5. Pitt, W.G. *Protein Adsorption on Polyurethanes (FTIR)*; University of Wisconsin Press: Madison, WI, USA, 1987.
6. Mittelstein, D.R.; Ye, J.; Schibber, E.F.; Roychoudhury, A.; Martinez, L.T.; Fekrazad, M.H.; Ortiz, M.; Lee, P.P.; Shapiro, M.G.; Gharib, M. Selective ablation of cancer cells with low intensity pulsed ultrasound. *Appl. Phys. Lett.* **2020**, *116*, 013701. [CrossRef]
7. Buckner, C.A.; Buckner, A.L.; Koren, S.A.; Persinger, M.A.; Lafrenie, R.M. Inhibition of cancer cell growth by exposure to a specific time-varying electromagnetic field involves T-type calcium channels. *PLoS ONE* **2015**, *10*, e0124136. [CrossRef]
8. Kang, C.; Li, Y.; Novak, D.; Zhang, Y.; Zhou, Q.; Hu, Y. Brain networks of maintenance, inhibition and disinhibition during working memory. *IEEE Trans. Neural Syst. Rehabil. Eng.* **2020**, *28*, 1518–1527. [CrossRef] [PubMed]
9. Leisman, G. On the Application of Developmental Cognitive Neuroscience in Educational Environments. *Brain Sci.* **2022**, *12*, 1501. [CrossRef]
10. Leisman, G.; Melillo, R. Front and center: Maturational dysregulation of frontal lobe functional neuroanatomic connections in attention deficit hyperactivity disorder. *Front. Neuroanat.* **2022**, *16*, 936025. [CrossRef] [PubMed]
11. Ma, Z.; Turrigiano, G.G.; Wessel, R.; Hengen, K.B. Cortical circuit dynamics are homeostatically tuned to criticality in vivo. *Neuron* **2019**, *104*, 655–664. [CrossRef] [PubMed]
12. Miller, R.A.; Miller, I. The Schumann's resonances and human psychobiology. *Nexus Mag.* **2003**, *10*, 43–49.
13. McCraty, R.; Al Abdulgader, A. Consciousness, the human heart and the global energetic field environment. *Cardiol. Vasc. Res* **2021**, *5*, 1–19. [CrossRef]
14. Liu, J.; Huang, J.; Li, Z.; Zhao, Z.; Zeren, Z.; Shen, X.; Wang, Q. Recent Advances and Challenges in Schumann Resonance Observations and Research. *Remote Sens.* **2023**, *15*, 3557. [CrossRef]
15. Kruglov, A.G.; Kruglov, A.A.; Utkin, V.N. Resonant Interaction of the Psyche, Circadian Rhythms and External Electromagnetic Fields. *Curr. J. Appl. Sci. Technol.* **2023**, *42*, 23–30. [CrossRef]
16. Leisman, G.; Machado, C. Many Paths to Consciousness or Just One? Life in a Bounded Continuum. *J. Conscious. Stud.* **2021**, *28*, 83–96.
17. Young, A.; Hunt, T.; Ericson, M. The slowest shared resonance: A review of electromagnetic field oscillations between central and peripheral nervous systems. *Front. Hum. Neurosci.* **2022**, *15*, 796455. [CrossRef] [PubMed]
18. Garvanova, M.; Garvanov, I.; Borissova, D. The influence of electromagnetic fields on human brain. In Proceedings of the 2020 21st International Symposium on Electrical Apparatus & Technologies (SIELA), Bourgas, Bulgaria, 3–6 June 2020; IEEE: Piscataway, NJ, USA, 2020; pp. 1–4.
19. Leisman, G.; Moustafa, A.A.; Shafir, T. Thinking, walking, talking: Integratory motor and cognitive brain function. *Front. Public Health* **2016**, *4*, 179575. [CrossRef]
20. Signorelli, C.M.; Szczotka, J.; Prentner, R. Explanatory profiles of models of consciousness-towards a systematic classification. *Neurosci. Conscious.* **2021**, *2021*, niab021. [CrossRef] [PubMed]
21. Toker, D.; Pappas, I.; Lendner, J.D.; Frohlich, J.; Mateos, D.M.; Muthukumaraswamy, S.; Carhart-Harris, R.; Paff, M.; Vespa, P.M.; Monti, M.M.; et al. Consciousness is supported by near-critical slow cortical electrodynamics. *Proc. Natl. Acad. Sci. USA* **2022**, *119*, e2024455119. [CrossRef] [PubMed]
22. Leisman, G.; Alfasi, R.; D'Angiulli, A. The development of fetal primary consciousness: An emergent transitions framework. *Curr. Opin. Behav. Sci.* **2024**, in press.
23. Hebb, D. *The Organisation of Behavior: A Neuropsychological Theory*; Wiley: New York, NY, USA, 1948.
24. Koch, P.; Leisman, G. A continuum model of activity waves in layered neuronal networks: Computer models of brain-stem seizures. In Proceedings of the Third Annual IEEE Symposium on Computer-Based Medical Systems, Chapel Hill, NC, USA, 3–6 June 1990; IEEE: Piscataway, NJ, USA, 1990; pp. 525–531.
25. Koch, P.; Leisman, G. Cortical Activity waves are the physical carriers of memory and thought. In Proceedings of the 2015 7th International IEEE/EMBS Conference on Neural Engineering (NER), Montpellier, France, 22–24 April 2015; IEEE: Piscataway, NJ, USA, 2015; pp. 364–367.

26. Leisman, G.; Koch, P. Networks of conscious experience: Computational neuroscience in understanding life, death, and consciousness. *Rev. Neurosci.* **2009**, *20*, 151–176. [CrossRef] [PubMed]
27. Hammerschlag, R.; Jain, S.; Baldwin, A.L.; Gronowicz, G.; Lutgendorf, S.K.; Oschman, J.L.; Yount, G.L. Biofield research: A roundtable discussion of scientific and methodological issues. *J. Altern. Complement. Med.* **2012**, *18*, 1081–1086. [CrossRef] [PubMed]
28. Hammerschlag, R.; Levin, M.; McCraty, R.; Bat, N.; Ives, J.A.; Lutgendorf, S.K.; Oschman, J.L. Biofield physiology: A framework for an emerging discipline. *Glob. Adv. Health Med.* **2015**, *4* (Suppl. S1), gahmj-2015. [CrossRef]
29. Ho, M.W. *The Rainbow and the Worm: The Physics of Organisms*; World Scientific: Singapore, 2008.
30. Finger, A.M.; Kramer, A. Mammalian circadian systems: Organization and modern life challenges. *Acta Physiol.* **2021**, *231*, e13548. [CrossRef]
31. Doelling, K.; Herbst, S.; Arnal, L.; van Wassenhove, V. *Psychological and Neuroscientific Foundations of Rhythms and Timing*; HAL Open Science: London, UK; Oxford, UK, 2023.
32. Crick, F.; Koch, C. Towards a neurobiological theory of consciousness. *Semin. Neurosci.* **1990**, *2*, 263–275.
33. Fries, P. A mechanism for cognitive dynamics: Neuronal communication through neuronal coherence. *Trends Cogn. Sci.* **2005**, *9*, 474–480. [CrossRef] [PubMed]
34. Fries, P. Rhythms for cognition: Communication through coherence. *Neuron* **2015**, *88*, 220–235. [CrossRef]
35. Koch, C. Qualia. *Curr. Biol.* **2004**, *14*, R496. [CrossRef] [PubMed]
36. Dehaene, S. *Consciousness and the Brain: Deciphering How the Brain Codes Our Thoughts*; Viking Penguin: New York, NY, USA, 2014.
37. Grossberg, S.T. Towards solving the hard problem of consciousness: The varieties of brain resonances and the conscious experiences that they support. *Neural Netw.* **2017**, *87*, 38–95. [CrossRef]
38. Freeman, W.J.; Vitiello, G. Nonlinear brain dynamics as macroscopic manifestation of underlying many-body field dynamics. *Phys. Life Rev.* **2006**, *3*, 93–118. [CrossRef]
39. Pockett, S. *The Nature of Consciousness: A Hypothesis*; Iuniverse: Bloomington, IN, USA, 2000.
40. Pockett, S. The electromagnetic field theory of consciousness a testable hypothesis about the characteristics of conscious as opposed to non-conscious fields. *J. Conscious. Stud.* **2012**, *19*, 191–223.
41. Bandyopadhyay, A. Resonance Chains and New Models of the Neuron. 2019. Available online: https://medium.com/@aramis720/resonance-chains-and-new-models-of-the-neuron-7dd82a5a7c3a (accessed on 15 May 2023).
42. Sahu, S.; Ghosh, S.; Ghosh, B.; Aswani, K.; Hirata, K.; Fujita, D.; Bandyopadhyay, A. Atomic water channel controlling remarkable properties of a single brain microtubule: Correlating single protein to its supramolecular assembly. *Biosens. Bioelectron.* **2013**, *47*, 141–148. [CrossRef]
43. Sahu, S.; Ghosh, S.; Hirata, K.; Fujita, D.; Bandyopadhyay, A. Multi-level memory-switching properties of a single brain microtubule. *Appl. Phys. Lett.* **2013**, *102*, 123701. [CrossRef]
44. Singh, P.; Ray, K.; Fujita, D.; Bandyopadhyay, A. Complete dielectric resonator model of human brain from MRI data: A journey from connectome neural branching to single protein. In *Engineering Vibration, Communication and Information Processing*; Springer: New York, NY, USA, 2019; pp. 717–733.
45. Strogatz, S.H. *Sync: How Order Emerges from Chaos in the Universe, Nature, and Daily Life*; Hachette: London, UK, 2012.
46. Craddock, J.A.; Hameroff, T.R.; Ayoub, S.T.; Klobukowski, M.; Tuszynski, A. Anesthetics act in quantum channels in brain microtubules to prevent consciousness. *Curr. Top. Med. Chem.* **2015**, *15*, 523–533. [CrossRef]
47. Keppler, J. A new perspective on the functioning of the brain and the mechanisms behind conscious processes. *Front. Psychol.* **2013**, *4*, 242. [CrossRef] [PubMed]
48. Hunt, T. Kicking the psychophysical laws into Gear a new approach to the combination problem. *J. Conscious. Stud.* **2011**, *18*, 96–134.
49. Schooler, J.W.; Hunt, T.; Schooler, J.N. Reconsidering the metaphysics of science from the inside out. In *Neuroscience, Consciousness and Spirituality*; Springer: Dordrecht, The Netherlands, 2011; pp. 157–194.
50. Hunt, T. *Eco, Ego, Eros: Essays in Philosophy, Spirituality and Science*; Aramis Press: Arcueil, France, 2014.
51. Goff, P. *Consciousness and Fundamental Reality*; Oxford University Press: Oxford, UK, 2017.
52. Koch, C. Ubiquitous minds. *Sci. Am. Mind* **2014**, *25*, 26–29. [CrossRef]
53. Tononi, G.; Koch, C. Consciousness: Here, there and everywhere? *Philos. Trans. R. Soc. B Biol. Sci.* **2015**, *370*, 20140167. [CrossRef] [PubMed]
54. Hunt, T. Calculating the boundaries of consciousness in general resonance theory. *J. Conscious. Stud.* **2020**, *27*, 55–80.
55. Griffin, D.R. *Unsnarling the World-Knot: Consciousness, Freedom, and the Mind-Body Problem*; University of California Press: Berkeley, CA, USA, 1998; ISBN 0-520-20944-3.
56. Hameroff, S. The "conscious pilot"—Dendritic synchrony moves through the brain to mediate consciousness. *J. Biol. Phys.* **2010**, *36*, 71–93. [CrossRef] [PubMed]
57. Jones, M. Electromagnetic-field theories of mind. *J. Conscious. Stud.* **2013**, *20*, 124–149.
58. McFadden, J. Synchronous Firing and its influence on the brain's electromagnetic field. *J. Conscious. Stud.* **2002**, *9*, 23–50.
59. McFadden, J. The conscious electromagnetic information (Cemi) field theory: The hard problem made easy? *J. Conscious. Stud.* **2002**, *9*, 45–60.

60. John, E.R. A field theory of consciousness. *Conscious. Cogn.* **2001**, *10*, 184–213. [CrossRef]
61. Wyart, V.; Tallon-Baudry, C. Neural dissociation between visual awareness and spatial attention. *J. Neurosci.* **2008**, *28*, 2667–2679. [CrossRef]
62. Whitehead, C. Cultural distortions of self-and reality-perception. *J. Conscious. Stud.* **2010**, *17*, 95–118.
63. Olsen, L.F.; Degn, H. Chaos in biological systems. *Q. Rev. Biophys.* **1985**, *18*, 165–225. [CrossRef] [PubMed]
64. Aon, M.A.; Cortassa, S.; Lloyd, D. Chaos in biochemistry and physiology. *Encycl. Biochem. Mol. Cell Biol. Mol. Med. Syst. Biol.* **2012**, 239–276.
65. Teuscher, C. Revisiting the edge of chaos: Again? *Biosystems* **2022**, *218*, 104693. [CrossRef] [PubMed]
66. Barbieri, S.; Gotta, M. Order from chaos: Cellular asymmetries explained with modelling. *Trends Cell Biol.* **2023**. [CrossRef] [PubMed]
67. Rattigan, B.; Noble, D.; Hatta, A. (Eds.) *The Language of Symmetry*; Chapman & Hall/CRC: Boca Raton, FL, USA, 2023.
68. Gutjahr, N.; Hövel, P.; Viol, A. Controlling extended criticality via modular connectivity. *J. Phys. Complex.* **2021**, *2*, 035023. [CrossRef]
69. Dunham, C.S.; Lilak, S.; Hochstetter, J.; Loeffler, A.; Zhu, R.; Chase, C.; Stieg, A.Z.; Kuncic, Z.; Gimzewski, J.K. Nanoscale neuromorphic networks and criticality: A perspective. *J. Phys. Complex.* **2021**, *2*, 042001. [CrossRef]
70. O'Byrne, J.; Jerbi, K. How critical is brain criticality? *Trends Neurosci.* **2022**, *45*, 820–837. [CrossRef]
71. Korchinski, D.J.; Orlandi, J.G.; Son, S.W.; Davidsen, J. Criticality in spreading processes without timescale separation and the critical brain hypothesis. *Phys. Rev. X* **2021**, *11*, 021059. [CrossRef]
72. Beggs, J.M. Addressing skepticism of the critical brain hypothesis. *Front. Comput. Neurosci.* **2022**, *16*, 703865. [CrossRef] [PubMed]
73. Valverde, S.; Ohse, S.; Turalska, M.; West, B.J.; Garcia-Ojalvo, J. Structural determinants of criticality in biological networks. *Front. Physiol.* **2015**, *6*, 141017. [CrossRef] [PubMed]
74. Calderon, D.P.; Kilinc, M.; Maritan, A.; Banavar, J.R.; Pfaff, D. Generalized CNS arousal: An elementary force within the vertebrate nervous system. *Neurosci. Biobehav. Rev.* **2016**, *68*, 167–176. [CrossRef] [PubMed]
75. Del Papa, B.; Priesemann, V.; Triesch, J. Fading memory, plasticity, and criticality in recurrent networks. *Funct. Role Crit. Dyn. Neural Syst.* **2019**, 95–115. [CrossRef]
76. Cocchi, L.; Gollo, L.L.; Zalesky, A.; Breakspear, M. Criticality in the brain: A synthesis of neurobiology, models and cognition. *Prog. Neurobiol.* **2017**, *158*, 132–152. [CrossRef] [PubMed]
77. Marinazzo, D.; Pellicoro, M.; Wu, G.; Angelini, L.; Cortés, J.M.; Stramaglia, S. Information transfer and criticality in the Ising model on the human connectome. *PLoS ONE* **2014**, *9*, e93616. [CrossRef] [PubMed]
78. Singh, S.P. The ising model: Brief introduction and its application. In *Solid State Physics-Metastable, Spintronics Materials and Mechanics of Deformable Bodies-Recent Progress*; IntechOpen: London, UK, 2020. Available online: https://www.intechopen.com/chapters/71210 (accessed on 17 March 2024).
79. Popiel, N.J.; Khajehabdollahi, S.; Abeyasinghe, P.M.; Riganello, F.; Nichols, E.S.; Owen, A.M.; Soddu, A. The emergence of integrated information, complexity, and 'consciousness' at criticality. *Entropy* **2020**, *22*, 339. [CrossRef]
80. Hidalgo, J.; Grilli, J.; Suweis, S.; Munoz, M.A.; Banavar, J.R.; Maritan, A. Information-based fitness and the emergence of criticality in living systems. *Proc. Natl. Acad. Sci. USA* **2014**, *111*, 10095–10100. [CrossRef]
81. Vilone, D.; Realpe-Gomez, J.; Andrighetto, G. Evolutionary advantages of turning points in human cooperative behavior. *PLoS ONE* **2021**, *16*, e0246278. [CrossRef]
82. Merker, B.; Williford, K.; Rudrauf, D. The integrated information theory of consciousness: A case of mistaken identity. *Behav. Brain Sci.* **2022**, *45*, e41. [CrossRef]
83. Seth, A.K.; Bayne, T. Theories of consciousness. *Nat. Rev. Neurosci.* **2022**, *23*, 439–452. [CrossRef] [PubMed]
84. Northoff, G.; Zilio, F. From shorter to longer timescales: Converging integrated information theory (IIT) with the temporo-spatial theory of consciousness (TTC). *Entropy* **2022**, *24*, 270. [CrossRef] [PubMed]
85. Kim, H.; Lee, U. Criticality as a determinant of integrated information Φ in human brain networks. *Entropy* **2019**, *21*, 981. [CrossRef]
86. Kim, M.; Kim, S.; Mashour, G.A.; Lee, U. Relationship of topology, multiscale phase synchronization, and state transitions in human brain networks. *Front. Comput. Neurosci.* **2017**, *11*, 55. [CrossRef] [PubMed]
87. Lee, H.; Golkowski, D.; Jordan, D.; Berger, S.; Ilg, R.; Lee, J.; Mashour, G.A.; The ReCCognition Study Group. Relationship of critical dynamics, functional connectivity, and states of consciousness in large-scale human brain networks. *Neuroimage* **2019**, *188*, 228–238. [CrossRef] [PubMed]
88. Lombardi, F.; Pepić, S.; Shriki, O.; Tkačik, G.; De Martino, D. Statistical modeling of adaptive neural networks explains co-existence of avalanches and oscillations in resting human brain. *Nat. Comput. Sci.* **2023**, *3*, 254–263. [CrossRef] [PubMed]
89. Beggs, J.M.; Timme, N. Being critical of criticality in the brain. *Front. Physiol.* **2012**, *3*, 163. [CrossRef] [PubMed]
90. Kloucek, M.B.; Machon, T.; Kajimura, S.; Royall, C.P.; Masuda, N.; Turci, F. Biases in inverse Ising estimates of near-critical behaviour. *Phys. Rev. E* **2023**, *108*, 014109. [CrossRef] [PubMed]
91. Girardi-Schappo, M. Brain criticality beyond avalanches: Open problems and how to approach them. *J. Phys. Complex.* **2021**, *2*, 031003. [CrossRef]
92. Liu, X.; Fei, X.; Liu, J. The Cognitive Critical Brain: Modulation of Criticality in Task-Engaged Regions. *bioRxiv* **2023**. [CrossRef]

93. Del Papa, B.; Priesemann, V.; Triesch, J. Criticality meets learning: Criticality signatures in. a self-organizing recurrent neural network. *PLoS ONE* **2017**, *12*, e0178683. [CrossRef] [PubMed]
94. Grigolini, P. Emergence of biological complexity: Criticality, renewal and memory. *Chaos Solitons Fractals* **2015**, *81*, 575–588. [CrossRef]
95. Leisman, G.; Koch, P. Continuum model of mnemonic and amnesic phenomena. *J. Int. Neuropsychol. Soc.* **2000**, *6*, 593–607. [CrossRef] [PubMed]
96. Grossberg, S. Adaptive Resonance Theory: How a brain learns to consciously attend, learn, and recognize a changing world. *Neural Netw.* **2013**, *37*, 1–47. [CrossRef] [PubMed]
97. Mormann, F.; Koch, C. Neural correlates of consciousness. *Scholarpedia* **2007**, *2*, 1740. [CrossRef]
98. Logothetis, N.K. Single units and conscious vision. *Philos. Trans. R. Soc. Lond. Ser. B Biol. Sci.* **1998**, *353*, 1801–1818.
99. Grossberg, S.; Yazdanbakhsh, A.; Cao, Y.; Swaminathan, G. How does binocular rivalry emerge from cortical mechanisms of 3-D vision? *Vis. Res.* **2008**, *48*, 2232–2250. [CrossRef] [PubMed]
100. Grossberg, S. Human and computer rules and representations are not equivalent. *Behav. Brain Sci.* **1980**, *3*, 136–138. [CrossRef]
101. Grossberg, S. *Conscious Mind, Resonant Brain: How Each Brain Makes a Mind*; Oxford University Press: Oxford, UK, 2021.
102. Bhatt, R.; Carpenter, G.A.; Grossberg, S. Texture segregation by visual cortex: Perceptual grouping, attention, and learning. *Vis. Res.* **2007**, *47*, 3173–3211. [CrossRef]
103. Reynolds, J.H.; Heeger, D.J. The normalization model of attention. *Neuron* **2009**, *61*, 168–185. [CrossRef]
104. Crisan, M. Adaptive Resonance Theory Neural Network for Phoneme Perception and Production. In Proceedings of the 2019 2nd International Conference on Mathematics, Modeling and Simulation Technologies and Applications (MMSTA 2019), Xiamen, China, 27–28 October 2019; Atlantis Press: Dordrecht, The Netherlands, 2019; pp. 213–216.
105. Dresp-Langley, B. Seven properties of self-organization in the human brain. *Big Data Cogn. Comput.* **2020**, *4*, 10. [CrossRef]
106. Freriks, L.W.; Cluitmans, P.J.M.; van Gils, M.J. *The Adaptive Resonance Theory Network:(Clustering-) Behaviour in Relation with Brainstem Auditory Evoked Potential Patterns*; Technische Universiteit Eindhoven: Eindhoven, The Netherlands, 1992.
107. LeCun, Y.; Chopra, S.; Hadsell, R.; Ranzato, M.; Huang, F.-J. A Tutorial on Energy-Based Learning. 2006. Available online: http://yann.lecun.com/exdb/publis/orig/lecun-06.pdf (accessed on 12 April 2024).
108. Leisman, G. Enigma Variations: Elegy for Neural Coding in Understanding Cognition. *J. Integr. Neurosci.* **2024**, *23*, 104.
109. Chapeton, J.I.; Haque, R.; Wittig, J.H.; Inati, S.K.; Zaghloul, K.A. Large-scale communication in the human brain is rhythmically modulated through alpha coherence. *Curr. Biol.* **2019**, *29*, 2801–2811. [CrossRef] [PubMed]
110. Margulis, L.; Sagan, D. *Origins of Sex: Three Billion Years of Genetic Recombination*; Yale University Press: New Haven, CT, USA, 1990.
111. Zeki, S.; Bartels, A. Toward a Theory of Visual Consciousness. *Conscious. Cogn.* **1999**, *8*, 225–259. [CrossRef] [PubMed]
112. Zeki, S. The disunity of consciousness. *Trends Cogn. Sci.* **2003**, *7*, 214. [CrossRef]
113. Steinke, G.K.; Galán, R.F. Brain rhythms reveal a hierarchical network organization. *PLoS Comput. Biol.* **2011**, *7*, e1002207. [CrossRef] [PubMed]
114. Hilgetag, C.C.; Goulas, A. 'Hierarchy' in the organization of brain networks. *Philos. Trans. R. Soc. B* **2020**, *375*, 20190319. [CrossRef] [PubMed]
115. Jiruska, P.; De Curtis, M.; Jefferys, J.G.; Schevon, C.A.; Schiff, S.J.; Schindler, K. Synchronization and desynchronization in epilepsy: Controversies and hypotheses. *J. Physiol.* **2013**, *591*, 787–797. [CrossRef] [PubMed]
116. Grossberg, S. *Studies of Mind and Brain: Neural Principles of Learning, Perception, Development, Cognition, and Motor Control*; Springer: New York, NY, USA, 2012; Volume 70.
117. Aboitiz, F.; Montiel, J.; Morales, D.; Concha, M. Evolutionary divergence of the reptilian and the mammalian brains: Considerations on connectivity and development. *Brain Res. Rev.* **2002**, *39*, 141–153. [CrossRef]
118. Wilson, H.R.; Cowan, J.D. A mathematical theory of the functional dynamics of cortical and thalamic nervous tissue. *Kybernetik* **1973**, *13*, 55–80. [CrossRef]
119. Destexhe, A.; Sejnowski, T.J. The Wilson–Cowan model, 36 years later. *Biol. Cybern.* **2009**, *101*, 1–2. [CrossRef] [PubMed]
120. Hermann, B.; Raimondo, F.; Hirsch, L.; Huang, Y.; Denis-Valente, M.; Pérez, P.; Engemann, D.; Faugeras, F.; Weiss, N.; Demeret, S.; et al. Combined behavioral and electrophysiological evidence for a direct cortical effect of prefrontal tDCS on disorders of consciousness. *Sci. Rep.* **2020**, *10*, 4323. [CrossRef]
121. Wang, Y.; Liu, W.; Wang, Y.; Ouyang, G.; Guo, Y. Long-term HD-tDCS modulates dynamic changes of brain activity on patients with disorders of consciousness: A resting-state EEG study. *Comput. Biol. Med.* **2024**, *170*, 108084. [CrossRef] [PubMed]
122. Zhang, Y.; Song, W.; Du, J.; Huo, S.; Shan, G.; Li, R. Transcranial direct current stimulation in patients with prolonged disorders of consciousness: Combined behavioral and event-related potential evidence. *Front. Neurol.* **2017**, *8*, 620. [CrossRef]
123. Koch, P.; Leisman, G. Wave theory of large-scale organization of cortical activity. *Int. J. Neurosci.* **1996**, *86*, 179–196. [CrossRef] [PubMed]
124. Golomb, D.; Amitai, Y. Propagating neuronal discharges in neocortical slices: Computational and experimental study. *J. Neurophysiol.* **1997**, *78*, 1199–1211. [CrossRef]
125. Ermentrout, B. The analysis of synaptically generated traveling waves. *J. Comput. Neurosci.* **1998**, *5*, 191–208. [CrossRef] [PubMed]
126. Koch, P.; Leisman, G. Effect of local synaptic strengthening on global activity-wave growth in the hippocampus. *Int. J. Neurosci.* **2001**, *108*, 127–146. [CrossRef] [PubMed]

127. Koch, P.; Leisman, G. Typology of nonlinear activity waves in a layered neural continuum. *Int. J. Neurosci.* **2006**, *116*, 381–405. [CrossRef] [PubMed]
128. Buzsaki, G. *Rhythms of the Brain*; Oxford University Press: Oxford, UK, 2006.
129. Neymotin, S.A.; Lee, H.; Park, E.; Fenton, A.A.; Lytton, W.W. Emergence of physiological oscillation frequencies in a computer model of neocortex. *Front. Comput. Neurosci.* **2011**, *5*, 19. [CrossRef]

Disclaimer/Publisher's Note: The statements, opinions and data contained in all publications are solely those of the individual author(s) and contributor(s) and not of MDPI and/or the editor(s). MDPI and/or the editor(s) disclaim responsibility for any injury to people or property resulting from any ideas, methods, instructions or products referred to in the content.

 information

Article

The Grossberg Code: Universal Neural Network Signatures of Perceptual Experience

Birgitta Dresp-Langley

Centre National de la Recherche Scientifique UMR 7357 CNRS, Strasbourg University, 67000 Strasbourg, France; birgitta.dresp@cnrs.fr; Tel.: +33-388119117

Abstract: Two universal functional principles of Grossberg's Adaptive Resonance Theory decipher the brain code of all biological learning and adaptive intelligence. Low-level representations of multisensory stimuli in their immediate environmental context are formed on the basis of bottom-up activation and under the control of top-down matching rules that integrate high-level, long-term traces of contextual configuration. These universal coding principles lead to the establishment of lasting brain signatures of perceptual experience in all living species, from *aplysiae* to primates. They are re-visited in this concept paper on the basis of examples drawn from the original code and from some of the most recent related empirical findings on contextual modulation in the brain, highlighting the potential of Grossberg's pioneering insights and groundbreaking theoretical work for intelligent solutions in the domain of developmental and cognitive robotics.

Keywords: multisensory perception; brain representation; contextual modulation; adaptive resonance; biological learning; self-organization; matching rules; winner-take-all principle

Citation: Dresp-Langley, B. The Grossberg Code: Universal Neural Network Signatures of Perceptual Experience. *Information* 2023, 14, 82. https://doi.org/10.3390/info14020082

Academic Editor: Gordana Dodig-Crnkovic

Received: 30 December 2022
Revised: 27 January 2023
Accepted: 29 January 2023
Published: 1 February 2023

Copyright: © 2023 by the author. Licensee MDPI, Basel, Switzerland. This article is an open access article distributed under the terms and conditions of the Creative Commons Attribution (CC BY) license (https:// creativecommons.org/licenses/by/ 4.0/).

1. Introduction

In his latest book [1], Grossberg discusses empirical findings and his own neural network models to illustrate and forecast how autonomous adaptive intelligence [2] is or may be implemented in artificial systems at unprecedentedly high levels of brain function [3–5]. His account of how the brain generates conscious cognition and, ultimately, individual minds provides mechanistic insights into complex phenomena such as mental disorders or the biological basis of morality and religion. The author's theoretical work clarifies why evolutionary pressure towards adaptation and behavioral success not only explains the brain but is also a source for model solutions to large-scale problems in machine learning, technology, and artificial intelligence. Adaptive brain mechanisms [6] are the key to autonomously intelligent algorithms and robots. They may be pre-determined by a universal developmental code, or "engram", that is channeled through the connectome by specific proteins/peptides embedded within pre-synaptic neuronal membranes [7] and corresponds to information provided by the electrical currents afferent to pre-synaptic neurons [8–10]. Grossberg's book [1] conveys a philosophical standpoint on shared laws of function in living systems, from the most primitive to the most advanced, showing how neurons support unsupervised adaptive learning in all known species and how such biological learning has enabled the emergence of the human mind across the evolutionary process. Bearing this in mind, the present concept paper draws from the beginnings of this journey into the mind, which is described by Grossberg's significant early work on neural processes for perception, perceptual learning, and memory, aimed at understanding how the brain builds a cognitive code of physical reality. Since perception is the first step through which a brain derives sense from the raw data of a physical environment, his account of how elementary signals in the physical environment are processed by the neural networks of the brain was a mandatory achievement for understanding how inner representations of the outside world may be generated [11,12]. The ability to derive meaning from complex sensory input requires the integration of information over space and time, as well as memory mechanisms to shape that integration [13] into the contents of experience. In mammals with intact visual systems, this relies on processes in the primary visual cortex of the brain [14], where neurons integrate visual input along shape contours into neural association fields [15]. The geometric selectivity of ensembles of functionally dedicated neural networks is progressively fine-tuned by contextual modulation and experience towards long-term memory representation of all the different configurations likely to be encountered in natural scenes. Horizontal cortical connections provide a broad domain of potential associations in this process, and top-down control functions dynamically gate these associations to switch the function of a given network [16]. Grossberg's work has provided a unified model of brain learning where horizontal cortical connections provide a broad range of potential, functionally specific neural associations through a mechanism called bottom-up activation [17], as will be explained and illustrated on the basis of examples. Mechanisms of adaptive resonance and top-down matching [17] then explain how the contextual modulation of visual and other sensory input drives dynamic brain learning to gate the links within and between neural association fields towards increasingly complex memory representations [16,18]. This concept paper uses two of the functional principles of adaptive resonance theory [19] to illustrate the implications for unsupervised brain learning and adaptive intelligence. The examples chosen here are drawn from the original models and related empirical findings. These are revisited under the light of some of the most recent advances in a conceptual discussion aimed at highlighting the potential of Grossberg's pioneering insights and groundbreaking theoretical work for intelligent solutions to some of the most difficult current problems in artificial intelligence (AI) and robotics. The following sections will elaborate on the biological principles of multisensory contextual modulation in the brain in Section 2 to illustrate the relevance of adaptive resonant learning as conceptualized in the Grossberg code, the functional principles of which are then explained further in Section 3. Section 4 provides a generic ART system with its mathematical definition and an example of neural network architecture that could be implemented on this basis for autonomous and self-organizing multiple event coding to help control object-related aspects of environmental uncertainty in robotics.

2. Contextual Modulation in the Brain

The brain processes local information depending on the context in which this information is embedded. The representation of contextual information peripheral to a salient stimulus is critical to an individual's ability to correctly interpret and flexibly respond to stimuli in the environment. The processes and circuits underlying context-dependent modulation of stimulus-response function have mostly been studied in vertebrates [20], yet well-characterized connectivity patterns are already found in the brains of lower-level species such as insects [21], providing circuit-level insights into contextual processing. Recent studies in flies have revealed neuronal mechanisms that create flexible and highly context-dependent behavioral responses to sensory events relating to threats, food, and social interaction. Throughout brain evolution, functional building blocks of neural network architectures with increasingly complex functional architectures have emerged across species, with increasingly complex long-range connectivity ensuring information encoding in processing streams that are anatomically segregated at a cellular level. The functional specificity of individual streams, long-range interactions beyond the classic receptive field of neurons and interneurons [22], and cortical feedback mechanisms [21,23] provide an excellent model for understanding the complex processing characteristics inherent to individual streams as well as the extent and mechanisms of their interaction in the genesis of brain representation. Contextual modulation in the sensory cortex coding for vision, hearing, somatosensation, and olfaction is partly under central control by the prefrontal cortex, as shown by some of the most recent evidence from neuroscience.

2.1. Vision

To be able to extract structure, form, and meaning from intrinsically ambiguous and noisy physical environments, the visual brain has evolved neural mechanisms dedicated to the integration of local information into global perceptual representations. This integration is subject to contextual modulation [23]. Mechanisms with differential sensitivity to relative stimulus orientation, size, relative position, contrast, polarity, and color operate within specific spatial scales to integrate local visual input into globally perceived structure [24–27]. The differential contextual sensitivity to color and luminance contrast in visual contextual modulation involves the luminance-sensitive pathways (M-pathways) and the color-sensitive pathways (P-pathways) of the visual brain [23,28] in a simple-to-complex-cells processing hierarchy at the level of the visual cortex, already predicted in Grossberg's early models of visual form representation [29–31]. The cooperative and competitive interactions between co-activating or mutually suppressive detectors in functionally dedicated neural networks suggested in the model were confirmed several years later in psychophysical and electrophysiological studies, taking into account response characteristics of orientation-selective visual cortical neurons as a function of the context in which visual target stimuli were presented [22,24,25]. Contextual modulation translates into effects where nearby visual stimuli either facilitate or suppress the detection of the targets (behavior) and increase or decrease the firing rates of the cortical neurons responding to the targets (brain). The cooperative and competitive brain-behavior loops depend on the geometry of so-called "perceptive fields" [22] within a limited range of size-distance ratios. The shorter temporal windows of achromatic context effects compared with chromatic contextual modulation [23,27] Cooperative mechanisms of contextual modulation in vision are subject to substantial practice (perceptual learning) effects, where top-down signals dynamically modulate neural network activities as a function of specific perceptual task constraints. Such top-down-mediated changes in cortical states reflect a general mechanism of synaptic learning [4,8], potentiating or suppressing neural network function(s) depending on contextual relevance.

2.2. Hearing

Sounds in natural acoustic environments possess highly complex spectral and temporal structures, spanning over a whole range of frequencies, with temporal modulations that differ within frequency bands. The auditory brain [32] is capable of reliably detecting one and the same sound in a variety of different sound contexts, as well as distinguishing between different sounds within a complex acoustic scene. Processing acoustic features like sound frequency and duration is highly dependent on co-occurring, acoustic, and other sources of stimulation and involves interactions between an auditory target's spectral and temporal context and individual behavioral states like arousal or expectation. Current findings suggest that sensory attenuation and neuronal modulation may happen during behavioral action as a consequence of disrupted memory expectations in the case of unpredictable concurrent sounds [33]. The auditory system demonstrates nonlinear sensitivity to temporal and spectral context, often employing network-level mechanisms, such as cross-band and temporally adaptive inhibition, to modulate stimulus responses across time and frequency [33–35]. How the auditory system modulates responses to sensory and behavioral contexts is not yet understood. The superior colliculus (SC) is a structure in the mammalian midbrain that contains visual and auditory neural circuits. In mice [34], auditory pathways from external nuclei of the inferior colliculus (IC) with direct inhibitory connections and excitatory signals driving feed-forward inhibitory circuits within the SC were found. The lateral posterior nucleus (LP) of the thalamus projects extensively to the sensory cortex, a previously unknown pathway. Bidirectional activity modulations in LP or its projection to the primary auditory cortex (A1) in awake mice reveal that LP improves auditory processing by sharpening neuronal receptive fields and their frequency tuning [34,35]. LP is strongly activated by specific sensory signals relayed from the superior colliculus (SC), contributing to the maintenance and enhancement of sound signal processing in the presence of auditory background noise and threatening visual stimuli, respectively. This shows that multisensory bottom-up pathways play a role in contextual [36] and cross-modality modulation of auditory cortical processing in mammals. Cross-modality modulation of sensory perception is necessary for survival. In a natural environment, organisms are constantly exposed to a stream of sensory input depending on the environmental context. The response properties of neurons dynamically adjust to contextual changes across all sensory modalities and at different stages of processing from the periphery to the cortex.

2.3. Somatosensation

Cross-modality modulation implies that coincident non-auditory (visual, tactile) processing influences the neural networks underlying contextual modulation of hearing or that non-visual (auditory, tactile) signals may reach the neural networks underlying contextual modulation of vision. Touch, for example, has a direct effect on visual spatial-contextual processing [37]. Contextual modulation and neuronal adaptation in the visual and auditory systems interact with sensory adaptation in the somatosensory system, but it is unclear which pathways and mechanisms are involved. The ability to integrate information from different sensory modalities is a fundamental feature of all sensory neurons across brain areas, which makes sense in light of the fact that visual, auditory, and tactile signals originate from the same physical object when actively manipulated. The synthesis of multiple sensory cues in the brain improves the accuracy and speed of behavioral responses [38]. In motor tasks, task-relevant visual, auditory, and tactile signals are experienced together [39], and pioneering work in neurophysiology from the 1960s demonstrated convergence of visual, auditory, and somatosensory signals at the pre-frontal cortex level in cats [40]. Also, visual signals can bypass the primary visual cortex to directly reach the motor cortex, which is immediately adjacent and functionally connected to the somatosensory cortex [41]. Effects of neuronal adaptation on response dynamics and the encoding efficiency of neurons at single-cell and population levels in the whisker-mediated touch system in rodents illustrate that sensory adaptation provides context-dependent functional mechanisms for noise reduction in visual processing [42]. Between integration and coincidence detection, cross-modality modulation achieves energy conservation and disambiguates the encoding of principal features of tactile stimuli. Sensory systems do not develop and function independently. Early loss of vision, for example, alters the coding of sensory input in the primary somatosensory cortex (S1) to promote enhanced tactile discrimination. Neural response modulation in S1 of mammals (opossums in this case) after elimination of visual input through bilateral enucleation early in development reveals the neural origins of tactile experience in naturally occurring patterns of exploratory behavior after vision loss [43]. In early blind animals, overall levels of tactile experience were similar to those of sighted controls, and their locomotion activity was unimpaired and accompanied by normal whisking. Early blind animals exhibit a reduction in the magnitude of neural responses to whisker stimuli in S1, combined with a spatial sharpening of the neuronal receptive fields. The increased selectivity of S1 neurons in early blind animals is reflected by improved population coding of whisker stimulus positions, particularly along the axis of the snout aligned with the primary axis of the natural whisker motion. These findings suggest that a functionally distinct form of tactile (somatosensory) plasticity occurs when vision is lost early in development. After sensory loss, compensatory behavior mediated through the spared senses is generated through the recruitment of brain areas associated with the deprived sense. Alternatively, functional compensation in spared modalities may be achieved through a combination of plasticity in brain areas corresponding to both spared and deprived sensory modalities.

2.4. Olfaction

Multisensory interactions in the brain are most strongly relied upon and, therefore, need to be optimal when the stimulus ambiguity in a physical environment is highest [44].

Sensorial as well as central cross-modal signaling mechanisms contribute to bottom-up and top-down contextual signaling. For example, both whisking and breathing are affected by the presence of odors in rodents, and the odors modulate activity in a small but significant population of barrel cortex neurons through distinct bottom-up and top-down mechanisms [45]. In the human brain, different aspects of olfactory perception in space and time have been identified by means of EEG recordings [46]. Sensorial (low-level) representations of smell expand into larger areas associated with emotional, semantic, and memory processing in activities significantly associated with perception. These results suggest that initial odor information coded in the olfactory areas evolves towards perceptual realization through computations (a long-range mechanism) in widely distributed cortical regions with different spatiotemporal dynamics [47]. Specific brain structures act as hubs for integrating local multisensory cues into a spatial framework [48], enabling short-term as well as long-lasting memory traces of odors, touch sensations, sounds, and visual objects in different dynamic contexts. Contextual modulation in the brain thus explains how olfactory and other sensory inputs translate into diverse and complex perceptions, such as the pleasurable floral smell of flowers or the aversive smells of decaying matter. The prefrontal cortex (PFC) plays an important role in this process. Recent evidence suggests that the PFC has dedicated neural networks that receive input from olfactory regions and that the activity of these networks is coordinated on the basis of selective attention, producing different brain alert states [49].

2.5. Prefrontal Control

In the mammalian brain, information processing in specific sensory regions interacts with global mechanisms of multisensory integration under the control of the PFC. Emerging experimental evidence suggests that the contribution of multisensory integration to sensory perception is far more complex than previously expected [42,43]. Associative areas such as the prefrontal cortex, which receive and integrate inputs from diverse sensory modalities, not only affect information processing in modal sensory pathways through down-stream signaling but also influence contextual modulation and multisensory processing (Figure 1).

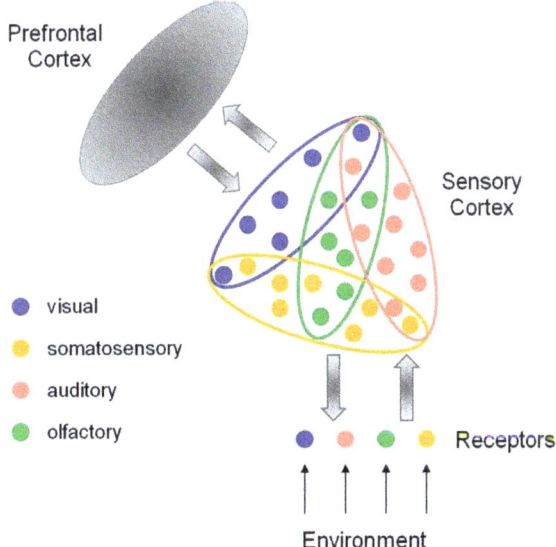

Figure 1. The prefrontal cortex receives and integrates signals from diverse sensory structures and pathways and controls information processing in, and interaction between, modal neural networks (visual, somatosensory, auditory, and olfactory) through down-stream signaling.

Developmental mechanisms account for the interaction between the neuronal networks involved [50], with relevance for brain-inspired intelligent robotics, as will be discussed further later herein. In animals and humans, prefrontal downstream control is necessary in cases of conflicting sensory information, where signals from different modalities compete or provide incongruent input data [51]. The brain then needs to reach a probabilistic decision on the basis of top-down control signals (perceptual experience). However, another remarkable ability of the brain is its capacity to rapidly detect unexpected stimuli. Living beings depend on rapid detection of the unexpected when it is relevant (i.e., an alarm going off, for example), because it enables them to adapt their behavior accordingly and swiftly. Prefrontal control also explains why irrelevant sounds are incidentally processed in association with the environmental context, even though the contextual stimuli activate different sensory modalities [52]. This is consistent with brain data showing that top-down effects of the prefrontal cortex on contextual modulation of visual and auditory processing depend on selective attention to a particular sensory signal [53] among several coincident stimuli. Attempts to understand how functional interaction between different brain regions occurs through multisensory integration constitute a leading-edge research area in contemporary neuroscience [54]. Low-level brain representation of information is not enough to explain how we perceive the world. To enable us to recognize and adaptively act upon objects in the physical world, lower-level sensory network representations need to interact with higher-level brain networks capable of coding contextual relevance.

3. Brain Signatures of Perceptual Experience

It is still unknown how the brain generates short- and long-term memory signatures of perceptual experience, or which mechanisms allow these traces to be retrieved and updated on a regular basis during life-long brain learning and development (ontogenesis). Well before contextual modulation and context-sensitive neural mechanisms were identified in neural circuits of different species, Grossberg understood that they must exist and, considering the principles of unsupervised synaptic (Hebbian) learning [8], which had been demonstrated in low-level species such as *aplysia* [55], that they would have to be universal. In his early work on adaptive resonance [19], he proposed universal functional principles for the generation of short-term and long-term memory traces and their activation in context-sensitive retrieval processes. These functional principles exploit two mechanisms of neural information processing in resonant circuits of the brain, referred to as "bottom-up automatic activation" and "top-down matching".

3.1. Bottom-Up Automatic Activation

Bottom-up automatic activation is a mechanism for the processing and temporary storage of perceptual input in short-term and working memory. Through bottom-up automatic activation, a group of cells within a given neural structure becomes potentiated and is eventually activated when it receives the necessary bottom-up signals. These bottom-up signals may or may not be consciously experienced. They are then multiplied by adaptive weights that represent long-term memory traces and influence the activation of cells at a higher processing level. Grossberg [17] originally proposed "bottom-up automatic activation" to account for the way in which pre-attentive processes generate learning in the absence of top-down attention or expectation. It appears that this mechanism is equally well suited to explain how subliminal signals may trigger supraliminal neural activities in the absence of phenomenal awareness [56,57]. Learning in the absence of phenomenal awareness accounts for visual statistical learning in newborn infants [58] and non-conscious visual recognition [59], for example. Bottom-up automatic activation may generate supraliminal brain signals, or representational contents with weak adaptive weights, as a candidate mechanism to explain how the brain manages to subliminally process perceptual input [60] that is either not directly relevant at a given moment in time or cannot be made available to conscious processing because of a local brain lesion [59].

Grossberg [9,12,17,19] suggested that bottom-up activation may automatically activate target cell populations at higher levels of processing, as in the bottom-up activation of the PCF by sensory cortices [47,49], for example.

3.2. Top-Down Matching

Top-down expectations are needed to consolidate traces of bottom-up representation through mechanisms that obey three properties: (1) they select consistent bottom-up signals, and (2) they suppress inconsistent bottom-up signals. Together, these properties initiate a process that directs attention to a set of critical features that are consistent with a learned expectation. However, (3) a top-down expectation by itself cannot fully activate target cells. It can only sensitize, modulate, or prime the cells to respond more easily and vigorously if they are matched by consistent and sufficiently strong (relevant) bottom-up inputs. If this were not the case, top-down expectation would produce hallucinations of events that do not exist. Top-down expectations therefore do not activate but only modulate representations, as discussed here above in 3.4. Top-down representation matching is a mechanism for the selective matching of bottom-up short-term or working memory representations to already stored and consolidated (learned) memory representations (Figure 2). Subliminal bottom-up representations may become supraliminal when bottom-up signals or representations are sufficiently relevant at a given moment in time to activate statistically significant top-down matching signals [60]. These would then temporally match the bottom-up representations (coincidence). A positive match confirms and amplifies ongoing bottom-up representation, whereas a negative match invalidates ongoing bottom-up representation. Top-down matching is a selective process where subliminal representations become embedded in long-term memory structures and temporarily accessible for recall, i.e., a conscious experience of remembering.

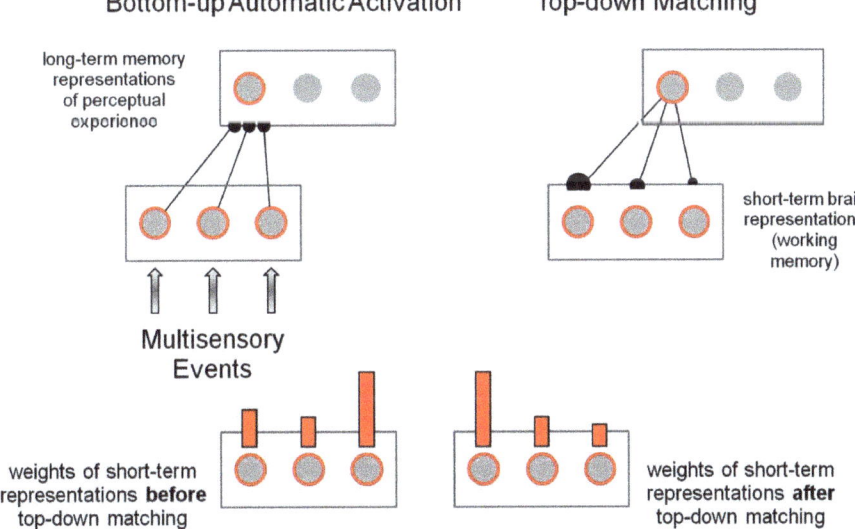

Figure 2. In the ART matching rules, bottom-up signals from the environment activate short-term memory representations in working memory, which then, in turn, send bottom-up signals towards a subsequent processing stage at which long-term memory representations are temporarily activated (top left). These bottom-up signals are multiplied by learned long-term memory traces, which selectively filter short-term representations and activate top-down expectation signals (top right) that are matched against the selected representations in working memory. The strength of the matches determines the weighting of short-term representations (bottom) after top-down matching.

3.3. Temporary Representation for Selection and Control

Grossberg's universal coding rules produce temporary and long-term brain signatures of perceptual experience. They address what he called the attention-pre-attention interface problem [9,12,17,19] by allowing pre-attentive (bottom-up) processes to use some of the same circuitry that is used by attentive (top-down) processes to stabilize cortical development and learning. Consistently, research on human cognition [61] has confirmed that attention ensures the selection of contents in working memory, controlled by mechanisms of filtering out irrelevant stimuli and removing no longer relevant representations, while working memory contributes to controlling perceptual attention as well as action by holding templates available for perceptual selection and action sets available to implement current goals [61]. Top-down matching in its most general sense generates feed-back resonances between bottom-up and top-down signals to rapidly integrate brain representations and hold them available for a consciousness experience at a given moment in time. Non-conscious semantic priming is explained on these grounds. Statistically significant positive top-down matching signals produced on the basis of strong signal coincidences explain why subliminal visual representations become conscious when presented in a specific context, especially after a certain amount of visual learning or practice [60]. Conversely, significant negative matches produced on the basis of repeated discrepancies generating strong negative coincidence signals could explain why a current conscious representation is suppressed and replaced by a new one when a neutral conscious representation is progressively and consistently weakened by association with a strongly biased representation, as in evaluative conditioning and contingency learning [57,58]. Some of the above-mentioned functional properties require long-range connectivity in cortical circuits capable of generating what Edelman [62] called "reentrant signaling". Bottom-up representations that activate specific structures of such circuits but do not produce sufficiently strong matches to long-term memory signals will remain non-conscious [60]. Strong positive top-down matching of selected representations will compete with weaker or negative matches and, ultimately, be suppressed from conscious experience, as, for example, in cases where the conscious integration of new input interferes with the conscious processing of anything else [35,50]. Specific instructions telling subjects what to look for, or what to attend to, in a visual scene may generate top-down expectation signals strong enough to inhibit matching of other relevant signals at the same moment in time [31]. Top-down matching generates neural computations of event coincidence [63]. Results from certain observations of motor behavior without awareness [64] highlight the potential implications of negative top-down matching for conscious control in learning. Individuals may become aware of unconsciously pursued goals of a motor performance or action when the latter does not progress well or fails. This could reflect the consequence of repeated negative top-down matching of the non-conscious bottom-up goal representation and top-down expectation signals in terms of either memory traces of previous successes or representations of desired outcomes. Repeated and sufficiently strong negative matching signals might thereby trigger instant consciousness of important discrepancies between expectation and reality [65]. Awake mammals can switch between alert and non-alert brain states hundreds of times every day. The effects of alertness on two cell classes in layer 4 of primary visual cortex, excitatory "simple" cells and fast-spike inhibitory neurons, show that for both cell classes, alertness increases their functional (excitatory or suppressive) strength and considerably enhances the reliability of visual responses [66]. In simple cells, alertness increases the temporal frequency bandwidth but preserves contrast sensitivity, orientation tuning, and selectivity for direction and spatial frequency. Alertness selectively suppresses the simple cell responses to high-contrast stimuli and stimulus motion orthogonal to their preferred direction of movement. This kind of conscious feedback control fulfills an important adaptive function and has evolved in response to the pressures of intrinsically ambiguous and steadily changing physical environments. The mathematical development and equations describing ART resonant learning in its most generic form were made explicit in the Cohen–

Grossberg model [67,68], which will be detailed further here below with respect to the development of adaptive intelligence in robotics.

4. Towards Adaptive Intelligence in Robotics

The concept of "resonant brain states" is central to ART. They arise from the self-organizing principles of biological neural learning, whereby our brains autonomously adapt to a changing world. Biological neural learning, unlike the learning algorithms that fuel artificial intelligence, is driven by evolution, with a remarkable pressure towards increasingly higher levels of consciousness across the phylogeny [69]. Pressure towards the development of increasingly autonomous and adaptively intelligent forms of agency also exists in the growing field of robotics, in particular neurorobotics [70]. Detailed descriptions and equations describing the full span of potential for the development of autonomously intelligent robots may be found in [71–74]. The most generic functional principle that ART aims for has been termed "hierarchical resolution of uncertainty". Hierarchical resolution of uncertainty means that multiple processing stages are needed for brains to generate sufficiently complete, context-sensitive, and stable perceptual representations upon which successful action by intelligent agents can be based. The mathematical development and equations describing ART resonant learning in its most generic form are inspired by the principles of Hebbian neural (synaptic) learning and are given by the Cohen–Grossberg model [67,68]. The latter is defined in terms of the following system of nonlinear differential equations describing interactions in time t among and between neural activities xi, or short-term memory (STM) traces, of any finite number of individual neurons or neuronal populations (networks)

$$dxi/dt = ai(xi)\,[bi(xi) - \sum j\, cij\, dj(xj)]. \tag{1}$$

With symmetric interaction coefficients $cij = cji$ for weak assumptions of state-dependent non-negative amplification functions $ai(xi)$, self-signaling functions $bi(xi)$, and competitive interaction functions $dj(xj)$. Magnitudes for $i, j = 1, 2, \ldots, n$ and n may be chosen arbitrarily. Each population in (1) can have its own functions $ai(xi)$, $bi(xi)$ and $dj(xj)$. One possible physical interpretation of the symmetric interaction coefficients $cij = cji$ is that the competitive interactions depend upon Euclidean distances between the populations. Defined as in (1), the ith population activity x can only grow to become momentarily a "winner" of the competition at times t where the competitive balance $[bi(xi) - \sum j\, cij\, dj(xj)] > 0$. When $[bi(xi) - \sum j\, cij\, dj(xj)] < 0$, the given population is "losing" the competition.

The ART-inspired neural network architecture for multiple event coding, represented schematically here above, can be implemented by exploiting the properties and parameters of the system described in (1). This would permit implementing robot intelligence with capacities beyond reactive behavior. The selective filtering of relevant sensory input from a multitude of external inputs and the ability to autonomously generate adaptive sequences of memory steps to identify and recognize specific visual objects in the environment permit the control of external perturbations acting on a robot–object system. This is possible in a system like the one depicted above solely because of the internal dynamics of the resonant network. The ability to correctly identify objects despite multiple changes across time is a competence required in many engineering applications that interact with the real world, such as robot navigation. Combining information from different sensory sources promotes robustness and accuracy in place recognition. However, mismatches in data registration, dimensionality, and timing between modalities remain challenging problems in multisensory place recognition [75]. We may, as ART stipulates, define intelligence as the ability to efficiently interact with the environment and to plan for adequate behavior based on the correct interpretation of sensory signals and internal states. This means that an intelligent agent or robot will be successful in accomplishing its goals, be able to learn and predict the effects of its actions, and continuously adapt to changes in real-world scenarios. Ultimately, embodied intelligence allows a robot to interact swiftly with the environment in a wide range of conditions and tasks [76]. The ART model made explicit here above in (1), a

Hebbian-learning-based and mathematically parsimonious system of non-linear equations, can be directly implemented to enable intelligent multi-event coding across time t (Figure 3) for robot control by adaptive artificial intelligence (neurons or neural populations).

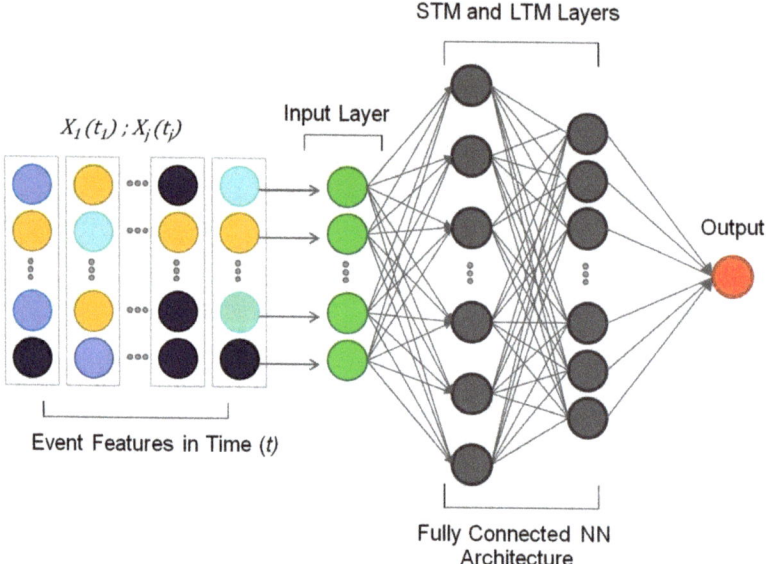

Figure 3. ART-inspired neural network architecture for adaptively intelligent event coding across time t.

5. Discussion

Grossberg's universal coding rules allow for learning in a non-stationary, unpredictable world, whereas the traditional machine learning approaches assume a predictable and controlled environment [2]. Unlike passive adaptive filters [77], they enable self-organized unsupervised learning akin to biological synaptic learning [2,4,5,8,55]. The ART matching rules actively focus attention to selectively generate short- and long-term brain signatures of critical features in the environment, which is achieved by dynamic, non-passive, steadily updated synaptic weight changes in the neural networks [9,12,17,19]. The top-down control of selective processing involves the activation of all memory traces to match or mismatch bottom-up representations globally using *winner-take-all* best-match criteria. Neural network architectures driven by the ART matching rules do not need labeled data to learn, as previously explained in [2]. In short, the Grossberg code overcomes many of the computational problems of back propagation and deep learning models. Equipping cognitive robots with artificial intelligence that processes and integrates cross-modal information according to such self-organized contextual learning ensures that they will interact with the environment more efficiently, in particular under conditions of sensory uncertainty [4,78]. The universal ART matching rules are directly relevant to a particular field in robotics that is motivated by human cognitive and behavioral development, i.e., developmental robotics. The goal is to probe developmental or environmental aspects of cognitive processes by exploring robotic capabilities for interaction using artificial sensory systems and autonomous motor capabilities on challenging environmental platforms [79]. As illustrated here in this paper, low-level sensory and high-level neural networks interact in a bottom-up and top-down manner to create coherent perceptual representations of multisensory environments. Similarly, bottom-up and top-down interactions for the integration of multiple sensory input streams play a crucial role in the development of autonomous cognitive robots by endowing agents with improved robustness, flexibility, and performance. In cases of ambiguous or incongruent cross-sensory inputs, for example, biological inspiration plays a major role. Autonomous robots with odor-guided navigation [80] can benefit from multisensory processing capabilities similar to those found in animals, allowing them to reliably discriminate between chemical sources by integrating associated auditory and visual information. Cross-modal interaction with top-down matching can enable the autonomous learning of desired motion sequences [81], matching expected outcomes from audio or video sequences, for example. Approaches to multisensory fusion in robotic systems directly inspired by the distributed functional architecture of the mammalian cortex have existed for some time [82]. Biological inspiration exploiting top-down cross-modal processing is mandatory for autonomous cognitive robots that acquire perceptual representations on the basis of active object exploration and groping. By actively processing geometric object information during motor learning, aided by tactile and visual sensors, it becomes possible to reconstruct the shape, relative position, and orientation of objects. Service robotics is a fast-developing sector that requires embedded intelligence in robotic platforms that interact with humans and the surrounding environment. One of the main challenges in this field is robust and versatile manipulation in everyday life. Embedding anthropomorphic synergies into the gripper's mechanical design [83] helps, but autonomous grasping still represents a challenge, which can be resolved by endowing robots with self-organizing multisensory adaptive capabilities, as discussed here above. Combining biological neural network learning with compliant end-effectors would not only permit optimizing the grasping of known deformable objects [84], but also help intelligent robots anticipate and grasp unforeseen objects. Bottom-up activation combined with top-down control gives robots the capability to progressively learn in an ever-changing multisensory environment by means of self-organizing interaction with the environment (Figure 4). Implementing multisensory memories in robotics in such a way permits equipping intelligent agents with sensory-cognitive adaptive functions that enable the agents to cope with the unexpected in complex and dynamic environments [85]. On the other hand, a lack of multisensory perceptive capabilities compromises the continuous learning of robotic systems because internal models of the multisensory world can then not be acquired and adapted throughout development.

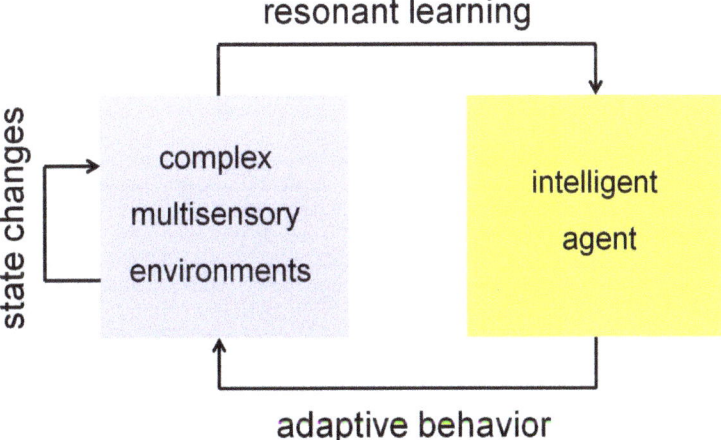

Figure 4. Adaptive resonance as a universal principle of biological learning gives intelligent agents the capability to cope and evolve with ever-changing multisensory environments on the basis of self-organizing adaptive behavior (interaction with the environment).

Adaptive resonance is a powerful concept that provides model approaches for a multitude of human interactions. The relationship between the physical mechanism of resonance and its biological significance in the genesis of perceptual experience in neural networks across all species, from mollusks to humans, makes it a powerful concept for human–robot interaction at all functional levels and within a wider cultural and scientific context. Resonant brain states, established on the basis of matching processes involving top-down expectations and bottom-up activation signals, drive all biological learning at lower and higher levels. Learning in biological neural networks is by nature unsupervised and best accounted for in terms of competitive *winner-take-all* matching principles [86,87]. A resonant state is predicted to persist long enough and at a high enough level of activity to activate long-term signatures of perceptual experience in dedicated neural networks. This explains how these signatures can regulate the brain's fast information processing, observed at the millisecond level, without any awareness of the signals that are being processed. Through resonance as a mediating event, the combination of universal matching rules and their attention-focusing properties makes learning and responding to arbitrary input environments stable. In the mammalian brain, such stability may be reflected by the ubiquitous occurrence of reciprocal bottom-up and top-down cortico-cortical and cortico-thalamic interactions [88].

6. Conclusions

Well before contextual modulation and context-sensitive mechanisms were identified in neural circuits of different species, Grossberg understood that they had to exist. The principles of unsupervised synaptic (Hebbian) learning had been demonstrated in low-level species such as *aplysia*, pointing towards universal principles of perceptual coding. In his earliest work on adaptive resonance, Grossberg laid the foundations of universal functional principles of neural network learning for the generation of brain traces of perceptual experience and their activation by context-sensitive, dynamic, self-organizing mechanisms producing resonant brain states. Equipping cognitive robots with artificial intelligence based on adaptive resonance and processing and integrating cross-modal information in self-organized contextual learning will produce intelligent robots that interact with complex environments adaptively and efficiently, in particular under conditions of sensory uncertainty.

Funding: This research received no external funding.

Acknowledgments: Support from the CNRS is gratefully acknowledged.

Conflicts of Interest: The author declares no conflict of interest.

References

1. Grossberg, S. *Conscious Mind, Resonant Brain: How Each Brain Makes a Mind*; Oxford University Press: Oxford, UK, 2021.
2. Grossberg, S. A path toward explainable AI and autonomous adaptive intelligence: Deep Learning, adaptive resonance, and models of perception, emotion, and action. *Front. Neurorobotics* **2020**, *14*, 36. [CrossRef] [PubMed]
3. Jadaun, P.; Cui, C.; Liu, S.; Incorvia, J.A.C. Adaptive cognition implemented with a context-aware and flexible neuron for next-generation artificial intelligence. *PNAS Nexus* **2022**, *1*, 206. [CrossRef] [PubMed]
4. Dresp-Langley, B. From Biological Synapses to Intelligent Robots. *Electronics* **2022**, *11*, 707. [CrossRef]
5. Dresp-Langley, B. Seven Properties of Self-Organization in the Human Brain. *Big Data Cogn. Comput.* **2020**, *4*, 10. [CrossRef]
6. Meirhaeghe, N.; Sohn, H.; Jazayeri, M. A precise and adaptive neural mechanism for predictive temporal processing in the frontal cortex. *Neuron* **2021**, *109*, 2995–3011.e5. [CrossRef]
7. Rosenberg, R.N. The universal brain code a genetic mechanism for memory. *J. Neurol. Sci.* **2021**, *429*, 118073. [CrossRef] [PubMed]
8. Hebb, D. *The Organization of Behaviour*; John Wiley & Sons: Hoboken, NJ, USA, 1949.
9. Grossberg, S. Self-organizing neural networks for stable control of autonomous behavior in a changing world. In *Mathematical Approaches to Neural Networks*; Taylor, J.G., Ed.; Elsevier Science Publishers: Amsterdam, The Netherlands, 1993; pp. 139–197.
10. Dresp-Langley, B.; Durup, J. A plastic temporal brain code for conscious state generation. *Neural Plast.* **2009**, *2009*, e482696. [CrossRef]
11. Churchland, P.S. *Brain-Wise: Studies in Neurophilosophy*; MIT Press: Cambridge, MA, USA, 2002.
12. Grossberg, S. *How Does a Brain Build a Cognitive Code?* Springer: Berlin/Heidelberg, Germany, 1982; Volume 87, pp. 1–52.
13. Connor, C.E.; Knierim, J.J. Integration of objects and space in perception and memory. *Nat. Neurosci.* **2017**, *20*, 1493–1503. [CrossRef]

14. Hubel, D.H.; Wiesel, T.N. Receptive fields and functional architecture of monkey striate cortex. *J. Physiol.* **1968**, *195*, 215–224. [CrossRef]
15. Chavane, F.; Monier, C.; Bringuier, V.; Baudot, P.; Borg-Graham, L.; Lorenceau, J.; Frégnac, Y. The visual cortical association field: A Gestalt concept or a psychophysiological entity? *J. Physiol. Paris* **2000**, *94*, 333–342. [CrossRef]
16. McManus, J.N.J.; Li, W.; Gilbert, C.D. Adaptive shape processing in primary visual cortex. *Proc. Natl. Acad. Sci. USA* **2011**, *108*, 9739–9746. [CrossRef] [PubMed]
17. Grossberg, S. How does the cerebral cortex work? Learning, attention, and grouping by the laminar circuits of visual cortex. *Spat. Vis.* **1999**, *12*, 163–185. [CrossRef]
18. Onat, S.; Jancke, D.; König, P. Cortical long-range interactions embed statistical knowledge of natural sensory input: A voltage-sensitive dye imaging study. *F1000Res* **2013**, *2*, 51. [CrossRef] [PubMed]
19. Grossberg, S. Adaptive Resonance Theory: How a brain learns to consciously attend, learn, and recognize a changing world. *Neural Netw.* **2013**, *37*, 1–47. [CrossRef]
20. Kim, L.H.; Sharma, S.; Sharples, S.A.; Mayr, K.A.; Kwok, C.H.T.; Whelan, P.J. Integration of descending command systems for the generation of context-specific locomotor behaviors. *Front. Neurosci.* **2017**, *11*, 581. [CrossRef]
21. Oram, T.B.; Card, G.M. Context-dependent control of behavior in Drosophila. *Curr. Opin. Neurobiol.* **2022**, *73*, 102523. [CrossRef] [PubMed]
22. Spillmann, L.; Dresp-Langley, B.; Tseng, C.H. Beyond the classical receptive field: The effect of contextual stimuli. *J. Vis.* **2015**, *15*, 7. [CrossRef]
23. Lankow, B.S.; Usrey, W.M. Contextual Modulation of Feedforward Inputs to Primary Visual Cortex. *Front. Syst. Neurosci.* **2022**, *16*, 818633. [CrossRef]
24. Gilbert, C.D.; Wiesel, T.N. The influence of contextual stimuli on the orientation selectivity of cells in the primary visual cortex of the cat. *Vis. Res.* **1990**, *30*, 1689–1701. [CrossRef]
25. Dresp, B. Dynamic characteristic of spatial mechanisms coding contour structures. *Spat. Vis.* **1999**, *12*, 129–142. [CrossRef]
26. Dresp, B.; Grossberg, S. Contour integration across polarities and spatial gaps: From contrast filtering to bipole cooperation. *Vis. Res.* **1997**, *37*, 913–924. [CrossRef] [PubMed]
27. Dresp, B.; Grossberg, S. Spatial facilitation by color and luminance edges: Boundary, surface, and attentional factors. *Vis. Res.* **1999**, *39*, 3431–3443. [CrossRef] [PubMed]
28. Hubel, D.H.; Livingstone, M.S. Color and contrast sensitivity in the lateral geniculate body and primary visual cortex of the macaque monkey. *J. Neurosci.* **1990**, *10*, 2223–2237. [CrossRef] [PubMed]
29. Grossberg, S.; Mingolla, E. Neural dynamics of perceptual grouping: Textures, boundaries, and emergent segmentations. *Percept. Psychophys.* **1985**, *38*, 141–171. [CrossRef]
30. Grossberg, S. 3-D vision and figure-ground separation by visual cortex. *Percept. Psychophys.* **1994**, *55*, 48–121. [CrossRef] [PubMed]
31. Li, W.; Piëch, V.; Gilbert, C.D. Learning to link visual contours. *Neuron* **2008**, *57*, 442–451. [CrossRef]
32. Angeloni, C.; Geffen, M.N. Contextual modulation of sound processing in the auditory cortex. *Curr. Opin. Neurobiol.* **2017**, *49*, 8–15. [CrossRef]
33. Paraskevoudi, N.; SanMiguel, I. Sensory suppression and increased neuromodulation during actions disrupt memory encoding of unpredictable self-initiated stimuli. *Psychophysiology* **2022**, *60*, e14156. [CrossRef]
34. Bednárová, V.; Grothe, B.; Myoga, M.H. Complex and spatially segregated auditory inputs of the mouse superior colliculus. *J. Physiol.* **2018**, *596*, 5281–5298. [CrossRef]
35. Chou, X.L.; Fang, Q.; Yan, L.; Zhong, W.; Peng, B.; Li, H.; Wei, J.; Tao, H.W.; Zhang, L.I. Contextual and cross-modality modulation of auditory cortical processing through pulvinar mediated suppression. *Elife* **2020**, *9*, e54157. [CrossRef]
36. Sutter, M.L.; Schreiner, C.E. Physiology and topography of neurons with multipeaked tuning curves in cat primary auditory cortex. *J. Neurophysiol.* **1991**, *65*, 1207–1226. [CrossRef] [PubMed]
37. Pérez-Bellido, A.; Pappal, R.D.; Yau, J.M. Touch engages visual spatial contextual processing. *Sci. Rep.* **2018**, *8*, 16637. [CrossRef]
38. Lohse, M.; Zimmer-Harwood, P.; Dahmen, J.C.; King, A.J. Integration of somatosensory and motor-related information in the auditory system. *Front. Neurosci.* **2022**, *16*, 1010211. [CrossRef] [PubMed]
39. Dresp-Langley, B. Grip force as a functional window to somatosensory cognition. *Front. Psychol.* **2022**, *13*, 1026439. [CrossRef] [PubMed]
40. Imbert, M.; Bignal, K.; Buser, P. Neocortical interconnections in the cat. *J. Neurophysiol.* **1966**, *29*, 382–395. [CrossRef]
41. Imbert MBuser, P. Sensory Projections to the Motor Cortex in Cats: A Microelectrode Study. In *Sensory Communication*; Rosenblith, W., Ed.; 2012 (re-edited); The MIT Press: Cambridge, MA, USA, 1961; pp. 607–628. [CrossRef]
42. Adibi, M.; Lampl, I. Sensory Adaptation in the Whisker-Mediated Tactile System: Physiology, Theory, and Function. *Front. Neurosci.* **2021**, *15*, 770011. [CrossRef]
43. Ramamurthy, D.L.; Krubitzer, L.A. Neural Coding of Whisker-Mediated Touch in Primary Somatosensory Cortex Is Altered Following Early Blindness. *J. Neurosci.* **2018**, *38*, 6172–6189. [CrossRef]
44. Raposo, D.; Sheppard, J.P.; Schrater, P.R.; Churchland, A.K. Multisensory decision-making in rats and humans. *J. Neurosci.* **2012**, *32*, 3726–3735. [CrossRef]
45. Renard, A.; Harrell, E.R.; Bathellier, B. Olfactory modulation of barrel cortex activity during active whisking and passive whisker stimulation. *Nat. Commun.* **2022**, *13*, 3830. [CrossRef]

46. Ezzatdoost, K.; Hojjati, H.; Aghajan, H. Decoding olfactory stimuli in EEG data using nonlinear features: A pilot study. *J. Neurosci. Methods* **2020**, *341*, 108780. [CrossRef]
47. Kato, M.; Okumura, T.; Tsubo, Y.; Honda, J.; Sugiyama, M.; Touhara, K.; Okamoto, M. Spatiotemporal dynamics of odor representations in the human brain revealed by EEG decoding. *Proc. Natl. Acad. Sci. USA* **2022**, *119*, e2114966119. [CrossRef] [PubMed]
48. Persson, B.M.; Ambrozova, V.; Duncan, S.; Wood, E.R.; O'Connor, A.R.; Ainge, J.A. Lateral entorhinal cortex lesions impair odor-context associative memory in male rats. *J. Neurosci. Res.* **2022**, *100*, 1030–1046. [CrossRef]
49. Cansler, H.L.; Zandt, E.E.; Carlson, K.S.; Khan, W.T.; Ma, M.; Wesson, D.W. Organization and engagement of a prefrontal-olfactory network during olfactory selective attention. *Cereb. Cortex* **2022**, bhac153. [CrossRef] [PubMed]
50. Xu, X.; Hanganu-Opatz, I.L.; Bieler, M. Cross-Talk of Low-Level Sensory and High-Level Cognitive Processing: Development, Mechanisms, and Relevance for Cross-Modal Abilities of the Brain. *Front. Neurorobotics* **2020**, *14*, 7. [CrossRef] [PubMed]
51. Botvinick, M.M.; Braver, T.S.; Barch, D.M.; Carter, C.S.; Cohen, J.D. Conflict monitoring and cognitive control. *Psychol. Rev.* **2001**, *108*, 624–652. [CrossRef]
52. Parmentier, F.B.R.; Gallego, L.; Micucci, A.; Leiva, A.; Andrés, P.; Maybery, M.T. Distraction by deviant sounds is modulated by the environmental context. *Sci. Rep.* **2022**, *12*, 21447. [CrossRef]
53. Mayer, A.R.; Ryman, S.G.; Hanlon, F.M.; Dodd, A.B.; Ling, J.M. Look Hear! The prefrontal cortex is stratified by modality of sensory input during multisensory cognitive control. *Cereb. Cortex* **2017**, *27*, 2831–2840. [CrossRef]
54. Skirzewski, M.; Molotchnikoff, S.; Hernandez, L.F.; Maya-Vetencourt, J.F. Multisensory Integration: Is Medial Prefrontal Cortex Signaling Relevant for the Treatment of Higher-Order Visual Dysfunctions? *Front. Mol. Neurosci.* **2022**, *14*, 806376. [CrossRef]
55. Walters, E.T.; Carew, T.J.; Kandel, E.R. Classical conditioning in Aplysia californica. *Proc. Natl. Acad. Sci. USA* **1979**, *76*, 6675–6679. [CrossRef]
56. Berns, G.S.; Cohen, J.D.; Mintun, M.A. Brain regions responsive to novelty in the absence of awareness. *Science* **1997**, *276*, 1272–1275. [CrossRef]
57. Wong, P.S.; Bernat, E.; Bunce, S.; Shevrin, H. Brain indices of non-conscious associative learning. *Conscious. Cogn.* **1997**, *6*, 519–544. [CrossRef] [PubMed]
58. Bulf, H.; Johnson, S.P.; Valenza, E. Visual statistical learning in the newborn infant. *Cognition* **2011**, *121*, 127–132. [CrossRef] [PubMed]
59. Rees, G.; Wojciulik, E.; Clarke, K.; Husain, M.; Frith, C.; Driver, J. Neural correlates of conscious and unconscious vision in parietal extinction. *Neurocase* **2002**, *8*, 387–393. [CrossRef] [PubMed]
60. Dresp-Langley, B. Why the brain knows more than we do: Non-conscious representations and their role in the construction of conscious experience. *Brain Sci.* **2011**, *2*, 1–21. [CrossRef] [PubMed]
61. Oberauer, K. Working Memory and Attention–A Conceptual Analysis and Review. *J. Cogn.* **2019**, *2*, 36. [CrossRef]
62. Edelman, G.M. Neural Darwinism: Selection and reentrant signaling in higher brain function. *Neuron* **1993**, *10*, 115–125. [CrossRef]
63. Judák, L.; Chiovini, B.; Juhász, G.; Pálfi, D.; Mezriczky, Z.; Szadai, Z.; Katona, G.; Szmola, B.; Ócsai, K.; Martinecz, B.; et al. Sharp-wave ripple doublets induce complex dendritic spikes in parvalbumin interneurons in vivo. *Nat. Commun.* **2022**, *13*, 6715. [CrossRef]
64. Fourneret, P.; Jeannerod, M. Limited conscious monitoring of motor performance in normal subjects. *Neuropsychologia* **1998**, *36*, 1133–1140. [CrossRef]
65. Mashour, G.A.; Roelfsema, P.; Changeux, J.P.; Dehaene, S. Conscious Processing and the Global Neuronal Workspace Hypothesis. *Neuron* **2020**, *105*, 776–798. [CrossRef]
66. Zhuang, J.; Bereshpolova, Y.; Stoelzel, C.R.; Huff, J.M.; Hei, X.; Alonso, J.M.; Swadlow, H.A. Brain state effects on layer 4 of the awake visual cortex. *J. Neurosci.* **2014**, *34*, 3888–3900. [CrossRef]
67. Cohen, M.A.; Grossberg, S. Absolute stability and global pattern formation and parallel memory storage by competitive neural networks. *IEEE Trans. Syst. Man Cybern.* **1983**, *13*, 815–821. [CrossRef]
68. Cohen, M.A. Sustained oscillations in a symmetric cooperative competitive neural network: Disproof of a conjecture about content addressable memory. *Neural Netw.* **1988**, *1*, 217–221. [CrossRef]
69. Dresp-Langley, B. Consciousness Beyond Neural Fields: Expanding the Possibilities of What Has Not Yet Happened. *Front. Psychol.* **2022**, *12*, 762349. [CrossRef] [PubMed]
70. Azizi, Z.; Ebrahimpour, R. Explaining Integration of Evidence Separated by Temporal Gaps with Frontoparietal Circuit Models. *Neuroscience* **2023**, *509*, 74–95. [CrossRef] [PubMed]
71. Grossberg, S. Towards solving the hard problem of consciousness: The varieties of brain resonances and the conscious experiences that they support. *Neural Netw.* **2017**, *87*, 38–95. [CrossRef] [PubMed]
72. Grossberg, S. The embodied brain of SOVEREIGN2: From space-variant conscious percepts during visual search and navigation to learning invariant object categories and cognitive-emotional plans for acquiring valued goals. *Front. Comput. Neurosci.* **2019**, *13*, 36. [CrossRef] [PubMed]
73. Grossberg, S. Toward autonomous adaptive intelligence: Building upon neural models of how brains make minds. *IEEE Trans. Syst.* **2021**, *51*, 51–75. [CrossRef]
74. Carpenter, G.A.; Grossberg, S. Adaptive resonance theory. In *Encyclopedia of Machine Learning and Data Mining*; Sammut, C., Webb, G., Eds.; Springer: Berlin/Heidelberg, Germany, 2016; pp. 1–17.

75. Pearson, M.J.; Dora, S.; Struckmeier, O.; Knowles, T.C.; Mitchinson, B.; Tiwari, K.; Kyrki, V.; Bohte, S.; Pennartz, C.M.A. Multimodal Representation Learning for Place Recognition Using Deep Hebbian Predictive Coding. *Front. Robot. AI* **2021**, *8*, 732023. [CrossRef]
76. Bartolozzi, C.; Indiveri, G.; Donati, E. Embodied neuromorphic intelligence. *Nat. Commun.* **2022**, *13*, 1024. [CrossRef]
77. Gong, X.; Wang, Q.; Fang, F. Configuration perceptual learning and its relationship with element perceptual learning. *J. Vis.* **2022**, *22*, 2. [CrossRef]
78. Parisi, G.I.; Kemker, R.; Part, J.L.; Kanan, C.; Wermter, S. Continual lifelong learning with neural networks: A review. *Neural Netw.* **2019**, *113*, 54–71. [CrossRef] [PubMed]
79. Wang, G.; Phan, T.V.; Li, S.; Wang, J.; Peng, Y.; Chen, G.; Qu, J.; Goldman, D.I.; Levin, S.A.; Pienta, K.; et al. Robots as models of evolving systems. *Proc. Natl. Acad. Sci. USA* **2022**, *119*, e2120019119. [CrossRef] [PubMed]
80. Gumaste, A.; Coronas-Samano, G.; Hengenius, J.; Axman, R.; Connor, E.G.; Baker, K.L.; Ermentrout, B.; Crimaldi, J.P.; Verhagen, J.V. A Comparison between Mouse, *In Silico*, and Robot Odor Plume Navigation Reveals Advantages of Mouse Odor Tracking. *Eneuro* **2020**, *7*, 212–219. [CrossRef]
81. Tekülve, J.; Fois, A.; Sandamirskaya, Y.; Schöner, G. Autonomous Sequence Generation for a Neural Dynamic Robot: Scene Perception, Serial Order, and Object-Oriented Movement. *Front. Neurorobotics* **2019**, *13*, 95. [CrossRef] [PubMed]
82. Axenie, C.; Richter, C.; Conradt, J. A self-synthesis approach to perceptual learning for multisensory fusion in robotics. *Sensors* **2016**, *16*, 1751. [CrossRef] [PubMed]
83. Holland, J.; Kingston, L.; McCarthy, C.; Armstrong, E.; O'Dwyer, P.; Merz, F.; McConnell, M. Service robots in the healthcare sector. *Robotics* **2021**, *10*, 47. [CrossRef]
84. Pozzi, L.; Gandolla, M.; Pura, F.; Maccarini, M.; Pedrocchi, A.; Braghin, F.; Piga, D.; Roveda, L. Grasping learning, optimization, and knowledge transfer in the robotics field. *Sci. Rep.* **2022**, *12*, 4481. [CrossRef]
85. Lomas, J.D.; Lin, A.; Dikker, S.; Forster, D.; Lupetti, M.L.; Huisman, G.; Habekost, J.; Beardow, C.; Pandey, P.; Ahmad, N.; et al. Resonance as a Design Strategy for AI and Social Robots. *Front. Neurorobotics* **2022**, *16*, 850489. [CrossRef]
86. Wandeto, J.M.; Dresp-Langley, B. Contribution to the Honour of Steve Grossberg's 80th Birthday Special Issue: The quantization error in a Self-Organizing Map as a contrast and colour specific indicator of single-pixel change in large random patterns. *Neural Netw.* **2019**, *120*, 116–128. [CrossRef]
87. Dresp-Langley, B.; Wandeto, J.M. Unsupervised classification of cell imaging data using the quantization error in a Self Organizing Map. In *Transactions on Computational Science and Computational Intelligence*; Arabnia, H.R., Ferens, K., de la Fuente, D., Kozerenko, E.B., Olivas Varela, J.A., Tinetti, F.G., Eds.; Springer-Nature: Berlin/Heidelberg, Germany, 2021; pp. 201–210.
88. Shepherd, G.M.G.; Yamawaki, N. Untangling the cortico-thalamo-cortical loop: Cellular pieces of a knotty circuit puzzle. *Nat. Rev. Neurosci.* **2021**, *22*, 389–406. [CrossRef]

Disclaimer/Publisher's Note: The statements, opinions and data contained in all publications are solely those of the individual author(s) and contributor(s) and not of MDPI and/or the editor(s). MDPI and/or the editor(s) disclaim responsibility for any injury to people or property resulting from any ideas, methods, instructions or products referred to in the content.

Article

The Psychometric Function for Focusing Attention on Pitch

Adam Reeves

Department of Psychology, Northeastern University, Boston, MA 02115, USA; reeves@neu.edu

Abstract: What is the effect of focusing auditory attention on an upcoming signal tone? Weak signal tones, 40 ms in duration, were presented in 50 dB continuous white noise and were either uncued or cued 82 ms beforehand by a 12 dB SL cue tone of the same frequency and duration as the signal. Signal frequency was either constant for a block of trials or was randomly one of 11 frequencies from 632 to 3140 Hz. Slopes of psychometric functions for detection in single-interval (Yes/No) trials were obtained from three listeners by varying the signal level over a 1–9 dB range. Plots of log(d') against signal dB were fit by linear functions. Slopes were similar whether signal frequency was constant or varied, as found by D. Green. Slopes for uncued tones increased by 14% to 20% more than predicted by signal energy (i.e., 0.10), as also found previously, whereas slopes for cued tones followed signal energy corrected for an 8 dB sensory threshold. That pre-cues help attention focus rapidly on signal frequency and permit listeners to act as near-ideal detectors of signal energy, which they do not do otherwise, supports a key hypothesis of Grossberg's ART model that attention guided by conscious awareness can optimize perception.

Keywords: attention; audition; energy; attention

1. Introduction

How well do listeners focus attention on a particular signal frequency? Green [1] and others [2–6] have shown that the threshold for detecting pure tones in broadband noise is higher, by about 3 dB, when listeners do not know at what frequency the signal will be presented than when they do know. The current research was undertaken to elucidate this improvement in perception due to foreknowledge. Here, the term 'frequency' describes the pitch in Hz, and 'level' describes the amplitude in decibels (dB). The term 'focusing attention' describes both the listener's objective task and his or her phenomenal awareness of the task, but not, in general, what focusing does. A general scheme for how attention can prime a signal by suppressing unwanted information is provided by Grossberg's ART theory [7] (p. 18); see Dresp-Langley [8]. ART requires the signal to be learnt, as resonance and top-down matching with memory is required, and in the psycho-acoustic literature cited here, this is the case: only experienced listeners who have memorized the possible tones are used. In the present context, it is possible to formulate a specific hypothesis, namely, that knowing the signal frequency allows the listener to focus attention in advance on the signal's *critical band* (CB), the band of tones around the signal which interact with it [9]. Focusing on the signal CB suppresses noise from non-signal CBs and so increases detectability (d') as compared to not knowing the signal in advance [10], a form of suppression which has been investigated physiologically in primates [11].

Experimentally, providing the same signal in every trial permits the listener to focus attention on the signal CB, whereas varying the signal at random across trials does not. Green [1] compared these two conditions, which I will term *const* when signal frequency is constant for a block of trials and *var* when signal frequency is varied. (In *var*, signal frequency is typically selected at random across trials from between 5 and 22 possible frequencies, each at least one CB from the next.) The listener's task in both *const* and *var* is to detect weak, brief (<350 ms) signals in continuously present wide-band noise that covers the range of possible signal frequencies. Such wide-band noise is convenient in that it elevates individual listeners' thresholds to the same level, within a dB or so, over a wide range of frequencies, making the experimental measurements possible in uniform conditions; this is not so for thresholds in silence, which vary idiosyncratically over individuals and frequencies.

How well attention can be focused in *const* has also been determined using the 'probe-signal' method of Greenberg and Larkin [12]. In this method, which differs from Green's, so-called 'probe' tones are occasionally presented at unexpected frequencies above or below the (constant) signal frequency. Signals and probes are near the threshold, and, apart from their frequencies, they are identical in duration and quality. Probes inside the signal CB are heard in proportion to their distance from the signal frequency, defining an 'attention band' around the signal [13–17]. Distant probe tones, those outside the signal CB, are not heard, being attenuated by up to 8 dB [17]. Although the close match between the attention band and the CB fails below 500 Hz, when the attention band more closely follows a narrower auditory filter [14], the argument of this paper will be phrased in terms of CBs as signals below 632 Hz were not used. When tones are very brief (20 ms), focusing fails to exclude neighboring CBs, and the attention band widens and peaks just below the signal frequency [15], but with longer durations, focusing on single CBs is successfully accomplished.

Proof that focusing primarily suppresses distant probe tones rather than enhancing the signal tone was provided by Scharf, Magnan, and Chays [18], who compared thresholds before and after vestibular neurotomy. This operation randomly severs the olivio-cochlear bundle, which mediates cortical feedback to the outer hair cells of the cochlear [19,20]. After neurotomy, patients lost the ability to suppress probes away from the signal CB but showed no change in signal threshold [18]. (Interestingly, the hearing of speech in noise is unaffected, speech being broadband so there is no particular 'signal' frequency.) Here, I assume that the suppression of non-signal CBs is the primary effect of attentional focusing, although Tan et al. [21] also reported a minor 2 dB signal enhancement due to focusing.

When a wide-band noise is applied, the listener who can focus on the signal CB (in *const*) will suppress noise from non-signal CBs, as evidenced by the probe-signal data just discussed, but a listener who attends to all possible signal frequencies (in *var*) cannot suppress noise, as all CBs potentially contain a signal. Thus, the detection mechanism in *var* will sum more noise than that in *const*, and the detectability of the signal (d') in *var* will fall below that in *const*.

Note that noise suppression may be total, exemplifying 'exclusion' in the terms of Lu and Dosher [22], or partial, exemplifying 'attenuation', as in Treisman [23]. As Green [1] pointed out, given the wide range of frequencies he employed, excluding all the noise in *var* predicts a 10 dB loss relative to *const*, not the 3 dB loss he obtained. Green's suggested explanation for this discrepancy was that listeners fail to focus completely on the signal CB even in *const*, so noise from non-signal CBs is attenuated rather than excluded.

One aim of the current research was to test Green's suggestion by validly pre-cuing the signal frequency. Frequency *var* versus *const* was crossed with validly cueing versus not cuing, a *var/const* × *valid cue/no cue* design adopted from Richards and Neff [24]. Validly cuing the signal frequency helps the listener focus on the signal frequency [2,10,16,25], so any uncertainty about the signal frequency should be reduced, perhaps even eliminated, by cuing.

Note: Richards and Neff [24] had crossed frequency certainty with cuing, as in the current study. They used an 'informational mask' consisting of a multitone array of tones all outside the signal CB. In *const*, the signal was always 1000 Hz, and the mean benefit of a valid pre-cue was 6.5 dB compared to no cue. In *var*, the signal was a random one of five tones, and the benefit of a valid pre-cue of the same frequency as the upcoming signal averaged 13.5 dB. They argued that attention can be focused within 50 ms, as longer cue-signal ISIs hardly increased the effectiveness of the cue. They did not measure slopes, but their cue effect (in dB) was encouragingly large. However, a multitone masker encourages attention to focus on non-signal CBs, as shown by their additional finding that pre-cuing the mask array helped the listener re-direct attention away from the mask and greatly aided detection. This would not apply to the broadband noise used here and Green [1].

Cues tones presented very close to the signal are not only informative but also interfere with detection [26,27] even when the cue is valid (i.e., has the same frequency as the signal). In the present work, valid cues were presented 82 ms before the signal, when interference is small, about 2 dB in both *const* and *var* [28].

Previous Studies: Energy Detection

The experimental literature contains several previous studies of the role of attention in detection, starting with Green [1], and I analyze these in the next section. (I provide new results from three listeners in the *var/const* × *valid cue/no cue* experiment.) My analyses show that the widely assumed 'energy detection' model of auditory threshold provides a rather poor approximation of the data.

Green [1] measured proportion correct detection (Pc) in two-alternative forced choice (2AFC) trials, for 800, 1250, 2250, and 3200 Hz signal tones, which were constant in each block of trials (*const*), and for 100, 300, 500, 1000, or 3500 Hz signal tones, randomized across trials (*var*). Cues were never provided. Tones were 100 ms in duration (and ramped on and off to avoid clicks, as is standard). Detection was measured over an 11 dB range of signal levels. Tones were presented in wide-band noise whose amplitude was constant at a 40 dB spectrum level. Pc's from all frequencies taken together are plotted in Figure 2 of his article.

Sound level in decibel (dB) units equals $10\log_{10}[(P/Po)^2]$, where Po is a reference level, either 0.0002 dynes/cm^2 in the case of dB SPL (sound pressure level) or the threshold in the case of dB SL (sensation level). Since thresholds in dB SPL varied with frequency, Green [1] plotted 2AFC accuracy (Pc) against signal dB SL, where at every frequency, 5 dB SL was defined to correspond to Pc = 75% (chance being 50%). Given the small numbers of recorded observations at each signal level, from 3 to 6, median (rather than mean) Pc's were read from Figure 2 in his work and are given below in Table 1 under the heads Pc *const* and Pc *var*.

Table 1. Data from Green [1], Figure 2. Pc const and Pc var are medians at each signal dB level. Amp = $10^{dB/20}$ is given for reference. Noise level was constant. Pcon and Pvar (converted to d'con and d'var) are the Pc's corrected for 2% lapsing.

Amp	dB	Pccon	Pcvar	Pcon	Pvar	d'con	d'var	log d'con	log d'var
1.12	1	0.54	0.55	0.541	0.551	0.145	0.181	−0.839	−0.741
1.26	2	0.55	0.58	0.551	0.582	0.181	0.291	−0.741	−0.535
1.41	3	0.64	0.66	0.643	0.663	0.518	0.596	−0.286	−0.225
1.58	4	0.66	0.68	0.663	0.684	0.596	0.676	−0.225	−0.170
1.78	5	0.78	0.76	0.786	0.765	1.120	1.023	0.049	0.010
2.00	6	0.87	0.82	0.878	0.827	1.644	1.330	0.216	0.124
2.24	7	0.91	0.91	0.918	0.918	1.972	1.972	0.295	0.295
2.51	8	0.97	0.93	0.980	0.939	2.893	2.184	0.461	0.339
2.82	9	0.98	0.97	0.990	0.980	3.279	2.893	0.516	0.461
3.16	10	0.98	0.95						
3.55	11	0.98	0.98			linear	slope	0.177	0.146

For signals above 9 dB SL, the mean error rate (E) did not depend on level, so it is likely that the few remaining errors, which averaged 2%, were due to lapses in attention [29,30]. Corrected for lapsing with E = 2%, the detection rates (Pc − 0.5E)/(1 − E) are listed in Table 1 under the headings Pconst and Pvar. Plotting these against signal dB SL yields slopes of 0.056 in *var* (r = 0.98) and 0.062 in *const* (r = 0.99), close to the slopes of 5% per dB reported in the auditory detection literature [5,6,31]. Table 1 gives d'const = $\sqrt{2}z$(Pconst) and d'var = $\sqrt{2}z$(Pvar), where z(P) is the standard Normal z-score of proportion P. The final two columns give these d's in $\log_{10}$ units. (Note: log(d') exists as all Ps exceeded 50%, or d' = 0.)

According to Green and Swets [32], a detector of sinusoidal signal tones obeys

$$d' = k(S/No) \qquad (1)$$

where S is the signal level, No is the noise level in the channel that detects the signal, and k is a constant of proportionality. They took No to equal the external noise provided by the experimenter, because there was no good evidence for internal auditory noise, and Brownian motion in air ensures No > 0 and so prevents division by zero in the quiet. For a *peak–trough* detector, S and No are in units of amplitude or sound pressure, P/Po. For an *energy* detector, S and No are in units of $(P/Po)^2$. Converting Equation (1) to dBs by canceling Po in the ratio S/No, and writing S_{dB} and No_{dB} for the Signal and Noise in dBs,

$$\log_{10}(d') = \log_{10}(k) + b(S_{dB} - No_{dB}) \qquad (2)$$

where the slope, b, is 1/20 for a peak–trough or amplitude detector and 1/10 for an energy detector [32].

The regression of $\log_{10}(d')$ on S_{dB} from Table 1 gave slopes (b) of 0.146 in *var* (r = 0.98) and 0.177 in *const* (r = 0.98). These slopes clearly reject the peak–trough detector (b = 1/20) but are also on average 16% steeper than the energy detector. Green [1] stated that the slope was 1/10 in both *var* and *const*, but he may have been misled, both because log(d') puts undue weight on near-zero d's, and because d' becomes unstable at high Pc's [30]. However, Green's claim has entered the literature and it is often taken for granted that his data showed that the ear is an energy detector.

Green, Birdsall and Tanner [33] had previously used uncued 1000 Hz signals in *const* and again reported slopes consistent with energy detection in wide-band noise for four listeners and three stimulus durations. However, interpolating the S_{dB} levels at d' = 0.5 and d' = 2.0 in all 12 of their plots, the average of the resulting log(d') versus S_{dB} slopes is again 14% steeper than the energy detector. Dai [31] also reported slopes of 0.14 in *const* and 0.15 in *var*, not 0.10, using an uncued 'profile' task in which listeners discriminated an array of 21 well-spaced tones from the same array plus a signal tone. It thus appears that for uncued tones of constant frequency, the log-log psychometric slopes are consistently around 14% too steep for pure energy detection.

As stated above, Green [1] concluded from his data that the listeners are uncertain about signal frequency, not only in *var* but also in *const*, because the thresholds in *var* and *const* were only 3 dB apart, not the 10 dB estimated from noise exclusion. The weakness of the uncertainty effect is too dramatic to be an artefact of the somewhat different frequency ranges Green employed in *const* and *var*. However, to obtain a steepening of 14% in *const* requires the listener to be uncertain about which of at least 32 channels contains the signal [29,32]. Such high channel uncertainty seems unlikely, given that the signal in *const* was fixed in every auditory parameter (lateralization, duration, onset time, and frequency). Alternatively, the noise level in *var* might be determined by the maximal noise in each CB, not the summed noise across CBs, an idea which correctly predicts a 3 to 4 dB uncertainty effect [32]. However, attention to all the possible signals in *var* implies attending to the noise in each of the possible signal CBs, rendering the max operator unrealistic. Scharf, Reeves, and Giovanetti [34] offered yet another explanation of the weak uncertainty effect. Attention can be focused on an unexpected signal frequency in less than 52 ms [24,28], and as Green [1] and Dai [31] used 100 ms tones, much of the noise from non-signal CBs in *var* could be excluded by shifting attention to the signal before it terminated. That is, rather than assuming uncertainty in *const*, Scharf et al. [34] assumed more certainty in *var*. They [34] estimated the true uncertainty effect as 9 dB in an overshoot experiment in which attentional focusing was completely disrupted by the onset of broadband noise, close to the predicted 10 dB. Thus, the conclusion that the normal listener excludes noise from all non-signal CBs when focusing may be correct after all.

The uncertainty effect in the current experiment was expected to be 3 dB, as the *const/var* method was used, rather than the overshoot procedure. It is the slopes that are of concern here. Given the earlier results [1,31,33], it seemed likely that with no cue, the present results would also show a steeper psychometric slope than the ideal energy detector. The question at issue was whether pre-cuing could help listeners focus attention and bring the slope closer to 1/10, the energy detector. If so, the claim can be made that attention to known sounds permits the ear to operate as an ideal receiver of signal energy.

2. Methods

The terms *var* and *const* will continue to be used for conditions in which frequency was varied unpredictably over trials or was constant for a block of trials. The *var* and *const* conditions were like Green's [1], except that tone duration was 40 ms, not 100 ms. The same frequencies were used in both conditions, since the uncertainty effect decreases with frequency [25]. Signals were preceded 82 ms earlier by a valid cue, also 40 ms in duration, or were, like Green's, uncued.

Participants. One male (MA) and two female (TA and NA) Northeastern University undergraduates, aged 19, 20, and 22, served as listeners. All three had normal audiograms and detection thresholds. Hour-long sessions were run over several weeks to obtain data. None reported using drugs (prescribed or otherwise) during the course of the study. The study was authorized by the human subjects committee of Northeastern University. Listeners gave informed consent. They were paid USD 10 per hour and were told they could leave the study at any time without loss of payment. They were informed that the study was undertaken to facilitate audiometry, but not that it was a study of focusing.

Apparatus. Listeners sat in a sound-attenuated booth (Eckel Industries) and heard sounds generated by a Tucker-Davis (Alachua, FL, USA) TDT System III signal processor (RP2.1) sampled at a rate of 48.83 kHz. A microcomputer (Dell Optiplex GX270; Dell Computers, Round Rock, TX, USA) programmed in Pascal controlled the processor and collected data via a response box (TDT BBOX). Sounds were sent through a headphone driver (TDT HB7) to Sony MDR-V6 cushioned headphones (Sony Corp, Tokyo, Japan). Waveforms, frequency content, and distortion were checked with a wave-analyzer and an oscilloscope. Digital filters were used to generate new wide-band 50 dB SPL noise on every trial, which resembled an analogue bi-quad bandpass filter flat from 200 to 6000 Hz.

Stimuli. Trials began with a warning signal appearing on a visual display screen. Half a second later, a 40 ms cue tone appeared in 'cued' trial blocks. In 'no-cue' blocks, the cue was set to zero amplitude to maintain timing by the program. The cue or silent cue interval was followed after 82 ms by a sinusoidal tone of 40 ms duration in half the trials, or no signal in the remaining trials. The 40 ms cues and signals were gated by cosine ramps (5.6 ms rise and 6.4 ms fall ms times), so each was 52 ms *in toto*.

Tone duration was 40 ms to reduce the chance that, in *var*, the listener could shift attention during the signal. An even briefer tone might reduce this chance even further, but at a cost; the attention band matches the critical band (the CB) for long duration tones but is considerably wider for 5 ms tones [17] and still somewhat wider even for the 40 ms tones used here [15]. Thus, to keep the attention band within reasonable limits, signal duration was not reduced to below 40 ms. The spectrum level of the 50 dB SPL broadband noise, namely 12.44 dB from 570 to 3400 Hz, was also chosen to be low since the attention band, unlike the CB, widens at higher levels [13].

Procedure. Signal and no-signal trials were intermixed at random, and listeners reported whether the signal was present or not (a single interval 'Yes/No' task). Blocks comprised 110 trials each. The cue condition was alternated after every trial block. A single-interval method was used rather than 2IFC to ensure that the cue signal interval was the same on every cued trial. Unless voluntarily delayed by the listener, the next trial began 500 ms after the response. In *const*, the same frequency tone was presented in every one of 55 signal trials. In *var*, the signal tone was selected at random from the same list of 11 frequencies as were employed in *const*, with each frequency appearing 5 times. These frequencies were spaced at least one CB apart [9].

Thresholds. To accommodate slight variations in sensitivity across sessions, the level of the middle (1266 Hz) tone was adjusted in 1 dB increments to reach 89% correct at the start of each session. All other signal tones were adjusted by adding the same amount to each listener's no-cue thresholds. These were measured in 3 initial sessions, for the 50 dB noise, at each of the 11 frequencies from 632 to 3140 Hz, using an adaptive procedure that converged on 79% correct. Table 2 lists the 11 frequencies and mean thresholds in dB SPL for each listener. (The expected increase in threshold from 632 to 3140 Hz, from the ratio of their ERBs, is 5.9 dB; actual increases for NA, TA and MA were 4.1, 7.3, and 3.3 dB.) The mean threshold at 1082 Hz was 35 dB, close to the 39 dB found by Baer, Moore and Glasburg [35] for 40 ms, 1000 Hz tones heard in background noise that was 3 dB higher than that used here. When presented, cues were 12 dB above the levels in Table 2. Experimental blocks were run after the levels were adjusted. At the start of each block, five additional (unrecorded) trials were run to notify the listener of the current condition.

Table 2. Thresholds of 40 ms tones in 50 dB SPL noise for each listener and frequency.

Hz	632	767	917	1082	1266	1481	1720	1994	2318	2693	3140
NA	36.2	36.3	36.3	36.3	36.1	36.0	36.8	37.6	38.4	39.2	40.3
TA	31.6	32.4	33.5	33.2	33.4	35.5	36.7	36.1	37.5	37.3	38.9
MA	36.2	36.6	36.9	37.2	37.6	38.0	38.3	38.6	38.9	39.2	39.5

Design. The four conditions obtained by crossing const versus var with no cue versus pre-cue were run on each of the 11 frequencies, at five signal levels (S_{dB}) spaced 2 dB apart. The order of signal levels, and of frequencies in *var*, was randomized within blocks. The order of conditions was randomized across blocks. Each listener ran in hour-long sessions over several weeks for a total of 60 blocks or 6600 experimental trials. The first week was devoted to obtaining no-cue signal thresholds. There followed two weeks of practice, during which the listeners became familiar with the Yes/No task, and with both cue and no-cue conditions in both *const* and *var*, before the experiment was run.

3 Results

Hit and false alarm rates in each trial block were converted to d' = z(Phit) − z(Pfa). In *const*, hit and false alarm rates were recorded for each frequency in each trial block. In *var*, the common false alarm rate was applied to each frequency; only the hit rates were frequency-specific. Detectabilities based on this assumption correlated well (r = 0.98) in pilot work with 2AFC detectabilities over the range of frequencies used, when measured with no cue, implying that listeners adopted the same criteria independent of frequency. This is not surprising since in *var*, the upcoming frequency was unknown. Note that 2AFC trials are normally preferred but cannot be used with a cue without unbalancing the two intervals.

The values of d' were tabulated for each signal level for each listener, signal frequency, and condition. Individual d's were between 0.03 and 4.0 (as logs, between −1.52 and +0.60), so errant floor and ceiling effects are possible. The d's and signal levels were therefore averaged into frequency groups, low (632–917 Hz), middle (1082–1720 Hz), and high (1994–3140 Hz), no consistent variation with frequency being apparent within each group. The rows in Table 3 give $\log_{10}(d')$, dB SPL, and dB SL, for each listener and frequency group (low fr, mid fr, and hi fr). The condition is specified by column headings from left to right, Cue *var*, Cue *const*, No cue *var*, and No cue *const*. Signal level in dB SL was obtained by subtracting from dB SPL the shifts given in Col. 1 below each listener. Thus, for TA low fr. in data row 1, dB SPL in cue var (row 1, col 2) was 38.90 and the shift (row 2, col 1) was 34.08, so dB SL (row 1, col 4) was 38.90 − 34.08 = 4.82. For TA low fr. cue const, dB SPL (row 1, col 5) was 39.0 and the shift (row 3, col 1) was 32.11, so dB SL (row 1, col 7) was 39.0 − 32.11 = 6.89, and so forth.

Table 3. Column 1 identifies the listener and frequency group. Successive columns identify dB SPL, log(d′), and signal dB SL, under the headings for the condition (cue var, cue const, no cue var, and no cue const). d's were obtained at 5 or 6 signal levels with the cue, and 4 or 5 signal levels with no cue.

Listener	Cue var			Cue const			No Cue var			No Cue const		
Fr.group	dB SPL	log(d)	dB SL	dB SPL	log(d)	dB SL	dB SPL	log(d)	dB SL	dB SPL	log(d′)	dB SL
TA Low	38.90	0.34	4.82	39.0	0.51	6.89	38.00	0.41	3.90	35.00	0.58	4.21
34.08	36.90	0.28	2.82	37.0	0.37	4.89	34.90	−0.08	0.80	33.00	0.55	2.21
32.11	34.90	0.18	0.82	35.0	0.27	2.89	32.90	−0.01	−1.20	31.00	0.29	0.21
34.10	32.90	−0.21	−1.18	33.0	0.08	0.89	29.90	−0.72	−3.20	29.00	−0.54	−1.79
30.79	30.90	−0.25	−3.18	31.0	−0.12	−1.11						
TA Med	43.80	0.43	6.80	42.0	0.54	5.47	39.80	0.54	7.31	39.00	0.53	4.72
36.99	41.80	0.41	4.80	40.0	0.36	3.47	37.80	0.32	5.31	37.00	0.48	2.72
36.53	39.80	0.32	2.80	39.0	0.32	2.47	35.80	0.26	3.31	35.00	0.43	0.72
32.49	37.80	0.12	0.80	38.0	0.22	1.47	33.80	−0.52	1.31	33.00	−0.09	−1.28
34.28	35.80	0.05	−1.20	37.0	−0.04	0.47				31.00	−0.77	−3.28
	33.80	−0.45	−3.20									
TA High	47.96	0.46	8.43	45.0	0.47	3.59	43.96	0.58	9.51	45.00	0.58	4.73
39.53	45.96	0.41	6.43	43.0	0.26	1.59	41.96	0.44	7.51	43.00	0.54	2.73
41.41	43.96	0.38	4.43	41.0	0.07	−0.41	39.96	0.34	5.51	41.00	0.38	0.73
34.45	41.96	0.17	2.43	39.0	−0.45	−2.41	37.96	0.19	3.51	39.00	−0.40	−1.27
40.27	39.96	0.06	0.43	37.0	−1.02	−4.41				37.00	−0.52	−3.27
	37.96	−0.18	−1.57									
NA Low	42.28	0.41	4.56	44.0	0.55	6.02	38.28	0.54	2.01	37.00	0.38	2.39
37.72	40.28	0.31	2.56	42.0	0.50	4.02	36.28	0.24	0.01	35.00	0.23	0.39
37.98	38.28	0.11	0.56	40.0	0.24	2.02	34.28	−0.77	−1.99	33.00	−0.33	−1.61
36.27	36.28	−0.44	−1.44	38.0	0.05	0.02	32.28	−1.50	−3.99	31.00	−0.77	−3.61
34.61	34.28	−0.12	−3.44	36.0	−0.28	−1.98						
	32.28	−0.50	−5.44									
NA Med	42.29	0.38	3.42	42.0	0.32	5.53	38.29	0.39	1.78	39.00	0.41	3.54
38.86	40.29	0.18	1.42	41.0	0.20	4.53	36.29	0.20	−0.22	37.00	0.33	1.54
36.47	38.29	0.03	−0.58	39.0	0.20	2.53	34.29	−0.78	−2.22	35.00	−0.19	−0.46
36.50	36.29	−0.24	−2.58	37.0	0.05	0.53	32.29	−1.22	−4.22	33.00	−0.27	−2.46
35.46	34.29	−0.88	−4.58	35.0	−0.12	−1.47						
	32.29	−0.58	−6.58									
NA High	44.84	0.42	4.65	44.0	0.34	3.14	40.84	0.44	1.54	39.00	0.33	1.30
40.19	42.84	0.31	2.65	42.0	0.07	1.14	38.84	0.04	−0.46	37.00	−0.17	−0.70
40.86	40.84	0.09	0.65	40.0	0.00	−0.86	36.84	−0.97	−2.46	35.00	−0.70	−2.70
39.31	38.84	−0.21	−1.35	38.0	−0.41	−2.86	34.84	−1.45	−4.46	33.00	−1.40	−4.70
37.70	36.84	−0.28	−3.35	36.0	−0.45	−4.86						
MA Low	38.57	0.44	3.47	41.0	0.44	8.23	40.57	0.55	7.06	39.00	0.55	7.00
35.09	36.57	0.41	1.47	39.0	0.39	6.23	38.57	0.38	5.06	37.00	0.52	5.00
32.77	34.57	0.15	−0.53	37.0	0.32	4.23	36.57	0.38	3.06	35.00	0.47	3.00
33.50	32.57	−0.59	−2.53	35.0	0.22	2.23	34.57	0.01	1.06	33.00	0.32	1.00
32.00	30.57	−0.90	−4.53	33.0	−0.08	0.23						
MA Med	39.79	0.48	4.82	41.0	0.51	5.08	41.79	0.53	4.84	39.00	0.58	3.55
34.97	37.79	0.39	2.82	39.0	0.44	3.08	39.79	0.44	2.84	37.00	0.46	1.55
35.92	35.79	0.15	0.82	37.0	0.24	1.08	37.79	0.36	0.84	35.00	0.22	−0.45
36.95	33.79	−0.26	−1.18	35.0	−0.02	−0.92	35.79	−0.34	−1.16	33.00	−0.78	−2.45
35.45	31.79	−0.30	−3.18	33.0	−0.50	−2.92						

Table 3. *Cont.*

Listener		Cue var			Cue const			No Cue var			No Cue const		
Fr.group		dB SPL	log(d)	dB SL	dB SPL	log(d)	dB SL	dB SPL	log(d)	dB SL	dB SPL	log(d′)	dB SL
MA High		41.03	0.42	3.83	41.0	0.38	3.05	43.03	0.47	5.93	43.00	0.60	5.88
37.20		39.03	0.20	1.83	39.0	0.23	1.05	41.03	0.37	3.93	41.00	0.51	3.88
37.95		37.03	−0.03	−0.17	37.0	−0.11	−0.95	39.03	0.14	1.93	39.00	0.25	1.88
37.10		35.03	−0.30	−2.17	35.0	−0.54	−2.95	37.03	−0.41	−0.07	37.00	0.07	−0.12
37.12		33.03	−0.39	−4.17	33.0	−0.65	−4.95				35.00	−0.34	−2.12

Regressions of $\log_{10}(d')$ against S_{dB}, as in Equation (2), were conducted separately for each frequency group, to determine if the slopes varied systematically with frequency. They did not, in agreement with Green [1], as shown by the averaged slopes plotted in Figure 1. Critically, the mean slope without a cue was 0.16 in *const* and 0.19 in *var*, close to the 0.16 slope found in Green [1] and the 0.14 slope in Dai [31], whereas the slopes with a cue averaged 0.107 in *const* and 0.102 in *var*, both close to 0.10. These data confirm Green's suggestion that the listener is uncertain about frequency in *const*, when—as in his experiment—there is no cue to guide attention. The new result is that *with* a cue, the listener is very close to an ideal detector of signal energy (slope: 0.10).

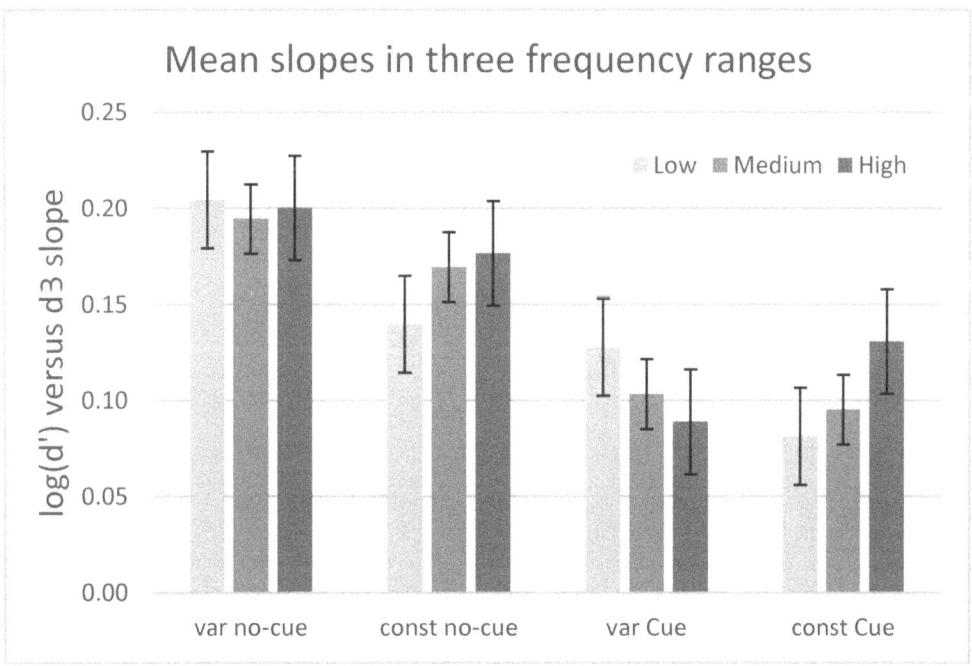

Figure 1. Mean slopes of $\log(d')$ versus dB in each condition: frequency uncertain ('var') or certain ('const') with no cue or validly cued 82 ms prior to the signal. Frequencies were in the low, middle, or high ranges (see text). Bars show ± SE of the mean.

This paper could stop here, given that the data—with a cue—conformed to Equation (1). However, data were also pooled across frequencies using the method of Green [1] with data shifted horizontally so $d' = 1$ ($\log_{10} d' = 0$) at 0 dB SL. (Without shifting, the dependence of dB SPL on threshold scatters the data.) Shifts (given in Table 3, col 1) were obtained by dividing the intercepts by the slopes of the linear fits to the $\log_{10}(d')$ versus dB SPL data, separately for each listener, frequency group, and condition. Plots of Green's type are shown in Figures 2–4 for listeners TA (top), NA (middle) and MA (bottom). Left panels show $\log_{10}$ (d′) against dB SL in *var*—right panels, in *const*. There was no cue (upper panels for each listener) or a cue (lower panels). Solid lines show linear regressions following Equation (2). Data were fit with quadratic regressions (dotted lines), for which the proportionality predicted by Equation (1) is not quite correct, despite the high linear r^2 (see Table 4, col 5). The r^2 s in the last two columns of Table 4 are lowered by the additional variability from shifting, but still show that the quadratic r^2 exceeds the linear r^2 by up to 12%. It is unlikely that the quadratic fits were random as all the bows faced downwards and had the same general form.

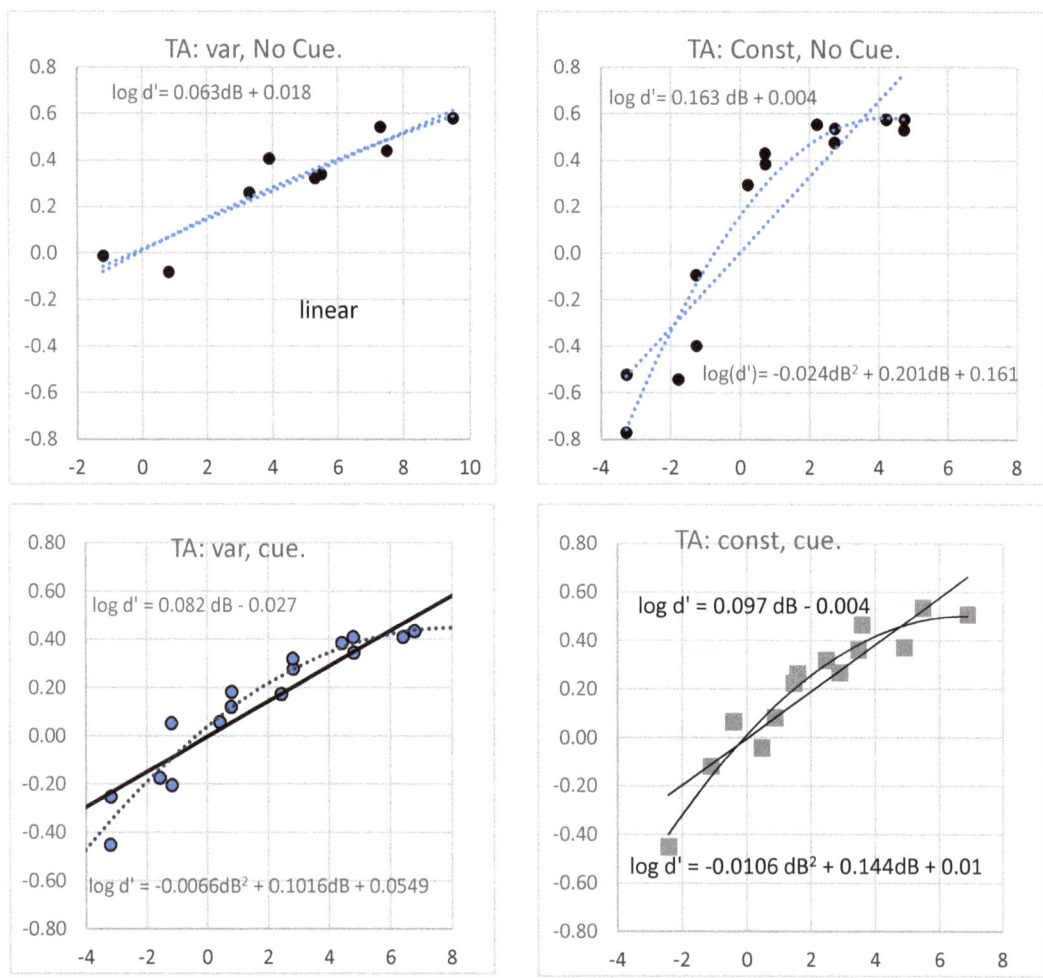

Figure 2. $\log_{10}$(d′) for all frequencies, plotted against dB SL. Listener TA. Frequency was uncertain in var (**left** panels) or certain in const (**right** panels). There was no cue (**upper** panels) or a cue (**lower** panels). Solid lines show linear regressions; mild bows were fit to the quadratic regressions shown by dotted lines.

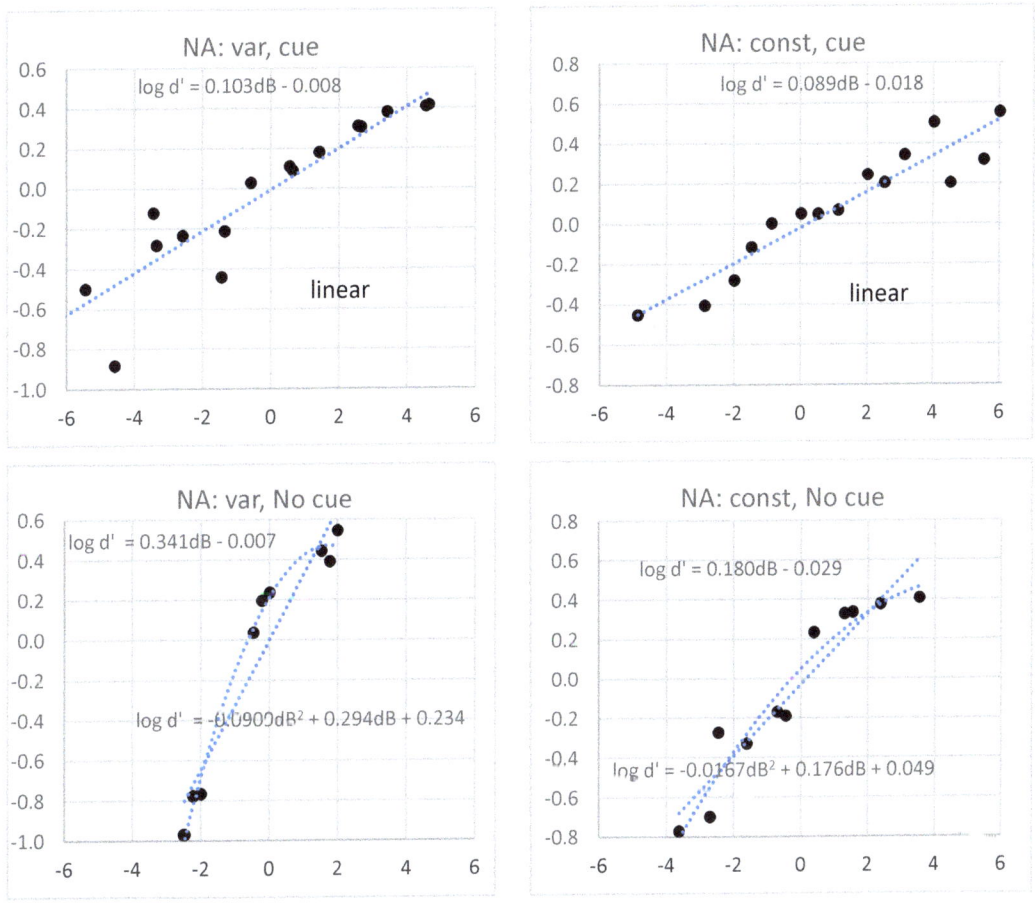

Figure 3. As in Figure 2, for listener NA.

Table 4. First three data columns: slopes, intercepts, and r^2 for linear regressions of log(d') on signal dB SL for each listener and condition, averaged over the three frequency groups. Last two columns: linear and quadratic r^2 for the shifted data shown in Figures 2–4.

Listener	Condition	Means over Frequencies			Shift	Shift
		slope	inter cpt	r^2 lin	r^2 lin	r^2 quad
TA	var No Cue	0.073	−2.46	0.88	0.86	0.87
	const NoC	0.165	−5.77	0.82	0.83	0.92
	var Cue	0.084	−3.08	0.89	0.86	0.98
	const Cue	0.110	−4.13	0.94	0.85	0.94
NA	var No Cue	0.340	−12.76	0.90	0.91	0.99
	const NoC	0.195	−7.05	0.95	0.89	0.93
	var Cue	0.102	−3.96	0.87	0.85	0.85
	const Cue	0.089	−3.43	0.94	0.89	0.90

Table 4. *Cont.*

Listener	Condition	Means over Frequencies			Shift	Shift
		slope	inter cpt	r^2 lin	r^2 lin	r^2 quad
MA	var No Cue	0.099	−3.57	0.85	0.69	0.81
	const NoC	0.125	−4.35	0.88	0.71	0.92
	var Cue	0.134	−4.76	0.94	0.87	0.89
	const Cue	0.109	−3.94	0.91	0.83	0.94
Mean	var No Cue	0.171	−6.26	0.88	0.82	0.89

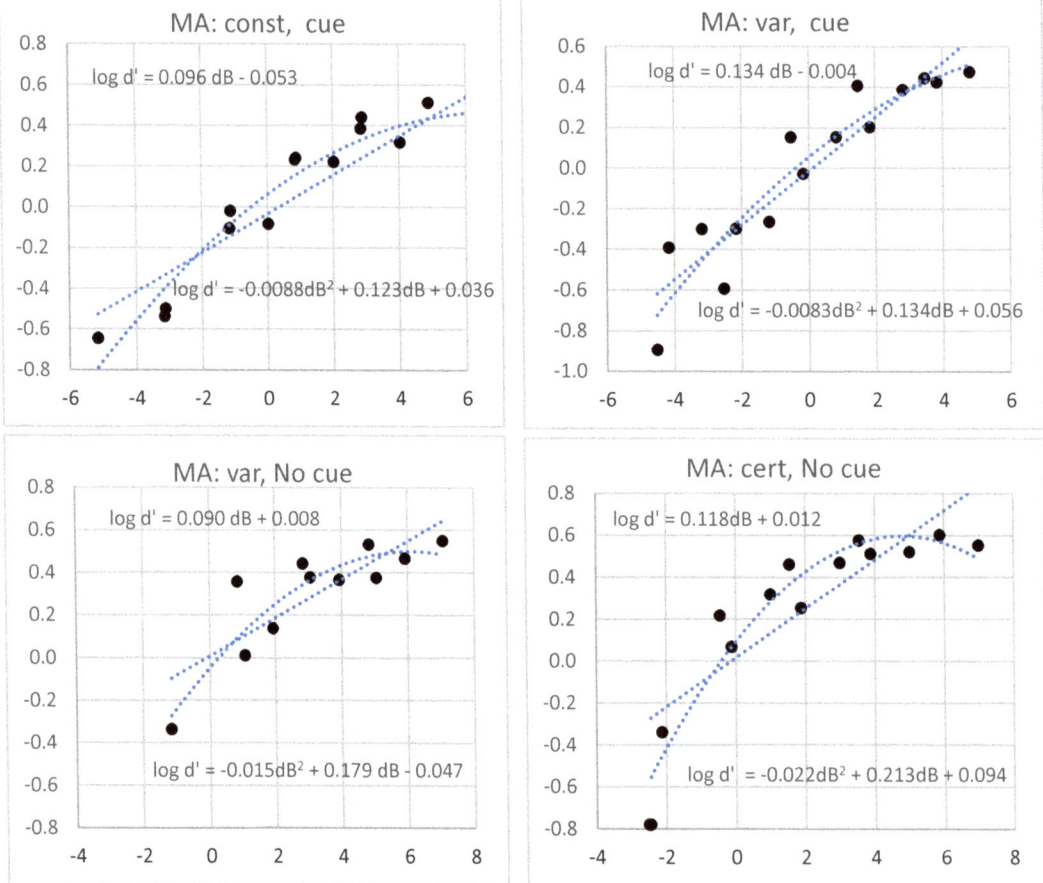

Figure 4. As in Figure 2, for listener MA.

A modification of Equation (1) to include a hard threshold, So, helps linearize these bows. Signals below the hard threshold are assumed to be inaudible. The *effective* signal is now defined as the signal level above So, so d' = 0 if S < So and

$$d' = k(S - So)/No, \text{ for } S > So. \tag{3}$$

The effective signal in dB, namely $20\log_{10}(S - So)$, is shifted further to the left at low than at high dBs, straightening out the bows. Figure 5 shows the quadratic fit to Green's [1] *const* data (with lapsing accounted for) on the left, and the linearized curve applied to the same data with So = 6 on the right.

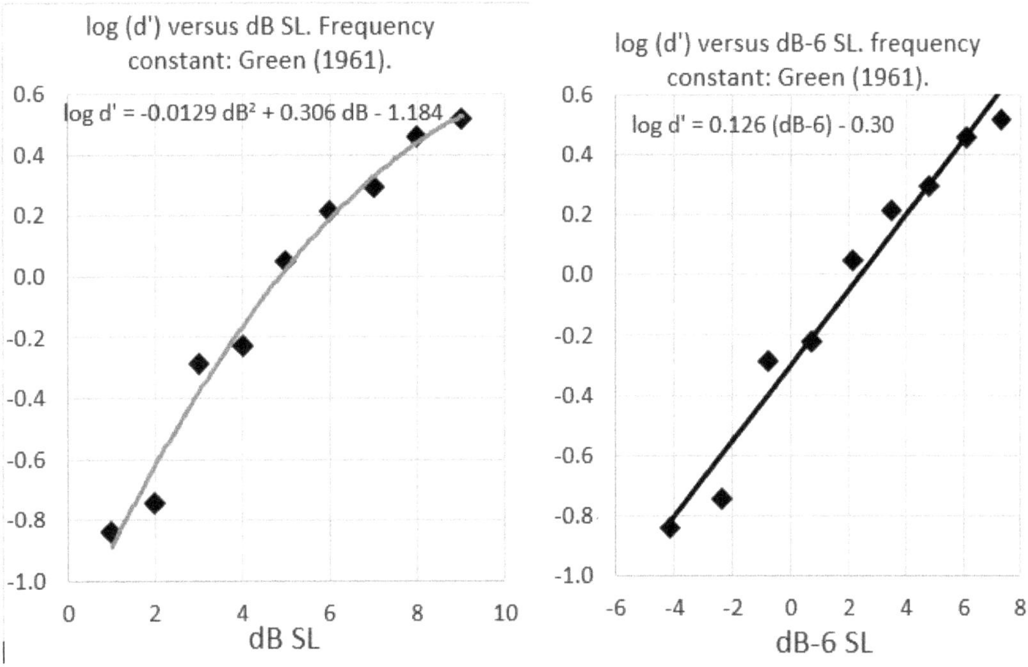

Figure 5. *Const* data from Green [1], taken from Table 1 above, plotted as log (d') versus signal dB SL (**left**), and after applying a hard threshold of 6 dB (**right**).

The same approach was taken for the present data (Figures 2–4). A value of So = 2.5, or 8 dB SPL, straightened out the quadratic bows and provided the best-fit linear regressions when applied to all three listeners and conditions. Note that So would be smaller, approaching 0 dB SPL, for the detection of long duration tones at absolute threshold. As Green and Swets [32] point out, ideally signal detection theory presumes that there is no sensory threshold. However, there is no obvious reason for a quadratic function, and a hard threshold may be more realistic.

4. Discussion

Listeners differ in the extent to which they benefit from cuing the frequency of the signal and knowing the frequency in advance. One explanation for the individual differences, as presented by Green [1], is that listeners vary in the degree to which they can voluntarily focus on a known frequency. However, there are no independent measurements here of focusing efficiency, so this remains speculative. A follow-up study with more listeners would be helpful in this respect, if the ability to focus could be independently assessed, perhaps using the probe-signal method of Greenberg and Larkin [12] or the overshoot method of Scharf et al. [34] on the same listeners. Here, one can only conclude that for this small sample, pre-cuing 82 ms beforehand *with a valid cue* let these listeners detect signals based on signal energy.

Green [1] compared known frequency to unknown as one way of assessing the effect of knowing the signal exactly by contrasting *const* with *var*. This procedure, also adopted here, may confound exogenous attention, controlled by the stimulus, with endogenous attention, controlled by the expectation or knowledge of the listener. In *const*, the same tone is repeated trial after trial, which can lead to two opposite effects; the priming of one tone on the subsequent one of the same frequency, which can increase stimulus salience, and inhibition or fatigue due to repeated stimulation, which can reduce the salience of weak stimuli [24]. These exogenous effects do not occur in *var*. Thus, the comparison of *const* with *var* may not be a simple comparison of known frequency versus unknown. Separating these two sources of attentional control would be useful.

The assumption that attention is paid equally to the signal as to the external noise in the signal critical band (the CB) in const is plausible for long-duration tones when the attention band has the same width as the CB. For the brief tones used here, the situation is more complex. Reeves [15] showed that the attention band for 40 ms tones is wider than the signal CB due to additional noise from adjacent CBs, which is progressively removed as signal duration increases. Unexcluded noise will have reduced the uncertainty effect. Scharf et al. [16] showed that, for 350 ms tones, the width of the attention band is equal to the CB whether the signal is cued or not, but no such evidence exists for 40 ms tones. A further issue is that the attention effect inferred here is untethered to other experimental methods of controlling attention. A final problem is that the temporal evolution of the cue and signal was ignored here, yet small differences in timing between the cue and the signal have large effects on signal detection [26]. Indeed, listeners can pick up temporal coherence in complex auditory streams even when paying attention elsewhere [36,37]. Knowing the temporal dynamics of focusing may aid understanding how attention suppresses noise and possibly enhances the signal.

5. Conclusions

In conclusion, uncued signals do not follow energy detection but generate steeper slopes, which may be partially accounted for by uncertainty even when stimulus frequency is known. Reducing uncertainty by pre-cuing, so that listeners can focus on the signal frequency and avoid including noise from irrelevant critical bands, demonstrates that the energy model assumed by Green [1] is correct after all. This finding comports well with the fundamental role of attention summarized by Grossberg [7], in which resonance with known information in long-term memory (here, pitch), followed by a successful match, aids perception.

Funding: AFOSR grant FA9550-04-1-0244 to Reeves and Scharf.

Data Availability Statement: Data are tabulated in the paper.

Acknowledgments: Zhenlan Jin programmed the experiments and Jennifer Olyjarchek helped run subjects and tabulate data. The late Bertram Scharf conceptualized the research program but did not plan these experiments or write the paper; any errors or misinterpretations are the sole responsibility of A.R.

Conflicts of Interest: The author and lab members have no conflict of interest.

References

1. Green, D.M. Detection of auditory sinusoids of uncertain frequency. *J. Acoust. Soc. Am.* **1961**, *33*, 897–903. [CrossRef]
2. Gilliom, J.D.; Mills, W.M. Information extraction from contralateral cues in the detection of signals of uncertain frequency. *J. Acoust. Soc. Am.* **1976**, *59*, 1428–1433. [CrossRef] [PubMed]
3. Green, T.J.; McKeown, J.D. Capture of attention in selective frequency listening. *J. Exp. Psychol. Hum. Percept. Perform.* **2001**, *27*, 1197–1210. [CrossRef]
4. Schlauch, R.S.; Hafter, E.R. Listening bandwidths and frequency uncertainty in pure-tone signal detection. *J. Acoust. Soc. Am.* **1991**, *90*, 1332–1339. [CrossRef]
5. Swets, J.A. Central factors in auditory frequency selectivity. *Psychol. Bull.* **1963**, *60*, 429–441. [CrossRef] [PubMed]
6. Hübner, R.; Hafter, E.R. Cuing mechanisms in auditory signal detection. *Percept. Psychophys.* **1995**, *57*, 197–202. [CrossRef]
7. Grossberg, S. *Conscious Mind, Resonant Brain*; Oxford University Press: Oxford, UK, 2021.
8. Dresp-Langley, B. The Grossberg Code: Universal Neural Network Signatures of Perceptual Experience. *Information* **2023**, *14*, 82. [CrossRef]
9. Scharf, B. Critical bands. In *Foundations of Modern Auditory Theory*; Tobias, J.V., Ed.; Academic Press: New York, NY, USA, 1970; Volume 1, pp. 157–202.
10. Swets, J.; Sewall, S.T. Stimulus vs Response uncertainty in recognition. *J. Acoust. Soc. Am.* **1961**, *33*, 1586–1592. [CrossRef]

11. Angeloni, C.; Geffen, M.N. Contextual modulation of sound processing in the auditory cortex. *Curr. Opin. Neurobiol.* **2018**, *49*, 8–15. [CrossRef]
12. Greenberg, G.Z.; Larkin, W.D. Frequency-response characteristics of auditory observers detecting signals of a single frequency in noise: The probe-signal method. *J. Acoust. Soc. Am.* **1968**, *44*, 1513–1523. [CrossRef]
13. Botte, M.-C. Auditory attentional bandwidth: Effect of level and frequency range. *J. Acoust. Soc. Am.* **1995**, *98*, 2475–2485. [CrossRef] [PubMed]
14. Dai, H.; Scharf, B.; Buus, S. Effective attenuation of signals in noise under focused attention. *J. Acoust. Soc. Am.* **1994**, *89*, 2837–2842. [CrossRef] [PubMed]
15. Reeves, A. The Auditory Attention Band: Data and model. In *Human Information Processing: Vision, Memory, and Attention*; Charles Chubb, C., Ed.; APA Books: Washington, DC, USA, 2013.
16. Scharf, B.; Quigley, S.; Aoki, C.; Peachey, N.; Reeves, A. Focused auditory attention and frequency selectivity. *Percept. Psychophys.* **1987**, *42*, 215–223. [CrossRef] [PubMed]
17. Wright, B.A.; Dai, H. Detection of unexpected tones with short and long durations. *J. Acoust. Soc. Am.* **1994**, *95*, 931–938. [CrossRef]
18. Scharf, B.; Magnan, J.; Chays, A. On the role of the olivocochlear bundle in hearing: 16 case studies. *Hear. Res.* **1997**, *103*, 101–122. [CrossRef]
19. Lesicko, A.M.H.; Geffen, M.N. Diverse functions of the auditory cortico-collicular pathway. *Hear. Res.* **2022**, *425*, 108488. [CrossRef]
20. Romero, G.E.; Russell, L.O. Central circuitry and function of the cochlear efferent systems. *Hear. Res.* **2004**, *425*, 108516. [CrossRef]
21. Tan, M.N.; Robertson, D.; Hammond, G.R. Separate contributions of enhanced and suppressed sensitivity to the auditory attentional filter. *Hear. Res.* **2008**, *241*, 18–25. [CrossRef]
22. Lu, Z.-L.; Dosher, B.A. External noise distinguishes attention mechanisms. *Vis. Res.* **1998**, *38*, 1183–1198. [CrossRef]
23. Treisman, A. Monitoring and storage of irrelevant messages in selective attention. *J. Verbal Learn. Verbal Behav.* **2004**, *3*, 449–459. [CrossRef]
24. Richards, V.M.; Neff, D.L. Cuing effects for informational masking. *J. Acoust. Soc. Am.* **2004**, *115*, 289–300. [CrossRef] [PubMed]
25. Scharf, B.; Reeves, A.; Suciu, J. The time required to focus on a cued signal frequency. *J. Acoust. Soc. Am.* **2007**, *121*, 2149–2157. [CrossRef] [PubMed]
26. Reeves, A.; Seluakumaran, K.; Scharf, B. Contralateral Proximal Interference. *J. Acoust. Soc. Am.* **2021**, *149*, 3352–3365. [CrossRef]
27. Zwicker, E. Dependence of post-masking on masker duration and its relation to temporal effects in loudness. *J. Acoust. Soc. Am.* **1984**, *75*, 219–223. [CrossRef] [PubMed]
28. Reeves, A.; Scharf, B. Auditory frequency focusing is very rapid. *J. Acoust. Soc. Am.* **2010**, *128*, 795–803. [CrossRef] [PubMed]
29. Kontsevich, L.L.; Chen, C.C.; Tyler, C.W. Separating the effects of response nonlinearity and internal noise psychometrically. *Vis. Res.* **2002**, *42*, 1771–1784. [CrossRef]
30. Buus, S.; Schorer, E.; Florentine, M.; Zwicker, E. Decision rules in detection of simple and complex tones. *J. Acoust. Soc. Am.* **1986**, *80*, 1646–1657. [CrossRef] [PubMed]
31. Dai, H. Signal-frequency uncertainty in spectral-shape discrimination: Psychometric functions. *J. Acoust. Soc. Am.* **1994**, *96*, 1388–1396. [CrossRef]
32. Green, D.M.; Swets, J.A. *Signal Detection Theory and Psychophysics*; Peninsular Publishing Inc.: Los Altos, CA, USA, 1988.
33. Green, D.M.; Birdsall, T.G.; Tanner, W.P. Signal Detection as a Function of Signal Intensity and Duration. *J. Acoust. Soc. Am.* **1957**, *29*, 523–531. [CrossRef]
34. Scharf, B.; Reeves, A.; Giovanetti, H. Role of attention in overshoot: Frequency certainty versus uncertainty. *J. Acoust. Soc. Am.* **2008**, *123*, 1555–1561. [CrossRef]
35. Baer, T.; Moore, B.C.J.; Glasberg, B.R. Detection and intensity discrimination of Gaussian-shaped tone pulses as a function of duration. *J. Acoust. Soc. Am.* **1999**, *106*, 1907–1916. [CrossRef] [PubMed]
36. Barascud, N.; Pearce, M.T.; Griffiths, T.D.; Friston, K.J.; Chait, M. Brain responses in humans reveal ideal observer-like sensitivity to complex acoustic patterns. *Proc. Natl. Acad. Sci. USA* **2016**, *113*, E616–E625. [CrossRef] [PubMed]
37. Dauer, T.; Nerness, B.; Fujioka, T. Predictability of higher-order temporal structure of musical stimuli is associated with auditory evoked response. *Int. J. Psychophysiol.* **2020**, *153*, 53–56. [CrossRef] [PubMed]

Disclaimer/Publisher's Note: The statements, opinions and data contained in all publications are solely those of the individual author(s) and contributor(s) and not of MDPI and/or the editor(s). MDPI and/or the editor(s) disclaim responsibility for any injury to people or property resulting from any ideas, methods, instructions or products referred to in the content.

Article

Accentuation as a Mechanism of Visual Illusions: Insights from Adaptive Resonance Theory (ART)

Baingio Pinna [1,*], Jurģis Šķilters [2] and Daniele Porcheddu [3]

[1] Department of Biomedical Science, University of Sassari, 07100 Sassari, Italy
[2] Laboratory for Perceptual and Cognitive Systems, Faculty of Science and Technology, University of Latvia, LV-1586 Riga, Latvia; jurgis.skilters@lu.lv
[3] Department of Economics and Business, University of Sassari, 07100 Sassari, Italy; daniele@uniss.it
* Correspondence: baingio@uniss.it

Academic Editors: Birgitta Dresp-Langley and Luiz Pessoa

Received: 1 October 2024
Revised: 13 February 2025
Accepted: 21 February 2025
Published: 25 February 2025

Citation: Pinna, B.; Šķilters, J.; Porcheddu, D. Accentuation as a Mechanism of Visual Illusions: Insights from Adaptive Resonance Theory (ART). *Information* 2025, 16, 172. https://doi.org/10.3390/info16030172

Copyright: © 2025 by the authors. Licensee MDPI, Basel, Switzerland. This article is an open access article distributed under the terms and conditions of the Creative Commons Attribution (CC BY) license (https://creativecommons.org/licenses/by/4.0/).

Abstract: This study introduces and examines the principle of accentuation as a novel mechanism in perceptual organization, analyzing its effects through the framework of Grossberg's Adaptive Resonance Theory (ART). We demonstrate that localized accentuators, manifesting as minimal dissimilarities or discontinuities, can significantly modulate global perceptions, inducing illusions of geometric distortion, orientation shifts, and apparent motion. Through a series of phenomenological experiments, we establish that accentuation can supersede classical Gestalt principles, influencing figure-ground segregation, shape perception, and lexical processing. Our findings suggest that accentuation functions as an autonomous organizing principle, leveraging salience-driven attentional capture to generate perceptual effects. We then apply the ART model to elucidate these phenomena, focusing on its core constructs of complementary computing, boundary–surface interactions, and resonant states. Specifically, we show how accentuation-induced asymmetries in boundary signals within the boundary contour system (BCS) can propagate through laminar cortical circuits, biasing figure-ground assignments and shape representations. The interaction between these biased signals and top–down expectations, as modeled by ART's resonance mechanisms, provides a neurally plausible account for the observed illusions. This integration of accentuation effects with ART offers novel insights into the neural substrates of visual perception and presents a unifying theoretical framework for a diverse array of perceptual phenomena, bridging low-level feature processing with high-level cognitive representations.

Keywords: visual perception; perceptual organization; dissimilarity; adaptive resonance theory; accentuation principle

1. Introduction

Kurt Koffka, one of the most influential scientists in Gestalt psychology, posed a fundamental question in perceptual science: "Why do things look as they do?" [1]. This inquiry encapsulates the essence of Gestalt psychology, which seeks to understand not just what we perceive, but the underlying mechanisms that shape our perception of the world. The principles of perceptual organization, first introduced by Max Wertheimer [2–5] (for comparative overviews and updates, see also [6,7]), now recognized as the foundational Gestalt principles, address this question by explaining how the brain organizes visual information into coherent structures. These principles have become central to vision science, offering phenomenological insights into our tendency to perceive elements within the visual field as parts of a unified whole, rather than as isolated entities.

Koffka's question arose from the specific inquiries addressed in Wertheimer's original work: What principles determine the appearance of objects? What governs the grouping of discrete visual elements into larger wholes? How do individual components organize to create holistic objects? What are the structured wholes that we perceive as objects? Thus, Koffka's question, "Why do things look as they do?" not only marks the advent of Gestalt psychology but also finds specific answers within the principles of perceptual organization.

Wertheimer identified several key principles: proximity, similarity, continuity, closure, symmetry, convexity, Prägnanz (simplicity), past experience, common fate, and parallelism. For instance, the proximity principle posits that, all else being equal, elements close together are perceived as part of a unified group. This principle can be illustrated by Figure 1a, where the proximity principle organizes dots along vertical and horizontal axes, resulting in a matrix of rows and columns. The equal proximities between the rows and columns facilitate a reversible perception, alternating between rows and columns, creating a strong sense of uniformity and vertical–horizontal stability. The high degree of homogeneity in the dot matrix generates a perception of a dotted surface on a gray background, despite the visibility of individual dots. At a foundational phenomenological level, the individual dots are perceived as a matrix, and at a more advanced level, as a dotted square surface. This demonstrates the different levels of phenomenological organization, from individual elements to their grouping based on proximity, culminating in the perception of a dotted square surface, thereby supporting the role of grouping principles.

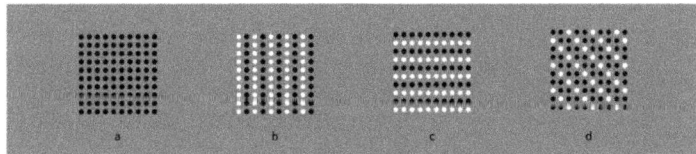

Figure 1. Proximity and similarity principles: all else being equal, the closest and most similar elements are grouped together creating columns (**a**,**b**), rows (**a**,**c**), and oblique arrangements (**d**).

Alternative groupings, such as zigzag patterns, can be formed through selective attention, although this is less likely because of the strong influence of the proximity principle. Even with intentional effort, perceiving diagonal groupings is difficult, as attention tends to focus on elements that are close together. The emphasis on rows and columns can be adjusted by altering the distances between them, thereby creating a variation in proximity (see [2–5]).

To modify the stability of Figure 1 while preserving the proximity principle, it is sufficient to introduce another type of dissimilarity between the rows and columns. In Figure 1b,c, the elements are grouped differently by reversing contrast polarity, using black and white elements on a gray background. Similar effects can be achieved by altering color, shape, or other perceptual features, although contrast polarity produces the most significant dissimilarity and change in perceptual organization due to the stark differences in luminance [8].

Subjects generally perceive alternating columns or rows consisting of white and black dots, respectively. As demonstrated in Figure 1d, the diagonal grouping of the dots can be emphasized by manipulating contrast polarity. In this case, the newly established grouping mechanism operates independently of, and even contrary to, the proximity principle, as the distances between elements along the diagonals are greater than those along the horizontal and vertical axes. According to Wertheimer, these last three groupings are governed by the similarity principle, which posits that, all else being equal, elements that are most similar are perceived as a cohesive group. This is evident in the perceptual formation of columns, rows, and diagonal structures composed of black and white dots in Figure 1b–d.

At first glance, Wertheimer's explanation for human descriptions seems straightforward, highly plausible, and consistent with empirical observations. It is no coincidence that the principle of similarity has rarely been contested (though see [9], for a notable exception). Some researchers have explored how varying levels of similarity and discontinuity facilitate the grouping and segmentation of regions [10–16].

Building on previous phenomenological descriptions, an initial observation reveals that introducing dissimilarities through reversed contrast effectively disrupts the uniform proximities among columns and rows, thereby favoring one arrangement over another. Simultaneously, the similarity in contrast polarity among the dots helps integrate them into distinct perceptual wholes. Dissimilarities assist in the segregation and differentiation of adjacent groups, while similarities enhance the internal cohesion of dots within each group.

Under these conditions, dissimilarities and similarities work together to enhance perceptual grouping by emphasizing the differences between groups and reinforcing the homogeneity within them. Therefore, a comprehensive understanding of a perceptual whole must consider at least two complementary dynamics: dissimilarities acting as divisive boundaries that highlight discontinuities within the visual field, and similarities reinforcing internal cohesion, contributing to the prominence of the segregated object. Essentially, dissimilarities define and separate the boundaries of emergent objects, while similarities enhance the perceived uniformity of their internal structures. The segregation caused by dissimilarity introduces discontinuities within the visual field, generating new information by reducing uncertainty, which is further supported by the principle of similarity. As a result, attention is naturally drawn to this emergent information, making alternative groupings that deviate from this perceptual organization highly unlikely. In short, the discontinuities introduced by dissimilarity serve as strong attractors for attention, functioning as salient features that capture and direct its focus. Dissimilarity restructures the prior perceptual organization. Dissimilarity also explains perceptual dynamics—although perception operates according to the canonical grouping principles, it is just a part of the overall dynamics of perceptual organization—and dissimilarity provides a new and stronger structure changing and constraining visual field.

In Figure 1, the synergistic interaction between similarity and dissimilarity, as predicted by Wertheimer, leads to the perception of rows, columns, or diagonals. But there is more. Returning to Figure 1b,c, by focusing attention on 3×3 sub-matrices within each global matrix, engaging in non-immediate perceptual processes, and comparing them, something not immediately apparent can be observed. This is an illusory phenomenon of elongation and widening, respectively, following the direction emerging from the grouping as reported by human subjects. Based on human descriptions, perceptual organization, contrary to Wertheimer's claim, does not end with grouping but can lead to other related phenomena.

To better visualize the illusions, observe the geometrically square patterns in Figure 2, which appear more clearly elongated or widened in the direction of the grouping. In these cases, groupings eliciting these illusions are due to both the principle of similarity and the principle of proximity. These groupings define the overall shape of the object, which in Figure 1a appears as a perfectly square matrix, and in Figure 1b, appears as a slightly vertically elongated rectangular matrix composed of alternating columns of black and white dots, and in Figure 1c as a horizontally oriented rectangular matrix composed of alternating rows of black and white dots.

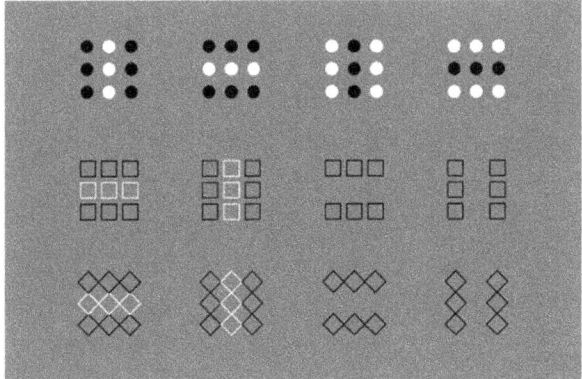

Figure 2. Despite the shape of each pattern has a geometrical square shape, it appears as a vertical or as a horizontal rectangle following the directions of the grouping.

These findings indicate that, in addition to grouping, which, as Wertheimer described, is undoubtedly perceptually significant, there are other forms of organization that are not necessarily linked to grouping alone. In Figure 2, the connection to grouping is evident, just as it is in the conditions illustrated in Figure 3, where the synergistic relationship between similarity and dissimilarity not only influences grouping but also other shape attributes (cf. [17–19]).

Figure 3. Proximity and similarity principles: all else being equal, the closest and most similar elements are grouped together, creating oblique (a–c) and vertical arrangements (d).

In addition to the deformations along the direction of grouping, there is another phenomenon, not clearly visible in Figure 1, more evidently noticeable in Figure 3, which is obtained by rotating the dot matrices of Figure 1 by 45 degrees.

Specifically, in Figure 3a,d, the matrices appear globally not as rotated squares but as diamonds, unlike the conditions illustrated in Figure 3b,c, which instead seem like squares rotated 45 degrees, the first rotated counterclockwise and the second clockwise. In the case of the diamonds, however, no orientation is perceived other than the canonical one, which belongs to the diamond, which is not a rotated square. Nevertheless, there is a substantial difference between Figure 3a,d regarding the grouping of the dots. In Figure 3a, they appear grouped according to the principle of proximity, while in Figure 3d, both black and white dots follow the larger distances along the diagonals. Thus, the appearance of Figure 3d as a diamond is significantly more pronounced compared to Figure 3a.

A similar effect, although much more pronounced, is illustrated in Figure 4, where the rotated square-diamond effect involves not only the overall matrix of elements, in this case composed of small squares, but also the individual elements themselves. More specifically, in Figure 4 (top row), the square elements are perceived as squares (left), and the diamond elements are perceived as diamonds (right). All these elements are embedded within a diamond-shaped whole, which is in both conditions perceived as a large diamond. This result is expected, as the direction of similarity emphasizes the sides of the squares on the left and the angles of the diamonds on the right, both for the individual elements and the overall shapes.

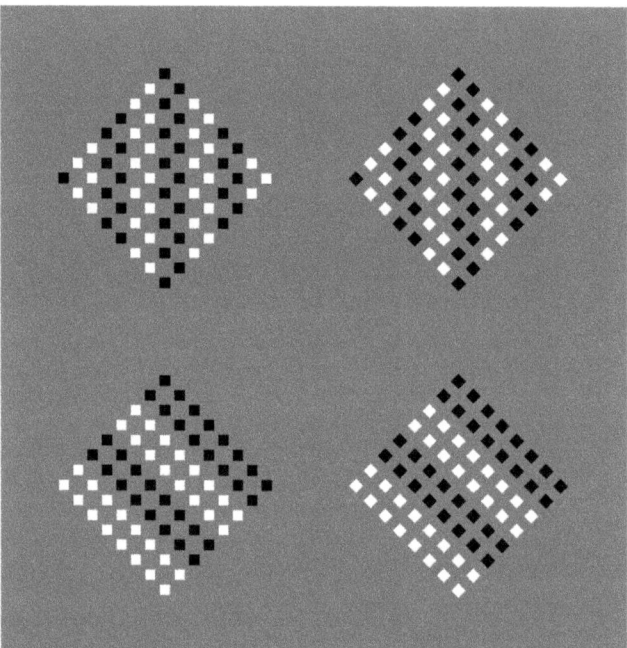

Figure 4. Squares perceived as squares (1st); diamond as diamonds (2nd); squares as diamonds (3rd) and diamonds as rotated squares (4th).

In Figure 4 (bottom row), the squares are perceived as diamonds (left), and the diamonds are perceived as rotated squares (right). Similarly, the global diamond shapes in both conditions are perceived as large rotated squares. In both cases, the direction of grouping highlights the attribute that contrasts with the geometrical shape, angles instead of sides, and sides instead of angles.

These preliminary results demonstrate that Wertheimer's principles, not only group elements, but through such groupings, they determine the directions that can influence dimensions, such as elongating and widening, as well as changing the apparent shape of both individual elements and wholes that encompass them. More simply, we could say that the resulting groupings accentuate directions and orientations that give rise to the shapes of objects. Even more briefly, the groupings seem to act as direction accentuators.

The limitations of Gestalt psychology mentioned here, which will become even more evident in the subsequent sections, are part of a broader context of the theory's shortcomings. Gestalt theory is often criticized for being too descriptive, focusing on how perceptual organization occurs (e.g., through principles like proximity, similarity, and closure) without providing mechanistic explanations for why these phenomena happen.

The theory is seen as lacking parsimony, as it introduces multiple principles without a unifying framework to explain their interplay or underlying mechanisms. Moreover, Gestalt theory does not clearly differentiate between perception and thought, leading to ambiguity in how higher-level cognitive processes influence perceptual organization.

The theory's focus on the holistic nature of perception sometimes overlooks the role of context and individual differences, which can significantly shape perceptual experiences. The theory does not address the neural and computational underpinnings of perception, which modern cognitive neuroscience has shown to be critical for understanding perceptual processes.

Despite these limitations, Gestalt theory's emphasis on experimental phenomenology and the qualitative aspects of perception remains influential and valuable.

In the following sections, we will explore what has been defined as the principle of accentuation, which, although it appears in these cases to be inextricably linked to or entirely identified with Wertheimer's principles, is in fact largely independent of them. Moreover, we will also examine all the illusory phenomena that can be generated from accentuation, much beyond the perceptual grouping studied by the Gestaltists. Finally, we will propose an explanatory theory capable of accounting for all the observed phenomena and explaining the effectiveness of this principle.

In summary, the primary aim of this study is to investigate the principle of accentuation as an innovative mechanism in perceptual organization, exploring its effects within the framework of Grossberg's Adaptive Resonance Theory (ART).

2. General Methods

2.1. Participants

Unless otherwise noted, each experiment detailed in the following sections involved different groups of 12 undergraduate students from fields such as linguistics, literature, human sciences, architecture, and design. These participants had limited knowledge of Gestalt psychology and were unaware of the specific phenomena being investigated or the objectives of the experiments. The groups consisted of both male and female students, all with normal or corrected-to-normal vision.

2.2. Stimuli

The stimuli were presented on a 21″ color CRT monitor (Sony GDM-F520, 1600 × 1200 pixels, 100 Hz refresh rate) (Sony Corporation, Tokyo, Japan) controlled by a MacBook computer. The testing environment was illuminated with an Osram Daylight fluorescent light (250 lx, 5600 K) (OSRAM Licht AG, Munich, Germany). All stimuli were displayed on a frontoparallel plane positioned 50 cm from the observer. Participants' head positions were stabilized using a chin rest, and stimuli were viewed binocularly.

The luminance of the white elements was 122.3 cd m^{-2}. Black components had a luminance value of 2.6 cd m^{-2}. The gray background luminance was 62.5 cd m^{-2}, about halfway between the white and black line components.

The stimuli were generated using a robust yet straightforward graphic design tool like Adobe Illustrator (v. 28.4.1), making them easily replicable. The figure dimensions, approximately 10° of visual angle, can be freely adjusted with minimal impact on their phenomenological clarity. The core methodology for stimulus creation relied on the simple but effective principle of introducing discontinuities or variations in specific regions near or along an object's contour, or by forming perceptual groupings that highlight different directional features of the stimulus or alter the symmetry of the object.

2.3. Procedure

The primary method used was a phenomenological free-report approach, where participants were asked, "What do you see?" Separate groups of 12 observers each described a single stimulus from the group of stimuli shown in the subsequent sections to prevent cross-stimulus interaction and contamination. The descriptions included in the paper are based on the spontaneous reports provided by at least 9 out of 12 participants in each group, with edits for conciseness and representativeness. To ensure unbiased representation and avoid interpretive bias, three independent graduate students in linguistics, who were unaware of the hypotheses, evaluated the descriptions [17,20–22]. These descriptions were then incorporated into the text to support the development of the arguments. All reports were spontaneous, and the presentation concluded once participants completed their descriptions. Participants viewed the stimuli during their reports, and the observation time was not restricted (see also [1,23–27]).

In future studies, we plan to incorporate specific quantitative methods, such as eye-tracking, reaction time measurements, or psychophysical tasks, to further enhance the rigor and robustness of our approach. These methodologies will allow for a more comprehensive analysis and provide additional insights into the phenomena under investigation.

During the experiment, participants were encouraged to reflect while observing and to perceive the stimuli in various ways. The experimenter also posed additional questions to prompt closer and deeper observation. Any potential variations that emerged during free exploration were recorded by the experimenter and are documented in the following sections. This documentation is essential for determining the optimal conditions for the emergence of the perceptions under investigation.

3. The Principle of Accentuation

3.1. Towards a Single Dot Accent

By modifying Figure 3 as shown in Figure 5, through a gradual reduction in perceptual groupings until reaching extreme conditions, such as those where the number of white dots is reduced to two, positioned at opposite corners of the dot matrix, or even to a single dot, as seen in the first and second stimuli of the second row in Figure 5, the change in the global shape from a diamond to a rotated square can be easily observed, similar to the effects perceived in Figure 3.

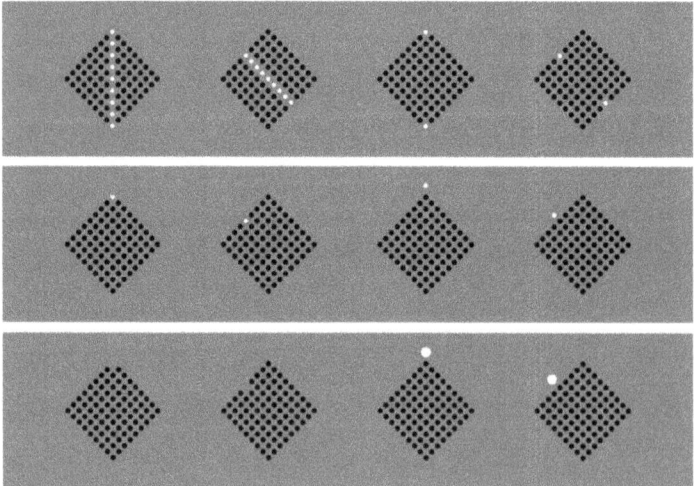

Figure 5. Rotated squares and diamonds from accentuation.

It is noteworthy that these effects persist even when a white dot of varying size is added outside the complete matrix or when one of the dots in the matrix is removed. Consequently, if the dissimilarity appears on one side of the matrix, a rotated square is perceived; if it appears at a corner or adjacent to it, a diamond is perceived. It seems as though the dissimilarities accentuate either the sides or the corners, thus emphasizing the flattening effect (sidedness) due to the phenomenological characteristics of the sides or the sharpness (pointedness) inherent to the corners and vertices of the matrix [17–19].

Note also that the grouping of the dots follows the accentuated directionality rather than proximity or similarity, as suggested by Wertheimer. Regarding similarity, the presence of a single dot or an external dot, even if of opposite polar contrast, should not fall under the principle of similarity. On the contrary, that single dot acts as a dissimilar element entirely independent of similarity (cf. [17–19]).

The rotated square-diamond phenomenon can also be accentuated as illustrated in Figure 6. In this case as well, the grouping of the individual dots follows the accentuated property and direction, that is, the rotated square or the diamond. This entails that it is the accentuation that determines the grouping of the individual dots, independently of and against Wertheimer's principles [19]. Accentuation provides the configuration of elements with an entirely new structure.

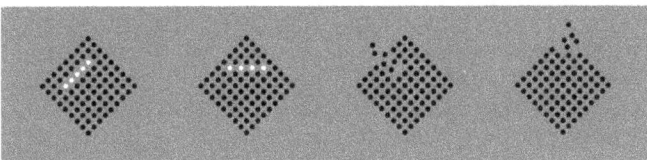

Figure 6. Rotated squares and diamonds from accentuation.

It is important to clarify the difference between a square rotated 45 degrees and a diamond. Geometrically, they are the same, but phenomenologically, they are entirely different, possessing different figural meanings. The former highlights and brings to the forefront one of its characteristics, namely being a square, and thus flattened along its side, while the latter accentuates the angles, the points, and the vertexes. A square is, in fact, composed of sides and angles that can be alternately emphasized through the methods we have discussed so far, as well as many others that we will explore later. It is as if the square contains within it two possible forms, one of which, independent of the other, can be brought out and emphasized through the principle of accentuation. We will return to this point in the next section with more complex figures involving small squares and dots.

Geometric squares can be easily switched in diamonds when their diagonals are grouped based on similarity (see Figure 7). The same elements can thus appear as squares or diamonds depending on the direction of the perceptual grouping based on similarity. The effect is even more evident in Figures 8 and 9.

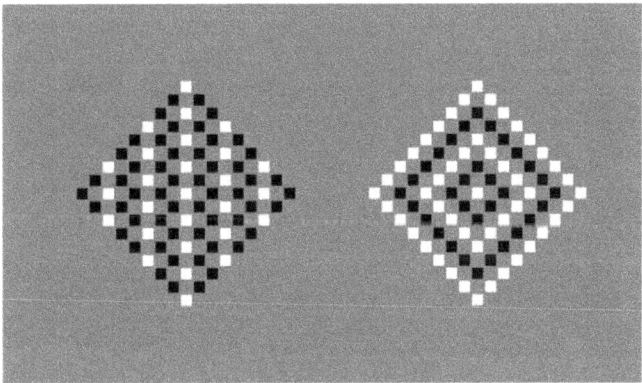

Figure 7. The same checks within the same whole perceived as squares or diamonds.

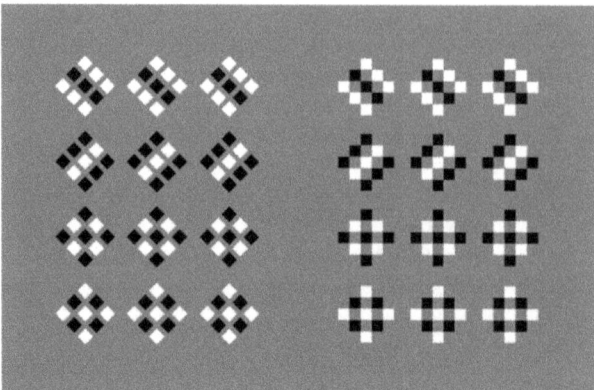

Figure 8. Diamonds perceived as rotated squares and squares perceived as diamonds.

Figure 9. Squares perceived as diamonds and diamonds perceived as rotated squares.

In Figure 8, the stimuli on the left half, despite containing geometrically identical elements, can appear as rotated squares in the upper part and as diamonds in the lower part. The opposite occurs in the stimuli illustrated on the right half, where, despite being identical to each other, they appear as diamonds in the upper part and squares in the lower part. It is worth noting the secondary effects of phenomenal transparency that arise due to the grouping of the contrast belonging to the individual elements, effects that are nonetheless unrelated to accentuation, which is the sole cause of the shape change [28].

A square-diamond switch, similar to those just described, is shown in Figure 9, where the spheres and their elements are identical in pairs along the vertical axis.

As with the dot matrices previously discussed, it is possible to achieve extreme conditions that are as independent as possible from the principle of similarity in the case of geometric squares, as illustrated in Figures 10–12.

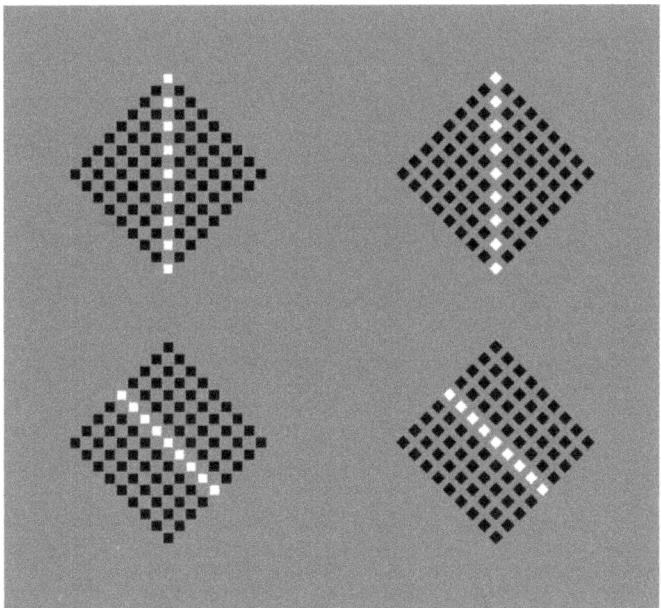

Figure 10. Diamonds and rotated squares from accentuation.

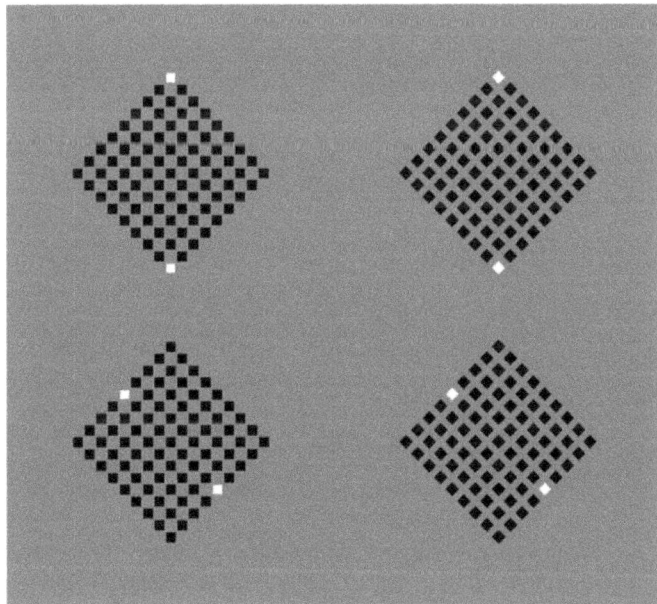

Figure 11. By reducing the vertical and oblique arrangements to only two checks placed at the antipodes, diamonds and rotated squares from accentuation.

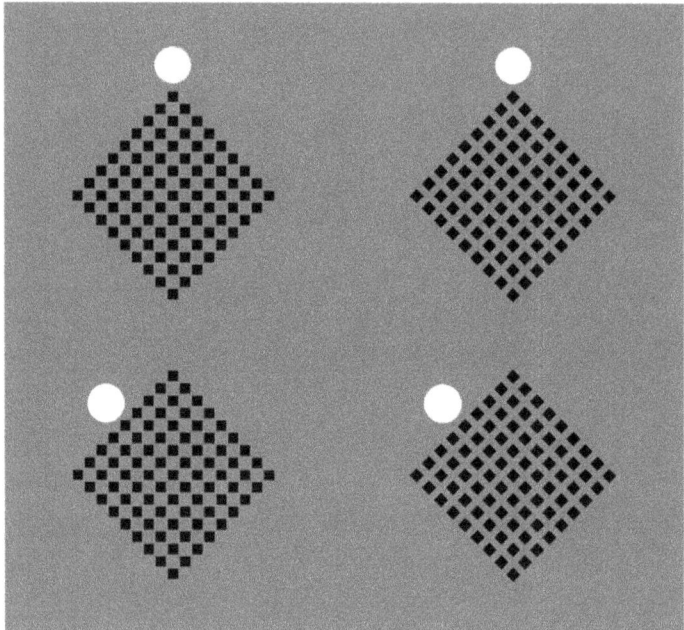

Figure 12. The white circles accentuate sides or angles within the checks and the large matrices thus switching their appearance as diamonds or rotated squares.

Figure 13 demonstrates the same effects, even in grids formed only by outlines, which can appear either crossed or parallel depending on the direction accentuated by similarity [28].

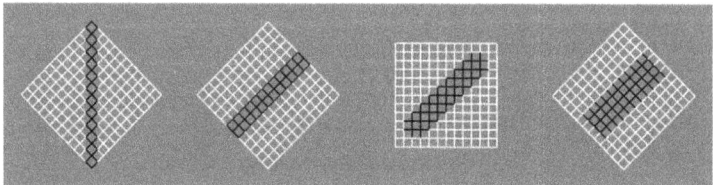

Figure 13. Crossed or parallel lines induced on a lattice by dissimilarity.

These changes in shape and orientation can cause noticeable distortions within the same homogeneous structure, especially when different directions along the sides or diagonals are accentuated, as demonstrated by Figure 14. Although the two matrices are identical and perfectly regular, they appear divided into two halves, with one part distorted along its diagonal while the other is oriented according to the vertical and horizontal directions of the space. The overall deformation is very evident. The deformation of individual elements and the global matrix in the two cases illustrated in Figure 15 is equally strong. The diamonds on the left appear wider and less tilted than those on the right. The same occurs with the two matrices as a whole, which are deformed differently.

So far, we have worked with groups of elements arranged in a matrix form. This implies a connection that is not entirely severed from Wertheimer's grouping principles, although the reduction to the extreme cases illustrated has demonstrated the possibility of making accentuation completely independent, allowing it to become a fully-fledged principle in its own right.

Figure 14. The same checks perceived as squares or diamonds.

Figure 15. The rhombi on the left are perceived to be bigger and less tilted and distorted than those on the right. Even the two matrices as a whole appear distorted in different ways.

To achieve a complete detachment, it is necessary to work on a single element rather than on groups. To this end, consider the conditions illustrated in Figure 16, where the introduction of dissimilar elements inside (black rectangles) or outside (dots) geometric squares results in the accentuation of direction or position relative to the geometric shapes along the sides or angles, giving rise to the rotated square-diamond effect.

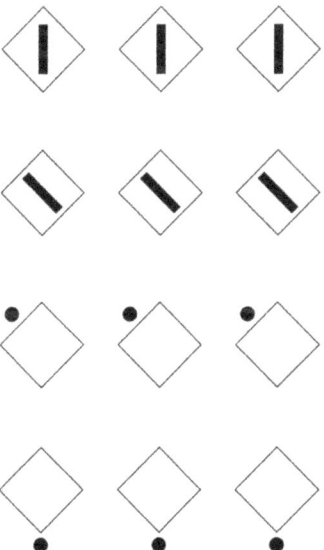

Figure 16. Accentuation of diamond (first and last rows) and rotated squareshapes (second and third rows) by introducing dissimilarity.

If we now replace the geometric squares with geometric diamonds or rhombuses (Figure 17), the accentuation leads to the perception of diamonds (first row) and parallelograms (second row), phenomenologically very different shapes despite being geometrically identical. The same effect is achieved if, instead of internal rectangles, external dots are used (not illustrated).

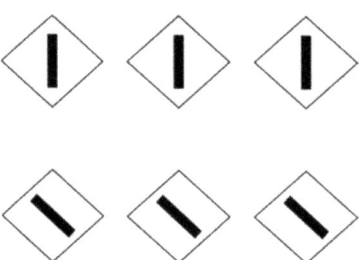

Figure 17. The rhombi of the two rows cannot be perceived as geometrically equal. The shapes of the second row are more clearly perceived as parallelograms.

The different degrees of distortion due to the presence of dots in different positions, which accentuate the different directions of the same figure, can be observed in Figure 18, where the overall deformation of the parallelogram is more intense in the first condition and partially compensated in the second.

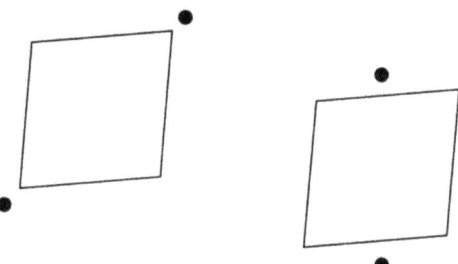

Figure 18. Different degrees of deformation of the same parallelogram.

Before proceeding, it is worth introducing some reflections. From a more theoretical perspective, accentuation is indeed a principle of organization, grouping, and form and structure generator that operates independently of Wertheimer's classic grouping principles. Moreover, it relies on dissimilarity, discontinuity, and the presence of changes. As dissimilarities, accents will be more effective on the elements and properties of both elementary and global objects to which they are applied, the more dissimilar they are. Dissimilarity implies phenomenal salience, and therefore greater power in attracting attention to a region or direction of the visual field where the processes of shape formation and object grouping are particularly decisive [19,28].

Finally, it is worth listing the effects obtained so far from the use of accentuators. Through the previous results, we observed elongations and widenings, shape switches between square-diamond or rhombus-parallelogram, deformations, and the segregations of portions within homogeneous wholes. These are not the only possible variations; we will explore others in the next section.

3.2. Illusions from Accents

In Figure 2, we observed how the accentuated direction suggested by grouping induces the global deformation of the set of elements. This result appears to be contrary to what is observed in the Helmholtz square illusion (Figure 19; see also [29]), where a square composed of horizontal segments appears taller and slimmer compared to the same square composed of vertical segments, which appears wider, like a sort of horizontal rectangle. In short, a square segmented horizontally appears as a kind of vertical rectangle, while one segmented vertically appears as a horizontal rectangle. If we now reconsider the conditions illustrated in Figure 2, we can notice an apparently opposite effect, where vertical groupings create a vertical rectangle, while horizontal groupings elicit an illusory horizontal rectangle. Seemingly, there is an unacceptable contradiction between these two conditions.

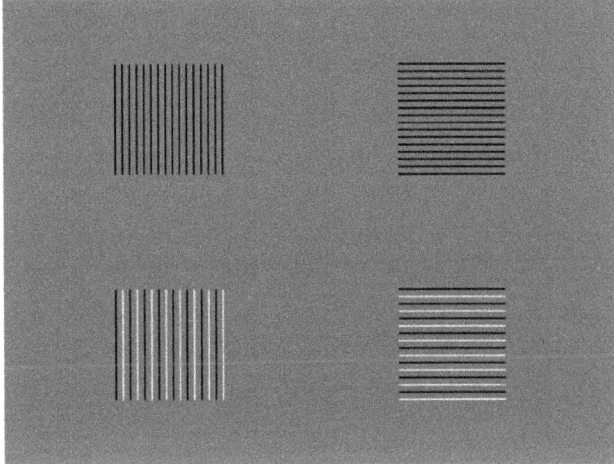

Figure 19. Helmholtz square illusion.

However, as suggested, the contradiction is only apparent. In fact, it is not just the horizontal or vertical segments of the Helmholtz square that determine the perceived shape, but the arrangement or grouping of elements that holistically defines the form. Whether they are segments, dots, squares, or diamonds, the result remains the same. Thus, since the arrangement of the horizontal segments in the Helmholtz square is vertical, the result will be a vertical rectangle. The opposite occurs in the case of vertical segments arranged horizontally. This is equivalent to the conditions illustrated in Figure 2 [18].

If all this is true, then we could easily achieve an even more intense effect of elongation or widening than those shown both in Figure 2 and in the Helmholtz square. It is simply a matter of multiplying the accentuated directions resulting from the grouping of elements, as illustrated in Figure 20 [18,19].

More specifically, the first row of Figure 20 presents two conditions where the horizontal and vertical directions and arrangements have been duplicated, respectively. In the top–left condition, two horizontal directions have been accentuated due to the arrangement of the individual vertical segments and the two horizontal bands composed of black and white vertical segments. In the top–right condition, the vertical directions have been accentuated instead. The result is a phenomenon of illusory widening and slimming that is much more intense than what is observed in the Helmholtz square. This effect can be further accentuated and amplified by adding elements (the red rectangle and the red dots) that further reinforces the directionality accentuated by the previous figural conditions (second and third row of Figure 20).

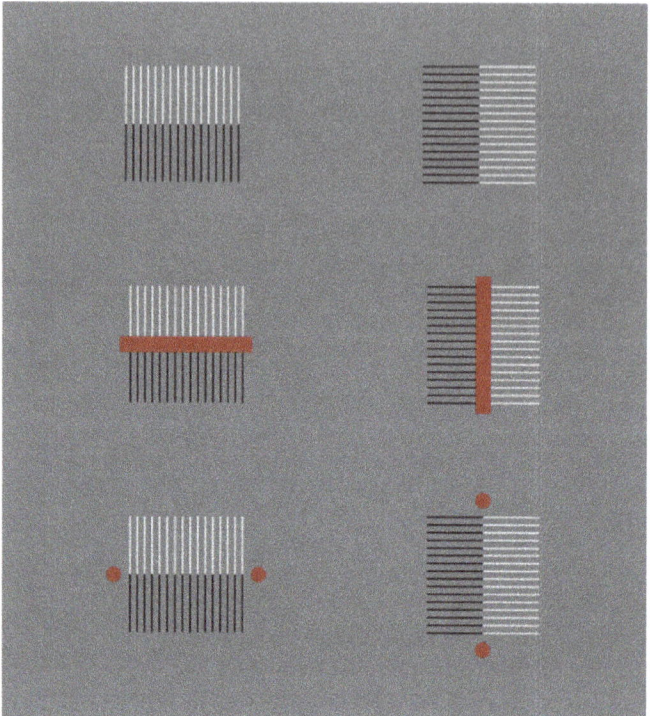

Figure 20. Improved Helmholtz square illusion.

Accents can therefore modify the shape to which they are connected, to which they belong, along the direction suggested, or the component of the figure that shows a discontinuity, dissimilarity, and, more generally, a change. This is the case with the paired conditions shown in Figure 21. Here, the individual conditions have been misaligned to prevent alignments from counteracting the illusory effect induced by discontinuity and dissimilarity or from activating visual analytical processes different from those associated with accentuation, which, after capturing attention, seems to generalize the information by spreading it globally, as we will see in the following figures. Nevertheless, even when the shapes are aligned, the effect persists unchanged.

In the first two conditions of Figure 21, the absence or cancellation of a portion of contour within the two opposite sides of the squares slims and elongates the overall square shape, in the first case, and shortens and widens the square, in the second. Similar effects are visible in the two subsequent rows, where different types of dissimilarity are present.

Similarly, we can extend the illusory phenomenon shown in the second row of Figure 20, which we can refer to as the 'tie effect', to other conditions. The presence of a vertical or horizontal strip (modal or amodal rectangle) causes a deformation of the square in the direction defined by the strip (Figure 22). Notice the strength of the induced deformation by analytically comparing the geometrically identical squares.

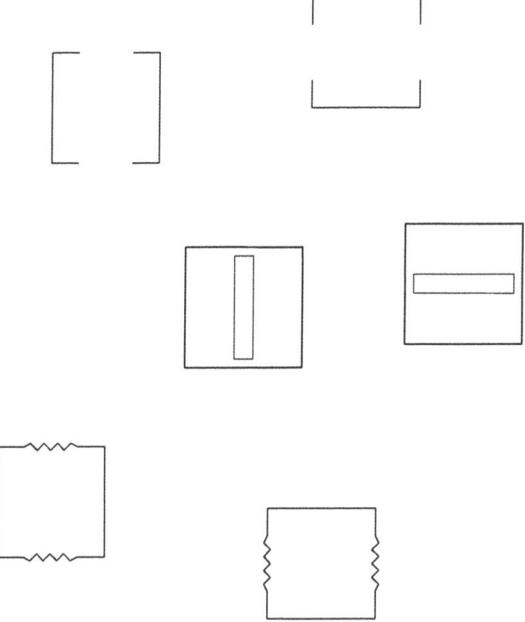

Figure 21. Vertical and horizontal rectangle following the directions of the accentuation.

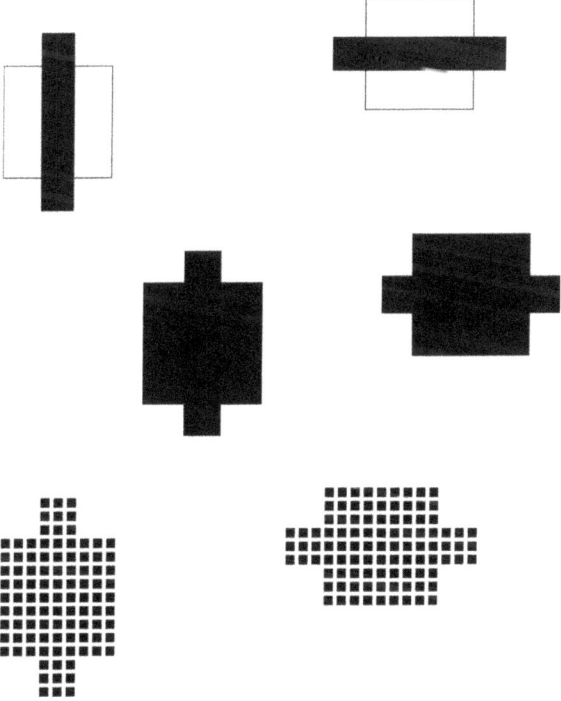

Figure 22. Vertical and horizontal rectangle following the directions of the accentuation.

Based on these results, it is possible to suggest that the use of ties in men's clothing, as well as necklaces, pendants, and necklines in women's fashion, may serve a similar function, namely elongating and slimming, thereby making the body and posture more elegant. Moreover, it is often mistakenly believed that shirts with horizontal stripes widen the body, making it appear heavier, while vertical lines elongate it. In fact, it is exactly the opposite, as demonstrated by the Helmholtz square. However, it is possible to make the desired effects much more intense than those of the Helmholtz square by using the variations suggested in Figure 20 [19].

Other conditions that appear very different at first glance, such as the emoji faces illustrated in Figure 23, show that a gradual disappearance of the eyes and mouth along the vertical or horizontal axis causes a significant illusory change in the dimensions of the face, which in all cases consists of an identical circumference. Comparing the first and last faces in both rows, one can immediately notice the different widths of the circle, which becomes increasingly deformed vertically in the first row and horizontally in the second.

Figure 23. Different widths of the circle, which becomes increasingly deformed vertically in the first row and horizontally in the second.

These last conditions suggest another illusory phenomenon of misalignment and variation in relative distance, as shown in Figure 24. Here, there are three rows of small circles, each containing a dot inside. In the first row, which serves as a control figure, the dot is placed at the center of each circle. In the second row, the dots are positioned differently, either higher or lower, but always within the circles. In the third row, the horizontal distance between the dots varies. The perceptual results are as follows: a perfect alignment of dots and circles in the first row, an apparent misalignment of the circles in the second row, and, finally, a perceived horizontal convergence or divergence of the circles in pairs in the third row, thereby altering the relative distance between them.

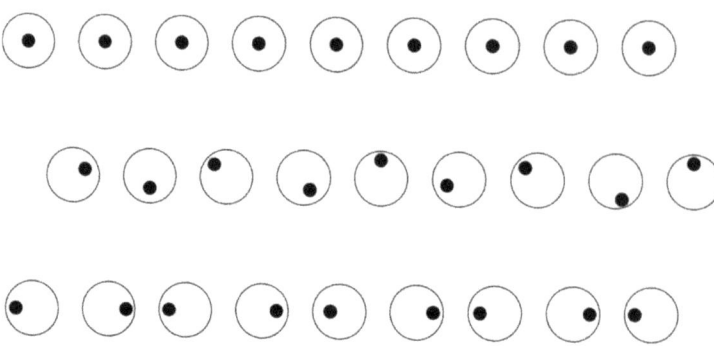

Figure 24. Illusory misalignment and variation in the relative distance of the circles.

More generally, it is as if the enclosing elements, whether circles or squares, are pushed in the relative direction defined by the dot. If this is true, it becomes possible to achieve additional illusory phenomena, such as those in Figure 25, where the presence of a dot determines the direction of the apparent motion tendency of the ball under static conditions. It is as if the ball is following the dot and not the other way around. In the first row, the ball seems to roll to the left in the first case and to the right in the second. In the second row, it appears to move upward and downward, respectively. In the third row, it seems to rise upward or fall downward, following the dot.

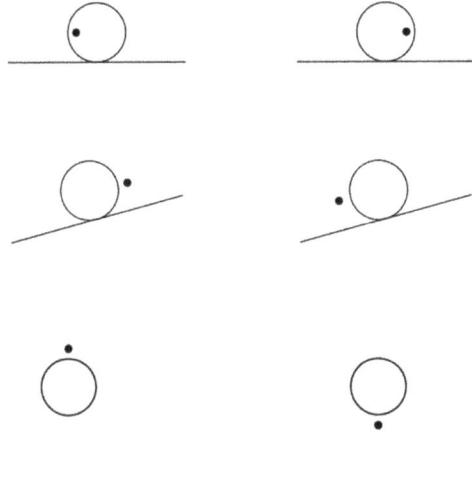

Figure 25. The ball is following the dot.

Thus, this implies that the accent can also determine the direction of pointing, even against the Configural Orientation Effect studied by Attneave [30] and Palmer [31] (see also [17,19]), who demonstrated that the arrangement of three equilateral triangles determines their pointing direction according to the overall configuration. In a sense, this could be considered an effect of accentuation due to their grouping, although, based on the previously presented phenomena, accentuation appears to be more of a local rather than a global phenomenon, dependent on a broader reference system. This is easily observable and therefore demonstrable in the conditions illustrated in Figure 26, where, despite the configural orientation effect pointing to the right, the equilateral triangles point upward in the first row and downward in the second.

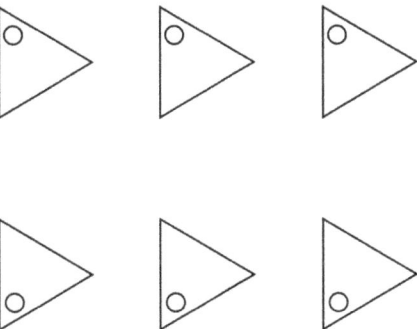

Figure 26. Illusory pointing.

There is more. If this is true, then we can make the phenomenon even more interesting, for example, by replacing the equilateral triangles with isosceles triangles synergistically oriented according to the configural orientation effect. If the accentuation of each triangle in a different direction is sufficiently noticeable, then we would expect that the shape of the isosceles triangles would also change or deform, transforming them into scalene triangles. This result is clearly demonstrated in Figure 27. Therefore, in addition to the pointing effect, there is also a shape change analogous to the switch between a rotated square and a diamond, as previously described.

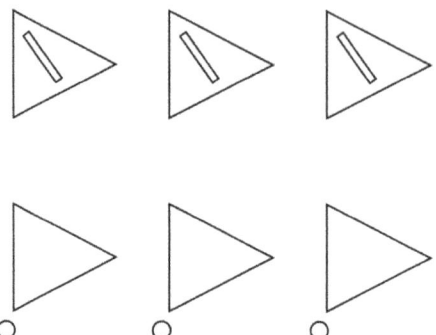

Figure 27. Illusory pointing and the scalene effect.

As previously mentioned, these accentuation-induced phenomena do not necessarily have to operate in each element of a configuration. It is sufficient for them to be present in a single component for the effect to propagate to all the others. This is the diffusion, filling-in or the generalization of an accentuated element that captures attention. The effect observed in this single element spreads to all the others, even across a very broad area (Figure 28). The effect can be compared to social conditions characterized by prejudice, where a single case is generalized to an entire population. Probably, the underlying processes in social contexts are analogous to those described by the principle of accentuation.

In the previous figures, we have seen how a single dot can not only modify a shape through deformation or a switch of its shape attributes, such as sides or angles, but also change the pointing direction, alignment, relative distance, and even alter the direction of apparent tendency to move despite being in a static condition. We will now explore how possible effects due to accentuation apply to different shapes beyond the square, circle, and triangle that we have worked with so far. We ask ourselves the following questions: If a square contains within it two potential forms that can be accentuated by a simple dot, what happens to an irregular quadrilateral with four different sides and four different angles? How many inner shapes can we accentuate given the diversity of its shape attributes? Based on our results, we can assume that all the present diversities or dissimilarities can give rise to different shapes, resulting in a total of eight possible forms. In Figure 29, for simplicity, three of the eight possible forms are shown, aligned in a way that contrasts with the configural orientation effect.

As can be easily observed, the elements in the first row appear as trapezoids, in the second as rhomboids, and in the third as shapes that are different from the previous ones. It is as if accentuation creates a sort of camouflage, making each shape different and almost unrecognizable compared to the actual geometric form present.

Figure 28. The accentuation effect of a single element spreads to all the others.

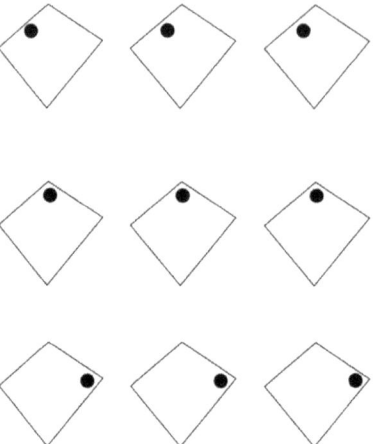

Figure 29. Trapezoids, rhomboids, and other shape within the same geometrical quadrilateral.

The phenomenon becomes even more evident when we move from a quadrilateral to a more complex irregular shape, like the first one illustrated in Figure 30, which at first glance appears as an irregularly undulating amoeboid shape, without any part being particularly prominent or more salient than others, except maybe for the left side, which is wider than the rest. However, at first sight, nothing seems to stand out significantly, with attention jumping from one part to another without lingering too long on any component. If we now add a dot, the accentuated region emerges in the foreground, characterizing all the other parts based on it (Figure 30, second row). Thanks to the dot, the irregular shape becomes a sort of organism moving in the direction of the dot, as seen in Figure 25. At the same time, all other components of each organism adapt to the properties of the accentuated part, making the illustrated shapes appear different from each other in many different attributes, not just expressively.

Figure 30. Different organic shapes from accentuation.

We might ask ourselves how many possible shapes can be accentuated. Certainly, many more than those of the square and the irregular quadrilateral. One might also wonder if the dot acts as a sort of eye, thereby attributing the characteristics of a head to the region where it is applied, from which the body follows. It is likely that this attribution is indeed the case, but not because it resembles an eye, as can be demonstrated by the examples illustrated in Figure 31, where the accents do not resemble eyes but still act similarly to the dot.

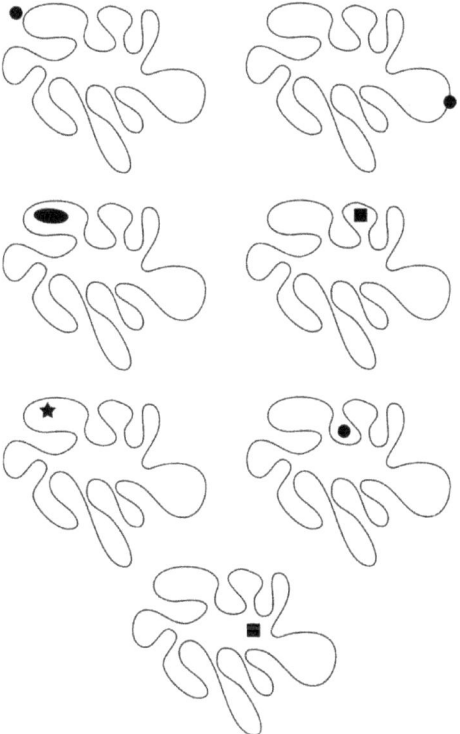

Figure 31. Different organic shapes from accentuation.

The use of accents cannot only render an irregular shape unrecognizable, as illustrated in Figure 32, where the four shapes correspond to the same one rotated progressively more, but also make it easily recognizable as the same rotated shape, as demonstrated in Figure 33 [19].

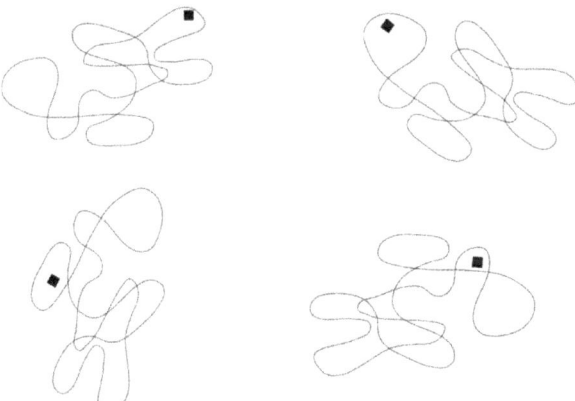

Figure 32. Rotated irregular shapes unrecognizable from accentuation.

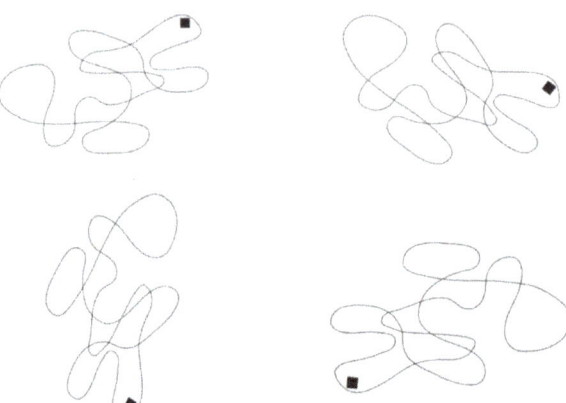

Figure 33. Rotated irregular shapes recognizable from accentuation.

In the same way that ties, necklaces, necklines, and other pendants elongate and slim the human body, it is highly likely that natural accentuators, known as ocelli, present in the markings of many organisms, starting with butterflies, operate to camouflage or modify the shape of the organism, helping to avoid predators while also deceiving prey, thereby improving adaptive fitness (see Figure 34) [17,19].

Figure 34. Accentuation in human fashion and animal markings (all pictures are sourced from publicly available sources).

Accentuation through single points can thus produce various illusory effects since it can be assumed that they highlight the figurality of the region where they are present, along with all the phenomenal attributes associated with that region. This means that the principle of accentuation, in addition to determining Wertheimer's perceptual grouping, as shown, may also be responsible for figure-ground segregation [32]. In Figure 35, several conditions demonstrate accentuation as a principle of figure-ground segregation to be added to the well-known principles studied by Rubin [33].

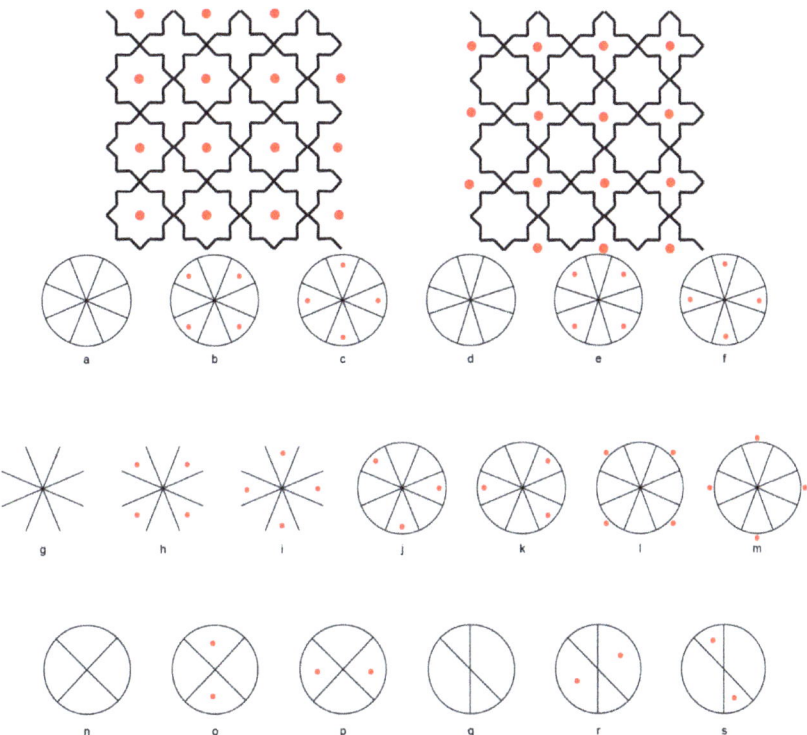

Figure 35. The role of accentuation in figure-ground segregation.

It is worth noting that accentuation with dots is just one of the many possible ways to accentuate the intrinsic properties of shapes. Figure 36 shows other methods to achieve similar effects to those previously discussed. What unites and makes accentuation effective, and what underlies the phenomenological notion of accentuation, is a simpler characteristic that, in harmony with Gestalt theory, has been termed dissimilarity. This corresponds to a discontinuity or the presence of a completely different element in proximity to a region carrying phenomenal attributes. Figure 36 contains discontinuities and dissimilarities of a different nature compared to those previously demonstrated.

In the first row, we once again observe the rotated square-diamond switch due to the removal of a corner and part of the upper side. In the second row, different vertices of the same pattern composed of isosceles triangles have been removed, which seem to point both locally and globally in a direction opposite to the geometrically privileged direction, that is, along the two equal sides of each small triangle and the overall composed triangle. As already observed in the case of Figure 27, this results in the isosceles triangles appearing both locally and globally as scalene triangles. In the third row, three identical octagons with the same orientation, due to the accentuation of vertices and sides in the second and third conditions, appear as two octagons rotated relative to each other, the first with vertices in the foreground and the second with sides emphasized, making them seem differently oriented.

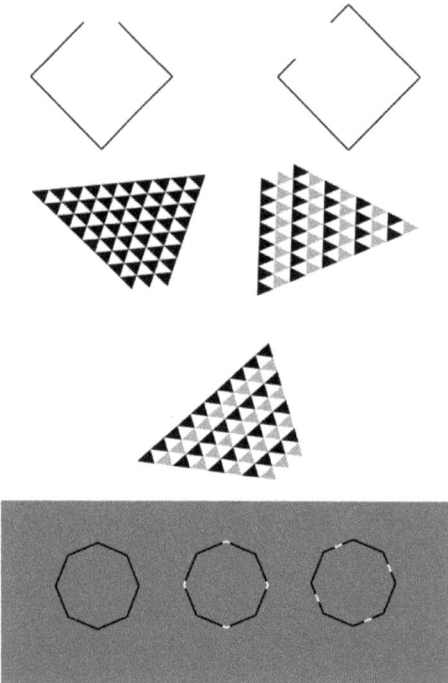

Figure 36. Different kinds of accentuation.

This last condition allows us to immediately take the next step, which addresses the question: what is the resulting effect if we accentuate different sides of the same square? The answer is demonstrated in Figure 37 [19,34]. In this case, white squares have one side accentuated in black. This is the dissimilar side and therefore responsible for the accentuation, which causes both a deformation of the squares, appearing as small rectangles oriented either vertically or horizontally, and an alternation in their orientation, up–down in the first case, and left–right in the second. In other words, while the elements of the first matrix appear alternately oriented upward and downward, as if moving in the direction suggested by the accent, those in the second matrix seem oriented and moving horizontally to the left and right. One can also notice the apparent misalignment of the small squares, as well as their deformation, as if they were small rectangles oriented vertically or horizontally.

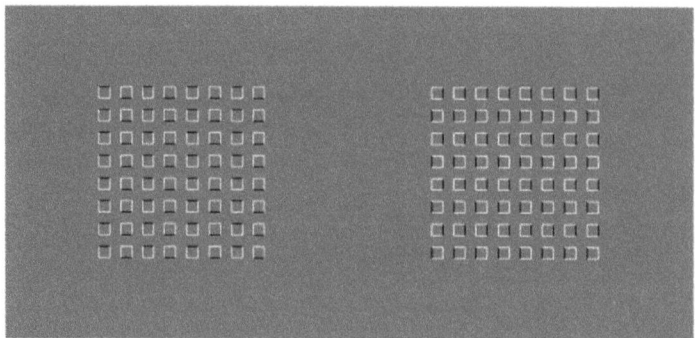

Figure 37. Apparent up and down and left and right motion from accentuation.

When shifting the gaze from one small square to another, an apparent movement is also observed, not just a tendency, but a kind of real movement or quick shift, as if the entire grid of alternating rows and columns were unstable and trying to reach an alignment that is impossible to achieve. This effect becomes even more evident if, while following the tip of a pen as it slowly moves up and down, left or right, within each matrix, one observes in peripheral vision what happens to the small squares around it. The previously described instability appears as a real movement of adjustment [19,34].

The phenomena just described can be amplified by accentuating the small squares in different ways, as shown in Figure 38 [19,34], where the accentuation involves two sides and therefore a different vertex, alternately from one small square to the adjacent one. First of all, one can notice the alternating deformation along the vertices of the individual elements, as if each were being pulled by an opposite vertex, creating a sort of rhomboid shape. Observing the figure as previously described, by focusing on the tip of a pen that slowly moves across the image, a kind of illusory movement can be noticed where each component seems to slide and partially rotate, just as if it were a real movement [19,34].

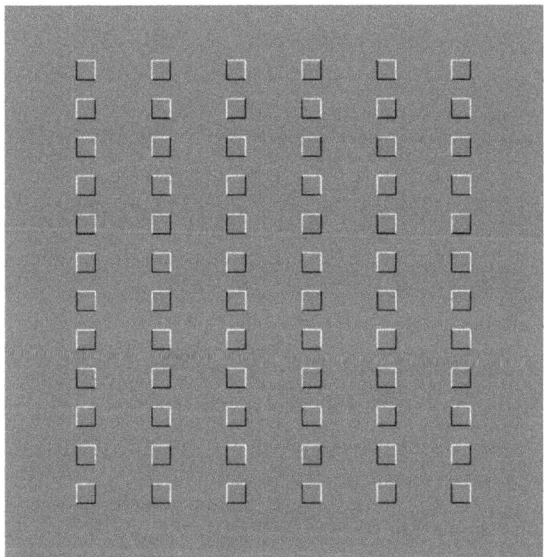

Figure 38. Shape deformations of the checks and apparent motion.

The apparent movement becomes even more evident when the conditions of similarity between the small squares allow it to be transmitted from one element to another, as illustrated in Figure 39. Observing the figure using the previously described technique results in a very noticeable horizontal motion when the pen is moved vertically, and a vertical motion when it is moved horizontally. Additionally, due to the accentuation of opposite vertices in the upper half of the pattern of small squares compared to those in the lower half, a loss of geometric alignment parallelism occurs, resulting in alternating columns that form concave and convex patterns in pairs [19,34].

It is not necessary to accentuate the entire vertex to achieve a similar effect, even if it is less pronounced than the previous one (Figures 40 and 41). A single dot is sufficient to observe the apparent motion using the previously described observation technique.

If the small squares are rotated by 45 degrees and two dots are placed on opposite sides, both within each individual square and between those that compose a column and the next, other interesting effects are observed (Figure 42). First, the apparent motion persists in a very noticeable way. Additionally, each small square appears elongated in the accentuated direction, as expected. Therefore, since they appear as small rectangles, if one were to try to visually align the elements of one column with another, perfect overlap would be impossible [19,28,34].

Figure 39. Global convex/concave effects and apparent motion.

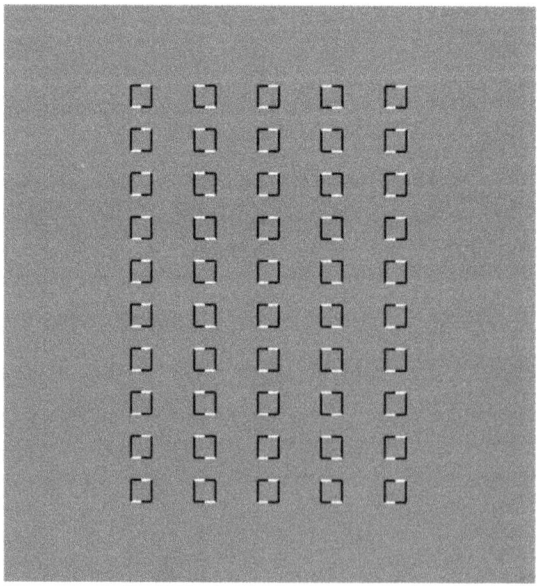

Figure 40. Apparent motion under more simple accentuation.

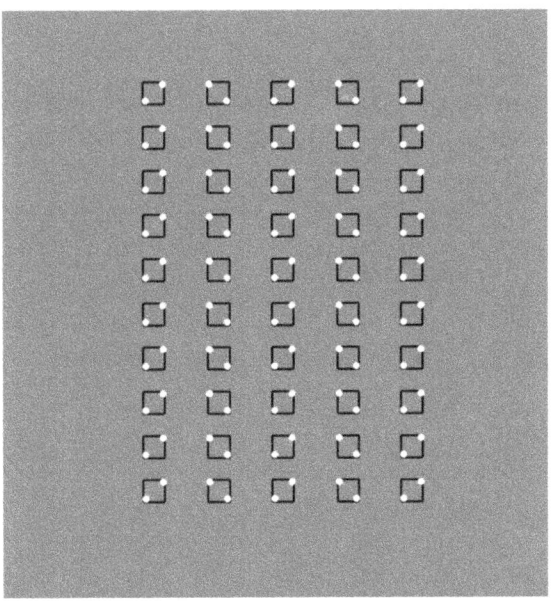

Figure 41. Apparent motion under simple accentuation.

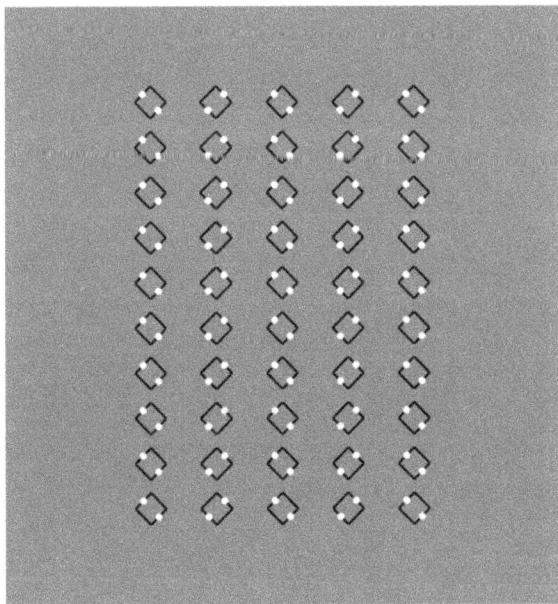

Figure 42. Apparent motion and shape deformations under simple accentuation.

Accentuation, in all its forms, proves to be particularly effective as a generator of illusions. But that is not all. Accentuation can also be useful in explaining other illusions that, at first glance, seem to be caused by phenomena and variables unrelated to accentuation. This is the case with the well-known Shepard's table [35], illustrated in Figure 43, where the tabletop on the left appears very different from the one on the right. The explanations provided so far focus on the different perspective orientations. However, reducing the stimulus to an extreme case, as shown in the lower part of Figure 43, suggests that the accentuation caused by pairs of dots is more than sufficient to generate the phenomenon. Figure 43a shows the exact relative distortion of Shepard's table, a distortion that appears inverted in Figure 43b when the accentuators are arranged in the opposite way. In Figure 43c,d, the two parallelograms appear almost identical, with the accents balancing each other out [19].

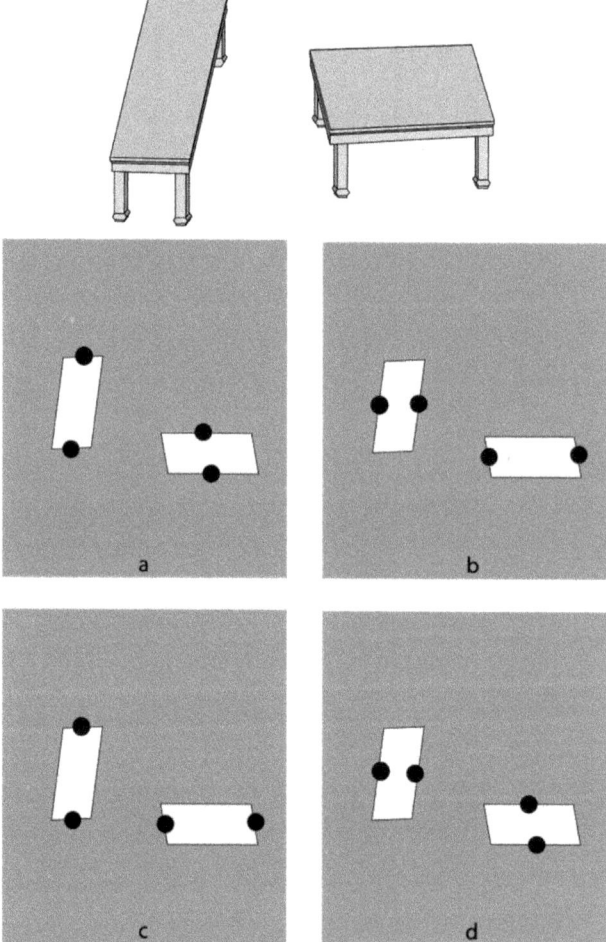

Figure 43. Shepard's table from accentuation.

One final effect, but no less important, is that accents can either facilitate or hinder the process of reading a text. In Figure 44, several conditions are shown where, by accentuating entire words or certain letters in different positions through polar contrast, whether or not spaces between words are present, the reading process can be made easier or more difficult, affecting the reading time or increasing errors. Similar results are obtained using different colors or placing dots above individual letters. The reader is invited to try reading the text in all the combinations presented here to confirm this effect.

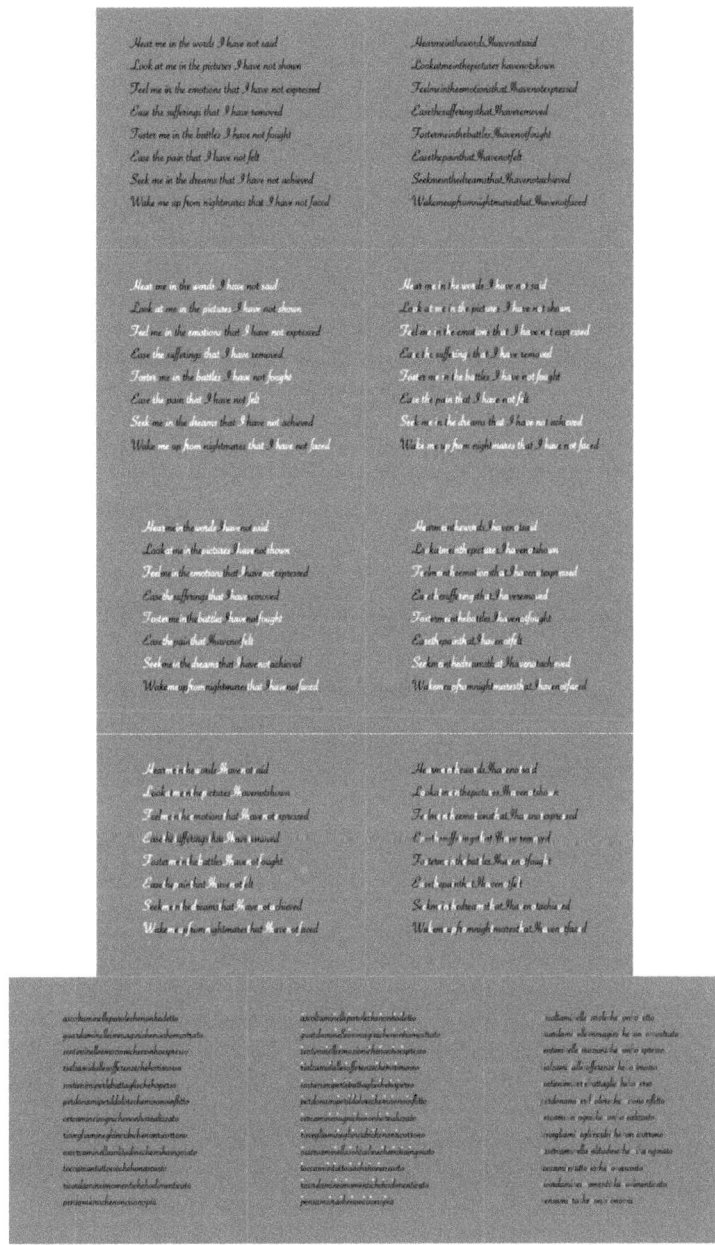

Figure 44. Accents can either facilitate or hinder the process of reading a text.

Given these visual illusions from accentuation, in the next section, we will explain both of them and the concept of accentuation itself in light of the Adaptive Resonance Theory (ART).

4. Accentuation in Light of the Adaptive Resonance Theory (ART)

4.1. Introduction

Stephen Grossberg's theory of visual perception stands as a cornerstone in our understanding of how the brain processes visual information, learns to recognize patterns, and generates conscious percepts. Developed over several decades, this comprehensive framework integrates multiple aspects of neural processing and has been instrumental in elucidating various phenomena in vision and cognition.

At the heart of Grossberg's theory lies the principle of complementary computing. This concept posits that the brain is organized into pairs of complementary subsystems, each specializing in different, often opposing, aspects of information processing. In vision, this principle is exemplified by two primary subsystems: the Boundary Contour System (BCS) and the Feature Contour System (FCS). The BCS is responsible for detecting and completing edges and boundaries, operating independently of contrast polarity and completing boundaries inwardly. Conversely, the FCS fills in surface properties like color and brightness, being sensitive to contrast polarity and spreading activation outwardly until stopped by boundaries. These systems, primarily associated with the interblob and blob streams in visual cortical areas V1 and V2, respectively, interact to allow the perception of coherent objects with well-defined boundaries and surfaces.

Central to Grossberg's theory is the Adaptive Resonance Theory (ART), which explains how the brain learns to categorize and recognize patterns while maintaining stability in its learned memories. ART describes a process where sensory inputs activate potential categorical representations in higher cortical areas through fast, bottom–up processing. These activated categories then send feedback signals to lower areas, representing learned expectations about the input. When bottom–up and top–down signals match sufficiently, a resonant state occurs, leading to conscious perception and learning. This mechanism elegantly solves the stability–plasticity dilemma, allowing the brain to remain plastic (able to learn new information) while also remaining stable (not forgetting previously learned information).

Grossberg's theory provides a detailed account of how visual processing is implemented in the layered structure of the visual cortex. It describes how different cortical layers perform specific functions: layer 4 receives bottom–up input and is modulated by top–down attention, layers 2/3 are the site of long-range horizontal connections involved in perceptual grouping, layer 6 provides modulatory feedback to layer 4, and layer 5 is involved in transmitting signals to other brain regions. This laminar organization explains phenomena like perceptual grouping, attention, and figure-ground segregation.

The theory extends to 3D vision and figure-ground perception through the FACADE (Form-And-Color-And-Depth) model. This model proposes that the visual system represents information at different depth levels, with 3D boundaries and surfaces interacting to create coherent percepts. Surface properties are filled in within depth-specific boundary representations, and figure-ground separation emerges from the interactions between boundaries and surfaces at different depths.

Attentional modulation plays a crucial role in Grossberg's theory. It distinguishes between spatial attention, which enhances processing in the specific regions of visual space, and object attention, which focuses on features and properties of specific objects. The concept of an attentional shroud, a form-fitting distribution of spatial attention, is introduced to explain how attention aids in object learning and recognition.

The ARTSCAN model, a further extension of Grossberg's theory, elucidates how the brain coordinates spatial and object attention during the learning and recognition of object categories. It explains processes such as view-invariant category learning, eye movement control during object exploration, and the formation and access of invariant object representations.

A key concept in Grossberg's theory is that conscious experiences are the emergent properties of resonant states in the brain. These resonances can occur between bottom–up features and learned categorical representations (feature-category resonance), between filled-in surface representations and spatial attention (surface-shroud resonance), and even between cognitive and emotional processes (cognitive-emotional resonance).

The theory incorporates several learning mechanisms, including self-organizing feature maps for learning the topographic representations of sensory inputs, adaptive filters for mapping between different levels of representation, competitive learning for categorization and pattern recognition, and match-based learning that occurs during resonant states to refine and stabilize learned representations.

Grossberg's framework also addresses the temporal aspects of visual processing, distinguishing between rapid feedforward processing and slower feedback and resonance. It explains phenomena like visual persistence and afterimages through the dynamics of neural activation and reset.

Importantly, this theory extends beyond vision, providing frameworks for understanding speech and language processing, cognitive–emotional interactions, decision making, action selection, working memory, and sequence learning. This broad applicability underscores the theory's power in providing a unified account of how the brain sees, learns, and adapts to its environment.

In summary, Grossberg's theory offers a comprehensive, biologically plausible framework for understanding visual perception and cognition. Its strength lies in its integration of multiple levels of analysis, from individual neurons to network dynamics to psychological phenomena, making it a powerful tool for explaining a wide range of perceptual and cognitive processes.

4.2. Applying Grossberg's Theory to Accentuation Phenomena

Grossberg's theory provides a comprehensive explanation for the perceptual effects observed in Figure 1. The alternating black and white dots create strong boundary signals in the Boundary Contour System (BCS). According to the principle of complementary computing, these boundaries interact with the Feature Contour System (FCS) to fill in surface properties [36]. In conditions b and c, the contrast polarity differences between adjacent columns or rows create stronger vertical or horizontal boundaries, respectively. This asymmetry in boundary strength leads to a bias in the resonant state formed between bottom–up sensory inputs and top–down expectations. The Adaptive Resonance Theory (ART) component of Grossberg's model suggests that this resonance reinforces the perception of elongation in the direction of stronger boundaries [11].

The attentional mechanisms described in ARTSCAN further enhance this effect [37]. The accentuated boundaries capture spatial attention, forming an attentional shroud that conforms to the elongated percept. This attentional modulation strengthens the resonant state, making the illusion of elongation more pronounced and stable.

The shape deformations and rotated square-diamond effects in these figures can be explained through the interaction of boundary completion and surface filling-in processes in Grossberg's model [38,39]. In Figure 2, the accentuation created by contrast polarity differences induces asymmetric activation in the BCS. This asymmetry biases the boundary completion process, leading to a perceptual elongation of the overall shape. The FCS then fills in surface properties consistent with these altered boundaries, reinforcing the illusion.

For the rotated square-diamond effect (Figures 3 and 4), Grossberg's theory of 3D vision and figure-ground separation becomes relevant [40]. The accents (dots or lines) create strong, localized boundary signals that influence the global interpretation of shape. In ART terms, these salient features rapidly activate categorical representations (corresponding to different figural meanings) of either "diamond" or "rotated square". The activated category then sends top–down expectations that enhance consistent features, creating a resonant state that stabilizes the chosen percept. The ARTSCAN model further explains how attention is deployed differently in each case. For the diamond percept, attention is drawn to the corners, while for the rotated square, it focuses on the sides. This attentional deployment reinforces the respective interpretations through feedback loops in the laminar cortical circuits described by Grossberg [41].

Figures 5–9 demonstrate how even minimal accentuation can dramatically alter perception. Grossberg's theory explains this through the concept of "symmetry-breaking" in neural networks [42]. A single accent creates an asymmetry in the BCS activation, which is then amplified through recurrent processing in the laminar cortical circuits. The ART component of the theory is crucial here [11,39]. The accent serves as a highly salient feature that rapidly activates a specific categorical representation (e.g., "diamond" or "rotated square"). Once activated, this category sends strong top–down signals that reshape the processing of the entire figure, even in regions far from the accent. The FACADE theory's explanation of figure-ground separation is also relevant [40]. The accent influences the assignment of border ownership, affecting how the visual system interprets the object's shape and its relation to the background.

Grossberg's theory offers a rich explanation for these complex phenomena of Figures 37–42. The apparent motion and shape instability arise from the interaction between boundary formation, surface filling-in, and attentional processes [43,44]. The alternating accents create ambiguous boundary signals in the BCS. As attention shifts (modeled by ARTSCAN's attentional shroud mechanism), these ambiguous signals interact with motion processing circuits. Grossberg's model of motion perception suggests that the visual system attempts to resolve this ambiguity by generating illusory motion percepts [45]. The shape instability can be understood through the concept of multi-stable resonances in ART [11]. Different interpretations of the stimuli compete, with slight shifts in attention or neural noise causing switches between alternative resonant states. Each state corresponds to a different perception of shape or motion.

Figure 35 demonstrates how accentuation influences figure-ground segregation, a process well explained by Grossberg's FACADE theory [40]. The accents create asymmetric boundary signals in the BCS, which bias the assignment of border ownership. This bias propagates through the laminar cortical circuits, influencing larger-scale figure-ground assignments. The ART component of the theory explains how these local accents can have global effects. The accented regions activate specific categorical representations, which then send top–down signals that reshape the interpretation of the entire image, reinforcing the figure-ground segregation initiated by the accent.

Grossberg's theory of 3D vision and surface perception provides a more inclusive account of the effect of Figure 43 [40]. The accents influence the BCS's interpretation of depth cues, biasing the perception of surface orientation. This bias is then reinforced through resonant interactions between boundary and surface representations in the FACADE model. The ARTSCAN model further explains how attention is deployed differently based on the accent placement, reinforcing either the "long" or "wide" interpretation of the table [37]. This attentional deployment creates a feedback loop that stabilizes the illusory percept.

Grossberg's ARTWORD model, an extension of ART principles to word recognition, explains the effects of Figure 44 [46]. The accents modify the saliency map of the text, altering how spatial attention (modeled by ARTSCAN) is deployed during reading. This affects the speed and accuracy of word form activation in the ventral visual stream. The theory suggests that accents falling on key letters or word boundaries may facilitate reading by rapidly activating appropriate word categories. Conversely, accents that disrupt normal word boundaries may interfere with the resonance formation necessary for fluent reading.

In short, Grossberg's comprehensive theory provides a unifying framework for understanding the illustrated accentuation effects. By considering how accentuation interacts with boundary formation, surface filling-in, attentional processes, and categorical learning, we can elucidate the neural mechanisms underlying these compelling visual phenomena. This synthesis not only explains existing illusions but also opens avenues for predicting and testing new perceptual effects based on the interplay between local accents and global percepts.

The comparison of Grossberg's theoretical explanations with other prominent theories in visual perception and cognitive neuroscience highlights the strengths and unique aspects of his approach.

While Gestalt theory provides intuitive explanations for many perceptual phenomena, Grossberg's approach offers a more mechanistic, neurally-grounded account [47]. For instance, in explaining the accentuation effects (Figures 1–4), this theory details how the similarity principle emerges from interactions between boundary and surface processing systems, providing a neural basis for Gestalt phenomena. It bridges the gap between phenomenological descriptions (like those in Gestalt theory) and underlying neural mechanisms.

While Feature Integration Theory [48–50] focuses on attentional processes in binding features, Grossberg's theory provides a more comprehensive account of how boundaries and surfaces interact to create object percepts [51]. For example, in explaining the rotated square-diamond effect (Figures 3 and 4), this theory addresses not just feature binding but also how categorical representations influence perception through top–down feedback. It offers a more integrated view of perception, linking low-level feature processing with high-level cognition and attention.

Predictive coding [52–54] suggests that the brain constantly generates predictions about sensory inputs and updates these predictions based on prediction errors. Grossberg's Adaptive Resonance Theory (ART) provides a more detailed account of how these expectations interact with bottom–up sensory information [11]. In explaining phenomena like the apparent motion illusions (Figures 37–42), this theory not only accounts for prediction but also describes how resonant states stabilize percepts, therefore providing a more comprehensive model of how learning, memory, and perception interact, and addressing issues like the stability–plasticity dilemma that predictive coding models often overlook.

While Bayesian models (see [55]) provide a mechanistic account of perceptual inference, Grossberg's theory offers a more biologically and evolutionary plausible implementation of how these inferences might occur in neural circuits [56]. For instance, in explaining figure-ground segregation (Figure 35), this theory details how laminar cortical circuits implement processes that could be described in Bayesian terms and bridges the gap between abstract computational principles and concrete neural mechanisms, providing testable predictions about brain function. In explaining the Shepard's table illusion (Figure 43), Grossberg's theory not only accounts for the effect but also explains how it arises from interactions between 3D boundary and surface processing systems [40]. It provides a bridge between the computational power of neural networks and the biological constraints and functional organization of the brain.

Grossberg's theory is particularly strong in terms of providing biologically plausible mechanisms for how the brain might implement complex perceptual and cognitive processes; integrating attention, learning, and memory with perceptual processes in a single coherent framework; offering detailed explanations for how complementary processes (like boundary formation and surface filling-in) interact to produce coherent percepts;

and addressing fundamental issues in neural computation, such as the stability–plasticity dilemma [46].

In conclusion, Grossberg's theory offers a powerful, biologically grounded framework for understanding visual perception and related cognitive processes. Its strengths lie in its comprehensiveness, biological plausibility, and ability to integrate multiple aspects of perception and cognition. However, these strengths also contribute to its main challenges: complexity, difficulty in empirical validation, and potential limitations in generalizability or integration with other cognitive theories.

In short, Grossberg's theory, while comprehensive and biologically grounded, faces several challenges. Its complexity, while a strength, can be a double-edged sword, making it difficult to fully grasp and implement. This complexity also poses challenges for experimental testing, as designing studies to conclusively test all aspects of the theory simultaneously can be problematic. The theory's unique mathematical formalization, though rigorous, is less widely adopted than other approaches, potentially limiting its accessibility. Computationally, implementing the full model can be resource-intensive, which may restrict its practical applications in certain contexts. In its attempt to explain a broad range of phenomena, the theory also lacks a strong evolutionary perspective, not always clearly accounting for why particular neural mechanisms evolved.

The choice between Grossberg's theory and other approaches often depends on the specific research question, the level of analysis required, and the balance between comprehensiveness and simplicity needed for a particular study or application. While Grossberg's theory provides deep macro-level insights into the mechanisms of perception and cognition, researchers may sometimes opt for simpler or more domain-specific theories when addressing particular questions or phenomena.

The complexity of Grossberg's theory makes it not particularly straightforward to apply and generalize, even in geometrically simple cases such as those illustrated in the present work. To better address these challenges and enhance the applicability of ART principles to the study of optical-geometric illusions, the following steps would be necessary:

Development of Simplified Models: Future research should focus on creating simplified ART-based models specifically designed for analyzing visual illusions. These models should prioritize key mechanisms such as boundary formation, surface filling-in, and perceptual grouping, which are essential for explaining how illusions arise. By reducing computational complexity while preserving the core principles of ART, these models would enable more straightforward empirical testing and wider adoption.

Establishment of Practical Guidelines: To help in applying ART to illusion studies, it would be necessary to provide clear, step-by-step guidelines. These guidelines should cover critical aspects such as experimental design, parameter selection, and interpretation of results within the ART framework.

Inclusion of Illustrative Examples: Our study represents a significant step forward in bridging the gap between theoretical principles and practical applications by incorporating concrete examples of how ART can explain specific illusions. These examples serve as clear, relatable illustrations of ART's explanatory power in the context of illusions, providing researchers with actionable insights into the mechanisms underlying perceptual phenomena. By grounding ART principles visual examples, our work not only enhances understanding but also paves the way for broader adoption and further exploration of ART's potential in visual perception research.

By implementing these strategies, ART could become more accessible and applicable to researchers studying illusions, fostering a deeper understanding of perceptual phenomena. These efforts would not only enhance the accessibility of ART-based approaches but also encourage a broader exploration of their potential in the field of visual perception and illusion research.

These limitations, however, should not overshadow the significant contributions of Grossberg's theory to our understanding of perception and cognition. Rather, they highlight areas where further development, simplification, or integration with other approaches could potentially enhance its already considerable explanatory power and practical applicability.

Author Contributions: Conceptualization and illusions: B.P.; Methodology, Data collection and analyses: B.P., J.Š. and D.P.; Writing and approving the final manuscript: B.P., J.Š. and D.P. All authors have read and agreed to the published version of the manuscript.

Funding: B.P. was supported by PRIN 2022 Missione 4—Componente C2—investimento 1.1, Fondo per il PRIN—del PNRR (Finanziamento dell'Unione Europea – NextGenerationEU) for the research project by the title: "Bayesian inference reconsidered in the light of new visual illusions" CUP J53D23007730006 and PRIN 2022 PNRR Missione 4 del PNRR—Componente C2—investimento 1.1 del PNRR for the project intitled: "Can the dynamics underlying face perception help prevent gender stereotypes" CUP J53D23016900001. B.P. and J.Š. were supported by Fundamental and Applied Research project, Republic of Latvia, "Development of an integrative approach to the assessment of cognitive abilities in patients with neurodegenerative diseases of the central nervous system" (project No. lzp-2022/1-0100).

Institutional Review Board Statement: In accordance with local laws and institutional policies, approval from an ethics committee was not required for this study as the experiments were limited to healthy individuals and did not involve invasive methods. The study adhered fully to local regulations and institutional standards and all procedures were carried out in line with the Declaration of Helsinki.

Informed Consent Statement: Informed consent was obtained from all subjects involved in the study. Participants did not receive course credit or financial compensation.

Data Availability Statement: The raw data supporting the conclusions of this article will be made available by the authors on request.

Acknowledgments: B.P. greatly acknowledges Rīga Stradiņš University and the Vice-Rector Agrita Kiopa for the visiting professor program, which gave him the chance to start and complete this research.

Conflicts of Interest: The authors declare no conflicts of interest.

References

1. Koffka, K. *Principles of Gestalt Psychology*; Lund Humphries: London, UK, 1935.
2. Wertheimer, M. Über das Denken der Naturvölker. *Z. Psychol.* **1912**, *60*, 321–378.
3. Wertheimer, M. Untersuchungen über das Sehen von Bewegung. *Z. Psychol.* **1912**, *61*, 161–265.
4. Wertheimer, M. Untersuchungen zur Lehre von der Gestalt. I. *Psychol. Forsch.* **1922**, *1*, 47–58. [CrossRef]
5. Wertheimer, M. Untersuchungen zur Lehre von der Gestalt II. *Psychol. Forsch.* **1923**, *4*, 301–350. [CrossRef]
6. Palmer, S.E. Perceptual Organization in Vision. In *Stevens' Handbook of Experimental Psychology*; Pashler, H., Yantis, S., Eds.; John Wiley & Sons Inc.: New York, NY, USA, 2002; pp. 177–234.
7. Wagemans, J.; Elder, J.H.; Kubovy, M.; Palmer, S.E.; Peterson, M.A.; Singh, M.; Von der Heydt, R. A century of Gestalt psychology in visual perception: I. Perceptual grouping and figure–ground organization. *Psychol. Bull.* **2012**, *138*, 1172–1217. [CrossRef] [PubMed]
8. Pinna, B.; Conti, L.; Porcheddu, D. On the role of contrast polarity in perceptual organization: A Gestalt approach. *Psychol. Conscious.* **2021**, *8*, 367–396. [CrossRef]
9. Vicario, G.B. On Wertheimer's principles of organization. *Gestalt Theory* **1998**, *20*, 256–269.
10. Chen, L. The topological approach to perceptual organization. *Vis. Cogn.* **2005**, *12*, 553–637. [CrossRef]
11. Grossberg, S.; Mingolla, E. Neural dynamics of form perception: Boundary completion, illusory figures, and neon color spreading. *Psychol. Rev.* **1985**, *92*, 173–211. [CrossRef]
12. Hojjatoleslami, S.; Kittler, J. Region growing: A new approach. *IEEE Trans. Image Process.* **1998**, *7*, 1079–1084. [CrossRef] [PubMed]

13. Julesz, B. A theory of preattentive texture discrimination based on first-order statistics of textons. *Biol. Cyber.* **1981**, *41*, 131–138. [CrossRef]
14. Julesz, B. Textons, the elements of texture perception, and their interactions. *Nature* **1981**, *290*, 91–97. [CrossRef] [PubMed]
15. Muir, A.; Warner, M.W. Homogeneous tolerance spaces. *Czech. Math. J.* **1980**, *30*, 118–126. [CrossRef]
16. Pavlidis, T.; Liow, Y.T. Integrating region growing and edge detection. *IEEE Trans. Pattern Anal. Mach. Intell.* **1990**, *12*, 225–233. [CrossRef]
17. Pinna, B. New Gestalt principles of perceptual organization: An extension from grouping to shape and meaning. *Gestalt Theory* **2010**, *32*, 11–78.
18. Pinna, B. Directional organization and shape formation: New illusions and Helmholtz's square. *Front. Hum. Neurosci.* **2015**, *9*, 92. [CrossRef] [PubMed]
19. Pinna, B. *La Percezione Visiva*; Il Mulino: Bologna, Italy, 2021.
20. Albertazzi, L. Philosophical background: Phenomenology. In *Oxford Handbook of Perceptual Organization*; Wagemans, J., Ed.; Oxford University Press: Oxford, UK, 2015; pp. 21–40. [CrossRef]
21. Pinna, B. Illusion and Illusoriness: New Perceptual Issues and New Phenomena. In *Handbook of Experimental Phenomenology*; Albertazzi, L., Ed.; Wiley-Blackwell: Hoboken, NJ, USA, 2013; pp. 317–341. [CrossRef]
22. Pinna, B.; Sirigu, L. The Accentuation Principle of Visual Organization and the Illusion of Musical Suspension. *Seeing Perceiving* **2011**, *24*, 595–621. [CrossRef]
23. Kanizsa, G. *Organization in Vision*; Praeger: New York, USA, 1979.
24. Kanizsa, G. *Grammatica del Vedere*; Il Mulino: Bologna, Italy, 1980.
25. Metzger, W. *Psychologie*; Steinkopff Verlag: Darmstadt, Germany, 1963.
26. Metzger, W. *Gesetze des Sehens*; Kramer: Frankfurt, Germany, 1975.
27. Spillmann, L.; Ehrenstein, W.H. Gestalt Factors in the Visual Neurosciences. In *The Visual Neurosciences*; Chalupa, L., Werner, J.S., Eds.; MIT Press: Cambridge, MA, USA, 2004; pp. 181–197. [CrossRef]
28. Pinna, B.; Porcheddu, D.; Skilters, J. Similarity and dissimilarity in perceptual organization: On the complexity of the Gestalt principle of similarity. *Vision* **2022**, *6*, 39. [CrossRef]
29. Thompson, P.; Mikellidou, K. Applying the Helmholtz illusion to fashion: Horizontal stripes won't make you look fatter. *I-Perception* **2011**, *2*, 69–76. [CrossRef] [PubMed]
30. Attneave, F. Triangles as ambiguous figures. *Am. J. Psychol.* **1968**, *81*, 447–453. [CrossRef]
31. Palmer, S.E. What makes triangles point: Local and global effects in configurations of ambiguous triangles. *Cogn. Psychol.* **1980**, *12*, 285–305. [CrossRef]
32. Pinna, B.; Reeves, A.; Koenderink, J.; van Doorn, A.; Deiana, K. A new principle of figure-ground segregation: The accentuaton. *Vis. Res.* **2018**, *143*, 9–25. [CrossRef]
33. Rubin, E. *Visuellwahrgenommenefiguren*; Gyldendalske Boghandel: Kobenhavn, Denmark, 1921.
34. Pinna, B. Pinna Illusion. *Scholarpedia* **2009**, *4*, 6656. [CrossRef]
35. Shepard, R.N. *Mind Sights: Original Visual Illusions, Ambiguities, and Other Anomalies, with a Commentary on the Play of Mind in Perception and Art*; W.H. Freeman & Co.: New York, NY, USA, 1990.
36. Grossberg, S. Cortical dynamics of three-dimensional figure-ground perception of two-dimensional pictures. *Psychol. Rev.* **1997**, *104*, 618–658. [CrossRef]
37. Grossberg, S.; Mingolla, E.; Ross, W.D. A neural theory of attentive visual search: Interactions of boundary, surface, spatial, and object representations. *Psychol. Rev.* **1994**, *101*, 470–489. [CrossRef]
38. Grossberg, S. The link between brain learning, attention, and consciousness. *Conscious Cogn.* **1999**, *8*, 1–44. [CrossRef]
39. Pinna, B.; Grossberg, S. Logic and phenomenology of incompleteness in illusory figures: New cases and hypotheses. *Psychofenia* **2006**, *9*, 93–135. [CrossRef]
40. Grossberg, S. How Does a Brain Build a Cognitive Code? In *Studies of Mind and Brain*; Boston Studies in the Philosophy of Science Series; Springer: Dordrecht, The Netherlands, 1980; pp. 1–52. [CrossRef]
41. Grossberg, S. Adaptive Resonance Theory: How a brain learns to consciously attend, learn, and recognize a changing world. *Neural Netw.* **2013**, *37*, 1–47. [CrossRef]
42. Grossberg, S. Towards a unified theory of neocortex: Laminar cortical circuits for vision and cognition. *Prog. Brain Res.* **2007**, *165*, 79–104. [CrossRef] [PubMed]
43. Grossberg, S.; Raizada, R.D. Contrast-sensitive perceptual grouping and object-based attention in the laminar circuits of primary visual cortex. *Vision Res.* **2000**, *40*, 1413–1432. [CrossRef] [PubMed]
44. Grossberg, S.; Pinna, B. Neural Dynamics of Gestalt Principles of Perceptual Organization: From Grouping to Shape and Meaning. *Gestalt Theory* **2012**, *34*, 399–482.
45. Grossberg, S. 3-D vision and figure-ground separation by visual cortex. *Percept. Psychophys.* **1994**, *55*, 48–120. [CrossRef] [PubMed]

46. Grossberg, S. Towards solving the hard problem of consciousness: The varieties of brain resonances and the conscious experiences that they support. *Neural Netw.* **2017**, *87*, 38–95. [CrossRef] [PubMed]
47. Grossberg, S. A path toward explainable AI and autonomous adaptive intelligence: Deep learning, adaptive resonance, and models of perception, emotion, and action. *Front. Neurorobot.* **2020**, *14*, 36. [CrossRef]
48. Treisman, A.M.; Gelade, G. A feature-integration theory of attention. *Cogn. Psychol.* **1980**, *12*, 97–136. [CrossRef]
49. Treisman, A.; Gormican, S. Feature analysis in early vision: Evidence from search asymmetries. *Psychol. Rev.* **1988**, *95*, 15–48. [CrossRef] [PubMed]
50. Treisman, A.; Souther, J. Search asymmetry: A diagnostic for preattentive processing of separable features. *J. Exp. Psychol. Gen.* **1985**, *114*, 285–310. [CrossRef] [PubMed]
51. Grossberg, S. *Conscious Mind, Resonant Brain: How Each Brain Makes a Mind*; Oxford University Press: Oxford, UK, 2021. [CrossRef]
52. Friston, K. A theory of cortical responses. *Phil. Trans. R. Soc. B* **2005**, *360*, 815–836. [CrossRef] [PubMed]
53. Friston, K. The free-energy principle: A unified brain theory? *Nat. Rev. Neurosci.* **2010**, *11*, 127–138. [CrossRef]
54. Rao, R.P.; Ballard, D.H. Predictive coding in the visual cortex: A functional interpretation of some extra-classical receptive-field effects. *Nat. Neurosci.* **1999**, *2*, 79–87. [CrossRef]
55. Knill, D.C.; Pouget, A. The Bayesian brain: The role of uncertainty in neural coding and computation. *Trends Neurosci.* **2004**, *27*, 712–719. [CrossRef] [PubMed]
56. Grossberg, S. The resonant brain: How attentive conscious seeing regulates action sequences that interact with attentive cognitive learning, recognition, and prediction. *Atten. Percept. Psychophys.* **2019**, *81*, 2237–2264. [CrossRef]

Disclaimer/Publisher's Note: The statements, opinions and data contained in all publications are solely those of the individual author(s) and contributor(s) and not of MDPI and/or the editor(s). MDPI and/or the editor(s) disclaim responsibility for any injury to people or property resulting from any ideas, methods, instructions or products referred to in the content.

Article

An ART Tour de Force on Mental Imagery: Vividness, Individual Bias Differences, and Complementary Visual Processing Streams

Amedeo D'Angiulli *, Christy Laarakker and Derrick Matthew Buchanan

Department of Neuroscience, Carleton University, Ottawa, ON K1S 5B6, Canada; christylaarakker@cmail.carleton.ca (C.L.); matthewbuchanan@cmail.carleton.ca (D.M.B.)
* Correspondence: amedeo.dangiulli@carleton.ca

Abstract: Grossberg's adaptive resonance theory (ART) provides a framework for understanding possible interactions between mental imagery and visual perception. Our purpose was to integrate, within ART, the phenomenological notion of mental image vividness and thus investigate the possible biasing effects of individual differences on visual processing. Using a Vernier acuity task, we tested whether indirect estimation of relative V1 size (small, medium, large) and self-reported vividness, in three subgroups of 53 observers, could predict significant effects of priming, interference, or more extreme Perky effects (negative and positive), which could be induced by imagery, impacting acuity performance. The results showed that small V1 was correlated with priming and/or negative Perky effects independently of vividness; medium V1 was related to interference at low vividness but priming at high vividness; and large V1 was related to positive Perky effects at high vividness but negative Perky effects at low vividness. Our interpretation of ART and related modeling based on ARTSCAN contributes to expanding Grossberg's comprehensive understanding of how and why individually experienced vividness may drive the differential use of the dorsal and ventral complementary visual processing pathways, resulting in the observed effects of imagery on concurrent perception.

Keywords: adaptive resonance theory; imagery; perception; vividness; visual cortex; visual priming; perky effect

1. Introduction: ART and Vividness of Visual Mental Imagery

Grossberg's adaptive resonance theory (ART) provides a robust framework for understanding how imagery–perception interactions occur in complementary dorsal and ventral cortical visual processing. The objective of this paper was to integrate within ART a phenomenological component based on the classic psychological notion of mental image vividness [1] to supplement the "how" explanation with a "why" explanation describing processing biases which are associated with individual anatomical differences.

The vividness of mental imagery has been studied for more than a century in psychology and is traditionally defined as a quasi-perceptual (predominantly *visual*) *phenomenological* experience [2–5]. In his comprehensive theory combining phenomenological and behavioral perspectives, Marks [3,6] posits vividness as a dynamic process guided by intentional, conscious, and voluntary executive and regulatory mechanisms embedded in generating and using visual mental imagery. This dynamic, processual view of vividness aligns with Grossberg's view of an "emerging theory of imagery" in the neuroscience domain as "...part of a larger neural theory of visual seeing and thinking" ([7], p. 195).

The rapid advancement of the neuroscience of vision (often inspired by Grossberg himself) has led to many new findings on mental images and has led to increased interest in vividness. For most people, generating visual mental images depends on the same neural and functional mechanisms involved in seeing. Imagery and perception involve not only similar mechanisms, but also similar synchronizations across brain areas [8].

Moreover, physical representations and imagined scenarios both influence the detection of target stimuli. Thus, studies have emphasized that early visual areas impact both the top-down generation of images during mental imagery and the vividness of images retrieved from memory [9]. While some findings suggest similar underlying mechanisms for visual imagery and visual perception, other findings suggest an overlap, and some research suggests equivalent mechanisms [9]. These overlaps in the top-down connectivity of neural mechanisms in perception and imagery—which are a necessary ingredient of ART—suggest a consistent relationship between mental imagery and the functional impact of conscious perception [10]. Using imagery, ambiguous stimuli can be formed into more precise and stable visual perceptions. As a paradigmatic example, vividness can induce bias, which determines the dominant perception of one of two binocularly different color patches [11]. Grossberg's approach, however, is an important advancement. Not only does it describe the contextually dependent differential variants of top-down connectivity and the influence of bottom-up processing on imagery, but also, it seamlessly integrates phenomenological components as a causally relevant and non-epiphenomenal aspect of consciousness within the same unitary model. Thus, Grossberg's idea of resonance in ART can be extended to create an implementable neural model of vividness of mental imagery. Following the ART rationale, vividness may depend on the complex functional links among the processes of consciousness, learning, expectation, attention, resonance, and synchrony (CLEARS) [12].

According to Grossberg [12], resonance occurs among different brain areas. The brain areas associated with perception and imagination communicate dynamically, resulting in the construction of mental images. In this process, resonance reflects the synchronization of neural activity between brain areas (particularly the ventral and dorsal streams), and increased resonance between such areas leads to stronger connections and the integration of more information [12]. Thus, the strength of resonance between areas involved in imagery and perception may be related to the vividness of the mental images. The top-down and bottom-up feedback recurrent connections utilizing the dorsal and ventral streams allow for the precision, refinement, and enhancement of the vividness of the image. Specifically, the high-level mechanisms that control the selective detection of change need a modulating factor that makes attention a phenomenologically vivid reality (as per William James's famous dictum: "...the taking possession by the mind, in clear and vivid form..." https://psychclassics.yorku.ca/James/Principles/prin11.htm, accessed on 1 September 2023). Consistent with the assumptions of ART [12,13], we argue that the top-down voluntary processing related to the vividness of imagery is important for distributing attention and contributes to the categorization, recognition, and prediction of objects. Externally and internally directed attention determines our ability to learn and adjust neural patterns [14]. While externally directed attention determines the objects, features, and spatial locations of what we see in our visual field, the mechanisms of internally directed attention are less known, and their connections to imagery and vividness have not yet been clarified [14]. An exception is a study by Gjorgieva et al. [15], who reported a clear relationship between attention and image vividness, showing that the latency of parietal ERP signatures of internally directed attention was inversely related to image vividness, replicating an earlier behavioral finding of D'Angiulli and Reeves [16], namely, that vividness was associated with faster processing.

1.1. Review of Related Imagery Research

In most individuals, visual mental images do not impact the accuracy of visual perception (i.e., how well an individual resolves external visual stimuli). In other individuals, however, concurrent mental images do impact perception by either augmenting or decreasing baseline visual performance. These facilitation and interference phenomena have been widely recognized and studied in the field of perception, where they are traditionally known as priming and interference, or negative and positive Perky effects, respectively [17]. However, negative and positive Perky effects are generally considered absolute changes in accuracy of approximately ±5% relative to the acuity baseline, while the corresponding priming and interference effects are relative within-subjects changes that could be empirically smaller but significant numerical deltas. Very recent findings from cognitive neuroscience studies (generally involving functional magnetic resonance imaging (fMRI)) have confirmed and extended previous findings (generally involving electroencephalography (EEG) or event-related potential (ERP) (see review in [18])) on the neural correlates of the VVIQ and trial-by-trial vividness ratings based on instructions that emphasize sensory strength (see reviews in [1,19]). Furthermore, other behavioral evidence has shown that vividness can prime stimulus detection [18], and several reports have shown that image vividness impacts visual sensitivity (see [17–21]).

Recent research has shown that the size of V1, the precision of visual acuity, and the vividness of mental imagery are related. The average or baseline accuracy of visual processing or visual precision can be assessed by tasks measuring accuracy in resolving detailed information in perceptual visual images, such as the Vernier acuity task, a standardized and validated paradigm [17]. In one version of this task, participants report the side of the visual hemifield (left or right) in which offset parallel line segments appear, either mono- or binocularly. By instructing participants to generate visual mental images while presenting Venier acuity targets, it is possible to empirically show whether imagery increases or decreases task performance (i.e., improves or hinders visual acuity, respectively) [16,17]. Importantly, Venier acuity is correlated with cortical magnification and the size of receptive fields in V1, making it a reliable behavioral proxy indicator of V1 size [22,23].

Bergmann et al. [21] showed that priming and interference depend on an individual's accuracy (i.e., visual precision); however, importantly, individual differences in visual precision differ from individual differences in sensory strength and can be associated with differences in the size of V1. Namely, when asked to create a concurrent visual mental image, individuals with a typical (medium) V1 size had average visual precision and showed no change in visual precision relative to baseline. However, individuals with larger V1 areas demonstrated above-average visual precision and with concurrent imagery, showed priming effects. In contrast, individuals with relatively smaller V1 regions demonstrated average visual precision and with concurrent imagery, showed "sensory" interference.

Although Bergmann et al.'s [21] study was successful in elucidating the neural early visual correlates of individual differences associated with mental imagery, they only partially clarified the neural substrate of vividness. Despite the finding that vividness was related to the prefrontal cortex (PFC) volume, they did not clarify how individual differences in vividness judgments reflect individual differences in V1 or how individual characteristics in early visual processing are driven by changes in PFC activity. Kosslyn and colleagues [24] suggested that during visual processing, the magnocellular pathway in the dorsal stream is recruited for spatial imagery tasks (locating objects), while the parvocellular pathway in the ventral stream is mainly recruited for object imagery tasks (identifying objects) [13]. The dorsal stream is recruited more in individuals with stronger sensory interference, while the ventral stream is recruited by individuals with stronger visual precision but weaker sensory interference (as per Bergman et al.) [21]. Based on this evidence, individual differences in the size of V1 might be correlated with recruitment of the dorsal and ventral pathways. D'Angiulli et al. [25] performed ERP and EEG studies, demonstrating hemispheric asymmetry during mental image generation, which reflects the differential distribution of activity in the dorsal and ventral pathways; magnocellular neurons associated with spatial precision ([24]) are mainly active in the right dorsal electrode sites, whereas parvocellular neurons associated with object shape ([24]) are mainly active in the left ventral electrode sites. Importantly, ERP activity and polarity in prefrontal regions were inversely correlated with those in the occipital regions. The latter finding cannot be explained according to EEG operation, as the inversely correlated activity was selectively identified only between those electrode sites and not within the other sites. The same electrode selectivity was also found for anticorrelated synchronization and desynchronization of EEG power involving alpha, beta, and theta band frequencies.

Kosslyn's work has been fundamental to the imagery research field. Nevertheless, it has also biased the field so that researchers now widely assume an underlying natural taxonomy of different mental representations matched with various neural systems or mechanisms. On this basis, individual differences are derived from the preferential mechanism or modules used and the characteristics of particular tasks that require images, which determines the alternate predominance of either the dorsal or ventral streams (for example, see [26]). In contrast, according to Grossberg [27], both the ventral and the dorsal streams always maintain complementary *parallel* cortical processes [27]. The dorsal stream includes the spatial and motor processes that control adaptation based on changing bodily parameters. Moreover, the dorsal stream involves spatial representations, whereas the ventral stream is specific and does not consider object views, positions, or sizes. Therefore, as Grossberg [27] described, the two streams operate in parallel to perform actions according to the specific object and scene, incorporating the processes of the ventral and dorsal streams accordingly. This corresponds to the key principle of complementary computation, according to which complementary cortical streams coordinate their activity reciprocally and dynamically to synergistically overcome their "weaknesses", namely, their limitations due to their modular rigidity and biomolecular boundedness in processing independent isolated aspects. He described the two coordination dynamics as *what-to-where* and *where-to-what* excitatory and inhibitory parallel interactive learning pathways. However, we suggest that image vividness may bias the weight of processing by recruiting one stream more than the other, acting as another complementary or competing process to the attention given to a visual object. That is, visual "images" are not the same as consciousness; they have a phenomenological gradient corresponding to the strength of resonance, which might reflect higher-level complementary dynamic processing from the top-down inputs to V1. Therefore, if the two streams are imbalanced, the view, position, or size of an object may be incorrect or unable to adapt to changing parameters; thus, the spatial context of the object may be unknown. The top-down interactions of these streams include object and spatial attentional processes that could influence whether imagery hinders or facilitates visual processes. Furthermore, the extent to which the dorsal and ventral streams influence the direction of internal attention may determine whether visual processes are hindered or facilitated by mental images [27].

To determine the nature of the vivid-is-fast relation, D'Angiulli and Reeves [28] modeled latencies of visual mental image generation under several visual angle (foveal and parafoveal) conditions to probe magnocellular (mainly dorsal) versus parvocellular (mainly ventral) pathways and measured concurrent trial-by-trial vividness ratings after instructing the observers to report sensory strength rather than details of the contents (see [5]). Based on the best available functional mapping of streams of information processing during image-related tasks [29], these data suggest that vividness ratings increase when they reflect fast judgments, presumably corresponding to the involvement of frontal areas based on input from ventral streams (ventralization), whereas ratings decline when the same observers make slower judgments (still presumably controlled by frontal areas) based on inputs from dorsal visual pathway streams (dorsalization) [28].

1.2. The Present Study: Hypotheses and Predictions

If, as the reviewed evidence suggests, individual differences in visual processing can bias how images are accessed and consciously self-reported, then more interference or priming could reflect disequilibrium between dorsal and ventral processes, which is linked with individual anatomical differences and levels of vividness. This is the central tenet we aim to investigate in the present study *from within* Grossberg's ART framework.

Following D'Angiulli and Reeves [27] and Kosslyn et al. [24], we hypothesize that a large V1 should correlate with top-down ventralization (top-down ventral dominance), whereas a small V1 should correlate with top-down dorsalization (top-down dorsal dominance). To test these hypotheses, we devised an experiment in which participants were asked to generate a visual mental image of their own choice (under strict image guidelines) and project those images onto a screen where the observers had to simultaneously detect a Vernier acuity target (i.e., an offset line). This experimental design allowed us to investigate the degree to which imagery influences the perception of fine acuity stimuli. The predicted outcome scenarios derived from the hypotheses are presented in Figure 1.

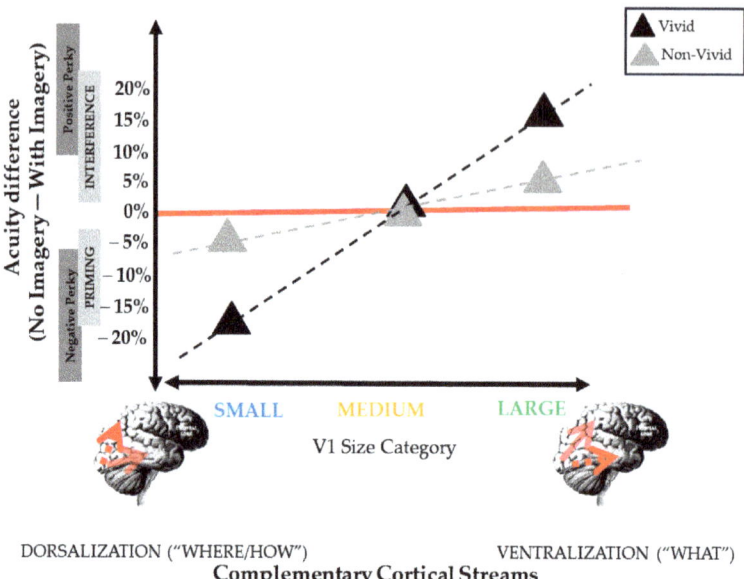

Figure 1. Schematic representation of the predicted outcomes for the interaction between visual mental imagery and target perception as a function of V1 size and complementary processing streams. Red line indicates no effect of imagery over acuity referencing baseline equilibrium between dorsal and ventral streams.

We expected that large, ventrally dominant V1 regions would direct attention internally within the ventral/what pathway (corresponding to Grossberg's "object shroud" [13]) in the case of high vividness, which should interfere with attentional resources directed externally to the position of the concurrently presented visual target (Grossberg's "spatial shroud" [13]), thereby disrupting the what-to-where stream. In this scenario, the what-to-where pathway should compete with where-to-what processing, resulting in reduced detection of the target spatial position (i.e., positive Perky effects). However, in the case of low vividness, the overlap in parvocellular processing between imagery and concurrent acuity would be minimal, and this competition among the pathways should be significantly reduced. In contrast, individuals with small, dorsally dominant V1 regions should perform mostly magnocellular processing and show minimal overlap between parvocellular processing and concurrent acuity, with this overlap further reduced in the case of low vividness. In this scenario, the what-to-where pathway should compete with where-to-what processing. Consequently, priming should occur at both vividness levels for small V1 processing, with more extreme priming (i.e., negative Perky effects) observed for low vividness. Finally, according to Bergman et al. [21], we predict that medium V1 regions should engage parvo- and magnocellular pathways approximately equally, balancing competition and cooperation among the two streams. Accordingly, in this case, vividness should bias attention by enhancing or reducing attention toward the target primarily through the what-to-where pathway; thus, we expect moderate priming effects for high vividness and moderate interference effects for low vividness, the opposite to what should occur for the case of large V1.

2. Materials and Methods

2.1. Participants

Initially, 60 first-year undergraduate psychology students aged 18 to 25 years (M = 22, SD = 1.75) were recruited to participate through Carleton University's Student Organization of North America (SONA) subject recruitment system. Inclusion in the study was conditional on signing a written informed consent form. The Institutional Behavioural Research Ethics Board of Carleton University approved this study (protocol code 111569 27 November 2019), which was conducted in conformity with the Declaration of Helsinki and Canada's Tri-Council Policy Statement.

Among the participants, 53% identified as male and 47% identified as female. In the preliminary phase of the study, the participants underwent personality and imagery screening using the VVIQ and the Big Five Inventory [30]. The VVIQ was the first questionnaire the participants completed. Participants practiced visualizing while completing this questionnaire. Following the standard procedure, the participants were presented with the 16 VVIQ descriptions and asked to rate the mental images that came to their minds on a scale of 1 (perfectly clear) to 7 (no image). Only data from participants who scored within the typical range (within 2 SD of the grand mean) in both questionnaires were included in the present study. Two candidates obtained the minimum possible score on the VVIQ, while five candidates scored below the norm on one of the items in the Big Five Inventory; therefore, their data were not included in the analysis. Finally, after screening, 53 participants were included; twenty-nine participants received a psychology course credit of 1.5%, whereas twenty-four participants were volunteers who did not receive any compensation. Preliminary inspection and analysis of the data did not reveal statistically significant differences between these two groups (multivariate test of the variance difference between the scores from the two samples in all eight no-imagery and imagery conditions yielded the following summary statistics: Hotelling's trace = 0.28 (df: 8, 51); $p \sim 0.20$).

2.2. Apparatus

The stimuli and background were projected onto a white screen mounted on a wall by a Sony Duocom LCD Data Projector (XGA VPL-CX1, Sony Electronics Inc., Park Ridge, NJ, USA). Projections were controlled by the experimenter using a keyboard connected to an LG Prosys computer, which also ran the computer program displayed by the projector and recorded the data for the visual acuity task. The stimuli were generated, displayed, and controlled using the Visual Basic program. The experimental setup is graphically represented in the right panel of Figure 2.

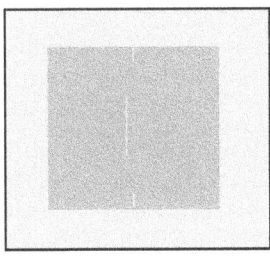
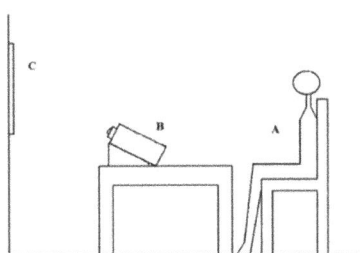

Figure 2. Schematic of the experimental setup. **Left** Panel: Actual screen appearance of the offset lines used for the acuity test. The particular offset in the shown trial is on the left visual hemifield (hence the correct response was "left"); note that the lines are not drawn to scale. **Right** panel: Participants (represented in (**A**)) were seated directly in front of the projected stimuli (represented in (**B**)) Stimuli were projected using a Sony Duocom LCD data projector (**B**). The stimuli were projected on a white screen mounted on a wall perpendicular to the participant's field of vision (represented in (**C**)).

2.3. Stimuli and Procedure

Participants were tested individually and seated in front of a table, upon which the projector rested (see Figure 2, right panel). The experimenter sat on the left of the table. Participants were asked whether they knew what mental imagery was and if they could generate one as an example. In the initial familiarization and subsequent practice phases, participants were encouraged to verbalize and describe their images.

Participants started the experimental session by completing the VVIQ and the TSDVI. The experimenter verbally explained the task instructions (adapted from the Appendix of ([28]; pp. 544–546); the modification concerned the response modality, which was changed in the present procedure). Vividness was defined as "the extent to which the imagined object is lifelike or resembles real seeing" ([28]; p. 545). Examples of vivid imagery (e.g., your mother's face) and nonvivid imagery (e.g., your kindergarten teacher's face) were provided, and participants were asked to provide some examples. The terms dynamic image ("something moving") and static image ("not moving" and "still") were described, and examples were provided (e.g., a Canadian flag blowing in the wind, a face not talking or moving at all). The latter was adapted from a previous protocol ([30]; Experiment 2). Participants were asked to generate other examples, verbalize and describe their experiences, and share their self-rating of vividness. To self-rate the vividness of their images, participants were asked to use the same 7-point Likert scale as the one used for the VVIQ items (i.e., from 1 = perfectly clear to 7 = no image). Following completion, both questionnaires were removed, and the participants started the visual acuity task trials.

The next phase of the experimental procedure for the actual acuity task session was adapted from the standard protocol for ERP and EEG data collection used by D'Angiulli et al. [25] (in the present experiment, only behavioral data were collected). Although the main focus of the present study was to compare vivid and nonvivid static visual mental images, two classic issues in the formation of imagery are the level of voluntary control and the incorporation of dynamic images. Both aspects may involve moving images. Previous research has shown that static imagery is significantly more vivid than dynamic imagery of the same content [31,32] and might be more difficult to voluntarily control. This might be due to the involvement of key areas of the dorsal stream, such as the MT [32]. Thus, we instructed the participants to generate vivid and nonvivid moving images, as a secondary objective was to explore whether asking participants to generate moving images might bias dorsal recruitment. Therefore, the instructions were changed according to the block of trials so that each participant was asked to produce images under previously validated instructions [28,32], yielding types of four mental image: *static vivid (SV)*, *dynamic vivid (DV)*, *static nonvivid (SNV)*, or *dynamic nonvivid (DNV)*. A fifth condition involved performing the acuity task without generating any mental image (no image, NI). In the static and dynamic conditions, participants were instructed to start the experiment by generating a small set of 2–3 images with consistent vividness self-ratings between 2 and 3 to define the vivid images, while another set of images with vividness ratings between 6 and 7 were used to define nonvivid images. To assess V1 size through neuropsychological methods, the NI condition and its associated visual acuity score served as indirect measures of an individual's V1 size, given that visual acuity is associated with the size of V1 [22,23]. One type of mental image or NI was used in each block of trials, and the order of the image types was randomly determined before the experiment using a free, online random number generator (http://www.random.org/ accessed on 17 January 2024). The NI and the four mental image types created 5 experimental conditions. There were 5 practice blocks (1 for each mental image type and 1 for the NI condition) of 5 trials each. The experimental trials consisted of 16 blocks of 10 trials each, with 8 blocks of mental images and 8 blocks of NI. (All executable programs for the experiment can be publicly viewed and downloaded from doi:10.5281/zenodo.10076451).

For the Vernier acuity task, the room was dimly lit at lighting settings approximating D'Angiulli et al. [25]. Participants were told that at any point, they could stop the experiment and take a break or have the lights turned on. A white screen measuring 1 ft × 1 ft was mounted on the wall, 4 ft. away from participants. The surface was painted on a black background, and a pair of thin, vertical white lines 5 mm long was placed at the center, with the lines stacked and separated by approximately 2.3 in (5.84 cm). A third thin, white vertical line (approx. 5 cm long) between, and slightly offset (approx. 2 mm left or right), from the two shorter lines was displayed for 68 ms by the experimenter for each trial on cue. This stimulus line was the target (see Figure 2, left panel). The complete line displays a subtended $2.62°$ visual angle. The line was displayed on a black background using a standard CRT monitor (11×19.5 cm). The contrast and brightness were set to a minimum, and the color was set to grayscale. The task corresponded to photopic conditions, with an approximate luminance of 50 cd/m^2 and a Weber contrast of 21:1 (as in [26]).

Cues came from the participant, either by verbally saying "ok" or clicking a retractable pen to indicate that a mental image was being generated. During each image trial, participants were asked to look between the two short lines and to imagine a specific image (as indicated by the experimenter). When the generated mental image was sufficiently stable, participants were asked to cue the experimenter, who then clicked the mouse; the experimenter's mouse click caused the long line (target) to flash for a duration of 67 ms, either to the left or right of the two short lines (presentation side was random). Participants, while holding onto their image, viewed the line and indicated which side they thought the line appeared on by saying "left" or "right" (see left panel of Figure 2). If uncertain, participants were instructed to give their best guess. *No image* (NI) trials proceeded similarly, but participants were instructed not to produce mental images during the acuity task. Participants took as much time as they needed between trials to ensure that their images were strong and reliable for each trial. If the patient was distracted or if an image was lost while completing a trial, the entire block was discarded, and the patient began a new trail.

Most participants had no difficulty understanding the different mental image types, as indicated by their own examples. Only three participants required extra practice. These participants were either given 5 extra practice trials for each image type or repeated the incomplete block. The experiment lasted approximately 1.5 h. Participants were debriefed following the visual detection task.

2.4. Analytical Approach

Participants' scores were recorded as a percentage of the total correct responses (accurately answering if the stimulus line was on the left or right side) in the visual detection task over each block of 10 trials. As the blocks for each mental image type were randomly selected to include two imagery blocks and two no-imagery blocks, the results yielded scores ≥ 20 for NI and >20 for each mental image type. These scores were then transformed into percentages of correct responses. The computer data acquisition program automatically rounded percent values to the closest integer real number without decimal places. The performance scores were calculated as NI % correct—image % correct. In other words, the image trial correct scores were subtracted from the NI trial correct scores to obtain a percentage, which was either negative or positive. Positive scores indicated interference, and negative scores indicated priming. Based on criteria similar to those used in the current literature [16], interference corresponding to a score difference of $\geq 5\%$ was defined as a *positive Perky* effect, while priming corresponding to a score difference of $\leq -5\%$ was defined as a *negative Perky* effect.

In the first analysis, we described the overall distribution of all effects without parametric (i.e., normality) assumptions. Performance scores were calculated for each participant for each mental image type (including dynamic images). No result (0% or "null" effects), interference (including positive Perky effects), and priming (including negative Perky effects) cases were subdivided into 3 categories, and each effect score (NI imagery) for each mental image type was subjected to the Kruskal–Wallis test (nonparametric repeated-measures ANOVA). Subsequently, for each mental image type, interference and priming data were compared using two independent sample tests (Mann–Whitney test) to explore possible post hoc differences following the initial Kruskal–Wallis test.

In the subsequent analysis, following confirmatory parametric diagnostics showing tolerable deviation from normality, we focused primarily on static imagery, and we regressed the effect of imagery on concurrent acuity accuracy (as % difference scores) against baseline acuity performance. As a secondary analysis for completeness, we performed the same analysis for the dynamic imagery to provide a comparison for reference. We converted the r coefficients to Zr scores as a polynomial contrast to test for trends. Multiple t tests with Simes–Bonferroni adjustment were applied to determine significant differences between mental image types, including polynomial linear pattern tests. Simes–Bonferroni adjustment yielded a threshold of $p < 0.03$, corresponding to a critical t value of 2.021 (df = 51).

Finally, to investigate the relationship between interference, priming and Perky effects, and the size of V1, we scaled all the measured percentage difference scores using the average NI collapsed on all blocks subtracted from each condition and tested between-subject effects using a three-way repeated measures hierarchical mixed model ANOVA with the following factors: V1 size (3 levels: small, medium, large) × vividness (vivid vs. nonvivid) × image type (static vs. dynamic). We included subjects as a covariate to control for individual subject variance. The categories of relative V1 size were extracted from the empirically observed distribution of baseline visual acuity performance scores, under the assumption derived from previously reviewed literature that visual sensitivity is a proxy for V1 size. There exists no accepted absolute partition of V1 size based on this indirect measurement method; therefore, we divided the observed interval of scores arbitrarily in three ordered bins of same data density. Based on the intervals of baseline acuity performance in the NI condition, V1 was categorized into three groups as follows: small, corresponding to a baseline performance interval between 20% and 45%; medium, corresponding to a baseline performance interval between 46% and 55%; and large, corresponding to a baseline performance interval between 56% and 90%. These defined the three relative size group categories used to empirically test the predictions represented in Figure 1.

3. Results

3.1. Interference and Priming Distributions

For all mental image types, effect scores by group were found to be significant (for SV: $\chi^2(2) = 35.02$, d = 2.79; for SNV: $\chi^2(2) = 36.41$, d = 2.96; for DV: $\chi^2(2) = 38.16$, d = 3.21; for DNV: $\chi^2(2) = 39.10$, d = 3.34; for all tests, N = 53 and $p < 0.0001$). The results showed that for all mental image types except DV, the proportion of participants who showed priming and/or negative Perky effects was greater than the proportion of participants who showed interference and/or positive Perky effects, and the distribution of the effect scores significantly differed, showing that the differences in the types of effects observed were not due to chance. The number of participants experiencing each effect, the proportion, and the mean rank for each image type are shown in Table 1.

Table 1. Proportions (and n) of participants experiencing interference/positive Perky effects, priming/negative Perky effects, or null effects for each type of imagery.

	Image Types			
	Static		Dynamic	
	Vivid	Nonvivid	Vivid	Nonvivid
Effect type				
Interference	32.1 (17)	43.4 (23)	45.3 (24)	39.6 (21)
Priming	58.5 (31)	49.1 (26)	41.5 (22)	43.4 (22)
Null	9.4 (5)	7.5 (4)	13.2 (7)	17 (9)

Note. N = 53. Effect Type refers to the resulting score after the NI trials. Negative scores were labeled as priming, including negative Perky effects; positive scores were labeled as interference, including positive Perky effects; and scores of 0 were considered null or no effect. All image types were found to be significant at the $p = 0.0001$ level. The numbers represent the proportions (%) of participants experiencing the effect, as calculated by N/53 × 100. All the numbers are rounded. The numbers in parentheses represent the number of participants out of N = 53 who experienced each effect for the SV image type (n indicates each image type).

Table 1 outlines the differences observed across mental image types. The largest difference between interference and priming within one image type was 14 participants, with more participants showing priming effects; this was observed for the SV image type (interference: $n = 17$, priming: $n = 31$). For SNV images, only 3 additional participants showed priming effects (interference: $n = 23$, priming: $n = 26$). For DV images, the difference was 2 participants, with more participants showing interference effects (interference: $n = 24$, priming: $n = 22$). For DNV images, 2 additional participants showed priming effects (interference: $n = 21$, priming: $n = 23$).

3.2. Positive and Negative Perky Effects

The Mann–Whitney U tests showed significant differences between the positive Perky and negative Perky effects for SV ($Z = -5.66$, $p = 0.000$, d = 2.47) and SNV ($Z = -5.53$, $p = 0.000$, d = 2.34) images. The results were similar for dynamic images (DV: $Z = -5.58$, $p = 0.000$, d = 2.39; DNV: $Z = -5.43$, $p = 0.000$, d = 2.24).

We then plotted all the Perky scores for each participant in the static vivid and nonvivid conditions to explain trends based on the image type. These data are presented in Figure 3.

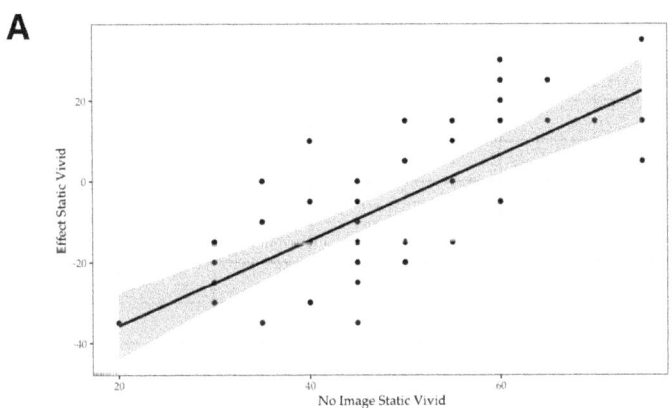

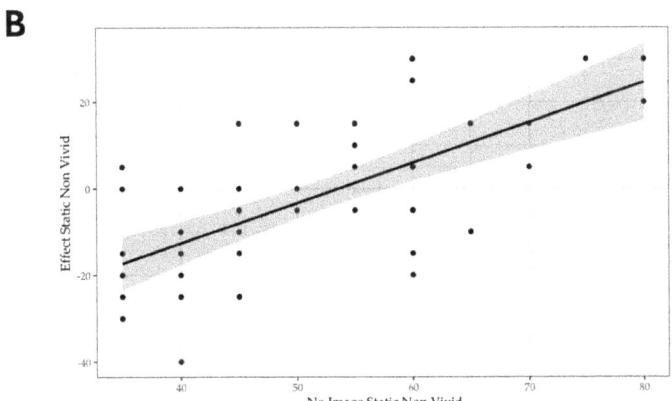

Figure 3. Effect of concurrent static imagery on acuity as a function of the baseline Vernier acuity performance for all participants for vivid (**A**) and nonvivid (**B**) images. Gray band indicates 95% confidence interval.

The correlation/regression coefficients for SV ($r^2 = 0.60$; $r = 0.78$) and SNV ($r^2 = 0.44$; $r = 0.66$) images showed significant differences between SV and SNV images ($t = 2.52$, $d = 0.49$), with a steeper slope for vivid images (i.e., higher interference and priming effects) than for nonvivid images. The same finding was observed for dynamic images: DV ($r^2 = 0.38$; $r = 0.62$) versus DNV ($r^2 = 0.36$; $r = 0.60$) ($t = 3.62$, $d = 0.71$). The graphs for this analysis are shown in Figure 4.

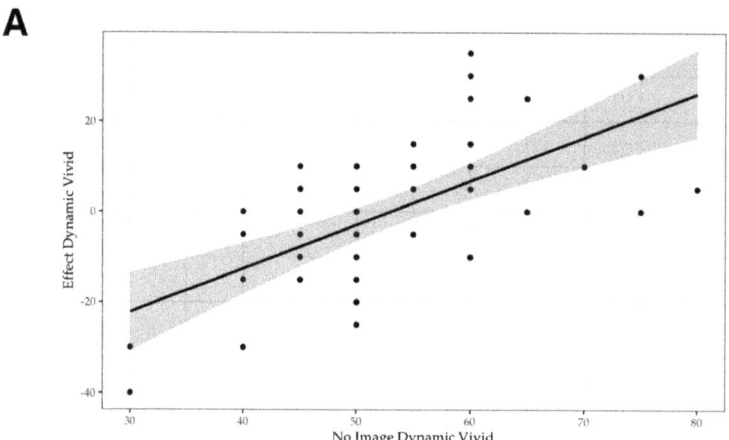

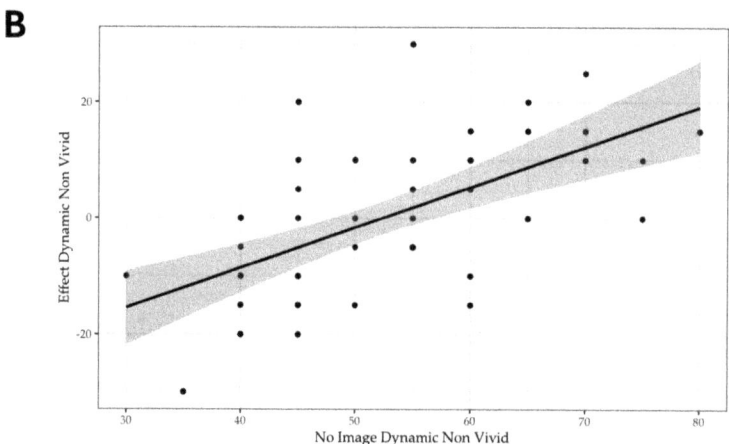

Figure 4. Effect of concurrent dynamic imagery on acuity as a function of the baseline Vernier acuity performance for all participants for vivid (**A**) and nonvivid (**B**) images. Gray band indicates 95% confidence interval.

Further pairwise t tests revealed significant differences between SV and DNV images ($t = 6.03$, $d = 1.18$) and between SNV and DNV images ($t = 3.34$, $d = 0.66$); however, nonsignificant differences were found between SV and DV images ($t = 1.96$, $d = 3.84$) and between SNV and DV images ($t < 1$). This reflects the trend SV > SNV = DV > DNV in terms of the r^2 value. To verify the significance of this pattern, the r coefficients were converted to Zr scores, which were subsequently subjected to polynomial contrast tests. The results confirmed that the trend SV > SNV = DV > DNV was reliable ($t(51) = 3.38$; $p = 0.0014$, $d = 0.66$). This finding suggested that there was a clear difference related to vividness, but there was some overlap between the effects of static and dynamic imagery. To determine the overall pattern, we next examined the possible confounding role of the size of V1.

3.3. Priming/Negative Perky Effects vs. Interference/Positive Perky Effects as a Function of V1 Size

In this analysis, we rescaled the effect using the average NI score subtracted from each condition separately (ISV, IDV, ISNV, and IDNV) since we assumed that the baseline remained the same for each subject (we did not find repeated measures of significant changes in NI across the blocks). The three-way V1 size x vividness x static/dynamic ANOVA showed that the only significant interaction with V1 size was vividness (see results in Table 2). The interaction can be analyzed according to Figure 5, which graphically represents the ANOVA results. Individuals with medium V1 sizes experienced modest interference with nonvivid images but priming with vivid images. In comparison, individuals with large V1s experienced priming and negative Perky effects with nonvivid images and interference and positive Perky effects with vivid images, while individuals with small V1s experienced priming irrespective of the vividness of the image (Figure 5).

Table 2. ANOVA results, showing the effects of concurrent imagery on Vernier acuity as a function of vividness and V1 size.

Source	Type III Sum of Squares	Df	Mean Square	F	p	Partial Eta Squared
Corrected Model	4319.311 [a]	12	359.943	2.405	0.006	0.127
Intercept	772.346	1	772.346	5.161	0.024	0.025
Vividness	419.980	1	419.980	2.806	0.095	0.014
Static/dynamic	4.871	1	4.871	0.033	0.857	0.000
Subject covariate	20.567	1	20.567	0.137	0.711	0.001
V1 size	2242.093	2	1121.047	7.491	<0.001	0.070
Static/dynamic X Vividness	70.489	1	70.489	0.471	0.493	0.002
Static/dynamic X V1 size	230.724	2	115.362	0.771	0.464	0.008
Vividness X V1 size	1192.185	2	596.093	3.983	0.020	0.038
Static/dynamic X Vividness X V1 size	21.749	2	10.875	0.073	0.930	0.001
Error	29,780.807	199	149.652			
Total	34,781.250	212				
Corrected Total	34,100.118	211				

[a] $R^2 = 0.127$.

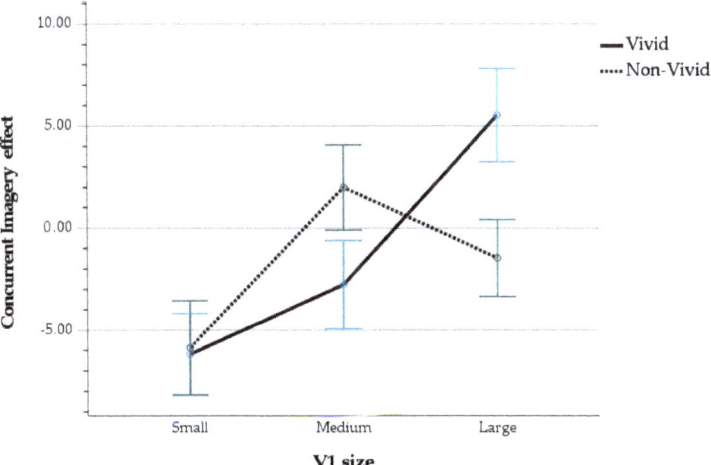

Figure 5. Effect of concurrent imagery on baseline visual acuity performance as a function of vividness and V1 size. Error bars represent standard errors. The data shown are controlled for subject covariates. Dots and bars in blue and green colors highlight data and standard errors for vivid and nonvivid V1 size categories, respectively.

4. Discussion
4.1. Summary of Findings and Interpretative Framework

In summary, we found that visual imagery can have priming and interference effects on visual perception depending on differences in individual neuroanatomy (i.e., V1 size). These findings are consistent with our original hypothesis that individual variability in V1 size may influence acuity precision, as V1 biases the differential activation of dorsal and ventral visual streams by directing the streams toward complementary cooperative or competitive interactions. In addition to the influence of V1 size, image vividness modulated perceptual acuity precision. More specifically, our results demonstrated that participants experienced interference, priming, Perky, and null effects across all the image types. Moreover, the priming and interference effects changed as a function of vividness, regardless of the image content (static vs. dynamic). Image vividness acted as a predictor of acuity performance, as reflected by the fact that the four imagery conditions interfered with perception according to our original hypothesis (see Figure 1). Specifically, the more vivid the imagery is, the more interference in the perception. Overall, our results replicate the findings of Reeves et al. [17] and are consistent with the classic "dipper" effect.

The trend of the imagery effects is compatible with classic theories in the experimental and cognitive psychology literature that suggest a functional equivalence between imagery and perception [26,33]. Specifically, adding mental imagery to a visual acuity task reduces the sensory and cognitive resources available for perception, particularly because the process of generating a visual image is related to the process of perceiving a visual image [24,33]. In other words, different image types can influence the working memory load imposed on perception by top-down mental image processing during concurrent imagery-perception tasks. Thus, images affect individuals' perception based on (1) sensory-based working memory capacity and (2) single processing pathways for imagery and perception. If perception and imagery share a common processing pathway and individuals are instructed to simultaneously use visual perception and visual imagery, the two processes must be balanced to achieve optimal performance. Furthermore, both tasks are governed by working memory and higher-order processes. Therefore, the extent to which perception and imagery processing are equilibrated, as well as the imposed working memory load distribution, largely determine the effect of concurrent imagery on perception. Thus, equilibrium between imagery and perception would be reflected by null effects, disequilibrium in favor of perception would be reflected by priming or negative Perky effects, and disequilibrium in favor of imagery would be reflected by interference or positive Perky effects. Thus, the vividness of mental imagery and the size of V1 can individually or jointly improve or reduce an individual's processing ability by priming or interfering with the perception of visual stimuli.

Here, what we refer to as resource competition and equilibrium can be related to Grossberg's ART logic. Namely, feature-category resonance involves the complementary integration of attended features and activated categories related to an object. Resources are reduced when, in the underlying neural networks, the weights of the connections are being learned during the dual task. Direct evidence and conceptualization of this process have been provided in a landmark study by Craver-Lemley and Reeves [34].

We clarify that Grossberg's conceptualization of imagery does not implicate a necessary role of V1. According to Grossberg, imagery is a "volitionally-mediated shift" that "enables top-down expectations, in the absence of supportive bottom-up inputs, to cause conscious experiences of imagery and inner speech, and thereby to enable fantasy and planning activities to occur". In addition, in certain conditions, tonically hyperexcited expectations can lead to conscious experiences in the absence of bottom-up inputs and volition. However, although "both bottom-up activation of visual percepts and top-down cognitively-activated and volitionally-modulated imagery are possible within the visual system" [12], visual representations underlying imagery are formed through hierarchical and interstream interactions in areas V2 to V4, and the final constructed and phenomenologically perceived visual representations are formed in V4 [12]. Imagery, conceived as "top-down expectations plus attention", operates across this hierarchy, thereby reorganizing bottom-level properties [12].

Furthermore, Grossberg argued that, only in some instances imagery should "have effects that are equivalent to bottom-up activation by visual scenes". This argument is supported with the example of imagery of bi-stable patterns (i.e., Necker cube) which should be already biased by top-down expectation and imagined according to one interpretation. We suggest that vividness influences the strength of resonance and individual differences, which, as shown by the literature, could involve resonance loops between the PFC and V1 and be linked to the bottom-up biasing of *spatial* attention (position of a target) without directly influencing bottom-up sensory or low-level effects. Thus, V1 involvement could be linked to the vividness of the level of consciousness or the level of resonance between complementary processes related to the mental image but not the content of the image (in the present context, static or dynamic), as has been recently shown for other features (i.e., object shape) in priming experiments [18]. Thus, activation of V1 during image-related tasks could be the result of top-down reentrant pathways such as indirect PCF feedback to A17 and A18 via A7 [35,36]. The resulting effects of these interactions could be observed in the what-to-where visual stream of processing, where "knowledge" of the features of an imagined object, i.e., the object shroud, influences the detection of a spatial bottom-up sensory target, as in our Vernier acuity task with concurrent imagery.

4.2. ARTSCAN Modeling of the Findings

In this section, we apply Grossberg's ART and, more specifically, its related ARTSCAN implementation [37,38] to explain the present findings with a descriptive graphical model. The outcomes of our task can be described in terms of the interactions between the what-to-where and where-to-what parallel processing streams, and these interactions can be examined by considering each of the cases corresponding to the V1 size (3) × vividness (2) factorial analysis (see Figure 5). The cases of vivid mental images with small and medium V1s, shown in Figure 6, can be considered together because the only critical difference is the extent to which parvocellular (P-cells) and magnocellular (M-cells) neuronal pools are recruited. In the small V1 case, more M cells than P-cells are activated. In contrast, for the medium V1 case, the activation of both pools should be approximately equal. This is the "combo" scenario modeled in Figure 6.

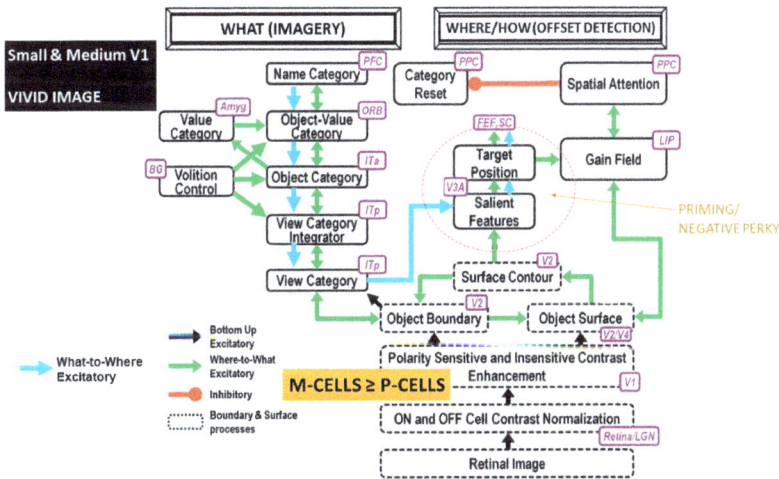

Figure 6. An ARTSCAN interpretation of the processes underlying the interaction between concurrent imagery and Vernier acuity line offset detection in the scenario where the observer has small or medium V1 and vivid imagery.

For the case of a small V1 with vivid imagery, the activation of M-cells largely exceeds that of P-cells. Thus, processing is biased toward the spatial pathway. This bias inhibits category reset according to the established attentional distribution. Because of the high vividness, however, the object characteristics are very and equally strong. The size of V1 is associated with the differential activity distribution of the M- and P-cell density. The cell density is directly related to the weight of excitation between and within the what and where/how streams. With a small or medium V1, due to the decreased density of P-cells, the focus is the object boundary of the mental image. Because of the perception of the image boundary and the contour in the periphery, in the small V1 case, or a weaker contour, in the medium V1 case, the object is perceived as fully transparent and/or in the background plane; therefore, the category or knowledge features of the imagined object receive more attention. With high vividness, the what stream is fully excited from bottom-up PCF recruitment, but it does not interfere with the where/how stream; in contrast, as the attentional distribution is biased toward the area of the possible target position, the image basically provides a background to better detect the gap between the offset lines. Thus, in the case of vivid images with small and medium V1s, spatial attention is strongly primed by two complementary excitatory influences from interacting systems in V3 and the frontal eye field (FEF). The M-cells allow for strong establishment of the mental image and inhibit the category reset mechanism in the posterior parietal cortex, shifting attention to the category features. The what stream focuses on the imagery present to "fill in" the gap in the spatial features. Thus, the target position is attended to. Without the category reset inhibitory action, the two systems remain complementary, and medium to strong priming (negative Perky effects) occurs.

The case of small V1 and nonvivid imagery, shown in the top panel of Figure 7, is similar to the case illustrated in Figure 6, except that the excitatory connections from the image are weaker than those in the case of high vividness. As a result, the imagined object is perceived as a faint background and receives less attention, which is firmly directed to the area containing the gap in the offset lines, leading to strong priming (negative Perky effects). In contrast, in the scenario depicted in the bottom panel of Figure 7, in which an individual has lower vividness but a large V1, the significant change is the predominant excitation of P-cell activity. This situation induces partial and weak activation of the inhibitory pathway linked with the category reset system since the object is relatively weak. Under these conditions, the object is in focus, and other images do not compete with the image through occluding surfaces. Therefore, in the low vividness condition, the brain focuses on the object boundary rather than the object surface. Imagery then facilitates the detection of the flashed line to "fill in" the boundary. The what stream is the dominant pathway due to P-cell excitation, and ultimately, this pathway is only weakly inhibited by the category reset mechanism. Although the attentional distribution should not be considerably altered, the extent of priming is much weaker than in the above cases, and priming may not occur.

In the large V1 condition with high vividness, as illustrated in the top panel of Figure 8, there is a greater density of P-cells than M-cells. With high image vividness, the brain focuses on the object rather than allowing interference from a competing perceived contour. This induces a discrepancy because more attention is removed from the possible target position and moved to the object, which triggers the where/how system to initiate the category reset mechanism and shift the spatial attention to stabilize perception. However, the boundary and surface of the mental image are both attended to since the object shroud is strong (due to high vividness). Phenomenologically, the image is no longer transparent due to competition between spatial attention and focusing on object category features; therefore, knowledge of its feature contents is similar to amodal perception, with a foreground surface occluding the area where the target and the offset gap appear. The latter results in strong interference in the perception and detection of the target (positive Perky effect). In the related scenario of medium-size V1 and nonvivid imagery, shown in the bottom panel of Figure 8, the density of P- and M-cells is the same, leading to equilibrium between the what and where/how streams. The size of V1 influences the density of P- and M-cells, impacting the bias or equilibrium between the what and where/how streams. Since there is bias toward the where stream in the low vividness case, the category reset mechanism is activated. The equal density of the P- and M-cells inhibits spatial attention, and the visual mental image is associated with a weak object shroud. This situation induces partial and weak activation of the inhibitory pathway linked with the category reset system since the stability and knowledge of the object are undermined. Under these conditions, the object is in focus amodally, and no other images compete with it on an occluding opaque surface. This leads to interference in the detection of the target.

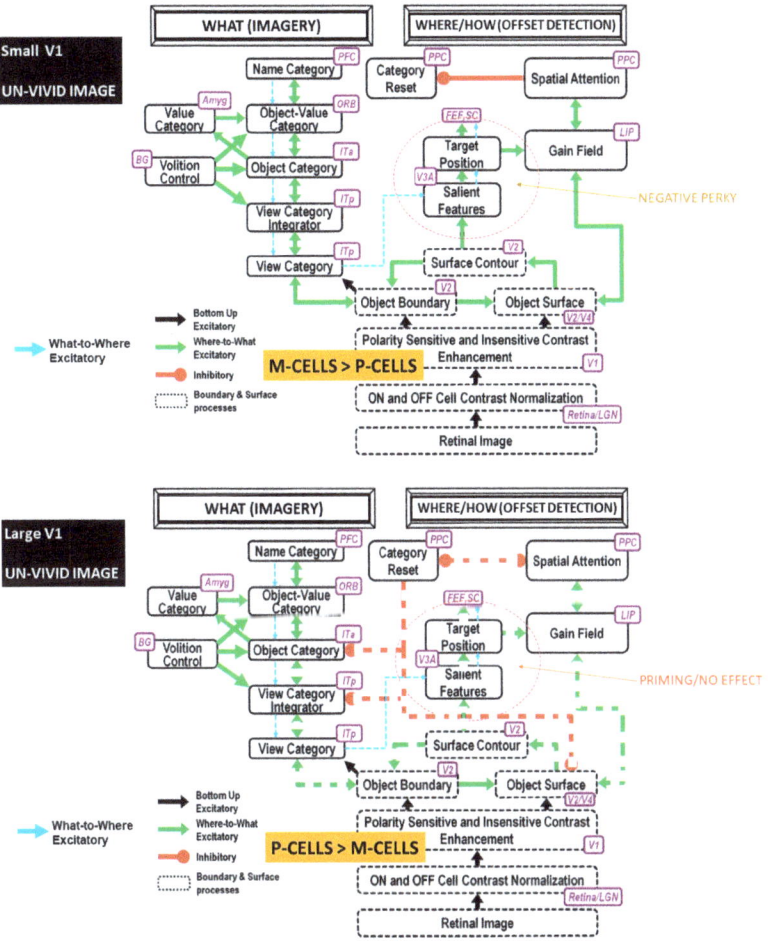

Figure 7. An ARTSCAN interpretation of the processes underlying the interaction between concurrent imagery and Vernier acuity line offset detection in two scenarios in which the observer has nonvivid imagery and either small V1 (**top** panel) or large V1 (**bottom** panel).

In summary, the two key factors that influence imagery–perception interactions are the equilibrium between the strength of resonance in the what system, which determines the extent to which the imagined object is phenomenologically "present" as evident conscious knowledge, and the stable activation of attention toward a spatial target through the control system guided by the object category reset mechanism. Table 3 describes in detail the 7 features that determine the different results.

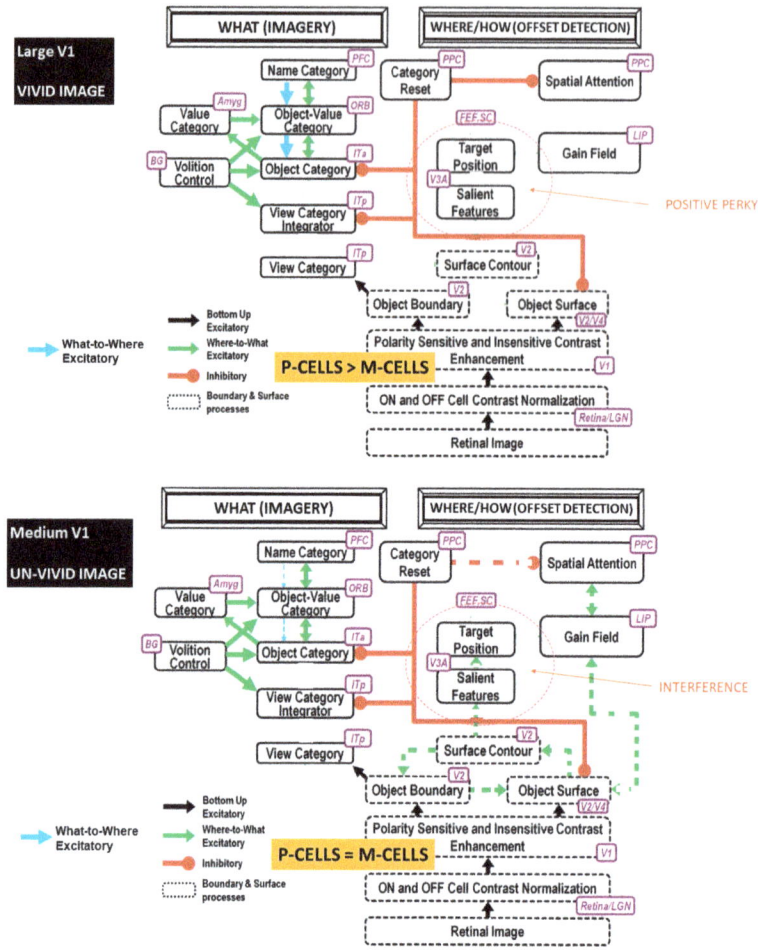

Figure 8. An ARTSCAN interpretation of the processes underlying the interaction between concurrent imagery and Vernier acuity line offset detection in two scenarios in which the observer has nonvivid imagery and either large V1 (**top** panel) or medium V1 (**bottom** panel).

Table 3. Summary of the key aspects of the complementary where-to-what and what-to-where pathways in the present experiment.

V1 Size × Vividness	Interacting Processes
Small V1, Vivid (see Figure 6)	<ul><li>M-cells > P-cells</li><li>Object shroud strong</li><li>Spatial shroud strong</li><li>Object category reset mechanism inhibited by the spatial shroud</li><li>Strong excitation at the target position</li><li>Visual phenomenology: object image boundary as background surface</li><li>Behavioral outcome: negative Perky (strong priming)</li></ul>
Medium V1, Vivid (see Figure 6)	<ul><li>M-cells = P-cells</li><li>Object shroud strong</li><li>Spatial shroud moderate</li><li>Object category reset mechanism inhibited by the spatial shroud</li><li>Strong what and moderate where excitation at the target position</li><li>Visual phenomenology: object image boundary as transparent or background, peripheral field</li><li>Behavioral outcome: variable priming</li></ul>

Table 3. Cont.

V1 Size × Vividness	Interacting Processes
Large V1, Vivid (see Figure 8, Top Panel)	• M-cells < P-cells • Object shroud strong • Spatial shroud weak • Object category reset mechanism inhibits what excitation to target position and spatial shroud • No excitation at the target position • Visual phenomenology: object image contour as occluding modal foreground surface • Behavioral outcome: positive Perky (strong interference)
Small V1, Non-Vivid (see Figure 7, Top Panel)	• M-cells > P-cells • Object shroud weak • Spatial shroud strong • Object category reset mechanism inhibited by the spatial shroud • Weak what and strong where excitation to the target position • Visual phenomenology: object boundary as amodal background • Behavioral outcome: variable priming
Medium V1, Non-Vivid (see Figure 8, Bottom Panel)	• M-cells = P-cells • Object shroud weak • Spatial shroud moderate • Object category reset mechanism inhibited by the spatial shroud and partially by Object Shroud • Weak where excitation to target position • Visual phenomenology: Amodal perception a foreground surface • Behavioral outcome: variable interference
Large V1, Non-Vivid (see Figure 7, Bottom Panel)	• M-cells < P-cells • Object shroud weak • Spatial shroud weak • Object category reset mechanism partially inhibits what excitation to target position and spatial shroud • Weak what and where excitation at the target position • Visual phenomenology: object image boundary as amodal background • Behavioral outcome: priming or no effect

4.3. Contributions of Present Work

4.3.1. The Primacy of Complementary Visual Cortical Streams

It is widely accepted that the dorsal visual processing stream is recruited for spatial perception (determining where an object is located), while the ventral stream is recruited for object perception (identifying what an object is) [39,40]. Since the dorsal nervous system determines the positions of visual stimuli in space, we suggest that this pathway is also involved in generating externally projected mental images (placing imagined images in particular spatial locations). Moreover, we theorize that the dual processing involved in detecting visual stimuli and externally projecting mental images may be responsible for creating interference (positive Perky effect) when detecting visual stimuli. Furthermore, given the role of the ventral visual system in object recognition, i.e., categorization, ventrally dominant individuals receive less interference from concurrent imagery, as ventral mediated imagery does not directly compete with the resources necessary for accurate perception of visual details in the external environment.

In agreement with Grossberg's theory, the "what" and "where/how" cortical streams seem to interact to determine the vividness and perception of visual objects. We observed that visual acuity scores were dependent on an individual's V1 size and vivid imagery ability. This influences the recruitment of the dorsal and ventral visual pathways. The involvement of the dorsal and ventral pathways determines whether the imagery is more sensory/category oriented or more detail oriented. Grossberg [25] described how visual cortical areas such as V1 enable our brains to consciously see. The ventral (what) and dorsal (where/how) streams interact through bottom-up, horizontal, and top-down interactions [25]. Top-down interactions use object and spatial attentional processes to engage consciousness. Top-down attentive matching creates synchronous resonant states that lead to bottom-up recognition of categories and top-down expectations [25]. Attentive matching may impact both mostly conscious (object shroud) and mostly unconscious (spatial shroud) seeing.

However, the size of V1 could introduce bias and change the dynamic interaction among the dorsal and ventral areas. As Grossberg [26] described, the architecture of the dorsal and ventral streams and the relationship between the two enables image recognition and determines appropriate actions. Furthermore, without bottom-up data, Grossberg's theory [13] describes how and why top-down interactions can lead to imagery with volitional modulation. Grossberg also suggested that imagery is not only an entity itself but also part of the complex dynamic system of seeing and thinking. In other words, in Grossberg's theoretical infrastructure, imagery is an important component in vision and thinking. Thus, imagery findings impact perception, and knowledge regarding perception can be applied to imagery. The vividness of an experience in the visual field, including light, color, and extra sensory information, draws human attention and necessarily activates both the ventral and dorsal streams. Within this system, we attempted to clarify the possible role of V1 through indirect measurements and suggested vividness as a possible bias guiding perception and imagery. Moreover, the novel aspect of this paper is the contribution and analysis of the role of V1. V1 is a high-level interaction region with the ventral and dorsal streams. An individual's V1 size may influence the individual's bias toward the dorsal or ventral stream through the reentrant loop. This would potentially contribute to reconcile why V1 activation during visual imagery is a ubiquitous find (e.g., in fMRI studies). Indeed, it should be expected that only imagery situations that induce extreme disequilibrium between dorsal and ventral processes *in certain individuals* (hence, usually a proportion of the sample) should reveal strong and clear evidence of V1 activation (or deactivation).

Kosslyn provided extensive independent supporting evidence demonstrating the importance of the dorsal and ventral pathways, as described in [40], and D'Angiulli and Reeves [28] described how vividness ratings reflect the strengths and weaknesses of the dorsal and ventral pathways. The vividness (or image strength) ratings and image latency could represent the combined action of the two pathways and their roles in both imagery and perception [6]. These two pathways are core mechanisms involved in image generation and high-level vision tasks that keep being rediscovered in current imagery research (see [19,41]), but no detailed model of their emerging dynamics has been previously proposed.

Although the role of the dorsal and ventral pathways has been described in the literature, the bias of V1 toward the dorsal or ventral pathway is another novel contribution of the present study. Importantly, we do not make any assumptions about the bias toward the dorsal or ventral streams, and we suggest that external bias, task demands, and individual differences (including V1 differences) impact responses to perceptual stimuli. What we call "voluntary" (for example, our unconscious bias) is a complex system of interactions. Rather than voluntary, this intertwining nature is autonomous in attending, categorizing, recognizing, and predicting objects, which is central to Grossberg's ART and the idea of the resonant brain. Our contribution emphasizes the primacy of the link among V1, the dorsal and ventral pathways, and visual phenomenology [12].

4.3.2. Limitations and Future Research Directions

In this context, a limitation of this work, and the literature, is the lack of understanding of exactly how attention affects unconscious and conscious bias toward the ventral and dorsal pathways. Future research should therefore focus on conscious and unconscious bias and how attention is linked to V1 and the dorsal and ventral pathways. Overall, the interaction among the dorsal and ventral pathways, vividness, and the size of V1 could improve our understanding of how individual differences in perception (sometimes major differences with influential consequences) occur. This understanding might be useful in educational applications. In particular, imagery training is a key application for this research. For example, young children with less acuity (who are cognitively less attentive to external stimuli) could benefit from imagery training. In this paper, we found that image vividness affects the perception of external stimuli. Generating imagery could lead to stronger priming of perceptual processing. More importantly, training and practice could be determined according to individual characteristics and task types, as some children may suffer unwanted interference and divided attention or distraction due to images that are too vivid. Similar applications could be considered for clinical, mental health, and psychotherapy settings, which routinely use mental imagery training and practice.

Some limitations of this paper include the relatively small sample size and the limited diversity of the participants. A larger, more diverse demographic would add more varied V1 size data as well as different imagery abilities. In light of these limitations, the interpretations and data are preliminary and should be considered an attempt to examine the impact of individual differences and phenomenology on dynamics that extends imagery research.

Our contribution should be considered a hypothetical extension of ART for future neurophysiological work on imagery and imagination. As mentioned, the present study is merely descriptive and limited to replicating Kosslyn's data and Grossberg's insights; however, connecting subjective and phenomenal results to actual empirical neural dynamics remains challenging. Ongoing investigations in our laboratory aim to extend the proposed framework using combined fMRI, EEG, and ERP techniques and deep learning simulations. We hope to elucidate the groundbreaking contributions of Grossberg's ART. The proposed approach might permit the prediction of phenomenology and subjectivity and individual differences starting from emerging complex properties of neural networks, in contrast to the large majority of research that, up to now, has proceeded in the opposite direction, going from insights driven from phenomenology and introspection to experimental phenomena and to cognitive and neural architectures (see [42,43]). The present proposed approach may considerably improve the current state-of-the-art in top-down attention, imagery, and consciousness research. In the most practical sense, the identification of the different possible scenarios of complex neural interactions between perception and imagery (as analyzed in Figures 6–8) and the reduction to a manageable set of system variables (as illustrated in Table 3) provide a testable and falsifiable computational working model of vividness which is amenable to further empirical and theoretical refinements, moving the bench from introspection to manipulation of objective variables within interacting complex systems, especially in terms validating implementations based on neural networks simulations. A far-reaching objective is that, through the advancement of multidisciplinary meta-theory, the present conceptualization of vividness might, in future research, be abstracted and generalized further, from the level of human domain to neuromorphic computing and neurorobotics to arrive at possible new forms of autonomous machine explainability (for more in depth discussions see [2]).

5. Conclusions

In conclusion, we showed that concurrent imagery can exert interference, priming, or no effects on perception depending on the interaction between image vividness and individual differences in neuroanatomy, including dynamic complementary parallel processing in ventral and dorsal visual streams. Our results suggest that highly vivid images and large (ventrally dominant) V1 interfere with perception, whereas weak imagery and small V1 (dorsally dominant) prime perception. A possible interpretation is that the size of V1 affects the neural synchronization between the connectivity of this region and other dorsal and ventral regions according to reentrant feedback from the PCF, thereby also influencing the vividness of the perception. Hence, under our static vivid imagery condition, the interference effects are greater than those under the static nonvivid and dynamic vivid conditions and more than double the effect than that under the dynamic nonvivid imagery condition.

Overall, we conclude that in most situations, imagery enhances perception, possibly because mental images are often processed by ventral pathways. The ventral network is beneficial for perception during imagery tasks because this network carries information that is less likely to compete with working memory and the attentional systems necessary for accurate visual-spatial prediction in the where/how system. However, despite these findings, there is still large individual variation among individuals, which appears to be due to the vividness of the image and the relative cortical size of the V1 area.

Our interpretation of ART and related descriptive modeling based on ARTSCAN contributes to expanding Grossberg's comprehensive account of how and why individually experienced vividness may influence the differential use of the dorsal and ventral complementary visual processing pathways, resulting in the reported effects of imagery on concurrent perception.

Author Contributions: Conceptualization, A.D.; methodology, A.D.; validation, C.L. and D.M.B.; formal analysis, A.D. and D.M.B.; investigation, A.D.; data curation, A.D. and D.M.B.; writing—original draft preparation, A.D., C.L. and D.M.B.; writing—review and editing, A.D.; supervision, A.D.; project administration, A.D. All authors have read and agreed to the published version of the manuscript.

Funding: This research was funded by the Natural Sciences and Engineering Research Council of Canada through the New Frontiers in Research Fund—Exploration Program (grant number NFRFE-2019-00503) to A.D.

Institutional Review Board Statement: The study was conducted in accordance with the Declaration of Helsinki, and approved by the Institutional Behavioural Research Ethics Board of Carleton University (protocol code 111569 27 November 2019).

Informed Consent Statement: Informed consent was obtained from all subjects involved in the study.

Data Availability Statement: The data presented in this study are available upon request from the corresponding author. The data are not publicly available because open data sharing was not included as an option for consent.

Acknowledgments: We thank Etienne Lefebvre for comments and editing the previous version of this manuscript. We thank Jennifer Goldberg and Leslie Lavoie for assisting with the data collection. We are indebted to Adam Reeves, whose two-decade discussions and guidance have shaped the empirical side of this research. This paper is also a celebration of his work and legacy. All remaining (inevitable) blunders are the responsibility of the first author. We thank the anonymous reviewers and the editors for helping us improve our manuscript.

Conflicts of Interest: The authors declare no conflicts of interest.

References

1. McKelvie, S. *Vividness of Visual Imagery: Measurement, Nature, Function & Dynamics*; Brandon House: Wexford, UK, 1995; Volume 5.
2. Molokopoy, V.; D'Angiulli, A. Multidisciplinary Intersections on Artificial-Human Vividness: Phenomenology, Representation, and the Brain. *Brain Sci.* **2022**, *12*, 1495. [CrossRef] [PubMed]
3. Marks, D.F. I Am Conscious, Therefore, I Am: Imagery, Affect, Action, and a General Theory of Behavior. *Brain Sci.* **2019**, *9*, 107. [CrossRef] [PubMed]
4. Runge, M.S.; Cheung, M.W.-L.; D'Angiulli, A. Meta-analytic comparison of trial- versus questionnaire-based vividness reportability across behavioral, cognitive and neural measurements of imagery. *Neurosci. Conscious.* **2017**, *2017*, nix006. [CrossRef]
5. Marks, D.F. Phenomenological Studies of Visual Mental Imagery: A Review and Synthesis of Historical Datasets. *Vision* **2023**, *7*, 67. [CrossRef] [PubMed]
6. Marks, D.F. The Action Cycle Theory of Perception and Mental Imagery. *Vision* **2023**, *7*, 12. [CrossRef]
7. Grossberg, S. Neural substrates of visual percepts, imagery, and hallucinations. *Behav. Brain Sci.* **2002**, *25*, 194–195. [CrossRef]
8. Ishai, A.; Sagi, D. Common Mechanisms of Visual Imagery and Perception. *Science* **1995**, *268*, 1772–1774. [CrossRef]
9. Dijkstra, N.; Bosch, S.E.; van Gerven, M.A.J. Vividness of Visual Imagery Depends on the Neural Overlap with Perception in Visual Areas. *J. Neurosci.* **2017**, *37*, 1367–1373. [CrossRef]
10. Kosslyn, S.M.; Thompson, W.L.; Ganis. *The Case for Mental Imagery*; Oxford University Press: Oxford, UK, 2006.
11. Pearson, J.; Clifford CW, G.; Tong, F. The Functional Impact of Mental Imagery on Conscious Perception. *Curr. Biol.* **2008**, *18*, 982–986. [CrossRef]
12. Grossberg, S. Adaptive Resonance Theory: How a brain learns to consciously attend, learn, and recognize a changing world. *Neural Netw.* **2013**, *37*, 1–47. [CrossRef]
13. Grossberg, S. *Conscious Mind, Resonant Brain: How Each Brain Makes a Mind*; Oxford Academic: New York, NY, USA, 2021. [CrossRef]
14. Chun, M.M.; Golomb, J.D.; Turk-Browne, N.B. A Taxonomy of External and Internal Attention. *Annu. Rev. Psychol.* **2011**, *62*, 73–101. [CrossRef] [PubMed]
15. Gjorgieva, E.; Geib, B.R.; Cabeza, R.; Woldorff, M.G. The influence of imagery vividness and internally-directed attention on the neural mechanisms underlying the encoding of visual mental images into episodic memory. *Cereb. Cortex* **2023**, *33*, 3207–3220. [CrossRef] [PubMed]

16. D'Angiulli, A.; Reeves, A. Generating Mental Images: Latency and Vividness are Inversely Related. *Mem. Cogn.* **2002**, *30*, 1179–1188. [CrossRef] [PubMed]
17. Reeves, A.; Grayhem, R.; Craver-Lemley, C. The Perky effect revisited: Imagery hinders perception at high levels, but aids it at low. *Vision. Res.* **2020**, *167*, 8–14. [CrossRef] [PubMed]
18. D'Angiulli, A.; Reeves, A. Experimental phenomenology meets brain information processing: Vividness of voluntary imagery, consciousness of the present, and priming. *Psychol. Conscious. Theory Res. Pract.* **2021**, *8*, 397–418. [CrossRef]
19. Pearson, J. The human imagination: The cognitive neuroscience of visual mental imagery. *Nat. Rev. Neurosci.* **2019**, *20*, 624–634. [CrossRef] [PubMed]
20. Pearson, J.; Rademaker, R.L.; Tong, F. Evaluating the mind's eye: The metacognition of visual imagery. *Psychol. Sci.* **2011**, *22*, 1535–1542. [CrossRef]
21. Bergmann, J.; Genç, E.; Kohler, A.; Singer, W.; Pearson, J. Smaller Primary Visual Cortex Is Associated with Stronger, but Less Precise Mental Imagery. *Cereb. Cortex* **2016**, *26*, 3838–3850. [CrossRef]
22. Duncan, R.O.; Boynton, G.M. Cortical magnification within human primary visual cortex correlates with acuity thresholds. *Neuron* **2003**, *38*, 659–671. [CrossRef]
23. Srinivasan, S.; Carlo, C.N.; Stevens, C.F. Predicting visual acuity from the structure of visual cortex. *Proc. Natl. Acad. Sci. USA* **2015**, *112*, 7815–7820. [CrossRef]
24. Kosslyn, S.M.; Pascual-Leone, A.; Felician, O.; Camposano, S.; Keenan, J.P.; Thompson, W.L.; Ganis, G.; Sukel, K.E.; Alpert, N.M. The role of area 17 in visual imagery: Convergent evidence from PET and rTMS. *Science* **1999**, *284*, 167–170. [CrossRef] [PubMed]
25. D'Angiulli, A.; Kenney, D.; Pham, D.A.T.; Lefebvre, E.; Bellavance, J.; Buchanan, D.M. Neurofunctional Symmetries and Asymmetries during Voluntary out-of- and within-Body Vivid Imagery Concurrent with Orienting Attention and Visuospatial Detection. *Symmetry* **2021**, *13*, 1549. [CrossRef]
26. Pearson, J.; Kosslyn, S.M. The heterogeneity of mental representation: Ending the imagery debate. *Proc. Natl. Acad. Sci. USA* **2015**, *112*, 10089–10092. [CrossRef]
27. Grossberg, S. The Embodied Brain of SOVEREIGN2: From Space-Variant Conscious Percepts During Visual. Search and Navigation to Learning Invariant Object Categories and Cognitive-Emotional Plans for Acquiring Valued Goals. *Front. Comput. Neurosci.* **2019**, *13*, 36. [CrossRef]
28. D'Angiulli, A.; Reeves, A. The relationship between self-reported vividness and latency during mental size scaling of everyday items: Phenomenological evidence of different types of imagery. *Am. J. Psychol.* **2007**, *120*, 521–551. [CrossRef] [PubMed]
29. De Borst, A.W.; Sack, A.T.; Jansma, B.M.; Esposito, F.; de Martino, F.; Valente, G.; Roebroeck, A.; di Salle, F.; Goebel, R.; Formisano, E. Integration of "what" and "where" in frontal cortex during visual imagery of scenes. *Neuroimage* **2012**, *60*, 47–58. [CrossRef] [PubMed]
30. Grossberg, S. Attention: Multiple types, brain resonances, psychological functions, and conscious states. *J. Integr. Neurosci.* **2021**, *20*, 197–232. [CrossRef] [PubMed]
31. D'Angiulli, A.; Runge, M.; Faulkner, A.; Zakizadeh, J.; Chan, A.; Morcos, S. Vividness of visual imagery and incidental recall of verbal cues, when phenomenological availability reflects long-term memory accessibility. *Front. Psychol.* **2013**, *4*, 1. [CrossRef]
32. Baddeley, A.D.; Andrade, J. Working memory and the vividness of imagery. *J. Exp. Psychol. Gen.* **2000**, *129*, 126–145. [CrossRef]
33. Kosslyn, S.M. *Image and Brain: The Resolution of the Imagery Debate*; The MIT Press: Cambridge, MA, USA, 1994; ISBN 978-0-262-11184-3.
34. Craver-Lemley, C.; Reeves, A. How Visual Imagery Interferes with Vision. *Psychol. Rev.* **1992**, *99*, 633–649. [CrossRef]
35. Ding, J.; Ye, Z.; Xu, F.; Hu, X.; Yu, H.; Zhang, S.; Tu, Y.; Zhang, Q.; Sun, Q.; Hua, T.; et al. Effects of top-down influence suppression on behavioral and V1 neuronal contrast sensitivity functions in cats. *iScience* **2022**, *25*, 1. [CrossRef] [PubMed]
36. Pan, H.; Zhang, S.; Pan, D.; Ye, Z.; Yu, H.; Ding, J.; Wang, Q.; Sun, Q.; Hua, T. Characterization of feedback neurons in the high-level visual cortical areas that project directly to the primary visual cortex in the cat. *Front. Neuroanat.* **2021**, *14*, 616465. [CrossRef] [PubMed]
37. Fazl, A.; Grossberg, S.; Mingolla, E. View-invariant object category learning, recognition, and search: How spatial and object attention are coordinated using surface-based attentional shrouds. *Cog. Psych.* **2009**, *58*, 1–48. [CrossRef] [PubMed]
38. Chang, H.-C.; Grossberg, S.; Cao, Y. Where's Waldo? How perceptual cognitive, and emotional brain processes cooperate during learning to categorize and find desired objects in a cluttered scene. *Front. Integr. Neurosci.* **2014**, *8*, 43. [CrossRef] [PubMed]
39. Mishkin, M.; Ungerleider, L.G. Contribution of striate inputs to the visuospatial functions of parieto-preoccipital cortex in monkeys. *Behav. Brain Res.* **1982**, *6*, 57–77. [CrossRef]
40. Borst, G.; Thompson, W.L.; Kosslyn, S.M. Understanding the dorsal and ventral systems of the human cerebral cortex: Beyond dichotomies. *Am. Psychol.* **2011**, *66*, 624–632. [CrossRef]
41. Dijkstra, N.; Bosch, S.E.; van Gerven, M.A. Shared neural mechanisms of visual perception and imagery. *Trends Cogn. Sci.* **2019**, *23*, 423–434. [CrossRef]

42. Spillmann, L. Phenomenology and neurophysiological correlations: Two approaches to perception research. *Vis. Res.* **2009**, *49*, 1507–1521. [CrossRef]
43. Hachen, I. Phenomenology and animal sensory systems: Asking "why". *Psychol. Conscious. Theory Res. Pract.* **2021**, *8*, 274–291. [CrossRef]

Disclaimer/Publisher's Note: The statements, opinions and data contained in all publications are solely those of the individual author(s) and contributor(s) and not of MDPI and/or the editor(s). MDPI and/or the editor(s) disclaim responsibility for any injury to people or property resulting from any ideas, methods, instructions or products referred to in the content.

Article

Analyzing Biomedical Datasets with Symbolic Tree Adaptive Resonance Theory

Sasha Petrenko [1,*], Daniel B. Hier [1,2], Mary A. Bone [3], Tayo Obafemi-Ajayi [4], Erik J. Timpson [5], William E. Marsh [5], Michael Speight [5] and Donald C. Wunsch II [1]

1. Department of Electrical and Computer Engineering, Missouri University of Science and Technology, Rolla, MO 65409, USA; hierd@mst.edu (D.B.H.); dwunsch@mst.edu (D.C.E.II)
2. Department of Neurology and Rehabilitation, University of Illinois at Chicago, Chicago, IL 60607, USA
3. Department of Science and Industry Systems, University of Southeastern Norway, 3616 Kongsberg, Norway; mary.bone@drmarybone.com
4. Engineering Program, Missouri State University, Springfield, MO 65897, USA; tayoobafemiajayi@missouristate.edu
5. Honeywell Federal Manufacturing & Technologies, Kansas City, MO 64147, USA; etimpson@kcnsc.doe.gov (E.J.T.); wmarsh@kcnsc.doe.gov (W.E.M.)
* Correspondence: petrenkos@mst.edu

Abstract: Biomedical datasets distill many mechanisms of human diseases, linking diseases to genes and phenotypes (signs and symptoms of disease), genetic mutations to altered protein structures, and altered proteins to changes in molecular functions and biological processes. It is desirable to gain new insights from these data, especially with regard to the uncovering of hierarchical structures relating disease variants. However, analysis to this end has proven difficult due to the complexity of the connections between multi-categorical symbolic data. This article proposes symbolic tree adaptive resonance theory (START), with additional supervised, dual-vigilance (DV-START), and distributed dual-vigilance (DDV-START) formulations, for the clustering of multi-categorical symbolic data from biomedical datasets by demonstrating its utility in clustering variants of Charcot–Marie–Tooth disease using genomic, phenotypic, and proteomic data.

Keywords: adaptive resonance theory; biomedical data; categorical data; ontologies; knowledge graphs

1. Introduction

Precision medicine depends upon a detailed unraveling of the relationships between diseases, phenotypes, genes, and the underlying proteins and biological pathways [1–7]. The ready availability of protein, disease, gene, phenotype, and biological pathway ontologies makes it possible to construct purpose-specific datasets for studying human disease. These can take the form of symbolic relationships that can be organized into formal ontologies that are instantiated as knowledge graphs defining the permissible relationships between classes and the instances within them [8].

However, many elements in these disease–gene–protein datasets are formatted as categorical rather than numerical variables, bringing a unique challenge to machine learning algorithms. Although tools exist to analyze and visualize categorical data [9], the tools for clustering these datasets depend heavily on recasting categories into real-valued spaces, which is largely unavoidable due to the definition of the problem statement; all modalities of machine learning assume distance metrics or similarity measures of their feature spaces, whereas categorical data contain symbols that do not belong to ordered sets, and thus, do not inhabit metric spaces. An important design choice then when working with mixed or fully categorical data is how to recast categorical features into spaces with similarity measures [10]. This recasting, whether by one-hot encoding, ordinal encoding, or another encoding scheme, can bring its own deleterious consequences; one-hot encoding of categories can generate large sparse feature vectors due to many different categories, while ordinal encoding can introduce measures of proximity between categories that do not intrinsically exist. Meta-analyses of symbolic datasets may yield similarity meta-metrics that are useful for clustering [11,12], but these meta-metrics require domain knowledge of the categories in the dataset, limiting both their transferability to other datasets and applicability to streaming learning. While statistical machine learning algorithms can compensate for some of these input feature space shortcomings through sophisticated machinery that relies on a large dataset size and a high degree of feature cardinality, these methods naturally suffer in regimes with small categorical datasets. Furthermore, these encoding schemes and the machine learning algorithms do not gracefully extend to instances of hierarchical or nested attributes such as occur with the variably sized association of diseases with phenotypes, genes, and proteins.

Adaptive resonance theory (ART) algorithms principally belong to the class of incremental neurogenesis clustering/unsupervised [13] algorithms, with many additional variants for use in supervised learning [14,15], reinforcement learning [16,17], and even self-supervised and multimodal applications [18]. The design of these algorithms allows them to update existing categories or create new ones from the data alone in a stable, incremental, and lifelong manner. With the notable exception of the binary-valued ART1 algorithm, most of these algorithms work upon real-valued preprocessed feature datasets via the use of fuzzy feature membership [19–23]. In contrast, the Gram-ART algorithm was designed for the meta-optimization of genetic algorithms, and thus, is designed to work with variable-length symbolic datasets [24], but it too has its shortcomings when tackling the large numbers of terminal symbols encountered in medical disease datasets.

With these myriad design challenges in mind, this article describes the design of a new ART algorithm named symbolic tree adaptive resonance theory (START) for the clustering of variable-length symbolic statements. This formulation of START also includes both dual-vigilance (DV-START) and distributed dual-vigilance (DDV-START) variants [25,26] along with their supervised modifications. This article also outlines methods for casting categorical disease–gene biomedical datasets into symbolic datasets for both unsupervised clustering and supervised training where labels are available.

The changes in START compared to the Gram-ART algorithm summarize the novel contributions of this article in addition to the use of this algorithm for the study of biomedical disease-variant data. START extends Gram-ART as a novel approach to analyzing biomedical disease-variant data in the following ways:

1. Both a match and activation function for the Gram-ART match rule.
2. Optimizations to the prototype-encoding scheme to mitigate memory complexity in grammars with large sets of terminal symbols.
3. A mechanism to grow prototype tree structures when novel production rule sets are encountered.
4. Both dual-vigilance and distributed dual-vigilance START variants [25,26].
5. A supervised modification for each unsupervised START variant.

This article is organized into the following sections: Section 2 provides a background of the literature pertinent to the formulation of START, while Section 3 describes the derivation and structure of START and its dual-vigilance and supervised variants. Section 4 outlines the datasets and experimental methodology utilized in the evaluation of START, including benchmark machine learning datasets and the target biomedical disease-variant datasets of the article, and Section 5 contains the results of these experiments. Section 6 discusses the experimental results and their biological plausibility, with Section 7 providing final conclusions on both START and the biomedical dataset analysis of the previous sections.

2. Background

2.1. Adaptive Resonance Theory

Adaptive resonance theory (ART) is a neurocognitive theory of how biological neural networks for self-stable representations learn without catastrophic forgetting, online and without supervision, through feedback and competitive dynamics [27–35]. Since its inception, a variety of machine learning models have been implemented using the theory as a basis [19,36–38]. Though these algorithms in large part belong to the class of incremental neurogenesis clustering/unsupervised algorithms, they have been adapted for applications in supervised, reinforcement, and even multimodal learning [19,39], tackling clustering issues from sample granularity [25,26] to distributed representations [40–42], pattern sequences [43], context recognition [44,45], and uncertainties [46–48]. Some algorithms based upon ART have even been combined with incremental cluster validity indices (ICVIs), metrics of clustering performance in the absence of supervised labels, to enable a variety of incremental, online, and multimodal clustering and biclustering applications [49–54]. ART algorithms are additionally well suited for lifelong learning (L2) applications because they are derived from theories on how biological neural networks address the stability–plasticity dilemma to mitigate catastrophic forgetting [55–57].

Nearly all ART formulations trade the explicit coarseness parameters of other clustering algorithms for a vigilance parameter ($\rho \in (0,1)$), which behaves as a threshold of agreement between a sample and expectations to determine whether to update existing knowledge or to create new categories altogether, a process known as the ART match rule [41]. Furthermore, nearly all ART formulations are intrinsically prototype-based machine learning algorithms, meaning that categories are defined by representative prototypes in the sample feature space. This has two important consequences: ART algorithms theoretically have unlimited memory because new prototypes may always be instantiated, but they generally have no representational capacity in the sense of manifold learning, relying instead on the assumption that the feature space being used for clustering is sufficiently well separated. Samples in this feature space are provided in a feature representation layer $F1$, which is compared with a category representation layer $F2$ containing these prototypes through ART competitive dynamics that include a check against this vigilance parameter.

2.2. Gram-ART

Gram-ART is a clustering algorithm, based on ART learning dynamics, that defines its prototypes and input features as trees of parsed statements adhering to a formal grammar [24]. Originally designed to tackle the problem of comparing similarity between symbolic expressions for the meta-optimization of genetic algorithms, it is capable of accepting statements of an arbitrary length according to a user-defined context-free grammar (CFG) expressed in the Backus–Naur form (BNF). In the original formulation, Gram-ART samples are statements adhering to a CFG that are parsed into rooted syntax trees. These parsed samples are then compared according to ART learning rules to Gram-ART prototypes that are themselves rooted trees containing distributions of terminal symbols that are encountered at each node during learning. Gram-ART answers the questions of how to formulate prototype trees of varied shape, compute similarities of sample statements to prototypes of differing shapes, and update the terminal symbol distributions at each node during learning.

Gram-ART is the first ART algorithm capable of clustering inputs samples of arbitrary length, but it also inherits some problems from working with symbolic data. Terminal symbols under a grammar have no fuzzy membership or relation without an additional embedding scheme. Gram-ART tackles this by updating distributions of terminal symbols at each position along the rooted prototype trees during learning. However, this technique quickly grows in space and subsequent time complexity in grammars with sets of terminal symbols larger than the algebraic expressions that they were originally designed for.

3. Method

3.1. START: Symbolic Tree Adaptive Resonance Theory

This paper introduces a new formulation of the Gram-ART algorithm called START for the clustering of symbolic datasets. START is a prototype-based unsupervised clustering algorithm that when presented with a new sample utilizes ART dynamics to determine whether to update an existing template or to instantiate a new one. START targets symbolic expressions adhering to a context-free grammar $CFG(\mathbf{T}, \mathbf{N}, \mathbf{P}, \mathcal{S})$ with a complete set of terminal symbols $\mathbf{T}$, non-terminal symbols $\mathbf{N}$, production rules $\mathbf{P}$, and a statement entry point $\mathcal{S}$. The prototypes of START are rooted trees containing learned distributions of the encountered terminal symbols at each node representing a non-terminal position, and symbolic statements are parsed into rooted constituency parse trees that are subsequently processed against these prototypes using ART learning dynamics. With such a formulation, the method is naturally extended to the clustering of purely categorical datasets of variable length sequences, such as in the myriad categorical fields of disease–gene–protein data.

3.1.1. Motivation

The realm of clustering, and indeed machine learning as a whole, requires a serious consideration and study of the various forms that data may take [10]. Datasets are often modeled as samples of the state space defined by some measuring device. Many samples of data are naturally real-valued, such as the readings from imaging sensors for the purposes of computer vision, while others are categorical in nature, such as descriptor labels of the color of an object (e.g., red, blue, yellow). Datasets may have one or more feature dimensions, and they may even be multimodal, containing a combination of real-valued and categorical data in each sample. A notion of the proximity of features is critical to machine learning algorithms that utilize similarity measures to model and interpret samples; metric spaces are defined as sets that can have such a similarity measure defining the distance between points in the set, and indeed even categorical features may sometimes have distance metrics if they have an ordering (e.g., low, medium, high), though they often only have a strict equivalence relation for comparing categories (e.g., red = red, red $\neq$ blue). The presence of a distance metric is especially important in unsupervised learning scenarios such as clustering where an algorithm has nothing available to model a dataset aside from the features themselves. As a consequence, the clustering of data with unordered categorical features is difficult, and many clustering algorithms are designed with the assumption that at least some ordered features exist in the data [10].

Nevertheless, purely categorical datasets such as those containing only label descriptors do exist, and it is desirable to cluster them to extract meaning and structure. It is even more challenging when such datasets contain a varying number of features for each sample; algorithms that tackle real-valued datasets of variable length such as time-series data utilize techniques like convolutions and pooling to turn a varying number of features at runtime into a fixed model size, but these techniques are ill-defined for purely categorical data, especially when individual symbols are sparsely populated throughout the dataset.

Purely categorical datasets of variable feature dimensions arise commonly in human-annotated datasets, such as those generated from medical research. Human-prescribed categories of diseases, their variants, and other ontological features can contain missing entries when data are missing or inapplicable, and categories can even be nested; for example, the presence or absence of the symptom of pain may be further qualified by pain in specific regions of the body or of varying intensity according to some pain scale.

One realm that specifically deals with categorical data of variable length is the study of languages [58,59]. Syntactically, sentences in a language are interpreted as statements that adhere to a formal grammar that determines the rules of what is or is not a valid statement in a given language. The study of language also applies in the design of lexers and parsers, which are used in computer science for the design of programming languages to structure valid symbolic statements of arbitrary length written by a programmer for compilation or interpretation. Parsers are especially important as a mechanism of applying the rules of a grammar to interpret strings of symbolic statements as syntax trees defining their structure. These grammar rules, however, do not define a notion of how similar or dissimilar two statements are, so a clustering algorithm working in this space must introduce a mechanism for comparing statement similarity.

Given that START shares the objective of Gram-ART to cluster variable-length symbolic expressions, the key design challenges of START's design are in how to formulate metrics of similarity between these symbolic expressions. In such a formulation, statements are collections of symbols sampled from unordered sets; individual symbols share no fuzzy membership, so similarity between symbols is dictated by strict equivalence in a set theoretic sense. Furthermore, though statements of equal length introduce a step-wise fuzziness when symbols in the same relative positions are identical, many datasets do not satisfy the assumption of equivalent non-terminal structure across all statements. In the pursuit of creating a clustering algorithm for variable-length symbolic datasets, START utilizes a prototype method as a proxy for direct comparison between statements, using ART-based competitive learning dynamics for determining when to update templates and when to instantiate new ones. As with all ART algorithms, START therefore inherits both the theoretically unlimited learning capacity of neurogenesis algorithms and the problems of category proliferation that they bring; though new prototypes can be instantiated for an arbitrary number of categories, this growing knowledge base incurs its own search time complexity [19,60].

3.1.2. START Algorithm

START shares the nomenclature of Gram-ART and other ART algorithms from its structure to its learning dynamics, so existing terminology is preferred where available. START also follows the procedure of most ART unsupervised clustering algorithms, with additional considerations for handling symbolic data. As in Gram-ART, START handles this symbolic data by working in the space of the syntactic trees representing the symbolic data as statements under a formal grammar. The shared notation of all START variants is listed in Table 1.

Table 1. Shared START notation. The learning dynamics of START and its variants follow the activation, competition, match, update, and initialization rules of unsupervised ART algorithms, so the notation here largely adheres to the elementary ART algorithm notation outlined in [19]. Dual-vigilance lower bound ρ_{lb} and upper bound ρ_{ub} follow the notation in DVFA [25] and DDVFA [26].

$\mathcal{R}$: set of prototype nodes.
R: a single prototype node.
$\mathcal{C}$: set of prototype node indices.
Λ: subset of active ART module node indices ($\Lambda \subset \mathcal{C}$).
ρ: START vigilance threshold, $\rho \in (0,1)$.
ρ_{lb}: dual-vigilance lower-bound vigilance threshold ($\rho_{ub} > \rho_{lb} > 0$).
ρ_{ub}: dual-vigilance upper-bound vigilance threshold ($1 > \rho_{ub} > \rho_{lb}$).
n: number of input dataset statements.
$\mathbf{X}$: statements parsed as syntax trees with terminal metadata.
$\texttt{Parser}(\cdot)$: syntactic parsing algorithm taking a set of statements and a grammar and producing rooted constituency parse trees.
$f_T(\cdot)$: activation function.
$f_M(\cdot)$: match function.
$f_N(\cdot)$: node initialization function.
$f_L(\cdot)$: node weight update function.
$f_V(\cdot)$: the vigilance test function.
$\mathcal{U}$: internal supervised category indices.
$\mathcal{L}$: set of cluster indices.

A START module is initialized to contain the $CFG(\mathbf{T}, \mathbf{N}, \mathbf{P}, \mathcal{S})$ rules of the target symbolic dataset statements. This grammar can be inferred from an existing dataset of statements if all relevant symbols and production rules are represented in the dataset. Statements from the dataset are parsed according to the production rules of the grammar into rooted constituency parse trees, the basic unit of which is known in Gram-ART and START as a TreeNode. Each parsed statement tree is presented incrementally to the START module, and each sample either mutates an existing prototype or is used to instantiate an entirely new prototype [19]. Prototypes in START are themselves rooted trees with a structure modified from the statement trees, the basic unit of which is known in Gram-ART as a ProtoNode. The stateful information of START TreeNodes and ProtoNodes can be seen in Tables 2 and 3, respectively.

Table 2. A simple UML diagram of the stateful information of one START TreeNode [24]. A symbol in a TreeNode in START is realized by either a terminal or non-terminal symbol at the syntax tree position of the node. A rooted tree of TreeNodes in this regard contains the minimum information necessary to describe the syntax tree of a statement parsed with a prescribed grammar.

TreeNode
Symbol: GrammarSymbol Children: Vector{TreeNode}

Table 3. A simple UML diagram of the stateful information of one START ProtoNode, which is the basic element of the rooted trees constituting the prototypes of START [24]. A rooted tree of START ProtoNodes encodes only through the non-terminal positions of the syntax tree of a TreeNode tree. Each ProtoNode encodes a PMF of terminal symbols encountered at and below the non-terminal position of the ProtoNode itself, with instance counts of each terminal encoded for the renormalization of the PMF when learning occurs at the node itself.

ProtoNode
Symbol: NonTerminalGrammarSymbol Distribution: Dictionary{TerminalGrammarSymbol, Float} InstanceCount: Dictionary{TerminalGrammarSymbol, Integer} Children: Vector{ProtoNode}

Here, START and Gram-ART differ on an important point in formulation: Gram-ART treats ProtoNodes and TreeNodes as modified dependency relation syntax trees where each node represents a terminal symbol, the children of which are the dependents of that symbol. This formulation is most apparent in the case of operators, such as in the algebraic statement $x + y$, where the operator terminal $+$ would have branch dependents x and y. In START, however, ProtoNodes and TreeNodes are defined as relation parse trees with non-terminal symbols representing non-terminal positions and terminal symbols at the leaves of the rooted tree. The same algebraic statement $x + y$ is then treated in START as a relation parse tree with non-terminal symbols for the operation and its three branches represent the operator and its two arguments, with leaf nodes realizing the terminal symbols at these non-terminal positions (Figure 1).

In START, sample symbolic statements are preprocessed into parse trees via a syntactic parser such as an Earley parser according to the production rules P of the grammar written most generally in an extended Backus–Naur form (EBNF) [61,62]. These syntax trees can be interpreted as concrete constituency relation parse trees belonging to constituency grammars, also known as phrase structure grammars, where branches of a parse tree are all non-terminal symbols in the grammar, including the statement entry point, and leaf nodes are terminal symbols [58,59]. These parse trees are then converted to statement trees via an inclusion of metadata at each node indicating the symbol to be terminal or non-terminal. Prototypes in START are rooted trees containing probability mass functions (PMFs) of terminal symbols encountered at and below the position of each ProtoNode on the tree. In contrast with Gram-ART, these START prototypes do not contain terminal symbol leaves; instead, the nodes of the prototypes represent the non-terminal positions of the grammar production rules applied to the node's position on the tree, which reduces the effective size of each prototype tree while still encoding the occurrence of terminal symbols at and below those positions via their PMFs.

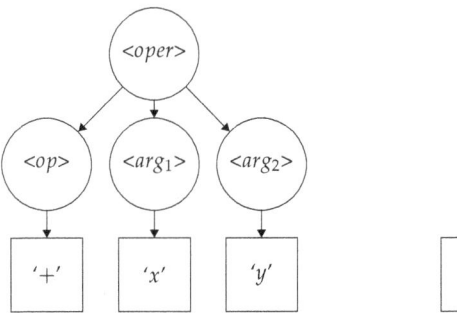 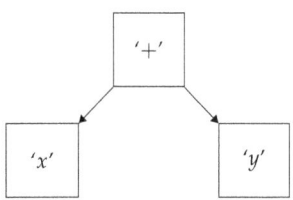

(**a**) START relation parse tree TreeNode. (**b**) Gram-ART syntax tree TreeNode.

Figure 1. Comparison of the constituency relation parse trees of START (**a**) to the dependency parsing syntax trees of Gram-ART (**b**) for the simple algebraic statement $x + y$. START TreeNodes are full constituency relation parse trees containing terminal symbols at the leaves of the tree, while START ProtoNodes contain only non-terminal symbols at non-terminal positions on the parse tree. As in the Grammar Listing 1, non-terminal symbols are surrounded by arrows <·> and terminal symbols are in single quotations. Here, <*oper*> denotes "operation," <*op*> denotes "operator", and <*arg*$_1$> and <*arg*$_2$> denote the two "arguments" of the operator.

Listing 1. Formal grammar for parsing Charcot–Marie–Tooth disease–protein flat-file data. EBNF syntax is used for production rules with the exception of the regular expression symbol '+', which is used to denote one or more occurrences of the preceding symbol. Statements are composed of a series of one or more categorical attributes, all of which are listed in the non-terminal symbol <attribute>. When an attribute is missing or otherwise unknown for a CMT variant, then it is not included in the parsed syntax tree and handled accordingly by START. The production rules for two notable multi-category attributes, <*phenotype*> and <*biologic_process*>, are listed to demonstrate how statements formulated from CMT disease-variant entries illustrate how a gene can be associated with multiple phenotypes and biologic processes. Other multi-category attributes are not listed for brevity.

⟨*S*⟩ ::= ⟨*attribute*⟩+ ;

⟨*attribute*⟩ ::= ⟨*num*⟩ | ⟨*gene_location*⟩ | ⟨*disease*⟩ | ⟨*disease_MIM*⟩ | ⟨*gene*⟩ | ⟨*gene_MIM*⟩
     | ⟨*inheritance*⟩+ | ⟨*protein*⟩ | ⟨*uniprot*⟩ | ⟨*chromosome*⟩ | ⟨*chromosome_location*⟩ |
     ⟨*protein_class*⟩+ | ⟨*biologic_process*⟩+ | ⟨*molecular_function*⟩+ | ⟨*disease_involvement*⟩+
     | ⟨*MW*⟩ | ⟨*domain*⟩+ | ⟨*motif*⟩+ | ⟨*protein_location*⟩+ | ⟨*length*⟩ | ⟨*disease_MIM2*⟩ |
     ⟨*phenotype*⟩+ | ⟨*weight_tag*⟩ | ⟨*length_tag*⟩ ;

⟨*phenotype*⟩ ::= 'ataxia' | 'atrophy' | 'auditory' | 'autonomic' | 'behavior' |
     'cognitive' | 'cranial_nerve' | 'deformity' | 'dystonia' | 'gait' | 'hyperkinesia'
     | 'hyperreflexia' | 'hypertonia' | 'hypertrophy' | 'hyporeflexia' | 'hypotonia' |
     'muscle' | 'pain' | 'seizure' | 'sensory' | 'sleep' | 'speech' | 'tremor' | 'visual' |
     'weakness' ;

⟨*biologic_process*⟩ ::= 'Apoptosis' | 'Mitosis' | 'Lipid_metabolism' | 'Symport'
     | 'Ubl_conjugation_pathway' | 'Glycolysis' | 'Glucose_metabolism'
     | 'Ion_transport' | 'Unfolded_protein_response' | 'Cell_division'
     | 'DNA_repair' | 'Cell_adhesion' | 'Notch_signaling_pathway' |
     'Protein_biosynthesis' | 'Stress_response' | 'Endocytosis' | 'Transcription'
     | 'Sodium_potassium_transport' | 'Transcription_regulation' |
     'Fatty_acid_metabolism' | 'Host_virus_interaction' | 'Antiviral_defense'
     | 'Lipid_degradation' | 'Autophagy' | 'Sodium_transport' | 'Immunity' | 'none'
     | 'Protein_transport' | 'Nucleotide_biosynthesis' | 'Calcium_transport'
     | 'Transport' | 'Phagocytosis' | 'Inflammatory_response' | 'DNA_damage'
     | 'Potassium_transport' | 'Carbohydrate_metabolism' | 'Cell_cycle' |
     'Innate_immunity' ;

3.1.3. Derivation of the START Match Rule

A fundamental characteristic of ART algorithms is the use of a match rule, whereby a process of bottom-up activations drive the evaluation of how much the input sample matches existing top-down categories [41]. Because of the origins of these algorithms lies in the analysis of the competitive dynamics of biological neural networks, these activation and match functions are frequently analogized with bottom-up prediction and top-down expectation, respectively.

Gram-ART utilizes an activation function, while START introduces separate activation and match functions. The distinction between the two lies in the normalization scheme of the activation and match functions; for example, in ART1 the match function (Equation (2)) is the activation function (Equation (1)) normalized by the size of the input [19].

$$T_j = \|x \cap w_j\|_1 \tag{1}$$

$$M_j = \frac{\|y^{(F_1)}\|_1}{\|x\|_1} = \frac{\|x \cap w_j\|_1}{\|x\|_1} \tag{2}$$

FuzzyART replaces the binary intersection with the fuzzy intersection in both equations and normalizes the activation by the magnitude of the weight vector [19]. When evaluated at a single node, an input terminal symbol can be interpreted as a one-hot binary vector encoding at the terminal symbol position, so the magnitude of the membership of sample x in weight w_j is indeed the fuzzy intersection $\|x \wedge w_j\|_1$. This is computed in START for the terminal distribution of each ProtoNode climbing up from the aligned leaf representing the terminal symbol. In statements with many branches arising from non-trivial production rules, this means the evaluation of the activation at each ProtoNode for potentially multiple terminal descendants.

The activation is then normalized by the size of the input pattern, which can be realized in multiple manners requiring a design decision; with the rooted tree definition of parsed input statements, the size of the input pattern could be interpreted as the number of nodes in the parsed statement, the number of terminal symbols in the unparsed statement, or a more complex function of the number of terminals that could be realized beneath the non-terminal position of the node in question according to the production rules of the grammar of the sample. For simplicity, the remainder of this study utilizes the length of the unparsed statement itself as a normalizing factor, having the effect of discounting the disproportional contributions to the match value of increasingly longer statements. In grammars where statements are of equal length, such as in the processing of tables with single-category data, each decision trivially scales the required vigilance values to satisfy the vigilance criterion.

The remainder of the match rule follows the activation, competition, match, and vigilance test of unsupervised ART algorithms, as can be seen in Algorithm 1, with the exception of the dual-vigilance variants of START, which can be seen in Section 3.1.5 and Algorithm 2.

3.1.4. Derivation of the Weight Update

When a prototype is selected for learning according to the START match rule, the input TreeNode and selected ProtoNode are root-aligned and compared, similar to in the activation and match processes. The terminal symbols contributing to the activation and match functions of the winning prototype are used for updating the PMF at each non-terminal symbol position at each ProtoNode up the prototype tree. The instance count of the observed terminal symbol is incremented, and the PMF update is weighted by the instance count of each terminal of the distribution to renormalize. In Equation (3), the weight value w of the PMF indexed at terminal T in node i is updated with instance count N and a Kronecker delta δ_T that is satisfied if the terminal symbol x being evaluated is equivalent to the PMF index T (Equation (4)).

$$w_i^T = \frac{w_i^T * N + \delta_{Tx}}{N+1} \qquad (3)$$

$$\delta_{Tx} = \begin{cases} 1 & \text{if } T = x \\ 0 & \text{otherwise} \end{cases} \qquad (4)$$

Algorithm 1: START algorithm. A set of symbolic statements under a formal context-free grammar are parsed into their syntax trees. Prototypes are defined as learning dynamics otherwise follow the activation, competition, match, update, and initialization rules of unsupervised ART algorithms [19]. ART dynamics notation here largely follow the elementary ART algorithm outlined in [19]. Inference during classification follows the same match rule dynamics without the instantiation of new categories; in the case of complete mismatch, either an "unknown" label or the best matching unit (the category that maximizes the match criterion) may be returned. Please see Table 1 for full notation

Data: Symbolic statements **S**; CFG grammar **G** with terminal symbols **T**, non-terminal symbols **N**, production rules **P**, and statement entry symbol $\mathcal{S}$.
Result: Cluster labels $\mathbf{Y} \in \mathbb{N}^n$
/* Parse statements into constituency parse trees   */
1 $\mathbf{X} \leftarrow \text{Parser}(\mathbf{S}, \mathbf{G})$
   /* Iteration over parsed statement trees   */
2 **foreach** $x \in \mathbf{X}$ **do**
      /* Compute activations for all nodes   */
3 $\quad T_j \leftarrow f_T(\mathbf{x}, \mathcal{R}_j), \forall j \in \mathcal{C}$
      /* Perform WTA competition for active nodes   */
4 $\quad J \leftarrow \underset{j \in \Lambda}{\arg\max} (T_j)$
      /* Compute match for the winning category   */
5 $\quad M \leftarrow f_M(\mathbf{x}, \mathcal{R}_J)$
      /* Vigilance test   */
6 $\quad$ **if** $M > \rho$ **then**
         /* Update category   */
7 $\quad\quad \mathcal{R}_J \leftarrow f_L(\mathbf{x}, \mathcal{R}_J)$
8 $\quad$ **else**
         /* Deactivate category   */
9 $\quad\quad \Lambda \leftarrow \Lambda - \{J\}$
10 $\quad\quad$ **if** $\Lambda \neq \emptyset$ **then**
            /* Continue match search   */
11 $\quad\quad\quad$ Goto Line 4
12 $\quad\quad$ **else**
            /* Create and initialize new category   */
13 $\quad\quad\quad K \leftarrow \|\mathcal{C}\|_1 + 1$
14 $\quad\quad\quad \mathcal{R}_K \leftarrow f_N(\mathbf{x}, \mathbf{G})$

If no prototype satisfies the vigilance criterion, a new one is instantiated. START prototypes do not encode all combinations of non-terminal production evaluations during instantiation, as this would quickly combinatorially explode towards the Catalan number of the non-terminal production rules, and it could be infinite in some recursive grammars. Instead, prototypes are instantiated as structural clones of the input TreeNode without the inclusion of the terminal symbols at their leaves. This design decision is made to mitigate the time and memory complexity of the ProtoNode evaluation given that the non-terminal node preceding a terminal leaf already encodes all of the instances that the terminal symbol encounters. The new structural clone prototype is then trained upon the input sample, updating the PMFs of each ProtoNode for the first time. In the case that an existing winning prototype does not contain the input TreeNode as a structural subset (i.e., it is missing a non-terminal production rule path describing the parsed TreeNode), these new non-terminal paths are instantiated on the winning prototype and updated as usual.

Algorithm 2: Dual-Vigilance START algorithm. This algorithm combines Algorithm 1 with the dual-vigilance procedure of DVFA [25]. The vigilance test is split into a cascade of two vigilance checks for the current match candidate node. Passing the upper vigilance check updates the current category node, while passing only the lower vigilance check creates a new category node belonging to the same cluster label. Failing to pass both vigilance checks results in the instantiation of a new category node belonging to an incrementally new cluster label. Please see Table 1 for full notation

Data: Symbolic statements **S**; CFG grammar **G** with terminal symbols **T**, non-terminal symbols **N**, production rules **P**, and statement entry symbol $\mathcal{S}$.
Result: Cluster labels $\mathbf{Y} \in \mathbb{N}^n$

```
/* Parse statements into constituency parse trees      */
```
1    $\mathbf{X} \leftarrow \text{Parser}(\mathbf{S}, \mathbf{G})$
```
/* Iteration over parsed statement trees              */
```
2   **foreach** $\mathbf{x} \in \mathbf{X}$ **do**
```
       /* Compute activations for all nodes              */
```
3        $T_j \leftarrow f_T(\mathbf{x}, \mathcal{R}_j), \forall j \in \mathcal{C}$
```
       /* Perform WTA competition for active nodes       */
```
4        $J \leftarrow \underset{j \in \Lambda}{\arg\max}\, (T_j)$
```
       /* Compute match for the winning category         */
```
5        $M \leftarrow f_M(\mathbf{x}, \mathcal{R}_J)$
```
       /* Dual-vigilance tests                           */
```
6   **if** $M > \rho_{ub}$ **then**
```
           /* Update current category                    */
```
7           $\mathcal{R}_J \leftarrow f_L(\mathbf{x}, \mathcal{R}_J)$
8   **else if** $M > \rho_{lb}$ **then**
```
           /* Create a new category within the same cluster */
```
9           $K \leftarrow \|\mathcal{C}\|_1 + 1$
10          $\mathcal{L}_K \leftarrow \mathcal{L}_J$
11          $\mathcal{R}_K \leftarrow f_N(\mathbf{x}, \mathbf{G})$
12   **else**
```
           /* Deactivate category                        */
```
13          $\Lambda \leftarrow \Lambda - \{J\}$
14   **if** $\Lambda \neq \emptyset$ **then**
```
               /* Continue match search                  */
```
15   Goto Line 4
16   **else**
```
               /* Create and initialize new category and cluster */
```
17             $K \leftarrow \|\mathcal{C}\|_1 + 1$
18             $\mathcal{L}_K \leftarrow \max(\mathcal{L}) + 1$
19             $\mathcal{R}_K \leftarrow f_N(\mathbf{x}, \mathbf{G})$

3.1.5. Dual-Vigilance and Distributed Dual-Vigilance START

The FuzzyART algorithm provides a foundation for how to adapt ART learning rules to real-valued datasets [19]. Like most ART modules, FuzzyART utilizes the ART match rule evaluated at a single threshold value that is either the vigilance hyperparameter ρ or a function thereof. Dual-vigilance FuzzyART (DVFA) utilizes instead two vigilance parameters for the match rule evaluation, a lower bound ρ_{lb} and upper bound ρ_{ub}, which separates prototypes in a many-to-one mapping from categories to clusters and introduces the ability to compensate for differing granularity both within and between clusters [25]. Distributed dual-vigilance FuzzyART (DDVFA) advances this idea by representing entire clusters with FuzzyART modules governed by a global FuzzyART module, compensating for even varying granularity within different clusters and enabling the ability to learn arbitrary cluster shapes [26]. Each node in the global F2 layer competes for assignment of a provided sample through modified activation and match linkage methods, defining the relevant proximity measures of the sample to an entire F2 FuzzyART module node.

The principles of dual-vigilance and distributed dual-vigilance are extended here for START. In the dual-vigilance formulation (DV-START), the same cascading technique as in DVFA is used for determining category–cluster assignments through upper- and lower-bound vigilance hyperparameters during the ART match evaluation:

1. $M_J > \rho_{ub}$: if the current match candidate satisfies the upper vigilance threshold, then the winning category is updated according to the START weight update rules.
2. $\rho_{ub} > M_J > \rho_{lb}$: if the current match candidate only satisfies the lower vigilance threshold but not the upper, then a new category prototype is instantiated that belongs to the same cluster as the winning node.
3. $\rho_{lb} > M_J$: if the current match candidate does not satisfy even the lower-bound vigilance threshold, then the normal mismatch procedure is followed, where a new category is instantiated belonging to an entirely new cluster.

In the distributed dual-vigilance formulation (DDV-START), additional modifications are made to accommodate the rooted tree structures of the prototypes. DDVFA utilizes a global FuzzyART module that represents nodes themselves as FuzzyART modules [26]. The basic units of DDV-START are the rooted ProtoNode trees, but global module dynamics are not restricted to their use; because the global module of DDV-START is largely agnostic to the formulation of the input samples, the global module may be approximated as a FuzzyART module coordinating the learning of its START F2 nodes. With the exception of the centroid linkage method, which in DDVFA is defined as a function of local FuzzyART weights, all other linkage methods from DDVFA can be utilized in DDV-START; by independently defining the activation and match values for each ProtoNode within an F2 START module, the global values can be compared using the hierarchical agglomerative clustering (HAC) methods of DDVFA, as can be seen in Table 4.

3.1.6. Supervised Variants

Most ART algorithms are designed as unsupervised clustering algorithms with variants and compositions of the elementary ART module motif providing supervised and reinforcement learning variants [19]. ARTMAP is a formulation of ART, comprised of two elementary ART modules and an inter-ART map field, that enables multidimensional mapping between two feature fields [63]. A simplified version of FuzzyARTMAP, where the second module ART_B is replaced with vectors representing class labels, provides a basic procedure for adapting unsupervised ART modules to simple supervised ARTMAP variants [64]. Though START is designed as an unsupervised clustering algorithm, it utilizes these supervised modifications for evaluation on the supervised machine learning benchmark datasets in Section 4.2 and in the Supplementary Materials of this paper. Algorithm 3 outlines this procedure of mapping the internal category representation labels to supervised labels for any START variant.

Because these supervised variants are derived from a procedure to modify an ART module to a simplified ARTMAP variant, their naming follows the same notation (e.g., START to Simplified STARTMAP).

Table 4. Distributed dual-vigilance START activation and match linkage methods where hierarchical agglomerative clustering (HAC) functions and distributed dual-vigilance notation are shared with DDVFA [26]. Global activation T_i^g and match M_i^g functions are defined via the generic function h_i^g for the global F2 node index i as a function of inner node indices $j = 1 \ldots k$, where k is the number of F_2 nodes in the local START module i. Each HAC method then is a "function of functions" evaluated at each F2 node in the global module to determine either the match or activation value in the global module match rule dynamics.

HAC Method	h_i^g
Single	$\max_j \left(f_j^i \right)$
Complete	$\min_j \left(f_j^i \right)$
Median	$\mathrm{median}_j \left(f_j^i \right)$
Average	$\frac{1}{k_i} \sum_{j=1}^{k_i} f_j^i$
Weighted [1]	$\sum_{j=1}^{k_i} p_j f_j^i$

[1] $p_j = \frac{n_j^i}{n_i^g}$, where n_j^i is the number of samples (i.e., instance count) encoded by j of the local START module at global F2 index i and $n_i^g = \sum_j n_j^i$.

3.1.7. Summary of START Variants

The previous sections have outlined three unsupervised algorithms for the clustering of categorical data of varying feature dimensionality: START, its dual-vigilance variant DV-START, and its distributed dual-vigilance variant DDV-START. The core START algorithm is outlined for clustering this categorical data using the incremental learning and update rules of ART algorithms with a single vigilance value; if a category match is found, that prototype is updated according to the ART match rule, and if there is instead a complete mismatch, a new category is instantiated. The dual-vigilance (DV-START) and distributed dual-vigilance (DDV-START) variants of this core algorithm follow as extensions of the algorithm through modifications of the prototype update method in a similar manner as FuzzyART is extended to DVFA and DDVFA [25,26]. In both dual-vigilance variants, two vigilance values (upper and lower) are instead used to determine how a single update should proceed, allowing for differing inter- and intra-cluster granularities. DV-START utilizes an internal category–cluster map for determining if a single prototype is updated, if a prototype is updated in an existing cluster, or if an entirely new cluster is instantiated. DDV-START, on the other hand, distinguishes between global and local nodes, where global nodes are themselves START modules and local nodes are their prototypes; this distinction necessitates the use of hierarchical agglomerative clustering (HAC) functions to determine the distance measures between START modules when evaluating the match and activation values of a sample, and the upper and lower vigilance values are used to determine which global and local nodes to update or instantiate.

Algorithm 3: Simplified supervised modification for all START variants (e.g., Simplified STARTMAP). The variation between START variants is captured in the evaluation of the vigilance test as a function f_V; if some node satisfies the match rule of the START variant, the sample is said to fall within the vigilance region of the prototype [19]. Complete mismatch instead occurs when no vigilance test is satisfied, and the prototype initialization procedure of the START variant is triggered. Inference after training is run through to the vigilance test procedure, reporting the supervised label mapping to the winning internal node category. In the case of complete mismatch, where no nodes satisfy the vigilance test of a supplied inference sample, either the supervised label mapping to the best matching unit (i.e., the node with the highest match value) or a custom mismatch signal may be reported depending on the desired application. Please see Table 1 for full notation.

Data: Symbolic statements **S**; supervisory labels Ω; CFG grammar **G** with terminal symbols **T**, non-terminal symbols **N**, production rules **P**, and statement entry symbol $\mathcal{S}$.
Result: Cluster labels $\mathbf{Y} \in \mathbb{N}^n$

```
  /* New supervised prototype initialization procedure taking
     supervised label ω                                            */
1 Function initialization(ω):
     /* Increment the count of unique internal categories          */
2  │  K ← ‖C‖₁ + 1
     /* Initialize a new prototype according the START variant with
        the new internal category label K                          */
3  │  R_K ← f_N(x, G)
     /* Map the supervised label the new internal category         */
4  │  U_K ← ω

  /* Parse statements into syntax trees                            */
5 X ← Parser(S, G)
  /* Iteration over parsed statement trees with supervised labels  */
6 foreach x, ω ∈ X, Ω do
     /* Instantiate a new prototype with the supervised label if the
        label is entirely novel                                    */
7  │  if ω ∉ U then
8  │  │    initialization(ω)
9  │  else
        /* Run the vigilance test specific to the START variant    */
10 │  │    V_J = f_V(R, x)
        /* Update winning node J if it correctly predicts label ω  */
11 │  │    if V_J ∧ (ω ∈ U) then
              /* Run START update procedure                        */
12 │  │    │    f_L(R_J, x)
13 │  │    else
              /* Otherwise, initialize a new category              */
14 │  │    │    initialization(ω)
```

Furthermore, these three unsupervised algorithms are extended to their own supervised variants using the procedure of Simplified FuzzyARTMAP to map internal category labels to supervised labels, and their nomenclature follows the same procedure (e.g., START to Simplified STARTMAP) [64]. Table 5 arranges the resulting six variants and their names in a table according to their learning modality and vigilance formulation.

Table 5. A summary of the START variants and their abbreviations. Three vigilance formulations are developed, starting with a core START algorithm and extending it with dual-vigilance and distributed dual-vigilance variants (Section 3.1.5). These three variants are intrinsically incremental, unsupervised clustering algorithms, but a supervised procedure in the vein of Simplified FuzzyARTMAP (summarized in Section 3.1.6) generates a supervised variant for each of these three algorithms as well.

Vigilance Formulation	Unsupervised	Supervised
Single-Vigilance	START	Simplified STARTMAP
Dual-Vigilance	DV-START	Simplified DV-STARTMAP
Distributed Dual-Vigilance	DDV-START	Simplified DDV-STARTMAP

3.1.8. Comparison of START Variants

Similar to the FuzzyART variants that they are inspired by, the six variants of START each have their own advantages and drawbacks according to the machine learning context at hand. Each algorithm is designed for learning upon purely categorical datasets where each sample may have a variable length; as a result, the use of these algorithms necessitates the design of a parser that may take such a dataset and transform it into a series of statements and their corresponding relation parse trees according to a context free grammar (CFG) that describes that dataset, which may be expressed in an a series of production rules in an extended Backus–Naur form (EBNF). When the entirety of the dataset is available, the CFG and its production rules may be immediately inferred from the data itself.

ART algorithms such as START are designed to completely learn upon a single sample at a time, which makes them suitable for streaming clustering applications. Because of its formulation, START tracks only distributions of symbols that it has encountered, without requiring full knowledge of the populations or distributions of symbols in advance, so new symbols may be added naturally in a streaming clustering context.

The unsupervised variants of START are naturally suited to symbolic clustering problems, and the supervised variants may be used in both supervised and multimodal contexts because the supervised modification is exterior to the weight update and instantiation process. When supervised labels are available, the label map is populated as a many-to-one mapping of internal categories to supervised labels, and when supervised labels are not available, updates to the label map correspond to updates to the internal labels. When no supervised labels are available in this scenario, the label map is populated as a one-to-one mapping of internal labels to supervised labels and is equivalent to running in the original unsupervised mode.

The selection of which vigilance formulation to use, however, is more nuanced; the original single-vigilance START formulation only has one hyperparameter to tune according to the application at hand, whereas DV-START and DDV-START have two. Furthermore, the use of dual-vigilance variants has a trade-off of variable cluster granularity versus computational and memory complexity; DDV-START, for example, is capable of capturing arbitrary cluster shapes, but this comes at the cost of the potential for prototype proliferation and the added computation necessary to compare global nodes. On the other hand, START is suited for capturing more globular clusters with fewer computations at the risk of excessive category proliferation when cluster densities vary. These considerations also apply to the supervised formulations of each variant, making the selection of which START variant to use dependent upon both the availability of supervised labels and the availability of *a priori* knowledge of the statistics of the dataset in question.

3.1.9. Comparison with Existing Methods

START is most directly comparable with Gram-ART for two important reasons: Gram-ART is the first and indeed only, prior to START, ART-based categorical data clustering algorithm, and the design of START uses Gram-ART as a basis with important modifications. Details on the design differences between START and Gram-ART can be seen in the Supplementary Materials section of this paper.

The related Cascade ARTMAP handles symbolic data rather than real-valued or binary input patterns, but it is designed to handle if–then rule-based knowledge datasets rather than the variable-length categorical data targeted by START [65].

4. Evaluation

START is evaluated here both on existing benchmark machine learning datasets with known labels (outlined in Section 4.2) and on a custom biomedical dataset (outlined in Sections 4.3 and Appendix A).

4.1. Software Implementation

The START algorithm and the experiments outlined in this paper are implemented in a version-archived software repository [66]. In this repository, the START algorithm is implemented in the Julia scientific programming language [67] and utilizes the Lerche.jl package for implementing parsers [62] and AdaptiveResonance.jl for ART post-processing and analysis tools [39]. Clustering result analysis was also performed on the CMT dataset using the Python SHAP library (detailed in Sections 4.5 and 5.3) [68]. Visualizations of the SHAP analysis and additional post-processing were performed with the Orange data mining toolbox [69] and the IBM SPSS toolbox.

All algorithms and tool dependencies are implemented in serial without parallel or GPU acceleration. Individual experiments involve parsing and clustering the dataset in question, and they are run on the scale of seconds with large vigilance parameter values and minutes with small vigilance parameter values when run with the single-thread performance of a desktop Ryzen 9 3950X CPU. This variation is a consequence of the variable number of categories instantiated, where small vigilance parameter values tend to over-partition the data into many categories and large vigilance parameter values tend to generalize the data as belonging to a small number of categories. These individual experiment iterations themselves were run in parallel on a university computing cluster for hyperparameter sweeps and for gathering performance statistics.

4.2. Benchmark Datasets

Purely categorical machine learning benchmark datasets are not as widespread and well-studied as real-valued benchmark datasets, and the START algorithm and its variants are not designed to handle real-valued data without modification. Therefore, START and its variants are evaluated on a combination of both real-valued clustering datasets and purely categorical datasets with caveats.

Gram-ART is originally verified upon a discretized version of the UCI Iris dataset, the UCI Mushroom dataset, and the UCI Unix User dataset [24,70–72]. For comparison, START is evaluated upon the following open-source machine learning benchmark datasets with existing labels: a set of real-valued clustering benchmark datasets [73,74], the categorical UCI Mushroom dataset [71], and a categorical lung cancer patient dataset [75]. Because benchmark datasets such as the Iris dataset's elements are real-valued, each feature is range-normalized and binned into a set of terminal symbols representing each bin.

Both the written procedures for accommodating real-valued benchmark datasets for evaluation and the results of all real-valued and categorical benchmark evaluations can be viewed in the Supplementary Material of this paper.

4.3. Charcot–Marie–Tooth Disease Dataset

To test the ability of START to cluster rows in a complex dataset with various multi-category fields of varying length, we created a test dataset based on Charcot–Marie–Tooth disease (CMT). CMT, also known as hereditary motor and sensory neuropathy, is one of the most common neurogenetic diseases, with a population prevalence of 1 in 2500 [76]. As a starting point, we began with 81 variants of CMT in the Online Mendelian Inheritance of

Man (OMIM) phylogenetic series. A known genetic mutation characterizes each variant. The protein associated with the mutation is known in all but three variants. For each CMT variant, we added a row to a flat file with the following columns: variant name, OMIM number, gene, gene location, chromosome, mode of inheritance, phenotype, protein name, UniProtKB number, protein location, biological process in which the protein participates, protein molecular function, protein length, and protein weight. External data sources were identified to populate the dataset (Table 6), including the Online Inheritance in Man (OMIM), the Human Phenotype Ontology (HPO), UniProtKB, and the Human Protein Reference Database (HPRD) [77–80]. The final dataset had 81 rows and 17 columns, as shown in (Table 6). Seven columns were multi-categorical. Gene number (OMIM), phenotype number (HPO), protein number (UniProtKB), and variant number (OMIM) were not used in the clustering.

Example production rules resulting from the interpretation of this dataset as statements sampled from a grammar can be found in Appendix A. The following clustering methodology and analysis was performed on this CMT dataset using the original START unsupervised variant.

Table 6. Table of features and their characteristics in CMT flat file. Protein numbers were from UniProtKB [79]. Variant and gene numbers were from OMIM [77]. The phenotype numbers were from HPO [1,81]. Since genes, proteins, and diseases have multiple names, the names were normalized to the standard form. Most of the features were categorical, and some were multi-categorical. The features were formatted as integers or strings of variable or fixed length.

Feature	Type	Format	Length	Multi-Category
variant name	categorical	string	variable	no
variant number	categorical	string	fixed	no
gene name	categorical	string	variable	no
gene number	categorical	integer	fixed	no
protein name	categorical	string	variable	no
protein number	categorical	string	fixed	no
protein length	numerical	integer	variable	no
protein weight	numerical	integer	variable	no
protein location	categorical	string	variable	yes
protein molecular function	categorical	string	variable	yes
protein biological process	categorical	string	variable	yes
protein class	categorical	string	variable	yes
mode of inheritance	categorical	string	variable	yes
phenotype	categorical	string	variable	yes
phenotype number	categorical	string	variable	yes
chromosome	categorical	string	variable	no
chromosome location	categorical	string	variable	no
chromosome location	categorical	string	variable	no

Each row of the flat file was interpreted as a statement of symbols corresponding to each column entry. In this manner, each statement was of variable length due to some rows missing entries while other entries contained more than one element. These statements of sequential symbols were then used to infer the grammar and production rules of the dataset; a statement could have one or more attributes (e.g., names of the columns containing data entries), which themselves could have one or more terminal symbols, to reflect how a disease variant could be associated with multiple different phenotypes, biologic processes, etc. The resulting grammar production rules seeded a parser that was used to process each statement into a parse tree. These trees were then interpreted as START TreeNodes (Figure 1) for clustering according to the prototype instantiation, comparison, and update procedures of the START algorithm (Figure 2, Algorithm 1), clustering in a single pass and updating weights or instantiating new prototypes at each incremental sample presentation. A hyperparameter sweep of the vigilance parameter with statistics generated by shuffled presentation order was performed to determine the most meaningful vigilance parameter selection for subsequent cluster analysis (Section 5.1).

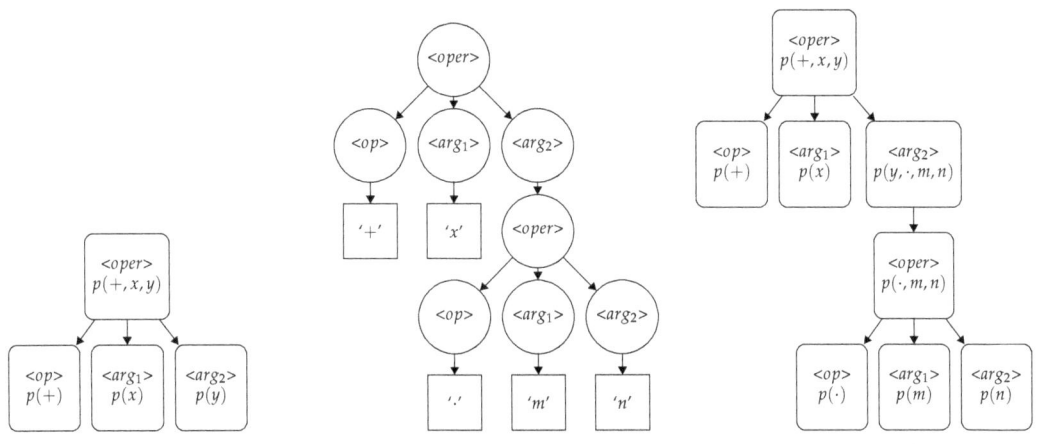

(a) START prototype before update. (b) Relation parse tree of $x + m \cdot n$. (c) START prototype after update.

Figure 2. A set of figures demonstrating the evaluation and update of a START prototype on a new sample. (**a** (left)) demonstrates a START prototype as a rooted tree of ProtoNodes instantiated on the algebraic statement $x + y$ (**a**). ProtoNodes are labeled by a non-terminal symbol, and they contain a probability mass function (PMF) of the terminal symbols generated both by that non-terminal and by any descendant non-terminals, where $p(x, y)$ is shorthand for the PMF of the set of outcomes $S = \{x_1, x_2, \ldots x_n\}$ that gives $p(x_1, x_2, \ldots x_n) = \{P(X = x) | x \in S\}$. (**b** (center)) demonstrates the relation parse tree of a new algebraic statement $x + m \cdot n$. The rooted trees of the prototype and parsed statement are aligned and compared as a graph intersection at the non-terminal positions. The START match rule (Section 3.1.3) then determines the activation and match values of this graph intersection as a function of the PMFs at each non-terminal position and the terminal symbols at the leaf nodes of the sample, and the hypothetical prototype of (**a**) is selected from a pool of other candidate prototypes. (**c** (right)) demonstrates the prototype after update, accommodating the new non-terminal symbol positions of the sample and updating the PMFs at each non-terminal position according to the START weight update rule (Equations (3) and (4)).

4.4. Cluster Feature Means and Heat Maps

After clustering by START, a cluster membership (between 1 and 9) was assigned to each row. Multi-categorical features (see Table 6) were flattened into individual features by one-hot encoding. Feature means for each cluster were calculated using the AGGREGATE procedure from SPSS (version 29.0, IBM). The features were visualized using heat maps from Orange 3.35 [69]. For the heat maps, raw feature means were used for the categorical variables, and normalized feature means (in the interval $[0, 1]$) were used for the numerical variables (see Table 6).

4.5. SHAP Values

SHAP summary values were calculated using the method of Lundberg et al. [68]. START cluster membership was added to the flattened feature array (see above). The cluster configuration was fitted to the HistGradientBoostingClassifier (scikit-learn). The shap.TreeExplainer and the shap.summary_plot procedures were used to compute SHAP values and create the SHAP summary plot.

5. Results

5.1. Selection of Cluster Configuration for the CMT Dataset

The vigilance parameter ρ was varied between 0.0 and 1.0 in a Monte Carlo of shuffled sample presentation order (Figure 3). To minimize the size of the largest cluster and minimize the number of clusters with one member, $\rho = 0.6$ was selected, yielding nine clusters (Figure 4).

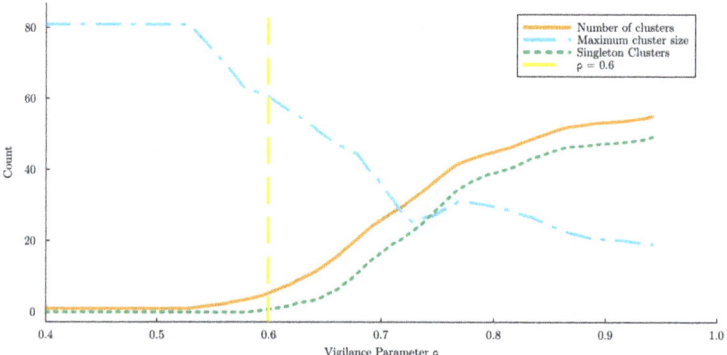

Figure 3. Effect of vigilance parameter ρ on number of clusters. A Monte Carlo of shuffled sample presentation order was run to generate 1σ intervals of the results at each vigilance parameter value. As ρ was increased from 0.0 to 1.0, the maximum cluster size decreased, the number of clusters increased, and the number of singleton clusters increased. A value of $\rho = 0.6$ (yellow dashed line) was selected to yield 9 clusters with only two singleton clusters. Larger ρ values gave too many singleton clusters, and smaller ones put too many cases into one cluster.

5.2. Cluster Characterization by Feature Composition

We used heat maps to visualize the features that characterized each cluster. The clusters differed in mode of inheritance, protein localization within the cell, protein participation in biological processes, protein length, molecular weight, motifs and domains in amino acid chains, phenotype, and protein molecular function (Figures 5–12). The heat maps were used to create a narrative summary of each cluster's most important feature characteristics (Table 7).

5.3. Identifying Features that Contributed the Most to Cluster Configuration

We used SHAP [68] to find the features that drove the cluster configuration. The SHAP summary plot (Figure 12) showed that protein length, chromosome number (autosomes 1 − 22 and X and Y), mode of inheritance (autosomal recessive and autosomal dominant), protein localization in the cell (cytoplasm and plasma membrane), and phenotype (hypertonia, auditory and cognitive) contributed the most to cluster formation.

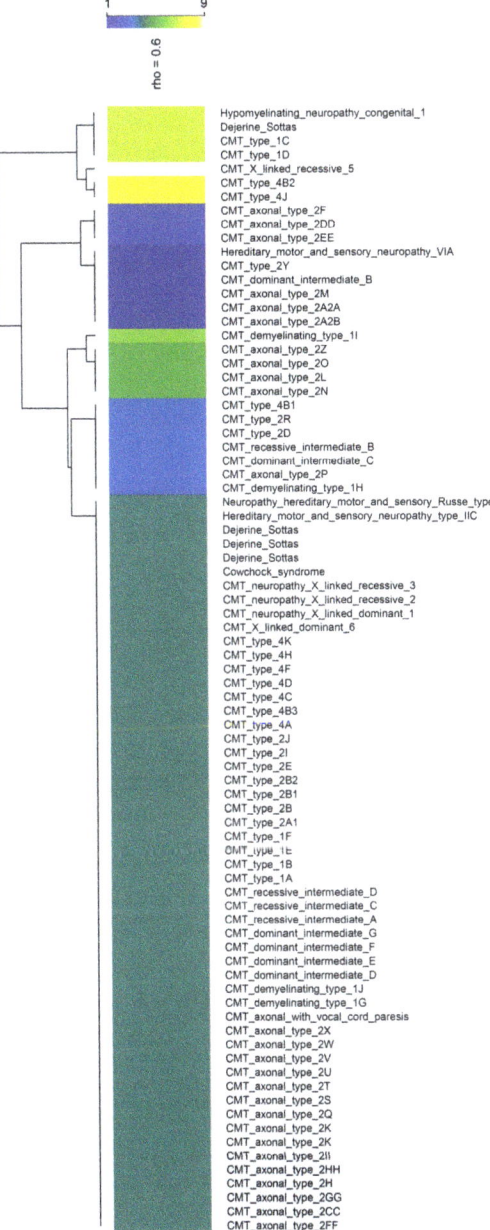

Figure 4. With $\rho = 0.6$, clustering by START yielded nine clusters from 81 variants of CMT. Each cluster is a different color on the heat map. Order of clusters on heat map is 7, 9, 8, 2, 1, 6, 5, 3, 4, with ordering by Euclidean distance between cluster centroids [69]. The largest cluster is 4 (dark green), with 53 members. Singleton clusters are 9 (white) and 6 (pea green). A shortened variant name is shown in the right margin. Dejerine–Sottas disease appears four times in the heat map because it is caused by four distinct mutations in the MPZ, PMP22, PRX, and EGR2 genes.

Table 7. Summary of features that characterize CMT clusters. **k** is the cluster number and **N** is the count of members in each cluster. Phenotype Plus lists signs and symptoms in addition to weakness, atrophy, deformities, sensory loss, and hyporeflexia that characterize most cases of CMT. AD is autosomal dominant inheritance; AR is autosomal recessive; XLR is X-linked recessive. TM is the transmembrane protein domain. GNRF is the guanine nucleotide-releasing factor. Note that some of the characteristics identified by the SHAP analysis, including cognitive, hypertonia, auditory, plasma membrane, autosomal recessive, and autosomal dominant (Figure 12), recur in this summary table.

k	N	Process	Function	Location	Domain	Inherit	Phenotype Plus
1	6	apoptosis	hydrolase			AD	auditory, visual
2	3			cytoplasm		AD	hypertonia
3	7	protein synthesis	transferase			AD, AR	
4	53			plasma membrane	TM	AD, AR	
5	4			plasma membrane	TM	AD	cognitive, auditory
6	1	immunity transcription	transferase	plasma membrane		AD	cognitive, ataxia, seizure, hypertonia, speech, hyperreflexia
7	4	transcription	DNA binding	plasma membrane		AD, AR	cognitive, hypotonia
			transferase				
8	2	autophagy apoptosis	hydrolase GNRF	nucleus		AR	cognitive, auditory, hypertonia
9	1		transferase	mitochondrion	TM	XLR	cognitive, auditory

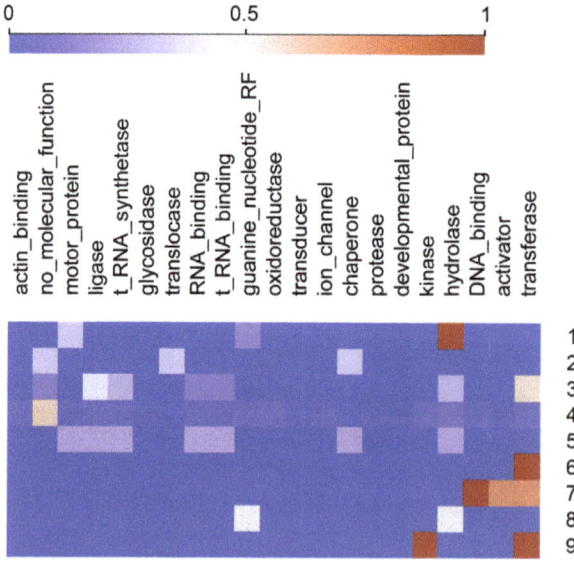

Figure 5. Heat map of molecular function for proteins in CMT clusters. Kinase function is associated with cluster 9, hydrolase function with clusters 1 and 8, DNA binding with cluster 7, activator function with cluster 7, and transferase function with cluster 9.

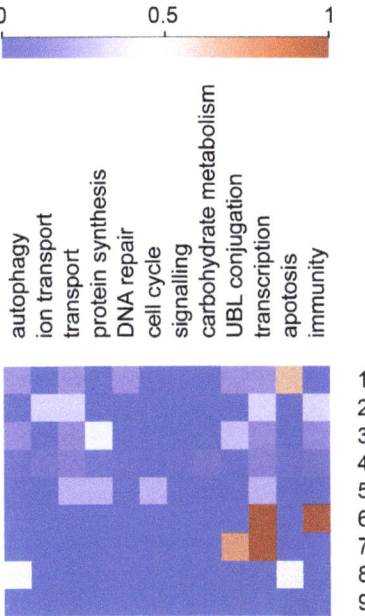

Figure 6. Heat map of biological process for proteins by CMT cluster. Cluster 1 is apoptosis, cluster 8 is autophagy and apoptosis, cluster 3 is protein synthesis, cluster 6 is transcription and immunity, and cluster 7 is UBL protein conjugation and transcription.

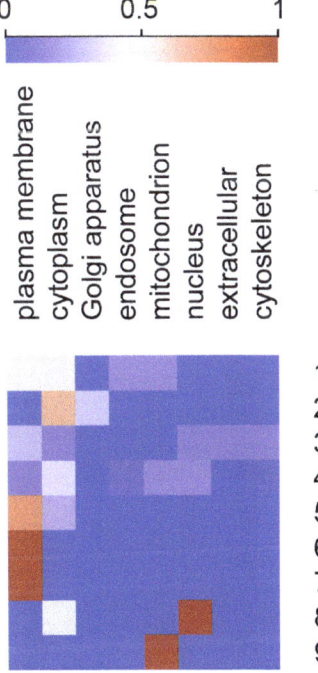

Figure 7. Heat map of protein locations by CMT cluster. Cluster 2 is cytoplasm, clusters 5, 6, and 7 are plasma membrane, cluster 8 is nucleus, and cluster 9 is mitochondrion.

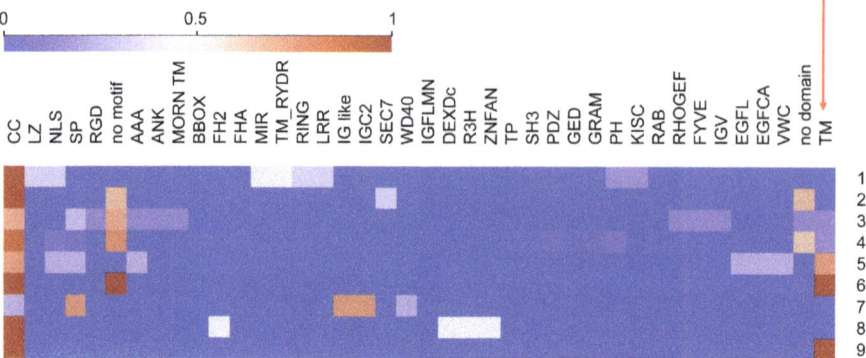

Figure 8. Heat map showing protein motifs and domains by CMT cluster. Motifs and domains are characteristics of configurations of the amino acid chains that make up proteins and are often associated with a specific function. Note the over-representation of the transmembrane (TM) domains in clusters 5, 6, and 9 (red arrow). The CC motif is found in most proteins except for cluster 7.

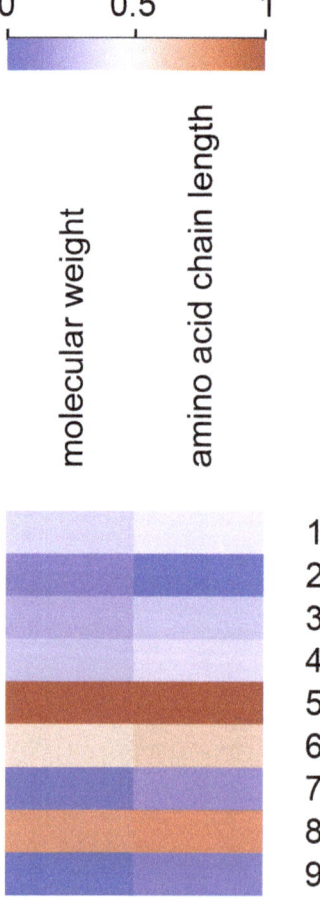

Figure 9. Heat map of molecular weights and amino acid chain lengths for proteins for CMT clusters.

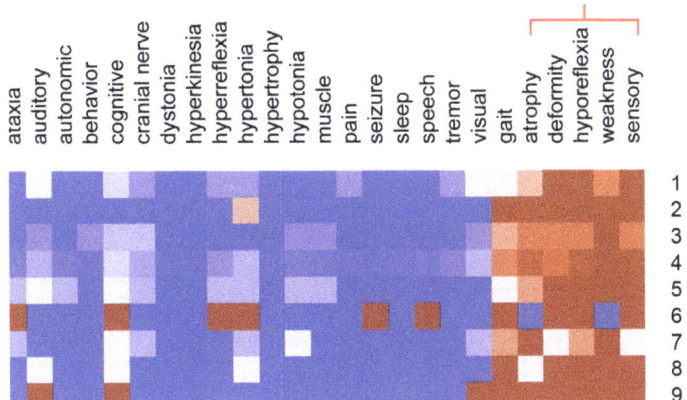

Figure 10. Phenotype scores for each of the nine clusters for the 81 variants of CMT. Scores have been normalized to the interval $[0, 1]$, where 1 indicates 100% and 0 indicates 0%. Note, as expected, that gait, atrophy, deformity, hyporeflexia, weakness, and sensory loss are common features in most cases (red bracket). Cluster 6 with one case and cluster 9 with one case are different because they manifest auditory and cognitive symptoms (cluster 9) or ataxia, cognitive, hyperreflexia, hypertonia, seizures, and speech symptoms (cluster 6). Cluster 6 is also of interest because it lacks weakness and atrophy, two of the core symptoms of CMT. Cluster 2 (3 cases) is also interesting because subjects have hypertonia. Cluster 4, with 53 cases, is the most common pattern and shows a typical phenotype of gait, atrophy, deformity, hyporeflexia, weakness, and sensory symptoms, which is characteristic of CMT.

Figure 11. Modes of inheritance for the nine CMT clusters. Cluster 8 is largely autosomal recessive. Cluster 9 is X-linked recessive. Clusters 5, 6, and 7 are autosomal dominant inheritance.

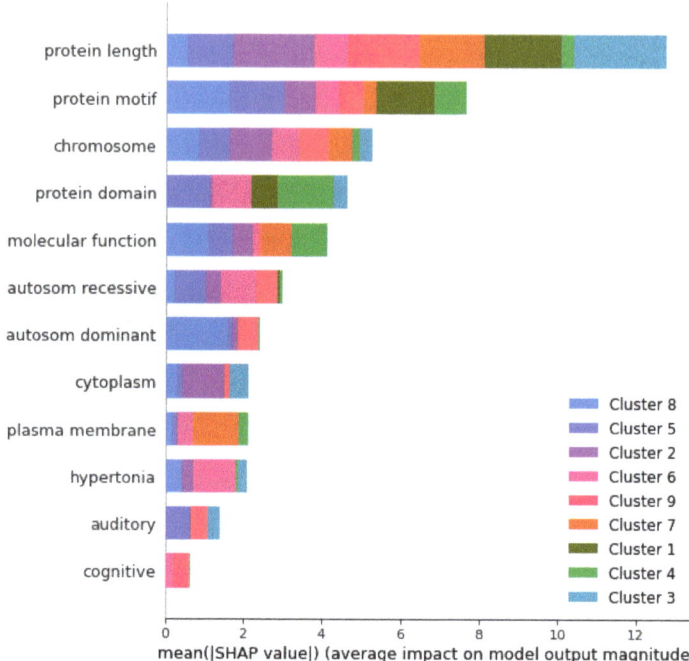

Figure 12. SHAP cluster summary plot for the 9 clusters derived from CMT dataset with $\rho = 0.6$. The SHAP plot shows which features contributed the most to the cluster configuration by cluster. Important features are protein length, chromosome, mode of inheritance (autosomal dominant and recessive), protein location (cytoplasm and plasma membrane), and certain phenotypes (auditory, cognitive, and hypertonia). The domain expert rated these features as highly biologically plausible. SHAP plots were created using the method of Lundberg et al. [68].

6. Discussion

6.1. Feasibility of Clustering Multi-Categorical Biomedical Data with START

START demonstrates several important capabilities that make it particularly useful for the clustering of multi-categorical data. Firstly, it directly represents the categorical data without an intermediate encoding representation and all the problems introduced therein; categorical data by definition does not define distance metrics or fuzzy membership between categories and feature dimensions. The problem is circumvented here by the definition of prototype parse trees tracking the distributions of symbols from learned statements using the ART match and learning rules.

Secondly, it naturally compensates for data points with missing elements entries in its fields; rather than requiring a special encoding scheme for missing fields or removing data points altogether, START can represent missing fields as unused non-terminal positions when representing multi-categorical datasets as statements containing one or more attributes, which has the effect of penalizing the degree to which samples with missing features match existing prototypes while still accommodating prototypes of varying sizes.

Thirdly, and as a consequence of the previous point, START can handle symbolic data of varying length when interpreted as statements under a grammar; in fact, this paper demonstrates an analysis of multi-categorical datasets of depth 2 due to the nature of the CMT data available, but categorical datasets of arbitrary depth can be analyzed with START when treating categories as themselves non-terminal symbols with production rules mapping to other sets of categories. This can be interpreted as processing hierarchical symbolic databases where individual fields can themselves link to other symbolic database tables.

6.2. Biological Interest and Plausibility of Derived Clusters

When the START vigilance parameter was set to $\rho = 0.6$ (Figure 3), we obtained nine clusters (Table 7). Cluster 4, the largest, had 53 members, and clusters 6 and 9 were singleton clusters. The fact that cluster 4 is large is not surprising since most cases of CMT are similar and have similar core symptoms of weakness, sensory loss, hyporeflexia, orthopedic abnormalities, atrophy, and gait abnormalities in common [76]. Although it is usual to differentiate clinically between axonal forms (involving the neuron axon) and demyelinating forms (involving the myelin sheath of the axon) of CMT, it is not surprising that we did not find axonal and demyelinating clusters of CMT since we did not input electromyographic data into the clustering algorithm. The finding of small clusters of CMT variants with auditory, hypertonic, or cognitive phenotypes is interesting and plausible biologically and is consistent with clinical observations.

The clusters differed in inheritance (Table 7) in biologically plausible ways and consistent with clinical practice. Since each variant of CMT was due to a gene mutation and since each gene coded for a unique protein, protein weight, protein length, protein configuration (motifs and domains), protein involvement in biological processes, protein molecular function, and protein locations could be examined for each CMT cluster and compared to the observed phenotype (Figures 5–12, and Table 7). Although these observations are intriguing, they do not offer a precise path to connect protein function, location, and process to the neurological phenotype in CMT. As an example of explainable AI [82], the SHAP plots in Figure 12 provide biologically plausible explanations for how START relied on certain features to form clusters.

6.3. Limitations

One limitation of this work is that START is used to cluster a small biomedical dataset without ground truth labeling. Although the diagnosis of each row (CMT disease variant) is known, cluster membership for the dataset as a whole is unknown. As a result, this work cannot contain an analysis of either truth in cluster membership and structure or performance of START with respect to such a ground truth. The reader is referred to the Supplementary Materials of this article for a study of the START algorithm on various other machine learning benchmark datasets, including fully symbolic and real-valued datasets including details of the procedure necessary to adapt the START algorithm to real-valued data.

Another limitation of this work is that all available features are used as inputs to the START clustering algorithm. A separate study is warranted to study how withholding some of the features as meta-features would allow potentially interesting cluster composition analyses.

Furthermore, the results of clustering and analyzing the CMT dataset with START has limited generalizability to other diseases datasets. It is seldom expected of clustering models or indeed machine learning models as a whole to generalize to distinct domains from which they were trained, outside of research areas such as lifelong machine learning that tackle this specific issue [83]. Nevertheless, some transferability should be expected to related datasets of the class of neurogenetic diseases that CMT belongs to, but this transferability is limited in two ways: by the format of the selected data and the START methodology itself. Biomedical data are themselves notoriously multifaceted, and the creation of generalizing models in this field depends on the narrowed problem statement and subsequent dataset at hand. For example, this work considers the clustering of data with categorical membership in specifically phenotype–gene relationships; with respect to the OMIM elements, each entry in the CMT dataset subsumes a variable number of clinical studies that generate the datapoints, discarding the qualitative aspects of the various individuals studied and the other clinical features that are inconsistently included between entries. This is a consequence not of the quality of the OMIM database but rather of the project of aggregating vastly disparate clinical data.

In addition to this, an ontological level of granularity is necessarily selected by the researcher when working with any clinical features; for example, a full hierarchy of pain may be studied as symptoms of a disease with respect to an individual patient from the location, duration/periodicity, and subjective intensity according to some pain scale, etc. Taking the location of pain as an example, some studies describe the location of pain with a varying degree of specificity; in the hierarchy of location on the human body, should one hypothetical study citing simply pain and another citing leg pain be considered the same by virtue of belonging on the same hierarchy or different by virtue of being two different points on that hierarchy? If neither is true, then what is the distance metric along this hierarchy until two points are considered distinct? Even clinical definitions of the term pain itself vary and are subject to debate [84]. As a result, simplifying assumptions must be made for any learned model of clinical data, such as the ontological subsumption of the phenotype of pain in this study, and the interpretation of clustering results and its usefulness for the treatment of a disease is tied to the selection of ontological granularity.

Lastly, the methodology of the START algorithm successfully tackles the clustering of the resulting variable-size categorical datasets, but it does so at the level of the symbols themselves without forming a feature-transformed intermediate representation of them. Additional similar phenotype–gene datasets could be clustered with an existing model trained on this CMT dataset, but relationships between them would only be found if they shared exactly the same symbols, such as gene locations and disease phenotypes. Completely disparate datasets with no shared symbols may indeed be clustered by the same START model after appropriate modifications to its parser's grammar, but this would be functionally equivalent to clustering with two separate START models; this benefit of START is also to its detriment, as if there are no shared symbols between data points, they are treated as having no shared features for computing similarities.

6.4. Future Work

This paper demonstrates that START can work with data from a knowledge graph or ontology when flattened into a rectangular file, even with missing or nested elements. Alternatively, knowledge graphs and ontologies can be converted into triplets as subject–object–predicate triplets, which retains the underlying graph architecture. In the future, we plan to determine whether START can successfully cluster these triplets derived from knowledge graphs into meaningful clusters.

Additional future work includes an evaluation of START clustering on large multi-categorical datasets with a known ground truth cluster membership and further experiments on datasets in which some features are withheld from input and retained as meta-features for post-clustering analysis.

7. Conclusions

This work introduces the START algorithm for the clustering of symbolic data with arbitrary length statements. This work also introduces dual-vigilance and distributed dual-vigilance variants of START along with a supervised modification for each. Because START is designed for symbolic datasets, it is naturally suited for the clustering of both categorical and multi-categorical datasets where each sample feature may realize multiple values. This multi-categorical clustering capability is demonstrated on a curated biomedical dataset of Charcot–Marie–Tooth disease variants and their disease–gene attributes, such as disease phenotypes and protein molecular functions.

For a dataset such as the CMT dataset used here, START is useful as a tool for studying structural relationships between disease variants for guiding future clinical research or in the formulation of useful models of those diseases via the hierarchies, clusters, and outliers identified during the clustering process; for example, distinct gene locations with shared phenotypes between two groups of disease variants may illustrate to a researcher some other shared molecular mechanism for future research, which could guide drug research in a data-driven manner.

Supplementary Materials: The following supporting information can be downloaded at: https://www.mdpi.com/article/10.3390/info15030125/s1, Listing S1: Discretized Iris dataset grammar illustrating the symbolic binning procedure of real-valued data used to evaluate START and GramART; Table S1: Hyperparameters for each START variant during supervised train/test evaluation. Table S2: Performance statistics of the supervised implementations of each START variant derived in the original paper on a set of benchmark real-valued and categorical machine learning datasets.

Author Contributions: Conceptualization, D.B.H., S.P. and D.C.W.II; methodology, S.P. and D.B.H.; software, S.P. and D.B.H.; validation, S.P.; formal analysis, S.P. and D.B.H.; investigation, S.P. and D.B.H.; resources, D.B.H. and D.C.W.II; data curation, D.B.H.; writing—original draft preparation, S.P. and D.B.H.; writing—review and editing, S.P., D.B.H., T.O.-A., M.A.B., E.J.T., W.E.M., M.S. and D.C.W.II; visualization, S.P. and D.B.H.; supervision, D.C.W.II; project administration, D.C.W.II and E.J.T.; funding acquisition, S.P. and D.C.W.II. All authors have read and agreed to the published version of the manuscript.

Funding: This work is funded by the Department of Energy's Kansas City National Security Campus, operated by Honeywell Federal Manufacturing & Technologies, LLC, under contract number DE-NA0002839.

Institutional Review Board Statement: Not applicable.

Informed Consent Statement: Not applicable.

Data Availability Statement: Disease–protein datasets are gathered from the openly available Online Mendelian Inheritance in Man (OMIM) knowledge base [85]. All data, code, and documentation related to the experiments outlined in this paper are contained in a version-archived repository [66].

Conflicts of Interest: The authors declare no conflicts of interest.

Abbreviations

The following abbreviations are used in this manuscript:

ART	Adaptive resonance theory
BNF	Backus–Naur form
CFG	Context-free grammar
CMT	Charcot–Marie–Tooth disease
DDVFA	Distributed dual-vigilance FuzzyART
DDV-START	Distributed dual-vigilance symbolic tree adaptive resonance theory
DVFA	Dual-vigilance FuzzyART
DV-START	Dual-vigilance symbolic tree adaptive resonance theory
EBNF	Extended Backus–Naur form
F1	ART Feature input layer (field 1)
F2	ART Category representation layer (field 2)
HAC	Hierarchical agglomerative clustering
L2	Lifelong learning
ML	Machine learning
PMF	Probability mass function
START	Symbolic tree ART
WTA	Winner-take-all

Appendix A. Charcot–Marie–Tooth Dataset Grammar

An analysis of the Charcot–Marie–Tooth (CMT) dataset *a posteriori* demonstrates the process used in this article for interpreting tabular multi-categorical data as statements sampled from a context-free grammar that can be expressed as a set of EBNF production rules, which can be seen in Grammar Listing 1. Gene–protein disease data are gathered for 81 variants of CMT with categorical attributes (Table 6). Categories such as phenotype are subsumed where hierarchically relevant to reduce attribute feature dimensionality (e.g., variants of "pain" symptomology are subsumed to one feature belonging to the "phenotype" attribute). This process results in a 81-row flat-file dataset of features with multi-categorical attributes represented as piped entries for each disease variant, including attributes with missing entries.

References

1. Robinson, P.N. Deep phenotyping for precision medicine. *Hum. Mutat.* **2012**, *33*, 777–780. [CrossRef]
2. Sonawane, A.R.; Weiss, S.T.; Glass, K.; Sharma, A. Network medicine in the age of biomedical big data. *Front. Genet.* **2019**, *10*, 294. [CrossRef] [PubMed]
3. Collins, F.S.; Varmus, H. A new initiative on precision medicine. *N. Engl. J. Med.* **2015**, *372*, 793–795. [CrossRef] [PubMed]
4. Carrasco-Ramiro, F.; Peiró-Pastor, R.; Aguado, B. Human genomics projects and precision medicine. *Gene Ther.* **2017**, *24*, 551–561. [CrossRef]
5. Phillips, C.J. Precision medicine and its imprecise history. *Harv. Data Sci. Rev.* **2020**, *2*, 1–10.
6. Ginsburg, G.S.; Phillips, K.A. Precision medicine: From science to value. *Health Aff.* **2018**, *37*, 694–701. [CrossRef]
7. Polster, A.; Cvijovic, M. Network medicine: Facilitating a new view on Complex Diseases. *Front. Bioinform.* **2023**, *3*, 47.
8. Healy, M.J.; Caudell, T.P. Ontologies and worlds in category theory: Implications for neural systems. *Axiomathes* **2006**, *16*, 165–214. [CrossRef]
9. Bezdek, J.C. *Elementary Cluster Analysis: Four Basic Methods That (Usually) Work*; River Publishers: Gistrup, Denmark, 2022.
10. Xu, R.; Wunsch, D.C. *Clustering*; John Wiley & Sons, Inc.: Hoboken, NJ, USA, 2009; pp. 1–21.
11. Gowda, K.; Diday, E. Symbolic clustering using a new similarity measure. *IEEE Trans. Syst. Man Cybern.* **1992**, *22*, 368–378. [CrossRef]
12. Chidananda Gowda, K.; Diday, E. Symbolic clustering using a new dissimilarity measure. *Pattern Recognit.* **1991**, *24*, 567–578. [CrossRef]
13. Carpenter, G.A.; Grossberg, S. The ART of adaptive pattern recognition by a self-organizing neural network. *Computer* **1988**, *21*, 77–88. [CrossRef]
14. Carpenter, G.A.; Grossberg, S.; Markuzon, N.; Reynolds, J.H.; Rosen, D.B. Fuzzy ARTMAP: A neural network architecture for incremental supervised learning of analog multidimensional maps. *IEEE Trans. Neural Netw.* **1992**, *3*, 698–713. [CrossRef]
15. Tan, A.H. Adaptive resonance associative map. *Neural Netw.* **1995**, *8*, 437–446. [CrossRef]
16. Subagdja, B.; Tan, A.H. iFALCON: A neural architecture for hierarchical planning. *Neurocomputing* **2012**, *86*, 124–139. [CrossRef]
17. Subagdja, B.; Tan, A.H. Planning with iFALCON: Towards a neural-network-based BDI agent architecture. In Proceedings of the 2008 IEEE/WIC/ACM International Conference on Web Intelligence and Intelligent Agent Technology, Sydney, Australia, 9–12 December 2008; IEEE: Los Alamitos, CA, USA, 2008; Volume 2, pp. 231–237.
18. Kim, T.; Hwang, I.; Lee, H.; Kim, H.; Choi, W.S.; Lim, J.J.; Zhang, B.T. Message passing adaptive resonance theory for online active semi-supervised learning. In Proceedings of the International Conference on Machine Learning. PMLR, Virtual, 18–24 July 2021; pp. 5519–5529.
19. Brito da Silva, L.E.; Elnabarawy, I.; Wunsch, D.C. A Survey of Adaptive Resonance Theory Neural Network Models for Engineering Applications. *Neural Netw.* **2019**, *120*, 167–203. [CrossRef] [PubMed]
20. Carpenter, G.A.; Grossberg, S.; Rosen, D.B. Fuzzy ART: Fast stable learning and categorization of analog patterns by an adaptive resonance system. *Neural Netw.* **1991**, *4*, 759–771. [CrossRef]
21. Bezdek, J.C.; Keller, J.; Krisnapuram, R.; Pal, N. *Fuzzy Models and Algorithms for Pattern Recognition and Image Processing*; Springer Science & Business Media: New York, NY, USA, 1999; Volume 4.
22. Ruspini, E.H.; Bezdek, J.C.; Keller, J.M. Fuzzy clustering: A historical perspective. *IEEE Comput. Intell. Mag.* **2019**, *14*, 45–55. [CrossRef]
23. Keller, J.M.; Yager, R.R.; Tahani, H. Neural network implementation of fuzzy logic. *Fuzzy Sets Syst.* **1992**, *45*, 1–12. [CrossRef]
24. Meuth, R.J. Adaptive Multi-Vehicle Mission Planning for Search Area Coverage. Ph.D. Thesis, Missouri University of Science and Technology, Rolla, MO, USA, 2007.
25. Brito da Silva, L.E.; Elnabarawy, I.; Wunsch, D.C. Dual vigilance fuzzy adaptive resonance theory. *Neural Netw.* **2019**, *109*, 1–5. [CrossRef]
26. Brito da Silva, L.E.; Elnabarawy, I.; Wunsch, D.C. Distributed dual vigilance fuzzy adaptive resonance theory learns online, retrieves arbitrarily-shaped clusters, and mitigates order dependence. *Neural Netw.* **2020**, *121*, 208–228. [CrossRef]
27. Grossberg, S. How Does a Brain Build a Cognitive Code? *Psychol. Rev.* **1980**, *87*, 1–51. [CrossRef] [PubMed]
28. Grossberg, S.; Grossberg, S. How does a brain build a cognitive code? In *Studies of Mind and Brain: Neural Principles of Learning, Perception, Development, Cognition, and Motor Control*; Springer: Dordrecht, The Netherlands, 1982; pp. 1–52.
29. Cohen, M.A.; Grossberg, S. Absolute stability of global pattern formation and parallel memory storage by competitive neural networks. *IEEE Trans. Syst. Man Cybern.* **1983**, *SMC-13*, 815–826. [CrossRef]
30. Grossberg, S. Nonlinear neural networks: Principles, mechanisms, and architectures. *Neural Netw.* **1988**, *1*, 17–61. [CrossRef]
31. Grossberg, S.T. *Studies of Mind and Brain: Neural Principles of Learning, Perception, Development, Cognition, and Motor Control*; Boston Studies in the Philosophy and History of Science Springer Dordrecht: Dordrecht, Holland, 1982; Volume 70.
32. Grossberg, S.; Versace, M. Spikes, synchrony, and attentive learning by laminar thalamocortical circuits. *Brain Res.* **2008**, *1218*, 278–312. [CrossRef]

33. Grossberg, S. Adaptive Resonance Theory: How a brain learns to consciously attend, learn, and recognize a changing world. *Neural Netw.* **2013**, *37*, 1–47. [CrossRef]
34. Grossberg, S. The resonant brain: How attentive conscious seeing regulates action sequences that interact with attentive cognitive learning, recognition, and prediction. *Atten. Percept. Psychophys.* **2019**, *81*, 2237–2264. [CrossRef]
35. Grossberg, S. *Conscious Mind, Resonant Brain: How Each Brain Makes a Mind*; Oxford University Press: Oxford, UK, 2021. [CrossRef]
36. Carpenter, G.A.; Grossberg, S. A massively parallel architecture for a self-organizing neural pattern recognition machine. *Comput. Vis. Graph. Image Process.* **1987**, *37*, 54–115. [CrossRef]
37. Carpenter, G.A.; Grossberg, S. *Pattern Recognition by Self-Organizing Neural Networks*; The MIT Press: Cambridge, MA, USA, 1991.
38. Carpenter, G.; Grossberg, S. *Adaptive Resonance Theory*; Technical report; Boston University Center for Adaptive Systems and Department of Cognitive and Neural Systems: Boston, MA, USA, 1998.
39. Petrenko, S.; Wunsch, D.C. AdaptiveResonance.jl: A Julia Implementation of Adaptive Resonance Theory (ART) Algorithms. *J. Open Source Softw.* **2022**, *7*, 3671. [CrossRef]
40. Park, G.M.; Kim, J.H. Deep Adaptive Resonance Theory for learning biologically inspired episodic memory. In Proceedings of the 2016 International Joint Conference on Neural Networks (IJCNN), Vancouver, BC, Canada, 24–29 July 2016; pp. 5174–5180. [CrossRef]
41. Carpenter, G.A. Distributed learning, recognition, and prediction by ART and ARTMAP neural networks. *Neural Netw.* **1997**, *10*, 1473–1494. [CrossRef]
42. Carpenter, G.A.; Milenova, B.L.; Noeske, B.W. Distributed ARTMAP: A neural network for fast distributed supervised learning. *Neural Netw.* **1998**, *11*, 793–813. [CrossRef]
43. Healy, M.J.; Caudell, T.P.; Smith, S.D. A neural architecture for pattern sequence verification through inferencing. *IEEE Trans. Neural Netw.* **1993**, *4*, 9–20. [CrossRef]
44. Grossberg, S.; Huang, T.R. ARTSCENE: A neural system for natural scene classification. *J. Vis.* **2009**, *9*, 6. [CrossRef]
45. Petrenko, S.; Brna, A.; Aguilar-Simon, M.; Wunsch, D. Lifelong Context Recognition via Online Deep Feature Clustering. *TechRxiv* **2023**, *14*, 1–15. [CrossRef]
46. Brna, A.P.; Brown, R.C.; Connolly, P.M.; Simons, S.B.; Shimizu, R.E.; Aguilar-Simon, M. Uncertainty-based modulation for lifelong learning. *Neural Netw.* **2019**, *120*, 129–142. [CrossRef] [PubMed]
47. Brown, R.; Brna, A.; Cook, J.; Park, S.; Aguilar-Simon, M. Uncertainty-Driven Control for a Self-Supervised Lifelong Learning Drone. In Proceedings of the IGARSS 2022—2022 IEEE International Geoscience and Remote Sensing Symposium, Kuala Lumpur, Malaysia, 17–22 July 2022; pp. 5053–5056. [CrossRef]
48. Aguilar-Simon, M.; Brna, A.; Brown, R.; Folsom, L.; Cook, J.; Park, S.; Yanoschak, A.; Shimizu, R.; Scientific, T.; Imaging, L. *Adaptive Learning Through Active Neuromodulation (ALAN)*; Air Force Research Laboratory, Sensors Directorate: Wright-Patterson Air Force Base, OH, USA, 2022.
49. Petrenko, S.; Wunsch, D.C. ClusterValidityIndices.jl: Batch and Incremental Metrics for Unsupervised Learning. *J. Open Source Softw.* **2022**, *7*, 3527. [CrossRef]
50. Brito da Silva, L.E.; Rayapati, N.; Wunsch, D.C. Incremental Cluster Validity Index-Guided Online Learning for Performance and Robustness to Presentation Order. *IEEE Trans. Neural Netw. Learn. Syst.* **2022**, *34*, 6686–6700. [CrossRef]
51. Brito da Silva, L.E.; Rayapati, N.; Wunsch, D.C. iCVI-ARTMAP: Using Incremental Cluster Validity Indices and Adaptive Resonance Theory Reset Mechanism to Accelerate Validation and Achieve Multiprototype Unsupervised Representations. *IEEE Trans. Neural Netw. Learn. Syst.* **2022**, *34*, 1–14. [CrossRef]
52. Yelugam, R.; Brito da Silva, L.E.; Wunsch, D.C. TopoBARTMAP: Biclustering ARTMAP with or without Topological Methods in a Blood Cancer Case Study. In Proceedings of the 2020 International Joint Conference on Neural Networks (IJCNN), Virtual, 19–24 July 2020; pp. 1–8. [CrossRef]
53. Yelugam, R.; Brito da Silva, L.E.; Wunsch II, D.C. Topological biclustering ARTMAP for identifying within bicluster relationships. *Neural Netw.* **2023**, *160*, 34–49. [CrossRef]
54. Some new indexes of cluster validity. *IEEE Trans. Syst. Man Cybern. Part B (Cybern.)* **1998**, *28*, 301–315. [CrossRef]
55. Chen, Z.; Liu, B. *Lifelong Machine Learning*; Morgan & Claypool Publishers: San Rafael, CA, USA, 2018; pp. 1–207.
56. Kudithipudi, D.; Aguilar-Simon, M.; Babb, J.; Bazhenov, M.; Blackiston, D.; Bongard, J.; Brna, A.P.; Chakravarthi Raja, S.; Cheney, N.; Clune, J.; et al. Biological underpinnings for lifelong learning machines. *Nat. Mach. Intell.* **2022**, *4*, 196–210. [CrossRef]
57. Baker, M.M.; New, A.; Aguilar-Simon, M.; Al-Halah, Z.; Arnold, S.M.; Ben-Iwhiwhu, E.; Brna, A.P.; Brooks, E.; Brown, R.C.; Daniels, Z.; et al. A domain-agnostic approach for characterization of lifelong learning systems. *Neural Netw.* **2023**, *160*, 274–296. [CrossRef]
58. Chomsky, N. *Syntactic Structures*; Mouton: Oxford, UK, 1957.
59. Chomsky, N. *On the Notion "Rule of Grammar"*; American Mathematical Society: Providence, RI, USA, 1961.
60. Wolpert, D.; Macready, W. No free lunch theorems for optimization. *IEEE Trans. Evol. Comput.* **1997**, *1*, 67–82. [CrossRef]
61. *ISO/IEC 14977:1996 (E)*; Information Technology-Syntactic Metalanguage-Extended BNF. ISO/IEC: Geneva, Switzerland, 1996.
62. Hester, J.R.; Shinan, E. Lerche: Generating data file processors in Julia from EBNF grammars. *J. Open Source Softw.* **2021**, *6*, 3497. [CrossRef]

63. Carpenter, G.A.; Grossberg, S.; Reynolds, J.H. ARTMAP: Supervised real-time learning and classification of nonstationary data by a self-organizing neural network. In Proceedings of the IEEE Conference on Neural Networks for Ocean Engineering, Miami, FL, USA, 9–11 December 1991; pp. 341–342. [CrossRef]
64. Kasuba, T. Simplified Fuzzy ARTMAP. *AI Expert* **1993**, *8*, 19–25.
65. Tan, A.H. Cascade ARTMAP: Integrating neural computation and symbolic knowledge processing. *IEEE Trans. Neural Netw.* **1997**, *8*, 237–250.
66. Petrenko, S. AP6YC/OAR: V0.1.0. *Zenodo*, 5 January 2024. [CrossRef]
67. Bezanson, J.; Edelman, A.; Karpinski, S.; Shah, V.B. Julia: A fresh approach to numerical computing. *SIAM Rev.* **2017**, *59*, 65–98. [CrossRef]
68. Lundberg, S.M.; Erion, G.; Chen, H.; DeGrave, A.; Prutkin, J.M.; Nair, B.; Katz, R.; Himmelfarb, J.; Bansal, N.; Lee, S.I. From local explanations to global understanding with explainable AI for trees. *Nat. Mach. Intell.* **2020**, *2*, 56–67. [CrossRef] [PubMed]
69. Demšar, J.; Curk, T.; Erjavec, A.; Črt Gorup.; Hočevar, T.; Milutinovič, M.; Možina, M.; Polajnar, M.; Toplak, M.; Starič, A.; et al. Orange: Data Mining Toolbox in Python. *J. Mach. Learn. Res.* **2013**, *14*, 2349–2353.
70. Fisher, R.A. *Iris*. UCI Machine Learning Repository: Irvine, CA, USA, 1988. [CrossRef]
71. *Mushroom*; UCI Machine Learning Repository: Irvine, CA, USA, 1987. [CrossRef]
72. Lane, T. *UNIX User Data*; UCI Machine Learning Repository: Irvine, CA, USA, 1988. [CrossRef]
73. Ilc, N. Datasets Package. Available online: https://www.researchgate.net/publication/239525861_Datasets_package (accessed on 5 January 2024)
74. Fränti, P.; Sieranoja, S. K-Means Properties on Six Clustering Benchmark Datasets. *Appl. Intell.* **2018**, *48*, 4743–4759 [CrossRef]
75. Ahmad, A.S.; Mayya, A.M. A new tool to predict lung cancer based on risk factors. *Heliyon* **2020**, *6*, e03402. [CrossRef]
76. Rossor, A.M.; Polke, J.M.; Houlden, H.; Reilly, M.M. Clinical implications of genetic advances in Charcot–Marie–Tooth disease. *Nat. Rev. Neurol.* **2013**, *9*, 562–571. [CrossRef]
77. Amberger, J.S.; Bocchini, C.A.; Scott, A.F.; Hamosh, A. OMIM.org: Leveraging knowledge across phenotype–gene relationships. *Nucleic Acids Res.* **2019**, *47*, D1038–D1043. [CrossRef]
78. Köhler, S.; Gargano, M.; Matentzoglu, N.; Carmody, L.C.; Lewis-Smith, D.; Vasilevsky, N.A.; Danis, P.; Balagura, G.; Baynam, G.; Brower, A.M.; et al. The human phenotype ontology in 2021. *Nucleic Acids Res.* **2021**, *49*, D1207–D1217. [CrossRef]
79. The UniProt Consortium. UniProt: The Universal Protein Knowledgebase in 2023. *Nucleic Acids Res.* **2023**, *51*, D523–D531. [CrossRef] [PubMed]
80. Keshava Prasad, T.; Goel, R.; Kandasamy, K.; Keerthikumar, S.; Kumar, S.; Mathivanan, S.; Telikicherla, D.; Raju, R.; Shafreen, B.; Venugopal, A.; et al. Human protein reference database—2009 update. *Nucleic Acids Res.* **2009**, *37*, D767–D772. [CrossRef] [PubMed]
81. Robinson, P.N.; Mungall, C.J.; Haendel, M. Capturing phenotypes for precision medicine. *Mol. Case Stud.* **2015**, *1*, a000372. [CrossRef] [PubMed]
82. Gunning, D.; Stefik, M.; Choi, J.; Miller, T.; Stumpf, S.; Yang, G.Z. XAI—Explainable artificial intelligence. *Sci. Robot.* **2019**, *4*, eaay7120. [CrossRef]
83. New, A.; Baker, M.; Nguyen, E.; Vallabha, G. Lifelong Learning Metrics. *arXiv* **2022**. arXiv:2201.08278.
84. Raja, S.N.; Carr, D.B.; Cohen, M.; Finnerup, N.B.; Flor, H.; Gibson, S.; Keefe, F.J.; Mogil, J.S.; Ringkamp, M.; Sluka, K.A.; et al. The revised International Association for the Study of Pain definition of pain: Concepts, challenges, and compromises. *Pain* **2020**, *161*, 1976–1982. [CrossRef]
85. Hamosh, A.; Scott, A.F.; Amberger, J.S.; Bocchini, C.A.; McKusick, V.A. Online Mendelian Inheritance in Man (OMIM), a knowledgebase of human genes and genetic disorders. *Nucleic Acids Res.* **2005**, *33*, D514–D517. [CrossRef]

Disclaimer/Publisher's Note: The statements, opinions and data contained in all publications are solely those of the individual author(s) and contributor(s) and not of MDPI and/or the editor(s). MDPI and/or the editor(s) disclaim responsibility for any injury to people or property resulting from any ideas, methods, instructions or products referred to in the content.

Review

From Information to Knowledge: A Role for Knowledge Networks in Decision Making and Action Selection

Jagmeet S. Kanwal

Department of Neurology, Georgetown University Medical Center, Washington, DC 20057, USA; kanwalj@georgetown.edu

Simple Summary: This perspective article examines the differences between memory, information, and knowledge. It is proposed that the creation of knowledge is not simply the extraction of information or sequencing and storage of memories, but its contextualization that offers a point of advantage for survival within a decision-making framework; outside these contexts there are no useful memories and therefore no relevant knowledge. A constellation of neural networks spread across multiple brain regions must work together to grow knowledge over time. Knowledge must be stored in such a way that it can be accessed by multiple tokens, or handles, at any time. The emergence of knowledge networks underlies the evolution of complex brains that can predict outcomes, induce imagination and expand knowledge. Attention and sleep play important roles in creating and protecting knowledge.

Abstract: The brain receives information via sensory inputs through the peripheral nervous system and stores a small subset as memories within the central nervous system. Short-term, working memory is present in the hippocampus whereas long-term memories are distributed within neural networks throughout the brain. Elegant studies on the mechanisms for memory storage and the neuroeconomic formulation of human decision making have been recognized with Nobel Prizes in Physiology or Medicine and in Economics, respectively. There is a wide gap, however, in our understanding of how memories of disparate bits of information translate into "knowledge", and the neural mechanisms by which knowledge is used to make decisions. I propose that the conceptualization of a "knowledge network" for the creation, storage and recall of knowledge is critical to start bridging this gap. Knowledge creation involves value-driven contextualization of memories through cross-validation via certainty-seeking behaviors, including rumination or reflection. Knowledge recall, like memory, may occur via oscillatory activity that dynamically links multiple networks. These networks may show correlated activity and interactivity despite their presence within widely separated regions of the nervous system, including the brainstem, spinal cord and gut. The hippocampal–amygdala complex together with the entorhinal and prefrontal cortices are likely components of multiple knowledge networks since they participate in the contextual recall of memories and action selection. Sleep and reflection processes and attentional mechanisms mediated by the habenula are expected to play a key role in knowledge creation and consolidation. Unlike a straightforward test of memory, determining the loci and mechanisms for the storage and recall of knowledge requires the implementation of a naturalistic decision-making paradigm. By formalizing a neuroscientific concept of knowledge networks, we can experimentally test their functionality by recording large-scale neural activity during decision making in awake, naturally behaving animals. These types of studies are difficult but important also for advancing knowledge-driven as opposed to big data-driven models of artificial intelligence. A knowledge network-driven understanding of brain function may have practical implications in other spheres, such as education and the treatment of mental disorders.

Keywords: neural network; learning and memory; attention; adaptive action; knowledge acquisition; education; artificial intelligence; decision making; goal-directed behavior; sleep

Citation: Kanwal, J.S. From Information to Knowledge: A Role for Knowledge Networks in Decision Making and Action Selection. *Information* **2024**, *15*, 487. https://doi.org/10.3390/info15080487

Academic Editors: Birgitta Dresp-Langley and Luiz Pessoa

Received: 7 June 2024
Revised: 5 August 2024
Accepted: 9 August 2024
Published: 15 August 2024

Copyright: © 2024 by the author. Licensee MDPI, Basel, Switzerland. This article is an open access article distributed under the terms and conditions of the Creative Commons Attribution (CC BY) license (https://creativecommons.org/licenses/by/4.0/).

1. Introduction

1.1. Motivation

Some humans are very good at memorizing facts and others have uncanny imaginative abilities that can be translated into beautiful works of art. Still others are very knowledgeable, i.e., they have a deep understanding in a particular information domain that can lead to insights on solving nontrivial problems. The term "knowledge" can be construed to represent a working model of a particular aspect of the real world. Acquiring this knowledge takes time and is built on processes involving cross-validation and justification in an attempt to arrive at the "truth". It is not merely a memory gained through sensory experience or through repeated association of a stimulus with a reward or punishment. Though typically applied to human domains of information, knowledge is equally important, however, for any organism to gain insights from their social and environmental interactions to make informed decisions.

In this perspective article, I extend neuroscientific findings on memory acquisition, storage and recall to propose a neurological framework within which to define knowledge as a wide-area neural network. Such a network can be referred to as a knowledge network (KN). KNs participate in creating and storing knowledge and have several key properties. These properties include interconnectivity between multiple brain regions, such as fronto-cortical cognitive and limbic emotive structures. KNs are considered to be highly dynamic networks, portions of which link up transiently depending upon the context, an explicit query or a physiological state or drive. KNs also need to transiently link up with attentional brain circuits to extract current information either from an incoming sensory stream or from memory. KNs eventually direct their output to decision-making and action-selection networks. Catastrophic events, such as "9–11" for humans in the US, can transiently crash KNs, causing confusion and the need to create a new real-world model.

Speech perception, reading and language can be considered as types of developmentally entrained, sapient KNs that acquire cross-validation via explicit instruction and are designed to rapidly gain new knowledge [1–6]. Acquiring a navigational map equates to developing a KN of one's surroundings within which to make quick decisions about escape from predators, foraging and to find mates. A navigational KN undergoes cross-validation and certainty or truth-seeking via repeated, direct interactions with the environment and has been partially elucidated for navigation in rodents [7,8]. KNs are important for decision making and survival. A navigational KN must be reliable for making split-second decisions for survival. This becomes obvious when observing a rabbit swerving in seemingly random directions to dodge a wild cat or a dog, and still able to find its rabbit hole while running at top speed on a rough terrain.

Below, I first briefly describe the philosophical idea and usage of the term "knowledge" and show how it relates to well-defined concepts of information and memory at the phenomenological level. I then elaborate on some of the neuroscientific attributes of knowledge and propose the building blocks and mechanisms for knowledge acquisition, storage and recall. Furthermore, I conceptualize the formation of KNs in an equation form and show where they fit in our current understanding of the evolution of the nervous system. Finally, building on recent studies on neural mechanisms for attention and sleep for memory formation and consolidation, I clarify their role in acquiring knowledge that gets embedded within KNs.

1.2. From Information to Knowledge

Ever since the formulation of information theory [9,10], a lot has been written on information processing from informational and neuroscientific perspectives [10–14]. Knowledge, however, remains less well defined from both a neurological and a computational perspective. Neither are there any mathematical definitions of knowledge or a knowledge theory. Lynn et al. [15,16] have recently provided a formulation of the perceived information (cross-entropy) within a communication system as being the sum of the large amount of information produced (having high entropy) and the efficiency of the observer's representation of that information (low divergence from expectations). The brain's ability to store and retrieve information, i.e., learning, memory and recall, is of fundamental importance for the elaboration of goal-directed behaviors that frequently involve decision making [17]. This requires querying the brain and extracting bits of relevant information simultaneously from various loci to direct and question decision-making and goal-setting tasks. We may term this contextualized information set as "knowledge". Neural networks that are required to perform these functions have not been clearly identified either in the neurobiological or computational domains. In this brief review, I provide a nonformal overview of the differences between information, memory and knowledge from a neurocognitive perspective. I propose a conceptual framework for describing KNs as a dynamic grouping of realistic neural networks different from those needed to extract information and create a memory.

A theory for information processing was first formulated to quantify the information load that the human mind can encode, store and retrieve over the short term, emphasizing capacity limits without external aids or techniques [18]. Its formulation was based on experimental data generated by others from the presentation of auditory, taste and visual stimuli to human subjects. Further mathematical elaboration was focused on the coding and decoding of signals for transmission and reception [19]. Work on cognitive and neural mechanisms for long-term storage capacity and the contextual linkage with existing information required animal experimentation using sophisticated techniques that were not available at that time. One way to do so is to integrate relevant information bits as synaptic connections whose strength or "weight" within local and global networks can be continuously modified. The configuration and patterns of activity generated by this network, when queried by inputs (in the form of either real or virtual stimuli), function as a model of the world in which an organism exists. This model can be equated to what we term as "knowledge" and the neural networks that participate in creating, consolidating and modifying knowledge can be referred to as knowledge networks or KNs. KNs incorporate the core memory networks described by others [20,21], but also include cross-validation (for truth seeking), organizational (sequencing and timing), contextualizing and attentional networks [22]. Parts of these nonmemory networks remain less well-defined anatomically but must come online via their interconnections during query (recall) and reflection. In this context, it is noteworthy that even simple memories need to be reactivated before they can be modified or erased, emphasizing the inbuilt labile nature of a KN [23–25].

1.2.1. Feature Extraction

Behavioral and cognitive psychology can go only so far in providing mechanistic insights into the way brain networks accomplish the task of developing and implementing a knowledge-based model of the world for decision making and action selection. For that, we need to take a step back and first understand how information is created from the sensory environment. A necessary step in the process of information creation via sensory perception is feature extraction. Naturalistic signals or stimuli in the environment are complex and typically have multiple elements and parameters by which they can be specified. From these, the brain uses parallel–hierarchical processing to extract features of varying levels of complexity [26]. Feature extraction is perhaps one of the most universal and useful aspects of sensory processing regardless of stimulus modality. Some of these features contain information that contributes to stimulus discrimination and object recognition [26–31]. A defining feature of an object does not solely depend on the physical properties of an object but also is the outcome of neural processing governed by the receptive fields of higher-order neurons [32–35]. A large amount of research on sensory processing and cognition has focused on feature identity and extraction and this is also a central theme of deep learning in artificial neural networks [13,36,37]. It should be noted that, at a more abstract level, cognition also involves terms like thinking, knowing, understanding, reasoning, judging and problem-solving. This review does not attempt to tackle all of these concepts from a neuroscientific perspective, though in some cases they may be intimately connected to and rely on knowledge embedded within KNs. An understanding of how neural networks learn, recognize and problem-solve has led to major advances in artificial intelligence (AI) models for face, handwriting and voice recognition—problems that were seemingly impossible to solve by conventional programming and engineering approaches [38–40].

Restating the argument made above more succinctly, a physical entity is intrinsically recognized as a feature depending on its relevance for a particular function or goal, such as for food and mate recognition or selection for reproduction [41,42]. A feature may consist of simpler elements that can be easily synthesized and experimentally tested, such as orientation columns in the visual cortex [34,43]. From a behavioral perspective, simple elements within a feature are referred to as information-bearing elements or IBEs [44,45]. They contain information that is critical for computing a feature and its variants. Non-IBEs within a signal can usually vary without affecting the perception of a particular feature but may carry other types of information. Furthermore, an IBE can be quantitatively defined based on any number of physical parameters. Those parameters that are behaviorally meaningful or communicate information to an organism (low surprise), and by design are extracted and encoded by the relevant sensory system are referred to as information-bearing parameters or IBPs [44,45]. IBEs and IBPs were first defined to provide a framework for identifying and studying the acoustic elements in the pulse–echo combinations in the vocalizations produced by bats for echolocation [45].

In the neuroethological studies of bats, empirical studies yielded putative IBEs that could be meaningfully attributed to the substructures or components of the acoustic structures of the naturalistic pulse–echo signals used for echolocation. These readily identifiable components, such as constant-frequency (CF) tones with harmonics, and frequency-modulated (FM) sweeps, were shown to play a critical role in the computation of important acoustic features, such as relative target velocity and distance, and wingbeat frequency and the amplitude of insects. Relative target velocity, wingbeat frequency and amplitude are IBEs for a bat tracking a target, such as an insect [46]. In our example, the IBPs would be the values of relative target velocity as a function of the Doppler-shifted frequency (60.6 to 62.3 kHz in mustached bats), with the wingbeat frequency resulting in an amplitude modulation rate of 50 to 500 Hz in the range of 48.2 ± 10.7 dB SPL, corresponding to particular insects that are a good (nontoxic) food source [47–49]. Key elements or putative IBEs and IBPs are also present in the sounds produced for social communication in bats and other species [50–52]. For vision, IBEs may corresponded to the combination of a particular shape, color and/or texture of an object, and for the olfactory system the combination of a mixture of odorants that can be used to identify a flower [53–56]. IBEs and IBPs can be determined by performing behavioral studies and estimated by determining receptive fields of neurons.

Neurophysiological and computational studies show that the IBEs are represented in the responses of neurons in many brain regions [57–61]. Cortical neurons and those present within hidden layers of multilayered, artificial neural networks exhibit high activation levels to either identifiable or abstract, low-dimensional representations corresponding to the principal components of the physical measures of an object [62,63]. They constitute IBE-like representations within real neurons and networks. Studies on the visual system of nonhuman primates identified a representation of IBE-like basis functions in the response of cortical neurons [64]. These basis functions do not necessarily represent easily identifiable elements within a naturalistic stimulus. Rather, they are statistical formulations of the real elements that are extracted as useful information. Features represent the building blocks of objects, and objects make up a scene [65,66] (Figure 1). Clearly, association between features is critical for computations that guide decision making and flight behavior, such as insect-tracking and capture, and the recognition of a food source. However, the memory of a feature that may help to identify a target or one that could be useful in identifying a social call does not in itself constitute knowledge.

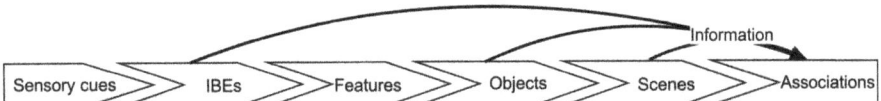

Figure 1. The parallel–hierarchical processing of sensory inputs leads to the extraction of information from features and objects defined by the information-bearing elements or IBEs. The physical proximity and/or temporal coherence of extracted features create objects, and that of objects within a scene creates perceptual associations or memories. Most of this processing is accomplished via ascending lemniscal pathways in the brain. Thalamocortical loops facilitate egocentric selection by neurons tuned to the parameters of an incoming stimulus, and signal amplification occurs via descending projections (see arrows) [67].

1.2.2. What Is Knowledge?

To be meaningful, information must exist in the form of knowledge. The study of knowledge borders the domains of educational science, cognitive science and philosophy [68,69]. Knowledge is mainly acquired from sensory inputs to the brain, though even at the very first step of sensory transduction of various forms of energy into electric or neural energy, knowledge acts like a filter, biasing what reaches the neural networks deep within the brain. In other words, the creation of new knowledge and learning is itself influenced by existing knowledge. Thus, knowledge is much more individualized than information. Two people may be given identical information, but the knowledge it creates in each of their brains may be quite different.

It is useful to also consider the meaning of knowledge from a philosophical perspective since a concept of knowledge has existed from a long time before a conception of mind and brain. Wikipedia defines human knowledge as "an awareness of facts, a familiarity with individuals and situations, or a practical skill" [70]. This type of definition of knowledge exists more within the domain of philosophy rather than neuroscience or information science. From an epistemological perspective, propositional or declarative knowledge has been proposed to have three essential features or components. These features are individually necessary and jointly sufficient for achieving a state of declarative knowledge [71]. Knowledge of facts, also called propositional knowledge, has been characterized as true belief that is distinct from opinion or guesswork by virtue of justification. Belief involves various levels of certainty about an observation or thought [72]. A low level of certainty of an event or a relationship may be equated to imagination by others, whereas an elevated level of certainty indicates a strong belief in a perception. If a belief happens to accurately represent reality, then it is taken to be true. The process of testing is important for obtaining evidence to justify that a belief is true. The process of justification protects against a lucky guess becoming knowledge. This suggests that KNs must involve neuronal processes that test for the level of certainty and establish certainty or belief in a perception go through a process of justifying that belief and check for the presence of evidence in memory circuits or find a way to seek that evidence. This makes knowledge, unlike memories, more robust and less prone to forgetting. In neural terms, this means that knowledge about an issue may have a fractured, distributed representation so that knowledge can be evoked in many different situations. In other words, there are multiple entry points to activating KNs or their subsets and their activation can impact decision making in many related circumstances. How exactly certainty is tested and justified at the neural level remains unclear (however, see [73]).

A KN's representation of knowledge, i.e., a species-specific model of the world, may guide decision making in many circumstances, e.g., the strategy an animal adopts to find food or to interact with conspecifics to facilitate various aspects of social behavior. Neural networks that represent knowledge are more difficult to define and usually require simultaneous recordings of the activity of neurons in multiple brain regions in awake-behaving animals exhibiting naturalistic behaviors. For example, neurobehavioral studies of a laboratory rat, mouse or a primate species maintained or placed within a small cage or apparatus where the animal has limited degrees of freedom of movement and decision making are not well-suited to explore their KNs. A naturally enriched environment offers a much greater opportunity for an organism to create and use KNs for action selection. Thus, the use of neuroethological approaches to study animals under natural or semi-natural environments has a greater potential to identify KNs and the neural mechanisms underlying knowledge processing [74–76]. With a few exceptions, such as social vocalizations in the house mouse and bats, and spatial navigation studies in rats and bats, neuroethological and neuro-ecological studies are easier to perform in invertebrate species. Advanced invertebrate brains likely contain rudimentary KNs, supporting limited reflection and justification processes that are difficult to extract. The technology to examine neural network activity at a large scale in vertebrate species has recently become available, however, and its application to study KNs via appropriately designed experiments should be feasible [77,78].

Knowledge of the environment in which an organism functions is critical for accomplishing multiple activities that are essential for survival. These include territorial, social and foraging forays on a regular basis. Figure 2 captures the periodic, behavior-driven incorporation of epistemological aspects (e.g., reinforcement, trust and belief) and mechanisms (associative memories) that define knowledge in general, within a navigational framework. During navigation, a cognitive route map within networks (e.g., using place and grid cells) is automatically created by an animal's behavior, and brain mechanisms (oscillations, excitation, inhibition, facilitation and spike-time-dependent plasticity) embed context-driven network properties within a navigational KN. Place cells fire maximally at a particular location based on multimodal sensory cues, whereas grid cells compute the vector from the starting to goal location. A cognitive map, typically created by strategic, free-exploration and probabilistic associations, is a neural model of the external spatial world which represents the distances and directions between locations.

Training animals on stereotypic actions, such as nose-pokes, within a constrained environment is important for examining the physiology and pharmacology of specific local circuits involved in either aversive or reward memories. Chronic neural recordings during free exploration behavior, such as for navigation, offer a more open-ended approach to finding key neuronal and network properties [79,80]. These types of studies led to the discovery of place neurons within the hippocampus and of grid cells within the entorhinal cortex (EC), important findings that were recognized with a Nobel prize [81]. In the last decade, research on networks and neurons underlying navigation continues to be a source of groundbreaking new findings, such as of ring and toroidal structures, border cells, stripe cells and head-direction cells in rats and free-flying bats [82,83] (Figure 3A). We still need to understand how navigational knowledge is generated, contextualized, and recalled within different contexts.

Within a KN concept, the understanding of navigation can be further advanced by adopting techniques of chronic recordings of positional information and neural activity from multiple brain regions while animals engage in navigation within different contexts (Figure 3B). Activity-dependent mapping, e.g., using c-FOS and ZENK as markers of early gene expression, has been used in songbirds to identify neurons for song discrimination and production [84–87]. The use of two-photon imaging and neural activity markers, such as CaMPARI, in freely behaving animals can also facilitate the identification of sensorimotor networks that are co-activated, and show how they engage a core KN to accomplish different phases of navigation [88]. These approaches can also explain how contextual queries are initiated and how they might reconfigure particular networks for multiple functions, e.g., shifting the excitatory–inhibitory balance in core networks and engaging new networks. This is important to know because the brain evolves as a whole, and while reductionist approaches are useful for identifying gene and receptor function and pharmacology, they also take us away from achieving a holistic understanding of the brain.

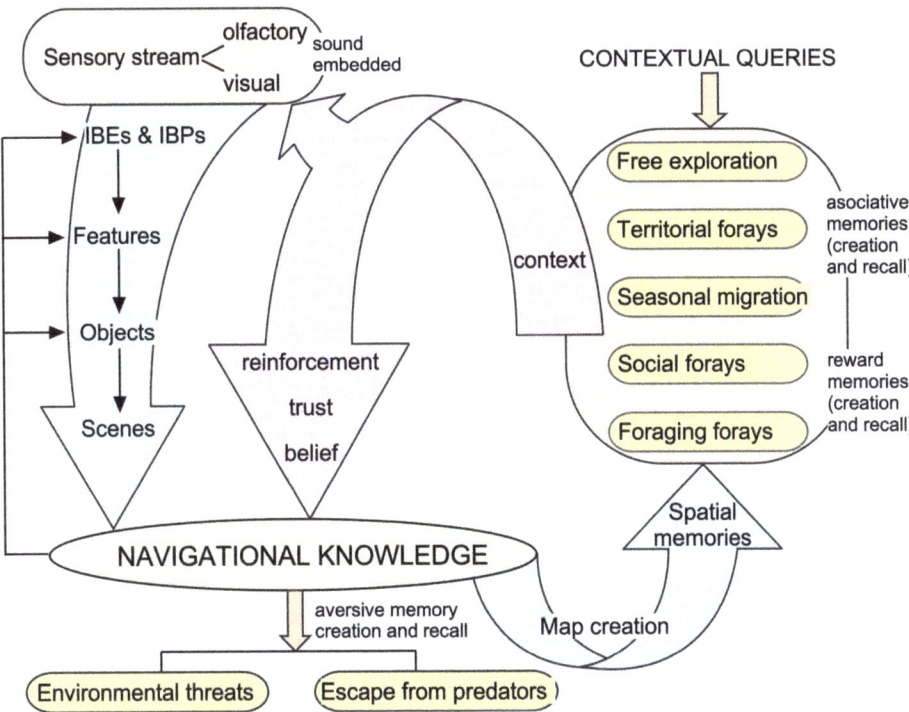

Figure 2. A schematic showing behavior-driven flow of information to extract object- and scene-specific cues for creating navigational knowledge. Associative memories are typically created via valence-driven idiothetic cues, or show statistically significant coincidence of occurrence in the form of allothetic cues. KNs are expected to play an important role in top-down modulation for sensory selection by sustaining attention at various levels of sensory processing and may be modified by reward- and aversion-driven associative memory mechanisms.

In common terms, knowledge is often understood as an awareness of facts (declarative knowledge) or as practical skills (procedural knowledge) and may also mean familiarity with objects or situations. The same terms have been used to categorize memories. Episodic memories require the activation of action-related networks that are associated with an activity or an event. For a long time, it was debated whether memories are stored within specific areas in the brain or distributed as information bits throughout the brain. Current data support the latter scenario [89,90]. If so, then, as in a computer, one also needs a directory of sorts to point to the address of each information bit. This means that to access a bit of information, one first needs to look up the registered address and then utilize the information in memory. This could mean first accessing another memory to locate the directory to in turn locate a bit of pertinent information. Theoretically, this sequencing of addresses and memories could lock up the neural access within an infinite loop. While loops are important components of information processing, they do not represent an efficient way to store information. Also, it is energetically costly to not only "remember" a certain bit of information but then also go to a location to recall where that information is stored. This further complicates recall by the number of instances or bits of information that need to be retrieved. In real life, one can equate this to finding a user manual for an electronic device, such as a television set. If one wants to obtain some information on the location or function of a port or connector, then it will be best if one can either look directly at that device or look up relevant information in a user manual sitting next to the television set rather than first locating and retrieving it from a different location. Moreover, this process involves the need for additional memory storage that can greatly increase the cost of obtaining information by a factor proportional to the number of bits accessed, slowing down recall. It may also trigger an infinite loop making the system crash. Alternately, directory information may be stored at a central location and automatically channeled to the source of the query. How this is accomplished within the brain without the involvement of an outside agent, as in the case of an individual using their brain to access the memory and physically locomoting to retrieve it, is still unclear.

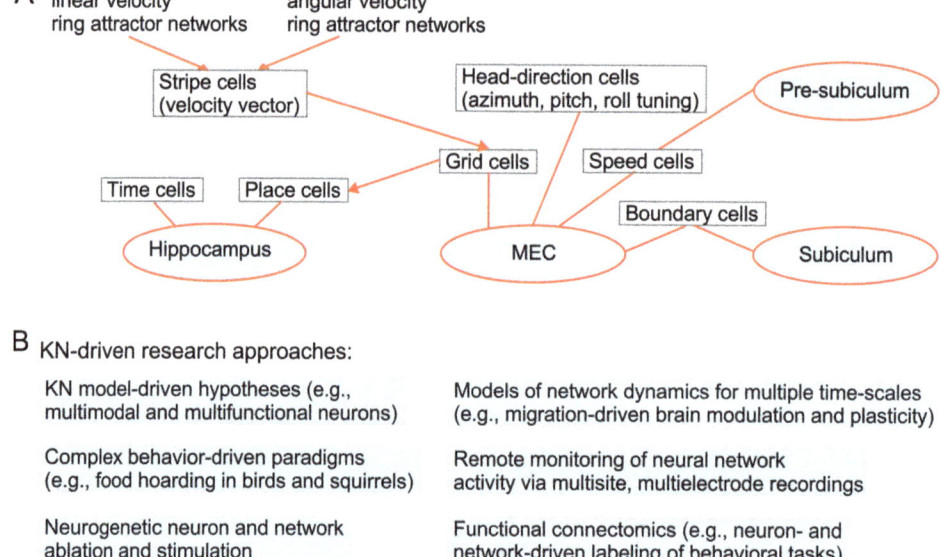

Figure 3. (**A**). Networks and cell types discovered for navigation in rodents, bats and primates, including humans. Lines connect to the brain structures where they are located and arrows show the directionality in which networks and one cell type carves the receptive field of another. (**B**). Examples of research questions that can be addressed using a KN-driven approach to provide a foundational understanding of the neuroscience of knowledge. These approaches can help us to define the physiological properties, configuration, extent and plasticity of KNs. MEC: medial entorhinal cortex.

1.2.3. Memory vs. Knowledge

Memory remains a vital component of knowledge, and considerable progress has been made towards understanding memory formation, consolidation and recall. Short-term memories are first transiently stored within the electrophysiologic activity of neurons and networks [91]. Some memories are then consolidated within neural networks throughout the brain via the modification of dendritic spines and synapses that are only just beginning to be delineated [92–95]. Over the long term, the relevant networks somehow become activated to access a specific memory each time a decision is to be made. It is as if the brain has the capacity to "dial-in" to different networks within a knowledge domain to extract information.

As a real-world example, to communicate with others to share and/or obtain information, one may access a digital phonebook and click on a number to be dialed. These actions require energy so that there is a cost–benefit ratio not only for movement but also of network usage within the brain. Many mental disorders, such as depression and schizophrenia, can be considered, respectively, as a high perceived cost of action and decision- making going array. These disorders can be triggered by chronic anxiety and stressful states that release hormones in the bloodstream via the activation of the hypothalamus and other endocrine organs, such as the adrenal glands [96]. Chronic release of these hormones can result in changes in the wiring of the brain [97–100]. It can also disrupt metabolic processes and deteriorate telomeres or the endcaps of chromosomes [101–103]. Knowledge not only lowers the basal state of energetic cost by providing access to previously obtained information, i.e., via experience, but also allows an organism to make decisions and take action in the interest of lowering energy consumption over the long term and increasing the probability of survival. But, what is knowledge in contrast to information and memory, and how is it created and stored in the brain? Semantic or conceptual knowledge has been defined and studied only loosely from a neurobiological perspective [69,104], and studied in a very limited way from a computational perspective [17]. Computationally, structured knowledge is thought to reside in long-term memory as a distributed activity pattern and accessed via partial retrieving cues. According to a proposed model, sequences of memories can be potentially stored as single attractors within recurrent neural networks [17,105]. To gain a more tangible sense of KNs, let us now consider brain structures that are well known to play a role in memory mechanisms.

1.3. Brain Structures Involved in Memory Formation and Recall

Memories, such as those used for face recognition, may be purely experiential [106], or they may be created via association with either reward or punishment [107]. Experimentally, memory formation can be studied in animals only via either reward or fear associations, i.e., within an emotive context. While an emotive context is a powerful mechanism of memory formation given the direct relationship of emotions with survival, not all memories are formed in this way. Associations can happen within any two temporally bound sensory inputs, provided those associations occur at a statistically significant level over other chance associations.

The hippocampus, a seahorse-shaped brain structure, stores information transiently until it is contextualized and stabilized, and then channeled to a neural network at a specific location for long term storage. In this scenario, memory may be accessed by reactivating the memory in a context-driven manner. In other words, context may activate a specific section of the "phonebook" to automatically "dial-in" to a particular network to access a specific memory and/or to transform it, given a new set of contextualized inputs. In the phonebook analogy, the same brain structure, the hippocampus, cannot however function both for long-term storage and as a pointer to the correct location of a phone number entry since the information represented by each phone number may change with time. We are, however, concerned less here with details of information storage and more about what that information represents and what it accomplishes for an organism's survival.

The hippocampi can be divided into a dorsal and a ventral subregion [108]. Whereas the ventral hippocampus receives information from the basal nucleus of the amygdala (BA), the dorsal hippocampus sends information to the basolateral nucleus of the amygdala, which also receives sensory information from the cortex and thalamus [109–111]. The reciprocal connectivity of the ventral hippocampus with the amygdala plays a central role in creating contextual memories, as summarized in Figure 4. The hippocampus binds together item and context information related to a study event. It receives information from the amygdala, an almond-shaped brain structure consisting of multiple nuclei, as well as the perirhinal and parahippocampal, including entorhinal, cortices. These structures transfer information to the hippocampus, respectively, about an event from the emotive value stream, and the "what" and "where" streams. The BA also projects to both the medial and lateral regions of the entorhinal cortex (EC). The BA receives projections back from the CA1 region and the subiculum as well as from the lateral EC (LEC). The LA sends excitatory output to the inferior colliculus (IC) that inhibits both the medial and lateral nuclei in the central amygdala (CeA). The LA also sends excitatory output to the BA, which in turn can excite both medial and lateral nuclei in the CeA. The baslolateral amygdala (BLA) has reciprocal connectivity with the prefrontal cortex [112]. Theta and gamma oscillatory activity within the hippocampus plays an important role in creating and retrieving navigational knowledge. Theta–gamma phase coupling encodes navigation-related functions, and spike timing within theta oscillations is important for memory consolidation and recall (Figure 3). With respect to navigation, e.g., during free exploration in a familiar environment (Figure 2), and during memory recall, CA1 pyramidal neurons respond most effectively to CA3 input [113]. Eventually, all information is transmitted to the central nucleus of the amygdala for action-related decisions.

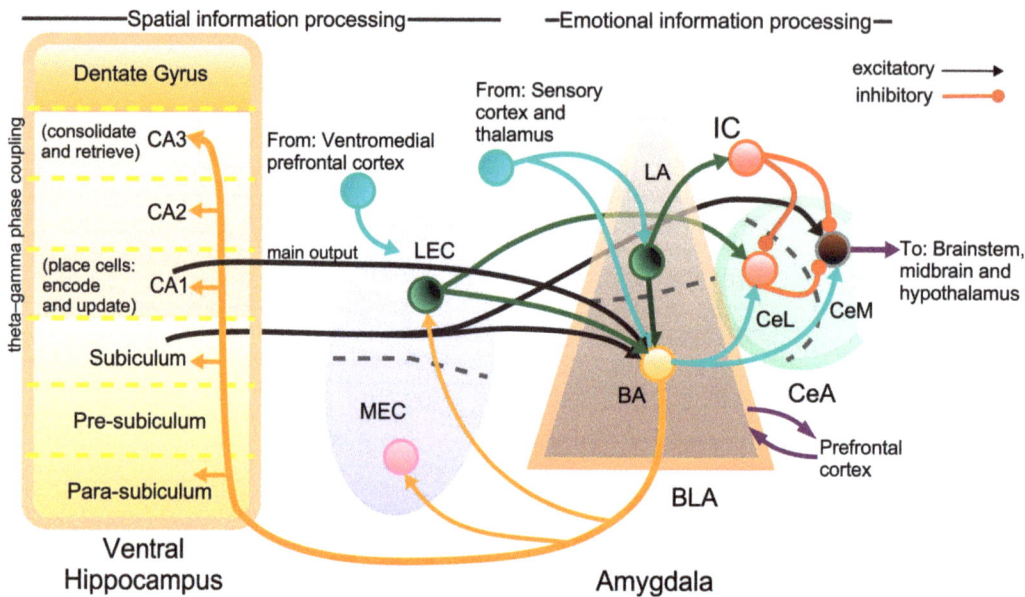

Figure 4. Schematic showing the localization of oscillatory activity (top-left) in the ventral hippocampus within a navigational context (see Figure 2) and for memory functions, and its complex interconnectivity with the amygdala for context-dependent associative learning. The lateral amygdala (LH) receives processed sensory inputs from the cortex and thalamus. These inputs contain information about features and objects in the sensory landscape. The subiculum, presubiculum and parasubiculum are extensions of the CA1, CA2 and CA3 regions of the hippocampus and they all receive outputs from the basal amygdala (BA). The basolateral amygdala (BLA) has reciprocal connections with the prefrontal cortex. Projections to the hypothalamus trigger hormonal changes, and those to the periaqueductal gray in the brainstem control respiration, heart rate and vocalization.

Finally, the prefrontal cortex (PFC), particularly the dorsolateral PFC, is heavily involved in working memory functions. It is also clearly important for maintaining and updating information, as well as for emotional regulation and motor control. The PFC, in general, plays a central role in orchestrating complex cognitive processes, such as executive functions, which include planning, decision making, problem solving, and controlling attention [114,115]. Therefore, KNs are expected to be intimately connected with and continuously interact with the PFC, though knowledge itself is likely distributed in wide-area networks extending to higher-order sensory cortices as well as diencephalic structures, such as the habenula.

Episodic memory for navigational and other tasks involves the conversion of sensory inputs into working memory. A working memory activity pattern in the hippocampus must be transferred to long-term memory stores, such as in the neocortex, to process the next set of events or sensory inputs. By definition, navigation is a sequential event. Therefore, it is not surprising that the hippocampus plays an important role in both functions and has been studied as such. Building on the adaptive resonance theory (ART) family of neural models, Grossberg and colleagues have advanced hypotheses to explain both the working memory and navigational functions of the hippocampus [116,117]. Their model stresses the importance of mass action-induced theta rhythms [118] in both mapping and extracting the information of an organism's spatial environment for navigation. As indicated earlier (see also Figure 3A), time- and distance-encoding cells, together with head-direction cells, project to grid cells in the entorhinal cortex (EC), which, in turn, project to place cells in the hippocampus [7,116]. In this scheme, the theta period represents a temporal metric for sequence learning [119] and also allows activity in widespread hippocampal and neocortical networks to be temporally coordinated [116]. The idea is that theta activity results in either gamma or beta oscillations, depending on match (resonance) and mismatch (reset) between expected vs. actual inputs. Altogether, the KN for navigation in mammals contains idio- and allothetic sensory, working memory, long-term memory, emotive–limbic, and action-selection modules. These reside in interconnected anatomical structures, namely, the thalamus, sensory and parietal cortex, hippocampus, subiculum and EC, amygdala, as well as the prefrontal cortex and subthalamic nucleus for action selection and the motor cortex/basal ganglia for motor output—for details see Figure 1 in Bermudez-Contreras et al. [120]. The retrosplenial cortex is a key structure that receives both head-direction and allocentric information. Most recently, Rolls and colleagues have expanded their quantitative theory of hippocampal function for short-term memory storage and recall without invoking mass action in the form of oscillations [121,122]. They include the orbitofrontal cortex as a source of reward-related input that is used to bind multimodal information within the hippocampal circuitry and invoke "concept" and "spatial view" cells within the hippocampus to explain goal-directed navigational behavior [121,123].

As with mirror neurons in Broca's area [124], it is becoming clear that the initial terminology developed to identify neurons and networks that conduct a specific function can usually explain a general class of functions. Thus, a part of the navigational network can also contribute to other cognitive processes based on associative thought [121]. This stresses the multifunctional nature of cortical, and possibly subcortical, neurons and networks [125–129]. Recent findings that expand the interconnectivity of a working memory module to its application to a task-directed navigation network are a prime example of the need to establish a viable and reliable KN where cross-validation can occur on a daily basis as an organism roams its environment under different environmental conditions and physiological states. Similar cross-validation and certainty-seeking processes can also occur via reflection-driven fronto-cortical activity.

2. Proposition

2.1. Knowledge Equation

The brain is essentially a complex and highly plastic network of neurons. Therefore, we presume that knowledge is stored as a state of synaptic interconnectivity within neural networks, partially as what we term as a memory of some information. To be meaningful (for survival), new information must be contextualized, linked up with existing information and tested for consistency or coherence before being stored as knowledge. In philosophical terms, knowledge of "facts" is often defined as true belief that is distinct from opinion or guesswork by virtue of justification. The process of justification is what delineates knowledge from a piece of factual information or a memory of it. The generation of knowledge involves the summation of cross-validated information over time and potentially across multiple timescales.

In this section, I propose a mathematical formulation of knowledge and of KNs. The motivation to do so is two-fold. First, it should allow those working in the domain of AI to incorporate a concept of KNs and develop new processes that go beyond using brute force, big data approaches to train artificial neural networks. Once established, the idea of KNs will allow systems and robots to learn from their interactions with the environment as humans and other animals do. Second, a mathematical conceptualization of KNs together with enabling technologies, in turn, can stimulate a more rigorous and comprehensive understanding of human cognition as well as predict the effects of neurological disorders, aiding in the development of diagnostic tools and treatments. I hope this will enable the simulation of knowledge-driven brain networks, such as for a better understanding of navigation, language learning and education in general (e.g., incorporating the role of emotional, motivational and movement networks to generate trust and belief). This will allow researchers to test hypotheses and explore the effects of different variables included in the mathematical formulation. Additional details of the mathematical extensions for these applications are beyond the scope of this review, but I hope will be picked up by others working in their respective fields.

First, let us try to formulate, in rigorous terms, the concept of knowledge residing within KNs. For knowledge to remain relevant, forgetting is as important as incorporating additional information. This is in fact critical for planning and efficient decision making. The state of knowledge at any time therefore can be given by a knowledge equation, where the information is updated by integrating new with existing information, and outdated or irrelevant information is deleted via forgetting to keep knowledge viable. Later, we will discuss how and when the forgetting happens in neurobiological terms.

To mathematize the idea that knowledge is a result of integrating new incoming information while forgetting old information, we can model knowledge as a dynamic system that changes with time. Some variables relevant to such a model are as follows:

1. $K(t)$: the cumulative knowledge at time "t";
2. $G(t)$: The rate of incoming new information at time "t". $G(t)$ is modeled as a function of time, depending on how information is received. For instance, it could be constant, exponentially growing or influenced by other factors like attention or exposure;
3. $L(t)$: The rate of loss or forgetting old information at time "t". This can be transient, triggered by distraction or change permanently via neuronal or synaptic degradation, as in Alzheimer's disease;
4. α: the integration rate constant, which determines how efficiently new information is integrated into the current knowledge state;
5. β: the forgetting rate constant, which determines how quickly old information is forgotten.

α and β are constants that quantify the efficiency of integration and the rate of loss of information via forgetting, respectively. In terms of memory, these can be determined either empirically from learning curves or theoretically based on the context.

The change in the state of knowledge over time, $dK(t)/dt$, can be expressed as a first-order linear differential equation, where

$$dK(t)/dt = \alpha G(t) - \beta K(t) \tag{1}$$

where $\alpha G(t)$ represents the gain in information or contribution of new information to knowledge, and, within the context of memory, $\beta K(t)$ represents the loss of information due to forgetting.

If we assume $G(t)$ for memory networks, we have to set up the initial condition where $M(0) = M_0$, and $K(0)$ is the initial knowledge at time $t = 0$. Then, we arrive at a form of the equation for memory:

$$M(t) = e^{-\beta t}(\alpha \int_0^t I(s)e^{\beta s}ds + M_0) \quad \text{(Memory equation)}$$

where the integral term, $\int_0^t I(s)e^{\beta s}ds + K_0$, represents the cumulative effect of incoming new information over time, adjusted for the forgetting rate. "s" represents a process reducing the contribution of memory modules' contribution weight. It should be noted, however, that knowledge is less prone to forgetting, and this equation applies strictly to the memory components of knowledge.

Assuming, for simplicity, that $G(t)$ is a constant G_0, we can find the explicit form of $K(t)$ by solving the differential equation

$$dK(t)/dt = \alpha G_0 - \beta K(t) \quad (2)$$

The general solution, using an integrating factor, $\mu(t)$, where $\mu(t) = e^{-\beta t}$ (an exponential nature of information decay over time, assuming $G(t)$ is not constant), is

$$K(t) = \alpha G_0/\beta + (K_0 - \alpha G_0/\beta) \ldots \text{(Knowledge equation)}$$

- The term $\alpha G_0/\beta$ represents the steady-state knowledge level when the rate of integrating new information and the rate of forgetting are balanced.
- The term $(K_0 - \alpha G_0/\beta)$ represents the transient behavior of knowledge over time, showing how it approaches the steady-state level. The rate at which $K(t)$ approaches the steady-state is governed by β.

Overall, the Knowledge Equation captures the dynamic nature of knowledge accumulation and decay over time. It provides a mathematical framework for understanding the dynamics of knowledge as a function of new information integration and forgetting. This model can be adapted or extended based on specific contexts or additional complexities in the real-world scenarios being modeled. The variables and constants used are intuitive and can be adjusted based on empirical data or specific scenarios to reflect different learning and forgetting processes.

2.2. Knowledge Networks

Within a neural net framework, it is presumed that knowledge is embedded within a network that, when activated, will produce a set of outputs different from what it might in its nascent or initial state. A network carries information by its activity and the properties of the neurons within the network, but the knowledge it imparts depends on the context within which it is queried. The same network can produce different sets of outputs depending on how it is queried, that is, how other inputs activate this network. Thus, a generic information network can be a storehouse of multiple knowledge sets. This conception of a knowledge network is supported by the multifunctional nature of many neurons and networks [127–130].

Locally re-afferent and looping circuits are much more likely to be a component of KNs that store category-specific object knowledge [131,132]. An example of this type of network is shown in Figure 5A. That means that KNs will likely have neurons that show either tonic firing or bursting as the information loops between different networks as a representation of knowledge. This indeed appears to be the case when recording single-unit activity from neurons in the frontal cortex in response to complex, naturalistic sounds [60,62,133,134]. In contrast, neural responses to the same sounds from the primary auditory cortex are phasic and time-locked to stimulus onset. Also, because of their dynamic nature, the representation of knowledge within neural networks requires an activity component that is difficult to define a priori and is best studied using naturalistic stimuli [135]. These properties are not yet incorporated within artificially trained, deep learning networks, but in time hopefully AI will utilize an integration between multiple networks, each of which is trained for a specific task but relies on inputs or knowledge from other networks for justification. The knowledge could be related to ethics and other such constraints that can be independently updated. Presumably, the next generation of artificially intelligent agents will rely on knowledge-based models rather than generative language ones that are driven largely by statistical features. KNs have been alluded to previously from the viewpoint of social networks. Within this context, "KNs" are collections of individuals and teams who come together across organizational, spatial and disciplinary boundaries to invent and share a body of knowledge [136]. From an educational perspective, a network that provides knowledge to an organism is more representative of what we think of as "understanding".

Therefore, KNs need to be continuously updated, are multifunctional and are more highly distributed than an information-extracting or a specific-memory network.

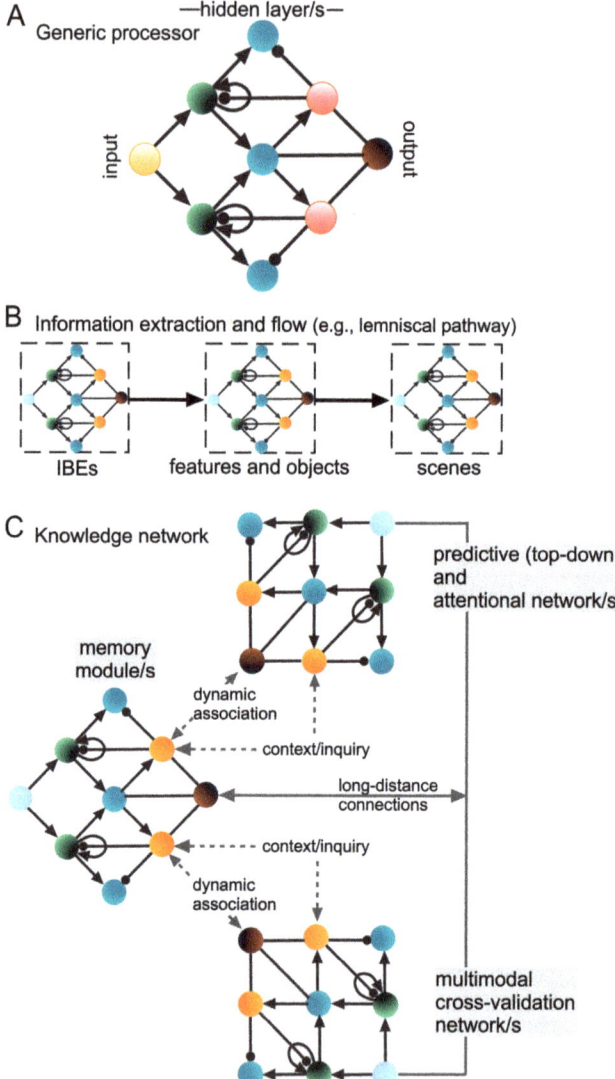

Figure 5. Knowledge network construction and distinction. (**A**) A generic multilayered network for signal extraction or associative learning, including recurrence (looping back arrows on green circles) that can be either excitatory or inhibitory, and feedforward (arrows) and feedback (filled circles) connections. The green, blue and orange circles belong to hidden layers of the network. (**B**) A series of modular networks showing the bottom-up flow of information to extract IBEs, features and objects from the sensory landscape (see Figure 1). (**C**) A putative knowledge network consisting of multiple distributed memory modules, predictive and attentional, and multimodal cross-validating networks as the basic components. This type of network contains multimodal representations, and has long-distance connections with inputs that can modify as well as query the network via sensory and cephalic triggers. Information is expected to flow bidirectionally (gray arrows) between these

networks for decision making and action selection. The entire network can be triggered by either query or contextual signals. Transient coupling between networks (dashed arrows) can occur via oscillatory activity (see text for details). Physical dissociation via synaptic degradation or temporal unbinding over time is also possible via the de-correlation of neural activity. Prediction mismatch triggers large mismatch negativity-evoked potentials, leading to error signals and potential re-learning that may result in a reconfiguration of the knowledge network.

KNs can be considered as both valance-driven and referential. A simple example of a contextualized KN involves circuits within both the hippocampus and the amygdala. For example, if one walks into a dark alley, the hippocampus provides spatial information, whereas the amygdala provides valence information from either past experiences or from "instructional" inputs. This "knowledge" then guides one's decision about a choice to enter the alley, or once there to leave it as soon as possible. If this knowledge is based on experience, then the hippocampus plays a role in embedding this in memory within the entorhinal cortex where valance appears to be represented within spatial coordinates. Figure 5B shows neural activity flowing through a sequence of generic information networks where each network holds a specific memory or bit of information. A KN would constitute a cluster of smaller networks that are typically accessible via a query or contextual input (Figure 5C). Intuition is a form of intrinsic knowledge that is spontaneously activated, and is less under the control of conscious inquiry and rational analysis. The components of intuitive KNs are expected to be present within the enteric nervous system and subcortical brain structures, such as the reticular formation.

Neural networks filter, process, code and decode signals as information either in the form of sensory, recurrent or feedback signals [137–139]. KNs, as formulated here, do not necessarily perform any of the low-level functions, but they can modulate, gate and facilitate activity within neural networks, including memory modules. KNs store the information as knowledge that can later prove useful to the organism. Hence, unless genetically encoded, KNs are created over time, taking into account the consequences of prior action and information processing. KNs tend to be distributed globally and need to be dynamically interconnected, especially when a decision needs to be made and/or an action taken. Whole brain networks have previously been constructed using graph theory [140,141]. Thus, KNs and the neurons within them can be thought of as being multifunctional. This is not a requirement for purely sensory neurons, though they may also process multiple types of signals. Information can reside within static networks. Knowledge, however, requires information to be stored in contextualized networks (Figures 2 and 5C). Since the context can change with every instance, knowledge cannot be represented by a static network.

2.3. Mathematical Formulation of KNs

As with knowledge, the state of a KN must also evolve with time. One can consider a KN to be a sum of multiple transient networks that are updated by new external (allothetic) and internal (idiothetic) sensory inputs and states. This may be represented symbolically as

$$KN_t = NN1_t + NN2_{t+1} + NN3_{t+2} + \ldots NNx_{t+x}. \qquad \ldots \text{(Network equation)}$$

where KN = knowledge network, NN = refers to a neural network and t = time at which the KN and NNs are accessed; NN's can be memory, cross-validation, context or organizational networks that are transiently linked during knowledge creation and access.

To mathematize the concept of KNs rigorously, we need to model the dynamics of these networks, their interactions and how they contribute to the overall knowledge state [142]. First, we make the following assumptions:

1. The activity of neural networks, including memory modules, can be described by continuous functions of time.
2. The connection weights between neural networks and memory modules are constant over time.

3. The contribution weights of neural networks and memory modules to the knowledge network are dynamic and vary with time.

The following components, including variables listed, are an integral part of model formulation:

1. Neural Networks and Modules:
   - $N_j(t)$: the activity level of the i-th NN at time t;
   - $M_j(t)$: the activity level of the j-th memory module at time t;
   - w_{ij}: the connection weight between the i-th NN, and the j-th memory module.
2. Knowledge Networks (KNs):
   - $K(t)$: total knowledge at time t;
   - $\alpha_i(t)$: the weight of the i-th NN's contribution to the KN at time t;
   - $\beta_j(t)$: the weight of the j-th memory module's contribution to the KN at time t.
3. Dynamics and Interactions:
   - $G(t)$: the rate of gain of new information at time t;
   - $F(t)$: the rate of forgetting old information at time t.

Furthermore, a mathematical model of KN has the following properties:

1. Neural Network Dynamics: The activity level of each NN, $Ni(t)$, represents the dynamic activity levels of different neural circuits that contribute to knowledge. This can be influenced by incoming information and interaction with memory modules.
2. Memory Module Dynamics: The activity level of each memory module $Mj(t)$ represents the activity levels of memory storage systems that interact with neural networks, which can be influenced by the activity of a neural network.
3. Connection Weights, (w_{ij}), represent the strength of interaction between neural networks and memory modules.
4. Contribution Weights Dynamics: the weights $\alpha i(t)$ and $\beta j(t)$ represent the dynamic importance of each neural network and memory module to the KN.
5. Total Knowledge Dynamics: The total knowledge at time t, after adjusting weights, is a function of the contributions from neural networks and memory modules. The final solution for total knowledge within a KN at time t, can be modeled as

$$K(t) = \sum_i \alpha_{ij}(t) Ni(t) + \sum_i \beta_j(t) M_j(t) \quad \text{(KN knowledge equation)}$$

A model incorporating the above features captures the dynamic nature of knowledge networks, integrating new information, and the forgetting process, with contributions from both neural networks and memory modules.

Using partial differential equations (PDEs) can make the model more realistic by capturing the spatial and temporal dynamics of KNs, reflecting how knowledge is dynamically structured and represented in the brain [143]. Specifically, sparse connectivity contributes efficiency, robustness and flexibility to the KN model [144]. Efficiency reduces the computational and energetic load on the brain by minimizing unnecessary connections. Robustness enhances the brain's ability to isolate damage or dysfunction, as fewer connections mean that problems in one area are less likely to propagate widely. Flexibility allows the brain to adapt and reorganize more easily in response to learning and new experiences, as specific pathways can be strengthened or weakened without affecting the entire network. The mathematization of a PDE model is beyond the scope of this review, but PDE equations allow one to model how knowledge, neural activity and memory activity evolve not only over time but also across different regions of the brain. Hence, as noted earlier, to test these types of models, it is necessary to record neural activity over time and across different regions of the brain in actively behaving animals.

2.4. Evolution of Knowledge Networks

The identification and quantification of naturalistic, unimodal stimuli and binary motor behaviors have played an important role in advancing neuroethological approaches to understanding neural organization and mechanisms. Although such approaches will continue to be of benefit, given the present-day technologies and those that will be available in the near-future, it is timely to consider neural organization within more complex, integrative multimodal frameworks. It is time to address the fundamental integrative unit of brain organization and potentially its evolution. This unit almost always has to be multimodal because organisms function and evolve within a multimodal environment even though sometimes one sensory system may play a dominant role, e.g., the auditory system in bats and dolphins, and the olfactory system in rodents. Dogs have excellent olfactory and auditory capabilities. Even within a single sensory modality, neurons can be multifunctional, switching their role depending on the context, such as for echolocation vs. communication in bats [129,145]. Similarly, memory networks may be transformed with context via neuromodulators, such as dopamine and oxytocin, as happens for pair bonding vs. maternal bonding in prairie voles [146]. The conceptualization of KNs offers a more robust, naturalistic and adaptive way that may govern not only the organization of brain networks but also its evolutions as such. A KN-based model emphasizes the acquisition and processing of information to gain knowledge as a real-world model and the primary and urgently needed goal for survival of a newborn. A KN must consist of and engage with multiple and multimodal networks for decision making and action selection. As the brain matures, specific memories may be lost or become inaccessible having served their function of creating knowledge and this knowledge is both essential and sufficient for an organism's survival in its adopted environment and ecological niche. Thus, one way to think about the evolution of the brain is to consider that it was gradually configured over millennia towards a dynamic, knowledge-directed system to enable information storage and processing over increasing timeframes.

KNs incorporate distant memories and the present context for building predictive models of the social and physical environment. In humans, knowledge can sustain motivation and goal-directed action over a timeframe of several years. A long-term goal stored within a separate network can periodically query KNs and act as a planning and "decision center" for action selection as needed. A query can be triggered by either a sensory cue in the environment (a physical change or a conspecific interaction) or an internally generated, imaginative signal. It may also be triggered by the physiological state of the body, such as sleep, arousal and hunger, driving the organism to retrieve information based on knowledge about the location of a food source and activate a behavioral algorithm that will bring that organism to its food source [147–149]. Thus, a KN may connect with components of sensory, attention, goal-setting/planning and motor networks that work together for decision making and action selection (Figures 2 and 6).

Foraging strategies and many other adaptive behaviors depend on the complexity and size of the information-processing and storage system that an organism is endowed with. Single-celled organisms and simple multicellular organisms, such as sponges and coelenterates, respond to stimuli by orienting and translational movements that are both directed and random [150–152]. These organisms require only a sensor and a motor element to react reflexively in a preprogrammed manner with a built-in, limited range of tolerance for environmental change (Figure 7). They do not require a knowledge network. Alternatively, in more complex organisms, particularly vertebrates as well as some invertebrate groups, such as cephalopods with a well-organized brain, a goal-driven process may involve querying many networks that can extract knowledge before triggering a sequential decision set that ultimately gets converted into a sequence of actions [153].

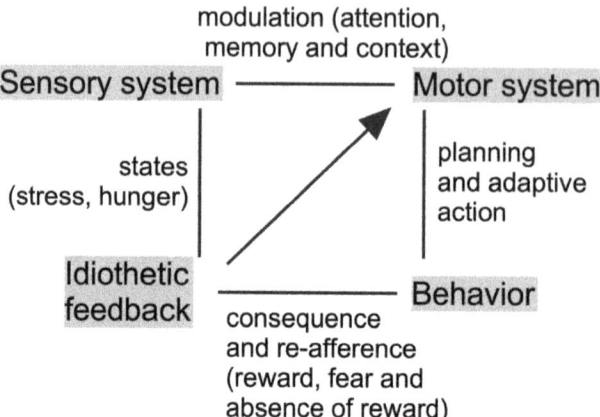

Figure 6. A line diagram depicting the relationship between sensory inputs, motor control and behavior within a sense of self (idiothethic) in both physical (time and space) and physiological terms. The reciprocal interconnectivity of the various functions emphasizes the importance of and role of various neural states and mechanisms that constitute components of KNs. The behavior or motor output is typically triggered in response to a query generated by signals from the internal or the external environment. Physiological states, such as hunger, drive an organism to attend to contextual or allothetic cues in its environment and activate central motor programs in the brain to trigger behavioral actions. These in turn become the source of sensory inputs that allow an organism to monitor its movement and location within its relevant region of space. Some of this feedback leads to contextual learning through motivational cues related to reward and fear. Direct idiothetic feedback (diagonal arrow) can modulate coordinated and directed motor activity.

In vertebrates, action sequences are embedded within brain structures, such as the basal ganglia and motor (including pre-motor) cortex for bodily movement, and the amygdala for autonomic functions and physiological activity of the internal organs [154,155]. Thus, neural networks are proposed as having gradually evolved from simple, non-overlapping reactive nerve nets, dedicated to specific functions of neuroids in sponges, to hydra-like organisms, more complex, bilateral brains in worms and to a multilobed, distributed central nervous system in insects and cephalopods. These advancements led to the emergence of primitive to advanced KNs present within proactive and imaginative brains, respectively (Figure 7). Some knowledge elements become embedded within neural networks through genetic encoding, especially in invertebrates and lower vertebrates [156,157]. Recent findings on the organization of the lamprey brain support this possibility [158,159]. Eventually, increases in complexity and connectivity led to the development of imaginative brains where scenarios could be simply imagined with or without follow-up with action selection [160]. Here, KNs became critical for providing top-down information via predictive computations [16,161–164]. Predictive networks enable "fact/error-checking" and the justification for decision making and action selection without reference to incoming sensory information [165].

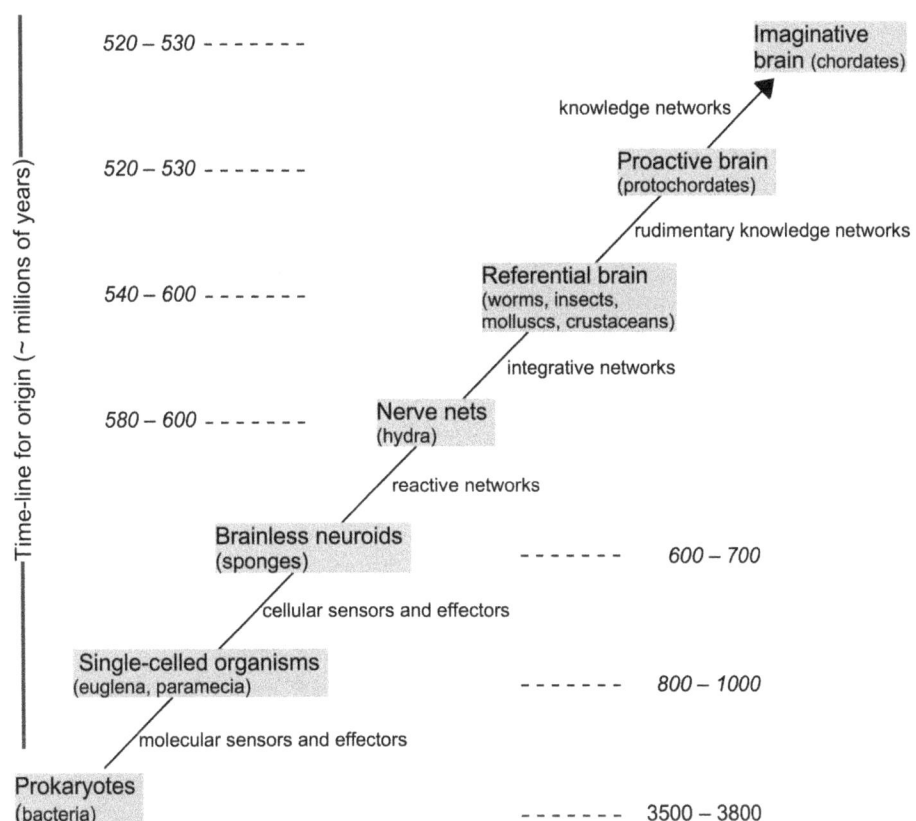

Figure 7. Flow-chart showing the evolution of organisms with or without "brains" (shaded boxes) within the animal kingdom. Early forms of life (over 540 million years ago) did not require knowledge to adapt to their environment. Their action selection was directly determined by sensors and effectors operating at either molecular, cellular or simple reflex levels. Later, as organisms and their brains became more complex, just-in-time information availability was supplanted by KNs that allowed a brain to be proactive in terms of evaluating its environment, goal-setting and action selection. Some molluscan species with large brains, such as the octopus, and protochordates are expected to have rudimentary KNs, whereas the neurally advanced species, such as cetaceans and primates, have the capacity of knowledge abstraction and manipulation. Humans are assumed to have the most advanced KNs capable of symbolic representation through cultural evolution and education.

3. Discussion

I have proposed here that a paradigm shift in our thinking is required to approach neurobiological research from a more comprehensive perspective. Despite numerous studies on learning and memory, we have barely elucidated the networks in which knowledge resides. Navigational systems represent an important frontier in this regard (see Figure 2). Below I discuss what we know about mechanisms for knowledge acquisition and, capitalizing on studies of memory consolidation, the important role of attention and sleep in the conversion of memory stores and contextual information into knowledge. As discussed later, an interdisciplinary approach promises to enhance the effectiveness of educational strategies and the sophistication of AI technologies, leading to better outcomes in both fields.

3.1. Knowledge Acquisition and Action Selection

Let us first examine in a little more detail the steps of information acquisition and processing within putative KNs. Exteroceptors, such as in eyes and ears, are designed to feed information about the external environment, whereas interoceptors, such as proprioceptors and carbon dioxide sensors, monitor and transmit information about the internal state of the body. These are a part of the peripheral division of the nervous system. These receptors send inputs to various parts of the brain where the inputs are consolidated and evaluated based upon experience and stored as "memory". Because sensory systems are adaptive, to some extent sensors at the level of the peripheral nervous system, and more so central sensory processing networks, are primarily designed to detect changes in the quantity and quality of the sensory profile of the external and internal environment over different time-windows. For example, the vestibular system in humans is activated by changes in linear and angular acceleration over an approximately 7 s time window [166]. Hence, when constructing rollercoasters to stimulate the vestibular system, a turn needs to be introduced for every 7 s of travel to satisfy the stimulus expectations of the customers. Let us now tackle the question of how knowledge is gained from these sensations.

Some neurons themselves function as sensors by having receptors on specialized segments of their cell membrane, such as olfactory receptors present on olfactory cilia that are specialized forms of dendrites. Similarly, intraspinal cord mechanosensory neurons within the spinal cord can detect axial bending of the body [167,168]. Neurons within the central nervous system can also be regarded as sensors that monitor the body's physiological, physical and emotive states by monitoring the activity of other neurons via receptors for neurotransmitters as well as for the hormonal and neuromodulator milieu within the extracellular space. Thus, changes in both externally driven and internally sensed neural activity eventually determine the behavior of an organism. Neuronal plasticity occurs at the synaptic level via both active and silent synapses that can control learning during critical periods [169,170]. Synaptic modification is less likely to occur during the elicitation of the reflexive type of responses, where a referential knowledge or prediction network is not invoked. During information gain, however, each new active synapse has the potential to significantly bias the output of a KN.

An ultimate goal of knowledge creation is to minimize perceived complexity and maximize predictability (minimizing entropy within an information-theoretic framework) without sacrificing accuracy. To achieve this, KNs may tolerate a certain amount of fuzziness, maximizing their applicability to real world scenarios that are rarely identical [171,172]. Neuro-fuzzy systems appear to be good at pattern recognition for solving real-world problems [173]. Feature extraction, cross-validation, synchronization and consensus finding are important components of such systems that have been implemented for knowledge discovery via artificial neural nets [174,175]. Consensus maps have been proposed to encode naturalistic smells via the odotopic mapping of odorants in the olfactory bulb and forebrain [176–179], and social calls via combination-sensitivity within the auditory cortex [50,61,180]. How cross-validation and synchronization is automatically accomplished within real neural networks is less clear. Oscillations in neural activity within different brain regions, such as the amygdala and hippocampus, may provide a mechanism for cross-validation, typically involving cross-modal processing, via temporal coherence, phase-amplitude coupling and other such mechanisms [137,181–186]. Oscillations in the form of traveling waves may also provide a mechanism for spreading information (memory encoding and recall) within the brain to strengthen multimodal consensus and the binding of common features within an information scene or landscape [187–190]. In this regard, the state of network dynamics and Hebbian plasticity appear to be essential for the optimization of network topology within real and artificial neural nets [191,192].

Action selection can occur at multiple timescales and involve different amounts of knowledge for action decisions. For fast reflexive activity, information is locally processed and triggers a quick (few milliseconds) reflexive action that can be monosynaptic. Other actions can take hundreds of milliseconds to minutes and even days to be planned and processed. Action decisions involve querying the KNs and extracting bits of relevant information from various parts to direct behavior. Navigation behavior involves both rapid and long-term decisions that must be sustained over time and during seasonal migration [193–196]. As indicated earlier, action selection involves the process of decision making that is a rapidly growing field of study in itself [197,198]. Decision making is a term that has been applied to the behavioral economy within the contexts of morality and commerce involving impulsiveness (risk-taking) vs. knowledge-based cognition [199–201]. The concept of the behavioral economy externally, however, is also relevant to the inner workings of the brain. We can think of decision making as a neural economy where neurons decide to fire or not to fire considering an energetic cost associated with bodily activity and for the generation of action potentials for processing information via neural networks within the brain [202].

Neurophysiological and imaging studies show that during decision making and task performance, the brain channels and loops neural activity through multiple regions of the brain [203] before channeling their output to brain regions that activate bodily patterns of movement. Within the basal ganglia, this is accomplished via disinhibition so that action patterns can be quickly sequenced and released without having to overcome the inertia of building up activity within a network [204,205]. Disinhibition is a good strategy for quickly translating knowledge-driven decisions into activity patterns.

Knowledge recall and action may be triggered by a few or even a single command neuron that, when activated, can bring multiple networks online to seek the justification of a decision [206,207]. When making intuitive decisions, one frequently relies on a "gut feeling", suggesting that these command neurons may literally reside within the enteric nervous system, freeing neural circuits within the brain to process new incoming information to create new memories to expand or modify existing knowledge [208,209]. Neurons that fire together wire together via synaptic stabilization. Over the long term, non-neural mechanisms involving glial cells and perineural nets can protect developed and established networks from being modified [210–212]. Perineural nets create a matrix of proteins that stabilize the network and prevent new synapses from forming easily [213]. Perineural nets have been mostly observed encapsulating inhibitory, parvalbumin neurons. In this way, stored knowledge can be protected from being changed by random inputs [214]. Next, we consider the role of attention, a perceptual attribute that is critical for forming associative memories and the role of sleep, which is important for the stabilization of memories and, as postulated here, for converting memories into knowledge.

3.2. Establishing and Retrieving Knowledge: Attention, Sleep and Oscillations

Vertebrate brains typically receive vast amounts of information at any moment through multiple sensory channels. Therefore, a major function of the brain is to select the most relevant information so that it can be processed quickly and at the required level of resolution as well as stored effectively to make informed decisions that maximize the probability of survival over the short- and long-term. This is achieved via attention (Figure 8). Attention is important for both learning and for modifying behavior via synaptic modification that can occur across brief timescales of <200 ms [215,216]. Mechanisms for selectively attending to and "making sense" of the available information are critical for creating and modifying KNs.

Attentional mechanisms remain largely unknown and difficult to study, partly because of the largely covert nature of attention in species with a well-developed forebrain, and because it is difficult to impossible to interrogate animals about their attentional focus as well as the nature and duration of their attention. A number of studies have focused on visual attention using eye tracking, but attentional control by other sensory modalities is more difficult to study [217,218]. The habenula, a highly conserved mid-diencephalic brain structure, is considered as the integrative switchboard for directing attention either to the self or to others [219]. Its circuit-level connectivity is ideally suited for channeling knowledge residing in the forebrain to influence decision making and action selection via circuits present within the brainstem, e.g., projections to the dorsal raphe.

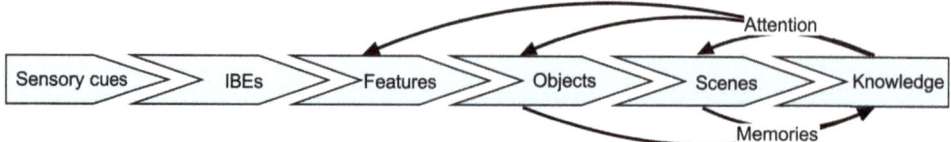

Figure 8. Information flow to extract object- and scene-specific information and create memories as well as knowledge. KNs are expected to play an important role in top-down modulation for sensory selection by sustaining attention at various levels of sensory processing.

KNs not only determine the process of adaptive behavior elaboration, but also direct attention towards the source of additional relevant information [218]. This occurs via alternating between sustained attention and attentional shifts. Attentional shifts are a likely outcome of intrinsic oscillations in neural activity at different timescales, depending on the mechanism at play—from cellular up/down states to circuit level excitatory/inhibitory balance to hormonal rhythms [220,221]. These fluctuations in neural activity can facilitate attentional shifts to enhance knowledge by providing a temporal framework within which bits of information, e.g., those that provide a context, can be coupled to create new knowledge [222]. Within this context, a knowledge network can sustain attention to one attentional set or periodically shift it across multiple attentional sets [223,224]. The neural mechanisms for and the brain regions involved in attentional-shifts are even less studied than those involved in sustaining attention. Periodically shifting attention appears to be a conserved mechanism that remains little appreciated [225–227]. Shifting attention may turn out to be a key mechanism allowing fact checking, and hence in the creation of knowledge, as opposed to simply memories of reward- or fear-associations.

All brains basically exist in one of two states– either an awake or a sleep state, with daily transitions between the two. A sleep state is required to gate most of sensory activity and allow the selective pruning and suppression of ongoing activity by pruning irrelevant synaptic connections, maintaining and updating KNs and preparing them for acquiring new information via interactions with the environment during the awake state [228,229]. For most species, these interactions occur via movement. Therefore, the restoration of muscle (both skeletal and cardiac) tissue are also essential functions of sleep. Sleep also plays a protective role for established KNs by insulating and protecting them from random inputs during day-to-day activities. A number of experimental studies over the last two decades have firmly established that sleep plays an important role in the maintenance of memories and the ability for organisms to acquire and store new memories [230].

During the awake state, the brain allows bodily interactions with the environment, gaining information and testing its validity for conversion to memories and potentially to knowledge. During sleep, memories are consolidated by identifying and strengthening knowledge-building connections, while weakening or disabling those connections that are inconsistent with the acquisition of new knowledge. This may happen by repeatedly activating a KN, presumably via increased slow oscillatory activity (0.85 to 2.0 Hz) in the brain, so that synaptic noise, represented by those synapses that are inconsistently activated during each iteration of the activation cycle, is eliminated [231]. The inconsistent activation of a particular synaptic connection may result from a build-up of inhibitory activity within a network and contribute to a lowering of the synaptic strength (probability of neurotransmitter release) at a particular locus. A large part of this processing happens during sleep. Multichannel electroencephalographic (EEG) recordings in zebra finches underscore an increase in functional connectivity between brain regions during development, likely correlated with learning and knowledge development [232]. Even in fruit flies, sleep duration and sleep–wake switch parameters influence decision making critical for reproductive output [233].

Both attention and sleep are strongly associated with oscillations in the total population activity of neurons. Therefore, oscillations must play a key role in knowledge creation and retrieval, although we do not yet quite understand the detailed mechanisms. A match in either amplitude or phase between the oscillatory activity of distant brain regions leads to coherence [234]. Coherent networks underlie both top-down and bottom-up information flow [235,236]. According to one study in rats, an increase in oscillatory (0.85 to 2.0 Hz) activity during slow wave (SW) sleep within the short-term memory retention interval (80 min in duration) was associated with significantly stronger recall of episodic-like memory [231]. This is particularly effective for spatial memory, but not for object or declarative memory.

The consolidation of object or declarative memory appears to be correlated with sleep spindle activity. Sleep spindles are bursts of neural oscillations (~11 to 16 Hz) generated during nonrapid eye movements (NREM). They are electrical surface correlates, observed in the EEG of thalamocortical oscillations with a duration of 0.5 to 1.5 s [237,238]. The thalamic reticular nucleus has a significant role in the generation of oscillations [239]. Spindles have been proposed to enable large-scale functional connectivity and plasticity involving the rerouting of wake-instated neuronal traces between brain areas, such as the hippocampus and cortex [238]. The presence of spindles in the upstate during theta band of SW oscillatory activity enhances memory consolidation, whereas their presence in the upstate during delta wave activity facilitates the suppression of consolidation [240,241]. Thus, the timing of spindle activity is thought to play a key role in the process of memory consolidation and forgetting.

The fragmented activation of neural networks during the process of memory consolidation and forgetting may play out as a narrative, or what we term as "dreams", some of which reach our conscious level, depending on the sleep state at which they occur [242]. Some dreams are triggered or contextualized by incoming sensory inputs during a light sleep state; others dreams are driven by intense emotive experiences during the awake state and lead to offline performance gain [243]. Dreams may also lead to mental/knowledge clarity during natural or induced recall as during hypnosis or psychoanalytic regression [244,245].

The question remains whether memory consolidation mechanisms also contribute to the process of building a knowledge network. For this to happen, sleep must also facilitate the processes of belief, justification and truth testing. Unfortunately, these concepts remain undefined in neural terms and therefore largely untested at the neurological level [246]. Oscillatory activity resulting in synaptic modification during sleep [247,248] could provide a mechanism for justification, or of obtaining evidence and testing certainty by perturbing neural networks, e.g., in the cingulate cortex, to bounce out of local minima until a new global state of stability (excitatory–inhibitory balance) is achieved that increases the level of certainty and hence strengthens belief [249]. Through this process, a new model of the real world or knowledge can be established within the networks (Figure 9).

Reaching a computational global minimum of neural activity while creating knowledge, especially during sleep, is consistent with and is an outcome of the Bayesian Free Energy Principle [16]. Free energy is an information-theoretic quantity that results from sensory inputs (data) and brain states. It provides a probabilistic representation coded by the brain, and a true conditional distribution of the causes of sensory input [251,252]. Within the context of knowledge, free energy allows the brain to minimize variational free energy as predicted by a model (knowledge network), by sampling and re-sampling information acquired during the awake state. This is best carried out during sleep when new sensory inputs are minimized, allowing re-entrant signaling and circuit manipulation. The state of achieving a global minimum each morning, assuming a sound sleep of adequate duration has occurred, may also explain the mental clarity experienced after waking up from a restful sleep. In short, sleep quiets the accumulated excitatory activity, or information overload, via a test of certainty, or justification, to arrive at a truth (elevated certainty) and eventually belief via multiple awake- and sleep-state cycles. These processes are central to knowledge building, as already discussed, and must occur in all species, though the exact mechanisms may differ, to improve decision making and chances of survival in the real world.

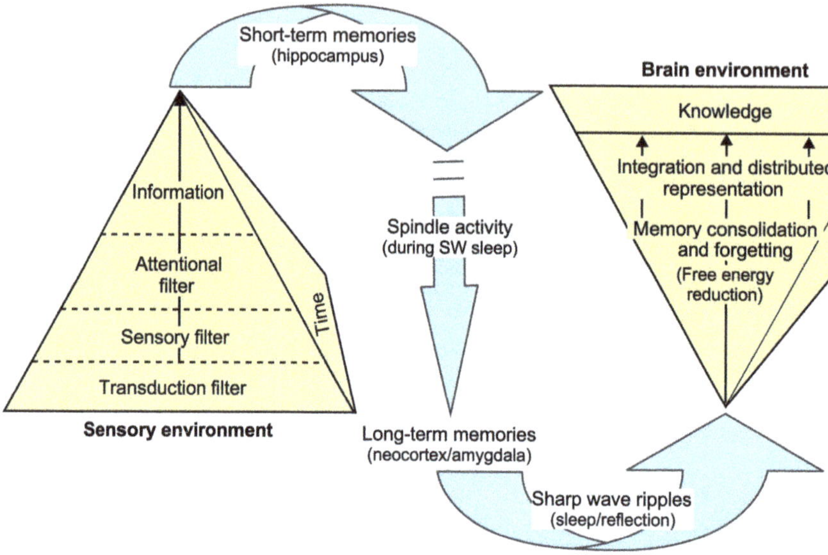

Figure 9. A diagrammatic representation of a "pyramid-inversion model" for the transfer of information over time from the sensory to the brain environment via a series of filters (**left**). The conversion to knowledge (**right**) occurs via oscillatory mechanisms (**middle**) involving the transfer of short-term to long-term memories. The theta band (0.2 to 0.8 Hz oscillations), during the up-state in nonREM sleep, consolidates memories and integrates them with contextual and cross-validated information as knowledge. Delta waves attenuate sleep spindle activity occurring during the down-state of sleep leading to the forgetting and incorporation of new memories [240]. Together with sharp wave ripples (140 to 200 Hz) during sleep and sustained reflection, this activity can modify memories stored within KNs [247,250].

Attention, together with attentional shifts, plays a crucial role in the efficiency and accuracy of knowledge creation, whereas sleep consolidates memories, trashing noise that may manifest itself as dreams. Together with reflection, that in some ways is functionally like a sleep state, sleep may be essential not just for its restorative capacity and memory consolidation, but also to minimize network traffic so that a viable and reliable generative model of the world can exist within KNs. Such models are essential for minimizing prediction errors [253,254]. Without a stable knowledge-based model, humans can become confused and suffer from anxiety/mental illness, leading to poor choices during decision making and action selection.

3.3. Future Directions

Having established the significance of KNs from a perspective covering the areas of philosophy, cognitive psychology, neuroscience and phylogeny, it is important to explore what this might mean for the future. Rather than using drugs that interact nonspecifically at multiple sites within the brain, a KN approach to understanding brain disorders and treatment may usher in the era of electroceuticals, a trend that is already gaining momentum with the use of deep brain stimulation and transcranial magnetic stimulation [255–257]. These interventions can reset and re-organize neural networks in an individual to either restore or bypass network deficits, e.g., in depression [258,259]. An in-depth understanding of how knowledge is embedded within brain networks can positively impact such approaches and lead to interventions to alleviate several brain disorders, such as dyslexia, ADHD and autism.

By integrating neuroscience perspectives, both education and AI can move from rote memorization and big data input, respectively, to systems that are more adaptive, efficient and aligned with the natural learning processes of the human brain. The educational implications of a KN-based approach include a greater acceptance of personalized learning, and an impact on cognitive skill development, as well as the adoption of neuroscientific approaches to early childhood education, and the tackling of emotional and social learning disabilities. A knowledge-driven approach can be used to tailor educational experience to individual learning styles and needs that align with how brain processes route information in different individuals. Cognitive skills could be improved by incorporating insights gained into executive functions like working memory, attention and cognitive flexibility. These insights could inform the development of curricula and teaching methods for strengthening learning skills and information retention.

With respect to AI, we need to create systems that will mimic human learning processes more accurately. This is possible by applying new insights into how the brain learns, e.g., by replicating synaptic plasticity, reinforcement learning and other neural processes embedded within a knowledge-based framework, including KN-inspired algorithms that are based on spike-timing-dependent plasticity and hierarchical processing [260–263]. This will lead to the development of a more robust and adaptive AI. In general, AI can be made more intuitive, and actions/decisions more reliable and meaningful, especially as related to human–AI interactions. In the context of navigation (see Figure 2), robots and autonomous systems that apply principles of sensorimotor integration and adaptive learning can engage in naturalistic interactions with the environment more effectively for various tasks. Many of the details still need to be worked out but this will not happen without incorporating a broader, knowledge-based point-of-view in contrast to a purely memory-driven one. In the end, one is left wondering if there are any limits to the amount of knowledge that can be stored within KNs. Theoretically, the brain's capacity may be infinite, bounded only by biological life time and by brain-size. If so, artificial KNs could easily overcome these limitations, providing practically boundless knowledge.

4. Conclusions

In conclusion, the creation and storage of knowledge in neural networks plays a crucial role in the functioning of the brain and likely a central theme guiding its evolution. Memories over a short term are stored in the hippocampus and distributed throughout the brain for long-term storage in the form of connection strengths within either a local or a distributed network of neurons. Once memories are consolidated and contextualized, they, together with parts of other relevant networks, constitute what is referred to here as a 'knowledge network'. The knowledge can then be accessed via a query for decision making that directs behavior at relevant times and over multiple timescales. Attentional and attention-shifting networks play a key role in the creation, selection and modification of knowledge, and sleep is necessary for establishing knowledge, clearing noisy activity, and readying the brain for the acquisition of new information and/or knowledge. Together, these processes allow organisms to adapt their behavior in response to changes in the environment and survive.

Funding: This research received no external funding.

Institutional Review Board Statement: Not applicable.

Acknowledgments: I thank J. K. Kanwal at Caltech, Pasadena, CA, for her thoughtful feedback from a careful read of the manuscript, and M. S. Kanwal at Stanford University, Palo Alto, CA, for discussions and assistance with the mathematical formulation of knowledge equations. I also wish to thank two anonymous reviewers whose feedback helped to greatly improve the manuscript.

Conflicts of Interest: The author declares no conflicts of interest.

References

1. Ge, J.; Peng, G.; Lyu, B.; Wang, Y.; Zhuo, Y.; Niu, Z.; Tan, L.H.; Leff, A.P.; Gao, J.-H. Cross-language differences in the brain network subserving intelligible speech. *Proc. Natl. Acad. Sci. USA* **2015**, *112*, 2972–2977. [CrossRef] [PubMed]
2. Poeppel, D. The maps problem and the mapping problem: Two challenges for a cognitive neuroscience of speech and language. *Cogn. Neuropsychol.* **2012**, *29*, 34–55. [CrossRef] [PubMed]
3. Si, X.; Zhou, W.; Hong, B. Cooperative cortical network for categorical processing of Chinese lexical tone. *Proc. Natl. Acad. Sci. USA* **2017**, *114*, 12303–12308. [CrossRef] [PubMed]
4. Hickok, G.; Poeppel, D. Dorsal and ventral streams: A framework for understanding aspects of the functional anatomy of language. *Cognition* **2004**, *92*, 67–99. [CrossRef] [PubMed]
5. Wahl, M.; Marzinzik, F.; Friederici, A.D.; Hahne, A.; Kupsch, A.; Schneider, G.-H.; Saddy, D.; Curio, G.; Klostermann, F. The human thalamus processes syntactic and semantic language violations. *Neuron* **2008**, *59*, 695–707. [CrossRef] [PubMed]
6. Cohen, L.; Billard, A. Social babbling: The emergence of symbolic gestures and words. *Neural Netw.* **2018**, *106*, 194–204. [CrossRef] [PubMed]
7. Moser, E.I.; Kropff, E.; Moser, M.-B. Place cells, grid cells, and the brain's spatial representation system. *Annu. Rev. Neurosci.* **2008**, *31*, 69–89. [CrossRef] [PubMed]
8. Solstad, T.; Boccara, C.N.; Kropff, E.; Moser, M.-B.; Moser, E.I. Representation of geometric borders in the entorhinal cortex. *Science* **2008**, *322*, 1865–1868. [CrossRef] [PubMed]
9. Shannon, C.E. A Mathematical Theory of Communication. *Bell Syst. Tech. J.* **1948**, *27*, 379–656. [CrossRef]
10. Nakamura, K.; Komatsu, M. Information seeking mechanism of neural populations in the lateral prefrontal cortex. *Brain Res.* **2019**, *1707*, 79–89. [CrossRef]
11. Nelken, I.; Chechik, G.; Mrsic-Flogel, T.D.; King, A.J.; Schnupp, J.W.H. Encoding stimulus information by spike numbers and mean response time in primary auditory cortex. *J. Comput. Neurosci.* **2005**, *19*, 199–221. [CrossRef] [PubMed]
12. Kayser, C.; Montemurro, M.A.; Logothetis, N.K.; Panzeri, S. Spike-phase coding boosts and stabilizes information carried by spatial and temporal spike patterns. *Neuron* **2009**, *61*, 597–608. [CrossRef] [PubMed]
13. Furukawa, S.; Middlebrooks, J.C. Cortical representation of auditory space: Information-bearing features of spike patterns. *J. Neurophysiol.* **2002**, *87*, 1749–1762. [CrossRef] [PubMed]
14. Averbeck, B.B.; Lee, D. Coding and transmission of information by neural ensembles. *Trends Neurosci.* **2004**, *27*, 225–230. [CrossRef] [PubMed]
15. Lynn, C.W.; Papadopoulos, L.; Kahn, A.E.; Bassett, D.S. Human information processing in complex networks. *Nat. Phys.* **2020**, *16*, 965–973. [CrossRef]
16. Lynn, C.W.; Kahn, A.E.; Nyema, N.; Bassett, D.S. Abstract representations of events arise from mental errors in learning and memory. *Nat. Commun.* **2020**, *11*, 2313. [CrossRef] [PubMed]
17. Steinberg, J.; Sompolinsky, H. Associative memory of structured knowledge. *Sci. Rep.* **2022**, *12*, 21808. [CrossRef] [PubMed]
18. Miller, G.A. The magical number seven, plus or minus two: Some limits on our capacity for processing information. *Psychol. Rev.* **1956**, *63*, 81–97. [CrossRef] [PubMed]
19. Shannon, C.E.; Weaver, W. *The Mathematical Theory of Communication*; The University of Illinois Press: Champaign, IL, USA, 1963.
20. Doeller, C.F.; Barry, C.; Burgess, N. Evidence for grid cells in a human memory network. *Nature* **2010**, *463*, 657–661. [CrossRef]
21. Ferreira, T.L.; Shammah-Lagnado, S.J.; Bueno, O.F.A.; Moreira, K.M.; Fornari, R.V.; Oliveira, M.G.M. The indirect amygdala-dorsal striatum pathway mediates conditioned freezing: Insights on emotional memory networks. *Neuroscience* **2008**, *153*, 84–94. [CrossRef]
22. Krauzlis, R.J.; Bogadhi, A.R.; Herman, J.P.; Bollimunta, A. Selective attention without a neocortex. *Cortex* **2018**, *102*, 161–175. [CrossRef] [PubMed]
23. Lai, C.S.W.; Franke, T.F.; Gan, W.-B. Opposite effects of fear conditioning and extinction on dendritic spine remodelling. *Nature* **2012**, *483*, 87–91. [CrossRef] [PubMed]
24. Nader, K. Memory traces unbound. *Trends Neurosci.* **2003**, *26*, 65–72. [CrossRef] [PubMed]
25. Gottfried, J.A.; Dolan, R.J. Human orbitofrontal cortex mediates extinction learning while accessing conditioned representations of value. *Nat. Neurosci.* **2004**, *7*, 1144–1152. [CrossRef] [PubMed]
26. Suga, N. Principles of auditory information-processing derived from neuroethology. *J. Exp. Biol.* **1989**, *146*, 277–286. [CrossRef] [PubMed]
27. Fujita, I.; Tanaka, K.; Ito, M.; Cheng, K. Columns for visual features of objects in monkey inferotemporal cortex. *Nature* **1992**, *360*, 343–346. [CrossRef] [PubMed]
28. von der Emde, G.; Fetz, S. Distance, shape and more: Recognition of object features during active electrolocation in a weakly electric fish. *J. Exp. Biol.* **2007**, *210*, 3082–3095. [CrossRef] [PubMed]
29. Ehret, G.; Haack, B. Ultrasound recognition in house mice: Key-Stimulus configuration and recognition mechanism. *J. Comp. Physiol.* **1982**, *148*, 245–251. [CrossRef]
30. Kanwal, J.S.; Fitzpatrick, D.C.; Suga, N. Facilitatory and inhibitory frequency tuning of combination-sensitive neurons in the primary auditory cortex of mustached bats. *J. Neurophysiol.* **1999**, *82*, 2327–2345. [CrossRef]
31. Esser, K.H.; Condon, C.J.; Suga, N.; Kanwal, J.S. Syntax processing by auditory cortical neurons in the FM-FM area of the mustached bat Pteronotus parnellii. *Proc. Natl. Acad. Sci. USA* **1997**, *94*, 14019–14024. [CrossRef] [PubMed]

32. Xiao, Z.; Suga, N. Reorganization of the auditory cortex specialized for echo-delay processing in the mustached bat. *Proc. Natl. Acad. Sci. USA* **2004**, *101*, 1769–1774. [CrossRef] [PubMed]
33. Fujita, K.; Kashimori, Y. Neural mechanism of corticofugal modulation of tuning property in frequency domain of bat's auditory system. *Neural Process. Lett.* **2016**, *43*, 537–551. [CrossRef]
34. Grossberg, S. On the development of feature detectors in the visual cortex with applications to learning and reaction-diffusion systems. *Biol. Cybern.* **1976**, *21*, 145–159. [CrossRef]
35. Nelken, I.; Fishbach, A.; Las, L.; Ulanovsky, N.; Farkas, D. Primary auditory cortex of cats: Feature detection or something else? *Biol. Cybern.* **2003**, *89*, 397–406. [CrossRef]
36. Chang, T.R.; Chiu, T.W.; Sun, X.; Poon, P.W.F. Modeling frequency modulated responses of midbrain auditory neurons based on trigger features and artificial neural networks. *Brain Res.* **2012**, *1434*, 90–101. [CrossRef] [PubMed]
37. Goldshtein, A.; Akrish, S.; Giryes, R.; Yovel, Y. An artificial neural network explains how bats might use vision for navigation. *Commun. Biol.* **2022**, *5*, 1325. [CrossRef]
38. Yang, L.; Zhan, X.; Chen, D.; Yan, J.; Loy, C.C.; Lin, D. Learning to cluster faces on an affinity graph. In Proceedings of the 2019 IEEE/CVF Conference on Computer Vision and Pattern Recognition (CVPR), Long Beach, CA, USA, 15–20 June 2019; IEEE: Piscataway, NJ, USA, 2019; pp. 2293–2301.
39. Mahadevkar, S.; Patil, S.; Kotecha, K. Enhancement of handwritten text recognition using AI-based hybrid approach. *MethodsX* **2024**, *12*, 102654. [CrossRef]
40. Diep, Q.B.; Phan, H.Y.; Truong, T.-C. Crossmixed convolutional neural network for digital speech recognition. *PLoS ONE* **2024**, *19*, e0302394. [CrossRef]
41. Suga, N.; O'Neill, W.E. Neural axis representing target range in the auditory cortex of the mustache bat. *Science* **1979**, *206*, 351–353. [CrossRef]
42. Ehret, G.; Bernecker, C. Low-frequency sound communication by mouse pups (Mus musculus): Wriggling calls release maternal behaviour. *Anim. Behav.* **1986**, *34*, 821–830. [CrossRef]
43. Hubel, D.H.; Wiesel, T.N. Receptive fields and functional architecture of monkey striate cortex. *J. Physiol.* **1968**, *195*, 215–243. [CrossRef]
44. Suga, N. Philosophy and stimulus design for neuroethology of complex-sound processing. *Philos. Trans. R. Soc. Lond. B Biol. Sci.* **1992**, *336*, 423–428. [CrossRef]
45. Suga, N. Analysis of information-bearing elements in complex sounds by auditory neurons of bats. *Audiology* **1972**, *11*, 58–72. [CrossRef] [PubMed]
46. Suga, N.; Niwa, H.; Taniguchi, I.; Margoliash, D. The personalized auditory cortex of the mustached bat: Adaptation for echolocation. *J. Neurophysiol.* **1987**, *58*, 643–654. [CrossRef]
47. Mendoza Nava, H.; Holderied, M.W.; Pirrera, A.; Groh, R.M.J. Buckling-induced sound production in the aeroelastic tymbals of Yponomeuta. *Proc. Natl. Acad. Sci. USA* **2024**, *121*, e2313549121. [CrossRef] [PubMed]
48. Baier, A.L.; Stelzer, K.-J.; Wiegrebe, L. Flutter sensitivity in FM bats. Part II: Amplitude modulation. *J. Comp. Physiol. A Neuroethol. Sens. Neural Behav. Physiol.* **2018**, *204*, 941–951. [CrossRef] [PubMed]
49. Kuwabara, N.; Suga, N. Delay lines and amplitude selectivity are created in subthalamic auditory nuclei: The brachium of the inferior colliculus of the mustached bat. *J. Neurophysiol.* **1993**, *69*, 1713–1724. [CrossRef]
50. Washington, S.D.; Kanwal, J.S. DSCF neurons within the primary auditory cortex of the mustached bat process frequency modulations present within social calls. *J. Neurophysiol.* **2008**, *100*, 3285–3304. [CrossRef]
51. Ma, J.; Naumann, R.T.; Kanwal, J.S. Fear conditioned discrimination of frequency modulated sweeps within species-specific calls of mustached bats. *PLoS ONE* **2010**, *5*, e10579. [CrossRef]
52. Andoni, S.; Pollak, G.D. Selectivity for spectral motion as a neural computation for encoding natural communication signals in bat inferior colliculus. *J. Neurosci.* **2011**, *31*, 16529–16540. [CrossRef]
53. Giraudet, P.; Berthommier, F.; Chaput, M. Mitral cell temporal response patterns evoked by odor mixtures in the rat olfactory bulb. *J. Neurophysiol.* **2002**, *88*, 829–838. [CrossRef] [PubMed]
54. Lindsay, S.M.; Vogt, R.G. Behavioral responses of newly hatched zebrafish (Danio rerio) to amino acid chemostimulants. *Chem. Senses* **2004**, *29*, 93–100. [CrossRef] [PubMed]
55. Sigala, N.; Logothetis, N.K. Visual categorization shapes feature selectivity in the primate temporal cortex. *Nature* **2002**, *415*, 318–320. [CrossRef] [PubMed]
56. Ramkumar, P.; Jas, M.; Pannasch, S.; Hari, R.; Parkkonen, L. Feature-specific information processing precedes concerted activation in human visual cortex. *J. Neurosci.* **2013**, *33*, 7691–7699. [CrossRef]
57. Romanski, L.M.; Averbeck, B.B.; Diltz, M. Neural representation of vocalizations in the primate ventrolateral prefrontal cortex. *J. Neurophysiol.* **2005**, *93*, 734–747. [CrossRef] [PubMed]
58. Romanski, L.M.; Averbeck, B.B. The primate cortical auditory system and neural representation of conspecific vocalizations. *Annu. Rev. Neurosci.* **2009**, *32*, 315–346. [CrossRef] [PubMed]
59. Washington, S.D.; Kanwal, J.S. Excitatory tuning to upward and downward directions of frequency-modulated sweeps in the primary auditory cortex. In Proceedings of the Society for Neuroscience, Washington, DC, USA, 12–16 November 2005; Volume 35.

60. Kanwal, J.S.; Gordon, M.; Peng, J.P.; Heinz-Esser, K. Auditory responses from the frontal cortex in the mustached bat, *Pteronotus parnellii*. *NeuroReport* **2000**, *11*, 367–372. [CrossRef] [PubMed]
61. Fitzpatrick, D.C.; Kanwal, J.S.; Butman, J.A.; Suga, N. Combination-sensitive neurons in the primary auditory cortex of the mustached bat. *J. Neurosci.* **1993**, *13*, 931–940. [CrossRef]
62. Averbeck, B.B.; Romanski, L.M. Probabilistic encoding of vocalizations in macaque ventral lateral prefrontal cortex. *J. Neurosci.* **2006**, *26*, 11023–11033. [CrossRef]
63. Wagatsuma, N.; Hidaka, A.; Tamura, H. Correspondence between Monkey Visual Cortices and Layers of a Saliency Map Model Based on a Deep Convolutional Neural Network for Representations of Natural Images. *eNeuro* **2021**, *8*, 1–19. [CrossRef]
64. Gallant, J.L.; Braun, J.; Van Essen, D.C. Selectivity for polar, hyperbolic, and Cartesian gratings in macaque visual cortex. *Science* **1993**, *259*, 100–103. [CrossRef]
65. Oliva, A.; Torralba, A. The role of context in object recognition. *Trends Cogn. Sci.* **2007**, *11*, 520–527. [CrossRef]
66. Stoll, J.; Thrun, M.; Nuthmann, A.; Einhäuser, W. Overt attention in natural scenes: Objects dominate features. *Vision. Res.* **2015**, *107*, 36–48. [CrossRef]
67. Suga, N.; Gao, E.; Zhang, Y.; Ma, X.; Olsen, J.F. The corticofugal system for hearing: Recent progress. *Proc. Natl. Acad. Sci. USA* **2000**, *97*, 11807–11814. [CrossRef]
68. Messinger, A.; Squire, L.R.; Zola, S.M.; Albright, T.D. Neural correlates of knowledge: Stable representation of stimulus associations across variations in behavioral performance. *Neuron* **2005**, *48*, 359–371. [CrossRef]
69. Patterson, K.; Nestor, P.J.; Rogers, T.T. Where do you know what you know? The representation of semantic knowledge in the human brain. *Nat. Rev. Neurosci.* **2007**, *8*, 976–987. [CrossRef] [PubMed]
70. Knowledge. Available online: https://en.wikipedia.org/wiki/Knowledge (accessed on 15 January 2024).
71. Kump, B.; Moskaliuk, J.; Cress, U.; Kimmerle, J. Cognitive foundations of organizational learning: Re-introducing the distinction between declarative and non-declarative knowledge. *Front. Psychol.* **2015**, *6*, 1489. [CrossRef]
72. Hansson, I.; Buratti, S.; Allwood, C.M. Experts' and novices' perception of ignorance and knowledge in different research disciplines and its relation to belief in certainty of knowledge. *Front. Psychol.* **2017**, *8*, 377. [CrossRef] [PubMed]
73. Howlett, J.R.; Paulus, M.P. The neural basis of testable and non-testable beliefs. *PLoS ONE* **2015**, *10*, e0124596. [CrossRef] [PubMed]
74. Sainburg, T.; Gentner, T.Q. Toward a computational neuroethology of vocal communication: From bioacoustics to neurophysiology, emerging tools and future directions. *Front. Behav. Neurosci.* **2021**, *15*, 811737. [CrossRef]
75. Wagner, H.; Egelhaaf, M.; Carr, C. Model organisms and systems in neuroethology: One hundred years of history and a look into the future. *J. Comp. Physiol. A Neuroethol. Sens. Neural Behav. Physiol.* **2024**, *210*, 227–242. [CrossRef]
76. Lambert, K. Wild brains: The value of neuroethological approaches in preclinical behavioral neuroscience animal models. *Neurosci. Biobehav. Rev.* **2023**, *146*, 105044. [CrossRef] [PubMed]
77. Roth, R.H.; Ding, J.B. From neurons to cognition: Technologies for precise recording of neural activity underlying behavior. *BME Front.* **2020**, *2020*, 7190517. [CrossRef] [PubMed]
78. Du, J.; Riedel-Kruse, I.H.; Nawroth, J.C.; Roukes, M.L.; Laurent, G.; Masmanidis, S.C. High-resolution three-dimensional extracellular recording of neuronal activity with microfabricated electrode arrays. *J. Neurophysiol.* **2009**, *101*, 1671–1678. [CrossRef]
79. O'Keefe, J. A computational theory of the hippocampal cognitive map. *Prog. Brain Res.* **1990**, *83*, 301–312. [PubMed]
80. Lever, C.; Wills, T.; Cacucci, F.; Burgess, N.; O'Keefe, J. Long-term plasticity in hippocampal place-cell representation of environmental geometry. *Nature* **2002**, *416*, 90–94. [CrossRef]
81. Moser, E.I.; Moser, M.-B.; McNaughton, B.L. Spatial representation in the hippocampal formation: A history. *Nat. Neurosci.* **2017**, *20*, 1448–1464. [CrossRef]
82. Finkelstein, A.; Derdikman, D.; Rubin, A.; Foerster, J.N.; Las, L.; Ulanovsky, N. Three-dimensional head-direction coding in the bat brain. *Nature* **2015**, *517*, 159–164. [CrossRef]
83. Geva-Sagiv, M.; Las, L.; Yovel, Y.; Ulanovsky, N. Spatial cognition in bats and rats: From sensory acquisition to multiscale maps and navigation. *Nat. Rev. Neurosci.* **2015**, *16*, 94–108. [CrossRef]
84. Mello, C.V.; Ribeiro, S. ZENK protein regulation by song in the brain of songbirds. *J. Comp. Neurol.* **1998**, *393*, 426–438. [CrossRef]
85. Jarvis, E.D.; Mello, C.V. Molecular mapping of brain areas involved in parrot vocal communication. *J. Comp. Neurol.* **2000**, *419*, 1–31. [CrossRef]
86. Chatterjee, D.; Tran, S.; Shams, S.; Gerlai, R. A Simple Method for Immunohistochemical Staining of Zebrafish Brain Sections for c-fos Protein Expression. *Zebrafish* **2015**, *12*, 414–420. [CrossRef]
87. Guthrie, K.M.; Anderson, A.J.; Leon, M.; Gall, C. Odor-induced increases in c-fos mRNA expression reveal an anatomical "unit" for odor processing in olfactory bulb. *Proc. Natl. Acad. Sci. USA* **1993**, *90*, 3329–3333. [CrossRef] [PubMed]
88. Fosque, B.F.; Sun, Y.; Dana, H.; Yang, C.-T.; Ohyama, T.; Tadross, M.R.; Patel, R.; Zlatic, M.; Kim, D.S.; Ahrens, M.B.; et al. Neural circuits. Labeling of active neural circuits in vivo with designed calcium integrators. *Science* **2015**, *347*, 755–760. [CrossRef]
89. Christophel, T.B. Distributed Visual Working Memory Stores Revealed by Multivariate Pattern Analyses. *J. Vis.* **2015**, *15*, 1407. [CrossRef]
90. Linden, D.E.J. The working memory networks of the human brain. *Neuroscientist* **2007**, *13*, 257–267. [CrossRef]
91. Sauseng, P.; Klimesch, W.; Heise, K.F.; Gruber, W.R.; Holz, E.; Karim, A.A.; Glennon, M.; Gerloff, C.; Birbaumer, N.; Hummel, F.C. Brain oscillatory substrates of visual short-term memory capacity. *Curr. Biol.* **2009**, *19*, 1846–1852. [CrossRef]

92. Fiebig, F.; Lansner, A. Memory consolidation from seconds to weeks: A three-stage neural network model with autonomous reinstatement dynamics. *Front. Comput. Neurosci.* **2014**, *8*, 64. [CrossRef] [PubMed]
93. Schafe, G.E.; LeDoux, J.E. Memory consolidation of auditory pavlovian fear conditioning requires protein synthesis and protein kinase A in the amygdala. *J. Neurosci.* **2000**, *20*, RC96. [CrossRef]
94. Gal-Ben-Ari, S.; Rosenblum, K. Molecular mechanisms underlying memory consolidation of taste information in the cortex. *Front. Behav. Neurosci.* **2011**, *5*, 87. [CrossRef]
95. Izquierdo, I.; Medina, J.H. Role of the amygdala, hippocampus and entorhinal cortex in memory consolidation and expression. *Braz. J. Med. Biol. Res.* **1993**, *26*, 573–589.
96. McEwen, B.S. Mood disorders and allostatic load. *Biol. Psychiatry* **2003**, *54*, 200–207. [CrossRef]
97. Toledo-Rodriguez, M.; Sandi, C. Stress during Adolescence Increases Novelty Seeking and Risk-Taking Behavior in Male and Female Rats. *Front. Behav. Neurosci.* **2011**, *5*, 17. [CrossRef]
98. Shekhar, A.; Truitt, W.; Rainnie, D.; Sajdyk, T. Role of stress, corticotrophin releasing factor (CRF) and amygdala plasticity in chronic anxiety. *Stress* **2005**, *8*, 209–219. [CrossRef]
99. Andersen, S.L.; Teicher, M.H. Stress, sensitive periods and maturational events in adolescent depression. *Trends Neurosci.* **2008**, *31*, 183–191. [CrossRef]
100. Krugers, H.J.; Lucassen, P.J.; Karst, H.; Joëls, M. Chronic stress effects on hippocampal structure and synaptic function: Relevance for depression and normalization by anti-glucocorticoid treatment. *Front. Synaptic Neurosci.* **2010**, *2*, 24. [CrossRef]
101. McEwen, B.S. Early life influences on life-long patterns of behavior and health. *Ment. Retard. Dev. Disabil. Res. Rev.* **2003**, *9*, 149–154. [CrossRef]
102. Evans, J.R.; Torres-Pérez, J.V.; Miletto Petrazzini, M.E.; Riley, R.; Brennan, C.H. Stress reactivity elicits a tissue-specific reduction in telomere length in aging zebrafish (Danio rerio). *Sci. Rep.* **2021**, *11*, 339. [CrossRef]
103. Cleber Gama de Barcellos Filho, P.; Campos Zanelatto, L.; Amélia Aparecida Santana, B.; Calado, R.T.; Rodrigues Franci, C. Effects chronic administration of corticosterone and estrogen on HPA axis activity and telomere length in brain areas of female rats. *Brain Res.* **2021**, *1750*, 147152. [CrossRef]
104. Maguire, E.A.; Frith, C.D. The brain network associated with acquiring semantic knowledge. *Neuroimage* **2004**, *22*, 171–178. [CrossRef]
105. Kotkat, A.H.; Katzner, S.; Busse, L. Neural networks: Explaining animal behavior with prior knowledge of the world. *Curr. Biol.* **2023**, *33*, R138–R140. [CrossRef]
106. Livingstone, M.; Hubel, D. Segregation of form, color, movement, and depth: Anatomy, physiology, and perception. *Science* **1988**, *240*, 740–749. [CrossRef]
107. Baumgärtel, K.; Genoux, D.; Welzl, H.; Tweedie-Cullen, R.Y.; Koshibu, K.; Livingstone-Zatchej, M.; Mamie, C.; Mansuy, I.M. Control of the establishment of aversive memory by calcineurin and Zif268. *Nat. Neurosci.* **2008**, *11*, 572–578. [CrossRef]
108. Moser, M.B.; Moser, E.I. Functional differentiation in the hippocampus. *Hippocampus* **1998**, *8*, 608–619. [CrossRef]
109. Fanselow, M.S.; Dong, H.-W. Are the dorsal and ventral hippocampus functionally distinct structures? *Neuron* **2010**, *65*, 7–19. [CrossRef]
110. White, N.M.; McDonald, R.J. Acquisition of a spatial conditioned place preference is impaired by amygdala lesions and improved by fornix lesions. *Behav. Brain Res.* **1993**, *55*, 269–281. [CrossRef]
111. Pikkarainen, M.; Rönkkö, S.; Savander, V.; Insausti, R.; Pitkänen, A. Projections from the lateral, basal, and accessory basal nuclei of the amygdala to the hippocampal formation in rat. *J. Comp. Neurol.* **1999**, *403*, 229–260. [CrossRef]
112. Ghashghaei, H.T.; Hilgetag, C.C.; Barbas, H. Sequence of information processing for emotions based on the anatomic dialogue between prefrontal cortex and amygdala. *Neuroimage* **2007**, *34*, 905–923. [CrossRef]
113. Fernández-Ruiz, A.; Oliva, A.; Nagy, G.A.; Maurer, A.P.; Berényi, A.; Buzsáki, G. Entorhinal-CA3 Dual-Input Control of Spike Timing in the Hippocampus by Theta-Gamma Coupling. *Neuron* **2017**, *93*, 1213–1226. [CrossRef]
114. Aoi, M.C.; Mante, V.; Pillow, J.W. Prefrontal cortex exhibits multidimensional dynamic encoding during decision-making. *Nat. Neurosci.* **2020**, *23*, 1410–1420. [CrossRef]
115. Knight, R.T.; Stuss, D.T. Prefrontal cortex: The present and the future. In *Principles of Frontal Lobe Function*; Stuss, D.T., Knight, R.T., Eds.; Oxford University Press: New York, NY, USA, 2002; pp. 573–598, ISBN 9780195134971.
116. Grossberg, S. A neural model of intrinsic and extrinsic hippocampal theta rhythms: Anatomy, neurophysiology, and function. *Front. Syst. Neurosci.* **2021**, *15*, 665052. [CrossRef] [PubMed]
117. Carpenter, G.A.; Grossberg, S.; Mehanian, C. Invariant recognition of cluttered scenes by a self-organizing ART architecture: CORT-X boundary segmentation. *Neural Netw.* **1989**, *2*, 169–181. [CrossRef]
118. Freeman, W.J. *Mass Action in the Nervous System*; Academic Press: New York, NY, USA, 1975; ISBN 9780122671500.
119. Buzsáki, G.; Moser, E.I. Memory, navigation and theta rhythm in the hippocampal-entorhinal system. *Nat. Neurosci.* **2013**, *16*, 130–138. [CrossRef] [PubMed]
120. Bermudez-Contreras, E.; Clark, B.J.; Wilber, A. The neuroscience of spatial navigation and the relationship to artificial intelligence. *Front. Comput. Neurosci.* **2020**, *14*, 63. [CrossRef] [PubMed]
121. Rolls, E.T.; Treves, A. A theory of hippocampal function: New developments. *Prog. Neurobiol.* **2024**, *238*, 102636. [CrossRef] [PubMed]
122. Treves, A.; Rolls, E.T. Computational analysis of the role of the hippocampus in memory. *Hippocampus* **1994**, *4*, 374–391. [CrossRef]

123. Rolls, E.T. Neurons including hippocampal spatial view cells, and navigation in primates including humans. *Hippocampus* **2021**, *31*, 593–611. [CrossRef] [PubMed]
124. Kohler, E.; Keysers, C.; Umiltà, M.A.; Fogassi, L.; Gallese, V.; Rizzolatti, G. Hearing sounds, understanding actions: Action representation in mirror neurons. *Science* **2002**, *297*, 846–848. [CrossRef]
125. Heyes, C. Where do mirror neurons come from? *Neurosci. Biobehav. Rev.* **2010**, *34*, 575–583. [CrossRef]
126. Keysers, C.; Gazzola, V. Hebbian learning and predictive mirror neurons for actions, sensations and emotions. *Philos. Trans. R. Soc. Lond. B Biol. Sci.* **2014**, *369*, 20130175. [CrossRef] [PubMed]
127. Briggman, K.L.; Kristan, W.B. Multifunctional pattern-generating circuits. *Annu. Rev. Neurosci.* **2008**, *31*, 271–294. [CrossRef] [PubMed]
128. Queenan, B.N.; Zhang, Z.; Ma, J.; Naumann, R.T.; Mazhar, S.; Kanwal, J.S. Multifunctional cortical neurons exhibit response enhancement during rapid switching from echolocation to communication sound processing. In Proceedings of the Society for Neuroscience, Abstract #275.21, San Diego, CA, USA, 13–17 November 2010.
129. Suga, N. Multi-function theory for cortical processing of auditory information: Implications of single-unit and lesion data for future research. *J. Comp. Physiol. A* **1994**, *175*, 135–144. [CrossRef] [PubMed]
130. Parker, J.; Khwaja, R.; Cymbalyuk, G. Asymmetric control of coexisting slow and fast rhythms in a multifunctional central pattern generator: A model study. *Neurophysiology* **2019**, *51*, 390–399. [CrossRef]
131. Mahon, B.Z.; Caramazza, A. What drives the organization of object knowledge in the brain? *Trends Cogn. Sci.* **2011**, *15*, 97–103. [CrossRef] [PubMed]
132. Martin, A.; Wiggs, C.L.; Ungerleider, L.G.; Haxby, J.V. Neural correlates of category-specific knowledge. *Nature* **1996**, *379*, 649–652. [CrossRef] [PubMed]
133. Eiermann, A.; Esser, K.H. Auditory responses from the frontal cortex in the short-tailed fruit bat *Carollia perspicillata*. *NeuroReport* **2000**, *11*, 421–425. [CrossRef] [PubMed]
134. Hage, S.R. Auditory and audio-vocal responses of single neurons in the monkey ventral premotor cortex. *Hear. Res.* **2018**, *366*, 82–89. [CrossRef] [PubMed]
135. Nicolelis, M.A.L. Computing with thalamocortical ensembles during different behavioural states. *J. Physiol.* **2005**, *566*, 37–47. [CrossRef]
136. Pugh, K.; Prusak, L. *Designing Effective Knowledge Networks*; MIT Press: Cambridge, MA, USA, 2013.
137. García-Rosales, F.; López-Jury, L.; González-Palomares, E.; Wetekam, J.; Cabral-Calderín, Y.; Kiai, A.; Kössl, M.; Hechavarría, J.C. Echolocation-related reversal of information flow in a cortical vocalization network. *Nat. Commun.* **2022**, *13*, 3642. [CrossRef] [PubMed]
138. Hackett, T.A. Information flow in the auditory cortical network. *Hear. Res.* **2011**, *271*, 133–146. [CrossRef]
139. Bowers, J.S.; Vankov, I.I.; Damian, M.F.; Davis, C.J. Why do some neurons in cortex respond to information in a selective manner? Insights from artificial neural networks. *Cognition* **2016**, *148*, 47–63. [CrossRef] [PubMed]
140. Bullmore, E.; Sporns, O. Complex brain networks: Graph theoretical analysis of structural and functional systems. *Nat. Rev. Neurosci.* **2009**, *10*, 186–198. [CrossRef] [PubMed]
141. Feldt, S.; Bonifazi, P.; Cossart, R. Dissecting functional connectivity of neuronal microcircuits: Experimental and theoretical insights. *Trends Neurosci.* **2011**, *34*, 225–236. [CrossRef] [PubMed]
142. Izhikevich, E.M. *Dynamical Systems in Neuroscience: The Geometry of Excitability and Bursting*; The MIT Press: Cambridge, MA, USA, 2006; ISBN 9780262276078.
143. Evans, L.C. *Partial Differential Equations (The Graduate Studies in Mathematics, 19)*, 2nd ed.; American Mathematical Society: Providence, RL, USA, 2022; p. 662, ISBN 978-1-4704-6942-9.
144. Sacramento, J.; Wichert, A.; van Rossum, M.C.W. Energy Efficient Sparse Connectivity from Imbalanced Synaptic Plasticity Rules. *PLoS Comput. Biol.* **2015**, *11*, e1004265. [CrossRef] [PubMed]
145. Kanwal, J.S.; Peng, J.P.; Esser, K.H. Auditory communication and echolocation in the mustached bat: Computing for dual functions within single neurons. In *Echolocation in Bats and Dolphins*; Thomas, J.A., Moss, C.J., Vater, M., Eds.; University of Chicago Press: Chicago, IL, USA, 2004; pp. 201–208.
146. Santiago, A.F. Plasticity in the Prairie Vole: Contextual Factors and Molecular Mechanisms Modulating Bond Plasticity in the Prairie Vole (*Microtus ochrogaster*). Doctoral Dissertation, Cornell University, Ithaca, NY, USA, 2024.
147. Cho, J.Y.; Sternberg, P.W. Multilevel modulation of a sensory motor circuit during C. elegans sleep and arousal. *Cell* **2014**, *156*, 249–260. [CrossRef] [PubMed]
148. Takeishi, A.; Yeon, J.; Harris, N.; Yang, W.; Sengupta, P. Feeding state functionally reconfigures a sensory circuit to drive thermosensory behavioral plasticity. *eLife* **2020**, *9*, e61167. [CrossRef] [PubMed]
149. Voigt, K.; Razi, A.; Harding, I.H.; Andrews, Z.B.; Verdejo-Garcia, A. Neural network modelling reveals changes in directional connectivity between cortical and hypothalamic regions with increased BMI. *Int. J. Obes.* **2021**, *45*, 2447–2454. [CrossRef] [PubMed]
150. Dupre, C.; Yuste, R. Non-overlapping Neural Networks in Hydra vulgaris. *Curr. Biol.* **2017**, *27*, 1085–1097. [CrossRef] [PubMed]
151. Keramidioti, A.; Schneid, S.; Busse, C.; von Laue, C.C.; Bertulat, B.; Salvenmoser, W.; Heß, M.; Alexandrova, O.; Glauber, K.M.; Steele, R.E.; et al. A new look at the architecture and dynamics of the Hydra nerve net. *eLife* **2024**, *12*, RP87330. [CrossRef]

152. Musser, J.M.; Schippers, K.J.; Nickel, M.; Mizzon, G.; Kohn, A.B.; Pape, C.; Ronchi, P.; Papadopoulos, N.; Tarashansky, A.J.; Hammel, J.U.; et al. Profiling cellular diversity in sponges informs animal cell type and nervous system evolution. *Science* **2021**, *374*, 717–723. [CrossRef]
153. Schnell, A.K.; Amodio, P.; Boeckle, M.; Clayton, N.S. How intelligent is a cephalopod? Lessons from comparative cognition. *Biol. Rev. Camb. Philos. Soc.* **2021**, *96*, 162–178. [CrossRef] [PubMed]
154. Parent, A.; Hazrati, L.N. Functional anatomy of the basal ganglia. I. The cortico-basal ganglia-thalamo-cortical loop. *Brain Res. Brain Res. Rev.* **1995**, *20*, 91–127. [CrossRef] [PubMed]
155. Braine, A.; Georges, F. Emotion in action: When emotions meet motor circuits. *Neurosci. Biobehav. Rev.* **2023**, *155*, 105475. [CrossRef] [PubMed]
156. Lettvin, J.; Maturana, H.; McCulloch, W.; Pitts, W. What the Frog's Eye Tells the Frog's Brain. *Proc. IRE* **1959**, *47*, 1940–1951. [CrossRef]
157. Maisak, M.S.; Haag, J.; Ammer, G.; Serbe, E.; Meier, M.; Leonhardt, A.; Schilling, T.; Bahl, A.; Rubin, G.M.; Nern, A.; et al. A directional tuning map of Drosophila elementary motion detectors. *Nature* **2013**, *500*, 212–216. [CrossRef] [PubMed]
158. Edens, B.M.; Stundl, J.; Urrutia, H.A.; Bronner, M.E. Neural crest origin of sympathetic neurons at the dawn of vertebrates. *Nature* **2024**, *629*, 121–126. [CrossRef] [PubMed]
159. Bedois, A.M.H.; Parker, H.J.; Price, A.J.; Morrison, J.A.; Bronner, M.E.; Krumlauf, R. Sea lamprey enlightens the origin of the coupling of retinoic acid signaling to vertebrate hindbrain segmentation. *Nat. Commun.* **2024**, *15*, 1538. [CrossRef] [PubMed]
160. Corominas-Murtra, B.; Goñi, J.; Solé, R.V.; Rodríguez-Caso, C. On the origins of hierarchy in complex networks. *Proc. Natl. Acad. Sci. USA* **2013**, *110*, 13316–13321. [CrossRef] [PubMed]
161. Watabe-Uchida, M.; Eshel, N.; Uchida, N. Neural circuitry of reward prediction error. *Annu. Rev. Neurosci.* **2017**, *40*, 373–394. [CrossRef]
162. Riceberg, J.S.; Shapiro, M.L. Orbitofrontal Cortex Signals Expected Outcomes with Predictive Codes When Stable Contingencies Promote the Integration of Reward History. *J. Neurosci.* **2017**, *37*, 2010–2021. [CrossRef]
163. Jordan, R. The locus coeruleus as a global model failure system. *Trends Neurosci.* **2024**, *47*, 92–105. [CrossRef]
164. Korzyukov, O.; Lee, Y.; Bronder, A.; Wagner, M.; Gumenyuk, V.; Larson, C.R.; Hammer, M.J. Auditory-vocal control system is object for predictive processing within seconds time range. *Brain Res.* **2020**, *1732*, 146703. [CrossRef]
165. Mikulasch, F.A.; Rudelt, L.; Wibral, M.; Priesemann, V. Where is the error? Hierarchical predictive coding through dendritic error computation. *Trends Neurosci.* **2023**, *46*, 45–59. [CrossRef]
166. Goldberg, J.M.; Fernandez, C. Physiology of peripheral neurons innervating semicircular canals of the squirrel monkey. I. Resting discharge and response to constant angular accelerations. *J. Neurophysiol.* **1971**, *34*, 635–660. [CrossRef]
167. Knafo, S.; Wyart, C. Active mechanosensory feedback during locomotion in the zebrafish spinal cord. *Curr. Opin. Neurobiol.* **2018**, *52*, 48–53. [CrossRef]
168. Henderson, K.W.; Menelaou, E.; Hale, M.E. Sensory neurons in the spinal cord of zebrafish and their local connectivity. *Curr. Opin. Physiol.* **2019**, *8*, 136–140. [CrossRef]
169. Bottjer, S.W. Silent synapses in a thalamo-cortical circuit necessary for song learning in zebra finches. *J. Neurophysiol.* **2005**, *94*, 3698–3707. [CrossRef]
170. Xu, W.; Löwel, S.; Schlüter, O.M. Silent Synapse-Based Mechanisms of Critical Period Plasticity. *Front. Cell. Neurosci.* **2020**, *14*, 213. [CrossRef] [PubMed]
171. Buhusi, C.V. The across-fiber pattern theory and fuzzy logic: A matter of taste. *Physiol. Behav.* **2000**, *69*, 97–106. [CrossRef] [PubMed]
172. Kanwal, J.S.; Ehret, G. *Behavior and Neurodynamics for Auditory Communication*; Cambridge University Press: Cambridge, UK, 2006.
173. Vlamou, E.; Papadopoulos, B. Fuzzy logic systems and medical applications. *AIMS Neurosci.* **2019**, *6*, 266–272. [CrossRef] [PubMed]
174. Cacciatore, S.; Luchinat, C.; Tenori, L. Knowledge discovery by accuracy maximization. *Proc. Natl. Acad. Sci. USA* **2014**, *111*, 5117–5122. [CrossRef] [PubMed]
175. Brede, M.; Stella, M.; Kalloniatis, A.C. Competitive influence maximization and enhancement of synchronization in populations of non-identical Kuramoto oscillators. *Sci. Rep.* **2018**, *8*, 702. [CrossRef] [PubMed]
176. Nikonov, A.A.; Finger, T.E.; Caprio, J. Beyond the olfactory bulb: An odotopic map in the forebrain. *Proc. Natl. Acad. Sci. USA* **2005**, *102*, 18688–18693. [CrossRef] [PubMed]
177. Fuss, S.H.; Korsching, S.I. Odorant feature detection: Activity mapping of structure response relationships in the zebrafish olfactory bulb. *J. Neurosci.* **2001**, *21*, 8396–8407. [CrossRef]
178. Stettler, D.D.; Axel, R. Representations of odor in the piriform cortex. *Neuron* **2009**, *63*, 854–864. [CrossRef] [PubMed]
179. Wang, F.; Nemes, A.; Mendelsohn, M.; Axel, R. Odorant receptors govern the formation of a precise topographic map. *Cell* **1998**, *93*, 47–60. [CrossRef] [PubMed]
180. Ohlemiller, K.K.; Kanwal, J.S.; Suga, N. Facilitative responses to species-specific calls in cortical FM-FM neurons of the mustached bat. *NeuroReport* **1996**, *7*, 1749–1755. [CrossRef] [PubMed]
181. García-Rosales, F.; López-Jury, L.; González-Palomares, E.; Cabral-Calderín, Y.; Hechavarría, J.C. Fronto-Temporal Coupling Dynamics During Spontaneous Activity and Auditory Processing in the Bat Carollia perspicillata. *Front. Syst. Neurosci.* **2020**, *14*, 14. [CrossRef] [PubMed]

182. Martin, L.M.; García-Rosales, F.; Beetz, M.J.; Hechavarría, J.C. Processing of temporally patterned sounds in the auditory cortex of Seba's short-tailed bat, *Carollia perspicillata*. *Eur. J. Neurosci.* **2017**, *46*, 2365–2379. [CrossRef] [PubMed]
183. Tseng, Y.-L.; Liu, H.-H.; Liou, M.; Tsai, A.C.; Chien, V.S.C.; Shyu, S.-T.; Yang, Z.-S. Lingering Sound: Event-Related Phase-Amplitude Coupling and Phase-Locking in Fronto-Temporo-Parietal Functional Networks During Memory Retrieval of Music Melodies. *Front. Hum. Neurosci.* **2019**, *13*, 150. [CrossRef]
184. Yang, L.; Chen, X.; Yang, L.; Li, M.; Shang, Z. Phase-Amplitude Coupling between Theta Rhythm and High-Frequency Oscillations in the Hippocampus of Pigeons during Navigation. *Animals* **2024**, *14*, 439. [CrossRef] [PubMed]
185. Vivekananda, U.; Bush, D.; Bisby, J.A.; Baxendale, S.; Rodionov, R.; Diehl, B.; Chowdhury, F.A.; McEvoy, A.W.; Miserocchi, A.; Walker, M.C.; et al. Theta power and theta-gamma coupling support long-term spatial memory retrieval. *Hippocampus* **2021**, *31*, 213–220. [CrossRef]
186. Daume, J.; Kamiński, J.; Schjetnan, A.G.P.; Salimpour, Y.; Khan, U.; Kyzar, M.; Reed, C.M.; Anderson, W.S.; Valiante, T.A.; Mamelak, A.N.; et al. Control of working memory by phase-amplitude coupling of human hippocampal neurons. *Nature* **2024**, *629*, 393–401. [CrossRef]
187. Mohan, U.R.; Zhang, H.; Ermentrout, B.; Jacobs, J. The direction of theta and alpha travelling waves modulates human memory processing. *Nat. Hum. Behav.* **2024**, *8*, 1124–1135. [CrossRef] [PubMed]
188. Aggarwal, A.; Brennan, C.; Luo, J.; Chung, H.; Contreras, D.; Kelz, M.B.; Proekt, A. Visual evoked feedforward-feedback traveling waves organize neural activity across the cortical hierarchy in mice. *Nat. Commun.* **2022**, *13*, 4754. [CrossRef] [PubMed]
189. Wu, Y.; Chen, Z.S. Computational models for state-dependent traveling waves in hippocampal formation. *BioRxiv* **2023**. [CrossRef]
190. Wu, J.Y.; Guan, L.; Bai, L.; Yang, Q. Spatiotemporal properties of an evoked population activity in rat sensory cortical slices. *J. Neurophysiol.* **2001**, *86*, 2461–2474. [CrossRef]
191. Erkol, Ş.; Mazzilli, D.; Radicchi, F. Influence maximization on temporal networks. *Phys. Rev. E* **2020**, *102*, 042307. [CrossRef]
192. Medvedev, A.V.; Chiao, F.; Kanwal, J.S. Modeling complex tone perception: Grouping harmonics with combination-sensitive neurons. *Biol. Cybern.* **2002**, *86*, 497–505. [CrossRef] [PubMed]
193. Aharon, G.; Sadot, M.; Yovel, Y. Bats Use Path Integration Rather Than Acoustic Flow to Assess Flight Distance along Flyways. *Curr. Biol.* **2017**, *27*, 3650–3657.e3. [CrossRef]
194. Merlin, C.; Gegear, R.J.; Reppert, S.M. Antennal circadian clocks coordinate sun compass orientation in migratory monarch butterflies. *Science* **2009**, *325*, 1700–1704. [CrossRef] [PubMed]
195. Shukla, V.; Rani, S.; Malik, S.; Kumar, V.; Sadananda, M. Neuromorphometric changes associated with photostimulated migratory phenotype in the Palaearctic-Indian male redheaded bunting. *Exp. Brain Res.* **2020**, *238*, 2245–2256. [CrossRef] [PubMed]
196. Irachi, S.; Hall, D.J.; Fleming, M.S.; Maugars, G.; Björnsson, B.T.; Dufour, S.; Uchida, K.; McCormick, S.D. Photoperiodic regulation of pituitary thyroid-stimulating hormone and brain deiodinase in Atlantic salmon. *Mol. Cell. Endocrinol.* **2021**, *519*, 111056. [CrossRef] [PubMed]
197. Glimcher, P.W.; Rustichini, A. Neuroeconomics: The consilience of brain and decision. *Science* **2004**, *306*, 447–452. [CrossRef] [PubMed]
198. Tversky, A.; Kahneman, D. Judgment under Uncertainty: Heuristics and Biases. *Science* **1974**, *185*, 1124–1131. [CrossRef] [PubMed]
199. Luo, J.; Yu, R. Follow the heart or the head? The interactive influence model of emotion and cognition. *Front. Psychol.* **2015**, *6*, 573. [CrossRef] [PubMed]
200. Fellows, L.K. The cognitive neuroscience of human decision making: A review and conceptual framework. *Behav. Cogn. Neurosci. Rev.* **2004**, *3*, 159–172. [CrossRef] [PubMed]
201. Pearson, J.M.; Watson, K.K.; Platt, M.L. Decision making: The neuroethological turn. *Neuron* **2014**, *82*, 950–965. [CrossRef] [PubMed]
202. Basten, U.; Biele, G.; Heekeren, H.R.; Fiebach, C.J. How the brain integrates costs and benefits during decision making. *Proc. Natl. Acad. Sci. USA* **2010**, *107*, 21767–21772. [CrossRef]
203. Floresco, S.B.; Ghods-Sharifi, S. Amygdala-prefrontal cortical circuitry regulates effort-based decision making. *Cereb. Cortex* **2007**, *17*, 251–260. [CrossRef] [PubMed]
204. Hikosaka, O.; Takikawa, Y.; Kawagoe, R. Role of the basal ganglia in the control of purposive saccadic eye movements. *Physiol. Rev.* **2000**, *80*, 953–978. [CrossRef] [PubMed]
205. Grillner, S.; Robertson, B. The basal ganglia over 500 million years. *Curr. Biol.* **2016**, *26*, R1088–R1100. [CrossRef] [PubMed]
206. Cregg, J.M.; Leiras, R.; Montalant, A.; Wanken, P.; Wickersham, I.R.; Kiehn, O. Brainstem neurons that command mammalian locomotor asymmetries. *Nat. Neurosci.* **2020**, *23*, 730–740. [CrossRef] [PubMed]
207. DiDomenico, R.; Nissanov, J.; Eaton, R.C. Lateralization and adaptation of a continuously variable behavior following lesions of a reticulospinal command neuron. *Brain Res.* **1988**, *473*, 15–28. [CrossRef] [PubMed]
208. Schemann, M.; Grundy, D. Electrophysiological identification of vagally innervated enteric neurons in guinea pig stomach. *Am. J. Physiol.* **1992**, *263*, G709–G718. [CrossRef] [PubMed]
209. Jing, J.; Vilim, F.S.; Horn, C.C.; Alexeeva, V.; Hatcher, N.G.; Sasaki, K.; Yashina, I.; Zhurov, Y.; Kupfermann, I.; Sweedler, J.V.; et al. From hunger to satiety: Reconfiguration of a feeding network by Aplysia neuropeptide Y. *J. Neurosci.* **2007**, *27*, 3490–3502. [CrossRef] [PubMed]

210. Nugent, M.; St Pierre, M.; Brown, A.; Nassar, S.; Parmar, P.; Kitase, Y.; Duck, S.A.; Pinto, C.; Jantzie, L.; Fung, C.; et al. Sexual Dimorphism in the Closure of the Hippocampal Postnatal Critical Period of Synaptic Plasticity after Intrauterine Growth Restriction: Link to Oligodendrocyte and Glial Dysregulation. *Dev. Neurosci.* **2023**, *45*, 234–254. [CrossRef] [PubMed]
211. Schreurs, B.G.; O'Dell, D.E.; Wang, D. The role of cerebellar intrinsic neuronal excitability, synaptic plasticity, and perineuronal nets in eyeblink conditioning. *Biology* **2024**, *13*, 200. [CrossRef] [PubMed]
212. Christensen, A.C.; Lensjø, K.K.; Lepperød, M.E.; Dragly, S.-A.; Sutterud, H.; Blackstad, J.S.; Fyhn, M.; Hafting, T. Perineuronal nets stabilize the grid cell network. *Nat. Commun.* **2021**, *12*, 253. [CrossRef]
213. Karetko, M.; Skangiel-Kramska, J. Diverse functions of perineuronal nets. *Acta Neurobiol. Exp.* **2009**, *69*, 564–577. [CrossRef]
214. Sorvari, H.; Miettinen, R.; Soininen, H.; Pitkänen, A. Parvalbumin-immunoreactive neurons make inhibitory synapses on pyramidal cells in the human amygdala: A light and electron microscopic study. *Neurosci. Lett.* **1996**, *217*, 93–96. [CrossRef] [PubMed]
215. Deco, G.; Rolls, E.T. Attention, short-term memory, and action selection: A unifying theory. *Prog. Neurobiol.* **2005**, *76*, 236–256. [CrossRef] [PubMed]
216. Jensen, O.; Kaiser, J.; Lachaux, J.-P. Human gamma-frequency oscillations associated with attention and memory. *Trends Neurosci.* **2007**, *30*, 317–324. [CrossRef] [PubMed]
217. Flechsenhar, A.; Larson, O.; End, A.; Gamer, M. Investigating overt and covert shifts of attention within social naturalistic scenes. *J. Vis.* **2018**, *18*, 11. [CrossRef] [PubMed]
218. Belardinelli, A.; Herbort, O.; Butz, M.V. Goal-oriented gaze strategies afforded by object interaction. *Vision. Res.* **2015**, *106*, 47–57. [CrossRef] [PubMed]
219. Okamoto, H.; Cherng, B.-W.; Nakajo, H.; Chou, M.-Y.; Kinoshita, M. Habenula as the experience-dependent controlling switchboard of behavior and attention in social conflict and learning. *Curr. Opin. Neurobiol.* **2021**, *68*, 36–43. [CrossRef] [PubMed]
220. Mohanty, A.; Gitelman, D.R.; Small, D.M.; Mesulam, M.M. The spatial attention network interacts with limbic and monoaminergic systems to modulate motivation-induced attention shifts. *Cereb. Cortex* **2008**, *18*, 2604–2613. [CrossRef] [PubMed]
221. Salmi, J.; Rinne, T.; Koistinen, S.; Salonen, O.; Alho, K. Brain networks of bottom-up triggered and top-down controlled shifting of auditory attention. *Brain Res.* **2009**, *1286*, 155–164. [CrossRef] [PubMed]
222. Tamber-Rosenau, B.J.; Esterman, M.; Chiu, Y.-C.; Yantis, S. Cortical mechanisms of cognitive control for shifting attention in vision and working memory. *J. Cogn. Neurosci.* **2011**, *23*, 2905–2919. [CrossRef]
223. Parker, M.O.; Gaviria, J.; Haigh, A.; Millington, M.E.; Brown, V.J.; Combe, F.J.; Brennan, C.H. Discrimination reversal and attentional sets in zebrafish (*Danio rerio*). *Behav. Brain Res.* **2012**, *232*, 264–268. [CrossRef]
224. Fodoulian, L.; Gschwend, O.; Huber, C.; Mutel, S.; Salazar, R.; Leone, R.; Renfer, J.-R.; Ekundayo, K.; Rodriguez, I.; Carleton, A. The claustrum-medial prefrontal cortex network controls attentional set-shifting. *BioRxiv* 2020. [CrossRef]
225. Buschman, T.J.; Miller, E.K. Shifting the spotlight of attention: Evidence for discrete computations in cognition. *Front. Hum. Neurosci.* **2010**, *4*, 194. [CrossRef]
226. Goldberg, M.E.; Bisley, J.; Powell, K.D.; Gottlieb, J.; Kusunoki, M. The role of the lateral intraparietal area of the monkey in the generation of saccades and visuospatial attention. *Ann. N. Y. Acad. Sci.* **2002**, *956*, 205–215. [CrossRef]
227. Amo, R.; Aizawa, H.; Takahashi, R.; Kobayashi, M.; Takahoko, M.; Aoki, T.; Okamoto, H. Identification of the zebrafish ventral habenula as a homologue of the mammalian lateral habenula. *Neurosci. Res.* **2009**, *65*, S217. [CrossRef]
228. Puentes-Mestril, C.; Roach, J.; Niethard, N.; Zochowski, M.; Aton, S.J. How rhythms of the sleeping brain tune memory and synaptic plasticity. *Sleep* **2019**, *42*, 1–14. [CrossRef] [PubMed]
229. Geva-Sagiv, M.; Mankin, E.A.; Eliashiv, D.; Epstein, S.; Cherry, N.; Kalender, G.; Tchemodanov, N.; Nir, Y.; Fried, I. Augmenting hippocampal-prefrontal neuronal synchrony during sleep enhances memory consolidation in humans. *Nat. Neurosci.* **2023**, *26*, 1100–1110. [CrossRef]
230. Capellini, I.; McNamara, P.; Preston, B.T.; Nunn, C.L.; Barton, R.A. Does sleep play a role in memory consolidation? A comparative test. *PLoS ONE* **2009**, *4*, e4609. [CrossRef]
231. Oyanedel, C.N.; Binder, S.; Kelemen, E.; Petersen, K.; Born, J.; Inostroza, M. Role of slow oscillatory activity and slow wave sleep in consolidation of episodic-like memory in rats. *Behav. Brain Res.* **2014**, *275*, 126–130. [CrossRef] [PubMed]
232. Yeganegi, H.; Ondracek, J.M. Multi-channel EEG recordings reveal age-related differences in the sleep of juvenile and adult zebra finches. *Sci. Rep.* **2023**. [CrossRef]
233. Buchert, S.N.; Murakami, P.; Kalavadia, A.H.; Reyes, M.T.; Sitaraman, D. Sleep correlates with behavioral decision making critical for reproductive output in Drosophila melanogaster. *Comp. Biochem. Physiol. Part A Mol. Integr. Physiol.* **2022**, *264*, 111114. [CrossRef]
234. Sauseng, P.; Klimesch, W.; Gruber, W.R.; Birbaumer, N. Cross-frequency phase synchronization: A brain mechanism of memory matching and attention. *Neuroimage* **2008**, *40*, 308–317. [CrossRef]
235. Engel, A.K.; Fries, P.; Singer, W. Dynamic predictions: Oscillations and synchrony in top-down processing. *Nat. Rev. Neurosci.* **2001**, *2*, 704–716. [CrossRef] [PubMed]
236. Drebitz, E.; Haag, M.; Grothe, I.; Mandon, S.; Kreiter, A.K. Attention configures synchronization within local neuronal networks for processing of the behaviorally relevant stimulus. *Front. Neural Circuits* **2018**, *12*, 71. [CrossRef]
237. Klimesch, W. EEG alpha and theta oscillations reflect cognitive and memory performance: A review and analysis. *Brain Res. Rev.* **1999**, *29*, 169–195. [CrossRef] [PubMed]

238. Fernandez, L.M.J.; Lüthi, A. Sleep spindles: Mechanisms and functions. *Physiol. Rev.* **2020**, *100*, 805–868. [CrossRef]
239. Macdonald, K.D.; Fifkova, E.; Jones, M.S.; Barth, D.S. Focal stimulation of the thalamic reticular nucleus induces focal gamma waves in cortex. *J. Neurophysiol.* **1998**, *79*, 474–477. [CrossRef] [PubMed]
240. Ngo, H.-V.V.; Born, J. Sleep and the Balance between Memory and Forgetting. *Cell* **2019**, *179*, 289–291. [CrossRef]
241. Kim, J.; Gulati, T.; Ganguly, K. Competing Roles of Slow Oscillations and Delta Waves in Memory Consolidation versus Forgetting. *Cell* **2019**, *179*, 514–526.e13. [CrossRef]
242. Nir, Y.; Tononi, G. Dreaming and the brain: From phenomenology to neurophysiology. *Trends Cogn. Sci.* **2010**, *14*, 88–100. [CrossRef]
243. Tamaki, M.; Berard, A.V.; Barnes-Diana, T.; Siegel, J.; Watanabe, T.; Sasaki, Y. Reward does not facilitate visual perceptual learning until sleep occurs. *Proc. Natl. Acad. Sci. USA* **2020**, *117*, 959–968. [CrossRef]
244. Schredl, M.; Doll, E. Emotions in diary dreams. *Conscious. Cogn.* **1998**, *7*, 634–646. [CrossRef]
245. Marzano, C.; Ferrara, M.; Mauro, F.; Moroni, F.; Gorgoni, M.; Tempesta, D.; Cipolli, C.; De Gennaro, L. Recalling and forgetting dreams: Theta and alpha oscillations during sleep predict subsequent dream recall. *J. Neurosci.* **2011**, *31*, 6674–6683. [CrossRef] [PubMed]
246. Wiswede, D.; Koranyi, N.; Müller, F.; Langner, O.; Rothermund, K. Validating the truth of propositions: Behavioral and ERP indicators of truth evaluation processes. *Soc. Cogn. Affect. Neurosci.* **2013**, *8*, 647–653. [CrossRef]
247. Joo, H.R.; Frank, L.M. The hippocampal sharp wave-ripple in memory retrieval for immediate use and consolidation. *Nat. Rev. Neurosci.* **2018**, *19*, 744–757. [CrossRef]
248. Roumis, D.K.; Frank, L.M. Hippocampal sharp-wave ripples in waking and sleeping states. *Curr. Opin. Neurobiol.* **2015**, *35*, 6–12. [CrossRef]
249. Remondes, M.; Wilson, M.A. Slow-γ Rhythms Coordinate Cingulate Cortical Responses to Hippocampal Sharp-Wave Ripples during Wakefulness. *Cell Rep.* **2015**, *13*, 1327–1335. [CrossRef]
250. Moser, M.-B.; Rowland, D.C.; Moser, E.I. Place cells, grid cells, and memory. *Cold Spring Harb. Perspect. Biol.* **2015**, *7*, a021808. [CrossRef]
251. Friston, K.; Kilner, J.; Harrison, L. A free energy principle for the brain. *J. Physiol. Paris* **2006**, *100*, 70–87. [CrossRef] [PubMed]
252. Friston, K. The free-energy principle: A rough guide to the brain? *Trends Cogn. Sci.* **2009**, *13*, 293–301. [CrossRef] [PubMed]
253. Krupnik, V. I like therefore I can, and I can therefore I like: The role of self-efficacy and affect in active inference of allostasis. *Front. Neural Circuits* **2024**, *18*, 1283372. [CrossRef]
254. Friston, K. The free-energy principle: A unified brain theory? *Nat. Rev. Neurosci.* **2010**, *11*, 127–138. [CrossRef] [PubMed]
255. Kammer, T.; Spitzer, M. Brain stimulation in psychiatry: Methods and magnets, patients and parameters. *Curr. Opin. Psychiatry* **2012**, *25*, 535–541. [CrossRef] [PubMed]
256. Wagle Shukla, A.; Vaillancourt, D.E. Treatment and physiology in Parkinson's disease and dystonia: Using transcranial magnetic stimulation to uncover the mechanisms of action. *Curr. Neurol. Neurosci. Rep.* **2014**, *14*, 449. [CrossRef]
257. Magsood, H.; Syeda, F.; Holloway, K.; Carmona, I.C.; Hadimani, R.L. Safety study of combination treatment: Deep brain stimulation and transcranial magnetic stimulation. *Front. Hum. Neurosci.* **2020**, *14*, 123. [CrossRef] [PubMed]
258. Holtzheimer, P.E.; Mayberg, H.S. Neuromodulation for treatment-resistant depression. *F1000 Med. Rep.* **2012**, *4*, 22. [CrossRef] [PubMed]
259. Bluhm, R.; Castillo, E.; Achtyes, E.D.; McCright, A.M.; Cabrera, L.Y. They affect the person, but for better or worse? perceptions of electroceutical interventions for depression among psychiatrists, patients, and the public. *Qual. Health Res.* **2021**, *31*, 2542–2553. [CrossRef]
260. Farries, M.A.; Fairhall, A.L. Reinforcement learning with modulated spike timing dependent synaptic plasticity. *J. Neurophysiol.* **2007**, *98*, 3648–3665. [CrossRef]
261. Detorakis, G.; Sheik, S.; Augustine, C.; Paul, S.; Pedroni, B.U.; Dutt, N.; Krichmar, J.; Cauwenberghs, G.; Neftci, E. Neural and Synaptic Array Transceiver: A Brain-Inspired Computing Framework for Embedded Learning. *Front. Neurosci.* **2018**, *12*, 583. [CrossRef]
262. Florian, R.V. Reinforcement learning through modulation of spike-timing-dependent synaptic plasticity. *Neural Comput.* **2007**, *19*, 1468–1502. [CrossRef]
263. Teng, T.-H.; Tan, A.-H.; Zurada, J.M. Self-organizing neural networks integrating domain knowledge and reinforcement learning. *IEEE Trans. Neural Netw. Learn. Syst.* **2015**, *26*, 889–902. [CrossRef]

Disclaimer/Publisher's Note: The statements, opinions and data contained in all publications are solely those of the individual author(s) and contributor(s) and not of MDPI and/or the editor(s). MDPI and/or the editor(s) disclaim responsibility for any injury to people or property resulting from any ideas, methods, instructions or products referred to in the content.

 *information*

Review

Global Realism with Bipolar Strings: From Bell Test to Real-World Causal-Logical Quantum Gravity and Brain-Universe Similarity for Entangled Machine Thinking and Imagination

Wen-Ran Zhang

Independent Researcher, Statesboro, GA 30460, USA; wrzhang@georgiasouthern.edu

Abstract: Following Einstein's prediction that *"Physics constitutes a logical system of thought"* and *"Nature is the realization of the simplest conceivable mathematical ideas"*, this topical review outlines a formal extension of *local realism* limited by the speed of light to *global realism with bipolar strings (GRBS)* that unifies the principle of locality with quantum nonlocality. The related literature is critically reviewed to justify GRBS which is shown as a necessary and inevitable consequence of the Bell test and an equilibrium-based axiomatization of physics and quantum information science for brain–universe similarity and human-level intelligence. With definable causality in regularity and mind–light–matter unity for quantum superposition/entanglement, *bipolar universal modus ponens (BUMP)* in GRBS makes quantum emergence and submergence of spacetime logically ubiquitous in both the physical and mental worlds—an unexpected but long-sought simplification of quantum gravity with *complete background independence*. It is shown that GRBS forms a basis for *quantum intelligence (QI)*—a spacetime transcendent, quantum–digital compatible, analytical quantum computing paradigm where bipolar strings lead to *bipolar entropy* as a nonlinear bipolar dynamic and set–theoretic unification of order and disorder as well as linearity and nonlinearity for energy/information conservation, regeneration, and degeneration toward *quantum cognition and quantum biology (QCQB)* as well as information-conservational blackhole keypad compression and big bang data recovery. Subsequently, GRBS is justified as a *real-world quantum gravity (RWQG)* theory—a bipolar relativistic causal logical reconceptualization and unification of string theory, loop quantum gravity, and M-theory—the three roads to quantum gravity. Based on GRBS, the following is posited: (1) life is a living bipolar superstring regulated by *bipolar entropy*; (2) thinking with consciousness and memory growth as a prerequisite for human-level intelligence is fundamentally mind–light–matter unitary QI logically equivalent to quantum emergence (entanglement) and submergence (collapse) of spacetime. These two posits lead to a positive answer to the question *"If AI machine cannot think, can QI machine think?"*. *Causal–logical brain modeling (CLBM)* for *entangled machine thinking and imagination (EMTI)* is proposed and graphically illustrated. The testability and falsifiability of GRBS are discussed.

Keywords: bipolar universal modus ponens (BUMP); global realism with bipolar strings (GRBS); axiomatization of physics and quantum information science; complete background independence; bipolar quantum graphs for entangled neural networks; causal–logical brain modeling (CLBM); quantum cognition and quantum biology (QCQB); mind–light–matter unity AI and QI; bipolar entropy; god/nature logic vs. human/mind logic; lost but found miracle

Citation: Zhang, W.-R. Global Realism with Bipolar Strings: From Bell Test to Real-World Causal-Logical Quantum Gravity and Brain-Universe Similarity for Entangled Machine Thinking and Imagination. *Information* **2024**, *15*, 456. https://doi.org/10.3390/info15080456

Academic Editors: Gabriel Luque, Luiz Pessoa and Birgitta Dresp-Langley

Received: 8 June 2024
Revised: 15 July 2024
Accepted: 19 July 2024
Published: 1 August 2024

Copyright: © 2024 by the author. Licensee MDPI, Basel, Switzerland. This article is an open access article distributed under the terms and conditions of the Creative Commons Attribution (CC BY) license (https://creativecommons.org/licenses/by/4.0/).

1. Introduction

Modern science holds many unsolved mysteries. One mystery is that machine learning can use powerful computation for significant commercial applications, but AI machines are widely deemed unable to reach human-level intelligence—a kind of biological intelligence (BI). Another mystery is that scientific reports have shown striking similarities between the human brain and the universe in structural organization, which has perplexed scientists with suspicion.

The 2022 Nobel Prize in Physics [1] was awarded jointly to three Nobel Laureates *"for experiments with entangled photons, establishing the violation of Bell inequalities and pioneering quantum information science"*. The Nobel award is epoch-making as it is the most authoritative vindication of quantum entanglement that formally opened the door to quantum information science on the long march toward **real-world quantum gravity (RWQG)** for **quantum cognition and quantum biology (QCQB)**—a step forward to quantum intelligence (QI) for human-level AI to resolve the brain–universe similarity puzzle.

Being most authoritative, the Nobel Prize vindicated Bell inequality violation but also led to a new mystery. Since quantum entanglement defied Einstein's locality and causality principle of realism limited by the speed of light, the Prize has been deemed by some scientists as the conclusion of the great debate of the 20th century: *Niels Bohr won, and Einstein lost*. The problem is that, without causality and realism, quantum entanglement would be unreal—the greatest mystery in science and philosophy that entails a causal–logical quantum gravity theory missing from mainstream quantum theories.

It is asserted [2] that *"The causality principle had been and will still be the cornerstone of science. Without cause–effect science would be religion. Specifically, the causality of quantum entanglement must be made clear in both experimental and logical terms. If it is not an effect of* **local realism** *limited by Einstein's speed of light, it must be an effect of* **global realism** *with logically definable causality that unifies local and global realities. . . ."*. Thus, the term *"global realism"* is coined as a prediction in physics for the unification of Einstein's local realism with Bohr's quantum nonlocality which leads to this topical review. (Note: The term *"Platonic global realism"* appeared in an earlier paper [3]).

It is a common view that without machine thinking [4] there would be no adaptive machine learning for human-level AI [5]. While cutting-edge AI technologies have been focused on machine learning from big data for commercial applications, they came short of reaching logically definable causality and mind–light–matter unity for entangled, quantum–digital compatible, and analytical machine thinking for QI [6]. Notably, the logical road to human-level intelligence leads to a dead-end [7]. It can be argued, however, that the so-called "dead-end" is the end of truth-based, being-centered, unipolar, human/mind logic [8] for symbolic AI in the classical world but not the end of Spinoza–Einstein's God/Nature logic for entangled QI that could be YinYang bipolar equilibrium-based in nature and entails open-world, open-ended exploration [2,6,9]. Thus, Einstein's assertion that physics constitutes a logical system of thought and the strikingly similar images of the human brain and the universe in structural organization [10] lead us to the valid questions: *Could human thinking as a brain function be logically equivalent to spacetime emergence and submergence through quantum entanglement/collapse? Could truth-based AI and BI be revealed by equilibrium-based QI?*

Based *on* ground-0 axioms [6] that unify the first principles and the second law, this work critically reviews the related literature on realism and extends Einstein's *local realism* limited by the speed of light to the formal theory of **global realism with bipolar strings (GRBS)**. GRBS introduces real-world **bipolar strings** [2,6,9,11–42] into realism with equilibrium-based, logically definable causality in regularity [9,11]. Supported by QI and mind–light–matter unity, GRBS is shown applicable in entangled machine thinking and imagination. Figure 1 shows the distinction between QI, AI, and BI that brings up the question [2] *"If AI machine cannot think, can QI machine think?"*. GRBS is used to provide an answer to the question.

It is shown that GRBS constitutes a real-world bipolar relativistic logical reconceptualization of string theory [43–46] loop quantum gravity (LQG) [47–49], and M-theory [46] toward a grand unification of general relativity and quantum mechanics with much-needed, long sought, but unexpected simplification. The simplification follows Einstein's predictions *"pure thought can grasp reality"* and *"Nature is the realization of the simplest conceivable mathematical ideas"* (re. [50–58]).

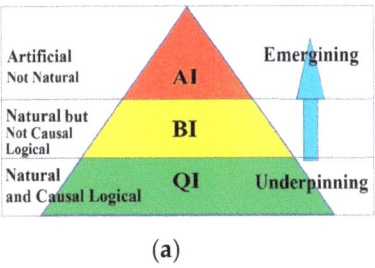 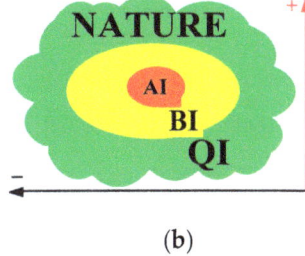

Figure 1. Quantum Intelligence (QI) as natural underpinning of artificial intelligence (AI) and biological intelligence (BI) (adapted from [2]): (**a**) three-layer closed view; (**b**) three-layer open world.

In physics, string theory as a theoretical framework replaced the point-like particles of particle physics with unipolar one-dimensional objects called strings. The theory describes how these strings propagate through space and interact with each other without definable or testable causality. Notably, it used to be the dominating theory of modern physics for years. It was once believed the theory of everything (TOE). Now the theory has faded significantly due to its lack of scalability and testability. It has been criticized as *"not even wrong"* [59], *"trouble with physics"* [60], and *"lost in math"* [61].

While strings are unipolar and truth-based, GRBS is an equilibrium-based bipolar dynamic string theory for a super symmetrical grand unification of Nature, agents, and causality [9,11,18,21,22]. While strings are not logical and not testable, ***bipolar strings*** as scalable dipoles such as input–output, action–reaction, and particle–antiparticle pairs are logical and observable everywhere in both the classical and quantum worlds as well as in the physical and mental worlds. (Remark: following [6], β+ and β− decay are taken in this work as part of Nature's "encryption" mechanism to conceal a positron in a proton to prevent its annihilation with an electron—a logical interpretation of matter–antimatter asymmetry.)

The aim of this work is to present GRBS as a logically different real-world unified field theory that reveals truth-based local reality with bipolar equilibrium-based QI. It is stated in [6] that the equilibrium-based mathematical abstraction assumes bipolar quantum agents (BQAs) in bipolar dynamic equilibria (BDEs) as its ontological basis that is extended to ***bipolar strings*** [9,11,18,21,22]. Fundamentally, bipolar strings as BDEs/BQAs are bipolar variables with bipolar values including but not limited to the basic states:

(i) Non-equilibrium state: $(-1, 0)$; //e.g., particle such as electron;
(ii) Non-equilibrium state: $(0, +1)$; //e.g., antiparticle such as positron;
(iii) Equilibrium state: $(-1, 0) \oplus (0, +1) = (-1, +1)$; //e.g., superposition/entanglement;
(iv) Non-existence: $(-1, 0) \& (0, +1) = (0, 0)$. //e.g., electron-positron annihilation.

Notably, a photon is its own antiparticle which can be in any of the four states, and electron–positron annihilation releases two photons. It is shown in [6] that a photon as a BQA provides a logically definable interpretation of quantum superposition/entanglement and leads to an analytical extension of quantum mechanics named QI for mind–light–matter unity AI.

Assuming that bipolar strings can be entangled and collapsed, GRBS further extends BQAs to a graphically visualizable causal–logical brain–universe similarity model with formal logically definable causality for mind–light–matter unity AI&QI [6,26–31]. It is shown that GRBS constitutes a philosophically different logical theory for quantum gravity and quantum information science [11] with hope for the ***lost but found miracle*** which states *"Lost in the beauty of truth-based singularity but found in the harmony of equilibrium-based bipolar relativity"*.

Since acceleration is equivalent to gravitation under general relativity [51,52], any physical, logical, socioeconomic, mental, or biological acceleration, growth, or degeneration with creative thinking is qualified to be a kind of quantum gravity [9,21]. Thus, causal–

logical quantum gravity leads to entangled machine thinking and imagination, a quantum extension of the resonant brain model [62–64].

Based *on* ground-0 axioms [6], GRBS starts with the following postulates:

Postulate 1. *Negative–Positive (−, +) bipolarity is the most fundamental property of the universe,* **bipolar dynamic equilibrium (BDE)** *(including both equilibrium and non-equilibrium states) of (−, +)* **bipolar energy/information** *is the fundamental regulating power of the universe and the human brain, from which spacetime emerges, and truths in spacetime are revealed. Without BDE the human brain cannot distinguish truth from falsity, and the universe cannot exist.*

Postulate 2. *Gravitational action–reaction, electromagnetic particle–antiparticle, or any energy/information input–output bipolarity is logically a BDE—a bipolar unification of all basic forces and matters discovered or to be discovered; a BDE can be characterized by a bipolar logical or algebraic variable in a bipolar lattice* $\{-1, 0\} \times \{0, +1\}$, $[-1, 0] \times [0, +1]$, *or* $[-\infty, 0] \times [0, +\infty]$ [6].

Postulate 3. *If* **quantum gravity** *is the grand unification, it must be a (−, +) bipolar unified field that forms a global* **bipolar quantum entanglement (BQE)** *where a* **bipolar quantum agent (BQA)** *or* **bipolar string** *as a quantum entanglement or superposition can form or collapse without the speed of light limitation at the generic or most fundamental level.*

Postulate 4. *Mind–light–matter unity is logically reachable with bipolar dynamic logic (BDL), bipolar dynamic fuzzy logic (BDFL), bipolar quantum linear algebra (BQLA), and bipolar quantum geometry (BQG) based on: (i) mind–light–matter in the forms of BDEs or bipolar strings form a unified field of physics and biophysics from which truths are revealed; (ii) BQG and BDL have been proven the geometry of light and the logic of photon, respectively; (iii) mind and matter are bridged by light in the form of bio-photonics/bioelectronics; (iv) bipolar universal modus pones (BUMPs) provides logically definable causality in regularity for bipolar reciprocal interaction and quantum superposition/entanglement. (Note: For detailed examples, readers are referred to [6]).*

The four postulates provide an equilibrium-based, bipolar dynamic logical basis for the unification of general relativity and quantum theory with or without graviton–antigraviton and dark matter or energy fully tested. Based on the logical basis, photons and electrons can be bipolar quantum entangled because (1) a photon, as its own antiparticle, is itself a BDE [6]; (2) an electron, as an electromagnetic particle, is part of particle–antiparticle (−, +) bipolarity; (3) any massive/massless pair may form a gravitational action–reaction or input–output pair including but not limited to dark matter and energy. Thus, with bipolar relativity or bipolar string theory [9,18], not only should GRBS be applicable in physical science, but also in computing/information science, brain science, life science, and social economics as well. This argument leads GRBS to a RWQG theory with *(i) physical quantum gravity, (ii) logical quantum gravity, (iii) mental quantum gravity, (iv) biological quantum gravity, and (v) social quantum gravity* [9,21].

It is proven that GRBS is an inevitable consequence of Bell inequality violation shown in Bell tests and a bipolar relativistic *axiomatization of physics and quantum information science*. On the one hand, GRBS provides a trouble-free real-world bipolar logical unification of string theory, loop quantum gravity (LQG), and M-theory—the three roads toward quantum gravity [65]; on the other hand, it provides a generalized basis for *mind–light–matter unity AI&QI* machinery [6]. It is shown that the key to a trouble-free testable solution lies in background-independent logically definable causality for bipolar equilibrium-based revealing of truths with quantum emergence and submergence of spacetime [6,9,20,23–25,27,28].

Following this introduction, the remaining work is organized as follows:

Section 2 presents a review of Einstein's principle of locality, realism, and the search for causality.

Section 3 presents GRBS as a real-world causal–logical theory of quantum gravity with **bipolar entropy** and QCQB. It is shown that GRBS is an inevitable consequence of the Bell test or Bell's inequality violation that constitutes a background-independent, equilibrium-based, bipolar set-theoretic, spacetime transcendent dynamic paradigm of physics and quantum information science for mind–light–matter unity QI—an analytical paradigm of quantum computing.

Section 4 presents a logically testable application of GRBS in causal–logical brain modeling for machine thinking and imagination.

Section 5 presents an analysis and discussion. It is shown that GRBS provides a bipolar axiomatization of physics and quantum information science with a background independent reconceptualization and unification for real-world quantum gravity. Testability and falsifiability are discussed.

Section 6 draws a few concluding remarks with distinctions.

2. Locality and Causality with Irregularity

2.1. The Principle of Locality or Local Realism

In physics, the *principle of locality* asserts that an object is influenced directly only by its immediate surroundings. Thus, "local theory" does not agree with quantum nonlocality. Locality evolved from classical field theories which assert that, for any causal action at one point to have an effect at another point, something between those points must mediate the action. To exert an influence, a wave or particle must travel through the space between the two points, carrying the influence.

In 1905 Albert Einstein's special theory of relativity [50] postulated that no material or energy can travel faster than the speed of light. This is the well-known *principle of locality*, which is also widely called *the principle of realism*. The principle limits any cause–effect relation between two points by the speed of light. Therefore, the principle of locality implies that an event at one point A cannot cause a simultaneous result at another point B in a time t less than $t = d/c$ where d is the distance between the two points and c is the speed of light in vacuum. Einstein later extended his special theory of relativity to the general theory of relativity, which still obeys the principle of locality [51,52].

The theory of quantum mechanics presents a challenge to the principle of locality. Einstein himself had helped to create the quantum theory. In 1935, in their EPR paper [57], the authors theorized that quantum mechanics might not be a local theory, because a measurement made on one of a pair of separated but entangled particles causes a simultaneous effect. Specifically, the collapse of the wave function as an effect exceeds the speed of light. If it is not local, it should be part of a global theory. However, Niels Bohr asserted that a causal description of a quantum process cannot be attained, and quantum mechanics must content itself with particle–wave complementary descriptions [66]. Thus, Bohr set up an insurmountable limitation on the definability of causality for quantum nonlocality until logically definable causality was formally defined with **bipolar universal modus ponens (BUMP)** for quantum entanglement [9,16–18] that made ***global realism*** possible.

Because of the probabilistic nature of wave function collapse, its violation of locality was once believed unable to transmit information faster than light. So, the EPR paradox challenged Bohr's Copenhagen interpretation with a thought experiment on quantum entanglement. Einstein once called quantum entanglement *"spooky action at a distance"* and argued that *"God does not play dice with the universe"*. That triggered the great debate of the 20th century with Bohr's tit for tat: *"Stop telling God what to do (with his dice)"*.

2.2. Truth-Based Causality—Experimental but Formally Undefinable in Regularity

According to Ben–Menahem [67], Einstein's concept of causality is comprised of (a) regularity; (b) locality; (c) symmetry considerations leading to conservation laws; (d) mutuality of causal interaction. It is well known that Einstein refused to accept Bohr's interpretation of quantum mechanics as a complete theory for its lack of causality for quantum nonlocality. However, after wrestling with definable causality for his entire life, Einstein's truth-based locality stopped short of reaching logical definability for causality, and modern science including classical and quantum mechanics (QM) has been relying on systematic experiments to find causal relationships.

Based on singularity and partial observability of truth-based reasoning, it is now a widely accepted theory that spacetime as well as the universe was created by a big bang and will end in one or more black holes. As far as we know, however, the Big Bang came from nowhere and was caused by nothing; a black hole goes nowhere [68]. To reconcile the inconsistency between singularity and the second law of thermodynamics, as critiqued in [69], Stephen Hawking proposed the remedy that a black hole should have particle and/or antiparticle emission or Hawking radiation [70,71].

It is noted ([9] Ch1) that, while Hawking radiation has been a hot topic of discussion in quantum theory, its far-reaching consequence was overlooked. The consequence is that, when the universe ends, matter–antimatter pairs will miraculously survive. Therefore, singularity is not a contradiction but a vindication of YinYang bipolarity—the only property that can survive the Big Bang and black hole singularity to provide equilibrium-based background-independence, logically definable causality, symmetry, and reciprocal interaction or mutuality. Notably, the vindication has been overlooked in science.

Notably, Bohr's YinYang in QM asserted "*Opposites are Complementary*" [66] (Figure 2, words in Latin). But Bohr's YinYang was based on truth–falsity, particle–wave, or real–imaginary that stopped short of reaching strict (−, +) bipolar opposites. Without strict bipolarity, truth-based unipolar logic and geometry failed to reach geometrical background independence and logically definable causality for spacetime emergence and submergence since ancient Greek times. It was reasonable to believe that the unfound logical foundation or axiomatization of physics sought by Hilbert [72] and Einstein [54] could be holding the key to quantum causality, quantum gravity, and quantum intelligence. *Could there be a formal YinYang bipolar causal–logical system hidden behind Niels Bohr's YinYang logo that could serve as a breakthrough to his own limitation on the definability of causality* [66]?

Figure 2. Particle–wave or real–imaginary complementarity: Bohr's coat of arms (Creative Commons file by GJo, 3 August 2010, Source: File: Royal Coat of Arms of Denmark.svg (Collar of the Order of the Elephant) + File: yinyang.svg).

2.3. Axiomatizing Physics—The Unreachable Goal with Truth-Based Thinking

Einstein wrestled with definable causality for his whole life searching for a logical foundation for physics. He stated [54]: "*Development of Western science is based on two great achievements: the invention of the formal logical system (in Euclidean geometry) by the Greek philosophers, and the discovery of the possibility to find out causal relationships by systematic experiment (during the Renaissance). In my opinion one has not to be astonished that the Chinese sages have not made those steps. The astonishing thing is that those discoveries were made at all*".

A few conclusions were drawn from the above quote [6]. First, the logic Einstein used was the truth-based formal logical system originated from Euclidean geometry. Secondly, the truth-based system does not provide logically definable causality with regularity. Thirdly, the causality he relied on was empirical causality in spacetime which is not a formal logical system. Fourthly, what he sought was a formal causal system for the grant unification. Although Einstein never believed in the theory of singularity and even regarded the theory as "bizarre", resisting the logic of his own theory right up to his final departure in 1955, his equations of general relativity did eventually lead to the flourishing of singularity after his death following the discovery of black holes.

It is well-known that Einstein was a friend and colleague of renowned mathematician Kurt Gödel at Princeton University, and, before fleeing from Nazi Germany to resettle in the United States, Einstein once visited German mathematician Hilbert by invitation. So, he was aware of Hilbert's program in mathematics for axiomatizing physics [72]. Einstein believed that it was possible to axiomatize physics. It is noted [36] that, in 1931, Gödel published his incompleteness theorems [73]. Many believe that these theorems proved Hilbert's mathematical program impossible and shattered his hope for axiomatizing physics. Three years after Gödel published his incompleteness theorems, however, Einstein reaffirmed [53] that *"pure thought can grasp reality"* and *"nature is the realization of the simplest conceivable mathematical ideas"*. In 1936 he asserted that [54] *"Physics constitutes a logical system of thought which is in a state of evolution, whose basis (principles) cannot be distilled, as it were, from experience by an inductive method, but can only be arrived at by free invention"*. In 1940, nine years after Gödel published his incompleteness theorems, Einstein asserted [55] that the grand unification of general relativity and quantum mechanics needs a new logical foundation: *"For the time being we have to admit that we do not possess any general theoretical basis for physics which can be regarded as its logical foundation"*.

Evidently, Einstein never wavered on a logical foundation for physics. Hilbert lived for twelve years after Gödel published his incompleteness theorems. Many wondered why Hilbert did not concede or officially respond to Gödel's findings. A sober view is that if Einstein refused to give up hope for the logic of physics with definable causality in regularity, why should Hilbert? [36].

Gödel's incompleteness theorems, Hilbert's effort in axiomatizing physics, and Einstein's assertion on a new logical foundation for physics were all giant steps. However, the three giants stopped short of pointing out the inevitable ([9] p. 92):

(1) The incompleteness of truth-based reasoning is due to its lack of syntax and semantics for the fundamental physical concepts of *"equilibrium"* and *"symmetry"*.

(2) A logical foundation for physics requires a philosophically deeper cosmology beyond spacetime and a different mathematical abstraction beyond classical being-centered, truth-based, unipolar cognition such that spacetime can emerge and truths can be revealed.

It is clear from the above analysis that a geometry transcending being, truth, and spacetime is the key to hosting the Spinoza–Einstein's God/Nature logic with **complete background independence**. However, what geometry could go beyond spacetime?

The long search reached bipolar quantum geometry (BQG) of equilibrium or supersymmetry of negative–positive energies/information for reciprocal and complementary YinYang bipolar interaction. Since no system can escape from equilibrium, an equilibrium-based bipolar dynamic logic that reasons on equilibrium and quasi-equilibrium or symmetry and broken symmetry will transcend spacetime as well as all beings and truths in spacetime as we say that the universe is a dynamic equilibrium but not a truth and/or falsity.

3. From Local to Global Realism—A Causal–Logical Theory of Real-World Quantum Gravity

3.1. From Truth-Based to Equilibrium-Based Reasoning

In 1964 physicist John Stewart Bell formulated the Bell inequality [74], which, if violated in actual experiments, would imply that quantum mechanics violates the *locality* or *realism* principle [74–76]. Thus, Bell introduced another principle on the values of *unmeasured quantities* or *counterfactual definiteness* which has been generally called the **Bell test** or **Bell inequality**. In the words of the author, for whom this family of results is named, *"If (a hidden-variable theory) is local it will not agree with quantum mechanics, and if it agrees with quantum mechanics it will not be local"* [76].

While the two principles of locality and realism are commonly referred to as a single principle named **local realism**, the Bell inequality violation opened the door to a new world of physics—**global realism** with logically definable causality in regularity. Beginning with

John Clauser and Alain Aspect's experiments in the 1970s to 1980s, the **Bell test** results show that quantum mechanics violated the inequality, so it must violate locality or (local) realism. However, critics have noted that these experiments included "loopholes", which prevented a definitive answer to the uncertainty. This problem was resolved in the 1990s when a "loophole-free" experiment was conducted by Anton Zeilinger of the University of Vienna who joined with John Clauser and Alain Aspect as a Nobel Laureate for the 2022 Nobel Award. The experimental findings, however, could not reach definable causality in regularity. (Note: This work presents a falsifiable causal–logical quantum-gravity theory that goes beyond the continuing debate on the Bell test).

Theorem 1. *Global realism is a necessary and inevitable consequence of the Bell inequality violation.*

Proof. It follows from the fact that (1) the Bell inequality is the general name for the values of unmeasured quantities or counterfactual definiteness [74] and, in the words of the author, for whom this family of results is named, "If (a hidden-variable theory) is local it will not agree with quantum mechanics, and if it agrees with quantum mechanics it will not be local" [76]; (2) the Bell inequality violation has been experimentally verified, and the experimental results have been vindicated by the 2022 Nobel Award in Physics; (3) If quantum non-locality or entanglement is not local but real it must belong to global realism [2,11]. □

Theorem 2. *Global realism must be a background-independent, equilibrium-based, spacetime transcendent, dynamic theory that unifies/reveals truth-based local reality/realism. Thus, quantum superposition/entanglement must be a dynamic equilibrium, and quantum nonlocality must be part of equilibrium-based global realism.*

Proof. It follows that (1) being in a spacetime geometry cannot be true in quantum terms due to spacetime expansion/shrinking; (2) dynamic equilibrium including equilibrium, quasi-equilibrium, and non-equilibrium states are essential and ubiquitous for all dynamic existence per the second law of thermodynamics [77]; (3) everything in the universe including the universe itself and the mind of human being is a dynamic equilibrium but not a truth, falsity, or contradiction; (4) quantum entanglement and/or superposition can be tested/observed as a dynamic equilibrium that can form (emerge) for quantum computing and collapse (submerge) when being measured; (5) the equilibrium-based system must be background-independent such that it can expand and shrink with dynamic quantum emergence or submergence of spacetime without boundary in spacetime; (6) equilibrium is real based on the second law of thermodynamics; (7) global equilibrium is real, and quantum nonlocality can naturally be part of global realism. □

Theorem 3. *Global realism constitutes a fundamentally bipolar equilibrium-based, dynamic, set-theoretic, background-independent, logical, geometrical, and algebraic system with logically definable causality and information/energy conservation that can reveal truth-based crisp logic, fuzzy logic, linear algebra, and local reality through quantum emergence or submergence of spacetime, where quantum superposition/entanglement is fundamentally a bipolar dynamic equilibrium or BDE, and quantum collapse is essentially the collapse of a BDE.*

Proof. It follows that, fundamentally, any multidimensional equilibrium in spacetime can be decomposed into a set of background-independent bipolar dynamic equilibria/quasi-equilibria. Global realism is then fundamentally a completely background-independent, bipolar equilibrium-based, set-theoretic, geometrical, logical, and/or algebraic system (see Figures 3–7). Without logically definable causality the formal equilibrium-based logical/algebraic basis (Figures 5 and 6) would not be able to reveal truth-based crisp and fuzzy logic for local reality. Without input–output, action–reaction, and particle–antiparticle bipolarity, formal logically definable causality in regularity would be impossible due to the lack of bipolar interactive dynamics for information/energy flow. Without formal logically definable causality in regularity, GRBS would be impossible. Furthermore, BQG must be completely background-independent such that BDEs are completely background-independent. Quantum superposition or entanglement is thus fundamentally a bipolar dynamic equilibrium, and quantum collapse is the collapse of a bipolar dynamic equilibrium [2,6] (Figure 7). □

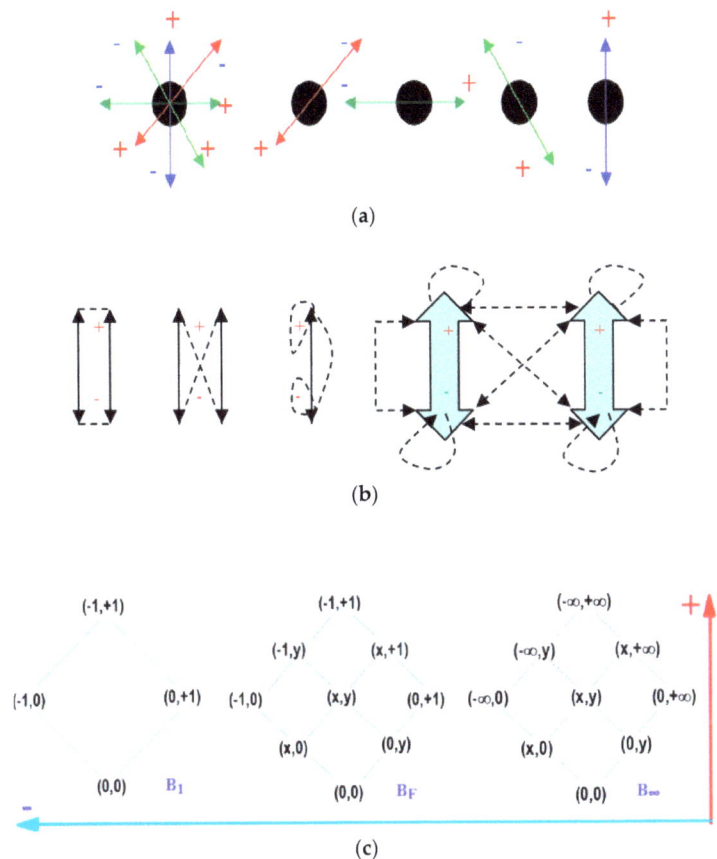

Figure 3. Background-independent mathematical abstraction (adapted from [9]: (**a**) M-bipolar equilibrium decomposed to a set of bipolar equilibria or bipolar strings; (**b**) bipolar interaction and entanglement; (**c**) Hasse diagrams of bipolar lattices.

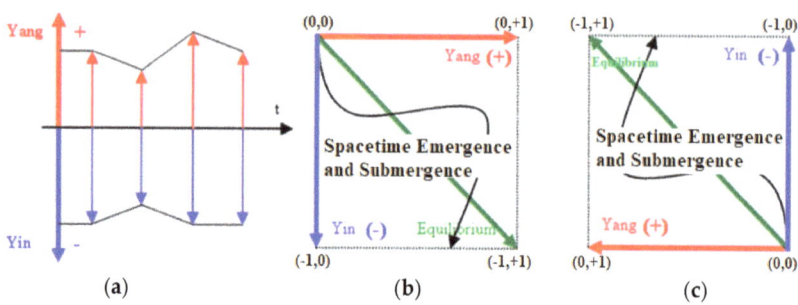

Figure 4. YinYang bipolar quantum geometry (BQG) (adapted from [9,20]: (**a**) magnitude with time t; (**b**,**c**) background-independent quantum unification of geometry and logic.

&	(0,0)	(-1,0)	(0,+1)	(-1,+1)
(0,0)	(0,0)	(0,0)	(0,0)	(0,0)
(-1,0)	(0,0)	(-1,0)	(0,0)	(-1,0)
(0,+1)	(0,0)	(0,0)	(0,+1)	(0,+1)
(-1,+1)	(0,0)	(-1,0)	(0,+1)	(-1,+1)

&⁻	(0,0)	(-1,0)	(0,+1)	(-1,+1)
(0,0)	(0,0)	(0,0)	(0,0)	(0,0)
(-1,0)	(0,0)	(0,0)	(0,+1)	(0,+1)
(0,+1)	(0,0)	(0,0)	(-1,0)	(-1,0)
(-1,+1)	(0,0)	(0,+1)	(-1,0)	(-1,+1)

⊕	(0,0)	(-1,0)	(0,+1)	(-1,+1)
(0,0)	(0,0)	(-1,0)	(0,+1)	(-1,+1)
(-1,0)	(-1,0)	(-1,0)	(-1,+1)	(-1,+1)
(0,+1)	(0,+1)	(-1,+1)	(0,+1)	(-1,+1)
(-1,+1)	(-1,+1)	(-1,+1)	(-1,+1)	(-1,+1)

⊕⁻	(0,0)	(-1,0)	(0,+1)	(-1,+1)
(0,0)	(0,0)	(0,+1)	(-1,0)	(-1,+1)
(-1,0)	(0,+1)	(0,+1)	(-1,+1)	(-1,+1)
(0,+1)	(-1,0)	(-1,+1)	(-1,0)	(-1,+1)
(-1,+1)	(-1,+1)	(-1,+1)	(-1,+1)	(-1,+1)

⊗	(0,0)	(-1,0)	(0,+1)	(-1,+1)
(0,0)	(0,0)	(0,0)	(0,+0)	(0,0)
(-1,0)	(0,0)	(0,+1)	(-1,0)	(-1,+1)
(0,+1)	(0,0)	(-1,0)	(0,+1)	(-1,+1)
(-1,+1)	(0,0)	(-1,+1)	(-1,+1)	(-1,+1)

⊗⁻	(0,0)	(-1,0)	(0,+1)	(-1,+1)
(0,0)	(0,0)	(0,0)	(0,0)	(0,0)
(-1,0)	(0,0)	(-1,0)	(0,+1)	(-1,+1)
(0,+1)	(0,0)	(0,+1)	(-1,0)	(-1,+1)
(-1,+1)	(0,0)	(-1,+1)	(-1,+1)	(-1,+1)

⊘	(0,0)	(-1,0)	(0,1)	(-1,+1)
(0,0)	(0,0)	(0,0)	(0,0)	(-1,+1)
(-1,0)	(0,0)	(-1,0)	(0,1)	(-1,+1)
(0,1)	(0,0)	(0,1)	(-1,0)	(-1,+1)
(-1,1)	(-1,1)	(-1,1)	(-1,1)	(-1,+1)

⊘⁻	(0,0)	(-1,0)	(0,+1)	(-1,+1)
(0,0)	(0,0)	(0,0)	(0,0)	(-1,+1)
(-1,0)	(0,0)	(0,+1)	(-1,0)	(-1,+1)
(0,+1)	(0,0)	(-1,0)	(0,+1)	(-1,+1)
(-1,+1)	(-1,+1)	(-1,+1)	(-1,+1)	(-1,+1)

Figure 5. Truth tables of eight BDL operators (adapted from [9]).

Bipolar Partial Ordering: (x,y)≥≥(u,v), iff |x|≥|u| and y≥v;	(a)
Complement: ¬(x,y)≡(-1,1)-(x,y)≡(¬x,¬y)≡(-1-x,1-y);	(b)
Negation: −(x,y) ≡ (−y,−x);	(c)
Implication: (x,y)⇒(u,v) ≡ (x→u,y→v) ≡ (¬x∨u, ¬y∨v);	(d1)
Entanglement Ω: {(x,y)Ω(u,v)} ≡{(x,y)⇔(u,v) or (x,y)⇔−(u,v)};	(d2)
Fission: fission(x,y) = {(x,0); (0,y)};	(d3)
Fusion: fusion((x,0); (0,y)) = (x,0)⊕(0,y) = (x, y);	(d4)
Bipolar least upper bound (blub):	
blub((x,y),(u,v))≡(x,y)⊕(u,v)≡(-(|x|∨|u|),y∨v);	(e)
-blub: blub⁻((x,y),(u,v))≡ (x,y)⊕⁻(u,v) ≡ (−(y∨v),(|x|∨|u|));	(f)
Bipolar greatest lower bound (bglb):	
bglb((x,y),(u,v)) ≡ (x,y)&(u,v) ≡ (-(|x|∧|u|),y∧v));	(g)
-bglb: bglb⁻((x,y),(u,v)) ≡ (x,y)&⁻(u,v) ≡ (− (y∧v), (|x|∧|u|)));	(h)
Cross-pole greatest lower bound (cglb):	
cglb((x,y),(u,v))≡(x,y)⊗(u,v)≡(-(|x|∧|v|∨|y|∧|u|),(|x|∧|u|∨|y|∧|v|));	(i)
-cglb: cglb⁻((x,y),(u,v)) ≡ (x,y)⊗⁻(u,v) ≡ −((x,y)⊗(u,v));	(j)
Cross-pole least upper bound (cglb):	
club((x,y),(u,v))≡(x,y)⊘(u,v)≡(-1,1)−(¬(x,y)⊗¬(u,v));	(k)
-club: club⁻((x,y),(u,v))≡(x,y)⊘⁻(u,v)≡ −((x,y) ⊘ (u,v)).	(l)

(**a**)

Excluded Middle (LEMs)	(x,y)⊕ −(x,y) ≡ (-1,+1); (x,y)⊕⁻ −(x,y) ≡ (-1,+1);
Non-Contradiction	¬((x,y)&¬(x,y)) ≡ (-1,+1); −((x,y)&⁻−(x,y)) ≡ (-1,+1);
Linear Bipolar DeMorgan's Laws	¬((a,b)&(c,d)) ≡ ¬(a,b)⊕¬(c,d); ¬((a,b)⊕(c,d)) ≡ ¬(a,b)&¬(c,d); −((a,b)&⁻(c,d)) ≡ −(a,b)⊕⁻−(c,d); −((a,b)⊕⁻(c,d)) ≡ −(a,b)&⁻−(c,d);
Non-Linear Bipolar DeMorgan's Laws	¬((a,b)⊗ (c,d)) ≡ ¬(a,b) ⊘ ¬(c,d); ¬((a,b) ⊘ (c,d)) ≡ ¬(a,b) ⊗ ¬(c,d); −((a,b)⊗⁻(c,d)) ≡ −(a,b) ⊘⁻ −(c,d); −((a,b)⊘⁻(c,d)) ≡ −(a,b) ⊗⁻ −(c,d)

(**b**)

Unipolar Axioms (UAs): UA1: ϕ→ (φ→ϕ); UA2: (ϕ→(φ→χ)) →((ϕ→φ)→(ϕ→χ)); UA3: (¬ϕ→φ)→((¬ϕ→¬φ)→ϕ); UA4: (a) ϕ∧φ→ϕ; (b) ϕ∧φ→φ; UA5: ϕ→(φ→ϕ∧φ);	Bipolar Linear Axioms: BA1: (ϕ⁻,ϕ⁺)⇒((φ⁻,φ⁺)⇒(ϕ⁻,ϕ⁺)); BA2: ((ϕ⁻,ϕ⁺)⇒((φ⁻,φ⁺)⇒(χ⁻,χ⁺))) ⇒(((ϕ⁻,ϕ⁺)⇒(φ⁻,φ⁺))⇒((ϕ⁻,ϕ⁺)⇒(χ⁻,χ⁺))); BA3: (−(ϕ⁻,ϕ⁺)⇒(φ⁻,φ⁺)) ⇒ ((−(ϕ⁻,ϕ⁺)⇒−(φ⁻,φ⁺)) ⇒ (ϕ⁻,ϕ⁺)); BA4: (a) (ϕ⁻,ϕ⁺)&(φ⁻,φ⁺)⇒(ϕ⁻,ϕ⁺); (b) (ϕ⁻,ϕ⁺)&(φ⁻,φ⁺)⇒(φ⁻,φ⁺); BA5: (ϕ⁻,ϕ⁺)⇒((φ⁻,φ⁺)⇒((ϕ⁻,ϕ⁺)&(φ⁻,φ⁺)));
Inference Rule – Modus Ponens (MP): UR1: (ϕ∧(ϕ→φ))→φ.	Non-Linear Bipolar Universal Modus Ponens (BUMP) BR1: IF ((ϕ⁻,ϕ⁺)∗(ψ⁻,ψ⁺)), [((ϕ⁻,ϕ⁺)⇒(φ⁻,φ⁺))&((ψ⁻,ψ⁺)⇒(χ⁻,χ⁺))], THEN [(φ⁻,φ⁺)∗(χ⁻,χ⁺)];
Predicate axioms and rules UA6: ∀x,ϕ(x) →ϕ(t); UA7: ∀x, (ϕ→φ)→ (ϕ→∀x,φ); UR2–Generalization: ϕ→∀x,ϕ(x)	Bipolar Predicate axioms and Rules of inference BA6: ∀x,(ϕ⁻(x),ϕ⁺(x))⇒(ϕ⁻(t),ϕ⁺(t)); BA7: ∀x,((ϕ⁻,ϕ⁺)⇒(φ⁻,φ⁺))⇒((ϕ⁻,ϕ⁺)⇒∀x,(φ⁻,φ⁺); BR2-Generalization: (ϕ⁻,ϕ⁺)⇒∀x,(ϕ⁻(x),ϕ⁺(x))

(**c**)

∀ϕ=(ϕ⁻,ϕ⁺)∈B₁ or B_F = [-1,0]×[0,+1],

[\|ϕ\| = (\|ϕ⁻\|∨\|ϕ⁺\|)] → (BUMP → MP) → (BDL → BL) → (BDFL → FL).

(**d**)

Figure 6. Bipolar axiomatization on BDL (adapted from [9]): (**a**) basic operations (has been extended to BDFL, ∀(x,y), (u,v)∈B_1 or B_F where (x,y)≡(−\|x\|,\|y\|) shows explicit bipolarity); (**b**) equilibrium-based laws; (**c**) equilibrium-based vs. truth-based axiomatization of BDL; (**d**) equilibrium-based revealing of truth.

> **Bipolar Universal Modus Ponens (BUMP) in IF-THEN Form:**
> IF [(ϕ⁻,ϕ⁺)⇒(φ⁻,φ⁺)]&[(ψ⁻,ψ⁺)⇒(χ⁻,χ⁺)]& [(ϕ⁻,ϕ⁺)*(ψ⁻,ψ⁺)]; THEN [(φ⁻,φ⁺)*(χ⁻,χ⁺)].
> **BUMP in Tautological Form:**
> [(ϕ⁻,ϕ⁺)⇒(φ⁻,φ⁺)] & [(ψ⁻,ψ⁺)⇒(χ⁻,χ⁺)] ⇒ {[((ϕ⁻,ϕ⁺)*(ψ⁻,ψ⁺)) ⇒ ((φ⁻,φ⁺)*(χ⁻,χ⁺))]}.
> **BUMP in Singleton Form:**
> IF [(ϕ ⇒ φ) & (ψ ⇒ χ)] and (ϕ * ψ), THEN (φ * χ), or (ϕ ⇒ φ) & (ψ ⇒ χ) ⇒ [(ϕ * ψ) ⇒ (φ * χ)] .
> **Bipolar Superposition/entanglement in Logical Form (Binding):**
> Binding{(−1,0), (0,+1)} = (−1,0)⊕(0,+1) = (−1,+1).
> **Bipolar Collapse in Logical Form (Separating):**
> Separating(−1,+1) = {(−1,0), (0,+1)}.
> **Single Entanglement:** (ϕ Ω φ) = (-1,+1) or (ϕ ⇔ φ) or (ϕ ⇔ − φ).
> ∀a,b,c,d, quantum spacetime emergence through BUMP:
> *[ψ(a(t_x,p_1))⇒χ(c(t_y,p_3))]&[ϕ(b(t_x,p_2))⇒φ(d(t_y,p_4))] ⇒ [ψ(a(t_x,p_1)) *ϕ(b(t_x,p_2))⇒χ(c(t_y,p_3)) *φ(d(t_y,p_4))];*
> Spacetime emergence through bipolar quantum entanglement with BUMP:
> *[ψ(a(t_x,p_1))⇔χ(c(t_y,p_3))]&[ϕ(b(t_x,p_2))⇔φ(d(t_y,p_4))] ⇒ [ψ(a(t_x,p_1)) *ϕ(b(t_x,p_2))⇔χ(c(t_y,p_3)) *φ(d(t_y,p_4))];*
> Or *[ψ(a)⇔χ(c)]&[ϕ(b)⇔φ(d)]⇒ [ψ(a)*ϕ(b)⇔χ(c)*φ(d)];*
> where a(t₁,p₁), b(t₁,p₂), c(t₂,p₃), d(t₂,p₄) are bipolar strings with k(t,p) standing for *"agent k at time t and space p"* (t_x, t_y, p_x and p_y can be the same or different points in time and space). An agent without time and space is assumed at any time t and space p such as non-local quantum entanglement.
>
> **Two-fold universal instantiation:**
> Operator instantiation: * as a universal operator can be bound to any commutative and bipolar monotonic (w.r.t. ≥≥) operator &, ⊕, &⁻, ⊕⁻, ⊗, ⊘, ⊗⁻, and ⊘⁻. (ϕ⇒φ) is designated bipolar true; ((ϕ⁻,ϕ⁺)*(ψ⁻,ψ⁺)) is not designated. Bipolar instantiation: ∀x, (ϕ⁻,ϕ⁺)(x) ⇒ (φ⁻,φ⁺)(x); (ϕ⁻,ϕ⁺)(A); ∴ (φ⁻,φ⁺)(A).

Figure 7. Bipolar quantum entanglement/superposition and quantum emergence or submergence of spacetime (adapted from [2,6,9]).

Theorem 4. *Global realism must be transcendent of spacetime, spacetime relativity, real–imaginary or particle–wave complementarity, and Dirac bra-ket standard for quantum mechanics. It must reach logically definable causality with global energy/information conservation. Thus, it must be necessarily a background-independent geometrical and logical unification of general relativity and quantum mechanics—a real-world quantum gravity (RWQG) theory.*

Proof. (1) General relativity is a physical theory about space and time. According to general relativity, spacetime is a four-dimensional object that must obey an Einstein equation, which explains how matter curves the spacetime. Without the geometry of light and logic of photons, however, it has been shown [6] that observer–observability formed a paradox in modern science, truth–equilibrium found no unification, and mind–light–matter unity was unreachable in spacetime.

(2) It is shown [6] that quantum mechanics has been shrouded with mysteries preventing itself from reaching definable causality for a general-purpose analytical quantum computing paradigm.

(3) Spacetime geometries and truth-based logics have been disqualified to be the geometry of light and logic of photons, and background-independent bipolar quantum geometry or BQG and bipolar dynamic logic or BDL have been identified as the geometry of light and logic of photons with logically definable causality for quantum emergence/submergence of spacetime with energy/information conservation in dynamic equilibrium and harmony.

(4) Following (1) and (3), **global realism** must necessarily be a background-independent geometrical and logical unification of general relativity and quantum mechanics—an RWQG theory for quantum emergence and submergence of spacetime. □

3.2. From Bipolar Dynamic Equilibrium to Bipolar Strings

To visualize global realism in graphical forms and physical terms, we introduce bipolar strings [9,21] as a real-world string theory that unifies the concept of BQAs [9,37] with QI [2,6].

Definition 1. *A bipolar string* is a BQA in BDE characterized by a bipolar logical/algebraic state (Re. Postulates 1–4) of a bipolar quantum entanglement or BQE.

Definition 2. *A bipolar generic string* is a string with elementary negative-positive (−, +) poles, each of which cannot be further decomposed. The two poles can be alternating until they collapse (such as when being measured).

Definition 3. *A bipolar superstring* is a composite and/or entangled set of multiple bipolar generic strings and/or bipolar superstrings.

Definition 4. Bipolar strings as generic or composite quantum superposition and/or entanglement can form (emerge) and collapse (submerge); **collapsed bipolar strings** as unbalanced bipolar strings remain part of the global BDE that can be entangled again.

Postulate 5. *Gravitation among cosmological objects is fundamentally a super symmetrical entanglement of bipolar strings with or without graviton-antigraviton pairs.*

Postulate 6. *The formation and collapse of bipolar strings are not limited by the speed of light but can show superluminal cause and effect in generic cases.*

Notably, among the basic forces of Nature, gravitation is the most difficult force to unify. The main reason is the physically different structures of the gravitational force from the other forces. Equilibrium-based bipolar strings lead to a completely background-independent RWQG theory—a bipolar unification that overcomes the difficulty.

Theorem 5. *Bipolar strings constitute the physical foundation for logically definable quantum emergence and submergence of spacetime.*

Proof. Following Theorems 1–4, Definitions 1–4, and Postulates 5 and 6, without bipolar strings there would be no bipolar dynamic equilibrium and no bipolar universal modus ponens (BUMP) for logically definable causality of quantum emergence and submergence of spacetime [6,9,20] (Figures 4–8). □

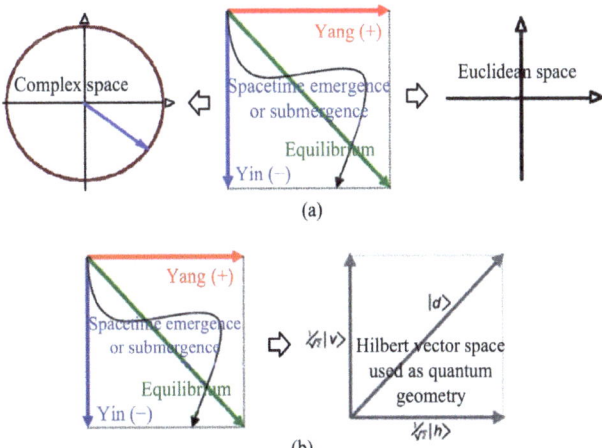

Figure 8. Spacetime emergence/submergence (adapted from [6,20]).

Theorem 6. *Bipolar strings constitute the physical foundation for the logically definable mind–light–matter unitary causal–logical human/machine thinking, learning, and imagination.*

Proof. It follows directly from Theorem 5. □

Postulate 7. *Thinking and imagination are fundamentally cognitive processes logically equivalent to quantum emergence (entanglement) and submergence (collapse) of spacetime in mind–light–matter unitary terms. Thus, quantum entanglement and collapse constitute the basic functionality of the physical and mental worlds with mind–light–matter unity.*

Postulate 8. *Machine thinking and imagination are the basis and prerequisite for adaptive machine learning and human-level intelligence.*

Based on Definitions 1–4 and Postulates 1–5, action–reaction and particle–antiparticle bipolarity, as well as mind–light–matter, are logically unified. Now, a quantum entanglement of two elementary particles forms a bipolar generic string; an atom, a neuron, a brain, a mind, a star, or a pair of interactive stars or universes form superstrings.

Theorem 7. *Global realism with bipolar strings (GRBS) as a theory of physics and information constitutes a scalable logical system of thought—a minimal but most general axiomatization of physics and quantum information science that is a necessary and inevitable consequence of the Bell inequality violation.*

Proof. Notably, the first principles of science and the second law of thermodynamics are unified with ground-0 axioms [6]. Following Theorems 1–6, Definitions 1–4, Postulates 5–8, and Ref. [6], without GRBS there would be no being, no truth, no first principles of science, no second law of thermodynamics, no reality, and no epistemology. □

3.3. Mind–Light–Matter Unity

Historically, mind–light–matter unity [6] was unreachable in spacetime. It is argued [2] that if $i = \sqrt{-1}$ can be used by Niels Bohr for real–imaginary complementarity in his Copenhagen interpretation of QM where opposites are said complementary, there is no reason to forbid the use of negative numbers as the direct opposites of positive numbers to reach logically definable causality and analytical quantum computing for global realism. It is shown in [2,6,9] that BDL, BDFL, and BQLA in the complete background independent geometry BQG have reached logically definable causality, information conservation, the geometry of light, and the logic of photon for mind–light–matter unity and quantum emergence (entanglement) or submergence (collapse) of spacetime. As a unification of the first principles of science with the second law of thermodynamics the equilibrium-based bipolar system [6] can serve as a logical resolution to the EPR and Schrödinger's Cat paradoxes where a quantum superposition/entanglement can be simply defined as a BDE.

It is noted in [6]: "While all interpretations in quantum mechanics have so far been commonly claimed leading to the same answers regarding observation and prediction, the bipolar equilibrium-based interpretation has led to fundamentally different answers. Arguably, the Einstein-Bohr debate of the 20th century has come to a logical settlement. While Bohr was right on the existence of quantum superposition and entanglement as well as their measurement in Hilbert space at his time, the geometry of light and logic of photon has revealed the logical nature of a deeper universe where quantum superposition/entanglement is neither Schrödinger's Cat nor spooky action at a distance. Indeed, Spinoza-Einstein's God does not play dice but plays a game of equilibrium and harmony with logically definable causality as Einstein stated: 'I believe in Spinoza's God, who reveals himself in the orderly harmony of what exists, ...'"

It is concluded in [2]: "Firstly, without negative numbers, there would be no imaginary numbers. Without imaginary numbers, there would be no Hilbert spacetime geometry, no Dirac bra-ket standard, no Niels Bohr's real-imaginary or particle-wave complementarity principle, and no QM. Secondly, without negative numbers, there would be no strict (−, +)-bipolarity, no bipolar crisp/fuzzy sets, no completely background-independent bipolar logical axiomatization for bipolar interaction and bipolar dynamic equilibrium. Without bipolar dynamic equilibrium, there would be no logically definable causality, no geometry of light, no logic of photon, no spacetime emergence or *submergence, no analytical quantum computing for QI, no imagination, no mind, no truth, and no mind–light–matter unity".*

It is well-known that the brain consists of billions of cells called neurons interconnected to form ensembles for the coordination and control of all physical and mental aspects of life. The nucleus of the cell body is structured like an atom but much larger in size and much more complex where I/O bipolarity is essential. Thus, mind–light–matter unity can be logically pictured with an equilibrium-based world of bipolar crisp or fuzzy sets where light bridges or illuminates mind and matter with the geometry of light and logic of photons in bioelectronics, biophotonics, or bioeconomics terms. Figure 9 illustrates a logical unification of matter and antimatter particles. Figure 10a shows a sketch of mind–light–matter unification where an equilibrium-based logic/algebra is both physical and logical. Figure 10b illustrates that different body functionalities can be coordinated by entangled (Ω) neural ensembles in the brain [6].

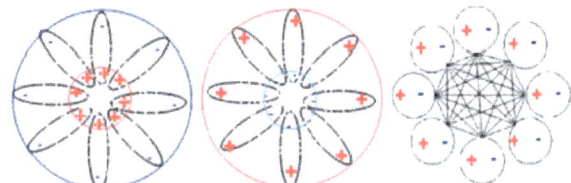

Figure 9. Bipolar unification of matter and antimatter (adapted from [21]).

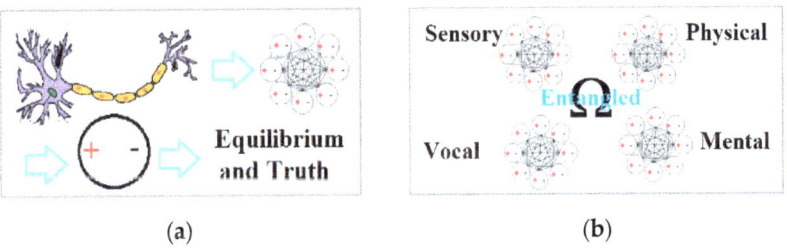

Figure 10. Mind–light–matter unity (adapted from [6]): (**a**) mind–light–matter unity in logical terms; (**b**) entangled (Ω) neural ensembles for the coordination of sensory, vocal, physical, and mental functionalities with mind–light–matter unity.

With QI, Turing's machine thinking puzzle [4] was revisited. It is stated in [2] that *"with strict (−, +)-bipolarity we have reached logically definable causality for mind–light–matter unity in equilibrium-based analytical terms. With the unpredicted new finding in thousands of years, Turing's thinking machinery puzzle [4] can be extended to a deeper and trickier question that is potentially closer to a definitive answer: 'If AI machine cannot think, can QI machine think?'"*

3.4. Bipolar Entropy for Equilibrium-Based Unification of Order and Disorder

While classical entropy is a measure of disorder, we define *bipolar entropy* and *bipolar entropy matrix* as a regulatory measure or relation.

Definition 5. *Bipolar entropy* is a regulatory bipolar measure in the bipolar (quantum) lattice $[-1, 0] \times [0, +1]$ (see Figure 3) for non-linear bipolar dynamic unification and regulation of Nature's elementary order and disorder. **The bipolar entropy matrix** is a holistic regulatory bipolar relational matrix of bipolar entropy measures for non-linear bipolar dynamic and set-theoretic unification and regulation of Nature's order and disorder or linearity and non-linearity.

With bipolar entropy matrix, it is shown [6,9,26] that bipolar energy/information can be conserved in an entangled bipolar quantum cellular automaton (BQCA) with BQLA. Equation (1a–c) provide the elementary equations for the transformation of bipolar quantum superposition to an entangled BQCA where E(t) is a bipolar column vector and M(t) a bipolar quantum logic gate (BQLG) as a specific type of BQLA matrix at time t. For $\forall (x, y), (u, v) \in B_\infty = [-\infty, 0] \times [0, +\infty]$, we have [21]:

Bipolar Elementary Multiplication/Interaction:
$$(x, y) \times (u, v) = (xv + yu, xu + yv); \tag{1a}$$

Bipolar Elementary Addition/Superposition:
$$(x, y) + (u, v) = (x + u, y + v) \tag{1b}$$

Bipolar Quantum Cellular Automaton (BQCA):
$$E(t + 1) = M(t) \times E(t). \tag{1c}$$

Why do we need BQLG, BQLA, and BQCA while linear algebra has been taught in college algebra classes for centuries? A simple answer is that classical linear algebra (LA) cannot accommodate the non-linear bipolar dynamic coexistence of equilibrium information. For instance, let $(-0.1, +0.1)$ and $(-1,000,000, +1,000,000)$ be different I/O bipolar balances, with LA we have the information loss $(-0.1 + 0.1) = (-1,000,000 + 1,000,000) = 0$. With BQLA, let the absolute bipolar elementary energy $|\varepsilon|(x,y) = |x| + |y|$ and let $|\varepsilon_{col}|M_{*j}(t)$ be the energy/information of the j column of a BQLG matrix $M(t)$, we have Equation (2a–c) for a BQCA [9,21,24,26]:

Energy/Information Conservation: $\forall j, |\varepsilon_{col}|M_{*j}(t) = 1.0$,
$$|\varepsilon|E(t + 1) = |\varepsilon|(M(t) \times E(t)) \equiv |\varepsilon|E(t); \tag{2a}$$

Energy/Information Regeneration: $\forall j, |\varepsilon_{col}|M_{*j}(t) > 1.0$,
$$|\varepsilon|E(t + 1) = |\varepsilon|(M(t) \times E(t)) > |\varepsilon|E(t); \tag{2b}$$

Energy/Information Degeneration: $\forall j, |\varepsilon_{col}|M_{*j}(t) < 1.0$,
$$|\varepsilon|E(t + 1) = |\varepsilon|(M(t) \times E(t)) < |\varepsilon|E(t). \tag{2c}$$

Based on Equations (1a–c) and (2a–c), M(t) forms a *bipolar entropy* matrix—a bipolar relational or algebraic matrix of bipolar entropy elements that makes the bipolar energy vector E(t) a regulated quantum entanglement. Different from unipolar entropy, bipolar entropy matrix as a holistic structure can play the forming and regulating roles of entanglement for energy/information conservation toward a global dynamic equilibrium with local regeneration (or growth) and degeneration (or aging) in physical, logical, mental, biological, and social-economical terms [6,9]. Thus, bipolar entropy leads to quantum cellular bioeconomics, equilibrium-based business intelligence, information conservational quantum-fuzzy cryptography, and other applications of RWQG for a Q5 (or QG-5) paradigm [2,6,9,21].

Notably, Schrödinger's book *What is Life?* [78] stimulated research in quantum biology. Schrödinger originally stated that life feeds on *negative entropy*, or *negentropy*, and, in a later edition, restated that the true source is *free energy*. Notably, negative entropy has led to important applications in physics and quantum information science [79–83]. Without bipolar dynamic equilibrium, however, negative entropy and free energy as unipolar concepts could not free Schrödinger from truth-based and being-centered singularity to reach logically definable causality. As a result, he stopped short of reaching *bipolar entropy* to unify order and disorder for bipolar coexistence/interaction of Nature. Similarly, Schrödinger's Cat paradox on quantum superposition remained a mystery for nearly two centuries (re. [6]).

With ground-0 axioms and *bipolar entropy*, BDL, BDFL, or BQLA can be alternatively named *bipolar entropy logic or algebra*. While truth-based entropy as a scientific concept as well as a measurable physical property is usually associated with a state of disorder, randomness, or uncertainty, it stopped short of going beyond the first principles and the second law to reach logically definable causality [6]. With bipolarity, the new entropy logic or algebra provides definable causality for bringing disorder, randomness, or uncertainty to an entanglement of equilibrium and harmony with mind–light–matter unity for AI&QI [6].

Ideas about the relationship between entropy and living organisms have inspired hypotheses and speculations in many contexts, including psychology, information theory, the origin of life, and the possibility of extraterrestrial life. It is evident that, however, *bipolar entropy* is the only way to unify negative and positive energies for bipolar dynamic equilibrium (BDE) through bipolar quantum entanglement with logically definable causality. Subsequently, the essence of life as a living bipolar superstring in BDE can be posited as quantum entanglement regulated by bipolar entropy. While the question *"which comes first, cognition or consciousness?"* is left open for further philosophical debate, GRBS with logically definable causality for quantum entanglement provides a unique scientific basis and a common starting point for both cognition and consciousness.

Theorem 8. *Bipolar entropy or bipolar entropy matrices can serve as a causal–logical regulatory measure for bringing bipolar strings in order or disorder to equilibrium-based energy/information conservation, regeneration, or degeneration states.*

Proof. While classical unipolar entropy is a measure of disorder in truth-based terms, bipolar entropy is a measure of order–disorder or symmetry–asymmetry in bipolar equilibrium-based terms. Since a perfect bipolar energy/information equilibrium can be characterized by the bipolar logical or bipolar entropy value $(-1, +1)$, its truth-based representation can be calculated as $|-1 + 1| = 0$, the lowest disorder measure for a perfect bipolar equilibrium. On the other hand, a bipolar non-equilibrium can be characterized by the value $(-1, 0)$ or $(0, +1)$, its truth-based representation can be calculated as $|-1 + 0| = 1$ or $|0 + 1| = 1$, the highest disorder measure for a bipolar non-equilibrium. While in the truth-based unipolar case, 0 shows no disorder but no representation of non-existence, (0,0) shows non-existence in the bipolar case. In the bipolar fuzzy case, order and disorder are unified. For instance,

$$(-0,5, +0.7) = \{(-0.5, +0.5) + (0, +0.2)\},$$

where $(-0.5, +0.5)$ shows the balance or order, and $(0, +0.2)$ shows the disorder. Equation (2a–c) shows that bipolar superstrings can be regulated by bipolar entropy matrices for energy/information conservation, regeneration (or growing), and degeneration (or aging). Proof of Equation (2a–c) is referred to as the Proof of Theorem 4 in [26]. □

Conjecture 1. *Life is a mind–light–matter unitary bipolar superstring regulated by bipolar entropy matrices; **thinking with consciousness and memory growth** is logically equivalent to mind–light–matter unitary quantum emergence of spacetime through quantum entanglement.*

Conjecture 2. *Energy/information can be conserved through dipoles including but not limited to black–white wholes that form an entangled wormhole or Einstein–Rosen bridge.*

Based on Equation (2a), Conjecture 2 can be illustrated with an example of information conservational security of large data sets. Figure 11a,b presents a sketch of the example. It is shown that the keypad of a huge data file can be compressed with "blackhole" keypad compression to a tiny minimum for encrypted data transmission to the receiver side. The data received can be decrypted using the keypad with "big bang (or white hole)" data recovery [30]. This approach can bring AI&QI into security to conceal large volumes of information in the post-quantum era for further integration with other systems.

Figure 11. Information conservational security (Adapted from [30]): (**a**) "Black Hole" Keypad Compression; (**b**) "Big Bang" Data Recovery.

4. Causal–Logical Brain Modeling (CLBM) for Entangled Machine Thinking and Imagination (EMTI)

4.1. Lost in Singularity but Found in Bipolar Relativity for Real-World Quantum Gravity

Quantum gravity (QG) as a field of theoretical physics seeks to describe gravity according to the principles of quantum mechanics. It deals with environments in which neither gravitational nor quantum effects can be ignored [49] such as in the vicinity of black holes or similar astrophysical objects. While QG as a truth-based paradigm so far avoided the historical topics of logically definable causality and mind–light–matter unity [6], the equilibrium-based approach brought QG to the real world.

It is noted [26] that "*Modern science is in urgent need for equilibrium-based bipolar unitary mathematical abstraction and knowledge representation due to the emergence of economic globalization, global climate change, and the mysterious phenomena of quantum nonlocality, which entail equilibrium-based visualization, rebalancing, and global regulation*".

The bipolar axiomatization (Figures 2–10) of GRBS presents a real-world logical unification of string theory, LQG, and M-theory—the three roads to quantum gravity [65]. Assuming action–reaction and particle–antiparticle bipolarity as the most fundamental properties of the universe, GRBS constitutes a minimal but most general axiomatization of physics and quantum information science—a logical basis of *YinYang Bipolar Relativity* that unifies the first principles of science and the second law of thermodynamics [6,9].

Bipolar relativity was identified as a scalable real-world, equilibrium-based bipolar string theory [9,18,21]. Now, the bipolar set–theoretic property is supported by the unique formal background-independent BQG and BDL/BDFL (Figures 2–10) identified as the geometry of light and logic of photon, respectively, to illuminate the classical and the quantum worlds as well as the mental and physical worlds [6]. While the equilibrium-based bipolar paradigm as a formal causal–logical system can reveal truths with quantum emergence/submergence of spacetime, string theory without bipolar modularity, scalability, and testability so far came short of providing a formal causal–logical basis even though it was once regarded as TOE.

The pitfall of string theory could be due to its lack of background independence as it is usually formulated with perturbation theory around a fixed background. The background-dependent property made it impossible to go beyond truth-based singularity within spacetime toward equilibrium-based bipolar geometrical and logical formulation for quantum emergence/submergence of spacetime with energy/information conservation. For instance, quantum entanglement and collapse can be easily represented with background-independent bipolar logical binding and separation, respectively, with spacetime-transcendent quantum nonlocality (re. Figures 7 and 8). However, that would be impossible with truth-based singularity in spacetime. This is shown in the following:

Emergence through superposition or entanglement:
$Binding\{(-1, 0), (0, +1)\} = (-1, 0) \oplus (0, +1) = (-1, +1)$;
Submergence or collapse:
$Separating(-1, +1) = \{(-1, 0), (0, +1)\}$.

While string theory got into a major controversy in science, GRBS logically reformulated string theory to a bipolar formal system for real-world causal–logical reasoning. On the other hand, LQG aims to merge quantum mechanics and general relativity by incorporating the matter of the Standard Model with posited spacetime structures as finite loops woven into spin networks or spin foam. However, the LQG theory came short of reaching definable causality for quantum emergence or submergence of spacetime even though it is claimed background-independent and non-perturbational. Notably, LQG has been formulated into a four-dimensional framework (with or without supersymmetry) while M-theory requires 11-dimensional supersymmetry. A direct comparison between the two has not been possible. Unexpectedly, bipolar strings as a unified logical/physical theory can not only provide a process model for fine loops at the spin foam level for LQG but also a process model for cosmological loops at the multiverse level for M-theory. Surprisingly, both levels can follow the same equilibrium-based geometrical and logical reasoning of BQG and BDL/BDFL to extend and unify the fundamentally different theories.

Different bipolar strings as dipoles are shown in Figures 12 and 13, which generalize strings to the real world at various levels including but not limited to multiverse cosmological, galaxy, atomic, and subatomic levels that assume *complete background independence*. Figure 12a shows a quantum emergence or submergence of spacetime at the Big Bang and blackhole level; Figure 12b shows a quantum emergence or submergence of spacetime at the particle–antiparticle level; Figure 12c shows unified loop quantum processes of multiverses and/or spin foams; Figure 12d shows a bipolar string in a logical circle. Figure 13a shows a bipolar generic string as a quantum entanglement; Figure 13b shows a bipolar superstring as a hypothetical wormhole of two entangled universes—one submerges in a black hole, and another emerges from a white hole; Figure 13c shows a composite of bipolar strings; Figure 13d shows a composite of bipolar superstrings or multiverses.

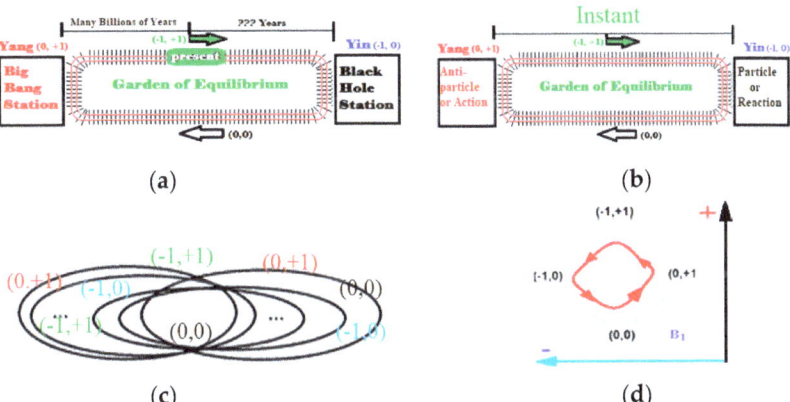

Figure 12. Background independent GRBS (adapted from [20]): (**a**) a cyclic process model of quantum emergence and submergence of spacetime; (**b**) a cyclic process model of quantum emergence and submergence of spin foam spacetime; (**c**) unified quantum processes of multiverses and/or spin foam loops; (**d**) the quantum logical and geometrical nature of a cyclic process model for bipolar strings or loops as an entangled-collapse-annihilation-reincarnation circle.

The bipolar strings under global realism as loop processes assume logically definable causality and information conservation. Thus, equilibrium-based GRBS provides a scalable and observable logical–physical and truth–equilibrium unification of the three roads to quantum gravity with different loops of back–forth logical entanglement (Figure 12c). The logical nature provides a basis for entangled machine thinking and imagination with or without a general direction. Under the condition of complete background independence, the + and −poles of a bipolar string can be alternating until one end is measured [21].

Note that, at all levels of composition (re. Figure 7), the following bipolar logical interactions form a *loop* process of bipolar states (Re. Figure Figure 12):

(1)　　$(0, +1) \oplus (-1, 0) = (-1, +1)$; //entangled bipolar string in superposition/BDE;

(2) (−1, +1)&(−1, 0) = (−1, 0); //equilibrium transiting to blackhole or particle;
(3) (−1, 0)⊗(−1, 0) = (0, +1); //blackhole transiting to big bang or particle action–reaction;
(4) (0, +1)&(−1, 0) = (0, 0); //annihilation or transformation;
(5) BUMP: [(A⇒B)&(C⇒D)]⇒[(A*C)⇒(B*D)]; [(A⇔B)&(C⇔D)]⇒[(A*C)⇔(B*D)].
//* bipolar interaction/integration.

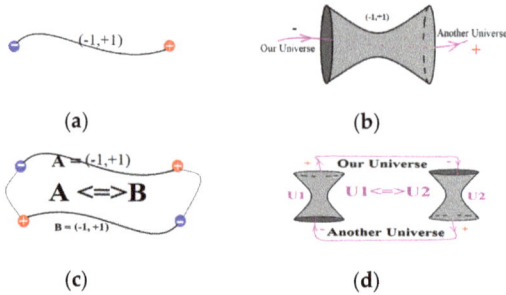

Figure 13. Bipolar strings: (**a**) quantum entanglement as a bipolar string (−1, +1) with spin down (−) and spin up (+); (**b**) hypothetical wormhole or Einstein–Rosen bridge as an entangled bipolar superstring (−1, +1) with input (black hole) (−) and output (white hole) (+); (**c**) entanglement of two bipolar strings A and B to a composite bipolar string; (**d**) entanglement of two bipolar superstrings U1 and U2 to multiverses.

4.2. Causal–Logical Brain Modeling for Entangled Machine Thinking and Imagination

While machine learning from data has been a focus, digital or quantum, for commercial applications with powerful computation, it is widely deemed unable to reach human-level AI because machines are deemed unable to think. *"If AI machine cannot think, can QI machine think?"*. That was the question asked in an earlier paper [2]. To give a potential answer to the question, a *causal–logical brain model (CLBM)* for *entangled machine thinking and imagination (EMTI)* is proposed in the following.

Figure 14 shows a bipolar superstring multiverse CLBM based on BUMP for EMTI. Following Postulate 7, we show that thinking can be modeled as a cognitive process logically equivalent to quantum emergence (entanglement) and submergence (collapse) of spacetime with mind–light–matter unity at the fundamental level.

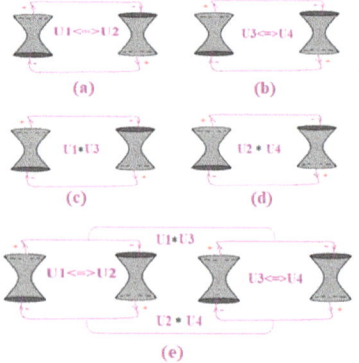

Figure 14. Illustration of a causal–logical brain model (CLBM) with entangled quantum neural networks based on bipolar universal modus ponens (BUMP) where a star * is any bipolar interaction: If (**a**) universes U1 and U2 are entangled, and (**b**) U3 and U4 are entangled, then (**c**) any interaction * between U1 and U3 must cause (**d**) the same interaction * of U2 and U4 or vice versa and leading to (**e**) all are entangled.

Let Figure 14 be elementary *bipolar quantum graphs (BQGs)* for *entangled neural networks (ENN)*, we have the concept of *entangled bipolar cognitive map (EBCM)*—an extension of bipolar cognitive map (BCM) or bipolar fuzzy cognitive map (BFCM) [9,12–17] of a college student. First, the student may wonder or imagine how multiverses be entangled logically with Hawking's negative–positive energies [84]. Based on the ubiquitous scalability and integrability of BUMP, we have:

Universal solution for entangled bipolar superstrings:

$$[(U1 \Leftrightarrow U2) \& (U3 \Leftrightarrow U4)] => [(U1*U3) \Leftrightarrow (U2*U4)]. \tag{3}$$

Next, if we let U1 be the concept of "**study**" and U2 be "**GPA**", the two concepts can be logically entangled in the student's mind. If we let U3 be the concept of "**degree**" and U4 be "**job**", the two concepts can be similarly entangled in the student's mind. Since U1 or "study" and U3 or "degree" can also be entangled in a normal thinking activity, the logic of BUMP as shown in Equation (3) (re. Figure 14) can be instantiated to different truth-based sentences. For instance, consider the following:

(a) *"If I study hard, I can get high GPA to get my degree and get a job after graduation"*.
(b) *"If I do not study hard, I cannot get high GPA to get my degree and get a job after graduation"*.

Unexpectedly, truths are revealed by bipolar dynamic equilibrium with bipolar strings in the mind of a human being or in the memory of a humanoid robot. While bio-photonics must play the bridge role between mind and matter in a human brain for revealing neurobiological functionalities, it is questionable whether that is possible for AI&QI thinking machinery. The answer is positive because mind–light–matter unity could be reached with the geometry of light and logic of photons in quantum–digital compatible terms [6] (re. Figures 3–10).

Could the entangled bipolar strings be further extended or scaled up for creative machine thinking and imagination with unlimited emerging new concepts from adaptive machine learning?

Conjecture 3. *Entanglement of bipolar strings can be scaled up for unlimited creative machine thinking and imagination assuming unlimited emergence of new concepts in memory through self-organizing adaptive/accumulative machine learning.*

The Postulate can be illustrated by further extending the above example. For instance, one day the student might be thinking about a high "GPA" (U2) from studying "hard" (U1) to be qualified for a "research assistantship" (U5) that would gain "research experience" (U6) for "graduate admission" (U7) into a "PhD program" (U8). Then we have the new entanglement $[(U5 \Leftrightarrow U6) \& (U7 \Leftrightarrow U8)] => [(U5*U7) \Leftrightarrow (U6*U8)]$. Adding the new entanglement to the earlier one in memory we have a bigger mental picture (Figure 15).

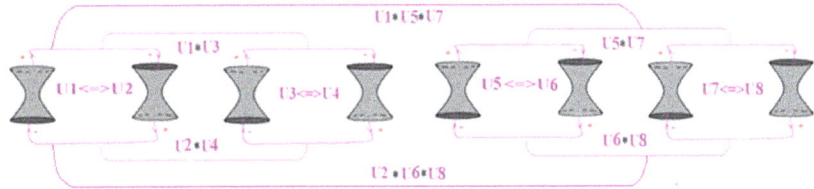

Figure 15. Entanglement of two different career paths for machine thinking.

Career Path 1 (job path):

$$[(U1(study) \Leftrightarrow U2(gpa)) \& (U3(degree) \Leftrightarrow U4(job))]$$
$$=>[(U1(study)*U3(degree)) \Leftrightarrow (U2(gpa)*U4(job))]; \tag{4}$$

Career Path 2 (graduate study path):

$$[(U1(study) \Leftrightarrow U2(gpa)) \& (U5(ra) \Leftrightarrow U6(re)) \& (U7(ga) \Leftrightarrow U8(phd))]$$
$$=> [(U1(study)*U5(ra)*U7(ga)) \Leftrightarrow (U2(gpa)*U6(re)*U8(phd))]. \quad (5)$$

Career Path 2 indicates the following: *"If I study hard, I can get high GPA, if I get a research assistantship I can get research experience, and if I get graduate admission, I can enroll in a PhD program. That implies (study hard & research assistantship & graduate admission) lead to high GPA & research experience & PhD program"*. (see Figure 15).

Theorem 9. *With bipolar universal modus ponens or BUMP, thinking and consciousness can be described as mind–light–matter unitary QI logically equivalent to quantum emergence (entanglement) and submergence (collapse) of spacetime.*

Proof. Thinking, consciousness, QI, and quantum emergence/submergence can follow the same logic of BDL/BDFL and BUMP for bipolar entangled causal–logical reasoning with logically definable, scalable, interactive, and integrative causality (re. Figure 7). □

A comparison of Equations (2a–c) and (3) with Figure 7 reveals the logical equivalence of EMTI to quantum emergence (entanglement) and submergence (collapse) of spacetime. For instance, let the concepts of "study" and "gpa" et al. be conceptual agents in any spacetime, Equations (2a–c) and (3) would be logically spacetime emergence/submergence in the mind as shown in Figure 7. Surprisingly, EMTI with a CLBM is unified with quantum gravity for QCQB. (Note: while new concepts can emerge in creative thinking/imagination, submerged concepts can be recalled from memory).

It should be noted that, while crisp bipolarity is so far used for illustration purposes, in fuzzy or algebraic cases there could be bipolar granularities to support focus generation in cognitive mapping or pattern recognition for adaptive machine learning from EBCMs, a typical task for a GPU. Figure 16 shows two separate foci corresponding to Career Path 1 and Path 2, respectively.

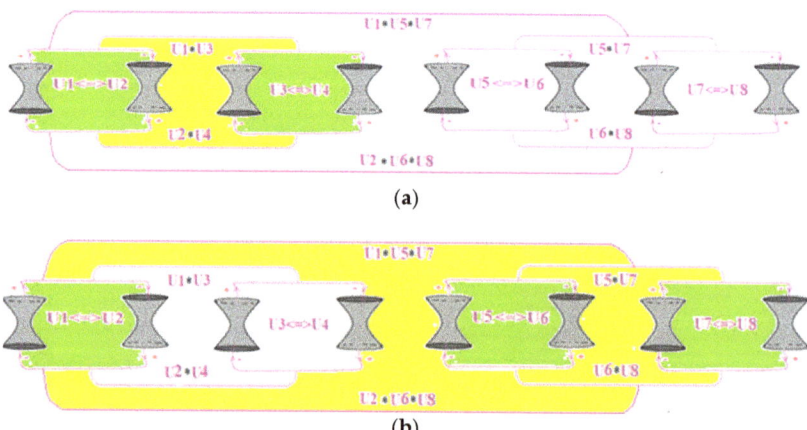

Figure 16. (**a**) Focus generation for Career Path 1; (**b**) focus generation for Career Path 2.

4.3. Road to Human-Level Intelligence

Now, career Path 1 and Path 2 in Figure 15 show two competitive options for further reasoning. Someone may wonder: *What are the differences between EMTI and rule-based reasoning?*

While if–then production rules are coded into machines by programmers based on truth-based unipolar Boolean logic (BL) or fuzzy logic (FL), EMTI is based on equilibrium-based bipolar strings that make reciprocal bipolar interaction possible—the key for resonant self-organization and consciousness with entangled thinking [62–64]. While truth in AI is static, GRBS asserts that everything in the universe or in the mind including the universe and the mind themselves form a dynamic equilibrium-based bipolar string or superstring that can be entangled for human-level AI&QI. While rule-based reasoning needs hard-coded production rules, entangled machine thinking assumes emerging concepts in the mind. While an if–then production rule has precedence and is a consequence following MP, any pair or group of concepts can be bipolar entangled for causal–logical thinking and imagination following BUMP that can reveal modus ponens (MP), but not vice versa. While MP supports programed reasoning and learning, BUMP supports adaptive, enactive, creative, accumulative, entangled, causal–logical reasoning and learning in a "growing up" process. Here, quantum emergence and submergence naturally lead to consciousness and unconsciousness, respectively, with mind–light–matter unity in logical terms [6,9,13,15,17]. Thus, EMTI forms a mind–light–matter unity CLBM for QCQB with QI that is theoretically different from AI. Bipolar distinctions include but are not limited to logically definable causality in regularity and global energy/information conservation.

The next question could be as follows: *How could spacetime emergence and submergence be ubiquitous in the physical and mental worlds?*

This is a tough question with a simple answer. Logically, BUMP as an equilibrium-based bipolar universal generalization of MP provides logically definable causality in regularity. Observably, when a balloon is warmed up, it gets bigger, and when it is cooled down, it gets smaller. Thus, with mind–light–matter unity the ubiquitous property is both logical and observable.

A follow-up question is as follows: *What are the differences between EMTI and entangled thought?*

While entangled thought is a mental problem in modern psychology, EMTI is for logical and creative thinking with equilibrium and harmony. Of course, EMTI can also be used to model or simulate mental problems with drastic bipolar oscillation, chaos, and dichotomy [6,9,16,19,34,35]. This is possible because **bipolar entropy** can unify order and disorder. Thus, EMTI is applicable in mind–light–matter unitary AI&QI but also in modern clinical psychiatry and cognitive psychology as well as in bio-electronics, bio-economics, and social economics.

The next question is as follows: *How could an emerging concept in the mind be bipolar dynamic?*

Without input–output or negative–positive bipolar energy/information, no concept can emerge or submerge in spacetime or in the mind. Thus, GRBS asserts that bipolar entangled thinking and imagination is fundamentally open-world, open-ended, ubiquitous quantum emergence or submergence of spacetime with logically definable causality for human-level mind–light–matter unity AI&QI (Re. Figure 7).

It can be further questioned as follows: *How could the multiverses or superstrings in Figures 14–16 be applicable while M-theory is still hypothetical?*

While entangled spacetime emergence/submergence is still a matter of debate, dipoles are observed everywhere. The James Webb Space Telescope is reshaping cosmology, and some evidence of cyclic cosmology has been reported [2]. Regardless of the unsettled nature of this issue, equilibrium-based bipolar strings and superstrings or multiverses as imaginary structures in the universe and the mind are both logical and physical that can conserve information and can reveal truths. With logically definable causality in regularity, BUMP can reveal MP and equilibrium can reveal truth. Such properties make them ideal for the mind–light–matter unitary creative thinking and imagination towards the development of human-level AI&QI machinery through quantum entanglement. Furthermore, without creative thinking and imagination for new theories, there would be no experimental observation. The observational proof of light bending around celestial objects was preceded by Einstein's prediction in his relativity theory; the actual observation of black holes did not come until decades later after the black hole theory was established; the Bell inequality violation could not have been tested without the Bell theorem. Regardless of all these, the logical nature of BUMP and QI with bipolar strings can enable a machine to think—a sufficient condition for the applicability of GRBS. That is comparable with any historical breakthroughs.

Yet another question is as follows: *What is the key difference between QI and cutting-edge AI?* Notably, the logical road to human-level AI has led to a dead-end [7], but QI = AI ∪ BI (re. Figure 1), as a quantum–digital compatible, analytical quantum computing paradigm with logically definable causality for quantum superposition/entanglement, makes mind–light–matter unity and entangled thinking logically possible. While cutting-edge AI technology has so far came short of finding a breakthrough on the origin of entangled causal–logical cognition and consciousness even though supervised and unsupervised machine learning from big data has been applied for major commercial applications using artificial neural networks, QI can be supported with *entangled quantum neural networks* where each concept can be matched to a physical/biological entity, and GPU pattern recognition can be used for causal–logical focus generation from a cognitive map. That has been impossible with existing AI technologies even though artificial neural networks show certain incremental learning abilities through training. Fundamentally speaking, BUMP can reveal MP, but not vice versa [6,9].

While the above machine thinking illustration is soft science for intuitive illustration, in hard science, such as in particle physics and quantum biology [70,71,84–88], bipolar interaction would be actual quantum emergence and/or submergence of spacetime logically defined with BUMP (Re. Figure 7). Thus, creative thinking and imagination with mind–light–matter unity are fundamentally the quantum emergence (entanglement) and submergence (collapse) of spacetime (Re. Theorems 6 and 7) either in the physical world or in the mental world. While a human's analytical and creative thinking can be continued (entangled), stopped (collapsed), or become psychologically illogical for varied reasons, quantum entanglement in a machine can emerge and submerge or collapse in quantum–digital compatible terms [2], and a machine will not get tired from creative thinking and imagination.

Thus, a causal–logical brain model provides a basis for adaptive machine learning. With quantum–digital compatibility [2,6], bipolar quantum entanglement becomes part of an analytical paradigm of QI where a multidimensional system consists of a set of bipolar strings in bipolar dynamic equilibrium states (Figure 3a). Thus, bipolar quantum entanglement provides both a logical and a physical basis for entangled machine thinking and imagination toward human-level intelligence.

Notably, while human thinking could be logical, less logical, or even illogical limited by individual neurobiological development and physical strength, machine thinking can be strictly logical but less flexible/intellectual—a gap between humanoid robots and human intelligence. Thus, we still have the following question:

Can a machine pass the Turing test?

Recall that the Turing Test [4] involves three players: a computer, a human respondent, and a human interrogator. All three are placed in separate rooms or in the same room but physically separated by terminals. The interrogator asks both players a series of questions and, after a period, tries to determine which player is the human and which is the computer.

Conjecture 4. *Existence is fundamentally a bipolar dynamic equilibrium or BDE. Thus, all existence is dynamic. Consciousness as a mental state is a dynamic existence with mind–light–matter unity.*

Conjecture 5. *The intellectual gap in creativity between humanoid robots and humans can be bridged with entangled machine thinking, imagination, and adaptive/accumulative machine learning through a "growing up" training process with sufficient learning examples. (Note: machine learning is not covered in this work).*

Conjecture 6. *Conjectures 4 and 5 lead to the possibility for a humanoid robot's causal–logical brain to reach human-level intelligence to pass the Turing test provided (i) mind–light–matter* unity AI/QI can be logically realized with GRBS, and (ii) examples are adequate or unlimited for adaptive/accumulative machine learning with EMTI.

5. Analysis and Discussion

5.1. God/Nature Logic vs. Human/Mind Logic

In 1925, on a walk with a young student named Esther Salama, Einstein shared his key guiding intellectual principle: *"I want to know how God created this world. I'm not interested in this or that phenomenon, in the spectrum of this or that element. I want to know His thoughts; the rest are just details"*.

Einstein asserted [54] that *"Physics constitutes a logical system of thought which is in a state of evolution"* and *"Evolution is proceeding in the direction of increasing simplicity of the logical basis (principles). We must always be ready to change these notions—that is to say, the axiomatic basis of physics—in order to do justice to perceived facts in the most perfect way logically"*.

It is noted [2] that, while the notion of "God logic" [36] might be irritating to some scientists, if God and Nature are for the same reality then *"God logic"* becomes a unified notion of God/Nature logic. That was exactly defined by the philosopher Spinoza [89]. Einstein famously stated later that *"I believe in Spinoza's God who reveals himself in the orderly harmony of what exists, not in a God who concerns himself with the fates and actions of human beings"*. Einstein also famously said *"Everyone who is seriously involved in the pursuit of science becomes convinced a spirit is manifest in the laws of the Universe—a spirit vastly superior to that of man, and one in the face of which we with our modest powers must feel humble. In this way the pursuit of science leads to a religious feeling of a special sort, which is indeed quite different from the religiosity of someone more naive"*.

While Einstein has been, for what he said, deemed as a God believer by some atheists but as an atheist by some God believers, following Einstein the phrase *"God's thoughts"* has been widely regarded by scientists, both theists and atheists, as the goal of modern physics to develop a logical understanding of the laws of Nature. However, that seemed to take researchers forever to accomplish unless God/Nature logic was found. Indeed, it has been impossible to reach the goal with truth-based "being qua being" logical thinking within spacetime geometry because spacetime as a being can emerge from or submerge to an equilibrium-based, completely background-independent geometry [6,9,20]. Fundamentally speaking [24], *"Truth-based logic is human logic; equilibrium-based logic is God (or Nature) logic. Mankind has been using human logic for thousands of years in seeking truths from the universe. Now, it is time for mankind to seek and accept God logic as a guiding light for scientific and technological endeavors"*.

Then, *what is the difference between the God logic of Gödel* [73] *and the God logic of Spinoza–Einstein?* While Gödel's God logic meant to use truth-based human logic to prove the existence of God as an exemplar Being, Spinoza–Einstein's God thought/logic meant to be the logic of Nature that can be equilibrium-based for revealing truth [2,6,36].

Although truth-based being qua being human mind logic has been widely regarded as God logic, GRBS is supported by numerous observations or historical facts in science and philosophy. The long search for ether and monad found no result, the modern quest for monopoles and strings turned out no concrete findings, but dipoles are everywhere. Without bipolar dynamic equilibrium, Platonic universals as well as the Dao of YinYang found no scientific logical basis [9,32,41]. Without bipolar dynamic logic or BDL to extend MP to BUMP, Aristotle's causality principle—the cornerstone of science—was logically undefinable for thousands of years [66,90–92], even with truth-based causal set [93], modern information theory [94], QM [66], and the second law of thermodynamics [77]—the paramount law of modern science.

It is noted [9,37] that, without definable causality in regularity, David Hume—an 18th-century Scottish philosopher and founder of empiricism—challenged Aristotle's causality principle and claimed it empirical, irreducible to pure regularity [90]; Bertrand Russell—a founder of analytic philosophy—deemed the law of causality as a relic of a bygone age [91]. Following Hume and Russell it is widely believed today by the scientific community that causality is no longer the only cornerstone of modern science. However, quantum entanglement needs the causality principle to come back with logical definability in regularity for equilibrium-based GRBS. Otherwise, quantum entanglement as a spacetime transcendent phenomenon cannot be logically real because it defied local realism.

Subsequently, we have the following historical observations:

(1) Without YinYang bipolarity, Hilbert as a great mathematician failed to solve his Problem 6 in spacetime geometry—axiomatizing all of physics [72].
(2) Without definable causality, Einstein as a great physicist stopped short of accomplishing his grand unification.
(3) While the renowned British scientist Paul Dirac once denied the foundational role of philosophy for scientific discovery (cf. [95]), without YinYang bipolarity for logically definable causality in regularity his real-imaginary bra-ket standard in QM found no logical exposition for his 3-polarizer experiment [96] and cannot serve as the geometry of light and the logic of photon for mind–light–matter unity [6,38–40].
(4) Without strict $(-,+)$ bipolar complementarity, Niels Bohr as a founding father of QM asserted that quantum causality is unattainable [66], but Einstein refused to accept QM as a complete theory.
(5) More recently, with truth-based reasoning American theoretical physicist Lee Smolin wrote the book titled *Three Roads to Quantum Gravity: A New Understanding of Space, Time and the Universe* [65], but that was followed by another book titled *The Trouble with Physics: The Rise of String Theory, the Fall of a Science, and What Comes Next* [60].

Notably, Lee Smolin is a foreseer in science and a strong advocate of background independence [60,97]. He is the first theoretical physicist who made the visionary prediction that the three approaches, namely, string theory, LQG, and M-theory, may be approximations of a single, underlying theory [65]. While the underlying theory should be background-independent, the insurmountable barrier had, however, been that, without bipolar dynamic equilibrium, being and truth as static unipolar concepts in the human mind could not go beyond spacetime to perform the causal–logical quantum gravity function of God/Nature with complete background independence for spacetime emergence—a distinction of GRBS from local realism.

Someone may argue that we do have the equilibrium concept in the second law of thermodynamics. Unfortunately, the second law is a unipolar truth-based first principle, not a bipolar dynamic ground-0 axiom [6]. Someone may further argue that the concept of entropy in modern information theory must be most fundamental. Similarly, truth-based unipolar entropy is not equilibrium-based bipolar entropy, and classical information science is not quantum information science. It is evident that the key concept of quantum entanglement and/or superposition of the latter is missing from the former. Logically, the latter can reveal the former or QI can reveal AI through ubiquitous spacetime emergence/submergence, but not vice versa. However, the ubiquitous concept remained a "spooky action" or Schrödinger's Cat through the 20th century.

Among the distinguished scientists, black hole theorist Steven Hawking was once near the equilibrium-based GRBS theory. His book *The Grand Design* ([84] p. 5) pronounced that *"Philosophy is dead" "M-theory predicts that a great many universes were created out of nothing"* and *"Their creation does not require the intervention of some supernatural being or God"*. It is noted in [20] that, *"when they advocated M-theory and nihilism, however, they also promoted the concept of negative-positive energies ([84] pp. 179–180) but stopped short of pointing out the unavoidable consequence that the two energies are respectively the Yin and Yang of Nature. And when they proclaimed the death of (truth-based and being-centered) philosophy, they were calling back a different (YinYang bipolar equilibrium-based and harmony-centered) philosophy"*.

Among the Nobel Laureates, 2020 Nobel Prize Winner in Physics Roger Penrose is the strongest advocate for cyclic cosmology and dipoles. He proposed the Conformal Cyclic Cosmology (CCC) model [98] that iterates through infinite cycles in the framework of general relativity. On the other hand, he suggested that dipoles [99] could serve as a physical basis of quantum gravity and quantum biology for consciousness [100] but pointed out the incompatibility with quantum measurement.

Arguably, quantum gravity as a fundamental theory needs a definitive battleground with the logic of photon in the geometry of light for resolving the observer–observability paradox [6]. The key here is not the details of measurement but logically definable causality in regularity [2,6,9] for global realism to reveal spacetime as emergence through ubiquitous quantum entanglement [101] in both physical and mental worlds [6,36]. Thus, we are faced with the deeper question: *Could equilibrium-based YinYang bipolar relativity serve as a formal geometrical and logical basis for spacetime emergence and submergence with mind–light–matter unity?*

5.2. Why YinYang?

Is YinYang not a kind of informal Eastern dialectic in philosophical terms?

It is noted [26] that Hegel—a founding father of dialectics after Heraclites made the famous assertion [102]: after his truth-based contradiction-centered dialectical logic it would henceforth be impossible to state a philosophical proposition that is both true and new—the proclaimed end of philosophy and history (cf. [103]). Now, after being the only one of its kind for truth-based logical deduction for thousands of years, MP can be revealed by the equilibrium-based BUMP in BDL. BUMP is evidently a logical and philosophical proposition that is both new and true. While all dialectical logic models are truth-based and contradiction-centered where a contradiction is both true and false and can be characterized by the value-pair (1, 1), YinYang bipolarity is equilibrium-based and harmony-centered and does not admit contradiction. For instance, (−pole, +pole) = (−1, +1) stands for bipolar true and shows a perfect input–output equilibrium that is syntactically, semantically, and fundamentally different from a contradiction in dialectics.

Is bipolarity not a modern physics or psychiatry concept in the West?

The term "YinYang Bipolar" was used in [9] to distinguish (−, +) bipolarity from the (0, 1) "bipolar" misnomer in digital logic design that meant to be bipolar transistor logic, where a transistor is NP or PN bipolar, but the logic implemented is (0, 1)-bivalent. While (0, 1) is considered normal, (−, +)-bipolarity is widely deemed abnormal. As noted in the preface of Ref. [9]: "*YinYang symbolizes the two energies of dynamic equilibrium, harmony, and complementarity; bipolarity without YinYang is often used in the West to indicate disorder, chaos, and dichotomy. Although disorder, chaos, and dichotomy are important aspects of Nature, they do not lead to a logical unification of Nature, agents, and causality like YinYang bipolar relativity in terms of equilibrium and harmony*". That is the reason that bipolarity without YinYang is unable to reach the geometry of light and the logic of photon for complete background-independence [6]. As stated by American linguist Alford [104], YinYang "*represents a higher level of formal operations, . . ., which lies beyond normal Western Indo-European development*".

For instances,

(1) in modern psychiatry, negative (−) is used to indicate depression, positive (+) is used to indicate mania, and zero (0) is used to indicate a normal mind, but the fundamental distinction of strong and weak mental equilibria, such as (−1, +1) and (−0.1, +0.1), are denied by the math (−1 + 1) = (−0.1 + 0.1) = 0;

(2) In modern psychology "entangled thought" is used for "intrusive thought", a mental condition that needs medical attention, but quantum entanglement as a key for QI should be a ubiquitous causal–logical concept in the classical and quantum worlds as well as in the mental and physical worlds.

(3) The misnomer "bipolar logic" in digital circuit design as "*binary logic implemented by bipolar transistors*" is a typical example of truth-based human/mind logic of the classical world revealed by equilibrium-based God/Nature logic.

While the binary digits 1 and 0 are used as sign bits in digital computers to indicate (−, +) bipolarity, respectively, negative numbers have been prohibited from entering logical formulation for logically definable causality due to the claim of (−, +) isomorphistry—a kind of sophistry on isomorphism (cf. [31,105,106]). It is commonsense, however, that without bipolar dynamic equilibrium of negative–positive energy/information to perform its regulating role, the human mind would be in total disorder, and the multiverses in M-theory would be completely isolated and collapsed [20]. With GRBS, the multiverses with order and chaos are unified in a global dynamic equilibrium in supersymmetry; the human mind may enjoy mental equilibrium or suffer from bipolar disorder as well [9,34].

Naturally, the Dao of YinYang has been widely influential in philosophy and science in Asia and the world (e.g., [66,107–110]). Without a unique formal geometrical and logical basis, however, it had been widely deemed an unscientific concept by the worldwide scientific community including but not limited to Chinese scientists in the homeland of negative numbers and YinYang bipolarity. It is noted in [27] that Chinese logician and philosopher Jin Yuelin almost failed to mention "YinYang" in his book *On Dao* [111]. Instead, he interpreted the Dao as Heisenberg's uncertainty principle in QM [112]. It is a typical example of some modern Chinese philosophers/scientists' effort to Westernize the Dao by denying YinYang bipolarity—the essence of the Dao in *Yijing—The Book of Change*, which asserts that *"One Yin and one Yang constitute what called the Dao"*.

Subsequently, few in modern science ventured to devote lifetime effort to the development of a unique formal equilibrium-based logical/mathematical system for YinYang bipolar reciprocal coexistence to reach logically definable causality in regularity. Such an effort would be and has been deemed "foolish", "futile", and "doomed" to fail. Notably, due to the $(-,+)$ isomorphism claim, negative numbers were forbidden to enter mathematics in the West for thousands of years until the Renaissance. Then, they were forbidden in both the East and the West to enter logical formulation even after Hilbert made i = $\sqrt{-1}$ as a basis for imaginary numbers in Hilbert space (cf. [113]), and Bohr used i = $\sqrt{-1}$ as part of his real–imaginary complementarity principle of the Copenhagen interpretation (cf. [2]). Ironically, with Leibniz's 01-binary interpretation [107] and Bohr's particle–wave or real–imaginary interpretation [66] to YinYang, no physicist would say electron and positron $(-e, +e)$ are isomorphic, no one dared to call Newton to wake up from his tomb to "correct" his action–reaction pair in physics textbooks from $(-F, +F)$ to $(+F, +F)$ or $(iF, +F)$, and no parents would be willing to ask their children to learn math in school without negative numbers (cf. [2,31,105,106]).

Nevertheless, starting in Ancient Greek times when negative numbers were forbidden in the West, isomorphism formed a scientific research area. While negative and positive numbers are not the same type ([9] Ch12) [31,105,106], now, in the worldwide fuzzy set community, it has been typical for some researchers to cite plagiarism as requested by a reviewer/plagiarizer and falsely claim $(-,+)$ isomorphism/equivalence repeatedly, disregarding logically definable causality in regularity, the geometry of light, the logic of photon, and Zadeh's recognition of bipolar fuzzy sets (re. [6,31,105,106]).

A key argument used to "support" the false claim is the so-called $(-,+)$ order-isomorphic property. The property is, however, only valid for linear, truth-based logics/sets of the same type and invalid for equilibrium-based, non-linear (or quantum linear) bipolar dynamic coexistence. For instance, self-negation $(-1,0) \otimes (-1,0) = (0,+1) \otimes (0,+1) = (0,+1)$ does not have a unique inverse mapping for the non-linear bipolar interactive operation $\otimes$. Such property leads to Yin adaptivity to bipolar equilibrium $(-1,0) \oplus [(-1,0) \otimes (-1,0)] = (-1,0) \oplus (0,+1) = (-1,+1)$, which is impossible for Yang—a logical basis for the secular "Yin-first" principle [9,31]. Thus, negative numbers and positive numbers are not the same type, and $(-,+)$ isomorphism/equivalence is a false claim.

It is obvious that without bipolar coexistence there would be no BUMP for quantum entanglement with logically definable causality in regularity. The effort of deriving a unipolar result from Nature's bipolar original and claiming the equilibrium-based original isomorphic or equivalent to the truth-based derivation must be a mathematical or philosophical joke like saying *"God/Nature logic is isomorphic or equivalent to my human/mind logic"*.

It is noted [31] that *"Without equilibrium truth cannot be revealed; without truth equilibrium cannot be identified. Equilibrium as holistic truth is not to replace truth but to extend it. With limited abilities humans should be forever humble in front of God (or Nature). We can get closer to God through scientific research but should never try to play God's role like a religious frenetic.*

Seeking God's logic is science; isomorphistry with truth-based supremacy might be a human play of God's role as we say: The universe is a dynamic equilibrium, not a truth or falsity. Thus, it is neither a (−, +)-equivalence nor a (−, +)-isomorphism". Fundamentally, truth-based logic as a human/mind unipolar linear logic should not or cannot be used to forbid scientists from seeking and accepting Spinosa–Einstein's God/Nature logic for open-world and open-ended scientific explorations, such as to find the causal relationships for equilibrium-based revealing of truths in sustainable development.

5.3. The "Championship"

Notably, bipolar fuzzy set theory [12,13] was repeatedly plagiarized before and after being recognized by Lotfi A. Zadeh [114]—founder of fuzzy logic [115]. In 2000, it was plagiarized by a researcher in an Eastern country to *"bipolar-valued fuzzy sets"* that denied the ontological basis of the theory as manifested by bipolar lattices (cf. [12,13,31]). Following the plagiarism in 2000, betting on (−, +) equivalence/isomorphistry to win, ignoring repeated warnings, focused on shallow copying/renaming and citation trading, with decade-long social construction and abduction effort, in a 2021 book a professor in another Eastern country boldly plagiarized YinYang bipolar crisp and fuzzy sets/logics in the lattices {−1, 0} × {0, +1} and [−1, 0] × [0, +1], respectively, to YangYin bipolar crisp/fuzzy sets/logics in the lattices {0, +1} × {−1, 0} and [0, +1] × [−1, 0] and renamed bipolar fuzzy equilibrium relation (or cognitive map) [15] to "bipolar fuzzy equivalence relation" (or graph). When he was caught engaging in academic theft, he argued that the bipolar fuzzy set was itself plagiarism due to (−, +) isomorphism and that he was, therefore, entitled to plagiarize it (cf. [2,31]).

Evidently, without a basic understanding of bipolarity and background independence, the YinYang-YangYin or (−, +)-(+, −) plagiarizer failed to realize that his decade-long effort would win him the "championship" for committing the most laughable plagiarism in the history of science and philosophy. Furthermore, the plagiarizer attempted to religionize and politicize YinYang in an effort to justify his plagiarism but "overlooked" the historical fact that the Dao of YinYang as an ancient Indigenous philosophy of Nature in Asia found its equilibrium-based formal logical basis in America thousands of years later with definable causality in regularity for quantum entanglement, mind–light–matter unity, and global realism beyond Leibniz and Bohr's interpretations, that would be a beautiful story in science philosophy in stark contrast to the "championship".

5.4. The Search for a Definitive Battleground of Quantum Gravity with Background-Independence

Background-independence has been a long-sought property in the quest for quantum gravity [60,97]. It is believed that *"an urgent issue in both physics and the philosophy of physics is to work out exactly what is meant by 'background independence' in a way that satisfies all parties, that is formally correct, and that satisfies our intuitive notions of the concept"* [116].

Logically, besides YinYang bipolar relativity [9], no other formal system has been reported for complete background independent reasoning with logically definable causality in regularity enabled by BQG as the geometry of light and BDL as the logic of photon [6]. While string theory lacks the background-independent property, the other two roads, namely, LQG and M-theory, are claimed to be background-independent. However, why did they also come short of finding a definitive battleground for quantum gravity?

The crux of the problem has been traced to the lack of a precise definition for *complete background independence*. It is asserted [24] that *"We need a minimum set of necessary and sufficient conditions for complete background independence. Without such a set of conditions, a unique logical foundation for quantum gravity cannot be developed"*.

Notably, until this day, a popular definition of background-independent geometry requires the unnecessary condition of being coordinate-free but does not require the imperative condition of supporting both reductionism and emergence [24]. For instance, according to Wikipedia (20 August 2023), *"Background independence is a condition in theoretical physics that requires the defining equations of a theory to be independent of the actual shape of the spacetime and the value of various fields within the spacetime. In particular this means that it must be possible not to refer to a specific coordinate system—the theory must be coordinate-free. In addition, the different spacetime configurations (or backgrounds) should be obtained as different solutions of the underlying equations".*

It is pointed out [24] that the above definition failed to realize that YinYang bipolar coordinate transcends spacetime and is completely background independent [9,20,21,38,39]. Without YinYang bipolarity, it would be impossible to reach any reciprocal, adaptive, creative, enactive, complementary, and/or affective interactions for reductionism, emergence, and submergence. After all, without bipolarity, the geometry of light and the logic of photons [6] would be unreachable for logically definable causality and background-independent causal–logical thinking and imagination to reveal truths in spacetime. Subsequently, spacetime geometry became the only choice without mind–light–matter unity for thousands of years. Remarkably, reductionism enabled the identification of YinYang bipolar coordinate as the most fundamental geometrical and logical basis of physical existence for quantum emergence and submergence with information conservation, where emergence enables bipolar strings to be entangled/composed to bipolar superstrings or multiverses with scalability, and submergence allows a string to collapse. Evidently, truth-based logic as a unipolar logic of the human mind cannot achieve such physical, reciprocal, adaptive, and creative properties without bipolar quantum interaction and entanglement.

Thus, the unnecessary coordinate-free condition inhibited the development of a truly background-independent geometry and a new formal logical foundation for quantum gravity. Subsequently, the quest for quantum gravity in physics has so far came short of finding a definitive logical battleground for quantum superposition and entanglement while YinYang bipolar relativity with bipolar strings reached the goal a decade earlier following the quantum information science path [9,16,17,20,21].

It is proposed in [6,24] that a geometry with complete background independence must satisfy the following minimum set of conditions:

(1) *It is shape-free, quadrant irrelevant, and spacetime transcendent* (e.g., both bar-shaped and u-shaped magnets are bipolar; import-export balance has no shape; equilibrium transcends spacetime);
(2) *It supports reductionism, emergence, and submergence;*
(3) *It is ubiquitous (e.g., a photon can be anywhere).*

In the above definition, the condition of *"coordinate-free"* was dropped from the popular definition (re. Wikipedia 20 August 2023). Subsequently, BQG as the geometry of light with the YinYang coordinate is shown to satisfy the conditions of complete background independence (re. Figures 4 and 8) and lead to quantum emergence and submergence of spacetime in both macroscopic cosmological multiverse level and microscopic spin foam level in logical terms (Figure 12) [2,6,9,20,21,31].

As a mathematically well-defined, non-perturbative, and background-independent quantization of general relativity, with its conventional matter couplings, LQG today forms a vast research area, ranging from mathematical foundations to physical applications. It is, however, critiqued as an incomplete theory and may not work out, just like its cousin string theory, which also claims to be a quantum theory of gravity. Hopefully, BQG and BDL will help the mathematics of LQG to reveal a workable solution.

Remarkably, while background independence has been sought in quantum gravity research, it has been overlooked in the search for mind–matter unitary cognition. The GRBS theory provides a new direction for quantum gravity with mind–light–matter unity in geometrical and logical terms. Notably, bipolar crisp/fuzzy sets have been applied in both the classical and the quantum worlds (re. [2,6,9,29,31]). Without the bipolar set theory, formal logically definable causality would be impossible. As a bipolar-set theoretic real-world string theory, GRBS provides the key to open the door to causal–logical quantum gravity and quantum information science with entangled thinking and imagination for adaptive and accumulative machine learning—a definitive battleground.

5.5. Axiomatizing Physics and Quantum Information Science for Mind–Light–Matter Unity AI/QI Machinery

While truth-based singularity is supported by the titanic Big Bang and black hole theories, quantum physicists overlooked the subtle but deeper fundamental, philosophical, and cosmological predictions [2]:

(1) Particles and antiparticles can be posited as the only things that survived a Big Bang and a black hole due to Hawking radiation or particle–antiparticle emission [70], and Newtonian action–reaction can be ubiquitous in the classical and quantum worlds in both crisp or fuzzy and soft or hard scientific terms, such as in decision science and mechanics.

(2) Without equilibrium-based bipolarity, truth-based singularity cannot provide complete background independence and the geometrical dynamics for cause and effect [6,9,20]. Thus, singularity alone is not qualified as a complete science theory to reach logically definable causality.

(3) While the Big Bang and black hole theory has been repeatedly questioned, we may assume that any pair of black holes and Big Bangs form a universe-wide or galaxy-wide dipole—an Einstein–Rosen Bridge [58] or wormhole [117]. Furthermore, such dipoles (or wormholes) can be generalized to any dipoles from the global cosmological levels to the atomic and subatomic levels. The generalization leads to YinYang bipolar relativity [9]. Subsequently, a one-directional flow of cosmological energy/information must be a long journey with many back–forth spinning cycles caused by bipolar interaction and entanglement at various levels. That may well explain why it has been a journey of many billions of years from the so-called Big Bang to our present time.

The above three observations and/or theoretical generalizations led to the theory of GRBS. That makes bipolar strings as bipolar dynamic equilibria in the real world are testable/observable at both the macroscopic and microscopic levels. Notably, the supersymmetry of negative–positive energies/information is different from that of boson-fermion particles. While boson-fermion supersymmetry is an unobserved theory, it is an observable fact that every action is matched with its reaction; dipoles are everywhere; every boson or fermion particle may have an antiparticle; parity non-conservation and CP-violation are observable; the universe is regulated by the dynamic equilibria of negative–positive energies. Thus, the Yin and the Yang of nature are non-isomorphic observable bipolar coexistence.

It might be argued that, in the Standard Model, the Higgs particle is a boson with no spin, electric charge, or color charge. That can be countered by the fact that the Higgs particle is a quantum excitation of one of the four components of the Higgs field with two neutral and two charged components constituting a scalar field. Each pair possesses either action–reaction or negative–positive bipolarity. Thus, bipolar dynamic equilibrium or bipolar strings, and bipolar symmetry or broken symmetry can be posited as the cause of boson-fermion symmetry or broken symmetry should the latter be observed, and GRBS can serve as a real-world theory of quantum gravity for the grand unification of action–reaction and particle–antiparticle pairs including the mysterious dark matter and dark energy to be further discovered. While the confirmation and unification of the two possible symmetries are left open for further research effort, the observable supersymmetry of negative–positive energies can be posited as more fundamental and general which governs the microscopic world as well as the macroscopic world in holistic physical, logical, biological, mental, and social terms.

Thus, with logically definable causality for mind–light–matter unity, GRBS provides a bipolar axiomatization of physics and quantum information science—a minimal but most general solution to Hilbert Problem 6 that has remained unsolvable for more than a century. As a logical system, the axiomatization is logically provable and analytically testable for mind–light–matter unity [6,9]. This fact leads to the Q5 (or QG5) paradigm of real-world causal–logical quantum gravities for quantum information science and human-level intelligence beyond the three roads toward quantum gravity [65].

(1) *Physical quantum gravity* (Examples: Re. [1,6,9,10,17,18,20,21,24,60,65,82,83,86–88,97, 99,100,109,110,117–119]);
(2) *Logical quantum gravity* (Examples: Re. [2,3,6,9,29,31,32,38,39,85,110,120–130]);
(3) *Mental quantum gravity* (Examples: Re. [2,6,16–19,22,23,25–29,62–64,100,131–133]);
(4) *Biological quantum gravity* (Examples: Re. [9,18,78,96,108,128,134]);
(5) *Social quantum gravity* (Examples: Re. [6,9,31,42,135–137]).

Q5 can be regarded as a paradigm of bipolar strings for quantum gravity. In this paradigm, *physical quantum gravity* as part of physics is concerned with the unification of general relativity and quantum mechanics; *logical quantum gravity* as part of quantum information science is focused on quantum computing, communication, and teleportation; *mental quantum gravity* as part of neural science is focused on the interplay of quantum physics and brain science for the mind–light–matter unitary quantum cognition and consciousness, a typical example is creative thinking and imagination; *biological quantum gravity* as part of quantum biology is focused on the interplay of quantum information science and life sciences; *social quantum gravity* as part of social science is focused on quantum economics, social dynamics, and decision making. Unexpectedly, information conservation and blackhole data compression as physical quantum gravity found their applications in logical quantum gravity for post-quantum cryptography [30].

It has been remarked [9,21] that, while the Q5 paradigm may sound like an impossible mission, it follows a single condition and an undisputable observation:

(1) Condition: a bipolar string as a bipolar dynamic equilibrium is a basic form of any multidimensional equilibrium from which nothing can escape (Figure 3);
(2) Observation: bipolar quantum entanglement as a bipolar string/superstring is testable/observable and logically definable (Figures 12–15).

While truth cannot be out there existing independently from the human mind [138], bipolar strings as bipolar dynamic equilibria are ubiquitous physical/logical existence that must unify gravity and quantum theory. These observations have led to ground-0 axioms—a unification of the first principles of science and the second law of thermodynamics for the mind–light–matter unity AI&QI [6]. Now, we are ready to ask the three gigantic questions [101,139]:

(1) Could equilibrium-based information conservational bipolar quantum computing be the key to revealing the ubiquitous effect of quantum entanglement [26,101]?
(2) Could logically definable causality be the foundation for small-scale quantum computing to understand the universe completely [26,139]?
(3) Could the human brain be structurally similar to the universe [10]?

The answers must be YES for all three questions. Otherwise, equilibrium-based energy/information conservation and logically definable causality could not be the paramount laws of modern science [26]. The two paramount laws make equilibrium-based GRBS logically attainable, ubiquitous, and applicable for programming the universe [139] and the mind [25,27] with a small-scale quantum computer. Thus, mind–light–matter unity has led to real-world quantum gravity and brain–universe similarity for AI&QI.

5.6. Testability and Falsifiability

Notably, the no-communication theorem [140] in QM implies the no-cloning theorem, which states that quantum states cannot be (perfectly) copied. The counterargument is that no-cloning as a technological limitation cannot deny quantum entanglement as a reality of Nature for entangled causal–logical machine thinking/imagination to enter quantum information science with quantum-digital compatibility in logical terms, not in quantum cloning terms.

While the search for ether and monopole has so far turned out no concrete result, dipoles are observed everywhere. As a basis of string theory, monopoles are too far away from reality. For instance, without bipolarity, it is not clear how monopoles and strings can form an atom with equilibrium or non-equilibrium [21]. In contrast, open-ended testability and falsifiability are provided for the equilibrium-based GRBS theory:

(1) Modus ponens or MP can be derived/revealed from bipolar universal modus ponens or BUMP [9,16] but not vice versa—a formal proof of bipolar equilibrium-based generalization of truth for ubiquitous, scalable, integrative, and interactive entanglement in an open world;

(2) Unlike the predicted but inconclusive existence of monopoles in string theory, dipoles are observable, scalable, and ubiquitous, bipolar quantum entanglement is both physical and logical and can reach GRBS with logically definable causality in regularity [2,6];

(3) BQG and BDL have been identified as the geometry of light and logic of photons, respectively, to reach a logical exposition [6,38,39] for the Dirac 3-polarizer experiment [96];

(4) Entangled photons have been logically proven to be an example of YinYang bipolar quantum entanglement in nature [6,38,39];

(5) The YinYang reciprocal quantum entanglement of two photons has been independently tested and observed [109];

(6) Bipolar atoms and neurons can reach mind–light–matter unity for AI&QI in logical and geometrical terms [6];

(7) Independent research in physics and neuroscience compared the network of neuronal cells in the human brain with the cosmic network of galaxies and found surprising similarities in their structural organization [10];

(8) GRBS can be falsified in the following cases: (i) should logically definable causality in regularity with BUMP in BDL/BDFL be falsified; (ii) should ether, monad, or monopole be observed as the most fundamental existence free from action–reaction, particle–antiparticle, and input–output bipolarity and causality; or (iii) should the Bell inequality violation and quantum nonlocality be both falsified.

6. Conclusions

Following Einstein's predictions, the theory of GRBS has been developed based on Ground-0 Axioms. GRBS constitutes a background-independent axiomatization of physics and quantum information science, which has been proven a necessary and inevitable consequence of the Bell inequality violation. With equilibrium-based bipolar strings, local realism has been formally extended to global realism supported with logically definable causality in regularity, where spacetime emergence/submergence is formally defined as quantum entanglement/collapse. With the brain–universe similarity, GRBS provides a logical and physical foundation for bipolar entropy, consciousness, and the mind–light–matter unity QCQB that has led to machine thinking and imagination. Thus, GRBS has brought conscious mind and resonant brain modeling closer to mind–light–matter unity AI and QI for human-level intelligence [2,62–64]. The testability and falsifiability of GRBS have been discussed.

GRBS extends Einstein's concept of causality from local realism to global realism comprised of eight criteria vs. those for local realism (re. Section 2.2):

(1) *Logically definable causality in regularity vs. undefinable causality;*
(2) *Unification of locality with quantum-nonlocality vs. no unification;*
(3) *Bipolar dynamic symmetry with mutuality vs. unipolar singularity;*
(4) *Energy/information conservation vs. observation;*
(5) *Background-independent spacetime emergence vs. background-dependent spacetime;*
(6) *Equilibrium-based God/Nature logic vs. truth-based human/mind logic;*
(7) *Open-world vs. closed-world;*
(8) *Brain–universe similarity vs. no similarity.*

Distinctions of GRBS from local realism include but are not limited to the following (in alphabetical order):

(1) Analytical quantum intelligence (QI) with formal logically definable causality vs. quantum mechanics with unattainable causality;

(2) Bipolar complementarity vs. real–imaginary or particle–wave complementarity;
(3) Bipolar dynamic fuzzy logic (BDFL) vs. unipolar fuzzy logic (FL);
(4) Bipolar dynamic logic (BDL) vs. unipolar Boolean logic (BL);
(5) Bipolar entangled quantum graph or cognitive map vs. bipolar isomorphism/equivalence;
(6) Bipolar entropy vs. unipolar entropy;
(7) Bipolar fuzzy sets vs. fuzzy sets;
(8) Bipolar G-CPT symmetry vs. unipolar CPT symmetry;
(9) Bipolar quantum geometry (BQG) vs. bra-ket quantum geometry;
(10) Bipolar quantum linear algebra (BQLA) vs. linear algebra (LA);
(11) Bipolar reflexivity vs. unipolar reflexivity;
(12) Bipolar relation vs. binary relation;
(13) Bipolar sets (crisp) vs. classical sets;
(14) Bipolar strings vs. one-dimensional strings;
(15) Bipolar superstrings vs. M-theory;
(16) Bipolar symmetry vs. unipolar symmetry;
(17) Bipolar transitivity vs. unipolar transitivity;
(18) Bipolar universal modus ponens (BUMP) vs. modus ponens (MP);
(19) Bipolarity vs. singularity;
(20) Causal–logical spin processes vs. spin loops;
(21) Complete background-independence vs. incomplete background dependence;
(22) Dynamic bipolar reciprocal interaction and self-organization vs. static unipolar coding;
(23) Entangled causal–logical machine thinking and imagination vs. programmed machine learning and computation;
(24) Equilibrium relation vs. equivalence relation;
(25) Equilibrium-based bipolar axiomatization of physics and quantum information science vs. unreachable truth-based unipolar axiomatization of physics
(26) Equilibrium-based bipolar quantum cellular automata vs. truth-based unipolar cellular automata;
(27) Equilibrium-based generalization of CPT symmetry vs. truth-based CPT symmetry;
(28) Equilibrium-based revealing of truths vs. truth-based reasoning;
(29) Fuzzy equilibrium relation vs. fuzzy similarity relation;
(30) Geometry of light and logic of photon vs. bra-ket standard;
(31) Geometry of light vs. geometry of spacetime;
(32) Global realism with bipolar strings (GRBS) vs. local realism limited by the speed of light;
(33) God/Nature logic vs. human/mind logic;
(34) Ground-0 axioms vs. first principles and second law;
(35) Information-energy conservation vs. observation;
(36) Logic of photon vs. logic of human mind;
(37) Logically definable causality vs. undefinable experimental/probabilistic causality;
(38) Mind–light–matter unity vs. mind–matter unity mystery;
(39) Order–disorder unification vs. order–disorder separation;
(40) Quantum emergence and submergence of spacetime vs. spacetime dominance;
(41) Quantum gravity for quantum information science vs. quantum gravity for blackholes;
(42) Quantum intelligence (QI) vs. artificial intelligence (AI);
(43) Real-world bipolar strings vs. untestable one-dimensional strings;
(44) Real-world quantum gravity vs. quantum gravity without a definitive battleground;
(45) Scalable bipolar strings vs. unscalable one-dimensional strings;
(46) Spacetime transcendent bipolar relativity vs. spacetime relativity;
(47) Ubiquitous effects of bipolar quantum entanglement vs. unknown effects of quantum entanglement;
(48) Yin-first principle vs. Yang-first;
(49) YinYang bipolar coordinate for complete background-independence vs. coordinate-free without definitive battleground;
(50) YinYang bipolar relativity vs. space-time relativity.

Remarkably, the GRBS theory as an equilibrium-based reconceptualization and unification of truth-based local reality with quantum nonlocality provides logically definable causality in regularity for quantum emergence or submergence of spacetime—a key for revealing the ubiquitous effects of quantum entanglement with mind–light–matter unity. Notably, GRBS does not exclude local reality but reveals it—the opening of a new research direction in science and philosophy. While the compatibility of GRBS with the Standard Model and the intertwining of different quantum gravity theories are left open for further research efforts, some unifying properties have been examined and illustrated in complete background-independent logical, algebraic, and physical terms. Thus, GRBS forms a real-world relativistic causal–logical quantum gravity theory with unexpected but much-needed simplification.

As a formal unified logical/physical theory, GRBS makes Nature–human unity/harmony a scientific topic for global environment protection, global economy regulation, and mind–light–matter unity QCQB. It is hoped that GRBS can help humanity in dealing with global climate change with sustainable scientific research/development. While this work has been focused on GRBS with illustrations in entangled causal–logical machine thinking/imagination, hopefully, as a basis for QCQB it has opened a new door toward human-level AI&QI in physical, logical, mental, biological, and social-economical quantum gravity terms.

It should be further clarified that GRBS is reached by following the quantum information science path instead of the one-dimensional string theory path in physics. It is dramatic but also normal because GRBS as an axiomatization of physics and quantum information science is supposed to be logician's work. As the first and only background-independent theory of its kind, GRBS happened to provide a reconceptualization and unification of string theory, loop quantum gravity, and M-theory—the three roads to quantum gravity [65]—with unexpected but much-needed simplification. Alternatively, GRBS could have been named as *global realism with bipolar dynamic equilibria (GRBDE)*. It can be observed that GRBS holds the advantage over GRBDE in terms of bipolar entangled quantum graph representation, information visualization, reconceptualization, and causal–logical unification for real-world applications.

Finally, with a formal logical and physical basis, GRBS is expected to be free from the *"Not Even Wrong"*, *"Trouble with Physics"*, and *"Lost in Math"* problems. While it is a matter of debate whether GRBS would be able to inject new life into the faded TOE, this work has shown the potential of the equilibrium-based theory for major scientific advances, especially for the sustainable development of mind–light–matter unitary AI/QI machinery toward human-level intelligence and beyond. Now, with entangled machine thinking and imagination, our AI&QI humanoid robots should keep the hope alive for the miracle of reaching human-level intelligence someday as string theory was once lost in the beauty of the truth-based singularity but found in the harmony of equilibrium-based bipolar relativity.

Funding: No funding for this research. It is purely curiosity-driven.

Data Availability Statement: The article is logical and theoretical in nature, not experimental. Illustrations are included as examples and figures. No additional data are available.

Conflicts of Interest: The author declares that the research was conducted in the absence of any commercial or financial relationship that can be construed as a potential competing interest of a financial or personal nature.

References

1. The Nobel Prize in Physics 2022. Press Release. Available online: https://www.nobelprize.org/prizes/physics/2022/press-release/ (accessed on 15 July 2024).
2. Zhang, W.R. If AI machine cannot think, can QI machine think?—From negative numbers to quantum intelligence for mind-light-matter unity. *Quantum Mach. Intell.* 2023, 5, 14. [CrossRef]

3. Zhang, W.R. Bipolar quantum logic gates and quantum cellular combinatorics—A logical extension to quantum entanglement. *J. Quantum Inf. Sci.* **2013**, *3*, 93–105. [CrossRef]
4. Turing, A.M. Computing machinery and intelligence. *Mind* **1950**, *49*, 433–460. [CrossRef]
5. McCarthy, J. From here to human-level AI. *Artif. Intell.* **2007**, *171*, 1174–1182. [CrossRef]
6. Zhang, W.R. Ground-0 Axioms vs. first principles and second law: From the geometry of light and logic of photon to mind-light-matter Unity-AI&QI. *IEEE/CAA J. Autom. Sin.* **2021**, *8*, 534–553. [CrossRef]
7. Mason, C. The Logical Road to Human Level AI Leads to a Dead End. In Proceedings of the Fourth IEEE International Conference on Self-Adaptive and Self-Organizing Systems, SASO 2010, Budapest, Hungary, 27–28 September 2010. Workshops Proceedings. [CrossRef]
8. Boole, G. *An Investigation of the Laws of Thought*; MacMillan: London, UK, 1854.
9. Zhang, W.R. *YinYang Bipolar Relativity: A Unifying Theory of Nature, Agents and Causality with Applications in Quantum Computing, Cognitive Informatics and Life Sciences*; IGI Global: New York, NY, USA, 2011.
10. Vazza, F.; Feletti, A. The Comparison between the Neuronal Network and the Cosmic Web. *Front. Phys.* **2020**, *8*, 525731. [CrossRef]
11. Zhang, W.R. Global Realism with Bipolar Strings: From Bell Test to Real World Causal-Logical Quantum Gravity and Brain-Universe Similarity for Entangled Machine Thinking and Imagination. *Qeios* **2023**. [CrossRef]
12. Zhang, W.R. Bipolar fuzzy sets and relations: A computational framework for cognitive modeling and multiagent decision analysis. In Proceedings of the 1st International Joint Conference North American Fuzzy Information Processing Society Biannual Conference, San Antonio, TX, USA, 18–21 December 1994; pp. 305–309.
13. Zhang, W.R. YinYang bipolar fuzzy sets. In Proceedings of the IEEE World Computational Intelligence, Anchorage, AK, USA, 4–9 May 1998; pp. 835–840.
14. Zhang, W.-R. Equilibrium energy and stability measures for bipolar decision and global regulation. *Int. J. Fuzzy Syst.* **2003**, *5*, 114–122.
15. Zhang, W.-R. Equilibrium relations and bipolar cognitive mapping for online analytical processing with applications in international relations and strategic decision support. *IEEE Trans. Syst. Man Cybern. B Cybern.* **2003**, *33*, 295–307. [CrossRef] [PubMed]
16. Zhang, W.R. YinYang Bipolar universal modus ponens (BUMP)—A fundamental law of non-linear brain dynamics for emotional intelligence and mental health. In Proceedings of the 10th Joint Conference Information Sciences, Salt Lake City, UT, USA, 18–24 July 2007; pp. 89–95.
17. Zhang, W.R. Six conjectures in quantum physics and computational neuroscience. In Proceedings of the 3rd International Conference in Quantum, Nano and Micro Technologies, Cancun, Mexico, 1–7 February 2009; pp. 67–72.
18. Zhang, W.R. YinYang bipolar relativity—A unifying theory of Nature, agents and life science. In Proceedings of the International Joint Conference on Bioinformatics, Systems Biology and Intelligent Computing, Shanghai, China, 3–5 August 2009; pp. 377–383. [CrossRef]
19. Zhang, W.-R.; Pandurangi, A.K.; Peace, K.E.; Zhang, Y.Q.; Zhao, Z.M. MentalSquares: A generic bipolar support vector machine for psychiatric disorder classification, diagnostic analysis and neurobiological data mining. *Int. J. Data Min. Bioinform.* **2011**, *5*, 532–557. [CrossRef] [PubMed]
20. Zhang, W.R. Beyond spacetime geometry—The death of philosophy and its quantum reincarnation. *J. Mod. Phys.* **2012**, *9*, 1272–1284. [CrossRef]
21. Zhang, W.R. YinYang bipolar atom—An Eastern road toward quantum gravity. *J. Mod.Phys.* **2012**, *3*, 1261–1271. [CrossRef]
22. Zhang, W.R.; Zhang, L. Soundness and Completeness of a 4-Valued Bipolar Logic. *J. Mult.-Valued Log. Soft Comput.* **2003**, *9*, 241–256.
23. Zhang, W.R. A geometrical and logical unification of mind, light and matter. In Proceedings of the 15th IEEE International Conference on Cognitive Informatics & Cognitive Computing, Palo Alto, CA, USA, 22–23 August 2016; pp. 188–197.
24. Zhang, W.R. G-CPT symmetry of quantum emergence and submergence—An information conservational multiagent cellular automata unification of CPT symmetry and CP violation for equilibrium-based many-world causal analysis of quantum coherence and decoherence. *J. Quantum Inf. Sci.* **2016**, *6*, 62–97. [CrossRef]
25. Zhang, W.R. Programming the mind and decrypting the universe—A bipolar quantum-neuro-fuzzy associative memory model for quantum cognition and quantum intelligence. In Proceedings of the International Joint Conference on Neural Networks, Anchorage, AK, USA, 14–19 May 2017; pp. 1180–1187.
26. Zhang, W.R. From equilibrium-based business intelligence to information conservational quantum-fuzzy cryptography—A cellular transformation of bipolar fuzzy sets to quantum intelligence machinery. *IEEE Trans. Fuzzy Syst.* **2018**, *26*, 656–669. [CrossRef]
27. Zhang, W.R. A logical path from neural ensemble formation to cognition with mind-light-matter unification: The eternal Dow can be told. *Int. J. Cogn. Inform. Nat. Intell.* **2018**, *12*, 20–54. [CrossRef]
28. Zhang, W.R. On the Nature of Natural Intelligence—A Revision of Laozi. In Proceedings of the 2018 IEEE 17th International Conference on Cognitive Informatics & Cognitive Computing (ICCI*CC), Berkeley, CA, USA, 16–18 July 2018; pp. 316–323. [CrossRef]
29. Zhang, W.R. The road from fuzzy sets to definable causality and bipolar quantum intelligence—To the memory of Lotf A. Zadeh. *J. Intell. Fuzzy Syst.* **2019**, *36*, 3019–3032. [CrossRef]

30. Zhang, W.R. Information Conservational Security with 'Black Hole' Keypad Compression and Scalable One-Time Pad—An Analytical Quantum Intelligence Approach to Pre- and Post-Quantum Cryptography. *Cryptol. Eprint Arch.* **2019**. Available online: https://eprint.iacr.org/2019/913 (accessed on 15 July 2024). [CrossRef]
31. Zhang, W.R. Science vs. sophistry—A historical debate on bipolar fuzzy sets and equilibrium-based mathematics for AI&QI. *J. Intell. Fuzzy Syst.* **2021**, *41*, 6781–6799. [CrossRef]
32. Zhang, W.R.; Zhang, L. YinYang Bipolar Logic and Bipolar Fuzzy Logic. *Inf. Sci.* **2004**, *165*, 265–287. [CrossRef]
33. Zhang, W.R.; Zhang, L. A multiagent data warehousing (MADWH) and multiagent data mining (MADM) approach to brain modeling and neurofuzzy control. *Inf. Sci.* **2004**, *167*, 109–127. [CrossRef]
34. Zhang, W.R.; Pandurangi, A.K.; Peace, K.E. YinYang dynamic neurobiological modeling and diagnostic analysis of major depressive and bipolar disorders. *IEEE Trans. Biomed. Eng.* **2007**, *54*, 1729–1739. [CrossRef] [PubMed]
35. Zhang, W.R.; Zhang, H.J.; Shi, Y.; Chen, S.S. Bipolar linear algebra and YinYang-N-Element cellular networks for equilibrium-based biosystem simulation and regulation. *J. Biol. Syst.* **2009**, *17*, 547–576. [CrossRef]
36. Zhang, W.R.; Peace, K.E. Revealing the ubiquitous effects of quantum entanglement—Toward a notion of god logic. *J. Quantum Inf. Sci.* **2013**, *3*, 143–153. [CrossRef]
37. Zhang, W.R.; Peace, K. Causality is logically definable—Toward an equilibrium-based computing paradigm of quantum agent and quantum intelligence (QAQI). *J. Quantum Inf. Sci.* **2014**, *4*, 227–268. [CrossRef]
38. Zhang, W.R.; Marchetti, F. A logical exposition of Dirac 3-polarizer experiment and its potential impact on computational biology. In Proceedings of the 6th ACM Conference on Bioinformatics, Computational Biology, and Health Informatics, Atlanta, GA, USA, 9–12 September 2015; pp. 517–518.
39. Zhang, W.R.; Marchetti, F. YinYang bipolar quantum geometry and bipolar quantum superposition Part I—A background independent geometrical and logical exposition of Dirac 3-polarizer experiment. *Fractal Geom. Nonlinear Anal. Med. Biol.* **2015**, *1*, 61–68. [CrossRef]
40. Zhang, W.R.; Marchetti, F. YinYang bipolar quantum geometry and bipolar quantum superposition Part II—Toward an equilibrium-based analytical paradigm of quantum mechanics and quantum biology. *Fractal Geom. Nonlinear Anal. Med. Biol.* **2015**, *2*, 69–77. [CrossRef]
41. Zhang, W.R.; Wang, P.; Peace, K.; Zhan, J.; Zhang, Y. On truth, uncertainty, equilibrium, and harmony—A taxonomy for YinYang scientific computing. *New Math. Nat. Comput.* **2008**, *4*, 207–229. [CrossRef]
42. Zhang, W.R.; Peace, K.E.; Han, H.J. YinYang bipolar dynamic organizational modeling for equilibrium-based decision analysis: Logical transformation of an indigenous philosophy to a global science. *Asia Pac. J. Manag.* **2016**, *33*, 723–766. [CrossRef]
43. Witten, E. Quantum Background Independence in String Theory. *arXiv* **1993**, arXiv:hep-th/9306122.
44. Witten, E. String theory dynamics in various dimensions. *Nucl. Phys. B* **1995**, *443*, 85–126. [CrossRef]
45. Susskind, L. *The Cosmic Landscape: String Theory and the Illusion of Intelligent Design*; Back Bay Books: New York, NY, USA, 2005; ISBN 978-0316013338.
46. Becker, K.; Becker, M.; Schwarz, J. *String Theory and M-Theory: A Modern Introduction*; Cambridge University Press: Cambridge, UK, 2007; ISBN 978-0-521-86069-7.
47. Rovelli, C.; Smolin, L. Knot Theory and Quantum Gravity. *Phys. Rev. Lett.* **1988**, *61*, 1155–1158. [CrossRef]
48. Rovelli, C. Black Hole Entropy from Loop Quantum Gravity. *Phys. Rev. Lett.* **1996**, *77*, 3288–3291. [CrossRef] [PubMed]
49. Rovelli, C. Loop Quantum Gravity. *Living Rev. Relativ.* **2008**, *11*, 5. [CrossRef] [PubMed]
50. Einstein, A. Zur Elektrodynamik bewegter Körper. *Ann. Phys.* **1905**, *17*, 891. [CrossRef]
51. Einstein, A. On the General Theory of Relativity. *Sitzungsber. Preuss. Akad. Wiss. Berlin (Math. Phys.)* **1915**, *1915*, 778–786.
52. Einstein, A. The foundation of the general theory of relativity. *Ann. Phys.* **1916**, *49*, 769–822. [CrossRef]
53. Einstein, A. On The Method of Theoretical Physics. In *Mein Weltbild*; Querido Verlag: Amsterdam, The Netherlands, 1934.
54. Einstein, A. Physics and reality. *J. Frankl. Inst.* **1936**, *221*, 349–382. [CrossRef]
55. Einstein, A. Considerations Concerning the Fundaments of Theoretical Physics. *Science* **1940**, *91*, 487–491. [CrossRef] [PubMed]
56. Einstein, A. Famous Letter to J. E. Switzer; 1953. In *Science Since Babylon*; de Solla Price, D.J., Ed.; Yale University Press: New Haven, CT, USA, 1961.
57. Einstein, A.; Podolsky, B.; Rosen, N. Can quantum-mechanical description of physical reality be considered complete? *Phys. Rev.* **1935**, *47*, 777–780. [CrossRef]
58. Einstein, A.; Rosen, N. The particle problem in the general theory of relativity. *Phys. Rev.* **1935**, *48*, 73. [CrossRef]
59. Woit, P. *Not Even Wrong: The Failure of String Theory and the Search for Unity in Physical Law*; Basic Book: New York, NY, USA, 2006.
60. Smolin, L. *The Trouble with Physics: The Rise of String Theory, the Fall of a Science, and What Comes Next?* Houghton Mifflin Harcourt: New York, NY, USA, 2006.
61. Hossenfelder, S. *Lost in Math: How Beauty Leads Physics Astray*; Basic Books: New York, NY, USA, 2018.
62. Grossberg, S. *Conscious Mind, Resonant Brain: How Each Brain Makes a Mind*; Oxford University Press: New York, NY, USA, 2021. [CrossRef]
63. Dresp-Langley, B. Seven Properties of Self-Organization in the Human Brain. *Big Data Cogn. Comput.* **2020**, *4*, 10. [CrossRef]
64. Pessoa, L. The Entangled Brain. *J. Cogn. Neurosci.* **2023**, *35*, 349–360. [CrossRef] [PubMed]
65. Smolin, L. *Three Roads to Quantum Gravity: A New Understanding of Space, Time and the Universe*; Basic Books: New York, NY, USA, 2001.

66. Bohr, N. On the notions of causality and complementarity. *Dialectica* **1948**, *2*, 312–319. [CrossRef]
67. Ben-Menahem, Y. Struggling with Causality: Einstein's Case. *Sci. Context* **1993**, *6*, 291–310. [CrossRef]
68. Hawking, S.; Penrose, R. The Singularities of Gravitational Collapse and Cosmology. *Proc. R. Soc. A* **1970**, *314*, 529–548. [CrossRef]
69. Susskind, L. *The Black Hole War: My Battle with Stephen Hawking to Make the World Safe for Quantum Mechanics*; Little, Brown and Company: Boston, MA, USA, 2008; ISBN 978-0-316-01641-4.
70. Hawking, S. Black Hole Evaporation. *Nature* **1974**, *248*, 30–31. [CrossRef]
71. Hawking, S. Particle Creation by Black Holes. *Commun. Math. Phys.* **1975**, *43*, 199–220. [CrossRef]
72. Hilbert, D. Mathematical problems. *Bull. Am. Math. Soc.* **1902**, *8*, 437–479. Available online: https://projecteuclid.org/journals/bulletin-of-the-american-mathematical-society-new-series/volume-8/issue-10/Mathematical-problems/bams/1183417035.full (accessed on 15 July 2024). [CrossRef]
73. Gödel, K. Über formal unentscheildbare Sätze der Principia Mathematica und verwandter Systeme, I. *Monatshefte Math. Phys.* **1931**, *38*, 173–189. [CrossRef]
74. Bell, J.S. On the Einstein-Podolsky-Rosen paradox. *Physics* **1964**, *1*, 195–200. [CrossRef]
75. Bell, J.S. On the problem of hidden variables in quantum mechanics. *Physics* **1966**, *38*, 447–452. [CrossRef]
76. Bell, J.S. *Speakable and Unspeakable in Quantum Mechanics*; Cambridge University Press: Cambridge, UK, 1987; p. 65.
77. Carnot, S. *Réflexions sur la Puissance Motrice du feu et sur les Machines Propres à Développer Cette Puissance*; Bachelier: Paris, France, 1824.
78. Schrödinger, E. *What Is Life?* Cambridge University Press: Cambridge, UK, 1994; ISBN 978-0-521-42708-1.
79. Cerf, N.J.; Adami, C. Negative entropy and information in quantum mechanics. *Phys. Rev. Lett.* **1997**, *79*, 5194–5197. [CrossRef]
80. Chatzidimitriou-Dreismann, C.A. Experimental Implications of Negative Quantum Conditional Entropy—H_2 Mobility in Nanoporous Materials. *Appl. Sci.* **2020**, *10*, 8266. [CrossRef]
81. del Rio, L.; Åberg, J.; Renner, R.; Dahlsten, O.; Vedral, V. The thermodynamic meaning of negative entropy. *Nature* **2011**, *474*, 61–63. [PubMed]
82. Horodecki, M.; Oppenheim, J.; Winter, A. Partial quantum information. *Nature* **2005**, *436*, 673–676. [CrossRef] [PubMed]
83. Horodecki, M.; Oppenheim, J.; Winter, A. Quantum state merging and negative information. *Commun. Math. Phys.* **2007**, *269*, 107–136. [CrossRef]
84. Hawking, S.; Mlodinow, L. *The Grand Design*; Random House Digital, Inc.: New York, NY, USA, 2010.
85. Xu, L.; Wang, M.; Qin, J. Quantum bit commitment without quantum memory. *Comput. J.* **2023**, *67*, 1163–1170. [CrossRef]
86. Sandler, U. Evolutionary quantization and matter-antimatter distribution in accelerated expanding of Universe. *Phys. A Stat. Mech. Its Appl.* **2023**, *611*, 128359. [CrossRef]
87. Sui, J.; Zhang, D.; Zhang, H. Logical OR operation and magnetic field sensing based on layered topology. *J. Phys. D Appl. Phys.* **2022**, *55*, 415001. [CrossRef]
88. Guo, S.; Hu, C.; Zhang, H. Unidirectional ultrabroadband and wide-angle absorption in graphene-embedded photonic crystals with the cascading structure comprising the Octonacci sequence. *J. Opt. Soc. Am. B* **2020**, *37*, 2678–2687. [CrossRef]
89. de Spinoza, B. *Ethics, Demonstrated in Geometrical Order (Latin: Ethica, Ordine Geometrico Demonstrata)*; Dutch Republic; 1677. Available online: https://en.wikipedia.org/wiki/Wikisource (accessed on 15 July 2024).
90. Hume, D. *A Treatise of Human Nature*; Norton, D.F., Norton, M.J., Eds.; Oxford University Press: Oxford, UK; New York, NY, USA, 1738.
91. Russell, B. On the Notion of Cause. *Proc. Aristot. Soc.* **1913**, *13*, 1–26. [CrossRef]
92. Zadeh, L.A. Causality Is Undefinable—Toward a Theory of Hierarchical Definability. In Proceedings of the 10th IEEE International Conference on Fuzzy Systems, Melbourne, Australia, 2–5 December 2001; pp. 67–68.
93. Bombelli, L.; Lee, J.; Meyer, D.; Sorkin, R.D. Spacetime as a causal set. *Phys. Rev. Lett.* **1987**, *59*, 521–524. [CrossRef] [PubMed]
94. Shannon, C.E. A mathematical theory of communication. *Bell Syst. Tech. J.* **1948**, *27*, 379–423. [CrossRef]
95. Kragh, H. *Simply Dirac (Great Lives Book 1), Kindle ed.*; Simply Charly: New York, NY, USA, 2016.
96. Dirac, P.A.M. *The Principles of Quantum Mechanics*; Oxford University Press: Oxford, UK, 1930.
97. Smolin, L. The case for background independence. *arXiv* **2005**, arXiv:hep-th/0507235.
98. Penrose, R. *Cycles of Time: An Extraordinary New View of the Universe*; The Bodley Head: London, UK, 2010.
99. Tuszynski, J.; Hameroff, S.; Sataric, M.; Trpisova, B.; Nip, M. Ferroelectric behavior in microtubule dipole lattices; implications for information processing, signaling and assembly/disassembly. *J. Theor. Biol.* **1995**, *174*, 371–380. [CrossRef]
100. Hameroff, S.; Penrose, R. Review Consciousness in the universe: A review of the 'Orch OR' theory. *Phys. Life Rev.* **2014**, *11*, 39–78. [CrossRef] [PubMed]
101. Penrose, R. *The Road to Reality: A Complete Guide to the Laws of the Universe*; Alfred A, Knopf: New York, NY, USA, 2005.
102. Hegel, G.W.F. *Science of Logic (German: Wissenschaft der Logik)*; Di Giovanni, G., Ed.; Di Giovanni, G., Translator; Cambridge University Press: Cambridge, UK, 2010. Available online: https://ia601006.us.archive.org/27/items/hegel-the-science-of-logic/georg_wilhelm_friedrich_hegel__the_science_of_logic.pdf (accessed on 31 July 2024).
103. Fukuyama, Francis. A Reply to My Critics. In *The National Interest*; JSTOR: New York, NY, USA, 1989; no. 18; pp. 21–28. Available online: http://www.jstor.org/stable/42894641 (accessed on 31 July 2024).
104. Alford, D.M. A Report on the Fetzer Institute-sponsored Dialogues Between Western and Indigenous Scientists. In Proceedings of the Annual Spring Meeting of the Society for the Anthropology of Consciousness, Sevilla, Spain, 7–11 April 1993.

105. PubPeer. Debate: PubPeer—YinYang bipolar logic and bipolar fuzzy logic. 2021. Available online: https://www.pubpeer.com/publications/B3E3DFF8C01E768287258E9FF9C46D# (accessed on 15 July 2024).
106. PubPeer. Debate: PubPeer—A Logical Exposition of Dirac 3-Polarizer Experiment and Its Potential Impact on Computational Biology. 2023. Available online: https://www.pubpeer.com/publications/39500D23472BC01EA3C785D7BA3D6F (accessed on 15 July 2024).
107. Leibniz, G.W. Explication de l'arithmétique binaire. *Mem. L'Acad. R.* **1703**, *1703*, 85–89.
108. Gore, J.; van Oudenaarden, A. Synthetic biology: The yin and Yang of nature. *Nature* **2009**, *457*, 271–272. [CrossRef] [PubMed]
109. Zia, D.; Dehghan, N.; D'Errico, A.; Sciarrino, F. Interferometric imaging of amplitude and phase of spatial biphoton states. *Nat. Photonics* **2023**, *17*, 1009–1016. [CrossRef]
110. Turner, B. Quantum 'yin-yang' shows two photons being entangled in real-time. *Science News (Quantum Physics)*, 24 August 2023.
111. Jin, Y. *On Dao*; Reprint by Commercial Press Ltd.: Hong Kong, China, 1987; (Originally published in 1940).
112. Heisenberg, W. Über den anschaulichen Inhalt der quantentheoretischen Kinematik und Mechanik. *Z. Phys.* **1927**, *43*, 172–198. [CrossRef]
113. Gautam, K. A visual, intuitive guide to number imagination. *Ymer* **2022**, *21*, 216–223.
114. Zadeh, L.A. Fuzzy logic. *Scholarpedia* **2008**, *3*, 1766. [CrossRef]
115. Zadeh, L.A. Fuzzy sets. *Inform. Control* **1965**, *8*, 338–353. [CrossRef]
116. Weinstein, S.; Rickles, D. Quantum Gravity. In *The Stanford Encyclopedia of Philosophy*; Summer 2023 ed.; Zalta, E.N., Nodelman, U., Eds.; The Metaphysics Research Lab, Philosophy Department, Stanford University: Stanford, CA, USA, 2023. Available online: https://plato.stanford.edu/archives/sum2023/entries/quantum-gravity/ (accessed on 15 July 2024).
117. Misner, C.W.; Wheeler, J.A. Classical physics as geometry. *Ann. Phys.* **1957**, *2*, 525. [CrossRef]
118. The Nobel Prize in Physics 2008. Press Release. Available online: https://www.nobelprize.org/prizes/physics/2008/summary/ (accessed on 15 July 2024).
119. Nishiyama, A.; Shigenori, T.; Tuszynski, J. Non-equilibrium $\varphi 4$ theory in a hierarchy: Towards manipulating holograms in quantum brain dynamics, Special Issue Recent Advances in Dynamic Phenomena. *Dynamics* **2023**, *3*, 1–17. [CrossRef]
120. Laipaporn, K.; Phibul, K.; Khachorncharoenkul, P. The Metallic Ratio of Pulsating Fibonacci Sequences. *Symmetry* **2022**, *14*, 1204. [CrossRef]
121. Sandler, U.; Tsitolovsky, L. (Eds.) *Neural Cell Behavior and Fuzzy Logic*; Springer US: Boston, MA, USA, 2008.
122. Wang, Y.; Yang, S.; Ren, X.; Guo, S.; Zhao, C.; Han, Q. WaterEdge: Edge–Cloud Collaborative Intelligent Coagulation System for Group-Level Water Treatment Plants. *IEEE Syst. J.* **2023**, *17*, 5346–5356. [CrossRef]
123. Laipaporn, K.; Khachorncharoenkul, P. Ideals in Bipolar Quantum Linear Algebra. *Symmetry* **2024**, *16*, 924. [CrossRef]
124. Marchetti, F. *Division and Power of Bipolar Quantum Linear Algebra*; 2016; pp. 1–5. Available online: https://www.researchgate.net/publication/309154224 (accessed on 15 July 2024).
125. Gao, C.J.; Sun, Y.Z.; Dong, H.Q.; Zhang, H.F. Achieving polarization control by utilizing electromagnetically induced transparency based on metasurface. *Waves Random Complex Media* **2022**, 1–23. [CrossRef]
126. Delgado, F.; Cardoso-Isidoro, C. Non-local parallel processing and database settlement using multiple teleportation followed by Grover post-selection. *Entropy* **2023**, *25*, 376. [CrossRef] [PubMed]
127. Zhao, Y.Y.; Xiao, F.Y.; Aritsugi, M.; Ding, W.P. A quantum Tanimoto coefficient fidelity for entanglement measurement. *IEEE/CAA J. Autom. Sin.* **2023**, *10*, 439–450. [CrossRef]
128. Xu, J.; Jarocha, L.E.; Zollitsch, T.; Konowalczyk, M.; Henbest, K.B.; Richert, S.; Golesworthy, M.J.; Schmidt, J.; Déjean, V.; Sowood, D.J.C.; et al. Magnetic sensitivity of cryptochrome 4 from a migratory songbird. *Nature* **2021**, *594*, 535–540. [CrossRef] [PubMed]
129. Avishai, Y. On Topics in Quantum Games. *J. Quantum Inf. Sci.* **2023**, *13*, 79–130. [CrossRef]
130. Pazar, V.B.; Malkoç, H. Bipolar Fuzzy Supra Topology via (Q-) Neighborhood and Its Application in Data Mining Process. *Symmetry* **2024**, *16*, 216. [CrossRef]
131. Gunji, Y.; Shinohara, S.; Basios, V. Connecting the free energy principle with quantum cognition. *Front. Neurorobot.* **2022**, *16*, 910161. [CrossRef] [PubMed]
132. Bahador, N.; Lankarany, M. Uncovering the Origins of Instability in Dynamical Systems: How Can the Attention Mechanism Help? *Dynamics* **2023**, *3*, 214–233. [CrossRef]
133. Fink, G.; Yolles, M. Affect and cognition, part 2: Affect types and mindset types. *Kybernetes* **2018**, *47*, 99–117. [CrossRef]
134. Shi, Y.; Seto, E.; Chang, L.-S.; Shenk, T. Transcriptional repression by YY1, a human GLI-Kruppel-related protein, and relief of repression by adenovirus E1A protein. *Cell* **1991**, *67*, 377–388. [CrossRef] [PubMed]
135. Jana, C.; Garg, H.; Pal, M.; Biswajit Sarkar, B.; Wei, G. MABAC framework for logarithmic bipolar fuzzy multiple attribute group decision-making for supplier selection. *Complex Intell. Syst.* **2023**, *10*, 273–288. [CrossRef]
136. Kure, J. Theoretical Construction and Empirical Study of the Paradigm of Integrated Strategic Research: Operational Analysis of SMEs and Organizations in Japan and China. Ph.D. Thesis, University of Marketing and Distribution Sciences Academic Repository, Kobe, Japan, 2023. (In Japanese).
137. Garg, H.; Mahmood, T.; Rehman, U.R.; Nguyen, G.N. Multi-attribute decision-making approach based on Aczel-Alsina power aggregation operators under bipolar fuzzy information & its application to quantum computing. *Alex. Eng. J.* **2023**, *82*, 248–259. [CrossRef]

138. Rorty, R. *Contingency, Irony, and Solidarity*; Cambridge University Press: Cambridge, UK, 1989.
139. Lloyd, S. *Programming the Universe*; Alfred A Knopf, Inc.: New York, NY, USA, 2006.
140. Park, J.L. The concept of transition in quantum mechanics. *Found. Phys.* **1970**, *1*, 23–33. [CrossRef]

Disclaimer/Publisher's Note: The statements, opinions and data contained in all publications are solely those of the individual author(s) and contributor(s) and not of MDPI and/or the editor(s). MDPI and/or the editor(s) disclaim responsibility for any injury to people or property resulting from any ideas, methods, instructions or products referred to in the content.

Article

Inter-Brain Hemodynamic Coherence Applied to Interoceptive Attentiveness in Hyperscanning: Why Social Framing Matters

Michela Balconi [1,2] and Laura Angioletti [1,2,*]

[1] International Research Center for Cognitive Applied Neuroscience (IrcCAN), Università Cattolica del Sacro Cuore, 20123 Milan, Italy
[2] Research Unit in Affective and Social Neuroscience, Department of Psychology, Università Cattolica del Sacro Cuore, 20123 Milan, Italy
* Correspondence: laura.angioletti1@unicatt.it; Tel.: +39-2-7234-5929

Abstract: Grossberg's classification of adaptive resonance mechanisms includes the cognitive-emotional resonances that support conscious feelings and recognition of them. In this regard, a relevant question concerns the processing of signals deriving from the internal body and their contribution to interpersonal synchronization. This study aims to assess hemodynamic inter-subject coherence in the prefrontal cortex (PFC) through functional near-infrared spectroscopy (fNIRS) hyperscan recording during dyadic synchronization tasks proposed with or without a social frame and performed in two distinct interoceptive conditions: focus and no focus on the breathing condition. Individuals' hemodynamic data (oxygenated and de-oxygenated hemoglobin (O2Hb and HHb, respectively)) were recorded through fNIRS hyperscanning, and coherence analysis was performed. The findings showed a significantly higher O2Hb coherence in the left PFC when the dyads performed the synchronization tasks with a social frame compared with no social frame in the focus condition. Overall, the evidence suggests that the interoceptive focus and the presence of a social frame favor the manifestation of a left PFC interpersonal tuning during synchronization tasks.

Keywords: interoceptive attentiveness; hyperscanning; fNIRS; lateralization; inter-brain coherence; interpersonal synchronization; social frame

1. Introduction

The term "social interoception" was introduced in the literature to describe the link and the potential influence of interoception (the process by which our brain receives and processes information derived from our body [1]) on a number of social processes, such as self-other differentiation [2], social cognition, social isolation and connectedness [3], and emotional experience [4–6].

The ability to intentionally focus attention on one's body signal for a determined span of time is defined as "interoceptive attentiveness" (IA) [7,8]. Weng and colleagues [9] showed that it is possible to modulate IA to observe positive outcomes in an individual's emotional and cognitive health. However, there has been little neuroscientific research conducted to date on how manipulating interoception can impact the interpersonal synchronization processes. Turn-taking, mimicry, and non-verbal social communication [10], as well as time and content synchronization [11], can be included in interpersonal synchronization processes.

Previously, single-brain studies were carried out to investigate the neural correlates of IA manipulation (operationalized as focused on breathing) on the inter-personal synchronization necessary for performing joint tasks [12–15]. In two recent studies, functional near-infrared spectroscopy (fNIRS) was used to record the oxygenated hemoglobin (O2Hb) changes during joint tasks involving motor and cognitive synchronization, while the participants were required to concentrate on their breathing to better understand the hemodynamic correlates of IA manipulation in interpersonal synchronization [12,14]. In the first study, the induction of explicit focus on breathing during a socially framed motor task requiring synchronization increased the responsiveness of the prefrontal cortex (PFC), which is involved in sustained attention, reorientation of attention, social responsiveness, and synchronization. In the absence of a broader and more explicit social frame, this effect was not significant in the motor task [14].

The PFC was shown to play a significant role in high-order functions, including social and cognitive functions, motor control, and attention. Grossberg [16] recently proposed an increasingly comprehensive attentive brain architecture in his predictive adaptive resonance theory (pART) and assigned to the PFC the control of high-order functions, including working memory, learned plans, predictions, and optimized action. As a part of a larger interoceptive network [17], the PFC is also crucial in initiating and maintaining focused attention on a target while regulating internal and external interferences [18]. Furthermore, the PFC supports sustained attention to breathing by increasing individuals' awareness of the mind wandering and enables them to bring their attention back to breathing [19]. Additionally, it has been associated with social functions, such as fully aware motor control and the ability to adapt to shifting rhythmic patterns [20], and also interpersonal coordination and cooperative interactions [21,22].

In the second fNIRS study, hemispheric lateralization was reported with an increase in O2Hb in the right PFC when intentional attention toward breathing was induced during a cognitive synchronization task, namely a linguistic task [12]. According to previous studies, the right PFC appears to support the execution of IA tasks [6,23,24] and sustained and goal-directed attention [18].

Although the above-mentioned fNIRS studies were the first to describe the effect of IA manipulation on individuals completing motor and cognitive tasks in synchronization with another partner and aiding in identifying the role of the PFC in this phenomenon at the intraindividual level, one obvious shortcoming consisted of the lack of assessments of the interactional dynamics between the two members of the dyad.

With the development of the hyperscanning paradigm [25], numerous works have calculated inter-agent synchronization and inter-brain coupling metrics that reflect the degree of social attunement based on the simultaneous recording of behavioral and hemodynamic responses from various agents involved in a joint task or a social exchange [22,26]. For instance, this made it possible to investigate how dyads' inter-individual brain synchronization changes depending on whether the participants are collaborating or competing [27,28].

In addition, hyperscanning studies were extensively used for deepening synchronization mechanisms during motor [29–31], linguistic, and cognitive tasks. Naturalistic paradigms including verbal collaboration and turn-taking have revealed a lateralization effect, with right-sided activations of the dorsolateral PFC and temporal areas [32].

However, it has also been established that the setting of the interaction affects interbrain synchrony. For example, facing the interacting partner appears to improve interbrain synchrony, as evidenced by more simultaneous increases in activity within the left inferior frontal cortex and the right temporal parietal junction (TPJ) in subjects who were singing [33] or playing interactive games while facing each other as opposed to a wall [34]. Additionally, face-to-face interactions showed increased inter-brain synchrony, but back-to-back ones did not [35].

Furthermore, inter-brain synchronization in the left PFC was discovered to predict the effectiveness of teaching, highlighting the significance of shared attention for the accomplishment of shared objectives [36]. Greater inter-brain synchrony in the left frontopolar region was also found in dyads with different social experience [37]. In regions connected to the social alignment loop, such as the left inferior frontal cortex, behavioral alignment was found to be mediated by inter-brain synchrony [38].

Nonetheless, these hyperscanning studies did not manipulate IA when individuals performed the tasks in synchrony. Moreover, the social framing was not explicitly emphasized. Therefore, it is also interesting to determine the impact of these two variables on intercerebral coherence in terms of lateralization.

With reference to the influence of a social frame on synchronization performance, before it was shown how, during a real-person, joint-tapping hyperscanning experiment, interpersonal sensorimotor performance and interbrain synchrony in the left TPJ was greater in a bidirectional than in a unidirectional condition, indicating the social effect of a more cooperative condition [39] or suggesting a potential neural mechanism for selective tuning in to a target speaker while tuning out others [40]. Additionally, as stated above, the presence of an explicit social frame during a motor synchronization task, executed while paying attention to breathing, augmented the O2Hb values in the PFCs of individuals [14]. Thus, it may be argued that even basic exercises of synchronization, if explicitly socially framed, may differently impact an individual's inter-brain coherence. This research used neural coherence indices to explore the hemodynamic correlates of between-brain interconnectivity by using a two-person neuroscience paradigm. In former fNIRS hyperscanning experiments, coherence indices were used to examine the synchronization of brain rhythms during cooperative and competitive joint activities [22,26,41,42], social exchanges [43], and gesture observation and reproduction [44].

Therefore, the primary aim of the present study is to assess hemodynamic intersubject coherence through fNIRS hyperscan recording during dyadic synchronization tasks, proposed with and without a social frame and performed in two distinct interoceptive conditions. Specifically, the experimental design examines two distinct conditions of presence and absence of interoceptive focus (i.e., when the attention of the participants is focused on breathing versus not focused on breathing), the specific synchronization task performed by the participants (cognitive versus motor), as well as the social frame applied at the beginning of the synchronization task (that could be socially framed or not).

Given previous evidence, we hypothesized observed higher inter-brain coherence in the PFC of the dyads during focusing on breathing compared with not focusing on the breathing condition for both synchronization tasks [12,14].

Secondly, regarding social frame manipulation, we expect to observe an increase in the inter-brain coherence effect for socially framed synchronization compared with non-socially framed synchronization. It is also supposed that an increased effect in response to the motor compared with the linguistic synchronization task will be present, given the effect of the social frame we previously observed specifically for the motor task in our previous research [14].

Thirdly, as indicated in the literature reported above, we aim to observe a potential lateralization effect even in terms of inter-brain coherence, with a potential right hemisphere lateralization effect connected to interoceptive focus [12,23,24] and a left hemispheric activation predominance for positive emotions derived from the synchronization.

Finally, taking into account that coherence indices were used before in fNIRS hyperscanning experiments to investigate PFC synchrony, we also intend to deepen whether inter-subject hemodynamic coherence indices can be exploited as a reliable indicator of dyads' neural synchronization in this context (i.e., when the interoceptive attention to breathing is manipulated).

2. Materials and Methods

2.1. Participants

A total of 32 university students were enlisted for the current fNIRS experiment using a non-probabilistic convenience sampling technique (14 females; age mean = 27.1; standard deviation = 3.19). Each dyad was composed of two individuals of the same sex matched for age, and they did not meet before the experiment. We have previously estimated the adequate sample size to detect medium effects via inferential statistics (f = 0.25), with the α error probability set at 0.05 and with 0.80 power (G*Power 3.1 software [45]). The analysis suggested that a total of 15 observations (i.e., in our case, dyads) would be sufficient. All participants were right-handed and had normal or corrected-to-normal eyesight. The criteria for exclusion included pregnancy, past meditative experience, severe physical and chronic illnesses, convulsions, persistent pain, and any mental or neurological disorders.

They signed written informed consent forms and willingly agreed to participate in the study after being advised they would not receive payment for their contributions. The Ethics Committee of the Department of Psychology (Catholic University of the Sacred Heart in Milan, Italy) gave its approval for this study (2020 TD-a.a.2020–2021), which was conducted in conformity with the Declaration of Helsinki.

2.2. Joint Synchronization Tasks Description

Two basic motor and cognitive synchronization tasks were adopted as joint tasks in the current study.

The participants in the motor synchronization task had to synchronize and coordinate their finger-tapping motion for three minutes with the other person in their dyad. The participants were instructed to sit in a chair with their elbows resting on a table and their dominant hand's fingers spread about a centimeter apart. They were instructed to use all of the fingers on their dominant hand to tap the table. They were not told to move at a certain speed or to extend their fingers as wide as they could. All they had to do was ensure their finger movements matched those of the participant sitting in front of them. The average number of loops—measured as the total number of times a finger-tapping pattern was repeated—was 60.

A modified version of the human-to-human alternating speech task was utilized for the cognitive synchronization test, requiring the participants to syllabicate in unison with the other participant in the dyad for a total of three minutes. The four syllables of "LA", "BA", "CA", and "DA" were to be spoken consecutively and alternately by the participants. To pronounce a syllable at the same time, for example, when one member of the dyad said "LA", the other member should have paired the syllable by saying "LA", and so on. The speech patterns were not chosen in advance. Without any breaks, each language synchronization task session lasted three minutes. The number of repetitions from "LA" to "DA" in each loop throughout the course of the three minutes was at least 45.

These tasks were employed in prior single-brain investigations [12,14] and were used for this hyperscanning study to ensure consistency in the experimental design.

2.3. Procedure and Experimental Manipulations

Each dyad was positioned such that the participants could comfortably interact with each other face to face. The participants received procedural instructions before the experiment started. They were informed that they were required to execute two joint synchronization tasks following different experimental conditions in which IA was manipulated.

In the first condition, IA was purposefully controlled by instructing the participants to concentrate on their breathing. The following directions were given in this focus on breathing: "During this task, we ask you to concentrate on your breathing. Try to pay attention to how you feel and whether your breathing changes as you complete the activity." The participants were not instructed to breathe at a certain pace. In contrast, no specific instructions were given in the no attention to breathing condition, which was regarded as the control condition, in which interoception was not manipulated, and the participants were only instructed to complete the joint tasks. The same interoceptive manipulation was used in earlier investigations to preserve the procedure's reliability, and it was shown to have an impact on the hemodynamic neural correlates [12,46].

For the social framing manipulation, we asked the participants to perform the same motor and cognitive synchronization tasks previously described, but they were socially framed by specifying that they needed to synchronize in order to develop greater teamwork skills. In this way, the absence of a social frame resulted from not emphasizing the sharing of intention, whereas stressing the shared intentionality explicitly served to introduce the social frame [14].

A 120 s baseline of each dyad member's hemodynamic resting state was gathered before the synchronization tasks began. The order in which the condition and the synchronization tasks were performed were randomized and counterbalanced to prevent any potential biases brought on by sequence effects. After completing the activities, there was a debriefing phase in which the participants rated their attention to their breathing, the other person, and the task on a scale of 0 to 10. The entire experimental procedure took one hour to be completed (Figure 1A,B).

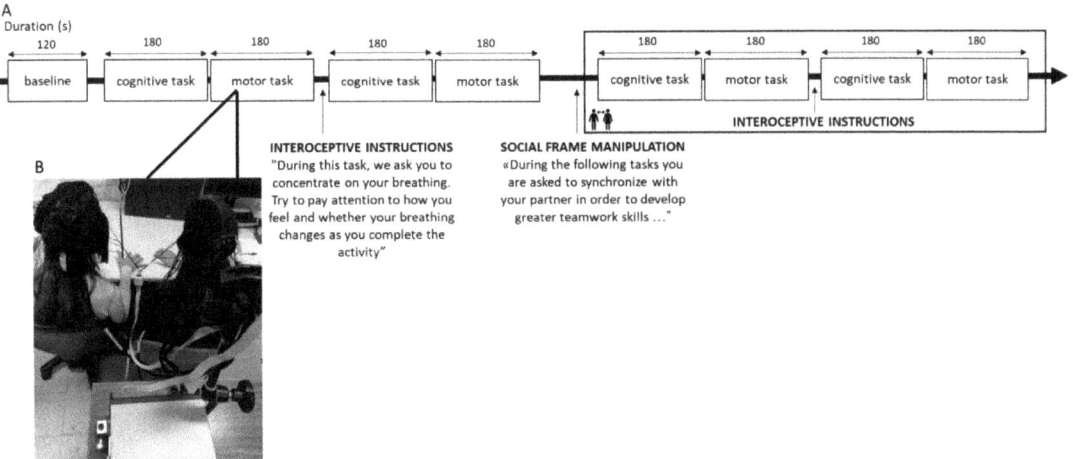

Figure 1. (**A**) Experimental procedure representing the setting for the joint task and (**B**) the fNIRS hyperscanning acquisition from the dyad. To avoid an order effect, the task execution was randomized and counterbalanced for the type of the task and the condition.

2.4. fNIRS Data Recording and Biosignal Data Analysis

The hemodynamic signal was recorded using a six-channel optode matrix of an NIRScout System (NIRx Medical Technologies, LLC, Los Angeles, CA, USA). This system measures fluctuations in the concentrations of oxygenated hemoglobin (O2Hb) and deoxygenated hemoglobin (HHb). Using an fNIRS cap, four light sources or emitters and four detectors were placed over the scalp in line with the worldwide standard 10/5 system [47].

For the montage, four emitters were installed at AF3, AF4, F5, and F6, and four detectors were installed at AFF1h, AFF2h, F3, and F4. The emitter-detector distance for consecutive optodes was kept at 30 mm, and two wavelengths of near-infrared light were used (760 and 850 nm). Six channels were acquired using this optode configuration: Ch1 (AF3-F3), Ch2 (AF3-AFF1h), and Ch3 (F5-F3), which corresponded to the left PFC, and Ch4 (AF4-F4), Ch5 (AF4-AFF2h), and Ch6 (F6-F4), which corresponded to the right PFC [6,48] (Figure 2). The sources, detectors, and space between them were placed in relation to the underlying functional region and the most appropriate Brodmann area according to online atlases [49,50].

2.5. Hemodynamic Data Reduction

NIRStar Acquisition Software (NIRx Medical Technologies LLC, 15 Cherry Lane, Glen Head, NY, USA) was used to continuously record the fluctuations in O2Hb and HHb concentrations during an initial 120 s resting baseline and the tasks. The signals from the six channels were collected at a sample rate of 6.25 Hz and then extracted and converted with nirsLAB software (v2014.05; NIRx Medical Technologies LLC, 15 Cherry Lane, Glen Head, NY, USA) based on their wavelengths and positions, producing mmol mm values that corresponded to the variations in the concentration of O2Hb and HHb per channel. Each channel's acquired raw O2Hb and HHb data were digitally band-pass filtered at 0.01–0.3 Hz [41,43].

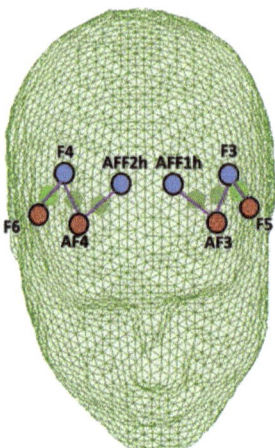

Figure 2. Head rendering with the fNIRS montage layout. Emitters and detectors are indicated in red and blue, respectively.

Both during the experimental phase and the signal analysis, raw time series were visually reviewed subject by subject to identify noisy channels caused by motion artifacts or amplitude variations (criterion for rejection: amplitude of hemoglobin (Hb) signal above or below ±5 SD; visual inspection). Artifacts caused 3% of the data to be removed. Channels with poor optical coupling and lack of heartbeat oscillations at 1 Hz were disregarded during this visual evaluation. Additionally, a linear-phase FIR filter on respiration was applied (0.3 Hz), which produced a symmetric impulse response [51,52].

Both during the experimental phase and the signal analysis, raw time series were visually inspected subject by subject to identify noisy channels caused by motion artifacts or amplitude variations. Here, 3% of the data were removed for artifacts.

The mean concentration of each channel for the tasks was determined following biosignal analysis. Based on the mean concentrations in the time series for each channel and subject, the effect size in each condition was calculated.

The effect sizes (Cohen's d) were calculated by dividing the difference between the baseline and trial means by the baseline standard deviation (SD) such that D = (m1 m2)/s, where m1 and m2 are the mean concentration levels for the baseline and trial, respectively, and s is the baseline SD. The effect sizes from the six channels were averaged in order to increase the signal-to-noise ratio. While raw fNIRS data were initially relative values that could not be directly averaged across people or channels, and the normalized effect sizes were averaged regardless of the unit, since the effect size is unaffected by the differential pathlength factor (DPF).

For the statistical analysis of the fNIRS data, the channels were grouped to compose the lateralization factor for the left (Ch1, Ch2, and Ch3) and right (Ch4, Ch5, and Ch6) hemispheres, corresponding to the left and right PFCs.

2.6. Coherence Value Analysis

A first analysis was conducted to obtain the inter-brain coherence by computing the partial correlation coefficient Π_{ij} for each dyad, applied to each channel and to the lateralization factor for both the O2Hb and the HHb. These indices were obtained by normalizing the covariance matrix's inverse:

$$\Gamma = \Sigma - 1$$

$\Gamma = (\Gamma_{ij}) = \Sigma - 1$ inverse of the covariance matrix

This analysis permits evaluating the relationship between two signals (i, j) independent of one another [53], and it was previously applied often in earlier fNIRS hyperscanning research [22,54].

2.7. Statistical Analysis

A second step of analysis was applied to the coherence values, considered as dependent measures of a repeated measures ANOVA with independent within the factors of condition (two: focus on breathing or no focus on breathing) × task (two: motor or cognitive) × lateralization (two: left or right) × frame (two: not social or social). For this analysis, IBM SPSS Statistics (version 25) was used. For all ANOVA tests, in case of significant effects, pairwise comparisons were conducted to explore the significant interactions between simple effects, and the Bonferroni correction was applied to lessen the possible bias of repeated comparisons. The degrees of freedom for all ANOVA tests were adjusted using the Greenhouse–Geisser epsilon where required. Using partial eta squared ($\eta2$) indices, the magnitudes of the statistically significant effects were calculated.

3. Results

Two sets of results corresponding to the two analyses performed on the hemodynamic dependent measures will be described below. The first step of analysis included the application of coherence analysis for each dyad. The second step concerned the application of an inferential statistical ANOVA test to the coherence values considered dependent measures.

3.1. First Step: Coherence Results

For the first step of analysis, we found the computed coherence values for each fNIRS channel in each experimental condition for both the O2Hb and HHb. A successive coherence analysis was applied to the lateralization factor for the left and right hemispheres, which were calculated as the average of the homologous channels for both the O2Hb and HHb, respectively. However, due to the limited significant values of coherence for the HHb, only the results for the O2Hb were considered and reported. In the graphs below, we have reported for this first step the mean trend of the coherence index for each dyad of participants (Figure 3A–D).

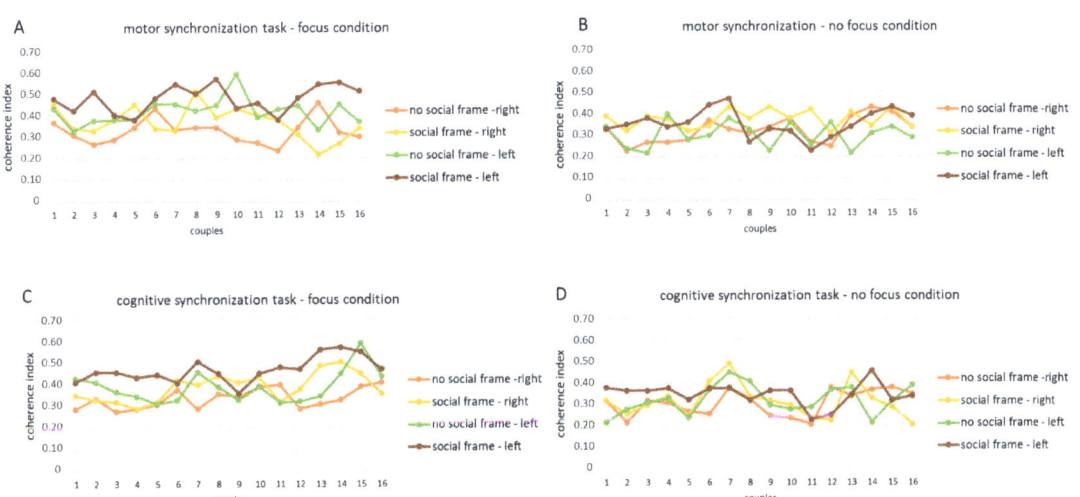

Figure 3. fNIRS coherence values for O2Hb. Trend of the coherence indices for the motor synchronization task in the focus (**A**) and no focus conditions (**B**) and for the cognitive synchronization task in the focus (**C**) and no focus conditions (**D**) in each dyad.

3.2. Second Step: ANOVA Results

The ANOVAs applied to the inter-brain coherence indices as dependent variables for each dyad revealed significant effects for the D values of the O2Hb hemoglobin. The following paragraphs report the significant results obtained for the ANOVAs.

A first significant main effect was observed for the lateralization (F [1, 15] = 7.09, $p = 0.01$, $\eta^2 = 0.421$), for which higher coherence for the O2Hb values was observed in the left compared with the right hemisphere.

Secondly, an interaction effect was detected for condition × task × lateralization (F [1, 43] = 8.09, $p = 0.01$, $\eta^2 = 0.498$). The pairwise comparison revealed an increase in coherence of the O2Hb values in the focus condition for both tasks (motor and cognitive) in the left compared with the right hemisphere (motor: F [1, 15] = 8.56, $p = 0.01$, $\eta^2 = 0.442$; linguistic; F [1, 15] = 8.11, $p = 0.01$, $\eta^2 = 0.432$).

Then, a third interaction effect was found for condition × task × lateralization × frame (F [1, 82] = 7.89, $p = 0.01$, $\eta^2 = 0.432$). A pairwise comparison revealed an increase in coherence in the left hemisphere when the participants in the focus condition performed the motor synchronization task with a social frame compared with no social frame (F [1, 15] = 8.98, $p = 0.01$, $\eta^2 = 0.408$) (Figure 4A). According to the pairwise comparison, greater coherence was observed in the left hemisphere when the participants in the focus condition performed the cognitive synchronization task with a social frame compared with no social frame (F [1, 15] = 8.04, $p = 0.01$, $\eta^2 = 0.391$) (Figure 4B).

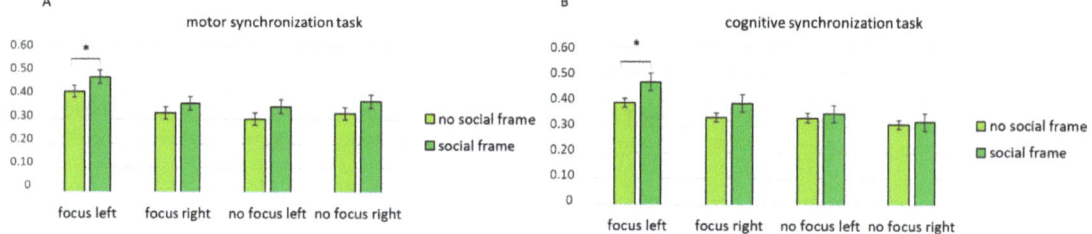

Figure 4. Mean coherence indices for the cognitive and motor synchronization tasks. All asterisks (*) mark statistically significant differences, with $p \leq 0.05$.

4. Discussion

In the present work, the hemodynamic interpersonal attunement of healthy participants during synchronization tasks with and without a social frame was explored and executed in two different experimental conditions. In particular, these tasks were executed in the presence or absence of explicit focus on breathing as interoceptive (IA) manipulation conditions. A social neuroscientific hyperscanning approach by fNIRS was applied to allow the recording of participants' hemodynamic responses related to the motor and cognitive synchronization tasks presented with or without a social frame. For the fNIRS signal, an analysis of the coherence indices and a comparison of the fNIRS coherence's strength for the conditions, tasks, and homologous PFC channels were performed.

The coherence analysis was computed to check the inter-subject neural hemodynamic coherence between the dyads for the left and right hemispheres considered in each experimental condition.

First, it was chosen to report the main significance results in graphs to describe the trend of synchronization within the dyads. In former fNIRS hyperscanning experiments, coherence indices were used to examine the synchronization of the hemodynamic signal during cooperative and competitive joint activities [22,26,41,42], social exchanges [43], and gesture observation and reproduction [44]. At the methodological level, the results of the present study proved that inter-subject hemodynamic coherence indices can be exploited as a reliable indicator of dyads' PFC tuning in this context, specifically when there is a focus on breathing and the social frame is manipulated.

Moreover, some relevant and significant outcomes were detected. In general, higher coherence for the O2Hb values was observed in the left compared with the right hemisphere when the participants were executing both synchronization tasks (motor and cognitive). This effect was especially observed during the condition of focusing on breathing (i.e., the interoceptive condition). Additionally, greater coherence for the O2Hb values was observed in the left hemisphere when the participants in the focus condition performed both synchronization tasks with a social frame compared with when they executed the same tasks without an explicit social frame.

The higher inter-brain coherence in the left compared with the right PFC observed for both synchronization tasks in the interoceptive condition can be explained by taking into consideration the role of the left PFC in synchronization. In fact, former studies reported a right hemisphere lateralization effect connected to interoceptive focus [12,23,24]. However, they did not apply IA to social synchronization tasks. Therefore, a possible explanation for this apparently counterintuitive result may consider the left PFC's role in relation to the positive impact of synchronization.

Past hyperscanning research on cooperation exploited fNIRS to assess subjects' brain activity during a cooperative dual task [41] which adopted the same computation for neural coupling. The fNIRS results revealed increased brain PFC activity and higher synchronization over the left PFC after feedback, in line with the perception of a positive dynamic of social synchronization and compatible with positive emotions and approach-related motivations. This finding can be explained by considering the left PFC's "emotional relevance" in comparison with the right PFC. As was previously noted, approach motivation, the capacity to control negative emotions, and general well-being are all correlated with the frontal cortical asymmetry favoring the left hemisphere [55–58]. According to converging data from evolutionary psychology and developmental research, cooperation is psychologically gratifying for the individual, and as a result, during cooperative conditions, frontal reward-processing regions may be more active than other cortical areas.

Therefore, it may be plausible that the synchronization per se, together with IA, may promote the left PFC's neural synchrony in dyads. Nonetheless, the effect of interoception on PFC lateralization, particularly during social processes, needs to be further explored in future studies.

Furthermore, this PFC left-lateralized synchrony was not only associated with the interoceptive condition but also with the social framework (compared with no social framework) for both synchronization tasks (motor and cognitive).

The PFC, together with the TPJ, has been previously considered a neuroanatomical region belonging to the so-called "mutual attention system", whose main characteristic is the mutual and synchronized activation aspect [40]. In particular, inter-brain synchrony in the left PFC was also found in several previous hyerscanning studies during simultaneous singing [33], face-to-face conversations [34], shared attention for the achievement of mutual goals [36], and also during a real-person, joint-tapping hyperscanning experiment in a bidirectional rather than unidirectional condition, indicating the social effect of a more cooperative condition [39] or suggesting a potential neural mechanism for selective tuning in to a target speaker while tuning out others [40]. Therefore, the present study adds to the existing body of knowledge evidence that even basic exercises of synchronization, which are also explicitly socially framed, may increase an individual's inter-brain coherence in the left PFC.

Interestingly, different from what was hypothesized in our second hypothesis, no differences were observed between the motor and cognitive synchronization tasks, since the increased effect of coherence in the left PFC was detected for both tasks in the condition of focusing on breathing when the tasks were socially framed compared with not being socially framed. This result suggests that the effect of the synchronization and the social frame affects both the motor [14] and cognitive synchronization.

Such evidence is also crucial from a neuroanatomical perspective, since the involvement of the left prefrontal areas has been associated with interoception during social synchronization.

While this study demonstrated the relevance of coherence indices as a marker of the focus on breathing as an interoceptive condition and of social frame manipulation in synchronization tasks, it also presents some limitations. In fact, given the focus of this study on the PFC, fNIRS channels were applied on the frontal locations only without covering the whole scalp, which would have included somatosensory cortical regions and other relevant structures, such as the TPJ. Future research should focus on these structures' roles in interoceptive processing [7] and social synchronization [39], respectively.

Furthermore, this basic research adopted some simplistic synchronization tasks that just required finger tapping or alternate syllable pronunciation. Future studies could (1) utilize more ecological and complex joint activities, such as dancing, playing an instrument, or communicating in a live interactive speech, as previously performed in prior hyperscanning studies, and (2) integrate multi-level measurements of the empathic resonance mechanisms, such as facial behavior analysis (to explore participants' facial feedback) [59] and self-reported measures, such as a scale to measure empathic behavior (e.g., the Balanced Emotional Empathy Scale) and individual differences in approach or avoidance motivational tendencies (e.g., the Behavioral Inhibition and Activation Scale) [60], to gather the complexity of this phenomenon. Moreover, an impfigureortant effect may be suggested for the gender factor in relation to the social synchronization. Indeed, as shown by Cheng, Li, and Hu (2015), "the presence of a homogender of a heterogender dyad" may modulate interbrain activity, and future enquiries could be formulated about the role of gender on the joint cognitive and brain strategies.

Finally, to increase the ecological validity of the findings, participants could receive less artificial and more contextually related instructions for the social frame.

5. Conclusions

Overall, this hyperscanning research shows how manipulating IA, which is attained by concentrating on breathing, and the social frame in a dyadic condition enhances the emergence of hemodynamic indicators of interpersonal tuning in the left PFC during basic synchronization tasks. The increase in coherence in the left PFC can be considered a neuroanatomic marker of the combination of IA and social synchronization. This evidence opens the way to also considering in Grossberg's pART model the contribution of interoception on high-level cognitive and emotional functions and on resonance mechanisms.

To the best of our knowledge, this is the first time that the effect of IA and the social frame on inter-brain neural synchrony has been explored during an interactive social dynamic involving two individuals. This experiment contributes to increasing the knowledge relating to those studies within the category of "social interoception", which intends to investigate the impact of interoception on social dynamics and processes.

Author Contributions: Conceptualization, M.B. and L.A.; methodology, M.B. and L.A.; software, L.A.; validation, M.B. formal analysis, M.B.; investigation, M.B.; resources, M.B.; data curation, M.B. and L.A.; writing—original draft preparation, L.A.; writing—review and editing, M.B. and L.A.; visualization, M.B.; supervision, M.B.; project administration, M.B.; funding acquisition, M.B. All authors have read and agreed to the published version of the manuscript.

Funding: This research received no external funding.

Data Availability Statement: The datasets generated and analyzed for this study are available from the corresponding author upon reasonable request.

Acknowledgments: The authors acknowledge Carlotta Acconito and Katia Rovelli for their assistance with data curation.

Conflicts of Interest: The authors declare no conflict of interest.

References

1. Khalsa, S.S.; Adolphs, R.; Cameron, O.G.; Critchley, H.D.; Davenport, P.W.; Feinstein, J.S.; Feusner, J.D.; Garfinkel, S.N.; Lane, R.D.; Mehling, W.E.; et al. Interoception and Mental Health: A Roadmap. *Biol. Psychiatry Cogn. Neurosci. Neuroimaging* **2018**, *3*, 501–513. [CrossRef] [PubMed]
2. Palmer, C.E.; Tsakiris, M. Going at the heart of social cognition: Is there a role for interoception in self-other distinction? *Curr. Opin. Psychol.* **2018**, *24*, 21–26. [CrossRef] [PubMed]
3. Arnold, A.J.; Winkielman, P.; Dobkins, K. Interoception and Social Connection. *Front. Psychol.* **2019**, *10*, 1–6. [CrossRef] [PubMed]
4. Burleson, M.H.; Quigley, K.S. Social interoception and social allostasis through touch: Legacy of the Somatovisceral Afference Model of Emotion. *Soc. Neurosci.* **2021**, *16*, 92–102. [CrossRef]
5. Balconi, M.; Angioletti, L. One's Interoception Affects the Representation of Seeing Others' Pain: A Randomized Controlled qEEG Study. *Pain Res. Manag.* **2021**, *2021*, 1–15. [CrossRef]
6. Balconi, M.; Angioletti, L. Interoception as a social alarm amplification system. What multimethod (EEG-fNIRS) integrated measures can tell us about interoception and empathy for pain? *Neuropsychol. Trends* **2021**, *29*, 39–64. [CrossRef]
7. Schulz, S.M. Neural correlates of heart-focused interoception: A functional magnetic resonance imaging meta-analysis. *Philos. Trans. R. Soc. B Biol. Sci.* **2016**, *371*, 20160018. [CrossRef]
8. Tsakiris, M.; De Preester, H. *The interoceptive Mind: From Homeostasis to Awareness*; Oxford University Press: Oxford, UK, 2018.
9. Weng, H.Y.; Feldman, J.L.; Leggio, L.; Napadow, V.; Park, J.; Price, C.J. Interventions and Manipulations of Interoception. *Trends Neurosci.* **2021**, *44*, 52–62. [CrossRef]
10. Charman, T. Commentary: Glass half full or half empty? Testing social communication interventions for young children with autism - Reflections on Landa, Holman, O'Neill, and Stuart (2011). *J. Child Psychol. Psychiatry Allied Discip.* **2011**, *52*, 22–23. [CrossRef]
11. Delaherche, E.; Chetouani, M.; Mahdhaoui, A.; Saint-Georges, C.; Viaux, S.; Cohen, D. Interpersonal Synchrony: A Survey Of Evaluation Methods Across Disciplines. *IEEE Trans. Affect. Comput.* **2012**, *3*, 349–365. [CrossRef]
12. Balconi, M.; Angioletti, L. Interoceptive attentiveness induces significantly more PFC activation during a synchronized linguistic task compared to a motor task as revealed by functional Near-Infrared Spectroscopy. *Brain Sci.* **2022**, *12*, 301. [CrossRef]
13. Angioletti, L.; Balconi, M. Delta-Alpha EEG pattern reflects the interoceptive focus effect on interpersonal motor synchronization. *Front. Neuroergonomics* **2022**, 1–10. [CrossRef]
14. Angioletti, L.; Balconi, M. The Increasing Effect of Interoception on Brain Frontal Responsiveness During a Socially Framed Motor Synchronization Task. *Front. Hum. Neurosci.* **2022**, *16*, 1–9. [CrossRef]
15. Angioletti, L.; Balconi, M. EEG brain oscillations are modulated by interoception in response to a synchronized motor vs. cognitive task. *Front. Neuroanat.* **2022**, *16*. [CrossRef]
16. Grossberg, S. Attention: Multiple types, brain resonances, psychological functions, and conscious states. *J. Integr. Neurosci.* **2021**, *20*, 197–232. [CrossRef]
17. Chen, W.G.; Schloesser, D.; Arensdorf, A.M.; Simmons, J.M.; Cui, C.; Valentino, R.; Gnadt, J.W.; Nielsen, L.; Hillaire-Clarke, C.S.; Spruance, V.; et al. The Emerging Science of Interoception: Sensing, Integrating, Interpreting, and Regulating Signals within the Self. *Trends Neurosci.* **2021**, *44*, 3–16. [CrossRef]
18. Kondo, H.; Osaka, N.; Osaka, M. Cooperation of the anterior cingulate cortex and dorsolateral prefrontal cortex for attention shifting. *Neuroimage* **2004**, *23*, 670–679. [CrossRef]
19. Dickenson, J.; Berkman, E.T.; Arch, J.; Lieberman, M.D. Neural correlates of focused attention during a brief mindfulness induction. *Soc. Cogn. Affect. Neurosci.* **2013**, *8*, 40–47. [CrossRef]
20. Stephan, K.M.; Thaut, M.H.; Wunderlich, G.; Schicks, W.; Tian, B.; Tellmann, L.; Schmitz, T.; Herzog, H.; McIntosh, G.C.; Seitz, R.J.; et al. Conscious and subconscious sensorimotor synchronization-Prefrontal cortex and the influence of awareness. *Neuroimage* **2002**, *15*, 345–352. [CrossRef]
21. Hu, Y.; Wang, Z.; Song, B.; Pan, Y.; Cheng, X.; Zhu, Y.; Hu, Y. How to calculate and validate inter-brain synchronization in a fnirs hyperscanning study. *J. Vis. Exp.* **2021**, *175*, 1–16.
22. Balconi, M.; Pezard, L.; Nandrino, J.-L.; Vanutelli, M.E. Two is better than one: The effects of strategic cooperation on intra- and inter-brain connectivity by fNIRS. *PLoS ONE* **2017**, *12*, e0187652. [CrossRef] [PubMed]
23. Zheng, Y.L.; Wang, D.X.; Zhang, Y.R.; Tang, Y.Y. Enhancing Attention by Synchronizing Respiration and Fingertip Pressure: A Pilot Study Using Functional Near-Infrared Spectroscopy. *Front. Neurosci.* **2019**, *13*, 1–18. [CrossRef] [PubMed]
24. Zhang, Z.; Olszewska-Guizzo, A.; Husain, S.F.; Bose, J.; Choi, J.; Tan, W.; Wang, J.; Tran, B.X.; Wang, B.; Jin, Y.; et al. Brief relaxation practice induces significantly more prefrontal cortex activation during arithmetic tasks comparing to viewing greenery images as revealed by functional near-infrared spectroscopy (fNIRS). *Int. J. Environ. Res. Public Health* **2020**, *17*, 8366. [CrossRef] [PubMed]
25. Montague, P.R.; Berns, G.S.; Cohen, J.D.; McClure, S.M.; Pagnoni, G.; Dhamala, M.; Wiest, M.C.; Karpov, I.; King, R.D.; Apple, N.; et al. Hyperscanning: Simultaneous fMRI during linked social interactions. *Neuroimage* **2002**, *16*, 1159–1164. [CrossRef]
26. Crivelli, D.; Balconi, M. Near-infrared spectroscopy applied to complex systems and human hyperscanning networking. *Appl. Sci.* **2017**, *7*, 922. [CrossRef]
27. Balconi, M.; Vanutelli, M.E. Cooperation and competition with hyperscanning methods: Review and future application to emotion domain. *Front. Comput. Neurosci.* **2017**, *11*, 1–21. [CrossRef]

28. Angioletti, L.; Vanutelli, M.E.; Fronda, G.; Balconi, M. Exploring the Connected Brain by fNIRS: Human-to-Human Interactions Engineering. *Appl. Mech. Mater.* **2019**, *893*, 13–19. [CrossRef]
29. Cheng, X.; Li, X.; Hu, Y. Synchronous brain activity during cooperative exchange depends on gender of partner: A fNIRS-based hyperscanning study. *Hum. Brain Mapp.* **2015**, *36*, 2039–2048. [CrossRef]
30. Baker, J.M.; Liu, N.; Cui, X.; Vrticka, P.; Saggar, M.; Hosseini, S.M.H.; Reiss, A.L. Sex differences in neural and behavioral signatures of cooperation revealed by fNIRS hyperscanning. *Sci. Rep.* **2016**, *6*, 1–11. [CrossRef]
31. Pan, Y.; Cheng, X.; Zhang, Z.; Li, X.; Hu, Y. Cooperation in lovers: An fNIRS-based hyperscanning study. *Hum. Brain Mapp.* **2017**, *38*, 831–841. [CrossRef]
32. Kelsen, B.A.; Sumich, A.; Kasabov, N.; Liang, S.H.Y.; Wang, G.Y. What has social neuroscience learned from hyperscanning studies of spoken communication? A systematic review. *Neurosci. Biobehav. Rev.* **2022**, *132*, 1249–1262. [CrossRef]
33. Osaka, N.; Minamoto, T.; Yaoi, K.; Azuma, M.; Shimada, Y.M.; Osaka, M. How two brains make one synchronized mind in the inferior frontal cortex: FNIRS-based hyperscanning during cooperative singing. *Front. Psychol.* **2015**, *6*, 1–11. [CrossRef]
34. Tang, H.; Mai, X.; Wang, S.; Zhu, C.; Krueger, F.; Liu, C. Interpersonal brain synchronization in the right temporo-parietal junction during face-to-face economic exchange. *Soc. Cogn. Affect. Neurosci.* **2015**, *11*, 23–32. [CrossRef]
35. Jiang, J.; Dai, B.; Peng, D.; Zhu, C.; Liu, L.; Lu, C. Neural synchronization during face-to-face communication. *J. Neurosci.* **2012**, *32*, 16064–16069. [CrossRef]
36. Davidesco, I.; Laurent, E.; Valk, H.; West, T.; Dikker, S.; Milne, C.; Poeppel, D. Brain-to-brain synchrony predicts long-term memory retention more accurately than individual brain measures. *bioRxiv* **2019**, 644047.
37. Sun, B.; Xiao, W.; Lin, S.; Shao, Y.; Li, W. Brain and Cognition Cooperation with partners of differing social experience: An fNIRS-based hyperscanning study. *Brain Cogn.* **2021**, *154*, 105803. [CrossRef]
38. Shamay-tsoory, S.G.; Saporta, N.; Marton-alper, I.Z.; Gvirts, H.Z. Herding Brains: A Core Neural Mechanism for Social Alignment. *Trends Cogn. Sci.* **2019**, *23*, 174–186. [CrossRef]
39. Dai, R.; Liu, R.; Liu, T.; Zhang, Z.; Xiao, X.; Sun, P.; Yu, X.; Wang, D.; Zhu, C. Holistic cognitive and neural processes: A fNIRS-hyperscanning study on interpersonal sensorimotor synchronization. *Soc. Cogn. Affect. Neurosci.* **2018**, *13*, 1141–1154. [CrossRef]
40. Gvirts, H.Z.; Perlmutter, R. What Guides Us to Neurally and Behaviorally Align With Anyone Specific? A Neurobiological Model Based on fNIRS Hyperscanning Studies. *Neuroscientist* **2020**, *26*, 108–116. [CrossRef]
41. Balconi, M.; Vanutelli, M.E. Interbrains cooperation: Hyperscanning and self-perception in joint actions. *J. Clin. Exp. Neuropsychol.* **2017**, *39*, 607–620. [CrossRef]
42. Balconi, M.; Vanutelli, M.E. Brains in competition: Improved cognitive performance and inter-brain coupling by hyperscanning paradigm with functional near-infrared spectroscopy. *Front. Behav. Neurosci.* **2017**, *11*, 1–10. [CrossRef] [PubMed]
43. Balconi, M.; Fronda, G.; Vanutelli, M.E. Donate or receive? Social hyperscanning application with fNIRS. *Curr. Psychol.* **2019**, *38*, 991–1002. [CrossRef]
44. Balconi, M.; Fronda, G.; Bartolo, A. Affective, Social, and Informative Gestures Reproduction in Human Interaction: Hyperscanning and Brain Connectivity. *J. Mot. Behav.* **2021**, *53*, 296–315. [CrossRef] [PubMed]
45. Faul, F.; Erdfelder, E.; Lang, A.G.; Buchner, A. G*Power 3: A flexible statistical power analysis program for the social, behavioral, and biomedical sciences. *J. Mater. Environ. Sci.* **2007**, *39*, 175–191. [CrossRef] [PubMed]
46. Balconi, M.; Angioletti, L. Aching face and hand: The interoceptive attentiveness and social context in relation to empathy for pain. *J. Integr. Neurosci.* **2022**, *21*, 1–13. [CrossRef]
47. Oostenveld, R.; Praamstra, P. The five percent electrode system for high-resolution EEG and ERP measurements. *Clin. Neurophysiol.* **2001**, *112*, 713–719. [CrossRef]
48. Balconi, M.; Vanutelli, M.E. Empathy in negative and positive interpersonal interactions. What is the relationship between central (EEG, fNIRS) and peripheral (autonomic) neurophysiological responses? *Adv. Cogn. Psychol.* **2017**, *13*, 105–120. [CrossRef]
49. Giacometti, P.; Perdue, K.L.; Diamond, S.G. Algorithm to find high density EEG scalp coordinates and analysis of their correspondence to structural and functional regions of the brain. *J. Neurosci. Methods* **2014**, *229*, 84–96. [CrossRef]
50. Koessler, L.; Maillard, L.; Benhadid, A.; Vignal, J.P.; Felblinger, J.; Vespignani, H.; Braun, M. Automated cortical projection of EEG sensors: Anatomical correlation via the international 10-10 system. *Neuroimage* **2009**, *46*, 64–72. [CrossRef]
51. Naseer, N.; Hong, M.J.; Hong, K.S. Online binary decision decoding using functional near-infrared spectroscopy for the development of brain-computer interface. *Exp. Brain Res.* **2014**, *232*, 555–564. [CrossRef]
52. Naseer, N.; Hong, K.S. Classification of functional near-infrared spectroscopy signals corresponding to the right- and left-wrist motor imagery for development of a brain-computer interface. *Neurosci. Lett.* **2013**, *553*, 84–89. [CrossRef]
53. Wheland, D.; Joshi, A.; McMahon, K.; Hansell, N.; Martin, N.; Wright, M.; Thompson, P.; Shattuck, D.; Leahy, R. Robust identification of partial-correlation based networks with applications to cortical thickness data. *Proc.—Int. Symp. Biomed. Imaging* **2012**, 1551–1554.
54. Balconi, M.; Vanutelli, M.E.; Gatti, L. Functional brain connectivity when cooperation fails. *Brain Cogn.* **2018**, *123*, 65–73. [CrossRef]
55. Balconi, M.; Mazza, G. Lateralisation effect in comprehension of emotional facial expression: A comparison between EEG alpha band power and behavioural inhibition (BIS) and activation (BAS) systems. *Laterality Asymmetries Body Brain Cogn.* **2010**, *15*, 361–384. [CrossRef]
56. Davidson, R.J. Anterior Cerebral Asymmetry and the Nature of Emotion. *Brain Cogn.* **1992**, *20*, 125–151. [CrossRef]

57. Koslov, K.; Mendes, W.B.; Pajtas, P.E.; Pizzagalli, D.A. Asymmetry in resting intracortical activity as a buffer to social threat. *Psychol. Sci.* **2011**, *22*, 641–649. [CrossRef]
58. Harmon-Jones, E.; Gable, P.A.; Peterson, C.K. The role of asymmetric frontal cortical activity in emotion-related phenomena: A review and update. *Biol. Psychol.* **2010**, *84*, 451–462. [CrossRef]
59. Balconi, M.; Canavesio, Y. Is empathy necessary to comprehend the emotional faces? The empathic effect on attentional mechanisms (eye movements), cortical correlates (N200 event-related potentials) and facial behaviour (electromyography) in face processing. *Cogn. Emot.* **2016**, *30*, 210–224. [CrossRef]
60. Balconi, M.; Bortolotti, A. Resonance mechanism in empathic behavior. BEES, BIS/BAS and psychophysiological contribution. *Physiol. Behav.* **2012**, *105*, 298–304. [CrossRef]

Disclaimer/Publisher's Note: The statements, opinions and data contained in all publications are solely those of the individual author(s) and contributor(s) and not of MDPI and/or the editor(s). MDPI and/or the editor(s) disclaim responsibility for any injury to people or property resulting from any ideas, methods, instructions or products referred to in the content.

Article

"We Will Let You Know": An Assessment of Digital vs. Face-to-Face Job Interviews via EEG Connectivity Analysis

Michela Balconi [1,2], Davide Crivelli [1,2] and Federico Cassioli [1,2,*]

[1] International Research Center for Cognitive Applied Neuroscience (IrcCAN), Università Cattolica del Sacro Cuore, 20123 Milano, Italy; michela.balconi@unicatt.it (M.B.); davide.crivelli@unicatt.it (D.C.)
[2] Research Unit in Affective and Social Neuroscience, Department of Psychology, Università Cattolica del Sacro Cuore, 20123 Milano, Italy
* Correspondence: federico.cassioli@unicatt.it

Abstract: We focused on job interviews as critical examples of complex social interaction in organizational contexts. We aimed at investigating the effect of face-to-face vs. computer-mediated interaction, of role (candidate, recruiter), and of the interview phase (introductory, attitudinal, technical, conclusive) on intra-brain and inter-brain connectivity measures and autonomic synchronization. Twenty expert recruiters and potential candidates took part in a hyperscanning investigation. Namely, electroencephalography (delta, theta, alpha, beta bands) and autonomic (skin-conductance, heart-rate) data were collected in candidate-recruiter dyads during a simulated job interview and then concurrently analyzed. Analyses highlighted a link between face-to-face condition and greater intra-/inter-brain connectivity indices in delta and theta bands. Furthermore, intra-brain and inter-brain connectivity measures were higher for delta and theta bands in the final interview phases compared to the first ones. Consistently, autonomic synchronization was higher during the final interview phases, specifically in the face-to-face condition. Finally, recruiters showed higher intra-brain connectivity in the delta range over frontal and temporoparietal areas, while candidates showed higher intra-brain connectivity in the theta range over frontal areas. Findings highlight the value of hyperscanning investigations in exploring social attunement in professional contexts and hint at their potential to foster neuroscience-informed practices in human resource management processes.

Keywords: job interview; remote vs. face-to-face; EEG hyperscanning; brain connectivity; autonomic synchronization

Citation: Balconi, M.; Crivelli, D.; Cassioli, F. "We Will Let You Know": An Assessment of Digital vs. Face-to-Face Job Interviews via EEG Connectivity Analysis. *Information* 2022, 13, 312. https://doi.org/10.3390/info13070312

Academic Editors: Khalid Sayood, Luiz Pessoa and Birgitta Dresp-Langley

Received: 6 May 2022
Accepted: 18 June 2022
Published: 27 June 2022

Publisher's Note: MDPI stays neutral with regard to jurisdictional claims in published maps and institutional affiliations.

Copyright: © 2022 by the authors. Licensee MDPI, Basel, Switzerland. This article is an open access article distributed under the terms and conditions of the Creative Commons Attribution (CC BY) license (https://creativecommons.org/licenses/by/4.0/).

1. Introduction

Social neuroscience investigates the neural mechanisms involved in the functioning of interpersonal behavior. The social brain comprehends the neurophysiological basis of interpersonal behavior and social cognition [1], mediated by certain neural networks that connect the limbic regions to the prefrontal cortex (PFC). For instance, the dorsal (DLPFC) and ventral portion of the lateral PFC support the components of social interaction and cooperative behavior [2–4]. These networks allow effective interpersonal interchanges.

In an organization, the social dimension appears critical for value and innovation developments, and in this light, cognitive neuroscience elicits the comprehension of the workers' cognitive and affective systems. Ongoing neuroscientific research refers to leadership, motivation, job assessment, and interviewing [5,6]. Its framework is referred to as neuromanagement, defined as that interdisciplinary approach that explores internal mechanisms of management by applying knowledge derived from neuroscience and cognitive sciences [7].

In this work, we focused on the job interview for the following reasons. First, psychologically, it represents the main social interaction between the organization and the candidate. Then, strategically, it was shown to be a good predictor of employability [8]

and a value-maximizer, as it limits cases of bad hiring and loss of virtuous workers. Lastly, according to the authors, available studies have never properly considered its social complexity. A job interview represents a subcomponent of the selection process, where a candidate is invited to meet and interact with a company representative, who aims at selecting the best-fitting candidate for a position [9].

Dimensions such as anxiety, self-efficacy, its predictive validity, performance outcome, and the impact of age, accent, age, and gender, were previously investigated [10,11]. Moreover, it was shown that anchoring-and-adjuments heuristics and associated motivational mechanisms drive bias against stigmatized people in interview decisions [12]. Stigmatized applicants receive lower interview judgments and have a lower probability to be selected for the job.

Through methodological lenses, research has adopted psychometric methods, via questionnaires, qualitative-verbal methods (i.e., focus groups, in-depth interviews), or behavioral approaches [12]. These methods are extremely valuable for investigating associations of meaning, concepts, events, or complex attitudinal constructs on a general scale, but they present weaknesses if covert cognitive and affective processes are the research object. In fact, they are mediated by the person's language, cognitive bias, and self-awareness. Social neuroscience's interest in the job interview appears evident as it represents a pivotal social moment, which can be easily stressful and demanding [5].

Furthermore, due to COVID-19, the employment of videoconferencing platforms proliferated. Therefore, the rise of digital forms is considered in this work. Historically telephone interviews were the first step toward technologized job interviews. Via the distribution of laptops, equipped with cameras, and a broadband internet connection, job interviews were firstly carried out in remote settings. In this sense, COVID-19 forced companies to switch to digitalized forms. Nowadays, many companies also include the use of machine learning approaches in the selection process, in particular for initial curricula screening purposes.

As many studies related to human-computer interaction have shown, a new medium generally determines different social responses, which are embodied at a neurophysiological and cognitive level. Communication platforms shape social relationships [13]. Unfortunately, existing evidence is ambiguous [14]. Computer-mediated interaction could act as a social connector or a separator. Remote communication has been linked to diminished levels of empathy [15], and factors such as age and technology habits are known to be significant mediators [14]. Conversely, face-to-face interaction is sometimes perceived as challenging and stressful [16].

Other approaches have focused on the behavioral dimension. The detection of nonverbal behaviors of the interviewee (gaze, facial expression, and posture) was investigated [17] aiming at signaling possible improvements to the candidate for training purposes [18]. Another study on job interviews found different gaze patterns between recruiters and candidates [19], in particular, the interviewer made more frequent and longer gaze contacts compared to the interviewee. Furthermore, automated video interview (AVI) analysis, via machine learning, using verbal, paraverbal, and nonverbal behavior from audio-video data was employed to assess personality traits [20]. Moreover, the positive effect of combined cognitive reappraisal (CCR) on stress levels, in terms of heart rate variability was considered, with the CCR group presenting less physiological stress, a speech better perceived by others, and more affiliative smile and hand gestures [21]. Besides these findings, it should be pointed out that the metrics used here are indirect proxies for cognitive and affective processes and only a few studies consider both interacting agents.

The complexity that arises in the social dimension can be efficiently approached only if all the agents are simultaneously considered [22]. For these reasons, among the available methods, hyperscanning is a proposed paradigm that allows the exploration of interpersonal brain mechanisms, generated by social interaction, via the consideration of inter-brain—besides intra-brain—connectivity [23]. In fact, hyperscanning consists of the simultaneous recording of cerebral activity of two or more subjects involved in a task.

EEG hyperscanning extends the research application in the domain of the social brain. Examples of applications were carried out and an electrophysiological synchronization occurs between the agents in terms of inter-brain connectivity [24] and intra-brain connectivity. Intra-brain connectivity refers to the synchronization and co-occurrence of neural activity between an individual's brain regions and is a proxy of the functional specialization of an individual's brain activity [25]. In contrast, inter-brain connectivity can be understood as functional connectivity between the individual's brain related to inter-personal coupling mechanisms during social exchanges [26]. The effects of increased inter-personal coupling could also result in a certain degree of synchronization of autonomic responses in interacting dyads [27].

Augmented portability, improved devices, and signal processing techniques are major factors that allowed the development of neuroscientific protocols for the organization [28]. Common techniques aim at assessing a stimulus (communication or advertising-related) or a medium (user experience of a product), training an individual (neuroempowering and neuro- and bio-feedback protocols), or assessing specific cognitive or affective dimensions within a group. An employed tool is non-invasive electroencephalography (EEG), which has been applied to investigate workers' mental workload [29], risk management [30], workers' trust [31], and emotion detection [32]. The power density data is extracted via Fourier's transformation [33] and then considered within specific spectral boundaries. The most commonly signal subcomponents are alpha (8–13 Hz), beta (13.5–30 Hz), delta (0.5–3.5 Hz), and theta (4–7.5 Hz). Each frequency wave is associated with a functional significance, which also depends on the activated cortical region where the pattern is detected. Concerning low-frequency waves, theta is considered correlated to long-term memory and emotional processing [34], and delta is linked to declarative, explicit memories, and other affective states [35]. Instead, alpha and beta are associated with attentional and conscious processing towards specific stimuli, or a general environment e.g., [36].

Together with central electrophysiological activity, peripheral autonomic parameters have been employed to determine the positive and negative emotional activation, the arousal, and the stress response in individuals and therefore they proved to be valuable in the assessment of cognitive-affective dimensions in social interactions [37]. Electrodermal activity (EDA) corresponds to the resistance and electrodermal potential that provoke alteration in the electrical characteristics of the skin and reflects a person's autonomic responses to internal and external stimuli. EDA is composed of skin conductance level (SCL) and skin conductance response (SCR). While the latter reflects short-lasting fluctuations, associated with attentional processing e.g., [38] SCL corresponds to the tonic activity of EDA and is linked to workload and arousal [39].

Given the methodological issues we underlined, and the known synergetic interaction between brain, body, and behaviors, composed of complex feedback and feedforward processes, we advocate and propose an integrated multi-method approach to study social dynamics during a job interview, adopting a dual hyperscanning paradigm [40]. Thus, central and peripheral parameters were applied to a qualitative evaluation of the job interview session to address set questions, where role (recruiter, candidate), setting (face-to-face vs. remote), and job interview phases (introductory, attitudinal, technical, and conclusive) are together considered.

Therefore, the following research questions were set. Is there a difference in intrapersonal and interpersonal connectivity levels depending on the face-to-face vs. computer-mediated setting of the job interview? Is electrophysiological connectivity in the dyads detected during a job interview? Does the connectivity emerge in specific interview phases?

Electrophysiological and autonomic parameters are simultaneously gathered during the task, in both participants. We hypothesized to observe specific patterns in the EEG and autonomic correlates, based on the considered factors. First, we expected to observe higher intra-brain connectivity in those job interview phases, which presented particular cognitive and emotional relevance such as the attitudinal and technical phases, where soft and hard skills are tested on the candidate. Conversely, regarding inter-brain connectivity, we expected to detect significantly increased activity in the last phases of the job interview process, due to a deeper social understanding within the dyad. Furthermore, we conjectured that the face-to-face condition might be an eliciting factor for both these predicted patterns we just introduced. Ultimately, as for the synchronization of autonomic indices (electrodermal activity and heart rate), we believed that it could mirror the trend expected for central activity, thus increasing during the final phases of the interview, resulting in it being higher in the face-to-face condition.

2. Method

2.1. Participants

Participants joined the experiment after signing the written informed consent. The research was carried out following the principles of the Helsinki Declaration and was further approved by the Ethical Committee, where the work was designed. The populations of interest were, on one side, human resource professionals, on the other, potential candidates who were actively seeking a job. A total of 20 subjects ($n = 20$, $M_{age} = 27.3$, $SD = 9.17$), 10 recruiters and 10 candidates, were successfully recruited. All subjects were right-handed, presenting normal/corrected-to-normal visual acuity. For all participants, the following exclusion criteria were considered: (i) history of neurology or psychiatry disorders; (ii) being involved in therapies with psychoactive drugs; (iii) presenting clinically relevant distress or burnout history.

Participants were then randomly divided into dyads while considering their role, and then randomly assigned to the condition (face-to-face vs. remote). For ethical reasons, the candidates were not real contenders, and have not been involved in other previous job interviews for this position. The following ad hoc inclusion criteria were considered: (i) being older than 18 years old; (ii) proficiency in online communication technologies; (iii) currently looking for a similar/equal job position in the experiment. For human resource professionals, the following ad hoc inclusion criteria were also considered: (a) being employed; (b) being regularly involved in the recruitment process and personally carrying out job interviews; (c) five or more years of professional experience in job interviewing.

2.2. Procedure

For the data acquisition, a dual-EEGs and autonomic activity hyperscanning paradigm was designed. In this work, simulated job interviews were carried out by participants. Every subject signed the written informed consent and was randomly assigned to one of the two experimental conditions: remote vs. face-to-face. Every dyad, composed of one recruiter and one candidate, underwent one interview. Every interview presented four different phases. Participants, one recruiter, and one candidate were introduced in a laboratory room by a researcher.

In the remote condition, two independent rooms were used. In one condition a face-to-face job interview was carried out, while in the other condition the task was conducted via the video teleconferencing software program *Microsoft Teams*, through personal computers. A member of the research team previously verified that every subject was familiar with the software. EEG and autonomic system devices were installed on both the subjects and a 2-min resting-state baseline was recorded. Data were simultaneously gathered from both agents. The research team previously briefed the recruiters regarding the conduction of the job interview to limit the impact of the interviewing style and maximize the standardization. All candidates were motivated to participate in the research protocol, as it represented a learning occasion for their professional future.

In line with the interviewers' experience, four phases were established, each one with an approximate duration of ~5 min. The interview lasted about 25 min, with the following phases: (i) introductory; (ii) attitudinal; (iii) technical; and (iv) conclusive. In the *introductory* phase, both actors shortly described themselves. The candidate's curriculum is discussed. Recruiters presented the company's profile, the aim of the process, and the job offer. In the *attitudinal* phase, candidates were questioned regarding their motivation and attitude.

A description of their soft skills was discussed. In the *technical* stage, recruiters investigated the candidate's hard skills, discussing how they would fit the job position and the overall company needs. Finally, in the *conclusive* phase, feedback was furnished, eliciting strengths and weaknesses. Once the job interview was concluded, tools were detached. A debriefing phase was conducted to assure that participants understood the research aim. Job interview phases are reported in Figure 1.

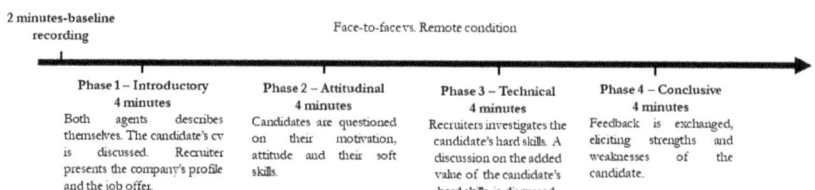

Figure 1. The four phases of the job interview. The four phases carried out during the experiment task by the dyads: introductory, attitudinal, technical, and conclusive.

To maximize the relevancy of the social interactions we checked each session to highlight not-pertinent time intervals, using audio-visual materials.

2.3. Signal Recording and Processing

2.3.1. EEG Signal

Recruiters' and candidates' EEG activity was recorded, according to the hyperscanning specifics, via two lean 15-channels EEG systems. Electrodes were placed in correspondence to F7, F3, Fz, F4, F8, T7, C3, Cz, C4, T8, P3, Pz, P4, O1, and O2 electrode sites (SI10) [41], using Ag/AgCl sensors with physical reference in the two earlobes. vEOG was monitored for subsequent signal processing. Electrodes impedance was kept below 5 kΩ. Data were sampled at 1000 Hz, with a 0.01–200 Hz bandpass input filter and a 50 Hz notch filter. During offline processing, a 0.5–50 Hz bandpass filter was applied to the raw data. Average reference was computed to limit the effect of situational biases on recorded data and improve the comparability between EEGs. Furthermore, to lower ocular movements and blinks noise, a regression-based ocular correction algorithm was applied. Data were then segmented according to the internal structure of the assessment interview (four phases) and manually screened for residual ocular and movement artifacts. Finally, power spectra were computed, via Fast Fourier Transform algorithm (resolution: 0.5 Hz; window length: 2 s) to extract power density data for the standard EEG bands, defined as follows: delta (0.5–3.5 Hz), theta (4–7.5 Hz), alpha (8–13 Hz), and beta (13.5–30 Hz). The average EEG power profile was computed and extracted for both resting and for each of the four phases (introductory, attitudinal, technical, and conclusive) of the interview plot, normalized based on the time lengths, and considering four main Regions of Interest (ROI): frontal (F7, F3, F4, F8), central (C3, C4), temporoparietal (T7, T8, P3, P4), and occipital (O1, O2).

2.3.2. Autonomic Activity

The autonomic activity was recorded in the dyads during the task through multi-use units. Recording sensors were positioned on subjects in correspondence with the distal phalanx of the second finger, on the non-dominant hand. The sensor monitored electrodermal and cardiovascular activity, in terms of skin conductance level (SCL), skin conductance response (SCR), and heart rate (HR). An accommodation phase took place before the recording session began. Data were sampled at 40 Hz. Moreover, to maximize accuracy, artifact rejection and data filtering were offline applied when needed. Heart Rate (HR, measured as beats per minute) was extracted via photoplethysmography, detecting blood volume changes in the microvascular tissues. Phasic SCR was computed using tonic EDA activity, via moving average. Mean HR, mean SCL, and SCR count were computed for each of the four phases of the job interview plot (introductory, attitudinal, technical, and conclusive).

2.4. Data Analysis

Here we described the data analysis process for the considered variables. For all ANOVA models, degrees of freedom were corrected by Greenhouse–Geisser epsilon when needed. No outliers were observed in that sample or subgroup. Post-hoc analysis (contrast analysis for ANOVA, with Bonferroni corrections for multiple comparisons) was successively applied. The size of statistically significant effects has been estimated via partial eta squared (η^2) indices.

2.4.1. EEG

In the first part of the analysis, we calculated the intra-brain and inter-brain connectivity index for every dependent variable (delta, theta, beta, and alpha power). The phase synchronization approach was not implemented in the preliminary analysis as it does not allow the further computation of correlation coefficients. Specifically, for the calculation of the functional intra-and inter-brain connectivity indices, the partial correlation coefficient Π_{ij} was computed, by normalizing the inverse of the covariance matrix $\Gamma = \Sigma^{-1}$:

$$\Pi ij = \vdash (\boxtimes \{-\Gamma ij)\} \{ \sqrt{\vdash (\Gamma ii \Gamma jj \dashv)} \} \dashv) \text{ Partial correlation matrix}$$

$$\Gamma = (\Gamma ij) = \Sigma - 1 \text{ Inverse of the covariance matrix}$$

This procedure [42] can quantify the relationship between two independent signals (i, j), for example within a dyad, known as inter-brain connectivity, and the neural connectivity between an individual's brain regions, defined as intra-brain connectivity.

For intra-brain connectivity, we applied a set of four ANOVA, one per every frequency band intra-brain connectivity index, considering the following factors: Role (2: recruiter, candidate) and Condition (2: face-to-face, remote) as between factors, and Interview phase (4: introductory, attitudinal, technical, and conclusive) and Region of Interest (ROI; 4: frontal, central, temporoparietal and occipital) as within factors.

Similarly, for inter-brain connectivity, we applied a set of four ANOVA, one per every frequency range inter-brain connectivity index, considering Condition (2: face-to-face, remote) as between factor, and Interview phase (4: introductory, attitudinal, technical, and conclusive) and Region of Interest (ROI; 4: frontal, central, temporoparietal and occipital) as within factors.

2.4.2. Autonomic Activity

In the first step of the analysis, we computed the synchronization indices using Pearson correlation coefficients [43] for each autonomic measure (HR, SCL, and SCR), with the same mathematical procedure previously described in the EEG section.

Then a set of three repeated-measures ANOVAs, one per each dependent variable, was run considering Condition (2: face-to-face, remote) as between factor and Interview phase (4: introductory, attitudinal, technical, and conclusive) as within factor.

3. Results

3.1. EEG

3.1.1. Intra-Brain Connectivity

Delta. Interview was found to be significant ($F[3,57] = 7.09$, $p \leq 0.05$, $\eta^2 = 0.43$). From post hoc analyses, higher intra-brain connectivity was found in the attitudinal phase compared to introductory phase ($F[1,19] = 7.13$, $p \leq 0.05$, $\eta^2 = 0.43$), and in the technical phase compared to the introductory phase ($F[1,19] = 8.07$, $p \leq 0.05$, $\eta^2 = 0.44$). Data is reported in Figure 2a. Moreover, Condition was found significant ($F[1,19] = 9.33$, $p \leq 0.05$, $\eta^2 = 0.48$), with higher intra-brain connectivity in the face-to-face compared to the remote condition. Data is reported in Figure 2b. Finally, the interaction effect Role*ROI resulted significant ($F[3,54] = 6.78$, $p \leq 0.05$, $\eta^2 = 0.40$). Post hoc analyses highlighted higher intra-brain connectivity for recruiters compared to candidates in the frontal region (F[1,19] = 6.70, $p \leq 0.05$, $\eta^2 = 0.40$) and in the temporoparietal region (F[1,19] = 6.78, $p \leq 0.05$, $\eta^2 = 0.40$). Data is reported in Figure 2c.

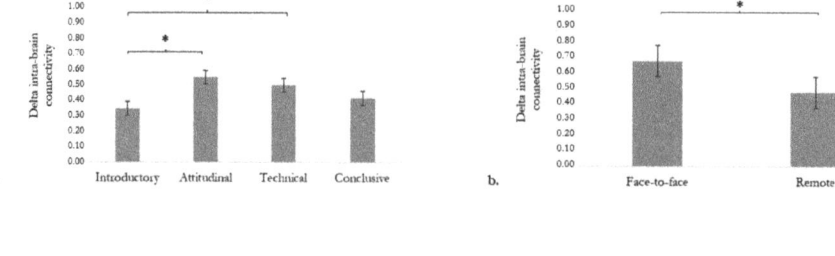

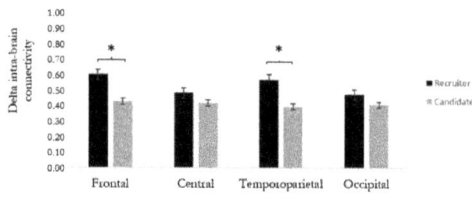

Figure 2. Delta intra-brain connectivity results. (a) Bar graph shows differences in Interview. Bars represent ±1 SE. Stars mark statistically significant pairwise comparisons. (b) Bar graph shows differences for Condition. Bars represent ±1 SE. Stars mark statistically significant pairwise comparisons. (c) Bar graph shows differences for Condition*Region of interest (ROI). Bars represent ±1 SE. Stars mark statistically significant pairwise comparisons.

Theta. The condition factor was found significant (F[1,19] = 8.45, $p \leq 0.05$, $\eta^2 = 0.45$), with increased intra-brain connectivity for the face-to-face condition compared to the remote one. Data is reported in Figure 3a. Furthermore, the interaction effect Role*ROI was found to be significant (F[3,54] = 6.70, $p \leq 0.05$, $\eta^2 = 0.40$). Post hoc analyses highlighted higher intra-brain connectivity in the candidates compared to the recruiters (F[1,19] = 6.16, $p \leq 0.05$, $\eta^2 = 0.38$) in the frontal region. Data is reported in Figure 3b. Moreover, the interaction effect Interview*ROI*Role was also found to be significant (F[9,162] = 7.65, $p \leq 0.05$, $\eta^2 = 0.44$). The post hoc analyses highlighted increased intra-brain connectivity in the frontal region for the candidates during the technical phase compared to the introductory (F[1,9] = 6.78, $p \leq 0.05$, $\eta^2 = 0.40$) and attitudinal (F[1,9] = 6.98, $p \leq 0.05$, $\eta^2 = 0.40$) phases, as well as during the conclusive phase compared to the introductory (F[1,9] = 9.14, $p \leq 0.05$, $\eta^2 = 0.46$) and attitudinal (F[1,9] = 7.74, $p \leq 0.05$, $\eta^2 = 0.40$) phases. Data is reported in Figure 3c.

No other significant results for intra-brain connectivity were detected.

3.1.2. Inter-Brain Connectivity

Delta. The factor Interview resulted in being significant (F[3,27] = 9.32, $p \leq 0.05$, $\eta^2 = 0.49$). Post hoc analyses highlighted higher inter-brain connectivity for the conclusive compared to the introductory phase (F[1,9] = 10.98, $p \leq 0.05$, $\eta^2 = 0.46$). Data is reported in Figure 4a. Furthermore, Condition resulted in being significant (F[1,9] = 9.32, $p \leq 0.05$, $\eta^2 = 0.48$), with higher inter-brain connectivity for the face-to-face condition compared to the remote condition. Data is reported in Figure 4b.

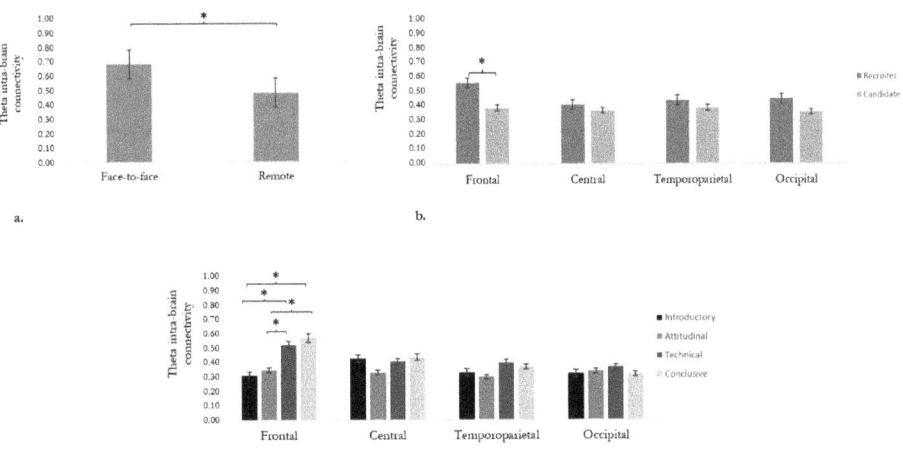

Figure 3. Theta intra-brain connectivity results (**a**) Bar graph shows differences in Condition (ROI). Bars represent ±1 SE. Stars mark statistically significant pairwise comparisons. (**b**) Bar graph shows differences considering Condition*ROI. Bars represent ±1 SE. Stars mark statistically significant pairwise comparisons. (**c**) Bar graph shows differences considering the interaction Interview*ROI*Role. Here are reported only candidate's data where significant differences were detected. Bars represent ±1 SE. Stars mark statistically significant pairwise comparisons.

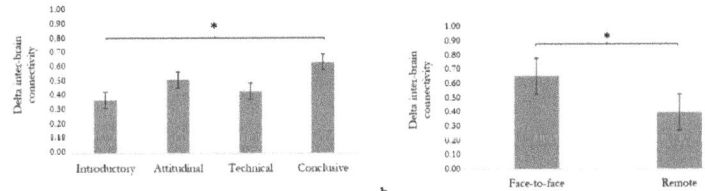

Figure 4. Delta inter-brain connectivity results. (**a**) Bar graph shows differences considering the factor Interview. Bars represent ±1 SE. Stars mark statistically significant pairwise comparisons. (**b**) Bar graph shows differences considering the Condition factor. Bars represent ±1 SE. Stars mark statistically significant pairwise comparisons.

Theta. The factor Condition was found to be significant ($F[1,9] = 8.80$, $p \leq 0.05$, $\eta^2 = 0.45$), with increased inter-brain connectivity in the face-to-face condition compared to the remote setting. Data is reported in Figure 5a.

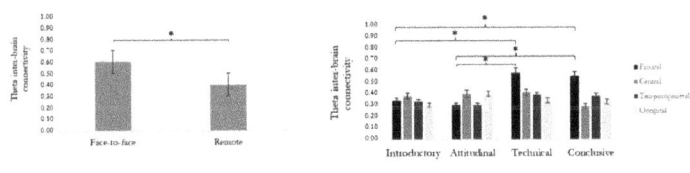

Figure 5. Theta inter-brain connectivity results. (**a**) Bar graph shows differences considering Condition. Bars represent ±1 SE. Stars mark statistically significant pairwise comparisons. (**b**) Bar graph shows differences considering Interview*ROI. Bars represent ±1 SE. Stars mark statistically significant pairwise comparisons.

The interaction effect Interview*ROI was also found to be significant (F[9,81] = 6.78, $p \leq 0.05$, $\eta^2 = 0.40$). Post hoc comparisons detected significant differences with increased inter-brain connectivity in the frontal area for technical and conclusion phases compared to introductory (respectively: F[1,9] = 6.04, $p \leq 0.05$, $\eta^2 = 0.37$; and F[1,9] = 6.11, $p \leq 0.05$, $\eta^2 = 0.36$) and attitudinal (respectively: F[1,9] = 7.13, $p \leq 0.05$, $\eta^2 = 0.41$; and F[1,9] = 6.93, $p \leq 0.05$, $\eta^2 = 0.37$) phases. Data is reported in Figure 5b.

No other significant results for inter-brain connectivity were detected from the statistical analysis.

3.2. Autonomic Data

HR. The interaction effect Interview*Condition was found to be significant (F[3,27] = 6.16, $p \leq 0.05$, $\eta^2 = 0.39$), revealing higher synchronization in the technical and conclusive phases compared to introductory (respectively: F[1,9] = 6.21, $p \leq 0.05$, $\eta^2 = 0.40$; and F[1,19] = 6.78, $p \leq 0.05$, $\eta^2 = 0.40$) and attitudinal (respectively: F[1,9] = 7.12, $p \leq 0.05$, $\eta^2 = 0.41$; and F[1,9] = 8.90, $p \leq 0.05$, $\eta^2 = 0.41$) phases in the face-to-face condition. Data is reported in Figure 6a.

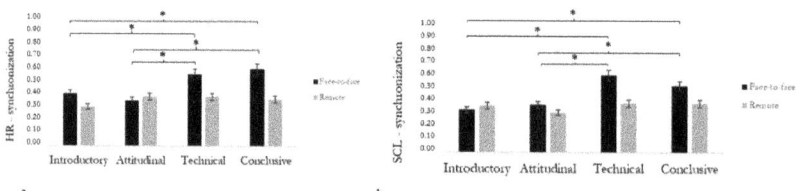

Figure 6. Heart rate (HR) and skin conductance level (SCL) significant results. (**a**) Bar graph shows the difference in HR considering the Condition*Interview interaction. Bars represent ±1 SE. Stars mark statistically significant pairwise comparisons. (**b**) Bar graph shows the difference in SCL considering the Condition*Interview interaction. Bars represent ±1 SE. Stars mark statistically significant pairwise comparisons.

SCL. The interaction effect Interview*Condition was found to be significant (F[3,27] = 8.23, $p \leq 0.05$, $\eta^2 = 0.42$). As revealed by post hoc analyses, synchronization was generally higher in the technical and conclusive phases compared to the introductory (respectively: F[1,9] = 8.90, $p \leq 0.05$, $\eta^2 = 0.44$; and F[1,9] = 8.98, $p \leq 0.05$, $\eta^2 = 0.42$) and attitudinal (respectively: F[1,9] = 6.09, $p \leq 0.05$, $\eta^2 = 0.40$; and F[1,9] = 9.04, $p \leq 0.05$, $\eta^2 = 0.40$) phases in the face-to-face condition. Data is reported in Figure 6b.

4. Discussion

In the present study, we focused on the job interview as a critical example of complex social interaction in organizational contexts. The research aimed at investigating the effect of face-to-face vs. remote computer-mediated interaction, of the phase of the job interview (introductory, attitudinal, technical, and conclusive), and of the role (candidate vs. recruiter) on neurophysiological and autonomic markers of inter-personal coupling between candidates and recruiters, as well as on intra-brain connectivity measures. Data analysis highlighted the influence of the investigated factors on both intra- and inter-brain connectivity measures and on autonomic synchronization of interlocutors.

Face-to-face interactions have systematically elicited higher intra-brain connectivity in delta and theta frequency ranges, mirroring a peculiarly coherent activation of neural networks likely involved in supporting the understanding of interlocutors' behavior [44]. It is worth noting that slower components of the EEG spectra are known to be linked to emotional processing and responsiveness, in particular when social reinforcements are present [45]. Greater intra-brain connectivity in lower frequency bands during face-to-face interviews, compared to remote ones, might hint at the greater information-processing demand imposed on social understanding and regulation processes by such a complex form of interaction. Namely, social exchanges occurring in face-to-face conditions are intrinsically connoted by richer social information deriving from the full set of verbal and non-verbal communication channels available for the dyadic exchange. Conversely, computer-mediated communication, due to setting and technical limitations, allows conveying only a part of non-verbal communication cues (e.g., degraded information on body posture, proxemics, and gestures in case a webcam is used, or loss of relevant information apart from verbal and vocal ones if no webcam is used). The greater presence of social cues in face-to-face interaction, while likely allowing the understanding of the interlocutor's motives and communication and fostering adaptive social regulation, increases processing effort. Furthermore, their multimodal nature plausibly requires the combined involvement of different neural structures.

Intra-brain connectivity in slower EEG bands changed with the progress of the job interview and was modulated by the phases and content of the interaction. In particular, the interview phases with higher delta connectivity indices appear to be the attitudinal and the technical ones. Those two phases were the most cognitively demanding during the interview and plausibly required peak attention from both the candidates—who were trying to provide the best presentation of their skills—and the recruiters—who were involved in checking matches and discrepancies in candidates' skills. The different observed levels of intra-brain connectivity might reflect the mediation of broad cortical networks for cognitive elaboration, with a more relevant impact and greater "echo effect" on the recruiter role e.g., [46]. At the same time, the peculiar pattern of increased intra-brain connectivity in the theta band specifically shown by candidates in the last phases of the interview compared to the first ones might mirror the progressive increase in cohesion among frontal structures involved in cognitive-affective control and behavior regulation in complex situations [47].

Then, higher intra-brain connectivity indices were observed in frontal and temporoparietal areas for the recruiters in the delta frequency range, while candidates showed higher intra-brain connectivity in frontal areas in the theta range. Intra-brain connectivity in the frontal and posterior regions is generally involved in mirroring mechanisms during action execution and the observation of similar actions and may be evidence of an interdependent synchronization at a cognitive level [48]. In fact, increased delta intra-brain connectivity was observed in the temporoparietal area while decoding informative gestures [23] and linked to the involvement of mirroring mechanisms e.g., [49]. Complementarily, delta intra-brain connectivity in frontal areas was associated with social-and affective- gesture encoding [23] and could be linked to the ability to respond to relational and social situations [50]. Building on such evidence, present findings might reflect the greater expertise of senior recruiters in decoding and understanding non-verbal language and socially relevant cues, compared to candidates. Yet, we acknowledge that this interpretation would benefit from additional testing and corroboration via focused investigations. The higher theta connectivity indices shown by candidates over the frontal region, instead, likely mark, as above mentioned, the shared neural effort imposed by the socially-salient situation in terms of cognitive-affective control and self-regulation.

Regarding inter-brain connectivity data, connectivity indices in both theta and delta ranges were higher in the face-to-face than in the remote condition. Such a pattern is consistent with the one emerging from the analysis of intra-brain connectivity measures. Decoding and encoding of affective non-verbal communication were previously linked to modulations of delta and theta frequency waves [51]. The response in slower EEG components might suggest a greater focus of the dyads on social processing and on the regulation of interpersonal interaction and its affective correlates during the face-to-face condition [52]. As above noted, the observed difference in neurophysiological indices of inter-brain coupling between face-to-face and remote computer-mediated interactions might plausibly reflect the intrinsic limitations in properly conveying part of non-verbal communication cues in remote interaction settings. The use of web-based communication platforms, indeed, leads to a greater focus on linguistic content and, among non-verbal communication channels, on non-verbal vocal cues (e.g., prosody), paralinguistic contents, eye behavior, and facial expressions, while neglecting other unavailable cues. The difference in the amount and in the source of information used to guide interpersonal regulation and sense-making processes during the interviews likely provides different socio-psychological contexts for engagement and interpersonal coupling.

In addition, inter-brain connectivity changed with the progress of the interview, with higher inter-brain connectivity measures in the delta range during the final phase than in the initial phase of social interaction. A similar pattern, though localized in frontal areas, for the theta frequency range was detected. Consistently, we observed greater autonomic synchronization during the final phases of the task, specifically in the face-to-face condition. This gradually increased interpersonal coupling pattern is consistent with the hypothesis that attunement in dyads increases by building on the progressive shared communication experience and fine-tuning processes aimed at optimizing the exchange and communication efficacy. Specifically, activity in the theta frequency range has been related to emotional tuning and encoding/recall processes [53], which might have happened more intensively in the last part of the job interview. Slow EEG activity predicts working memory, navigation, and encoding [54] during the wake. Furthermore, the implicit/explicit exchange of feedback during social interaction enhances emotional elaboration, shapes adaptation, and self-regulation mechanisms, and boosts long-term memory formation, modulating the degree of syntonization between inter-agents. Again, recent perspectives see inter-brain synchronization correlated to the degree of the sense of joint agency in communicative and shared actions e.g., [55]. Previous studies found that brain activities in the frontal region were synchronized in dyads engaged in joint actions [56] and, in particular, that inter-brain theta synchronization in the prefrontal cortex was especially associated with collaborative tasks between individuals that strongly involve executive functions [57].

In addition, being involved in a collaborative or a social communication task proved to elicit greater autonomic synchronization between the involved individuals, with a greater inter-personal correlation between cardiovascular and electrodermal activities.

5. Conclusions

This study explored the benefits of applying neuroscience methods in the investigation of human resource management (HRM), with a focus on job interviews. Given their strategic value and their psychological salience for both candidates and company representatives, such a form of social interaction typically elicits remarkable recruitment of cognitive resources and requires high levels of engagement in both inter-agents, which in turn modulate social attunement and interactional dynamics. Present findings highlight the value of hyperscanning investigations as a methodology to explore the quality of social dynamics and attunement even in real-life social exchanges, point out the feasibility of such investigations at the workplace, and hint at their potential to foster the development of neuroscience-informed evidence-based practices in HRM processes.

Indeed, some initial guidelines, in the form of practical implications can be derived from the acquired data. Firstly, job interviewing is a two-way process, but recruiters are more emotionally in control of the situation. Therefore, they should foster an emphatic connection with the candidate. For a reliable assessment, a successful tuning in the first phases of the interaction before proceeding into technical assessment is advisable. Secondly, the setting condition is relevant. Especially for positions that require social skills, available data suggests the employment of a face-to-face interview, in which the richness of social cues allows for a deeper attunement between recruiter and candidate and, therefore, for a more reliable evaluation.

The study is, however, not exempt from limitations. Firstly, the strength of current results would benefit from replication and investigation with bigger samples. Furthermore, interviews were simulated and the use of research tools might have impacted the setting and the individuals' interaction (i.e., observer bias) in terms of ecological validity. Psychometric data (e.g., personality traits) were not gathered in this work. Further research could use them to confront self-report measures and neurophysiological correlates. In replications studies, other factors could also be employed as covariates to ensure higher internal validity such as the recruiter's experience, interviewing style, and job position. Furthermore, in the future, other potentially relevant factors modulating the quality and efficacy of mediated vs. presence communication could be considered in addition. For instance, individual and socio-demographic factors play a role in acceptance and user experience with technology-mediated communication and should be explored. Moreover, the use of a deep-learning-based job interview solution was recently proposed [58], based on voice and video data. Personality, aptitude, and neurophysiological data could be further fed into the algorithm.

Author Contributions: M.B., D.C. and F.C. designed the research paradigm, carried out the data collection and analysis, and wrote the article. All authors have read and agreed to the published version of the manuscript.

Funding: This work was supported by "D.3.2. Fund (ricerche di particolare interesse per l'Ateneo) 2020" at Università Cattolica del Sacro Cuore.

Institutional Review Board Statement: Research was conducted following the principles and guidelines of the Helsinki Declaration and was approved by the local Ethical Committee institution where the work was carried out.

Informed Consent Statement: Informed consent was obtained from all subjects involved in the study.

Data Availability Statement: The data that support the findings of this study are available from the corresponding author, [F.C.], upon reasonable request. The data are not publicly available due to privacy reasons.

Conflicts of Interest: The authors declare no conflict of interest.

References

1. Toppi, J.; Borghini, G.; Petti, M.; He, E.J.; de Giusti, V.; He, B.; Astolfi, L.; Babiloni, F. Investigating Cooperative Behavior in Ecological Settings: An EEG Hyperscanning Study. *PLoS ONE* **2016**, *11*, e0154236. [CrossRef] [PubMed]
2. Balconi, M.; Pagani, S. Social hierarchies and emotions: Cortical prefrontal activity, facial feedback (EMG), and cognitive performance in a dynamic interaction. *Soc. Neurosci.* **2014**, *10*, 166–178. [CrossRef] [PubMed]
3. Chiao, J.Y.; Harada, T.; Komeda, H.; Li, Z.; Mano, Y.; Saito, D.; Parrish, T.B.; Sadato, N.; Iidaka, T. Neural basis of individualistic and collectivistic views of self. *Hum. Brain Mapp.* **2009**, *30*, 2813–2820. [CrossRef]
4. Baker, J.M.; Liu, N.; Cui, X.; Vrticka, P.; Saggar, M.; Hosseini, S.M.H.; Reiss, A.L. Sex differences in neural and behavioral signatures of cooperation revealed by fNIRS hyperscanning. *Sci. Rep.* **2016**, *6*, 26492. [CrossRef]
5. Zito, M.; Bilucaglia, M.; Fici, A.; Gabrielli, G.; Russo, V. Job Assessment through Bioelectrical Measures: A Neuromanagement Perspective. *Front. Psychol.* **2021**, *12*. [CrossRef]
6. Crivelli, D.; Balconi, M. Agentività e competenze sociali: Riflessioni teoriche e implicazioni per il management [Agency and social skills: Theoretical remarks and implications for management]. *Ric. Psicol.* **2017**, *40*, 349–363. [CrossRef]
7. Balconi, M.; Gatti, L.; Vanutelli, M.E. Cooperate or not cooperate EEG, autonomic, and behavioral correlates of ineffective joint strategies. *Brain Behav.* **2018**, *8*, e00902. [CrossRef]
8. Hogan, R.; Chamorro-Premuzic, T.; Kaiser, R.B. Employability and Career Success: Bridging the Gap between Theory and Reality. *Ind. Organ. Psychol.* **2013**, *6*, 3–16. [CrossRef]
9. McCarthy, J.M.; Truxillo, D.M.; Bauer, T.N.; Erdogan, B.; Shao, Y.; Wang, M.; Liff, J.; Gardner, C. Distressed and distracted by COVID-19 during high-stakes virtual interviews: The role of job interview anxiety on performance and reactions. *J. Appl. Psychol.* **2021**, *106*, 1103–1117. [CrossRef]
10. Nikolaou, I.; Georgiou, K. Fairness Reactions to the Employment Interview. *Rev. Psicol. Trab. Las Organ.* **2018**, *34*, 103–111. [CrossRef]
11. Kroll, E.; Ziegler, M. Discrimination due to Ethnicity and Gender: How susceptible are video-based job interviews? *Int. J. Sel. Assess.* **2016**, *24*, 161–171. [CrossRef]
12. Buijsrogge, A.; Duyck, W.; Derous, E. Initial impression formation during the job interview: Anchors that drive biased decision-making against stigmatized applicants. *Eur. J. Work. Organ. Psychol.* **2020**, *30*, 305–318. [CrossRef]
13. Bašnáková, J.; van Berkum, J.; Weber, K.; Hagoort, P. A job interview in the MRI scanner: How does indirectness affect addressees and overhearers? *Neuropsychologia* **2015**, *76*, 79–91. [CrossRef]
14. Waytz, A.; Gray, K. Does Online Technology Make Us More or Less Sociable? A Preliminary Review and Call for Research. *Perspect. Psychol. Sci.* **2018**, *13*, 473–491. [CrossRef]

15. Wellman, B.; Quan-Haase, A.; Boase, J.; Chen, W.; Hampton, K.; Díaz, I.; Miyata, K. The Social Affordances of the Internet for Networked Individualism. *J. Comput. -Mediat. Commun.* **2006**, *8*, JCMC834. [CrossRef]
16. Shalom, J.G.; Israeli, H.; Markovitzky, O.; Lipsitz, J.D. Social anxiety and physiological arousal during computer mediated vs. face to face communication. *Comput. Hum. Behav.* **2015**, *44*, 202–208. [CrossRef]
17. Beisel, R.V. The Effect of High-Power Nonverbal Communication in the Job Interview for Ex-Prisoners. Ph.D. Thesis, Universidade Católica Portuguesa, Lisbon, Portugal, 2021; pp. 1–134. Available online: http://hdl.handle.net/10400.14/35536 (accessed on 5 May 2022).
18. Takeuchi, N.; Koda, T. Initial Assessment of Job Interview Training System using Multimodal Behavior Analysis. In Proceedings of the 9th International Conference on Human-Agent Interaction, Nagoya, Japan, 9–11 November 2021. [CrossRef]
19. Acarturk, C.; Indurkya, B.; Nawrocki, P.; Sniezynski, B.; Jarosz, M.; Usal, K.A. Gaze aversion in conversational settings: An investigation based on mock job interview. *J. Eye Mov. Res.* **2021**, *14*. [CrossRef]
20. Hickman, L.; Saef, R.; Ng, V.; Woo, S.E.; Tay, L.; Bosch, N. Developing and evaluating language-based machine learning algorithms for inferring applicant personality in video interviews. *Hum. Resour. Manag. J.* **2021**, 1–20. [CrossRef]
21. Santos, A.C.; Arriaga, P.; Simões, C. Catching the audience in a job interview: Effects of emotion regulation strategies on subjective, physiological, and behavioural responses. *Biol. Psychol.* **2021**, *162*, 108089. [CrossRef]
22. Hasson, U.; Ghazanfar, A.A.; Galantucci, B.; Garrod, S.; Keysers, C. Brain-to-brain coupling: A mechanism for creating and sharing a social world. *Trends Cogn. Sci.* **2012**, *16*, 114–121. [CrossRef]
23. Balconi, M.; Fronda, G. Intra-Brain Connectivity vs. Inter-Brain Connectivity in Gestures Reproduction: What Relationship? *Brain Sci.* **2021**, *11*, 577. [CrossRef] [PubMed]
24. Lindenberger, U.; Li, S.C.; Gruber, W.; Müller, V. Brains swinging in concert: Cortical phase synchronization while playing guitar. *BMC Neurosci.* **2009**, *10*, 22. [CrossRef] [PubMed]
25. Balconi, M.; Caldiroli, C. Semantic violation effect on object-related action comprehension. N400-like event-related potentials for unusual and incorrect use. *Neuroscience* **2011**, *197*, 191–199. [CrossRef]
26. Kawasaki, M.; Yamada, Y.; Ushiku, Y.; Miyauchi, E.; Yamaguchi, Y. Inter-brain synchronization during coordination of speech rhythm in human-to-human social interaction. *Sci. Rep.* **2013**, *3*, 1692. [CrossRef] [PubMed]
27. Balconi, M.; Gatti, L.; Vanutelli, M.E. EEG functional connectivity and brain-to-brain coupling in failing cognitive strategies. *Conscious. Cogn.* **2018**, *60*, 86–97. [CrossRef]
28. Crivelli, D.; Fronda, G.; Venturella, I.; Balconi, M. Stress and neurocognitive efficiency in managerial contexts: A study on technology-mediated mindfulness practice. *Int. J. Workplace Health Manag.* **2019**, *12*, 42–56. [CrossRef]
29. Aghajani, H.; Garbey, M.; Omurtag, A. Measuring Mental Workload with EEG + fNIRS. *Front. Hum. Neurosci.* **2017**, *11*. [CrossRef] [PubMed]
30. Duan, R. Cognitive Mechanism of Economic Management Risk Based on EEG Analysis. *NeuroQuantology* **2018**, *16*. [CrossRef]
31. Shayesteh, S.; Ojha, A.; Jebelli, H. Workers' Trust in Collaborative Construction Robots: EEG-Based Trust Recognition in an Immersive Environment. *Autom. Robot. Archit. Eng. Constr. Ind.* **2022**, 201–215. [CrossRef]
32. Hwang, S.; Jebelli, H.; Choi, B.; Choi, M.; Lee, S. Measuring Workers' Emotional State during Construction Tasks Using Wearable EEG. *J. Constr. Eng. Manag.* **2018**, *144*, 04018050. [CrossRef]
33. Bhardwaj, H.; Tomar, P.; Sakalle, A.; Ibrahim, W. EEG-Based Personality Prediction Using Fast Fourier Transform and DeepLSTM Model. *Comput. Intell. Neurosci.* **2021**, *2021*, 6524858. [CrossRef] [PubMed]
34. Khader, P.H.; Jost, K.; Ranganath, C.; Rösler, F. Theta and alpha oscillations during working-memory maintenance predict successful long-term memory encoding. *Neurosci. Lett.* **2010**, *468*, 339–343. [CrossRef] [PubMed]
35. Hobson, J.A.; Pace-Schott, E.F. The cognitive neuroscience of sleep: Neuronal systems, consciousness and learning. *Nat. Rev. Neurosci.* **2002**, *3*, 679–693. [CrossRef] [PubMed]
36. Huang, J.; Sekuler, R. Alpha oscillations and the fidelity of visual memory. *J. Vis.* **2010**, *10*, 715. [CrossRef]
37. Lindquist, K.A.; Wager, T.D.; Kober, H.; Bliss-Moreau, E.; Barrett, L.F. The brain basis of emotion: A meta-analytic review. *Behav. Brain Sci.* **2012**, *35*, 121–143. [CrossRef]
38. McClenahan, E.L. Essays in Social Neuroscienceedited by John T. Cacioppo and Gary G. Berntson; Cambridge, Massachusetts, The MIT Press, 2004, 168 pages, $32. *Psychiatr. Serv.* **2007**, *58*, 421–422. [CrossRef]
39. Greene, S.; Thapliyal, H.; Caban-Holt, A. A Survey of Affective Computing for Stress Detection: Evaluating technologies in stress detection for better health. *IEEE Consum. Electron. Mag.* **2016**, *5*, 44–56. [CrossRef]
40. Balconi, M.; Fronda, G.; Cassioli, F.; Crivelli, D. Face-to-face vs. remote digital settings in job assessment interviews: A multilevel hyperscanning protocol for the investigation of interpersonal attunement. *PLoS ONE* **2022**, *17*, e0263668. [CrossRef]
41. Chatrian, G.-E.; Lettich, E.; Nelson, P.L. Modified nomenclature for the "10%" Electrode System. *J. Clin. Neurophysiol.* **1988**, *5*, 183–186. [CrossRef]
42. Wheland, D.; Joshi, A.; McMahon, K.; Hansell, N.; Martin, N.; Wright, M.; Thompson, P.; Shattuck, D.; Leahy, R. Robust identification of partial-correlation based networks with applications to cortical thickness data. In Proceedings of the 2012 9th IEEE International Symposium on Biomedical Imaging (ISBI), Barcelona, Spain, 2–5 May 2012. [CrossRef]
43. Hernandez, J.; Riobo, I.; Rozga, A.; Abowd, G.D.; Picard, R.W. Using electrodermal activity to recognize ease of engagement in children during social interactions. In Proceedings of the 2014 ACM International Joint Conference on Pervasive and Ubiquitous Computing, Washington, DC, USA, 13–17 September 2014. [CrossRef]

44. Rizzolatti, G.; Craighero, L. The mirror-neuron system. *Annu. Rev. Neurosci.* **2004**, *27*, 169–192. [CrossRef]
45. Balconi, M.; Pezard, L.; Nandrino, J.L.; Vanutelli, M.E. Two is better than one: The effects of strategic cooperation on intra- and inter-brain connectivity by fNIRS. *PLoS ONE* **2017**, *12*, e0187652. [CrossRef] [PubMed]
46. Fronda, G.; Balconi, M. What hyperscanning and brain connectivity for hemodynamic (fNIRS), electrophysiological (EEG) and behavioral measures can tell us about prosocial behavior. *Psychol. Neurosci.* **2021**, *15*, 147–162. [CrossRef]
47. Cavanagh, J.F.; Shackman, A.J. Frontal midline theta reflects anxiety and cognitive control: Meta-analytic evidence. *J. Physiol. Paris* **2015**, *109*, 3–15. [CrossRef] [PubMed]
48. Dick, B.; Stringer, E.; Huxham, C. Theory in action research. *Action Res.* **2009**, *7*, 5–12. [CrossRef]
49. Rizzolatti, G.; Sinigaglia, C. The functional role of the parieto-frontal mirror circuit: Interpretations and misinterpretations. *Nat. Rev. Neurosci.* **2010**, *11*, 264–274. [CrossRef]
50. Rameson, L.T.; Lieberman, M.D. Empathy: A Social Cognitive Neuroscience Approach. *Soc. Personal. Psychol. Compass* **2009**, *3*, 94–110. [CrossRef]
51. Rimmele, J.M.; Gross, J.; Molholm, S.; Keitel, A. Brain Oscillations in Human Communication. *Front. Hum. Neurosci.* **2018**, *12*. [CrossRef]
52. Harmon-Jones, E.; Gable, P.A.; Peterson, C.K. The role of asymmetric frontal cortical activity in emotion-related phenomena: A review and update. *Biol. Psychol.* **2010**, *84*, 451–462. [CrossRef]
53. Hutchison, I.C.; Rathore, S. The role of REM sleep theta activity in emotional memory. *Front. Psychol.* **2015**, *6*. [CrossRef]
54. Kahana, M.J.; Seelig, D.; Madsen, J.R. Theta returns. *Curr. Opin. Neurobiol.* **2001**, *11*, 739–744. [CrossRef]
55. Shiraishi, M.; Shimada, S. Inter-brain synchronization during a cooperative task reflects the sense of joint agency. *Neuropsychologia* **2021**, *154*, 107770. [CrossRef] [PubMed]
56. Liu, D.; Liu, S.; Liu, X.; Zhang, C.; Li, A.; Jin, C.; Chen, Y.; Wang, H.; Zhang, X. Interactive Brain Activity: Review and Progress on EEG-Based Hyperscanning in Social Interactions. *Front. Psychol.* **2018**, *9*. [CrossRef] [PubMed]
57. Müller, C.; Remy, S. Septo–hippocampal interaction. *Cell Tissue Res.* **2017**, *373*, 565–575. [CrossRef] [PubMed]
58. Lee, B.C.; Kim, B.Y. Development of an AI-Based Interview System for Remote Hiring, International. *J. Adv. Res. Eng. Technol.* **2021**, *12*, 654–663.

MDPI AG
Grosspeteranlage 5
4052 Basel
Switzerland
Tel.: +41 61 683 77 34

Information Editorial Office
E-mail: information@mdpi.com
www.mdpi.com/journal/information

Disclaimer/Publisher's Note: The title and front matter of this reprint are at the discretion of the Guest Editors. The publisher is not responsible for their content or any associated concerns. The statements, opinions and data contained in all individual articles are solely those of the individual Editors and contributors and not of MDPI. MDPI disclaims responsibility for any injury to people or property resulting from any ideas, methods, instructions or products referred to in the content.